CHARMING PLACES TO STAY

1 000 Charming Hotels
and Guesthouses
in France

SUMMARY

ALSACE
AQUITAINE
AUVERGNE
BURGUNDY
BRITTANY
CENTRE AND UPPER LOIRE VALLEY
CHAMPAGNE-ARDENNE
CORSICA
FRANCHE-COMTÉ
ÎLE-DE-FRANCE AND PARIS
LANGUEDOC-ROUSSILLON
LIMOUSIN
LORRAINE
MIDI-PYRÉNÉES
NORD-PAS-DE-CALAIS
NORMANDY
PAYS-DE-LA-LOIRE
PICARDY
POITOU-CHARENTES
PROVENCE-ALPS - FRENCH RIVIERA
RHÔNE-ALPES

Symbols used in the guide

12 **Number of the establishment**
in the guide and on the regional map:
blue for hotels
red for maisons d'hôte

 Hotel

 Maison d'hôte

 Hotel or maison d'hôte offering rooms
for under €50 per night
for a double room

 The little extra that makes the hotel
or maison d'hôte different

The guide

Michelin's 1000 Charming Hotels and Guesthouses features a selection of establishments at reasonable prices throughout France, chosen by our inspectors for their authenticity, character, warmth and setting. The most expensive rooms cost no more than €120, most of the prices are below €80 and a quarter of the establishments offer rooms for less than €50.

A few words, indicated by our ☺ symbol, highlight the little extra that we particularly liked: "Exploring the underwater depths of Scandola nature reserve", for example.

How the Guide works

The guide is divided into 21 French regions. Within these regions, the establishments are listed in ascending order of the number of the département: Aquitaine, for example, is split into the départements of Dordogne 24), Gironde (33), Landes (40), Lot-et-Garonne (47) and Pyrénées-Altantiques (64). Within the département, towns or villages where we list an establishment are given in alphabetical order and the establishments are numbered in this order. Hotels are marked in blue 🏨 and maisons d'hôte in red 🏛.

Maps

The map of France at the beginning of the guide shows the 21 regions and their départements.

At the beginning of each chapter is a regional map with the hotels marked as blue dots and the maisons d'hôte as red dots; each dot has a number which corresponds to the number at the top of the establishment's description. The maps and directions in this guide use the metric system for reasons of practicality; as a reminder 1km = c0.6miles.

Please note: The route nationale and route departementale road numbers are currently being changed in France

Maisons d'hôte

Maisons and chambres d'hôte are, loosely speaking, bed & breakfast establishments with between three and six rooms. Often converted mills, country houses, farmsteads or hunting lodges, and typically in quiet countryside or the residential area of a town, they are also the private homes of the people who will welcome you and endeavour to make your stay as pleasant as possible. We definitely recommend booking ahead, particularly during the summer or the long spring weekends. You should also call if you think you may arrive late in the evening.

Hotels

Many of our hotels are in converted castles, mansions, convents, abbeys and the like. As with the chambres d'hôte, all have been selected for their character, tranquillity and hospitality. There is no point, however, in attempting to compare a simple seaside holiday home with rooms at under €50 with accommodation in a luxurious medieval château: each has its own distinctive charm. Most hotels have a restaurant and offer half-board rates (i.e. for dinner and accommodation). If they do, we point this out: the establishment will confirm the details. Remember to confirm your reservation if you're running late – guests are usually expected to arrive by 6pm.

The information provided by the maisons d'hôte and hotels and reproduced in good faith should be considered as an indication only. Despite our best efforts, it is always possible that some of the information is not complete or accurate. Michelin Travel Publications cannot be held responsible for such changes.

Tables d'hôte

If a hotel or restaurant has dining facilities, we say so. Some maisons d'hôte offer a "table d'hôte". This home-cooked set menu at a fixed price may be served to you at your own table, or you may join the rest of the guests at a communal table.

Prices

All prices are inclusive of tax and service, the prices indicated in this guide were supplied to us by the proprietors of the hotels in 2006 for the year 2007 and may thus be liable to change during the year. Prices refer to the high season. Such prices are not contractual and Michelin Travel Publications may under no circumstances be held responsible for any possible changes.

Rooms: The prices given are the highest and lowest rates for a double room in high season. Always confirm the price when booking. Out of season, many establishments offer special deals; again, its best to ask when making the reservation.

Breakfast: Breakfast is sometimes included in the price of the room. Whenever this is not the case, we have indicated the price of breakfast per person.

Deposit and Instalments

Visitors should be aware of the conventional difference between a deposit ('arrhes' in French) and an instalment ('acompte'). In the first case, the customer may cancel his booking and so forfeit his deposit; if the hotelier is unable to provide his guest with the room, he repays double the amount his customer paid. An instalment, on the other hand, is considered a binding commitment to pay the whole tariff.

Credit Cards

If an establishment does not accept credit cards, we indicate this in its entry. Note that in giving your credit card number to secure your reservation, you are entitling the hotelier or owner of the maison d'hôte either to charge an instalment equal to the minimum tariff for your stay, to be reckoned against your final bill, or to take payment for what you have ordered and reserved, in such cases where the reservation is not cancelled within the time determined by the hotelier or the owner of the maison d'hôte.

Access and Facilities

For each establishment we give details of
• how to get there from the nearest town.
• facilities including television, swimming-pool, tennis court, sauna, children's games and an indication of whether dogs are allowed.
• handicapped access where special adaptations or arrangements have been made.

Places with that little bit extra

Three themed indexes can be found at the back of the book:

Low price: this index lists all the establishments which offer double rooms at under €50 a night.

Activity breaks: this includes all the establishments which have a swimming pool and also offer at least one other sport (hiking, riding, tennis, golf, canoeing etc.).

Discovery breaks: establishments that offer courses or theme weekends in a variety of areas.

Index

Alphabetical list of localities.

Exploring France?

Don't forget to stock up with the latest Michelin REGIONAL and LOCAL maps and titles from The Green Guide Collection. Michelin also offers an online route-planning service at www.ViaMichelin.com.

Your viewpoint

We have aimed to make this guide practical and readable and trust that it will accompany you on family outings and romantic weekends: it's written for you and you can help to make the next edition even better. Please point out any errors and omissions you spot and fill in the questionnaire at the back of the guide: all your comments and suggestions for new addresses are very welcome.

Alsace is perhaps the most romantic of France's regions, a place of fairy-tale castles guarding the foothills of the mountains, gentle vine-clad slopes and picturesque dolls' house villages perched on rocky outcrops or nestling in lush green valleys. From Colmar's Little Venice with its flower-decked balconies and famous storks to Strasbourg's Christmas market whose multi-coloured lights illuminate the magnificent cathedral or the half-timbered houses of Little France reflected in the meanders of the River Ill, an inner warmth radiates from Alsace that even the cold winter winds cannot chill. So make a beeline for the boisterous atmosphere of a brasserie and sample a real Alsace beer or head for a picturesque *winstub* – wine bar – and tuck into a steaming dish of choucroute – sauerkraut with smoked pork – and a huge slice of *kugelhof* cake, all washed down with a glass of fruity Sylvaner or Riesling wine.

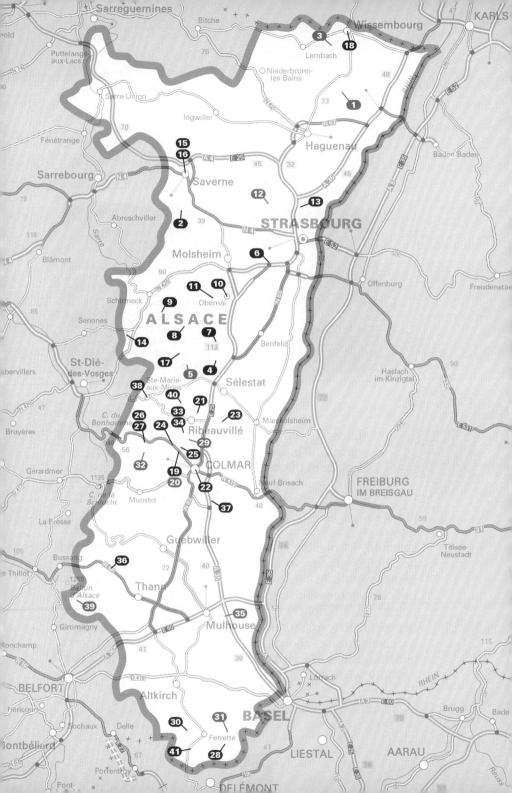

BETSCHDORF - 67660

KRUMEICH
M. Krumeich

23 rue des Potiers
67660 Betschdorf
Tel. 03 88 54 40 56
Languages : Eng., Ger.

Open all year • 3 rooms • €48 to €53, breakfast included • No table d'hôte • Garden, car park. Credit cards not accepted. Dogs not admitted • Pottery courses

The warm welcome from the owner, who is also a potter.

Situated in the heart of a village renowned for its stoneware pottery, this large property provides clean, quiet rooms decorated with elegant period furniture – including beautiful wardrobes – and a lovely shaded flower garden. The owner, the proud descendant of a long line of potters, organises introductory pottery courses all year long.

Pottery courses

Access : *15km north-east of Haguenau, towards Wissembourg on the D 263 then the D 243*

BIRKENWALD - 67440

AU CHASSEUR
M. Gass

7 rue de l'Eglise
67440 Birkenwald
Tel. 03 88 70 61 32
hotel.au-chasseur@wanadoo.fr
chasseurbirkenwald.com
Languages : Eng., Ger., Sp.

Closed in Jan • 24 rooms with bath/WC or shower/WC and television • €65 to €120; breakfast €12; half-board available • Non-smoking restaurant closed Mon and Tue and Thu lunchtimes; menus €12 (weekday lunchtimes) to €65 • Terrace, garden, car park • Heated indoor swimming pool, sauna, jacuzzi

Taking the time to enjoy the covered heated swimming pool, sauna, Jacuzzi and solarium.

This family-run hostelry, hidden behind an inviting flower-decked façade, dominates the village of Birkenwald, guaranteeing nights of peaceful slumber to even the lightest sleepers. The rooms are comfortable, pleasant and extremely well kept; a few command a view over the Vosges mountains. The owner takes pleasure in concocting tasty dishes which are a happy blend of classical and regional cooking, served in a dining room whose multicoloured wainscoting is the work of a local artist.

Game weekend in November, cooking lessons from Mar-Apr and Nov, gastronomic weekends all year

Access : *In the centre of the village between Saverne and Molsheim*

CLEEBOURG - 67160

KLEIN
Mme Klein

59 rue Principale
67160 Cleebourg
Tel. 03 88 94 50 95
annejp.klein@laposte.net

www.chez.com/cleebourg
Languages : Ger.

Open all year • 4 rooms • €42, breakfast included; half-board available • Table d'hôte €14, including drinks (evening only, closed Sundays) • Garden, car park. Credit cards not accepted. Dogs not admitted

 The lovingly preserved, authentic Alsatian décor.

This 18C-19C Alsatian house in the heart of an acclaimed wine-growing village could well prove irresistible: there's no mistaking the true Alsatian style. The peaceful rooms, all on the ground floor, are decorated with pristine antique furniture; wood is the predominant feature of the dining room which serves typical regional cuisine. Guests can relax in the pretty garden to the rear.

Access : *7km south-west of Wissembourg on the D 7, in the centre of the village*

DAMBACH-LA-VILLE - 67650

LE VIGNOBLE
M. Martin

1 rue de l'Église
67650 Dambach-la-Ville
Tel. 03 88 92 43 75
Languages : Eng., Ger., Sp.

Closed in Jan • 7 rooms, one of which has disabled access, most have bath/WC, all have television • €55; breakfast €7 • No restaurant • Private car park. Dogs not admitted

Walking along the Dambach wine path.

This hotel's architecture is characteristic of the modest winegrowers' houses dotted along the Wine Route. A narrow façade facing onto the street, only the upper residential storey of which has the traditional half-timbering, and a ground floor devoted to grape pressing equipment and the cellar. The rooms with their original oak beams are peaceful, even though the bells of the neighbouring church ring during the night! Family breakfast room.

Access : *In the centre of the village*

DIEFFENBACH-AU-VAL - 67220

LA ROMANCE
M. Geiger

17 route de Neuve-Église
67220 Dieffenbach-au-Val
Tel. 03 88 85 67 09
corinne@la-romance.net
www.la-romance.net

Open all year • 6 rooms, one of which is split-level, two have sitting rooms • €75 to €85, breakfast included • No table d'hôte • Garden, car park. Credit cards not accepted, dogs not admitted • Sauna and spa

 The modern comfort of this pretty regional residence.

Although rather difficult to find, this snug house is so comfortable that, once over the threshold, you may not want to leave! Warm welcome and spotless interior. The well-appointed, tastefully decorated rooms are named after flowers and trees and two of them overlook the valley. Add to this a warm welcome, spotless housekeeping and a garden on the edge of the forest which is the perfect spot for breakfasts in the summertime.

Access : 12km north-west of Sélestat on the N 59 and the D 424, towards Villé

ENTZHEIM - 67960

PÈRE BENOIT
M. Massé

34 route de Strasbourg
67960 Entzheim
Tel. 03 88 68 98 00
hotel.perebenoit@wanadoo.fr
www.hotel-perebenoit.com
Languages : Eng., Ger.

Closed from 30 Jul to 21 Aug and from 24 Dec to 2 Jan • 60 rooms on 2 floors, 4 of which have disabled access, all have bath/WC and television • €62 to €80; breakfast €8.50 • Air-conditioned restaurant; menu €19 to €24 • Terrace, garden, private car park. No dogs admitted in restaurant • Fitness room, sun deck

 A farmhouse full of character near Strasbourg airport.

Behind the half-timbered, red façade of this genuine 18C Alsatian farmhouse, a range of dining choices reveals a real love of good food. Take your pick from a family dining room, the adorable balcony-cum-terrace installed under a wooden gallery, a snug "winstub" – literally a "wine room", with paintings, wood panelling and earthenware stove – or a vaulted cellar serving local tartes flambées. Snug rooms, most overlooking a peaceful flowered courtyard.

Access : 12 km from Strasbourg on the A 35 (exit no 8), then take the D 400 and D 392

ITTERSWILLER - 67140

LE HOHWALD - 67140

HÔTEL WINSTUB ARNOLD
M. et Mme Simon

98 route des vins
67140 Itterswiller
Tel. 03 88 85 50 58
arnold-hotel@wanadoo.fr
www.hotel-arnold.com
Languages : Eng., Ger.

Closed 25 and 26 Dec • 29 rooms, 10 of which are in a separate wing, 1 with disabled access; all have bath/WC or shower/WC and television • €90 to €111 (€77 to €99 low season); breakfast €12; half-board available • Menus from €23 (weekdays) to €58 • Terrace, garden, car park

Filling up our shopping basket from the regional produce boutique.

The Arnold Hotel epitomises Alsace from its vineyard landscape to its spruce half-timbered façades and smart, immaculately cared-for interior. Recent renovations have added to guests' comfort and well-being without detracting from the regional character of its three buildings. The comfortable welcoming rooms overlook either the picturesque village or the vineyards. As for the winstub, its typical local décor and regional cuisine are an invitation to sample its excellent fare.

Access : *In the heart of the village, south of Obernai*

LA PETITE AUBERGE
M. Hubrecht

6 rue Principale
67140 Le Hohwald
Tel. 03 88 08 33 05
hrpetiteauberge@aol.com
www.lapetiteauberge-hohwald.com
Languages : Ger.

Closed 2 Jan to 7 Feb • 7 rooms with bath/WC and television • €61; breakfast €8; half-board available • Non-smoking restaurant; menus €15 to €27 • Terrace, car park

The split-level rooms are wonderfully spacious.

The accommodation wing of La Petite Auberge is located behind a long brand-new wooden façade. The rooms are most pleasant: 36m^2 in size, a private terrace, tastefully decorated with light wooden furniture, functional bathrooms and a sleeping area upstairs under the timber-framed roof. Meals are served in a more traditionally-inspired house with a choice of classical cuisine in the restaurant or regional dishes in the Caveau le Relais.

Access : *In the heart of the village*

NATZWILLER - 67130

OBERNAI - 67210

AUBERGE METZGER
M. Metzger

55 rue Principale
67130 Natzwiller
Tel. 03 88 97 02 42
auberge.metzger@wanadoo.fr
www.hotel-aubergemetzger.com
Languages : Eng., Ger.

Closed from 3 to 24 Jan, 21 June to 4 July, Sun evening and Mon • 16 rooms all with bath/WC or shower/WC and television • €59 to €73; breakfast €9; half-board available • Menus €13 (weekdays) to €53 • Garden

COLOMBIER
M. Baly

6/8 rue Dietrich
67210 Obernai
Tel. 03 88 47 63 33
info@hotel.colombier.com
www.hotel.colombier.com
Languages : Eng., Ger.

Open all year • 44 air-conditioned rooms with bathrooms and television; 2 have disabled access • €83 to €111; breakfast €10.50 • No restaurant • Garage

 The exquisite lush garden filled with flowers.

Set in the heart of a peaceful village in the midst of Alsace's green countryside, everything about this appealing country inn conjures up an image of peace and quiet. The rooms are tastefully and individually decorated in a modern decorative style, which provides the backdrop to period and contemporary furniture and paintings by artist friends of the family. Appetising, liberally-served regional cuisine is served in a welcoming dining room or in the shade of a pleasant terrace.

 Leave your car in the hotel garage and discover the charm of Obernai on foot.

The Colombier is proof that regional architecture and contemporary interior design can coexist happily. The flower-decked façade, which fits so perfectly into the lovely Alsace city, hides a surprising interior which is a mixture of designer furniture, modern light fittings, metal structures, half-timbered walls and bare beams. Most of the rooms are spacious and a few boast a balcony overlooking the street.

Access : *In the upper reaches of the village*

Access : *In the heart of the village*

OTTROTT-LE-HAUT - 67530

À L'AMI FRITZ
M. Fritz

8 rue des Châteaux
67530 Ottrott-le-Haut
Tel. 03 88 95 80 81
ami-fritz@wanadoo.fr
www.amifritz.com
Languages : Ger., Eng.

Closed from 18 Jan to 4 Feb • 22 rooms, 11 are air-conditioned, with bath/WC or shower/WC and television • €71 to €103; breakfast €12; half-board available • Menus €23 to €60 • Terrace, park, private car park, garage

 Sipping the red wine of Ottrot while digging into one of the chef's tasty dishes.

The hotel's name, taken from a novel by Erckmann-Chatrian, also refers to the owner of this trim Alsace house located on the heights of the village. Personalised, cosily comfortable, impeccably-kept and stunningly quiet bedrooms set the scene of the establishment. The chef's tasty regional fare is served in a pleasant dining room or in a picturesque winstub. The annex (Le Chant des Oiseaux), located 500m away in the heart of the countryside, is home to simply furnished small rooms.

Access : *4km to the west of Obernai on D 426*

PFETTISHEIM - 67370

LA MAISON DU CHARRON
M. et Mme Gass

15 rue Principale
67370 Pfettisheim
Tel. 03 88 69 60 35
mdc67@free.fr
www.maisonducharron.com
Languages : Ger.

Open all year • 5 rooms, 2 are split-level and 2 are gîtes • €44 to €53, breakfast included • No table d'hôte • Garden. Credit cards not accepted, dogs not admitted

 The personalised decoration of each room.

The owners of these two 1858 houses enthusiastically took a hand in their renovation. The master-carpenter husband undertook the individual decoration of the rooms, each of which takes its inspiration from a different type of tree - birch, maple, larch, among others - while his wife, a gifted seamstress, decorated the house with her patchworks. The small garden is very pleasant in the summer and the horses are always popular with children.

Access : *13km north-west of Strasbourg on the D 31*

REICHSTETT - 67116

AIGLE D'OR
Mme Jung

5 rue de la Wantzenau
67116 Reichstett
Tel. 03 88 20 07 87
info@aigledor.com
www.aigledor.com
Languages : Eng., Ger., It.

Closed from 24 Dec to 7 Jan and 3 to 20 Aug
• 17 rooms with bath/WC or shower/WC and
television • €65 to €99; breakfast €10 • No
restaurant • Car park • Nearby: walks along the
banks of the canal from the Marne to the Rhine

A deliciously sophisticated small family establishment.

The attractive white, half-timbered façade of
the Aigle d'Or Hotel stands near the church of
this picturesque market town near Strasbourg.
Original stained-glass windows flood the hall
with light and the breakfast room, in the
basement, is most appealing. Upstairs,
wrought-iron or Louis XVI-style furniture, wainscoting and warm fabrics more than make up
for the small size of the bedrooms.

Access : *7km northbound of Strasbourg on the
D 468 and D 37, or via the A 4 and the D 63*

SAULXURES - 67420

LA BELLE VUE
Mme Boulanger

36 rue Principale
67420 Saulxures
Tel. 03 88 97 60 23
labellevue@wanadoo.fr
www.la-belle-vue.com
Languages : Eng.

Closed from 20 to 28 Mar, 26 Jun to 5 Jul, 13 to
28 Nov and 24 to 26 Dec • 11 rooms, 7 split-level,
with shower/WC and television • €84 to €122;
breakfast €10.50; half-board available • Restaurant closed Tue and Wed, non-smoking
room; menus €19.50 to €53 • Terrace, car park
• Tennis

The delightful interior decoration, an intelligent mix of old and new.

This village inn founded in the 19C and run by
the same family for five generations has
evolved admirably over the decades. The
present-day accommodation features modern,
spacious fittings and personalised decoration
with bright woodwork, original paintings and
brightly-coloured curtains; the split-level
rooms have a pleasant sitting room. The inventive cuisine is served in a non-smoking restaurant which sports exposed timberwork and
contemporary frescoes.

Cooking lessons

Access : *In the village*

SAVERNE - 67700

LE CLOS DE LA GARENNE
Mme Schmitt

88 route du Haut-Barr
67700 Saverne
Tel. 03 88 71 20 41
clos.garenne@wanadoo.fr

www.closgarenne.com
Languages : Eng., Ger.

Open all year • 15 rooms with bath/WC or shower/WC and television • €48 to €86; breakfast €10; half-board available • Menus €16 (weekdays) to €75 • Car park, park

😊 *We most liked* **The landscaped gardens.**

This early 20C family residence is peacefully located on the edge of a forest of fir trees. It is impossible to resist the temptation to snuggle up in the individually decorated rooms furnished in a tasteful period or country style. The all-wood, snug dining room is reminiscent of an old mountain inn. The terrace overlooks a landscaped park on a hillside.

Access : *From place des Dragons take the road to Haut-Barr Castle*

L'HÔTEL EUROPE
M. Kuhry

7 rue de la Gare
67700 Saverne
Tel. 03 88 71 12 07
info@hotel-europe-fr.com
www.hotel-europe-fr.com
Languages : Eng., Ger.

Closed 21 Dec to 6 Jan • 28 rooms, 20 of which have shower/WC, 8 have bath/WC, all have television • €60.50 to €120; breakfast €9.30 • No restaurant • Garage, public car park nearby • Visits to the nearby Château des Rohan

😊 *We most liked* **The individual decoration of each room.**

Near the castle on the banks of the canal that links the Marne to the Rhine, this family-owned business has recently been partly refurbished. In keeping with the hotel's namesake, each spacious room features a different European style: the choice includes "Scandinavian", "French", "English" and "contemporary". A delightful sitting room decorated with frescoes and a Jugendstil-style breakfast room.

Access : *Near the railway station*

VILLÉ - 67220

LA BONNE FRANQUETTE
M. Schreiber

6 place du Marché
67220 Villé
Tel. 03 88 57 14 25
bonne-franquette@wanadoo.fr
hotel-bonne-franquette.com
Languages : Eng., Ger.

Closed from 25 Feb to 12 Mar, 24 June to 2 July and 28 Oct to 12 Nov • 10 rooms, 2 non-smoking, all with bath/WC or shower/WC and television • €39 to €54; breakfast €6.80; half-board available • Menus €8 (weekdays) to €39

 Being so close to the Regional Park of the Ballons des Vosges.

The white façade, hidden by flowers during the summer, invites you to venture inside this aptly named country inn, which roughly translates as "A good, simple meal". The owner's kindness and friendly welcome immediately make it clear that he has his guests' welfare at heart. Unpretentious, practical and spotlessly clean rooms. The restaurant - a favourite with the locals, which is always a good sign - has a basement and an upper room, both serving traditional fare.

Access : *In the town centre*

WISSEMBOURG - 67160

AU MOULIN DE LA WALK
M. Roger Schmidt

2 rue de la Walk
67160 Wissembourg
Tel. 03 88 94 06 44
info@moulin-walk.com
www.moulin-walk.com
Languages : Eng., Ger.

Closed from 2 to 23 Jan and from 18 Jun to 3 Jul • 25 rooms, one of which has disabled access, with bath/WC or shower/WC and television • €55 to €70; breakfast €7; half-board available • Menus €30 to €55 • Terrace, garden, car park. Dogs not admitted in rooms

 Breakfast time!

This cluster of buildings built on the foundations of an old mill, whose well-preserved wheel is still in working order, stands on the banks of the Lauter on the outskirts of the town. Most of the rooms have been refurbished with modern fittings and brand new bathrooms. Tasty, traditional fare is served in a cosy, wainscoted dining room and a pretty flower-decked terrace.

Access : *Out of the town centre, on the banks of the Lauter*

AMMERSCHWIHR - 68770

AUX ARMES DE FRANCE
M. Gaertner

1 Grand' Rue
68770 Ammerschwihr
Tel. 03 89 47 10 12
aux.armes.de.france@wanadoo.fr
www.aux-armes-de-france.com
Languages : Eng., Ger.

Closed Wed and Thu • 10 rooms with bath/WC and television • €67 to €82; breakfast €12 • Menus €25 to €45 • Garden, private car park • Located in the heart of the Alsace vineyards. Golf 1km away

 Good taste abounds in this warm Alsatian inn.

Numerous famous chefs have learnt their craft in this handsome house rebuilt after the air raids of the Second World War. Its long culinary tradition dates back to the Thirties, when the grandmother of the present chef ruled the kitchen. Spacious rooms and a bourgeois-style dining room where mouth-watering dishes are served under the watchful eye of ancestors' portraits. Definitely worth tasting!

Personal and group cooking lessons

Access : *At the entrance to the town centre*

MAISON THOMAS
Famille Thomas

41 Grand'Rue
68770 Ammerschwihr
Tel. 03 89 78 23 90
info@maisonthomas.fr

www.maisonthomas.fr
Languages : Ger.

Open all year • 4 rooms with a kitchenette and bath/WC • €44 to €47, breakfast included • No table d'hôte • Garden, car park. Credit cards not accepted • Sauna

Extremely well-appointed rooms.

This former wine-grower's house – painted an unmissable turquoise – stands in the most picturesque part of the village. Each of the spacious, well-equipped rooms carries a name and all have kitchenettes. The well thought-out garden has something for everyone: a shaded corner for afternoon naps, bower, barbecue, swings, table-tennis and boules, not forgetting the view over the vineyards. The house also boasts a sauna and keep-fit equipment.

Access : *In the village*

BERGHEIM - 68750

CHEZ NORBERT
M. Moeller

9 Grand'Rue
68750 Bergheim
Tel. 03 89 73 31 15
labacchante@wanadoo.fr
www.cheznorbert.com
Languages : Eng., Ger.

Closed from 11 to 19 Jan, 5 to 31 Mar and 2 to 9 Jul • 12 rooms and 1 apartment, all are air-conditioned, most have bath/WC and television • €75 to €110; breakfast €15; half-board available • Air-conditioned restaurant, closed Wed lunchtime, Thu and Fri lunchtime; menus €22 (weekdays) to €48 • Terrace, courtyard, private car park

Home-made cakes and jams for breakfast.

The cachet of this group of wine-growers' farms is undeniable. The colourful, half-timbered façades (14C) vie for pride of place with the other picturesque houses of this town on the Alsace Wine Route. Some of the contemporary, practical rooms are located under the eaves; avoid those overlooking the road, which are noisier. Good country fare served in a typically Alsatian restaurant or on a pleasant terrace, bedecked with geraniums in the summer.

Access : *On the main street in the centre of the village*

COLMAR - 68000

ALSACE

TURENNE
M. et Mme Helmlinger

10 route de Bâle
68000 Colmar
Tel. 03 89 21 58 58
infos@turenne.com
www.turenne.com
Languages : Eng., Ger.

Open all year • 85 rooms, 42 of which are non-smoking, all have bath/WC or shower/WC, air-conditioning and television • €62 to €72; breakfast €8 • No restaurant • Garage • Wifi internet access

A convenient distance from the old town.

Conveniently located two minutes away from the picturesque Little Venice district, you can't miss the distinctive pink and yellow façade of this large house. Spacious, refurbished double rooms some of which have traditional regional furniture. Smaller, single rooms, equally well-kept and soundproofed, are also available. Breakfasts are served in a typically Alsatian dining room. Wainscoted sitting room and bar, heaven-sent private garage and friendly family welcome.

Access : *Coming from the railway station, head for the A 35 motorway and turn left at the Elf petrol station*

LES HIRONDELLES
M. et Mme Muller

33 rue du 25-Janvier
68970 Illhaeusern
Tel. 03 89 71 83 76
hotelleshirondelles@wanadoo.fr
www.hotelleshirondelles.com
Languages : Eng., Ger.

Closed 28 Jan to 17 Mar • 19 rooms, most have shower/WC, all have television • €72 to €80, breakfast included • No restaurant • Garden, private car park • Outdoor swimming pool

L'ARBRE VERT
Famille Kieny-Wittner

1 rue Haute du Rempart
68240 Kaysersberg
Tel. 03 89 47 11 51
http://perso.orange.fr/arbrevertbellepromenade/
Languages : Ger.

Closed from 7 Jan to 15 Feb • 20 rooms with bath/WC or shower/WC and television, 14 in a separate wing • €64 to €73 (€61 to €70 low season); breakfast €8; half-board available • Non-smoking restaurant; menus €24 to €39 • Dogs not admitted in restaurant

 The swallows, which really do make the summer.

Rustic painted furniture and oak beams set the tone of the relatively soberly-decorated rooms which overlook a flowered inner courtyard or a picture-book landscape of kitchen gardens. The recent swimming pool, complete with teak sun-deck and air-conditioning in the adjacent accommodation building makes the hotel very pleasant during the hot summer months.

 A walk round this tiny Alsatian town rich in points of interest.

The birthplace of the humanitarian Dr Schweitzer, the most famous inhabitant of Kayserberg, stands side by side this hostelry comprised of two Alsace houses located on either side of a square of greenery. The low-key countrified rooms and the restaurant, renowned for its regional-inspired classical cuisine, are located in the main house. The other, called the Belle Promenade, offers more spacious, pleasant accommodation, furnished in particular with pieces painted by the lady of the house.

Access : *6km westbound of Colmar in the centre of the village*

Access : *In the centre of the village*

KIENTZHEIM - 68240

HOSTELLERIE SCHWENDI
M. et Mme Schillé

2 place Schwendi
68240 Kientzheim
Tel. 03 89 47 30 50
hotel@hotel-schwendi.com
www.hotel-schwendi.com
Languages : Eng., Ger.

Open all year (by reservation from 24 Dec to 15 Mar) • 25 rooms all with bath/WC and television, 9 with air-conditioning • €78 to €98; breakfast €9; half-board available • Restaurant closed Wed all day and Thu lunchtime and from 24 Dec to 15 Mar; menus €22 to €59 • Terrace, private car park

 The delightful welcome of the hotel owners-cum-winegrowers.

An old well, around which the terrace is laid in the summer, stands in the paved courtyard of this 17C inn with its elegant, pale yellow facade. Guests are accommodated in renovated rooms with original timber ceilings. A likeable blend of classical Louis XIII chairs and bare stone walls adds a cosy combination of rustic and bourgeois to the dining room, where wholesome country cooking is served with delightful home-made wines.

Access : *3km to the east of Kaysersberg on the D 28*

LAPOUTROIE - 68650

LES ALISIERS
M. et Mme Degouy

Lieu-dit Faudé
68650 Lapoutroie
Tel. 03 89 47 52 82
hotel@alisiers.com
www.alisiers.com
Languages : Eng., Ger.

Closed 6 Jan to 6 Feb, 21 to 25 Dec, Mon, Tue (except evenings in season) • 16 rooms, 5 are non-smoking. Rooms have bath/WC or shower/WC • €50 to €122; breakfast €9; half-board available • Menus €15 to €46 • Terrace, garden, car park

 The kindness of the staff and the owners.

All the windows of this extended farmhouse built in 1819 overlook the pleasant, rolling countryside of the Béhine Valley, whether it be from the snug and countrified or more contemporary rooms; you can choose your favourite on the hotel's website. The veranda restaurant shares the same great view; generous helpings of regional cooking, with an accent on local produce, are served in the non-smoking dining room. Pleasant garden overlooking the village of Lapoutroie.

Access : *In the upper reaches of the village, 3km to the south-west on a minor road*

LAPOUTROIE - 68650

LUTTER - 68480

DU FAUDÉ
M. et Mme Baldinger

 28 rue du Général-Dufieux
68650 Lapoutroie
Tel. 03 89 47 50 35
info@faude.com
www.faude.com
Languages : Eng., Ger.

Closed from 4 to 23 Mar and from 4 to 23 Nov • 32 rooms, 2 of which are apartments, with bath/WC or shower/WC, all have television • €62 to €92; breakfast €13; half-board available • Restaurant closed Tue and Wed; menus €20 to €75, children's menu €9 • Garden, terrace, private car park • Indoor swimming pool, fitness room, hammam, jacuzzi, skiing

 A riverside country garden.

The Baldinger family has run this traditional country inn for over 40 years during which time they have certainly mastered the art of making guests feel at home. Well-soundproofed bedrooms are spacious and comfortable. At mealtimes, you have a choice between the Faudé Gourmet, with classical fare in a muted atmosphere or the Grenier Welche, for tasty, locally sourced food served by staff in traditional costume. Attractive indoor swimming pool and fitness facilities.

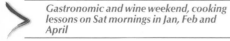

Gastronomic and wine weekend, cooking lessons on Sat mornings in Jan, Feb and April

Access : *In the centre of the village*

AUBERGE PAYSANNE
Mme Guérinol

 1 rue de Wolschwiller
68480 Lutter
Tel. 03 89 40 71 67
aubergepaysanne2@wanadoo.fr
 www.auberge-hostellerie-paysanne.com
Languages : Eng., Ger.

Closed for 2 weeks late Jan-early Feb, 2 weeks early Jul • 16 rooms at the Auberge and 9 in the separate wing, bath/WC or shower/WC, all have television • €49 to €69; breakfast €7; half-board available • Restaurant closed Tue lunchtime out of season and Mon; menus from €9.50 (weekdays) to €38.50 • Terrace, garden, car park

 The picturesque, unspoilt landscapes of the Sundgau.

This establishment does offer its own modern accommodation, but most people prefer the annexe, 200m away: a 1618 farmhouse typical of the Sundgau region, which was actually taken apart brick by brick and rebuilt here, a short distance from the Swiss border. Some of the rooms, of varying quality it must be said, have oak beamed ceilings, and a pretty flowered garden leads out towards the fields. Check-in at the main inn and sample the regional specialities and seasonal game in its dining room.

Access : *Leave Ferrette south-east bound on the D 23, at Sondersdorf take the D 21B, then at Raedersdorf go back onto the D 23*

MITTELWIHR - 68630

DOMAINE DU BOUXHOF
M. et Mme Edel

Rue du Bouxhof
68630 Mittelwihr
Tel. 03 89 47 93 67

Closed Jan to 15 Feb • 3 rooms with television and fridge; bath/WC or shower/WC • €53, breakfast included • No table d'hôte • Garden, car park. Credit cards not accepted, dogs not admitted

 Staying in a wine-growing property and trying a glass – it would be impolite to refuse!

This 17C castle flanked with square towers seems to rise out of a sea of vines. Guests can choose between two types of accommodation: modern, spotless rooms or very well-equipped cottages; those with a balcony overlooking the vineyards are the most attractive. The superb breakfast room is housed in a 15C chapel. Don't pass up a chance to visit the cellar and its oak vats where the estate's wine is made, finishing with a wine-tasting session.

Access : *In the upper part of the village, on the wine-growing estate*

MOERNACH - 68480

AUX DEUX CLEFS
Mme Enderlin

218 rue Hennin Blenner
68480 Moernach
Tel. 03 89 40 80 56
auxdeuxclefs@wanadoo.fr
 Languages : Eng., Ger.

Closed for two weeks in February, one week early Nov and from late Jul to early Aug • 7 rooms with shower/WC and television • €42 to €47; breakfast €7; half-board available • Restaurant closed Wed evening and Thu; menus €19 to €47 • Garden, car park, garage

 An afternoon nap in the pretty tree-lined garden.

A handsome half-timbered and gabled country house, characteristic of the Sundgau; look for its attractive wrought-iron sign of two crossed keys. Taste the local delicacy, fried carp, in the welcoming wood-panelled dining room, tastefully decorated with paintings. Comfortable, inviting rooms, which are being progressively renovated, occupy a wing which dates from the Sixties.

Access : *At Vieux-Ferrette leave the D 432 for the D 473 which goes through Koestlach and Moernach*

OLTINGUE - 68480

ORBEY - 68370

MOULIN DE HUTTINGUE
M. Thomas Antoine

68480 Oltingue
Tel. 03 89 40 72 91
Languages : Eng., Ger., Sp.

Closed in Jan and Feb • 4 rooms • €55 to €85, breakfast included • Car park, garden, terrace. Credit cards not accepted. Dogs not admitted

FERME DU BUSSET
Mme Batôt

33 lieu-dit Busset
68370 Orbey
Tel. 03 89 71 22 17
fabienne.batot@wanadoo.fr
www.fermedubusset.com
Languages : Ger., Eng.

Closed 24 Dec to 1 Jan • 6 rooms • €48, breakfast included • No table d'hôte • Garden, car park. Credit cards not accepted. Dogs not admitted

 The panoramic view over the Orbey Valley.

A steep road winds its way up to this farmhouse, which still breeds its own poultry and sheep, high on a lush green plateau at an altitude of 600m. Choose from self-catering cottages or bed and breakfast rooms: the latter are lined in wood and while not enormous are very well-kept and quiet. Before leaving, make sure you stock up on cheese, cooked meats and home-made jams.

 The decorative features which bear witness to the mill's long history.

The Franco-Swiss border is only a short distance from this 17C wheat mill on the banks of the Ill, which is little more than a stream here. The rooms, all upstairs, are quite simply appointed on the whole. The superb loft under the eaves has been fitted with a useful kitchenette. Breakfast is served in a dining room complete with magnificent wooden pillars or on the terrace when the weather permits.

Access : *1km to the east of Orbey on a minor road*

Access : *1.5km south of Oltingue on the D 21e*

RIQUEWIHR - 68340

L'ORIEL
Mme Wendel

3 rue des Écuries-Seigneuriales
68340 Riquewihr
Tel. 03 89 49 03 13
info@hotel-oriel.com
www.hotel-oriel.com
Languages : Eng., Ger.

Open all year • 22 rooms, 3 of which are split-level, with shower/WC or bath/WC, all have television • €67 to €97; breakfast €9.50 • No restaurant • Shaded terrace • Wifi internet access

 Breakfast served in the inner courtyard in summertime.

The frontage of this 16C country home is adorned with a handsome two-storey oriel window and an amusing wrought-iron sign; the delightful maze of corridors and staircases bear witness to the house's old age. The rooms, in the progress of being renovated, are decorated in a variety of styles, ranging from rustic to more modern – families generally prefer one of the split-level rooms.

Access : *From the town hall take Rue du Général de Gaulle then the first street on the right*

RIQUEWIHR - 68340

LE SARMENT D'OR
M. et Mme Merckling

4 rue du Cerf
68340 Riquewihr
Tel. 03 89 86 02 86
info@riquewihr-sarment-dor.com
www.riquewihr-sarment-dor.com
Languages : Eng., Ger.

Closed from 8 Jan to 4 Feb and 1 week in Jul • 9 rooms, 2 of which are split-level, most have bath/WC, all have television • €60 to €80; breakfast €8 • Restaurant closed Sun evening, Mon and Tue lunchtime; menus €20 to €48 • No dogs admitted in rooms

 The owners' attentive welcome.

The Sarment d'Or – or golden vine – has put down its roots in a quiet street lined with handsome 16C houses. A spiral staircase leads up to the cosy, modern bedrooms. The snug, warm dining rooms are characteristic of Alsatian interior decoration with pine panelling and dark beams lit up by the crackling flames of a welcoming log fire.

Access : *From the town hall square, drive to the end of Rue du Général de Gaulle and turn left (pedestrian street)*

SAINT-AMARIN - 68550

RIXHEIM - 68170

AUBERGE DU MEHRBÄCHEL
M. et Mme Kornacker

Route de Geishouse
68550 Saint-Amarin
Tel. 03 89 82 60 68
kornacker@wanadoo.fr
Languages : Eng., Ger.

LE CLOS DU MÛRIER
Mme Volpatti

42 Grande-Rue
68170 Rixheim
Tel. 03 89 54 14 81
Languages : Ger., It.

Open all year • 5 rooms with kitchenettes, bathrooms with separate WC • €64; breakfast €8 • No table d'hôte • Garden, car park. Dogs not admitted

Closed for one week early Nov, Mon evening, Thu evening and Fri • 23 rooms located in 2 buildings, with bath/WC or shower/WC • €55 to €60; breakfast €9; half-board available • Air-conditioned restaurant; menus €20 (weekdays) to €46 • Car park. Dogs not admitted • Ideal for rests and walking

 Toasting your toes by the warm stove after a hard day's trekking.

 The spacious, comfortable rooms.

This venerable 16C Alsatian house has been tastefully renovated. Old beams blend well with a modern décor and each bedroom has its own kitchenette. On the leisure side, the house has a pleasant walled courtyard and the owners are happy to lend bicycles to guests.

This old farmhouse built on the edge of a forest of fir trees, so characteristic of the Vosges scenery, has been in the family since 1886. Half the simple but spacious and well-kept rooms have balconies and most of them overlook the wonderful Rossberg mountain range. Game and regional dishes are served in the air-conditioned dining room, its walls are adorned with hunting trophies. A hiking trail runs past the inn, ideal for walkers!

Access : *Between Thann and Bussang, drive for 4km on the Mehrbächel road*

Access : *6km eastbound from Mulhouse, drive towards Basle, in the centre of Rixheim*

SAINTE-CROIX-EN-PLAINE - 68127

37

AU MOULIN
M. et Mme Woeffle

Route d'Herrlisheim
68127 Sainte-Croix-en-Plaine
Tel. 03 89 49 31 20
hotelaumoulin@wanadoo.fr
www.aumoulin.net
Languages : Eng., Ger.

Open from 1 Apr to 3 Nov • 16 rooms with bath/WC, almost all have television • €58 to €80; breakfast €8 • Menus from €15 to €30 (closed Sun) • Garden, car park • Small museum about Alsace in the inner courtyard

 Lingering over breakfast in the enchanting flowered courtyard.

With its flowered courtyard and half-timbered buildings, this former flour-mill, built in 1880, represents a haven of peace and quiet, just a short distance from an interchange on the A 35! The sizeable rooms are practical and tastefully decorated with cane furniture. Some overlook the peaks of the Vosges, while others look down on the plain; all are wonderfully quiet. Interesting mini-museum on the Alsace of yesteryear.

Access : *10km southbound from Colmar on the D 201, then at Sainte-Croix-en-Plaine take the D 1*

SAINTE-MARIE-AUX-MINES - 68160

38

AUX MINES D'ARGENT
Mme Willmann

8 rue du Docteur-Weisgerber
68160 Sainte-Marie-aux-Mines
Tel. 03 89 58 55 75
Languages : Ger.

Open all year • 9 rooms with shower/WC and television • €45 to €55; breakfast €6; half-board available • Menus €10 to €32 • Terrace

 The busy atmosphere surrounding the famous Mineral, Gem And Fossil Show (June).

The mullioned windows of the façade testify to the old age of this house, said to have been built in 1596 by a miner who would appear to have struck it rich! The original spiral staircase leads up to the rooms, graced with large windows and furniture dating from 1900 or thereabouts. The family dining room, in the "winstub" style, is embellished with wood carvings which depict the miners' lives: the seam at Ste Marie was mined from the 9C to the 18C.

Access : *In the centre, in the street parallel to the main road*

SEWEN - 68290

LA VILLA DU LAC
Mme Rioual

2 route du Ballon
68290 Sewen
Tel. 03 89 82 98 38
villadulac.sewen@tv-com.net
 www.villa-du-lac-alsace.com
Languages : Ger.

Closed Jan • 6 non-smoking rooms, all with bath/WC or shower/WC • €48 to €58, breakfast included • Table d'hôte €22 (closed Sun) (evenings only) • Garden, library, television room, car park. Credit cards not accepted, dogs not admitted in restaurant

The pleasant peaceful environment of the house.

This 1930's style villa, at the foot of the Ballon d'Alsace and opposite Lake Sewen, makes a perfect departure point for walking trips. On your return, dig into the tasty Alsatian dishes prepared by the mistress of the house with local farm produce. Then, after a good night's sleep in one of the rooms overlooking the lake or the forest, devour a generous breakfast, composed of, depending on the season, strudel, Christmas cake or fruit pie.

Access : *400m outside the village, towards Ballon d'Alsace on the D 466 opposite Lake Sewen*

THANNENKIRCH - 68590

AUBERGE LA MEUNIÈRE
M. et Mme Dumoulin

30 rue Sainte-Anne
68590 Thannenkirch
Tel. 03 89 73 10 47
info@aubergelameuniere.com
 www.aubergelameuniere.com
Languages : Ger., Eng., It., Sp.

Closed 20 Dec to 20 Mar • 25 rooms at the rear of the building. Rooms have bath/WC or shower/WC, all have television • €50 to €90; breakfast €7; half-board available • Restaurant closed Mon-Wed lunchtimes; menus €13 (weekdays) to €38 • Terrace, car park, garage • Sauna, fitness room, table-tennis, billiards

The restful view of the forest, from some of the bathrooms!

The imposing flowered façade of this inn conceals a host of attractions. Almost all the rooms are rear-facing – avoid those overlooking the street – with a view of the Bergenbach Valley and the towers of Haut-Koenigsbourg Castle, which film buffs may recognise as the location of Jean Renoir's anti-war masterpiece "La Grande Illusion". The restaurant is decorated in a delightful rustic style and the terrace opens out onto the splendid Vosges scenery.

Access : *Between Ribeauvillé and Sélestat, in a village very near Haut-Koenisbourg*

WINKEL - 68480

41

AU CERF
M. Koller

76 rue Principale
68480 Winkel
Tel. 03 89 40 85 05
g.koller@tiscali.fr

Closed 6 to end of Feb • 6 rooms upstairs with bath/WC, some have television • €46 to €59; breakfast €6.50; half-board available • Menus €12 to €25 • Dogs not admitted in rooms • Hiking

The family atmosphere behind these red walls.

The smart red frontage of this inn near the Swiss border cannot be missed. The rather bare rooms are tiled and furnished practically; nearly all have been recently renovated and the proverbial Swiss obsession with cleanliness has clearly made it over the border here. Family dining rooms in an up-to-date "winstub" style. Bring a rucksack and walking stick and explore the beautiful Sundgau region and the source of the Ill along countless footpaths.

Access : *In the centre of the village*

AQUITAINE

Friendly Aquitaine has welcomed mankind since pre-historic times. Its varied mosaic of landscapes is as distinctive as its inhabitants' dedication to hospitality, invariably spiced with a generous sprinkling of forthright rural humour. No stay in Aquitaine would be complete without visiting at least one of Bordeaux' justly famous châteaux and vineyards. Afterwards head for the "Silver Coast", prized by surfers and rugby fans alike, and sample delicious Basque gâteau, have a drink in a tapas bar or even take ringside seats for a bullfight! This rugged yet sunny land between the Pyrenees and the Atlantic has always been fiercely proud of its identity and the inhabitants of the Basque country still celebrate their time-honoured traditions in truly vigorous style. If you spend a little time in one these sleepy Basque villages, all of which sport the region's colours, red and green, you will be astounded by the ease with which they suddenly burst into spirited song and games.

ANNESSE-ET-BEAULIEU - 24430

CHÂTEAU DE SIORAC
M. Serrano

Route de Périgueux
24430 Annesse-et-Beaulieu
Tel. 05 53 07 64 53
serrano@chateaudesiorac.com
www.chateaudesiorac.com
Languages : Eng., Sp.

Closed Jan to Feb • 6 non-smoking rooms, 5 of which are upstairs, all have shower/WC • €80 to €100, breakfast included • Table d'hôte €30 (evenings only) • Park, car park. Credit cards not accepted, dogs not admitted • Outdoor swimming pool

 Staying in this chateau that dates from 1550 is a unique experience.

It must have taken a great deal of patience and work to restore this castle, but the result is well worth the effort. The superb studded front door opens onto an impressive sitting room and dining room lined in wood from ceiling to floor. The rooms are all generously proportioned and adorned with fine old furniture and king-size beds. Those in the towers have huge bathrooms. Table d'hôte meals in the evenings with Spanish or Périgord specialities, by request.

Access : *7km eastbound from St-Astier, on the D 3 and Périgueux road*

BADEFOLS-SUR-DORDOGNE - 24150

CÔTÉ RIVAGE
Mme de Roton-Couderc

Au bourg
24150 Badefols-sur-Dordogne
Tel. 05 53 23 65 00
coterivage@online.fr
www.cote-dordogne.com
Languages : Eng.

Open 30 Apr to mid-Oct, closed Sun • 7 air-conditioned rooms • €55 to €95; breakfast €9; half-board available • Menu €25 to €32 including beverages • Terrace, garden. No dogs admitted

 Cutting through the garden to walk along the banks of the Dordogne.

This welcoming, restored house is located between the presbytery and a fishermen's house, a few steps from the Dordogne River. Spotless walls, colourful curtains, antique furniture and air-conditioning make the rooms very pleasant. The bar and sitting room are decorated with old advertising gadgets, while beams, bare stone walls and wrought iron furniture set the contemporary tone of the dining room which leads into a pleasant terrace. Fresh, local produce and a fine wine menu of local vintages.

Access : *On the banks of the Dordogne*

BAYAC - 24150

LE RELAIS DE LAVERGNE
Mme Pillebout

« La Vergne »
24150 Bayac
Tel. 05 53 57 83 16
relaisdelavergne@wanadoo.fr
Languages : Eng.

Open all year • 5 rooms upstairs, one apartment with disabled access, all have bath or shower • €60 to €65, breakfast included • Table d'hôte €23 (evenings only) • Park, terrace, car park. Credit cards not accepted, no dogs admitted • Outdoor swimming pool, games room

The tranquillity of this handsome 17C manor house.

The peaceful appeal of this house is such that guests often wish they had planned to stay longer. The attentive welcome of the two hostesses, the tranquil atmosphere and mouth-watering smells wafting from the kitchen never fail to enchant. Light, airy bedrooms combine the charm of yesteryear with modern-day comforts. The spacious restaurant and inner courtyard provide a perfect setting for elegant dining.

Access : *3km to the south-west of Bayac on the D 27, then Issigeac road and path on the left*

BOURDEILLES - 24310

CHAMBRE D'HÔTE L'AMBROISIE
M. Joch

Grand'Rue
24310 Bourdeilles
Tel. 05 53 04 24 51
jc.joch@wanadoo.fr
www.best-of-perigord.tm.fr
Languages : Eng.

Closed 1 week in Feb • 5 rooms, all have bath/WC or shower/WC • €58 to €70, breakfast included • Table d'hôte €23 to €30, drinks included (evenings only) • Terrace, garden, television room. Credit cards not accepted, no dogs admitted

The availability and kindness of the owners.

The spirit and charm of Périgord reign throughout this handsome 18C property located in the town centre just a few steps from the castle. The rooms, furnished with antiques, sport the fresh tangy colours of the spices after which they are named (Curry, Paprika, Anis, etc.); some have retained the original bare walls and beams. The tasty dishes concocted by the lady of the house are served in the garden under the shade of olive trees in fine weather.

Theme stays on oenology and golf

Access : *In the town centre*

BOURG-DES-MAISONS - 24320

DOMAINE DE TEINTEILLAC
M. Pin

Route de Chapdeuil
24320 Bourg-des-Maisons
Tel. 05 53 91 51 03
www.teinteillac.com

Open all year • 4 non-smoking rooms, all have bathrooms • €60, breakfast included • Table d'hôte €18 to €30 • Terrace, park, private car park. Credit cards not accepted, no dogs admitted

The authentic beauty of the château, parkland and surrounding countryside.

This immense estate tucked away in the countryside and removed from the bustle of urban life, is home to a remarkable 15C château, currently undergoing renovation. The elegantly furnished bedrooms further enhance the appeal of the location. The farm-inn serves excellent regional dishes made from locally grown organic produce. The untamed parkland is perfect for long country walks.

Access : *2km northbound on the D 99 and D 106, Chapdeuil road*

BRANTÔME - 24310

LES HABRANS
M. Falcoz

Les Habrans
24310 Brantôme
Tel. 05 53 05 58 84
leshabrans@aol.com
 Languages : Eng.

Closed from 30 Oct to 1 May • 5 rooms, 4 of which are on the first floor; all have bath/WC or shower/WC • €50, breakfast included • No table d'hôte • Terrace, garden, kitchen available for guests, internet access. Credit cards not accepted

 Boating down the Dronne.

The riverside setting of this unpretentious little house is without question its main asset. The simple rooms are tastefully decorated; those on the first floor under the eaves have sloped ceilings and windows overlooking the river. The ground-floor room has direct access outdoors. When the weather is fine, guests can tuck into breakfast on the delightful terrace under a vine arbour.

Access : *In the lane opposite the gendarmerie (police station)*

BRANTÔME - 24310

LA MAISON FLEURIE
Mme Robinson

54 rue Gambetta
24310 Brantôme
Tel. 05 53 35 17 04
info@maisonfleurie.net
www.maisonfleurie.net
Languages : Eng.

Open all year • 5 non-smoking rooms • €65 to €90, breakfast included • No table d'hôte • No dogs admitted • Outdoor swimming pool

 Staying in the heart of the hometown of the 16C court chronicler Brantôme.

This 19C property, in the shadow of the elegant Romanesque belfry of the abbey, boasts a number of attractions: a convenient town centre location, exemplary welcome, excellent value for money and above all, its charming, comfortable rooms. Whenever the weather permits, generous breakfasts are served in the flowered courtyard and the small swimming pool is always appreciated during the hot weather.

Access : *In the town centre*

BUSSEROLLES - 24360

DOMAINE DE LEYMERONNIE
M. Zucchi

À Leymeronnie
24360 Busserolles
Tel. 05 53 56 89 08

 contact@domainedeleymeronnie.com
http://www.domainedeleymeronnie.com

Open all year • 5 rooms and 3 gîtes, with shower/WC • €48 to €58, breakfast included • Table d'hôte €16 • Park, terrace. Credit cards not accepted • Outdoor swimming pool, games field

 The relaxing tranquillity of a walk in the countryside under the chestnut trees.

It is difficult to believe that this old farmhouse was completely in ruins just a few years ago, such is the quality of restoration that has revived its charm of yesteryear without detracting from its appeal. Modern fixtures and fittings blend in perfectly with the setting, whether in the gîtes or in the rooms. The spacious rooms are adorned with functional furniture. The site is surrounded by 9ha of greenery, with a swimming pool and a multi-sports ground. Table d'hôte meals by reservation.

Access : *In the centre of the hamlet*

CARSAC-AILLAC - 24200

LA DÉSIRADE
M. Paul François

Route de Gourdon
24200 Carsac-Aillac
Tel. 05 53 29 52 47
contact@ladesirade-dordogne.com
www.ladesirade-dordogne.com

Open all year • 2 rooms and 1 gîte, all with
bath/WC or shower/WC • €75, breakfast
included • No table d'hôte • Park. Credit cards
not accepted, dogs not admitted • Outdoor
swimming pool, bicycles rented

DOMAINE LACOSTE
Mme Antoine et M. Pasche

« Lacoste »
24200 Carsac-Aillac
Tel. 05 53 59 58 81
domaine.lacoste@wanadoo.fr
www.domainelacoste.com

Open all year. • 4 rooms upstairs, all have
bathrooms • €60 (€56 low season), breakfast
included • Table d'hôte €18 • Terrace, garden,
car park. Credit cards not accepted, no dogs
allowed • Outdoor swimming pool

**The distinguished charm of the
French-style garden.**

Within the stone walls of this impressive Perigord home, beautifully restored to its former
glory, are very attractively decorated rooms.
Some are almost daring in style, as in the dining
room where the glass and wrought-iron table
rubs shoulders with a huge fireplace and an
unusual pebble stone floor. The rooms, all of
which are new, sport tastefully chosen matching fabrics and they all have direct access to the
splendid park and swimming pool. Faultlessly
looked after, friendly welcome.

**Lazing by the swimming pool and enjoying
the view of the valley.**

Located in the upper part of town, this traditional old Périgord townhouse, renovated and
extended, enjoys a sumptuous view over the
Dordogne and Montfort Castle. A harmonious
colour scheme of blue, beige and yellow adorns
the bedrooms, decorated with a tasteful combination of classical furniture. In a recently
extended wing, the new owners, chefs by
trade, deploy their talents and experience to
the delight of gourmets.

Access : *In the upper part of the village*

Access : *On the Gourdon road*

CÉNAC-ET-SAINT-JULIEN - 24250

LA GUÉRINIÈRE
M. et Mme Demassougne

« Baccas »
24250 Cénac-et-Saint-Julien
Tel. 05 53 29 91 97
contact@la-gueriniere-dordogne.com
www.la-gueriniere-dordogne.com
Languages : Eng.

Closed from 2 Nov to 1 Apr • 6 rooms upstairs, all with shower/WC and 2 gîtes • €75 to €90, breakfast included, half-board available • Table d'hôte €21 • Terrace, park, car park. Credit cards not accepted, no dogs admitted • Outdoor swimming pool, tennis, bicycles, golf

 Sampling the tasty meals made with fresh farm produce.

This 18C manor farm, extensively remodelled over the centuries, is reminiscent of a charterhouse. Each of the extremely spacious rooms - with bare stone walls, period furniture and tasteful fabrics - is named after a flower. Cats, dogs and farmyard animals enjoy the run of the extensive grounds, to the invariable delight of children.

Access : *On the D 46 road to Gourdon*

CÉNAC-ET-SAINT-JULIEN - 24250

LA TOUILLE
M. et Mme Barry

Route de l'Église
24250 Cénac-et-Saint-Julien
Tel. 05 53 28 35 25
sbarry.latouille@wanadoo.fr

 www.sarlat-en-perigord.com/latouille

Open all year • 4 rooms, 1 of which is upstairs, all with bathrooms • €31 to €36; breakfast €5 • No table d'hôte • Garden, car park

 The immaculately cared for rooms.

The rooms of this villa tucked away in one of the village's peaceful streets, have all been renovated: those on the ground-floor feature the simple charm of iron bedsteads and pretty fabrics, while the one upstairs is slightly cosier with wooden country-style furniture. Depending on the season, breakfast is served in the veranda or under the pergola. Children's play area in the garden. Friendly welcome.

Access : *5km southeast of La Roque-Gageac on the D 703 and D 46, towards Gourdon then the D 50 towards Saint-Cybranet, at Cénac*

LA ROQUE-GAGEAC - 24250

CHERVAL - 24320

LES POUYADES
M. et Mme Truffaux

24320 Cherval
Tel. 05 53 91 02 96

Open all year • 3 non-smoking rooms upstairs, with bath/WC or shower/WC • €75 to €85, breakfast included • No table d'hôte • Park, car park. Credit cards not accepted, dogs not admitted

LA BELLE ÉTOILE
M. Ongaro

Le bourg
24250 La Roque-Gageac
Tel. 05 53 29 51 44
hotel.belle-etoile@wanadoo.fr
 Languages : Eng.

Open from late Mar to early Nov • 15 rooms with bath/WC and television • €50 to €75; breakfast €8.50; half-board available • Menus €25 to €40 • Terrace, garage • Canoeing, swimming, fishing

 Floating down the Dordogne in a "gabarre".

This fine old creamy-coloured stone house perched on the cliff commands a wonderful view over the peaceful meanders of the Dordogne. The bedrooms have been painted white and most are furnished in a period style. The typical Périgordian repertoire, served in two pleasant dining rooms, or in the summer, under a trellis, will tempt even the most refined of palates. Numerous nearby leisure activities, including canoeing, swimming and fishing.

 The mixture of elegance and simplicity.

Set in a vast park with age-old trees, this handsome mansion has an immense hall adorned with four pillars. A staircase leads up to three tastefully decorated rooms, each of which has a comfortable new bathroom. The most spacious room is equipped with a desk set off by light-coloured wall coverings and lit up by two windows. Breakfasts are served in a period dining room furnished with family heirlooms. Guests are greeted with a friendly smile.

Access : *On the D 703, between the cliff and the river*

Access : *10km southwest on the D708, Verteillac road, then a minor road*

LANQUAIS - 24150

15

DOMAINE DE LA MARMETTE
Mme Rose

 « La Crabe », à Bournazel
24150 Lanquais
Tel. 05 53 24 99 13
lamarmette@aol.com
http://www.bergerac-tourisme.com/
annonces/chbmarmette.asp

Open mid-Mar to late Oct • 5 rooms on garden level, all with shower/WC • €59 to €69, breakfast included; half-board available • Table d'hôte €18 to €23 (evenings only) • Garden, terrace, car park. Credit cards not accepted, no dogs admitted • Outdoor swimming pool

 Back to basics in a land of open fields.

This 16C farm and outbuildings dotted with lawns and countless clumps of flowers is almost a little hamlet in itself. The former loose-boxes have been turned into bedrooms on the ground floor and each one is decorated with a personalised fabric, chest of drawers and a wrought-iron bed. A sitting room, library and dining room-conservatory are located in the main house. A kitchen is also available for use by guests.

Access : *Take the Faux road along the D 27, then turn left towards Bournazel and continue for 200m after leaving town*

LE BUGUE - 24260

16

MAISON OLÉA
Mme Nardou

 La Combe-de-Leygue
24260 Le Bugue
Tel. 05 53 08 48 93
info@olea-dordogne.com
www.olea-dordogne.com
Languages : Eng., Sp.

Open all year • 5 rooms, all with bath/WC or shower/WC • €70 to €85 (€60 to €75 low season); breakfast included • No table d'hôte • Garden, car park. Credit cards not accepted, dogs admitted by request • Heated outdoor swimming pool

 Lazing about on terraces of the rooms, overlooking the swimming pool and valley.

Though recently built, this house has faithfully upheld the style and tradition of local architecture. South-facing, it overlooks a superb overflow saltwater swimming pool with the Vézère Valley in the distance. On the ground floor you will be met with Moorish touches, murals, red-brick floor tiles and a stunning veranda-cum-winter garden. The immense (air-conditioned) rooms upstairs feature immaculate walls, pedestal tables draped in lace, antique furniture and exquisite bedding. Blissfully calm!

Access : *5km to the east of Le Bugue on the D 703, towards Sarlat-la-Canéda and then a minor road on the left*

LE FLEIX - 24130

LES EYZIES-DE-TAYAC - 24620

LES TROIS CHÊNES
M. Bernard

24130 Le Fleix
Tel. 05 53 24 15 89
les-trois-chenes@wanadoo.fr

Open all year • 5 rooms, one of which has disabled access, all with bath/WC or shower/WC • €55 to €62, breakfast included • Table d'hôte €13 including drinks • Garden, sitting room with television, car park. Credit cards not accepted, dogs not admitted

HOSTELLERIE DU PASSEUR
M. Brun

Place de la Mairie
24620 Les Eyzies-de-Tayac
Tel. 05 53 06 97 13
hostellerie-du-passeur@perigord.com
www.hostellerie-du-passeur.com
Languages : Eng., Sp.

Open early Apr to early Nov • 19 rooms on 3 floors, most have shower/WC, some have bath/WC, all have television • €65 to €120; breakfast €8; half-board available • Restaurant closed Mon and Tue lunchtimes (low season); menus €17 to €50 • Terrace, car park

The home-made foie gras which can be bought in the hotel or from its website.

This handsome stone house covered in Virginia creeper stands in the heart of the Périgord capital, known for its prehistoric heritage. The stylish, cheerful rooms all sport bright colours; some overlook the cliffs dotted with oak trees. Diners can choose from a traditional dining room complete with an attractive stone fireplace, a bright conservatory or a country terrace under lime-trees facing the Vézère, in all of which guests can relax and savour the hotel's renowned regional dishes.

The intimacy of the small walled park and its three oak trees.

Almost hidden behind its gates, this blue-shuttered house on the outskirts of the town is home to five rooms decorated in matching colours. The blue room, with direct access outside, has been designed for disabled guests. The others, accessible via a handsome wooden staircase, vary between elegance and cosy charm, but all are equally well kept. Breakfasts are served in the dining room amid antique furniture or on a shaded terrace.

Access : *In the town centre, not far from La Vézère*

Access : *In the town*

LES EYZIES-DE-TAYAC - 24620

19

LE MOULIN DE LA BEUNE
M. Soulié

2 rue du Moulin-Bas
24620 Les Eyzies-de-Tayac
Tel. 05 53 06 94 33
contact@moulindelabeune.com
moulindelabeune.com
Languages : Eng., Hungarian

Open from Apr to Oct • 20 rooms with bath/WC or shower/WC, all have television • €59; breakfast €7; half-board available • Menus €29 to €55 • Terrace, garden, car park. No dogs admitted in restaurant

 Talking into the early hours of the morning on the riverside terrace.

The attractive stone walls of this former seed and sawmill now house a charming hotel-restaurant. All the pleasant, tastefully decorated rooms enjoy peace and quiet and the stylish wood-panelled dining room commands views of the wonderfully preserved paddle wheel and the garden and river. The setting, on the banks of the Beune, is quite idyllic in fine weather.

Access : *In the town centre, off the road on the banks of the Beune*

LISLE - 24350

20

LE PIGEONNIER DE PICANDINE
M. et Mme Lacourt

La Picandine
24350 Lisle
Tel. 05 53 03 41 93
picandine@aol.com
www.picandine.com

Closed 15 Nov to 15 Feb • 5 rooms with shower/WC or bath/WC • €51, breakfast included; half-board available • Table d'hôte €21 • Terrace, car park. Credit cards not accepted, no dogs admitted • Outdoor swimming pool

 The sweeping view over the Périgord countryside.

This lovely 17C farmhouse is graced with two-hundred-year-old chestnut trees in the inner courtyard. Stone walls and wood beams set the tone for the bedrooms in the main wing, while two suites in the renovated barn are well suited to families. It's an ideal place to unwind: snuggle up with a good book in the cosy sitting room-library or treat yourself to a game of billiards.

Access : *From Lisle, take D 1 towards Périgueux, then take the third turning on the right*

MARNAC - 24220

MEYRALS - 24220

LA GRANDE MARQUE
Mme Cockcroft

24220 Marnac
Tel. 05 53 31 61 63
grande.marque@perigord.com
www.lgminfrance.com

Open all year • 6 rooms with bathrooms, 1 with disabled access • €70 to €75; breakfast €7 • Table d'hôte €28 to €32 • Terrace, park, car park. Credit cards not accepted, no dogs allowed in restaurant • Outdoor swimming pool

LA BÉLIE
Mme Baltzer

L'Abeille
24220 Meyrals
Tel. 05 53 59 55 82
contact@perigord-labelie.com
www.perigord-labelie.com
Languages : Eng., Sp.

Closed 1 Feb to 30 Mar • 3 non-smoking rooms, 1 in a separate wing, all have shower/WC • €80 to €120, breakfast included • Table d'hôte €25 (evenings only) • Terrace, garden, car park. Credit cards not accepted, dogs not admitted

 The owners' affable hospitality.

This traditional Perigord house has been beautifully renovated by a young architect, who endeavoured to retain the site's original appeal whilst adding contemporary touches: the bathrooms combine modern wash basins with old beams and the bedrooms sport a tasteful mixture of unusual objects and furniture and extremely tasteful fabrics. The table d'hôte is essentially regional in inspiration, but the owner also adores preparing dishes gleaned from her well-travelled past.

 Strolling round the magnificent ten-acre park.

This wonderful 17C Périgord estate, perched on the upper reaches of Marnac, commands a sumptuous view of the Dordogne Valley and the quaint village of Siorac-en-Périgord. The three rooms and the apartment under the eaves are a pleasant combination of simplicity and good taste. Two rooms are available in another wing, as well as two gîtes, a cottage and a studio. The estate offers a wide range of leisure activities, with a fitness room, sauna and tennis court.

Access : *8km along the Sarlat road, towards Meyrals and a place known as l'Abeille*

Access : *9km to the north-east on the D 703, take the road to Sarlat and then turn right*

NONTRON - 24300

LA MAISON DES BEAUX ARTS
Mme Delia

7 avenue du Général-Leclerc
24300 Nontron
Tel. 05 53 56 39 77
delia@deliacavers.co.uk
www.la-maison-des-beaux-arts.com

Open all year • 5 rooms and 1 gîte with bath/WC or shower/WC • €65 to €79, breakfast included, • No table d'hôte • Garden. Credit cards not accepted, dogs not admitted • Outdoor swimming pool

 A little whiff of Britain in the heart of green Périgord.

An artist who enjoys sharing her passion, the lady of the house happily welcomes guests to her blue-shuttered home. On the ground floor, the workshop, which doubles as a showroom, welcomes budding artists during painting courses. Furnished with a splendid ancient farm table where breakfast is served, the veranda commands a matchless view of the valley. The rooms are very colourful, sometimes surprisingly so; our favourite is the one whose superb terrace overlooks the Garden of Arts.

Access : *Next door to the Tourist office*

PAULIN - 24590

CHAMBRE D'HÔTE LA NOYERAIE
Mme Tribier

24590 Paulin
Tel. 05 53 28 81 88
pleinefage@free.fr
www.pleinefage.com

Open all year • 4 non-smoking rooms and 1 apartment upstairs, two of which are air-conditioned; all have bath/WC and television • €40, breakfast included • Table d'hôte €13 drinks included • Park, car park. Credit cards not accepted, dogs not admitted • Outdoor swimming pool

 The 40ha of farmland, walnut trees and a truffle grove.

Despite its recent foundation, this establishment has already earned itself the fame of television. Nothing could be less surprising in view of the quality of the five rooms with wooden floors and light wall coverings installed in the restored stone barn. Three of the rooms boast a view of the Périgord Noir. A vast terrace overlooks the pool and meals are served in the walnut grove. Farm produce takes pride of place on the table. Courses in preparing duck dishes are organised out of season.

Access : *In the centre of the town*

SAGELAT - 24170

LE BRANCHAT
M. et Mme Ginioux

Lieu-dit de Branchat
24170 Sagelat
Tel. 05 53 28 98 80
info@lebranchat.com
www.lebranchat.com
Languages : Eng., Sp.

Open Apr to Oct • 8 rooms, all with bath/WC or shower/WC • €65 to €72 (€53 to €63 low season); breakfast included • Table d'hôte €25 • Children's play area, park, car park. Dogs not admitted • Outdoor swimming pool, ponies

 The two rooms with a private terrace and a view of the lofty village of Belvès.

The quality of the restoration lavished on the sheepfold, cowshed, barn and farmhouse, now turned into chambres d'hôte, is quite outstanding. White walls and parquet flooring and wooden furniture set the tone. Surrounded by some 12 acres of valleys, woods and hazel trees, you won't have time to count the sheep at night! On the leisure side: swimming pool, walks in the park or pony riding.

Access : *3km south of Belvès on the D 710, towards Fumel and then a minor road on the left*

SAINT-CRÉPIN-ET-CARLUCET - 24590

LES CHARMES DE CARLUCET
M. et Mme Edgar

Carlucet
24590 Saint-Crépin-et-Carlucet
Tel. 05 53 31 22 60
lescharmes@carlucet.com
www.carlucet.com
Languages : Eng.

Closed from 1 Dec to 1 Feb • 4 non-smoking rooms on two floors, one with disabled access, and 1 gîte, all have bath/WC or shower/WC and television • €75 to €99 (€65 to €89 low season), breakfast included • No table d'hôte • Terrace, park, car park. Dogs not admitted • Outdoor swimming pool, sauna, wifi internet access

 The peace and quiet which reigns in this superb Périgord property.

This handsome property set in 2 hectares of grounds is home to spacious bedrooms, two of which are under the eaves. The rooms are decorated simply, but warmly and carefully with rustic or modern furniture, pastel colours, wooden floors and paintings. An extremely comfortable gîte for up to 8 people, complete with private terrace and swimming-pool, has been created in the pigeon-house. Faultless hospitality extended by the English-born owners.

"Foie gras" courses

Access : *13km northbound of Sarlat-la-Canéda, on the D 704 Montignac road and right onto the D 60*

SAINT-CRÉPIN-ET-CARLUCET - 24590

27

LES GRANGES HAUTES
M. Fauste

Le Poujol
24590 Saint-Crépin-et-Carlucet
Tel. 05 53 29 35 60
fauste@netcourrier.com
www.les-granges-hautes.fr
Languages : Eng., Sp.

Closed 15 Nov to 28 Feb • 5 non-smoking rooms, all have bath/WC or shower/WC • €74 to €87 (€67 to €78 low season); breakfast €7 • Table d'hôte €30 • Garden, car park. No dogs admitted

The sophisticated charm of a French country house.

It is hard to resist the charm of this 18C-19C Périgord country house, surrounded by superb gardens and a salt-water swimming pool. The stylish rooms feature oak beams, warm, sunny colours and immaculate bathrooms. The sitting room, whose central feature is a large fireplace, is the perfect place to relax and read. The charming owners are delighted to recommend interesting places to visit in the region.

Access : *12km to the north-east of Sarlat towards Brive then Salignac*

SAINTE-ALVÈRE - 24510

28

LE MOULIN NEUF
MM. Chappell et Shippey

Paunat
24510 Sainte-Alvère
Tel. 05 53 63 30 18
moulin-neuf@usa.net
www.the-moulin-neuf.com
Languages : Eng., Ger.

Closed from 15 to 31 Oct, 25 to 31 Dec • 6 rooms with bathrooms • €64.20 to €68.20; breakfast €10 • No table d'hôte • Terrace, garden. Credit cards not accepted, no dogs admitted

The relaxing murmur of the little stream running through the estate.

This attractive mill house is hidden in the heart of a country estate complete with pond. The cosy, English-inspired interior features light colours, sofas and floral print fabrics. The modest-sized rooms are tastefully decorated and located in a beautifully restored old barn. In summer, breakfast is served under an arbour and in winter, by the fireside in the sitting room.

Access : *Take the D 2 southbound*

SAINT-JULIEN-DE-CREMPSE - 24140

LE MANOIR DU GRAND VIGNOBLE
M. Scotti

Le grand vignoble
24140 Saint-Julien-de-Crempse
Tel. 05 53 24 23 18
grand.vignoble@wanadoo.fr
www.manoirdugrandvignoble.com
Languages : Eng., Sp.

Open from late Mar to mid-Nov • 44 rooms with bath/WC and television • €83 to €111 (€59 to €81 low season); breakfast €10; half-board available • Menus €24 to €46 • Park, car park • Swimming pool, tennis, golf practice, sauna, jacuzzi, fitness, riding centre, wine tasting lessons

 A canter around the estate thanks to the riding school on site.

This 17C manor house enjoys a wonderfully tranquil setting in the midst of over 100 acres of parkland. In the main wing are the reception, sitting room and pleasantly unassuming dining room, where guests are invited to sample regional fare and wines (Bergerac, Pécharmant). A dozen or so rooms, some with four-poster beds, can also be found in this wing. The other wing of the hotel is located in the outbuildings where the extra space has given rise to a more contemporary feel.

Wine courses

Access : *16km northbound from Bergerac on the N 21 as far as Campsegret, then left on a minor road towards Saint-Julien-de-Crempset*

SAINT-MARTIAL-VIVEYROLS - 24320

HOSTELLERIE LES AIGUILLONS
M. Beeuwsaert

Le Beuil
24320 Saint-Martial-Viveyrols
Tel. 05 53 91 07 55
lesaiguillons@aol.com
Languages : Eng., Ger.

Open 1 May to 1 Oct • 8 rooms, one of which has disabled access, all have bath/WC and television • €62 to €107; breakfast €8; half-board available • Menus €20 to €42 • Terrace, park, car park • Outdoor swimming pool

 Woods, hills and open fields for as far as the eye can see.

Here you will find total peace and quiet and a place in the sun, disturbed only by the twittering of birds and the occasional distant murmur of country life. Built on the ruins of an old farmhouse, this hotel offers fresh, spacious rooms, a restaurant in hacienda style and a terrace overlooking the grounds, surrounded by countryside. If you find yourself suffering withdrawal symptoms, the traffic jams, pollution and stress of Paris are a mere 500km stone's throw away!

Access : *5km to the north-west of Verteillac on the D 1, then right on the D 101, then the C 201*

SAINT-PIERRE-DE-CÔLE - 24800

DOUMARIAS
M. et Mme Fargeot

24800 Saint-Pierre-de-Côle
Tel. 05 53 62 34 37
doumarias@aol.com

Closed from 30 Sep to 31 Mar • 6 rooms with bath/WC or shower/WC • €60, breakfast included • Table d'hôte €16 (Mon, Wed and Fri) • Garden, car park. No dogs admitted • Outdoor swimming pool

 Hooking a fish in the River Côle just a step away.

The branches of a great lime tree shade the courtyard of this pleasant country property covered in Virginia creeper, at the foot of the crumbling towers of Bruzac Castle; the charm of the Périgord Vert at its best. The stylish, peaceful rooms are adorned with period furniture, ornaments and paintings. The impressively restored old mill is home to one of the two gîtes with a private pool. Another swimming pool and the garden are most appreciated, as is the staff's friendly welcome.

Access : *2km eastbound from Brantôme on the St-Jean-de-Côle road*

SAINT-RÉMY - 24700

DOMAINE DE LA MOUTHE
M. Caignard

La Mouthe
24700 Saint-Rémy
Tel. 05 53 82 15 40

Open all year • 5 non-smoking rooms with shower/WC • €55 to €70, breakfast included • No table d'hôte • Park, car park. Credit cards not accepted • Outdoor swimming pool

The respect for authenticity.

This old farm, tucked away in the countryside, has recently changed management. The original buildings have been turned into gîtes and the owner, a builder by trade, has built a house in the same style. The result is so harmonious that it is difficult to tell which is which. The three ground floor rooms are light and pleasant despite their modest dimensions. We preferred those in the adjacent wing which are larger and each of which has its own private terrace and fitted kitchenette.

Access : *11km northbound from Ste-Foy-la -Grande on the D 708*

SARLAT-LA-CANÉDA - 24200

SAINT-VINCENT-SUR-L'ISLE - 24420

CHAMBRE D'HÔTE LA CALMADE
M. Margo Collin

Le Bourg
24420 Saint-Vincent-sur-l'Isle
Tel. 05 53 07 87 83
margo@lacalmade.com
www.lacalmade.com

Open all year • 5 rooms one of which has disabled access, all have bathrooms • €60; breakfast included • No table d'hôte • Garden, car park. Credit cards not accepted • Outdoor swimming pool

CHAMBRE D'HÔTE LE CLOS-VALLIS
M. Delanoë

Le Clos Vallis
24200 Sarlat-la-Canéda
Tel. 05 53 28 95 64
closvallis@wanadoo.fr
www.leclosvallis.com

Open all year • 5 non-smoking rooms, 3 of which are upstairs, all have bathrooms • €60; breakfast included • No table d'hôte • Garden, car park. Credit cards not accepted, no dogs admitted • Outdoor swimming pool

 The calm of the countryside just a few kilometres outside Sarlat.

The buildings and outhouses of this carefully restored farmhouse are laid out around a pleasant Périgord-style courtyard. An old barn is now home to light, airy rooms, decorated in a refreshingly simple style with bare stone or white-washed walls, tiles or coconut matting and pine furniture. The sitting room, complete with fireplace, displays the same welcoming simplicity as does the teak-furnished breakfast room. Discreetly cordial welcome.

 The warm, simple family welcome.

This farm located on the town's doorstep is said to date back to 1750. The tastefully decorated rooms, located in the main wing and in a restored barn, are furnished with a combination of family heirlooms, antiques and modern pieces. Pastimes include a library complete with piano and board games and swings for the children in the garden under the shade of a superb chestnut tree.

Access : *15km north-east on the N 21 towards Limoges and then right on the D 705*

Access : *3km north-east of Sarlat-la-Canéda on the D 47 Sainte-Nathaléne road and then a lane to the left*

SARLAT-LA-CANÉDA - 24200

HÔTEL DES RÉCOLLETS
M. Larequie

4 rue Jean-Jacques-Rousseau
24200 Sarlat-la-Canéda
Tel. 05 53 31 36 00
contact@hotel-recollets-sarlat.com
www.hotel-recollets-sarlat.com
Languages : Eng., Ger., Sp.

Open all year • 18 rooms with bathroom and television • €43 to €63; breakfast €6.90 • No restaurant • Car park

 The tranquillity of this hotel in the heart of the medieval city.

The cloister of the Récollets convent, which dates back to the 17C, is now home to a characterful hotel, whose attractive stone walls are covered in wisteria and climbing roses. A narrow staircase leads up to small, well-restored rooms. Each one is different, but all feature the same happy blend of contemporary furniture and original beams and walls. Breakfast is served in a handsome room, where stone prevails, or on a delightful patio. Baggage service available from the public car park.

Access : *In the old town*

SARLAT-LA-CANÉDA - 24200

LE MAS DE CASTEL
Mme Charpenet-Castalian

Sudalissant
24200 Sarlat-la-Canéda
Tel. 05 53 59 02 59
info@hotel-lemasdecastel.com
www.hotel-lemasdecastel.com
Languages : Eng.

Open from Easter to 11 Nov • 13 rooms, half of which are on garden level, with bath/WC or shower/WC and television • €58 to €80 (€45 to €60 low season); breakfast €7 • No restaurant • Garden, car park. Dogs not admitted • Outdoor swimming pool

 The enchanting countryside feel of this authentic farmhouse.

Located in the heart of an unspoilt countryside, this farmhouse has been turned into a welcoming hostelry with rustic rooms upstairs or level with the garden (our favourites). A cockerel, the last remaining survivor of the hen house, joyfully serenades guests with a not-too-early morning call. Enjoy the relaxed pace of a traditional Périgord home and take a dip in the swimming pool before breakfast. The nights are so peaceful that you'll even be philosophical about the rooster's morning chorus.

Access : *3km from Sarlat-la-Canéda on the D 704 towards Gourdon, right onto the Canéda road, then take a minor road*

SORGES - 24420

37

TOURTOIRAC - 24390

38

CHAMBRE D'HÔTE AU VILLAGE
M. Valentini

Le Bourg
24420 Sorges
Tel. 05 53 05 05 08
valentini-camille@wanadoo.fr

Closed in Oct • 3 rooms with shower/WC and television • €39; breakfast €5 • No table d'hôte • Terrace, garden. Credit cards not accepted

L'ENCLOS
M. et Mme Ornsteen

Pragelier
24390 Tourtoirac
Tel. 05 53 51 11 40
rornsteen@yahoo.com
www.hotellenclos.com
Languages : Eng., Sp.

Closed from Oct to Apr • 6 rooms with shower/WC • €70 to €145; breakfast €9 • Table d'hôte €15 to €30 • Park, car park. Credit cards not accepted • Outdoor swimming pool

An unusual little hamlet of cottages.

You too will fall under the charm of this sumptuously restored old Périgord farmhouse and its outhouses, set in a pretty garden. The main house and the former chapel, bakery and estate manager's house, turned into independent, individually decorated rooms are furnished with antiques and lovely Provençal fabrics; all offer a delightful sophisticated charm, both inside and out. Direct access to the garden or the orchard, near a swimming pool.

Sampling the "black diamond" that has made Sorges famous.

This tiny village house, probably built in the 15C, is just next door to the Tourist Office and the Truffle Museum, devoted to the local "black diamonds". Bedrooms in a charming rural style feature wooden floorboards, stone walls, wooden ceilings and antique furniture. In the summer, breakfast is served in the lovely inner courtyard under the welcome shade of an enormous lime-tree.

Access : *In the village*

Access : *5km westbound from Hautefort on the D 62, then the D 67*

VALOJOULX - 24290

39

VAUNAC - 24800

40

LA LICORNE
Mme Bosse

24290 Valojoulx
Tel. 05 53 50 77 77
licornelascaux@free.fr
www.licorne-lascaux.com

Closed from Nov to Mar • 4 non-smoking rooms and 1 apartment, all with bath/WC or shower/WC • €60 to €72, breakfast included • Table d'hôte €20 • Garden, car park. Credit cards not accepted, dogs not admitted • Outdoor swimming pool, table tennis, mountains bikes lent

FERME DES GUEZOUX
M. Fouquet

Les Guezoux
24800 Vaunac
Tel. 05 53 62 06 39
escargot.perigord@wanadoo.fr
www.escargotduperigord.com
Languages : Eng., Sp.

Open all year • 3 rooms with shower/WC • €30 to €35; breakfast €4.50 • No table d'hôte • Garden, car park • Outdoor swimming pool; excursions to farms organized 1st Sun of each month

Playing the sorcerer's apprentice during a course on medicinal plants.

This authentic 17C and 19C Perigord house, opposite the church of the small town, invites you on a bewitching journey betwixt old stones and lush greenery. The five bedrooms are a harmonious blend of sobriety and tasteful decoration. Two of them, the "Mélilots" and the "Templerie" combine wrought-iron furniture and a four-poster bed with the charm of exposed beams. Large rustic dining room downstairs and outdoors a wide expanse of greenery with arbour and orchard.

Delicious homemade walnut cake served at breakfast time.

Hidden by dense woodland, this stone farmhouse was restored in 1990 and makes a wonderfully peaceful retreat for anyone hoping to get away from it all. Whitewashed walls, tiled floors and pine furniture set the scene of the simple, but impeccably kept bedrooms. A kitchen is available for the use of guests in the breakfast room. Also two gîtes, one in the former barn, the other in a wooden chalet. The genial proprietor loves showing his guests his snail farm.

Cultural and gourmet walks from farm to farm on 1st Sunday of each month

Access : *3km eastbound of Vaunac*

Access : *In the town*

ARÈS - 33740

ANDERNOS-LES-BAINS - 33510

LE GRAIN DE SABLE
M. Recullez

37 avenue de la Libération
33740 Arès
Tel. 05 56 60 04 50
hotel.legraindesable@wanadoo.fr
www.hotelgraindesable.com
Languages : Eng.

Open all year • 14 rooms, all have bath/WC or shower/WC, television and telephone • €68 (€52 low season); breakfast €7 • No restaurant • Garden, car park

LES ALBATROS
M. et Mme Malfère

10 bd de Verdun
33510 Andernos-les-Bains
Tel. 05 56 82 04 46
jmalfere@club-internet.fr
www.lesalbatros.com
Languages : Eng., Ger.

Closed Nov to Jan • 3 non-smoking rooms with shower/WC • €60 to €68 (€54 to €61 low season), breakfast included • No table d'hôte • Garden. Credit cards not accepted, dogs not admitted

A matchless location between the Atlantic and the Regional Nature Park of the Landes de Gascogne.

This enchanting recently restored house has retained the stylish regional character in its interior decoration where the theme of evasion takes pride of place. The spacious rooms are personalised on a variety of themes ranging from "Ouarzate" and "Bali" to "Cottage". The breakfast room and sitting room, inspired by the Arcachon basin, are a happy marriage of sandy colours and cane furniture.

The owners who bend over backwards for their guests.

This attractive white house surrounded by a beautifully cared-for garden full of flowers is ideally located just 100m from the beach and town. Each of three personalised rooms bears an evocative name, "Romantic", "Sea" and "Safari"; the latter is the most spacious and perfect for longer stays. Generous breakfasts, complete with home-made jams, are served on a covered terrace or in the dining room which boasts a crystal chandelier and cosy furniture.

Access : *On the church square in the town centre, head towards Arcachon/Andernos, the hotel is 400m further on to the left*

Access : *100m from the beach, near the town*

BERNOS-BEAULAC - 33430

43

DOUSUD
M. et Mme Chapdelaine

33430 Bernos-Beaulac
Tel. 05 56 25 43 23
info@dousud.fr
www.dousud.fr
Languages : Eng.

Open all year • 6 non-smoking rooms, all with bath/WC or shower/WC and television • €80 (€65 low season), breakfast included • Table d'hôte (evenings only) €20 • Terrace, park, kitchenette, car park • Outdoor swimming pool, riding, walking, canoeing, kayaks, bicycles

We most liked **The peace and quiet surrounding this lovely Landes farmhouse.**

Nature is the centre of attraction of this farmhouse set in the heart of immense grounds and the perfect departure point for walking, cycling and even riding excursions. The attractive rooms, each with its own individual outdoor access, are located in the renovated riding stables. A small kitchen and barbecue are available to guests, unless you wouldn't rather prefer putting your feet under the table and tucking into the dishes concocted by the owner, who trained as a chef.

Access : *In the town*

BOMMES-SAUTERNES - 33210

44

PEYRAGUEY MAISON ROUGE
M. et Mme Belanger

33210 Bommes-Sauternes
Tel. 05 57 31 07 55
belanger@club-internet.fr
www.peyraguey-sauternes.com
Languages : Eng., Sp., Port.

Open all year • 3 non-smoking rooms, 2 of which are on the ground floor with private entrance and 1 upstairs, all have shower/WC • €75 to €83 (€72 to €81 low season), breakfast included • No table d'hôte • Garden, car park. Credit cards not accepted, dogs not admitted • Outdoor swimming pool

We most liked **Each room has its own independent entrance.**

The mouth-watering names, "Sauternes", "St-Émilion" and "Médoc", of these enchanting spacious guestrooms located in the heart of the Sauternes vineyards set the stage for your stay. A bottle of Bordeaux is offered to each guest on arrival and tasting sessions are organised in the evenings, all of which is guaranteed to make you feel at home. What's more the house itself is full of character with its regional stone façade, red tile floors and antique furniture.

Oenology, discovering Bordeaux wines

Access : *Sauternes road*

BORDEAUX - 33000

UNE CHAMBRE EN VILLE
M. Labory

35 rue Bouffard
33000 Bordeaux
Tel. 05 56 81 34 53
ucev@bandb-bx.com
www.bandb-bx.com
Languages : Eng., Ger., Sp., Du.

Open all year • 5 non-smoking rooms, all with bath/WC or shower/WC and television • €79 to €89; breakfast €8 • No table d'hôte • No dogs admitted

 The tasteful, understated contemporary decoration.

This building in the heart of the historic district of Bordeaux has been fully restored and the old stone walls and staircase now make a handsome setting for modern furniture and fittings. The rooms are personalised and immaculately cared for: the "Bordelaise" apartment features warm colours and period furniture, the "Nautique" is decorated on a maritime theme while the "Orientale" sports the bright colours and furniture of North Africa...

Access : *In the town centre*

CAPIAN - 33550

CHÂTEAU DE GRAND BRANET
Mme Mainvielle

859 Branet-Sud
33550 Capian
Tel. 05 56 72 17 30
chateaugrandbranet@entredeuxmers.com
www.entredeuxmers.com/chateaugrandbranet

Closed in Jan • 5 non-smoking rooms upstairs, all have bathrooms • €65, breakfast included • Table d'hôte €18 (by reservation) • Park, car park. Credit cards not accepted, no dogs allowed

 A tour of the restored spirit store houses.

This handsome 17C castle, renovated in the 19C, stands in the heart of grounds planted with trees, some of which are several hundred years old. The ground-floor dining room commands a fine view of the surrounding vineyards. Upstairs, five rooms – bare stone walls and antique furniture – can accommodate 3 or 4 people each. The charming owner can generally be depended on to take guests on a guided tour and explanation of his estate and store houses, followed by a tasting session of course!

Access : *9km south of Créon towards Cadillac*

CASTELNAU-DE-MÉDOC - 33480

DOMAINE DE CARRAT
Mme Péry

Route de Sainte-Hélène
33480 Castelnau-de-Médoc
Tel. 05 56 58 24 80
Languages : Eng.

Closed Dec 25 • 4 rooms with shower/WC • €55 to €61, breakfast included • No table d'hôte • Park, car park. Credit cards not accepted

 Romance pervades this country estate.

This red-shuttered country seat, built in 1885, nestles in its own grounds, surrounded by 50 acres of woodland. Formerly the stables of the neighbouring castle, it now houses comfortable, quiet bedrooms, graced with family heirlooms. The most pleasant, on the ground floor, open directly onto the lawn. A roaring open fire welcomes guests in the winter, while the summer months ring to the voices of children swimming in the Jalette. Extremely attentive staff.

Access : *1km to the south-west of Castelnau-de-Médoc*

GENSAC - 33890

LES REMPARTS
M. Parker

16 rue du Château
33890 Gensac
Tel. 05 57 47 43 46
info@lesremparts.net
www.lesremparts.net
Languages : Eng.

Closed Jan and 2 weeks in Nov • 7 rooms, one of which has disabled access; all have bath/WC or shower/WC and television • €62 (€58 low season); breakfast €7.50; half-board available • Menus €18 to €35 • Car park, garden

The warm, friendly welcome from the whole family.

Exceptionally well-located, this house stands on the site of the former ramparts, dominating the old village and the surrounding countryside. The 11C presbytery now houses simple, but appealing rooms furnished in a rustic style and hung with bright, colourful fabrics. The dining room, which affords a splendid panoramic view of the Durèze Valley, lies on the other side of a delightful little garden.

Access : *Very close to the church*

LIBOURNE - 33500

LESTIAC-SUR-GARONNE - 33550

LA TOUR DU VIEUX PORT
M. Segonzac

23 quai Souchet
33500 Libourne
Tel. 05 57 25 75 56
latourduvieuxport@free.fr
http://atourduvieuxport.com
Languages : Eng.

Open all year • 14 rooms, all with bath/WC, telephone and television • €48 to €55; breakfast €6; half-board available • Menus €15 to €29 • Terrace

LES LOGIS DE LESTIAC
M. Dejean

71 route de Bordeaux
33550 Lestiac-sur-Garonne
Tel. 05 56 72 17 90
philippe@logisdelestiac.com
www.logisdelestiac.com
Languages : Eng., Sp.

Open all year • 5 non-smoking rooms on two levels, all have bath/WC or shower/WC (1 has a power shower) television and internet access • €80 to €95, breakfast included; half-board available • Table d'hôte €25 to €30 (evenings only) • Terrace, garden, car park. Credit cards not accepted, dogs not admitted • Outdoor swimming pool

 The interior decoration, both understated and elegant, of this mansion.

The young owner of this magnificent 18C manor house clearly indulged himself when he began restoring his home. A keen antiques collector and interior decorator, he has already restored four rooms on the theme of the seasons: "Autumn Loft" for example is an exquisite combination of burgundy-red fabrics and unusual objects (sewing machine, old suitcases); the equally unusual "Chambre de Philippe" will soon be finished. An immense garden and heated salt-water swimming pool complete the picture.

The personalised decoration of each room.

This hotel-restaurant next to the Tour du Port and opposite the Dordogne welcomes guests into a pleasant tastefully restored setting, full of imagination and comfort. The decoration of the spacious, personalised rooms is the work of the owner who has adorned each bed-head with a fresco which matches the room's fabrics. A traditional menu made from fresh market produce is served in one of three dining rooms.

Access : *In the town centre*

Access : *In the town centre*

MARGAUX - 33460

51

MARTILLAC - 33650

52

LE PAVILLON DE MARGAUX
Mme Laurent

3 rue Georges-Mandel
33460 Margaux
Tel. 05 57 88 77 54
le-pavillon-margaux@wanadoo.fr
www.pavillondemargaux.com
Languages : Eng.

Open all year • 14 rooms with bath/WC and television, 5 in a separate wing, 10 are air-conditioned • €84 to €115 (€63 to €95 low season); breakfast €12; half-board available • Restaurant closed Tues-Wed from 1 Nov to 31 Mar; menus €15 to €51 • Private car park • Surrounded by vineyards

 The hotel's remarkable wine cellar.

As you contemplate this entrancing 19C abode on the edge of the vineyards, it is difficult to imagine that it was formerly home to the village school. The shouts and laughter of the playground have given way to sophisticated decoration and a much calmer atmosphere. Each room is named after and decorated in the spirit of a Médoc château; those in the new wing are smaller but just as comfortable as the others. Elegant dining room and veranda overlooking the vineyards.

Cooking course, golf weekend

Access : *On the way into the village of Margaux*

CHÂTEAU LANTIC
Mme Ginèbre

10 route de Lartigue
33650 Martillac
Tel. 05 56 72 58 68
mginebre@wanadoo.fr
www.chateau-de-lantic.com
Languages : Eng., Sp., It.

Open all year • 11 non-smoking rooms, all have bath/WC or shower/WC, small kitchen, some have a television • €79 to €159, breakfast included • No table d'hôte • Terrace, garden, car park • Outdoor swimming pool

 The charm of this small restored castle.

Murielle Ginèbre, owner of the premises since 2003, has restored her 18C property with faultless taste. The splendid rooms, some of which with a kitchenette, all boast antique furniture and matching fabrics. The immense "Romeo and Juliet" suite with its sumptuous four-poster bed is the height of romanticism. Whatever your purpose, business trip or honeymoon night, you are sure to full in love with this delightful château.

Access : *Turn left before the church, the castle is on the left beyond the vineyards*

MAUBUISSON - 33121

VILLA ASHRAM
Mme François

18 rue des Genêts-d'Or
33121 Maubuisson
Tel. 05 56 03 49 19
Languages : Eng., Sp.

Open all year • 3 rooms, all have shower/WC • €60 to €70 (€55 to €60 low season); breakfast €6 • No table d'hôte • Terrace, garden. Credit cards not accepted, no dogs admitted

 The proximity of the forest and the ocean.

If you are in search of a quiet relaxing stay, Madame François has just what you need: a haven of peace and quiet in a residential neighbourhood just 500m from Lake Hourtin-Carcans. The three guest-rooms and self-contained gîte have been masterfully decorated by the lady of the house who has added her own artistic works here and there. Breakfasts can be taken either in the villa or on one of the countless café terraces which line the neighbouring beach.

Access : *500m from the lakeside and the town centre*

PAREMPUYRE - 33290

DOMAINE DU MASCARET
M. Marin

44 avenue de Labarde
33290 Parempuyre
Tel. 05 56 95 66 70
chambres@domainedumascaret.com
www.domainedumascaret.com
Languages : Eng.

Open all year • 6 rooms with private access, all have bath/WC and television • €80 to €110, breakfast included • No table d'hôte • Terrace, park, car park. Credit cards not accepted

Each room offers a glimpse of distant lands.

When he took over this 18C building located on the banks of the Garonne, Jean-Bernard Marin deployed his talents to turning each of the 6 bedrooms into a bona fide invitation to voyage: red walls, coconut matting and round bathtub for the "Asian", warm African fabrics and pearls for the "Moroccan", etc. Whatever your "destination", you will be invited to breakfast in the country-style dining room or charming terrace.

Access : *8km north of Bordeaux on the D 210 then right on a minor road*

PUJOLS - 33350

55

LES GUÉS RIVIÈRES
M. et Mme Bernard

5 place du Général-de-Gaulle
33350 Pujols
Tel. 05 57 40 74 73
margotte.olivier@wanadoo.fr
http://perso.wanadoo.fr/margotte.olivier
Languages : Eng., Sp.

Open all year • 3 non-smoking rooms upstairs, all have bathrooms • €58 to €65, breakfast included • Table d'hôte €23 (by reservation) • Terrace, garden. Credit cards not accepted, dogs not admitted • Nearby: tennis, golf, swimming pool, mountain bikes, cycling paths, rowing, canoeing

Relaxing on the panoramic terrace.

This handsome property full of character stands on the main village square, commanding a splendid view of the vineyards of the Entre-Deux-Mers from its terrace. Take the time to savour the view on a deckchair or seated in front of a generous breakfast table laden down with cakes and home-made jams. Upstairs the three simply but tastefully decorated rooms all sport a romantic air. Regional produce takes pride of place on the table d'hôte, booking essential.

Access : *6km southbound of Castillon-la-Bataille on the D 17*

RIMONS - 33580

56

LE GRAND BOUCAUD
M. Levy

4 l'Aubrade
33580 Rimons
Tel. 05 56 71 88 57
grandboucaud@free.fr
http://grandboucaud.free.fr

Open from Feb to 1 Oct • 3 non-smoking rooms upstairs, two with bath/WC and 1 with shower/WC • €65, breakfast included • Table d'hôte (evenings only) €23 to €35 • Terrace, garden, car park. Credit cards not accepted, dogs not admitted • Outdoor swimming pool

Strolling around this haven of greenery.

Swimming pool, shaded garden, cosy rooms with bare stone walls... This handsome 18C property extends an invitation to relax in a pleasant landscape of wooded hills and vineyards. The gourmet couple of owners pay equal attention to the quality of the meals. While Monsieur waxes lyrical on the marriage between local produce and wine, offering to accompany guests to local wine-growers should they so fancy, Madame invites guests to try their hand at local recipes in her kitchen.

Access : *3km west of Rimons on the D 230, Monségur road and a left turning*

58

57

CHAMBRE D'HÔTE MME FAVARD
Mme Favard

La Gomerie
33330 Saint-Émilion
Tel. 05 57 24 68 85
chateau.meylet@free.fr
www.chateau.meylet.free.fr
Languages : Eng., Sp.

Open all year • 4 rooms with bathrooms • €52 to €58, breakfast included • No table d'hôte • Garden, car park. Credit cards not accepted

CHÂTEAU MONLOT
M. et Mme Rivals

33330 Saint-Hippolyte
Tel. 05 57 74 49 47
mussetrivals@chateaumonlot.com
www.chateaumonlot.com
Languages : Eng., Ger.

Open all year • 5 rooms with bath/WC • €75 to €120, breakfast included • No table d'hôte • Garden, car park

 The personalised decoration of the rooms.

This château, with its chalk façade and lovely tiled roof is typical of the many stately homes of the region. Each room, stylishly furnished with antiques, paintings and old photos, is named after a variety of grape: Merlot, Cabernet, Sauvignon and so on. The vine theme is also prominent in the pleasant breakfast room. The lovely shaded garden is at its most idyllic in summer.

> *Discovering and tasting wine*

Access : *3km eastbound from St-Émilion, towards Castillon on the D 245*

 The rustic charm of the rooms.

A five-acre vineyard surrounds this elegant 1789 property. The rooms boast polished parquet floors and lovely 18C furniture inherited by the family or unearthed in the local flea markets. Some bedrooms enjoy a view of the vineyard, while others overlook the garden's magnificent Indian bean tree. Breakfast is served in the conservatory in the winter and under the arbour in the summer.

Access : *1.5km westbound from Saint-Émilion on the Libourne road (D 243)*

SAINT-MACAIRE - 33490

LES FEUILLES D'ACANTHE
Mme Bielsa

5 rue de l'Église
33490 Saint-Macaire
Tel. 05 56 62 33 75
info@feuilles-dacanthe.fr
www.feuilles-dacanthe.fr
Languages : Eng.

Closed from 18 Dec to 18 Jan • 12 rooms and 1 apartment, all with disabled access and bathrooms • €70 to €120; breakfast €8 • Menus €19 to €29 • Car park. American Express and Diners not accepted • Jacuzzi

The charm of this old merchant's house.

This handsome 14C and 17C house, located in the heart of the medieval district of Saint-Macaire, has been faultlessly restored, both inside and out. The rooms and the apartment are enchanting: Gironde tile floors, oak furniture, bare stone or orange roughcast walls. On the leisure side, a counter-current swimming pool and Jacuzzi surrounded by loungers await guests in the inner courtyard.

Access : *In the historic town*

SAINT-MARTIN-DE-LERM - 33540

LA LÉZARDIÈRE
M. et Mme Mattei

Boimier-Gabouriaud
33540 Saint-Martin-de-Lerm
Tel. 05 56 71 30 12
lalezardiere@free.fr
www.lalezardiere.free.fr
Languages : Eng., It.

Open 1 Mar to 31 Dec • 4 rooms and one gîte with shower/WC or bath/WC • €65, breakfast included; half-board available • Table d'hôte €20 • Garden, car park. Credit cards not accepted • Outdoor swimming pool, bicycles, children's games, petanque, table tennis

Lazing by the swimming pool in the immense garden.

A beautifully restored 17C farmhouse enjoying a stunning view over the Dropt Valley. Stone and wood add warmth to the welcoming rooms in the renovated cowsheds. The exposed beams, terracotta tiled floor, huge table and fireplace and original mangers lend the breakfast room a real country character. Ask to see the owner's fine collection of works on the local wines and produce.

Oenology, walking and bicycling

Access : *8km to the south-east of Sauveterre-de-Guyenne on the D 670, the D 230 and then the D 129*

SAINT-PALAIS - 33820

LA SAUVAGEONNE
M. Bienfail

2 les Mauvillains
33820 Saint-Palais
Tel. 05 57 32 92 15
marc@relax-in-gironde.com
www.relax-in-gironde.com
Languages : Eng., Ger.

Open all year • 4 non-smoking rooms all have bath/WC or shower/WC and television; 2 gîtes • €90 (€70 low season), breakfast included • Table d'hôte €30, drinks included (evenings only) • Terrace, park, car park. Credit cards not accepted, dogs not admitted • Outdoor swimming pool, Jacuzzi, sauna

 The elegance of this 18C property tucked away in the heart of the countryside.

This establishment's name, which roughly translates as wilderness, used to suit the property very well with its former abandoned garden... However things have changed with the arrival of the new owners and the surrounding woodland and vineyards now add to the charm of this well-tended property. The elegant bedrooms are gracefully proportioned and in the kitchen, garden produce takes pride of place in the dishes rustled up by one of the partners, a former pastry chef.

Access : *200m from the town*

VILLENAVE-DE-RIONS - 33550

LES BATARELLES
M. Tandonnet

103 Deyma
33550 Villenave-de-Rions
Tel. 05 56 72 16 08
tandonnet.danielle@wanadoo.fr
 http://lesbatarelles.free.fr

Open all year • 4 rooms, 2 of which are upstairs, all have bathrooms • €50 to €60, breakfast included • Table d'hôte €30 • Terrace, garden, car park. Credit cards not accepted, dogs not admitted

 The warmth of this house is most contagious.

Fancy a cosy jaunt into the heart of Bordeaux's vineyards? Les Batarelles is the place for you! The attractive comfortable rooms have been tastefully fitted out by the owner who bends over backwards to make sure her guests' stay is as pleasant and relaxing as possible. On the breakfast table you will be treated to homemade jams and honey, served by the fireside in winter or on a terrace lined in vines in summer.

Access : *1.5km westbound on the D 237*

ANGRESSE - 40150

BETBEZER-D'ARMAGNAC - 40240

TY-BONI
M. et Mme Boniface

1831 route de Capbreton
40150 Angresse
Tel. 05 58 43 98 75
info@ty-boni.com
www.ty-boni.com

Open all year • 3 rooms • €80 (€65 low season),
breakfast included • No table d'hôte • Park, car
park. Credit cards not accepted, no dogs admitted • Outdoor swimming pool

LE DOMAINE DE PAGUY
M. et Mme Darzacq

Domaine de Paguy
40240 Betbezer-d'Armagnac
Tel. 05 58 44 81 57
albert.darzacq@wanadoo.fr

Closed Wed from 1 July to 15 Sep • 6 rooms
• €40 to €68, breakfast included • Table d'hôte
from €15 (weekdays) to €33 • Park, terrace, car
park. Credit cards not accepted, dogs not
allowed in rooms • Outdoor swimming pool.
Guided tours of the Armagnac cellars

The owners' warm, generous welcome.

Only the chirping of birds and gentle breezes
rustling through the pine trees interrupt the
peace and quiet of this contemporary house in
regional style. The soberly decorated rooms
are very pleasant. Guests can cook their own
meals in a guest kitchen. The park and swimming pool next to the pond are particularly
pleasant during the summer months. An ideal
situation within easy reach of the beach and
the lively seaside village of Hossegor.

**The tour and commentary of the
Armagnac cellars.**

This 16C manor house stands in the centre of a
vast wine-growing estate overlooking the
Douze Valley. Spacious, attractive rooms,
partly renovated, open onto the landscaped
park and the vineyards, where hens and ducks
roam free. Fine local Landes cuisine takes pride
of place in the kitchen of this handsome property.

Visit to wine cellar

Access : *3km eastbound from Hossegor on the
D 133*

Access : *5km to the north-east of
Labastide-d'Armagnac on the D 11 then the D 35*

CRÉON-D'ARMAGNAC - 40240

LE POUTIC
M. Subra

Route de Cazaubon
40240 Créon-d'Armagnac
Tel. 05 58 44 66 97
lepoutic@wanadoo.fr

www.lepoutic.com
Languages : Eng.

Open all year • 3 non-smoking rooms upstairs, all with shower/WC • €47 to €58, breakfast included • Table d'hôte €19, including drinks • Terrace, park, car park. Credit cards not accepted, dogs not admitted • Library-sitting room, jacuzzi. Theme weekends

The theme weekends.

The restoration of this old regional farmhouse has enhanced the appeal of its old stone walls, beams and timber frame. The same attention to detail has been lavished on the tastefully decorated and well-tended rooms. A spa and a 100m^2 summer room, located in converted outhouses, further encourages guests to relax. The owners also organise theme weekends: horse-riding, golf, woodpigeon shooting...

Duck cooking courses

Access : *On the way out of Créon-d'Armagnac, on the D 51 Cazaubon road*

HAGETMAU - 40700

LES LACS D'HALCO
M. et Mme Demen

Route de Cazalis
40700 Hagetmau
Tel. 05 58 79 30 79
contact@hotel-des-lacs-dhalco.fr
www.hotel-des-lacs-dhalco.com
Languages : Eng., Sp., It.

Open all year • 24 air-conditioned rooms with bath/WC and television • €75 to €98 (€70 to €85 low season); breakfast €10; half-board available • Air-conditioned restaurant; menus €27 to €50 • Car park. No dogs admitted in restaurant • Indoor swimming pool, tennis, bicycle rentals

The resolutely futuristic architecture blends in perfectly with the Landes countryside.

Steel, glass, wood and stone comprise the surprising modern architecture overlooking the lakes and forest. The countless bay windows of this semi-circular construction invite guests to gaze out on the countryside. A spacious hall, contemporary bar and unusual dining room, built on a rotunda which seems to float on the water, are located on the ground-floor. Upstairs, the ample, modern bedrooms are decorated in a pleasantly unfussy style. Covered swimming pool, rowing boats and crazy golf.

Access : *3km south-west of Hagetmau on the Cazalis road*

HOSSEGOR - 40150

BARBARY-LANE
M. Duclau

156 avenue de la Côte-d'Argent
40150 Hossegor
Tel. 05 58 43 46 00
barbary-lane@wanadoo.fr
www.barbary-lane.com
*Languages : Eng., Sp., Ger., Russ.,
Norw., Sw.*

Closed Jan and Feb • 18 rooms, including
2 apartments, all with bathroom and television
• €75 to €100 (€48 to €65 low season); breakfast
€8 • Menus €13 • Terrace, wifi internet access
• Outdoor swimming pool

Lounging around the swimming pool.

This regional-style house, in a quiet tree-lined
residential neighbourhood, has been renovated from top to bottom. The personalised,
prettily-decorated rooms sport colourful fabrics, antique furniture, old box beds fixed to
the wall and painted chinaware. In summer,
the establishment offers a half-board formula
and breakfast – served until midday – becomes
brunch.

Access : *In the town*

MIMBASTE - 40350

CAPCAZAL DE PACHIOU
M. François Dufourcet-Alberca

606 route de Pachiou
40350 Mimbaste
Tel. 05 58 55 30 54
www.capcazaldepachiou.com
Languages : Eng., Sp.

Open all year • 5 rooms with shower/WC • €50 to
€70, breakfast included • Table d'hôte €20 • Car
park. Credit cards not accepted, no dogs
allowed in restaurant

**The authenticity of the house and the
welcome.**

This wonderful old house has been in the same
family since it was built in the 17C. Its loving
restoration has preserved countless traces of
its illustrious past, such as a dovecote, bird
cage, original panelling and parquet floors. The
house exudes history, as the canopied beds,
carved fireplaces and old prints illustrate, and
this same proud commitment to tradition is in
evidence in the kitchen, where duck and goose
feature prominently in mouth-watering local
dishes.

Access : *11km on the N 947 towards Dax-Orthez*

ST-MICHEL-D'ESCALUS - 40550

SABRES - 40630

LA BERGERIE ST-MICHEL
M. Verdoux-Loustau

40550 St-Michel-d'Escalus
Tel. 05 58 48 74 04
www.cybevasion.com
Languages : Sp.

Closed 30 Sep to 31 May • 3 rooms, all with bath/WC, television, direct access to rooms • €90 to €125 (€80 to €105 low season), breakfast included • No table d'hôte • Garden, car park. Credit cards not accepted, no dogs admitted

LES ARBOUSIERS
Mme Labri

Le Gaille
40630 Sabres
Tel. 05 58 07 52 52
lesarbousiers@aol.com
www.chambres-landes.com
Languages : Eng., Sp.

Open all year • 6 rooms with shower/WC • €52 (€48 low season), breakfast included; half-board available • Table d'hôte €20 (evenings only) • Park, car park. Credit cards not accepted, dogs not admitted in restaurant

 The enchanting picture of this half-timbered house.

Set in a clearing in a pine forest, this half-timbered home, typical of the region, never fails to attract admiring glances. The comfortable new rooms are bright and airy. The large bay windows of the restaurant also flood the dining room with light, while diners can enjoy the view of a park which makes no secret of the owner's passion for wildlife and ornithology. What's more, the owner's simple, unaffected welcome is quite irresistible.

> *"Greylag goose" weekends from Nov to Feb, "confit/foie gras" weekend by reservation with a producer and duck breeder*

Access : *7.5km westbound from Sabres on the D 44*

Being greeted by the owner's smile and his sumptuous breakfasts in the morning!

This magnificently restored former sheepfold is tucked away deep in the Landes forest not far from the 12C church of St Michael. The rooms, situated in the outhouses, boast lovely antiques, splendid hi-tech bathrooms and a private terrace. The largest, fully independent, was for a time the studio of an American artist. Breakfasts are served in the main house, which has a lovely half-timbered façade, or in the garden.

Access : *5km eastbound from St Michel d'Escalus on the D142, opposite the church*

TARNOS - 40220

BARBASTE - 47230

CHAMBRE D'HÔTE M. LADEUIX
M. et Mme Ladeuix

26 avenue Salvador-Allende
40220 Tarnos
Tel. 05 59 64 13 95
heleneladeuix@hotmail.com
www.enaquitaine.com

Open all year • 5 rooms with shower/WC and
one gîte • €55 to €75, breakfast included • No
table d'hôte • Park, car park. Credit cards not
accepted • Outdoor swimming pool

 The pleasant surprise of the woodland to
the rear of the house.

From the road, it is impossible to imagine that
this house covered in wisteria opens onto such
a sumptuous park of oak, chestnut, maple,
mimosa, banana and pear trees. Most of the
rooms are relatively simply decorated, except
one which has a distinctly Basque accent.
Guests have the use of a laundry room and a
kitchen. Children will love the sheep pen, as
well as the nearby rabbit and poultry cages.

Access : *5km northbound from Bayonne on the
N 10*

LA CASCADE AUX FÉES
Mme Mazurier

La Riberotte - Chemin du Moulin des
Tours
47230 Barbaste
Tel. 05 53 97 05 96
gmazurier@aol.com
www.cascade-aux-fees.com

Closed Jan and Feb • 4 non-smoking rooms
upstairs, all have bath/WC or shower/WC
• €90 to €110 (€72 to €88 low season); breakfast
€7; half-board available • Table d'hôte €25 to
€35 • Sitting room, garden, terrace, car park.
Credit cards not accepted • Swimming pool,
petanque, angling and mountain bikes

 The view of the restored Moulin des Tours.

This 18C property, partly built into the rock,
commands a view of magnificent flowered
grounds and the shady banks of the Gélise. The
wide range of facilities include a swimming
pool, hammock, riverside summer dining room
and bar. Indoors, the bedrooms and sitting
rooms, furnished with period pieces, are all
refreshingly simple and understated in style.
The overall impression of charm is further
enhanced by the delightful welcome extended
by the mistress of the house.

Access : *6km northwest of Nérac on the D 930
and D 655 Casteljaloux road*

NÉRAC - 47600

LE DOMAINE DU CAUZE
SCI du Cause- Mlle Isabelle Pope

47600 Nérac
Tel. 05 53 65 54 44
cauze.pope@wanadoo.fr
www.domaineducauze.com
Languages : Eng., Ger.

Closed from 23 Dec to 2 Jan • 5 rooms with shower/WC • €53 to €70, breakfast included; half-board available • Table d'hôte €24 in evening • Car park. Dogs not admitted • Outdoor swimming pool

The tranquillity of this hundred-year-old establishment.

This superbly restored old farmhouse has it all. First and foremost, an idyllic situation on a hillside with sweeping views of the dense forests of the Landes and the Gers on fine days. Add to this the tranquillity of the tastefully decorated rooms and last, but not least, the meals, served under the arbour in the summer and whipped up with rare enthusiasm by the imaginative owner-chef. Friendly, hospitable hosts.

Access : *2.5km eastbound from Nérac towards Agen (D 656)*

MONCLAR-D'AGENAIS - 47380

CHÂTEAU DE LA SEIGLAL
M. et Mme Decourty

47380 Monclar-d'Agenais
Tel. 05 53 41 81 30
la.seiglal.47@wanadoo.fr
www.chateau-de-la-seiglal.fr

Open all year (by reservation) • 5 rooms with shower/WC • €65, half-board available • Table d'hôte €20 including beverages (evening only) • Park, car park. Credit cards not accepted, dogs not admitted • Outdoor swimming pool, table-tennis, table football, football pitch, angling, cycling

The friendly atmosphere of this 19C castle.

Hidden by a park planted with ancient trees, this small château built in 1820 is a haven of peace and quiet. The renovated, well-proportioned, comfortable rooms, named after the owner's five sisters, overlook the park and the surrounding meadows. The dining room is a treasure trove of period furniture, carved hunting scenes and a superb fireplace. Not to be outdone, the menu boasts garden- and farm-produce as well as delicious home-made pastries.

Access : *6km northbound from Fongrave on the D 238 then left onto the D 667 Miramont-de-Guyenne road*

SAINT-EUTROPE-DE-BORN - 47290

75

MOULIN DE LABIQUE
Mme Boulet

47290 Saint-Eutrope-de-Born
Tel. 05 53 01 63 90
moulin-de-labique@wanadoo.fr
www.moulin-de-labique.fr
Languages : Eng., Sp.

Open all year (by reservation) • 6 non-smoking rooms on 2 floors, all have bath/WC or shower/WC • €90 to €140; breakfast €10; half-board available • Table d'hôte €31 • Garden, car park. No dogs allowed • Sitting room-library, tennis, outdoor swimming pool, ponies

The immaculate interior decoration.

The delicious inner courtyard planted with high plane trees is at the heart of this estate. The bedrooms, created in former barns and stables and the main house, which sports a Colonial-style façade, are all located off the courtyard. The personalised bedrooms feature a tasteful blend of furniture, objects and paintings. After a bout of angling, a dip in the pool or a read in the sitting room, you will be ready to do justice to the tasty dishes rustled up by the talented lady of the house...

Golf, adventure park in forest

Access : *4km southeast of Saint-Eutrope-de-Born on the D 153*

SAMAZAN - 47250

76

CHÂTEAU CANTET
M. et Mme Raitrie

47250 Samazan
Tel. 05 53 20 60 60
jbdelaraitrie@wanadoo.fr

Closed 15 Dec to 30 Jan • 3 rooms and 1 apartment with bath/WC or shower/WC • €59 to €75, breakfast included • Table d'hôte €25, including beverages (by reservation) • Park, car park. Credit cards not accepted, dogs not admitted • Outdoor swimming pool. Children's games room

The wide range of leisure activities.

An elegant 16C manor house set in well-tended grounds in the heart of the countryside. The bright colour scheme of the rooms sets off a smart but homely interior, with a hint of rustic style. Meals are served in the Louis XIII-style dining room or under the arbour around the pool. The choice of leisure activities is vast: play room, bicycles, lawn croquet, billiards, table-tennis, basketball, pétanque and only 10km away, a golf course and tennis courts.

Access : *10km southbound from Marmande towards Casteljaloux*

SAUVETERRE-LA-LÉMANCE - 47500

77

ASCAIN - 64310

78

LA CARETTE
M. Delong

47500 Sauveterre-la-Lémance
Tel. 05 53 01 63 04

Open all year • 4 rooms with bath/WC or shower/WC • €65 to €75, breakfast €6 • Table d'hôte €30 • Park, car park. Credit cards not accepted • Television room, outdoor swimming pool

CHAMBRE D'HÔTE ARRAYOA
M. Ibarburu

Ferme "Arrayoa"
64310 Ascain
Tel. 05 59 54 06 18
Languages : Eng., Sp.

Open all year • 4 rooms with bathrooms • €52, breakfast included • No table d'hôte • Living room with a kitchen and library. Credit cards not accepted

The square tower and thick drystone walls.

A little lost in a partly wooded park, this faultlessly kept Périgord house can guarantee that you will enjoy absolute peace and quiet. Former antiques dealers, the owners have decorated their home with antiques and other knick-knacks. All the ground floor rooms are as comfortable as they are tasteful and each has its own fully equipped bathroom. The delicious meals, served in fine chinaware, will delight epicureans.

Getting away from it all without entirely forgoing the social whirl of the Basque coast.

This lovely house seems to have been designed with the good life in mind, from the charming countrified rooms to the tempting home-made foie gras and other delicacies served in the former cowshed. If your waistband feels a little tight, you can try your hand on the establishment's private pelota court or don your walking boots and hike up the Rhune. The superb view is more than worth the effort, but those with fewer calories to burn may prefer to catch the little train from the Col de St Ignace.

Access : *800m from the pelota court*

Access : *15km northbound from Fumel on the D 710*

BIARRITZ - 64200

LA FERME DE BIARRITZ
Mme Fermé

15 rue d'Harcet
64200 Biarritz
Tel. 05 59 23 40 27
info@fermedebiarritz.com
www.fermedebiarritz.com

Closed from 2 to 15 Jan and 1 to 15 Dec
• 6 rooms, all with bath/WC or shower/WC
• €50 to €80, breakfast €7 • No table d'hôte
• Garden, car park. Credit cards not accepted,
dogs not admitted

 The lady of the house's warm welcome.

Among one of the oldest of the Basque Coast,
this farm built in the 17C enjoys a matchless
location between the beach and the forest.
Accessible via an outdoor stone staircase, the
rooms, all with sloping ceilings, are located in
the former barn. Pretty and well furnished,
they combine the charm of yesteryear with
modern-day facilities. Outside a small garden
and lawn await guests wishing to doze in the
sunshine. Faultless upkeep and reasonable
prices.

Access : *In the centre of the Ilbarritz district, in
the south of Biarritz*

BIARRITZ - 64200

NERE-CHOCOA
Mme Cadou

23 rue Larreguy
64200 Biarritz
Tel. 06 08 33 84 35
maryse.cadou@wanadoo.fr
www.nerechocoa.com

Open all year • 5 rooms with bath/WC and
modem • €60 to €97, breakfast €8 • No table
d'hôte • Garden, terrace, car park. Credit cards
not accepted, dogs not admitted • Music room,
keep-fit track

 **Staying in the former abode of Empress
Eugénie and Miss Stuart.**

Built in the tradition of Basque Spanish architecture, with roofs which are less sloping than
in France, this large white house stands in the
middle of a park planted with age-old oak
trees. Artist friends have adorned its white
walls with their works. A vast sitting room
opens out onto the garden. Upstairs, the five
relatively spacious rooms are comfortable and
well kept, decorated with matching carpets
and fabrics. Private concerts organised from
time to time. Delightful welcome.

Access : *Near Lake Marion*

BUZY - 64260

MAÏNADE
Mme Augareils

6 place Cazenave
64260 Buzy
Tel. 05 59 21 01 01
rolandeaugareils@free.fr

Closed in Jan • 6 rooms with shower/WC • €55 to €60, (€53 to €55 low season), breakfast included; half-board available • Table d'hôte €18 to €22 • Car park. Credit cards not accepted, dogs not admitted

 The warm welcome extended by the lady of the house, Rolande, and her staff.

This attractive Béarn farmhouse with its wrought-iron gate, flowered window boxes and courtyard, lies in the heart of the village. Don't stand on ceremony, just sit down with the other guests and Rolande's family at the huge open-air table, which can seat up to 25, and enjoy a wonderful meal, invariably accompanied by a song or two. The rooms are lovingly decorated with old lace and family heirlooms, but, beware, none are heated. 100% authentic Béarn cooking.

Access : *4km northbound from Arudy on the D 920*

FÉAS - 64570

LE CHÂTEAU DE BOUES
Mme Dornon

64570 Féas
Tel. 05 59 39 95 49
Languages : Eng., Sp.

Closed from mid-Oct to Apr • 4 rooms with bath/WC • €62, breakfast included • No table d'hôte • Garden, car park. Credit cards not accepted, dogs not admitted • Outdoor swimming pool

 The kindness of the hospitable owners.

On the doorstep of Baretous Valley, the pristine walls of this lofty 18C castle dominate the surrounding Béarn countryside. The bedrooms, located in the central wing - the owners occupy the towers - enjoy views of the garden, swimming pool and superb kitchen garden. Breakfast is a lively, friendly affair and guests are made to feel like friends of the family.

Access : *8km to the south-west of Oloron-Ste-Marie on the D 919*

GUÉTHARY - 64210

83

BRIKÉTÉNIA
M. et Mme Ibarboure

142 rue de l'Église
64210 Guéthary
Tel. 05 59 26 51 34
Languages : Sp.

Open from 15 Mar to 15 Nov • 16 rooms, 12 of which have balconies, 1 has disabled access, all have bath/WC and television • €60 to €65 (€58 to €60 low season); breakfast €8 to €10 • No restaurant • Car park

 Grab a "makhila" – a traditional Basque walking stick – and explore this seaside resort.

The coaching inn, built in 1680 on the heights of Guéthary, is a fine example of traditional Basque architecture: steep tiled roof, balcony, whitewashed walls, timber frames and red shutters. Perhaps it was the ocean view from some of the rooms that appealed to one Napoleon Bonaparte, an illustrious former guest? Be that as it may, the energetic proprietors are not the sort to rest on their laurels and the inn has recently been renovated from top to toe.

Access : *Near the church*

ISPOURE - 64220

84

FERME ETXEBERRIA
M. Mourguy

64220 Ispoure
Tel. 05 59 37 06 23
domainemourguy@hotmail.com
www.domainemourguy.com

Open all year • 4 rooms with shower/WC • €46 to €48, breakfast included • No table d'hôte • Car park. Credit cards not accepted, no dogs admitted • Tour of the cellars and wine-tasting

 Donkey rides through Irouleguy's vineyards.

What better way to really get to know the Basque country than by staying in this attractive farmhouse surrounded by vineyards. The converted barn houses modern, soberly decorated and very pleasant rooms. Guests have the use of a kitchenette, an attractive breakfast room and a conservatory which overlooks the vines. The owners, who also produce wine and raise donkeys, are happy to help guests organise hikes throughout the region.

Visit to wine cellar and tasting

Access : *0.8km to the north-east of Saint-Jean-Pied-de-Port on the D 933*

ITXASSOU - 64250

ISSOR - 64570

HÔTEL DU CHÊNE
Mme Salaberry

64250 Itxassou
Tel. 05 59 29 75 01
Languages : Sp.

Closed in Jan and Feb, Tue from Oct to Jun, and Mon • 16 rooms with bath/WC, some have television • €49, breakfast €6.50; half-board available • Menus €16 to €40 • Terrace, garden, car park. Dogs not admitted in restaurant

LA FERME AUX SANGLIERS
M. Delhay-Cazaurang

Micalet
64570 Issor
Tel. 05 59 34 43 96
Languages : Sp., It.

Open all year • 5 rooms with bathrooms • €45 to €55, breakfast included • Table d'hôte €15 to €22 (evenings only) • Car park. Credit cards not accepted, dogs not admitted • Tasting and sale of homemade "charcuterie"

 The stunning view from all the bedrooms.

A narrow road winds its way up to this lovingly restored Béarn farmhouse. You can be sure of a warm, generous welcome, together with comfortable rooms, all of which command sweeping views of the valley and the Pyrenean peaks. The focus is on healthy, local produce and the owner, who breeds animals, adores taking visitors round his boar parks, to the delight of children.

The superb Villa Arnaga, nearby, one-time home to Edmond Rostand, creator of Cyrano de Bergerac.

The doors of this hospitable country inn have been open, greeting guests warmly, since 1696. The bedrooms, graced with old Basque furniture, overlook the cherry trees of Itxassou – a sight to behold in spring! Make sure you sample the famous black cherry jam and the gras-double with cèpes, a house speciality, served under the colourful blue beams of the dining room or in the shade of the sweet-scented wisteria.

Access : *Near the church*

Access : *10km westbound from St-Christau on the D 918 as far as Asasp, then the N 134 and the D 918 towards Arette*

ITXASSOU - 64250

87

SOUBELETA
Mme Régérat

64250 Itxassou
Tel. 05 59 29 78 64

Open all year • 5 rooms with shower/WC • €49 to €55, (€48 to €52 low season), breakfast included • No table d'hôte • Garden, car park. Credit cards not accepted, dogs not admitted

> The tranquil mood of this peaceful 17C mansion.

This imposing mansion, built in 1675, certainly makes the most of a lovely spot in the upper part of the village. The generously proportioned rooms, graced with gleaming family antiques, look over meadows and the orchard; two have marble fireplaces. The light, airy sitting room is very pleasant and children will love visiting the cows in the neighbouring dairy farm.

Access : *In the village, stay on the D 918 until the Nive bridge, then turn right*

IZESTE - 64260

88

M. ET MME ASNAR
M. Asnar

4 avenue Georges-Messier
64260 Izeste
Tel. 05 59 05 71 51
jean-lili.asnar@tele2.fr

www.vallee-ossau.com/hebergement/asnar
Languages : Eng., Sp.

Closed 2 weeks in Oct • 3 rooms, all with shower/WC and television • €45, breakfast included • No table d'hôte • Terrace, garden, car park. Credit cards not accepted, no dogs allowed

> A simple smiling welcome.

A beautifully tended garden planted with flowers and plane, linden, palm and fruit trees, surrounds this handsome stone house facing the mountain. The owner offers a gîte and three rooms, all on the ground-floor, with an independent entrance; each room is different and all are furnished simply but with no lack of modern comforts.

Access : *In the town*

LANNE EN BARÉTOUS - 64570

MAISON RACHOU
Mme Évelyne Masero

64570 Lanne-en-Barétous
Tel. 05 59 34 10 30
www.gites64.com/maison-rachou
Languages : Eng., It.

Open all year • 5 rooms, 1 with disabled access, all with shower/WC • €48, breakfast included • Table d'hôte €18, drinks included • Terrace, garden, car park. Credit cards not accepted, no dogs allowed • Outdoor swimming pool

 The view of the village and the Pyrenees.

The owners of this old farmhouse located on the heights of the town have taken great care to ensure that you will be welcomed in an immaculately maintained establishment: renovated façade, vast dining room with fireplace and timber beams... The rooms are all more or less identical with wooden ceilings and floors, white walls and functional bathrooms. The master of the house, formerly a chef, prepares dinner himself.

Access : *In the village, opposite the baker's, follow the signposts*

LESCAR - 64230

LA GRANGE DU MOULIN
Mme Dubosc

Moulin du Batan
64230 Lescar
Tel. 06 88 25 39 20
lagrangedumoulin@club-internet.fr
www.lagrangedumoulin.com

Open all year • 4 non-smoking rooms upstairs, all with shower/WC and modem access • €90 (€68 low season), breakfast included • No table d'hôte • Terrace, park, library, private car park. Credit cards not accepted, dogs not admitted

 Relaxing in the heavenly garden by the water's edge.

The owners welcome their guests in their exquisitely restored former water mill. The personalised and tastefully decorated rooms are full of charm, as is the breakfast room with its bare stone walls, large fireplace and inviting table. If you then add the owners' warm welcome, you will have all the ingredients for a memorable stay in the Béarn region.

Access : *At Lescar, go towards Bayonne on the N 117 and a minor road to the left*

PAGOLLE - 64120

MAISON ELIXONDOA
M. et Mme Walther

64120 Pagolle
Tel. 05 59 65 65 34
jean.walther@wanadoo.fr
www.elixondoa.com
Languages : Eng.

Open all year • 4 rooms with shower/WC • €48, breakfast included • Table d'hôte €20 (evening only) • Garden, car park. Credit cards not accepted

 The pastoral charm of this remote spot.

Those in need of a serious break should head for this 17C farm, set among open fields, on one of the old pilgrim roads to Santiago de Compostela. The bedrooms, recently fitted-out with all the modern comforts, overlook the surrounding hillsides. Meals are taken in the vast dining room where the exposed stone work and timbers cannot fail to catch the eye. Friendly service.

Access : *13km westbound from Mauléon-Licharre on the D 918 then the D 302*

SAINT-JEAN-DE-LUZ - 64500

VILLA ARGI-EDER
M. Basset

Avenue Napoléon III
64500 Saint-Jean-de-Luz
Tel. 05 59 54 81 65
villa-argi-eder.@wanadoo.fr
www.chambresdhotes-argi-eder.com
Languages : Eng., Ger.

Open all year • 4 rooms with shower/WC • €50; breakfast €5 • No table d'hôte • Terrace, garden, car park. Credit cards not accepted

 Admire the reckless surfers braving the giant waves.

This handsome Basque villa, recently spruced up with a new coat of paint, has something for everyone: tranquillity, a well-tended lawn lined in flowers and a superb location just 100m from the surfing beach. The brand-new spacious bedrooms are an invitation to meditation and those overlooking the garden have private terraces. The bathrooms are neat and well appointed. One of the resort's most pleasant hotels.

Access : *5km to the north-east of Saint-Jean-de-Luz on the N 10 towards Biarritz, then take a minor road*

SALIES-DE-BÉARN - 64270

LA CLOSERIE DU GUILHAT
Mme Potiron

Le Guilhat
64270 Salies-de-Béarn
Tel. 05 59 38 08 80
guilhat@club-internet.fr
www.holidayshomes.com/guilhat
Languages : Eng.

Open all year • 4 rooms with shower/WC and one gîte • €53 to €58, breakfast included; half-board available • Table d'hôte €21.50 (evenings only except Thu) • Park, car park. Credit cards not accepted, dogs not admitted

LA DEMEURE DE LA PRESQU'ÎLE
M. Sclafer

22 avenue des Docteurs-Foix
64270 Salies-de-Béarn
Tel. 05 59 38 06 22
info@demeurepresquile.com
www.demeurepresquile.com
Languages : Eng., Sp.

Open all year • 4 rooms upstairs, all with bath/WC or shower/WC, 2 have a television • €65, breakfast included • Table d'hôte €23 (drinks included) • Terrace, park, library, garage. Credit cards not accepted, no dogs allowed in restaurant

 Whiling away the evenings on the terrace facing the Pyrenees.

It is difficult to find a fault with such a lovely old country house, especially one with a sumptuous landscaped park and an exquisite terrace overlooking the valley, set against a backdrop of Pyrenean peaks. A bold colour scheme distinguishes the quiet, well-dimensioned rooms, each of which is named after a flower. The mistress of the house makes guests feel truly welcome and dining on the winter veranda or summer terrace is an unforgettable experience.

 The mouth-watering home-made pastries.

This 18C abode, a short walk from the town centre, is home to an authentic interior full of character: lovely tiles in the entrance hall, a period dining room lined in mirrors in which the pretty wooden fireplace is reflected and a delightful sitting room-library. A handsome staircase leads up to the spacious elegant rooms furnished with period pieces. Regional influences feature prominently in the kitchen. Splendid magnolia in the immense grounds.

Access : *In the town*

Access : *4km northbound from Salies towards Puyoo, in the upper reaches of Salies*

SALIES-DE-BÉARN - 64270

95

MAISON LÉCHÉMIA
Mme Camougrand

Quartier du Bois
64270 Salies-de-Béarn
Tel. 05 59 38 08 55
www.gites64.com/maison-lechemia

Open all year • 3 non-smoking rooms, 2 in a separate wing, all with bath/WC or shower/WC • €50 to €53, breakfast included • Table d'hôte €23, including drinks • Terrace, garden, private car park. Credit cards not accepted, no dogs allowed in restaurant

 The owner's unaffected friendly welcome.

This old farm hidden in the country has been faultlessly restored. We recommend booking one of the two attractive rooms in the converted stables. At mealtimes, after choosing between the winter dining room, complete with fireplace, or the covered terrace in summer, you will be served delicious country fare made with home-made and home-grown produce: garden vegetables, home-made jams with fruit from the orchard, etc.

Access : *In the town, take the Carresse road by the D 17 and turn right onto a minor road at the Quartier du Bois*

SARE - 64310

96

ARRAYA
M. Fagoaga

64310 Sare
Tel. 05 59 54 20 46
hotel@arraya.com
www.arraya.com
Languages : Eng., Sp.

Closed 2 Nov to 30 Mar • 20 rooms, most have bath/WC, some have shower/WC, all have television • €94 to €120; breakfast €10; half-board available • Restaurant closed Sun evening and Mon lunchtime (except 3 Jul to 12 Sep); menus €21 to €31 • Terrace, garden. No dogs admitted in rooms • Shop with Basque linen and local produce

Chugging up the Rhune in an old train (1924).

This village, nestling at the foot of the Rhune, is a treasure chest of Basque heritage. In keeping with its historic past, the 17C coaching inn, which formerly welcomed pilgrims of St James, is a fine example of regional interior design with dark timbers, old furniture and colourful fabrics. The surrounding countryside, a former "smugglers' paradise" is now heaven on earth: footpaths criss-cross the region, winding through meadows where the local ponies and sheep graze peacefully.

Access : *In the heart of the village, near the main square, next to the pelota court*

AUVERGNE

Allier - 03
Cantal - 15
Haute-Loire - 43
Puy-de-Dôme - 63

Shh! Auvergne's volcanoes are dormant and have been for many millennia, forming a natural rampart against the inroads of man and ensuring that this beautiful wilderness will never be entirely tamed. If you listen very carefully, you may just make out a distant rumble from Vulcania, where spectacular theme park attractions celebrate the sleeping giants. The region's windswept domes and peaks, sculpted by long-extinguished fires, are now the source of countless mountain springs that cascade down the steep slopes into brooks, rivers and crystal-clear lakes. Renowned for the therapeutic virtues of its waters, the region has long played host to countless well-heeled *curistes*, come to take the waters in its elegant spa resorts. It has to be said that many find it impossible to follow doctor's orders when faced with the enticing aroma of a country stew or a full-bodied Cantal cheese.

CHARROUX - 03140

LA MAISON DU PRINCE DE CONDÉ
M. Speer

Place d'Armes
03140 Charroux
Tel. 04 70 56 81 36
jspeer@club-internet.fr
www.maison-conde.com
Languages : Eng., It.

Open all year • 6 non-smoking rooms, including 1 apartment in tower, all have bath or shower and WC and television • €56 to €89, breakfast included • No table d'hôte • Garden. Dogs not admitted

> We most liked
> **Chatting with the owner, ever available for guests.**

The tiny medieval city of Charroux is home to this delightful guesthouse run by a couple of retired Canadians. Five of the six rooms are situated in the main building, but the "Porte d'Orient", a split-level apartment with balneo bathtub and four-poster bed is tucked away in a tower up a narrow irregular staircase. Meals are served in an unusual and attractive 13C vaulted dining room.

Access : *In the centre of the village*

COULANDON - 03000

LE CHALET ET MONTÉGUT
M. Navarro

28 route du Chalet
03000 Coulandon
Tel. 04 70 46 00 66
chalet.montegut@wanadoo.fr
www.hotel.lechalet.com
Languages : Eng., Sp., Port.

Closed from 15 Dec to 15 Jan • 28 rooms, 19 of which are in a separate wing, one has disabled access. Rooms have bath/WC or shower/WC and television • €66 to €81; breakfast €9; half-board available • Menus €18 (weekdays) to €41 • Terrace, park, car park • Outdoor swimming pool

> We most liked
> **Generous breakfasts with a distinctly Alpine flavour; the landlord is Swiss.**

A cluster of three buildings make up this 10-acre country estate, complete with a large pond for fishing, hundred-year-old parkland and a swimming pool. The rooms are situated in the "chalet", which also houses the reception and in the former stables, while the restaurant is in a more recent building. Savour the pleasure of waking up in the heart of the peaceful Bourbon countryside.

Access : *7km to the south-west of Moulins on the D 945 (towards Souvigny), then right on a minor road*

COULANDON - 03000

LA GRANDE POTERIE
M. Pompon

9 rue de la Grande-Poterie
03000 Coulandon
Tel. 04 70 44 30 39
jcpompon@lagrandepoterie.com
www.lagrandepoterie.com

Closed in Jan • 4 rooms, 1 on ground floor, all have bathrooms • €60 to €65, breakfast included • Menu €20 • Terrace, garden, car park, small kitchen. Credit cards not accepted, no dogs allowed • Outdoor swimming pool, bicycles on request

 The kindness and availability of the owner.

Extremely well-kept tree-lined and flower-decked grounds surround this restored farmhouse, perfect for a peaceful halt. The refreshingly simply decorated yet sophisticated rooms are particularly pleasant and attractive. Local Auvergne produce takes pride of place on the table d'hôte in the form of mouth-watering specialities: pâté bourbonnais, pompe aux pommes, brioche aux grattons... Don't worry though – you can burn off those excess calories in the heated swimming pool!

Access : *From Coulandon, take the Savigny road, after the level crossing, continue for 600m then take the first left and follow the signs*

LA FERTÉ-HAUTERIVE - 03340

DEMEURE D'HAUTERIVE
M. Lefebvre

03340 La Ferté-Hauterive
Tel. 04 70 43 04 85
j.lefebvre@demeure-hauterive.com
www.demeure-hauterive.com
Languages : Eng.

Open all year • 5 rooms, one of which is on the ground floor, all have shower/WC • €80 (€75 low season), breakfast included • Table d'hôte €22 to €28 • Park, car park • Swimming pool, horse-drawn carriage outings possible

 Strolling through the park bedecked in autumn colours.

It would be difficult to find a more gracious establishment than this opulent mansion, built in 1850 in the heart of an 8-acre park. The exquisitely decorated rooms, particularly those on the ground floor, are spacious. The house also provides its guests with a wide range of leisure activities, including billiards, badminton and table tennis, but the most pleasant of all is a stroll through parkland dotted with ornamental pools and follies. Highly friendly atmosphere.

Access : *12km northbound from St-Pourçain-sur-Sioule on the N 9 then the D 32*

LE THEIL - 03240

CHÂTEAU DU MAX
M. Mazet-Pesar

03240 Le Theil
Tel. 04 70 42 35 23
chateaudumax@club-internet.fr
www.chateaudumax.com
Languages : Eng.

Open all year • 4 rooms with private bathrooms and television • €75, breakfast included • Table d'hôte €25, drinks included • Garden, car park. Credit cards not accepted

This magnificent castle still boasts its original moat.

The entrance to this 13C and 15C castle is through a porch, which used to be a drawbridge in former times. A spiral staircase in the paved courtyard leads up to the medieval style dining room and rooms. Each of the different coloured rooms has been tastefully decorated by the owner, a former Parisian theatre set designer. Her ebullient personality and excessive kindness make it a pleasure to join her at dinner time and taste the local produce.

Painting, pottery and sculpture courses

Access : *West of Theil, 2.5km on the D 235*

POUZY-MÉSANGY - 03320

MANOIR LE PLAIX
Mme Raucaz

03320 Pouzy-Mésangy
Tel. 04 70 66 24 06
leplaix@yahoo.fr
Languages : Eng.

Closed 15 Dec to 15 Mar • 4 non-smoking rooms, all have bathrooms • €46, breakfast included; half-board available • Table d'hôte €18 (evenings only, by reservation) • Sitting room, car park. Credit cards not accepted • Nearby: tennis, mini golf

Walking along the banks of the Bieudre, which meanders its way through the immense property.

This welcoming 16C stronghold stands in the heart of a working farm. One of the chambres d'hôte is reached by a handsome spiral staircase. Red-brick floor tiles, wooden beams, old furniture and stone fireplaces set the scene for a pleasantly, relaxed stay. In the evenings, don't miss the chance to sample the delicious local produce, including the tender Charolais beef raised on the estate. Depending on the season, you can go walking, fishing or mushroom picking.

Guided tour of neighbouring Romanesque churches, by reservation

Access : *D 234, drive for 1.5km to the north-west on a minor road*

VALIGNAT - 03330

CHÂTEAU DE L'ORMET
M. et Mme Laederich

 Lieu-dit l'Ormet
03330 Valignat
Tel. 04 70 58 57 23
lormet@wanadoo.fr
http://chateaudelormet.com
Languages : Eng., Ger.

Closed 18 Nov to 29 Mar • 4 non-smoking rooms on two floors, all with bathrooms • €63 to €83, breakfast included • Table d'hôte €25, Fri and Sat by reservation • Garden, park, car park. Credit cards not accepted, dogs not admitted • Outdoor swimming pool

 The toing-and-froing of the small trains that run through the garden in the evenings.

At an altitude of 465m on a plateau dominating the Limagne plain, this 18C manor house, altered countless times over the years, has lost none of its original class. The tastefully decorated personalised rooms overlook the park, the saltwater swimming pool and the amusing "garden trains" built by the railway enthusiast owner. Meals begin with a glass of Birlou (local aperitif made from white wine and sweet chestnut liqueur), followed by a main course, Auvergne cheeses and home-made desserts.

Access : *8km eastbound of Charroux on the D 183, at Valignat, L'Ormet*

YGRANDE - 03160

LE CHALET DE LA NEVERDIÈRE
M. et Mme Vrel

 Les Ferrons
03160 Ygrande
Tel. 04 70 66 31 67

Open all year • 5 rooms with shower/WC located in a small house 100m from the farm • €45, breakfast included • No table d'hôte • Garden, car park. Credit cards not accepted, dogs not admitted

 The gargantuan breakfasts.

This early 20C house with its ochre edged façade and steep roof nestling in the heart of the Bourbon countryside, looks nothing like the chalets the region abounds in, but who cares? Its well-proportioned and well thought-out rooms overlook lush, green countryside. Tronçais Forest, 12km away, is perfect to walk off the extremely generous breakfasts. Very friendly staff.

Access : *10km to the south-west of Bourbon-l'Archambault on the D 953, then a minor road*

CHAMPS-SUR-TARENTAINE - 15270

AUBERGE DU VIEUX CHÊNE
Mme Moins

34 route des Lacs
15270 Champs-sur-Tarentaine
Tel. 04 71 78 71 64
danielle.moins@wanadoo.fr

Closed 15 Oct to 15 Apr, Sun and Mon out of season • 15 rooms on 2 floors with bathrooms, some have television • €60 to €82 (€54 to €74 low season); breakfast €9 • Menu €23 • Terrace, garden, car park

The picturesque Artense region, somewhat reminiscent of Scandinavia.

The frontage of this historic 19C farmhouse is almost hidden by Virginia creeper and flowers. The pretty, cosy rooms overlook a pleasant, peaceful garden. Exposed beams, thick stone walls and a huge fireplace add character to the dining room in the converted barn. Relax on the shaded terrace and admire the beautiful countryside of hills and meadows where the owners' horses graze.

Access : *Not far from the centre of the village*

FONTANGES - 15140

AUBERGE DE L'ASPRE
M. Landau

15140 Fontanges
Tel. 04 71 40 75 76
auberge-aspre@wanadoo.fr
www.auberge-aspre.com
Languages : Eng., Sp.

Closed 17 Nov to 4 Feb; Sun and Wed evenings and Mon from Oct to May • 8 rooms, one of which has disabled access. All have unusual split-level bathrooms and television • €52; breakfast €8; half-board available • Menus €17.50 to €34 • Terrace, garden, car park • Outdoor swimming pool

The tinkling of the cow-bells.

This old farmhouse with its beautiful stone-shingled roof lies in a secluded hamlet of the Aspre Valley not far from the village of Salers. The modern, brightly-coloured bedrooms, each of which has an unusual split-level bathroom, are situated in the old barn. Savour the traditional, tasty Auvergne menu in the rustic-style dining room, the veranda or on the pleasant terrace overlooking the garden.

Access : *5km southbound from Salers on the D 35*

GIOU-DE-MAMOU - 15130

DE BARATHE
M. et Mme Breton

15130 Giou-de-Mamou
Tel. 04 71 64 61 72
barathe@wanadoo.fr
barathe.monsite.orange.fr

Open all year • 5 rooms with shower/WC • €48, breakfast included, half-board available • Table d'hôte €13 (evenings only except Sun) • Garden, car park. Credit cards not accepted, dogs not admitted

We most liked **The authentic character of this country setting.**

If you like the idea of waking to the sound of the cow-bells from the Salers cattle grazing in the lush, green meadows, then make a beeline for this place! Simple, yet comfortable rooms, ideal for families. Exposed stonework, old furniture, a fireplace, wood benches and a sink set the scene of the authentic dining room. Meals are, of course, prepared using produce grown and reared on the farm.

Access : *7km eastbound from Aurillac on the N 122 then the D 58*

JOURSAC - 15170

LA BARAJADE
M. Alain Nicolleau

Lieu-dit Recoules
15170 Joursac
Tel. 04 71 20 59 12
barajade@wanadoo.fr
chambres-hotes-cantal.com

Closed from 1 Nov to Easter, except during Feb school holidays • 5 rooms with shower/WC • €43, breakfast included • Table d'hôte €13 • Garden, car park. Credit cards not accepted • Sitting room-library

We most liked **The unspoilt setting of this village characteristic of the southern Cézallier region.**

At an altitude of 1120m, the cowshed of this old farmstead, built in 1820, has been turned into an entrance hall, stocked with an impressive selection of tourist information. The table d'hôte, served in a splendid dining room with fireplace, is a feast for lovers of Auvergne cuisine, 100% homemade. Upstairs, five comfortable rooms, named after wild flowers that grow in the vicinity.

Access : *7km northbound from Neussargues on the N 122*

LANAU - 15260

AUBERGE DU PONT DE LANAU
M. et Mme Kergoat

15260 Lanau
Tel. 04 71 23 57 76
aubergedupontdelanau@wanadoo.fr
www.lanau.fr

Languages : Eng.

Closed mid-Dec to Jan; Wed lunchtime and Tue out of season • 8 rooms on 2 floors, all have bath/WC or shower/WC • €45 to €60; breakfast €9; half-board available • Menus €15 (weekdays) to €50 (by reservation only) • Terrace, garden, car park

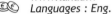

 The endless meanders of the River Truyère.

This former coaching house, built in 1821, spans one of the rare crossing-places over the Truyère. Good, solid furniture adorns the well-maintained rooms. The typical, Auvergne-style decoration of the dining room with its well-worn panelling, exposed beams and huge stone fireplaces, has been preserved by successive owners over the years. Guests have the run of a small garden and a pleasant, shaded terrace.

Access : *4.5km from Chaudes-Aigues on the D 921 (Saint-Flour road)*

LE FALGOUX - 15380

LA MICHIE
M. et Mme Supersac

15380 Le Falgoux
Tel. 04 71 69 54 36
guyll.supersac@wanadoo.fr
http://perso.wanadoo.fr/guy.supersac

Open from Easter to 1 Nov • 5 rooms with bathrooms • €49 to €57, breakfast included • Table d'hôte €18 • Park, car park. Credit cards not accepted, dogs not admitted

 Surprising a chamois leaping over the rocks.

Built in the late 19C by locals who had made it rich in Paris, this building has been entirely restored by the owner, a DIY fanatic. On the ground floor are a splendid living room with lounge area around a fireplace and a dining room adorned with antiques. Upstairs, the five spacious, light rooms are named after wild flowers. Regional cuisine with products supplied by local growers.

Access : *In the village*

SAINT-ÉTIENNE-DE-CARLAT - 15130

MURAT - 15300

HOSTELLERIE LES BREUILS
M. et Mme Rochès

34 avenue Docteur Mallet
15300 Murat
Tel. 04 71 20 01 25
info@hostellerie-les-breuils.com
www.hostellerie-les-breuils.com

Open late May to 15 Oct • 10 rooms, most have bath/WC, some have television • €65 to €77; breakfast €7.20 • No restaurant • Garden, private car park. No dogs admitted • Indoor swimming pool, sauna, leisure area

LOU FERRADOU
M. et Mme Balleux

Caizac
15130 Saint-Étienne-de-Carlat
Tel. 04 71 62 42 37
balleux@louferradou.com
 www.louferradou.com

Open all year • 5 non-smoking rooms with bathrooms • €44 to €54, breakfast included; half-board available • Table d'hôte €14 (evening only) • Car park, garden, terrace. Credit cards not accepted, no dogs admitted • Games room

 The friendly, personalised welcome.

All the rooms of this small 19C mansion backing onto the historic town, have recently been treated to a facelift of bright, bold colours and some have retained their Louis XVI furniture. The roomy bathrooms are well fitted-out. Attractive reading room with fireplace and piano. A building to the rear of the garden houses an indoor swimming pool.

 Dining and breakfasting in the enchanting garden in fine weather.

The typically austere Auvergne façade of this old farm cannot fail but impress. The eye is also drawn to the recently restored beams, bare stone walls and fireplace indoors. One of the rooms in the main wing has its own sitting room and an outhouse is home to two split-level rooms, all are furnished in a regional style. Large games room. At mealtimes, sample the vegetables fresh from the garden and other local delicacies, such as the famous truffade, a dish of potatoes, cheese, bacon and garlic.

Access : *Drive for 4km on a minor road*

Access : *Outside the ramparts, by the main road*

SAINT-JACQUES-DES-BLATS - 15800

LE GRIOU
M. Troupel

15800 Saint-Jacques-des-Blats
Tel. 04 71 47 06 25
hotel.griou@wanadoo.fr
www.hotel-griou.com
Languages : Eng.

Closed 5 to 20 Apr, and 10 Oct to 20 Dec
• 16 rooms all with bath/WC or shower/WC, one
has disabled access, some have television
• €42 to €52; breakfast €7; half-board available
• Menus €14 to €29 • Car park, garden

 **Admiring the natural and architectural
wealth of the Regional Volcano Park.**

Built in two stages, the hotel offers guests a
choice of accommodation; recent rooms, furnished in a Louis-Philippe style or others in
more classical vein. All are quite spotless and
most have a balcony. If unsure about which of
the two dining rooms to choose, we recommend the one with the large bay windows that
offers a delightful view over the village steeple
and Cantal mountains.

Access : *On the way out of the village*

SALERS - 15140

LE BAILLIAGE
M. et Mme Gouzon

Rue Notre-Dame
15140 Salers
Tel. 04 71 40 71 95
info@salers-hotel-bailliage.com
www.salers-hotel-bailliage.com

Closed from 15 Nov to 6 Feb • 23 rooms, 4 in a
separate wing (La Demeure Jarriges, 300m
away), all have bath/WC and television • €59 to
€85; breakfast €9.50; half-board available
• Menus €15 to €45 • Terrace, garden, garage,
car park • Outdoor swimming pool

 **Strolling past the historic buildings of
Salers.**

The stone walls of this 1960s farmstead stand in
one of the region's most enchanting medieval
villages. The spacious, comfortable rooms
overlook either the garden, the town or the
slopes of the nearby Puy Violent. Soft lighting,
cane furniture and red and orange drapes adorn
the stylish redecorated restaurant. Gourmets
come from miles around to enjoy the cuisine in
which the region's famous Salers beef naturally
takes pride of place, as does its namesake
cheese. Pleasant garden-terrace.

*Gastronomic weekend, relaxation and
balneotherapy weekend*

Access : *At the entrance to the village next to
the large car park*

SALERS - 15140

CHAMBRE D'HÔTE M. PRUDENT
M. et Mme Prudent

Rue des Nobles
15140 Salers
Tel. 04 71 40 75 36
claudine@chezprudent.com

www.chezprudent.com
Languages : Eng., Ger.

Open all year • 6 rooms with shower/WC and separate entrances • €45, breakfast included • No table d'hôte • Garden

Contemplating the exceptional panorama of the volcanic peaks of the Cantal.

This 17C house is idyllically situated in the heart of the picturesque medieval village of Salers. All the simply decorated yet comfortable rooms have their own private entrance and some command a fine view over the volcanoes. Treat yourself to breakfast in bed or venture downstairs and admire the attractive Auvergne dining room or the wonderful view from the terrace in fine weather. Souvenir shop in the hotel.

Access : *In the town centre*

TRIZAC - 15400

LE COUVENT
M. et Mme Belaiche

Le Bourg
15400 Trizac
Tel. 04 71 78 67 51
le-couvent@wanadoo.fr
www.lecouvent.fr
Languages : Eng.

Open from Easter to 31 Oct • 4 apartments with bath/WC • €90 to €95; breakfast €10 • No table d'hôte • Park. Credit cards not accepted, dogs admitted on request

Relaxing in the peaceful garden between the former convent and the village's Romanesque church.

Ask your friendly hosts to tell you the long story of this ancient abode and its slightly forbidding façade. You will find it all the easier to appreciate the efforts deployed since 1995 to turn it into a delightful house, whose comforts are now the antithesis of its former monastic vocation. A fine staircase leads up to the master bedroom and to three suites, each unique, and all comfortably and tastefully decorated and extremely peaceful.

Access : *In the centre of the village, on the D 678 between Mauriac and Riom-ès-Montagne*

VIC-SUR-CÈRE - 15800

AUBERGE DES MONTAGNES
M. et Mme Combourieu

15800 Vic-sur-Cère
Tel. 04 71 47 57 01
info@auberge-des-montagnes.com
www.auberge-des-montagnes.com
Languages : Eng.

Closed from 12 Oct to 20 Dec except weekend of 1 Nov • 23 rooms, 10 of which are in a separate wing and one has disabled access. Rooms have bath/WC or shower/WC, some have television • €55 to €64 (€48 to €55 low season); breakfast €6.50; half-board available • Restaurant closed Tue out of season; menus €18.50 (weekdays) to €33 • Terrace, car park, garage • 2 swimming pools, mountain bikes

LES CÈDRES BLEUS
M. et Mme Duverney

Route de la Rivière
43110 Aurec-sur-Loire
Tel. 04 77 35 48 48
www.lescedresbleus.com
Languages : Eng., Sp.

Closed from 2 Jan to 2 Feb, Sun evening and Mon lunchtime • 15 rooms, one has disabled access, most have bath/WC, some have shower/WC, all have television • €60 to €62; breakfast €8; half-board available • Air-conditioned restaurant; menus €20 (weekdays) to €78 • Terrace, garden, car park. No dogs admitted

 Visiting the farm where the film "With a friend like Harry" was shot.

The still waters of a pond reflect this picture-book hotel comprised of a handsome old farmstead with a stone-shingled roof, a more recent house flanked by a tower and a spacious stone terrace. The vast rooms are decorated in a rustic or a contemporary style. Swimming pool, mountain bikes, hiking, horse-drawn carts, fishing, skiing: the extensive range of activities illustrates the owners' get-up-and-go personality. Delicious feasts of Auvergne cooking.

Trying your hand at water-skiing on Lake Grangent.

Even though the site may lack the giant redwood trees, grizzly bears and log cabins of America's national parks, the same spirit reigns in this lakeside spot. The reception and restaurant are installed in the old family house, while three modern "chalets" house functional rooms, all of which overlook the garden and cedars. A well cared-for flowered terrace adds the final touch to this pastoral picture of unspoilt countryside.

Access : *At Vic-sur-Cère leave the N 122 (Aurillac-Murat road) and take the D 54 for Pailherols*

Access : *To the south-west of Saint-Étienne on the D 46, then at Aurec-sur-Loire towards Bas-en-Basset*

LA CHAISE-DIEU - 43160

CHASPINHAC - 43700

LA PARAVENT
M. Jourde

43700 Chaspinhac
Tel. 04 71 03 54 75
michel-jourde@wanadoo.fr
Languages : Eng.

Open all year • 5 rooms with shower/WC • €44 to €48, breakfast included • Table d'hôte €16 • Garden. Credit cards not accepted, no dogs admitted

LA JACQUEROLLE
Mme Chailly

Rue Marchédial
43160 La Chaise-Dieu
Tel. 04 71 00 07 52
lajacquerolle@hotmail.com
www.lajacquerolle.com
Languages : Eng., Sp., It.

Open all year • 4 rooms, one with bathroom • €57 to €60, breakfast included, half-board available • Table d'hôte €24 (evening only) • Car park. Credit cards not accepted, no dogs admitted

 Going mushrooming for cèps in the surrounding forest.

Entirely built out of local stone, this characterful house stands in the lower part of town. Countless family heirlooms, including a beautiful Louis-Philippe wardrobe and elegant looking mirrors grace the tastefully decorated, predominantly wood interior. A roaring log fire, lit in the dining room's magnificent stone fireplace, takes the chill off the short autumn and winter days.

The warm atmosphere of this handsome early-20C house.

The sterling welcome, constant attention to detail and eagerness to please immediately strike the visitor to this country house, just a few minutes' drive from Le Puy-en-Velay. The rustic-style interior decoration is full of character. Some of the cosy rooms have their own small sitting room and all have a private entrance. In the winter the lady of the house runs patchwork courses.

Access : *In the lower part of town*

Access : *10km to the north-east of Le Puy on the D 103 towards Retournac, then take the D 71*

RETOURNAC - 43130

LES REVERS
M. et Mme Chevalier

43130 Retournac
Tel. 04 71 59 42 81
jean-pierre.chevalier6@libertysurf.fr
www.lesrevers.fr.st
Languages : Eng.

Closed from Oct to Apr • 4 rooms with shower/WC • €45, breakfast included • Table d'hôte (evenings only and by reservation) €16 • Garden, car park. Credit cards not accepted, dogs not admitted

 The unspoilt countryside of this rural hideaway.

Those on a quest for silence, nature and authenticity will swoon at the sight of this extraordinarily secluded spot, wedged in between field and forest. The capacious, well-appointed rooms are furnished with comfortable bedding and all overlook the unspoilt countryside. Two rooms are on split-levels. The owner breeds horses and can organise rides for guests. A perfect hideaway for a relaxed, peaceful break.

Horse-riding, hiking weekends

Access : *8km to the south-east of Retournac on the D 103, then follow the signs*

SAINT-FRONT - 43550

L'HERMINETTE
Mme Mathieu

Bigorre - Les Maziaux
43550 Saint-Front
Tel. 04 71 59 57 58
lherminette@wanadoo.fr
www.auberge-lherminette.com
Languages : Eng.

Closed 3 weeks in Jan, 1 week in Sep and 1 week in Mar • 6 rooms with bathrooms • €72 to €76 (€54 to €58 low season) breakfast included; half-board available • Restaurant closed Sun evening and Mon; menus €12 (weekdays) to €23 • Garden, car park. No dogs admitted • Museum of local life nearby

 The change of scenery offered by this hamlet.

An enchanting hamlet of stone farmsteads topped with well-combed thatched roofs forms the backdrop to this typical Auvergne inn. Large, airy bedrooms, two on split-levels, regional-style dining rooms and delicious country cooking at unbeatable prices. If you're interested in finding out more about daily life in years gone by and how thatched roofs are made, stop by the Ecomuseum, and all will be revealed.

Access : *5km to the north-west of Saint-Front on the D 39, then take the lane on the right*

SAUGUES - 43170

LES GABALES
M. Gauthier

Route du Puy-en-Velay
43170 Saugues
Tel. 04 71 77 86 92
contact@lesgabales.com

www.lesgabales.com
Languages : Eng.

Closed 1 Dec to late Feb • 5 non-smoking rooms with shower/WC • €50, breakfast included, half-board available • Park, car park. Credit cards not accepted, no dogs admitted

We most liked — Finding out more about the legendary Beast of Gévaudan.

The legend of the Beast of Gévaudan is far from dead as you will find out when you listen to the tales related by the owner of this good-sized 1930s house. His other passion is walking and he is happy to share tips. Once safely back inside the hotel's walls, relax in the cosy sitting room-library; the wood panelling in the dining room is original. In the morning, after a well-earned night's sleep in one of the charmingly "retro" personalised rooms, guests can also enjoy a walk in the park.

Access : *On the road from Le Puy-en-Velay*

TENCE - 43190

LES PRAIRIES
M. et Mme Bourgeois

1 rue du Pré Long - Salettes
43190 Tence
Tel. 04 71 56 35 80
thomas.bourgeois@freesbee.fr
www.lesprairies.com
Languages : Eng.

Open all year (by reservation from 1 Nov to 15 Apr) • 5 non-smoking rooms, one with disabled access, all have bath/WC or shower/WC • €70, breakfast included • No table d'hôte • Terrace, garden, car park, television room and library. Credit cards not accepted • Children's play room and table-tennis

We most liked — The owners' faultless hospitality.

This handsome stone property (1850), nestling in a well-tended park planted with century-old trees, is just a stone's throw from the town. It is made up of two wings, one for the owners and one for guests with an independent entrance. On the ground-floor is a room with disabled access equipped with a large bathroom, while four other rooms are available upstairs. All are simply decorated and furnished with handsome pieces picked up in antique fairs and shops.

Access : *In the town*

BEAUREGARD-VENDON - 63460

CHAMBRE D'HÔTE MME BEAUJEARD
Mme Beaujeard

8 rue de la Limagne à Chaptes
63460 Beauregard-Vendon
Tel. 04 73 63 35 62
Languages : Eng.

Open all year, by reservation only from Nov to Mar • 3 non-smoking rooms with shower/WC • €68 to €75, breakfast included • No table d'hôte • Garden. Credit cards not accepted, no dogs admitted

 The enchanting, old-fashioned decoration.

This handsome late-18C country seat is the epitome of charm and tranquillity. The tastefully furnished rooms, all non-smoking, are perfect for winding down at the end of the day. The cosy sitting room with its fireplace, lavishly flowered garden in the summer, generous breakfasts, excellent welcome and moderate prices all add to the appeal.

Access : *9km northbound from Riom on the N 144 then the D 122*

CEILLOUX - 63520

DOMAINE DE GAUDON
M. et Mme Bozzo

63520 Ceilloux
Tel. 04 73 70 76 25
domainedegaudon@wanadoo.fr
www.domainedegaudon.fr

Open all year • 5 non-smoking rooms, including 1 family room, all have bath/WC or shower/WC and telephone • €98, breakfast included • No table d'hôte • Terrace, park, garage. Credit cards not accepted, no dogs admitted

 Being welcomed as if you were a friend of the family.

Park and woodland surround this handsome 19C property. A splendid wooden staircase leads up to superb rooms, each of which is poetically named: "Esther's dressing-table", "Garden of Love" or "Birds' Nest". Breakfasts are served in a lovely wood-panelled room or on the terrace in fine weather with the Puy de Dôme mountain range in the distance. Private fishing possible on the estate.

Access : *From Saint-Dier-d'Auvergne, head towards Domaize. 3km further on at "Les Palles", turn right towards Ceilloux, Gaudon is 1km away*

DAVAYAT - 63200

LA MAISON DE LA TREILLE
M. et Mme Honnorat

25 rue de l'Église
63200 Davayat
Tel. 04 73 63 58 20
honnorat.la.treille@wanadoo.fr
http://honnorat.la.treille.free.fr
Languages : Eng.

Open all year • 4 rooms including one family apartment, all with bath/WC or shower/WC • €72 to €87, breakfast included • No table d'hôte • Park, car park. Credit cards not accepted, no dogs admitted

 Tucking into the jams made with fruit from the orchard at breakfast time.

Italian Neoclassicism clearly inspired this smart bourgeois property built in 1810. A pleasant sitting room with piano and breakfast room, lit by a stone fireplace, make up the ground floor. Guests are accommodated in the orangery, an elegant outhouse which stands in the enchanting garden. The names of the trim, well-tended rooms give guests an idea of each room's decorative style: wheat, birds, grapes and beehive (for four people).

Tapestry and upholstery courses

Access : *7km northbound from Riom on the N 144*

LAQUEUILLE - 63820

AUBERGE DE FONDAIN
Mme Demossier

lieu-dit Fondain
63820 Laqueuille
Tel. 04 73 22 01 35
auberge.de.fondain@wanadoo.fr
www.auberge-fondain.com

Closed for 10 days in Mar and Nov • 6 rooms with bath/WC or shower/WC • €76 (€66 low season); breakfast €8; half-board available • Menus €12 (weekdays) to €23 (by reservation) • Terrace, garden, car park • Fitness room with sauna, hiking, mountain biking

 Signposted footpaths on themes such as fauna, flora and crater lakes.

This elegant 19C country house lost among fields and meadows is said to have belonged to the inventor of a local blue cheese: Laqueuille. The recently renovated rooms, named after flowers, combine a light, airy colour scheme with contrasting dark timbers, discreetly modern fittings and in some cases, a view of the Banne d'Ordanche. A fitness room, sauna and a dozen or so mountain bikes will make sure you work up an appetite for the tasty Auvergne cooking served in a welcoming rustic dining room.

Access : *2km to the north-east of Laqueuille, on the D 922 then a minor road*

LE MONT-DORE - 63240

33

LA CLOSERIE DE MANOU
Mme Larcher

Au Genestoux - BP 30
63240 Le Mont-Dore
Tel. 04 73 65 26 81
lacloseriedemanou@club-internet.fr
www.lacloseriedemanou.com
Languages : Eng.

Closed from 15 Oct to 30 Mar; open Sat-Sun early Mar • 5 non-smoking rooms with shower/WC • €75 to €80, breakfast included • No table d'hôte • Garden, car park. Credit cards not accepted, dogs not admitted

 The wealth of information about the region.

Nestling in the countryside, this traditional 18C Auvergne house with its stone walls and white shutters is quite enchanting. The decoration of the spacious rooms wavers between modern-uncluttered and snug; all are non-smoking. The sitting and dining rooms, furnished with antiques, provide a wonderful backdrop to the delicious breakfasts. The charm and attention of your hostess will be another reason why you won't want to leave.

Access : *3km westbound from Mont-Dore, take the Avenue des Belges D 996 towards Murat-le-Quaire on the A 89*

MONTPEYROUX - 63114

34

CHAMBRE D'HÔTE MME BOISSIÈRE
Mme Boissière

Rue de la Poterne
63114 Montpeyroux
Tel. 04 73 96 69 42
jules.boissiere@wanadoo.fr
www.chambres-boissiere.com
Languages : Eng.

Open all year • 5 non-smoking rooms with shower/WC • €55 to €60, breakfast included • No table d'hôte • Car park. Credit cards not accepted

 Exploring this historic village overlooking the Allier River.

Set at the foot of a 13C keep, this pretty sandstone house is well worth the short climb up the hill from the town car park; there are a few parking spaces in front of the house if needed. Each of the bedrooms boasts its own little extra bonus: terrace, fireplace, canopied bed or jacuzzi bath. After taking refreshments in the vaulted dining room, set off round the narrow lanes and meet the painters and potters who have replaced the wine-growers of yesteryear.

Access : *8km to the south-west of Vic-le-Comte on the A 75, exit no 7*

MONTPEYROUX - 63114

LES PRADETS
Edith Grenot

Les Pradets
63114 Montpeyroux
Tel. 04 73 96 63 40
claude.grenot@wanadoo.fr
www.auvergne.maison-hotes.com

Open all year • 3 rooms with bathrooms • €72, breakfast included • No table d'hôte • Garden. Credit cards not accepted

Edith Grenot's faultless welcome.

This delightful house lies in a secluded lane of the picturesque fortified village of Montpeyroux. Relax in the cosy ground floor sitting room strewn with well-used furniture, a piano and books on the Auvergne region. In fine weather, you will no doubt make a beeline for the inner courtyard garden where breakfast is served. Parquet floors, rugs, paintings by local artists and rustic furniture add character to the well-decorated rooms.

Access : *In the heart of the village*

NÉBOUZAT - 63210

LES GRANGES
Mme Gauthier

Recoleine
63210 Nébouzat
Tel. 04 73 87 10 34
gauthier.jocelyne@free.fr
lesgranges.free.fr

Closed from 15 Nov to 1 Feb • 3 rooms with shower/WC • €44 to €48, breakfast included; half-board available • Table d'hôte €16 • Credit cards not accepted, dogs not admitted

The pastoral scene just two minutes from the Dôme mountain range.

A warm welcome awaits visitors inside this old barn, beautifully renovated by a farming couple. The comfortable, tasteful rooms all enjoy views of the surrounding countryside. An immense living-sitting room and spacious sofa are most appreciated. Your charming, talkative hostess will be more than happy to point out walks and hikes. Ideal for nature lovers.

Access : *3km from Randanne on the N 89*

ORCINES - 63870

DOMAINE DE TERNANT
Mme Piollet

 5 route de Durtol à Ternant
63870 Orcines
Tel. 04 73 62 11 20
domaine.ternant@free.fr
http://domaine.ternant.free.fr
Languages : Eng.

Closed from 15 Nov to 15 Mar • 5 non-smoking rooms with shower/WC • €78 to €90, breakfast included • No table d'hôte • Sitting room, park, car park. Credit cards not accepted, no dogs admitted • Tennis, billiard room

 The sheltered environment of this old building.

This elegant 19C property stands in 25 acres of grounds at the foot of the Dôme mountain range. A profusion of family heirlooms scattered throughout the bedrooms, sitting room, library and games room creates a warm, lived-in feel. The personal touch and taste of the lady of the house, a patchwork artist, can be felt everywhere. Tennis court in the grounds and other sports facilities nearby, including Vulcania, the Regional Volcano Park.

Access : *11km north-west of Clermont-Ferrand on the D 941A and the D 90*

PERRIER - 63500

MAISON GEBRILLAT
M. Gebrillat

 Chemin de Siorac
63500 Perrier
Tel. 04 73 89 15 02
 gebrillat@club.fr
 www.maison-gebrillat.com
Languages : Eng., Du.

Closed 1 Dec to 31 Jan • 3 rooms and one apartment with shower/WC • €47 to €58, breakfast included • No table d'hôte • Garden, car park. Credit cards not accepted, dogs welcome on request

Strolling in the park bounded by the Couze de Pavin River.

This handsome 18C country house is perfect for those wishing to get to know the Dore Mountains a little better. The tastefully decorated rooms marry charm and comfort. As soon as the first rays of sun appear, the breakfast table is laid outdoors under a heated awning which overlooks a delightful inner courtyard; warm sweaters advisable. You host, Paul, is a gold mine of useful tourist tips.

> *Flower arranging weekend, cooking "differently" weekend*

Access : *3km westbound from Issoire on the D 996*

ROYAT - 63130

ROCHEFORT-MONTAGNE - 63210

CHÂTEAU DE CHARADE
M. et Mme Gaba

63130 Royat
Tel. 04 73 35 91 67
gaba@chateau-de-charade.com
www.chateau-de-charade.com
Languages : Eng.

Closed from early Nov to late Mar • 5 rooms with bathrooms • €78 to €86, breakfast included • No table d'hôte • Park, car park. Credit cards not accepted, no dogs admitted

CHÂTEAU DE VOISSIEUX
M. et Mme Phillips

Saint-Bonnet-d'Orcival
63210 Rochefort-Montagne
Tel. 04 73 65 81 02
Languages : Eng.

Closed from Oct to late Feb • 3 rooms with bathrooms • €57 to €65, breakfast included • No table d'hôte • Terrace, park, car park. Credit cards not accepted • Mountain biking, horse-riding, swimming, golf, paragliding, hot-air ballooning and skiing nearby

The country house feel of this whimsical castle just two minutes from the regional capital.

This castle which borders the Royat golf course extends a majestic welcome. High ceilings, a stone staircase and the antique furniture in the bedrooms and bathrooms all bear witness to an illustrious past. As for the present, guests are invariably charmed by the appeal of the lady of the house's gracious welcome, the tinkling of the piano playing in the sitting room or the click of billiard balls. If you don't feel like visiting the town, head for the nearby Dôme mountains.

Being treated like the lord or lady of the manor in the heart of the Auvergne Regional Park.

Volcanic stone was of course used to build this 13C castle, it was also used to restore it to its present-day state. In the park a 400-year-old lime tree keeps watch over the estate's quiet solitude. You have a choice between two soberly furnished rooms or a more exuberant rococo style in the third. Breakfasts are served in the kitchen by the fireside or on the flowered terrace overlooking the park. It isn't possible to lunch or dine in the castle, but restaurants are hardly in short supply.

Access : *6km to the south-west of Royat on the D 941C and the D 5, towards the racing track and golf course*

Access : *4km to the north-east of Orcival on the D 27*

SAINT-ANTHÈME - 63660

AU PONT DE RAFFINY
M. et Mme Beaudoux

Raffiny
63660 Saint-Anthème
Tel. 04 73 95 49 10
hotel.pont.raffiny@wanadoo.fr
www.hotel-pont-raffiny.com
Languages : Eng.

Closed from 8 Jan to 7 Mar, Sun evening and Mon (except Jul-Aug), Fri to Sun in Mar • 11 rooms and 2 small wooden chalets with private gardens. All rooms have bath/WC or shower/WC, television • €44 to €47; breakfast €7; half-board available • Menus €16.50 to €32 • Car park • Swimming pool, sauna, Jacuzzi, billiards, hiking, mountain bike rental

A ride in the panoramic "Livradois-Forez" train.

Two chalets designed for families, complete with kitchenette and private gardens, have recently been added to the hotel's amenities. The bedrooms in the main wing – a former village café – are more simply furnished, even if those on the second floor, lined in wood, do have a certain alpine charm. A rockery fountain lends an amusing touch to the rustic dining room. All in all, we were quite won over by the charm of this country hotel.

Hiking excursions with luggage transported, bicycling excursions

Access : *Leave Saint-Anthème southbound on the D 261 and drive for 5.5km*

SAINT-GERVAIS-D'AUVERGNE - 63390

CASTEL HÔTEL 1904
M. Mouty

Rue du Castel
63390 Saint-Gervais-d'Auvergne
Tel. 04 73 85 70 42
castel.hotel.1904@wanadoo.fr
www.castel-hotel-1904.com
Languages : Eng.

Open from Mar to Dec • 17 rooms with bath/WC or shower/WC, all have television • €65 to €75; breakfast €9; half-board available • Menus €15 to €54 • Garden, car park. No dogs admitted

The rather quaint old-fashioned atmosphere.

The carved "1616" over the fireplace bears witness to the age of these walls. This private residence, built for the Marquis of Maintenon, passed into the hands of a religious community in the 19C before it became a coaching inn at the turn of the 20c. Beams, creaky floorboards, well-worn furniture, gleaming silver and 1900 statuettes and lights bestow an almost nostalgic feel to this "castel". Sample the excellent home cooking of the Comptoir à Moustaches, a nearby country bistro.

Access : *In the centre of the village*

SAINT-GERVAIS-D'AUVERGNE - 63390

43

MONTARLET
M. et Mme Pelletier

Lieu-dit Montarlet
63390 Saint-Gervais-d'Auvergne
Tel. 04 73 85 87 10
montarlet@libertysurf.fr
www.montarlet-chambresdhotes.com

Closed 1 Jan to 29 Feb • 3 rooms with bathrooms • €46, breakfast included • No table d'hôte • Park, car park. Credit cards not accepted

 The enchanting natural site of this farmhouse.

Guests are often in raptures over the charm and tranquillity of this renovated farmhouse in the middle of the countryside. The rooms illustrate how much the owners have their guests' welfare at heart, from the sponge-painted walls and antique furniture gleaned in local flea markets to the matching bed-linen and curtains and roomy bathrooms. The sitting room is graced with a fireplace and floor made out of Volvic stone and the landscaped parkland commands a fine view over the Auvergne mountains.

Access : *3km westbound from St-Gervais-d'Auvergne on the D 532 towards Espinasse and take the lane on the left*

SAINT-RÉMY-DE-CHARGNAT - 63500

44

CHÂTEAU DE LA VERNÈDE
M. et Mme Chauve

63500 Saint-Rémy-de-Chargnat
Tel. 04 73 71 07 03
chateauvernede@aol.com
www.chateauvernedeauvergne.com
Languages : Eng.

Open all year • 5 non-smoking rooms, all have bath/WC or shower/WC • €65 to €90, breakfast included • No table d'hôte • Park, garage • Sitting room with billiards

 Discovering the charm of the "Tuscany of Auvergne".

This enchanting castle restored in the 19C in a Neo-Gothic style was originally a hunting lodge which belonged to Queen Margot. The interior still bears the trace of its splendid heritage: wainscoting, fireplaces, antique furniture, lovely sitting and dining rooms and elegant bedrooms. The park which boasts a stream, an old mill, a dovecote, well-tended flower beds and shady paths is equally inviting. A must at excellent value for money.

Access : *6km southeast of Issoire on the D 996, then the D 123 for 1km*

SAINT-RÉMY-DE-CHARGNAT - 63500

45

CHÂTEAU DE PASREDON
Mme Marchand

63500 Saint-Rémy-de-Chargnat
Tel. 04 73 71 00 67
Languages : Eng.

Closed from 16 Oct to 14 Apr • 5 non-smoking rooms, all have bathrooms • €70 to €90, breakfast included • No table d'hôte • Park, library, garage. No dogs admitted • Tennis

Sleeping in a castle steeped in history.

This 17C and 19C castle stands in a handsome park facing the Puy mountain range. The interior is equally appealing with spacious personalised bedrooms (Louis Philippe furniture or the "Polish" bed in the middle of one of the rooms, etc.), a splendid sitting room complete with coffered ceiling and wainscoting and the richly stocked library. But let us not forget the mouth-watering breakfasts...

Access : *8km southeast of Issoire on the D 996 and D 999*

TEILHÈDE - 63460

46

CHÂTEAU DES RAYNAUDS
M. et Mme Simon

63460 Teilhède
Tel. 04 73 64 30 12
info@chateau-raynauds.com

Open all year • 4 non-smoking rooms on 2 floors, all with bath/WC and shower/WC • €67 to €75, breakfast included, half-board available • Table d'hôte €24, drinks included, evenings only • Sitting room, garage. No dogs admitted

The owners' passion for their home.

In the heart of the Auvergne volcanic region stands this 17C abode flanked by two towers and surrounded by greenery – heaven for nature lovers. A magnificent spiral staircase leads up to generously proportioned, comfortable bedrooms. Delicious, hearty breakfasts served on carefully prepared tables. Regional produce takes pride of place on the table d'hôte menu: cold meats, cheese and wine from Auvergne.

Access : *2km westbound from Teilhède on the D 17*

THIERS - 63300

47

VARENNES-SUR-USSON - 63500

48

LE PARC DE GEOFFROY
M. Brugere

49 avenue du Général-de-Gaulle
63300 Thiers
Tel. 04 73 80 87 00
reservation@parc-de-geoffroy.com
www.parc-de-geoffroy.com
Languages : Eng., Ger.

Closed in Jan • 31 rooms on 3 floors. Rooms have bath/WC and television • €67 to €95; breakfast €8; half-board available • Menus €13 (weekdays) to €41 • Terrace, garden, car park

LES BAUDARTS
Mme Verdier

7 les Beaudards
63500 Varennes-sur-Usson
Tel. 04 73 89 05 51
Languages : Eng.

Closed from 1 Oct to 15 May • 3 rooms with shower/WC • €70 to €80, breakfast included • No table d'hôte • Garden, car park. Credit cards not accepted, dogs not admitted

 Enjoying a cutting-edge visit to the House of Cutlery-makers.

A luxurious walled garden protects the residence from the bustle of the nearby busy shopping centre. The comfortable reception and dining rooms decorated with frescoes are housed in a former cutlery workshop. The rooms, located in a quiet, modern wing, are light, airy and practical. The well-provisioned breakfast table provides guests with the energy necessary to embark on the "ascent" of the upper town.

 The unadulterated sophistication of every room.

Tucked away in the countryside, this establishment may not be easy to find, but it is well worth persevering because its dusty pink walls contain a marvel of sophistication, calm and comfort. The superb, spacious rooms are exquisitely decorated in light, warm tones. The sitting room, lit in the winter by a roaring log fire, is crammed with books. Who could resist Mrs Baudart's delightful welcome?

Access : *5km along the N 89 towards Clermont-Ferrand*

Access : *On leaving Varennes take the first right (D 123), then turn into the wooded drive at the first bend*

BURGUNDY

Côte-d'Or - 21
Nièvre - 58
Saône-et-Loire - 71
Yonne - 89

A visit to Burgundy takes travellers back through time to an era when its mighty Dukes rivalled even the kings of France. Born of an uncompromising desire for perfection, their stately castles and rich abbeys bear witness to a golden age of ostentation and prestige. As we look back now, it is difficult to reproach them for the flamboyance which has made Dijon a world-renowned city of art. And who would dispute Burgundy's claim to the "best wines in Christendom" when one sees how the hordes of today continue to lay siege to the region's cellars, where cool and canny wine-growers guard the secret of their finest vintages? This dedication to time-honoured traditions also rules the region's steadfast homage to the culinary arts, from strong-smelling époisses cheese to gingerbread dripping with honey. After sinning so extravagantly, you may be tempted to make amends and take a barge trip down the region's canals and rivers to digest in peace amidst the unspoilt countryside.

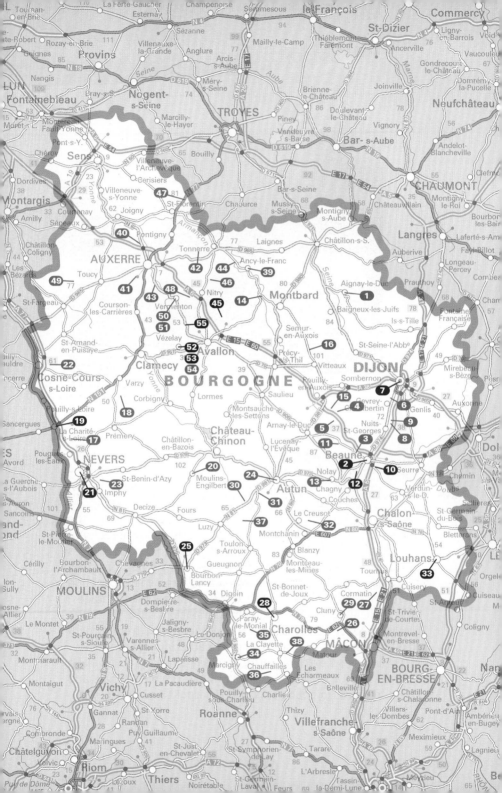

AIGNAY-LE-DUC - 21510

1

BEAUNE - 21200

2

MANOIR DE TARPERON
M. de Champsavin

Route de Saint-Marc
21510 Aignay-le-Duc
Tel. 03 80 93 83 74
manoir-de-tarperon@wanadoo.fr
Languages : Eng., Ger.

Closed from Nov to Mar • 5 rooms with bathrooms • €65 to €70, breakfast included • Table d'hôte €25 (evenings) • Terrace, garden. Credit cards not accepted, no dogs admitted • Stabling, concerts, exhibitions

GRILLON
M. et Mme Grillon

21 route de Seurre
21200 Beaune
Tel. 03 80 22 44 25
joel.GRILLON@wanadoo.fr
www.hotel-grillon.fr
Languages : Eng., Ger.

Closed from 29 Jan to 12 Mar • 18 air-conditioned rooms, most of which have bath/WC and television. Several are non-smoking • €52 to €65; breakfast €9 • No restaurant • Garden, terrace, private car park • Swimming pool

 We most liked
The beautiful "Wind in the Willows" feel to this location.

A unique charm emanates from this manor and its superb riverside setting on the banks of the Coquille. The bedrooms, of varying sizes, are colourfully and tastefully furnished. The sitting room, complete with library, leads onto a pleasant veranda overlooking the garden. Fly fishing enthusiasts are in for a treat with a private stream all of their own. Those otherwise inclined will enjoy boat trips and an excursion to the source of the Seine.

 We most liked
A haven of greenery close to the Hospices de Beaune.

This spruce pink house with light-green shutters is almost hidden in the summer by a thick curtain of chestnut trees, but we highly recommend venturing past the wrought-iron gate and inside the comfortable 19C mansion. The rooms vary between light and airy or cosy and some feature interesting old pieces of furniture picked up in local antique shops. The vaulted cellar has been turned into a sitting room and bar. Breakfast is served on a pretty flowered terrace.

Access : *Take the small road towards Saint-Marc*

Access : *At the entrance to Beaune, from Seurre (D 973, Dôle road)*

BOUZE-LES-BEAUNE - 21200

LA CADOLLE
M. Pawlowski

Grande-Rue
21200 Bouze-les-Beaune
Tel. 03 80 26 08 99

Closed Dec and Jan • 3 rooms with shower/WC • €50, breakfast included • No table d'hôte • Terrace. Credit cards not accepted, no dogs admitted

The charm of this tiny wine-growing village.

Be prepared to wind down and enjoy the friendly atmosphere of this beautifully restored old stone house. One of the twin buildings is home to three rooms accessible via an outside staircase. The two most spacious rooms (one of which boasts a marble fireplace) have their own balcony. The third, under the eaves, is cosier. All the rooms are comfortable and have original wooden floorboards. Their appeal is enhanced by the obvious care lavished by the discreet welcoming owners.

Access : *6km northwest bound from Beaune on the D 970*

CHÂTEAUNEUF - 21320

CHAMBRE D'HÔTE MME BAGATELLE
Mme Bagatelle

Rue des Moutons
21320 Châteauneuf
Tel. 03 80 49 21 00
jean-michel.bagatelle@wanadoo.fr
www.chateauneuf.net/bagatelle
Languages : Eng.

Closed during the February holidays • 4 rooms with shower/WC • €55 to €65, breakfast included • Garden, car park. Credit cards not accepted, no dogs admitted

Wandering through the narrow streets of this lovely fortified village.

This old stone sheepfold stands in the centre of the medieval village on the banks of the Burgundy Canal. Stone and wood take pride of place in this tastefully decorated house. Guests immediately feel at home in the welcoming bedrooms, one of which has a fireplace, while the split-level rooms are perfectly suited to families.

Access : *In the village*

CHAUDENAY-LE-CHÂTEAU - 21360

5

LE COTTAGE DU CHÂTEAU
M. Touflan

Le Bourg
21360 Chaudenay-le-Château
Tel. 03 80 20 00 43
le.cottage@libertysurf.fr
Languages : Eng.

Closed from 14 Dec to 30 Jan • 4 rooms with private entrance, all have bath/WC or shower/WC • €52 to €62, breakfast included • No table d'hôte • Terrace, garden, car park • Nearby: riding centre, angling, walking, hot-air balloons, golf, water sports

We most liked The view of the medieval tower and the surrounding countryside.

Ideal for a quiet break on the edge of a forest. The cleverly restored house and former sheepfold are today home to four spacious bedrooms, each of which has its own independent entrance. The rooms' generous proportions are enhanced by carefully chosen furnishings and fabrics. On sunny days breakfast is served in the flower-decked garden. Lovely walks in the vicinity.

Access : *15km westbound on the D 17 and D 115B*

COUCHEY - 21160

6

CHAMBRE D'HÔTE LES BRUGÈRES
M. et Mme Brugère

7 rue Jean-Jaurès
21160 Couchey
Tel. 03 80 52 13 05
brugeref@aol.com
www.francoisbrugere.com
Languages : Eng., Ger.

Closed from Dec to Mar • 4 rooms with shower/WC • €58 to €66, breakfast included • No table d'hôte • Car park. No dogs admitted

We most liked Soak up the atmosphere of a wine estate.

This charming 17C establishment, the property of a Marsannay wine-grower, provides a perfect opportunity to get to know more about the region's wine. The attractively restored rooms are decorated with exposed beams and prize finds from the local antique dealers: one bedroom even has a piano. In the winter, roaring log fires light up the breakfast room, hung with tapestries. The cellar is open for visits and wine-tastings.

Access : *2km southbound from Marsannay on the D 122*

DIJON - 21000

WILSON
Mmes Descaillot et Etievant

1 rue Longvic
21000 Dijon
Tel. 03 80 66 82 50
hotelwilson@wanadoo.fr
www.wilson-hotel.com
Languages : Ger., Eng., It.

Open all year • 27 rooms, (13 are air-conditioned), 18 of which have bath/WC, 9 have shower/WC, all have television • €74.50 to €103; breakfast €11 • No restaurant • Garage

 Snug as a bug in this house of character.

Lovingly and tastefully restored, this 17C coaching inn has now added the bonus of modern comforts to its beautifully preserved Burgundian architecture. The exposed beams and cosy, lived-in feel of the well-sound-proofed rooms, laid out round an inner courtyard, never fail to win over guests. Breakfast is served by an open fire in winter.

Access : *From the town centre, drive to Place du Théâtre and then along Rue Chabot-Charny*

FLAGEY-ECHÉZEAUX - 21640

CHAMBRE D'HÔTE LE PETIT PARIS
Mme Buffey

Rue du Petit-Paris
21640 Flagey-Echézeaux
Tel. 03 80 62 84 09
petitparis.bourgogne@free.fr
www.petitparis.bourgogne.free.fr
Languages : Eng.

Open all year • 4 rooms, 3 of which are upstairs, all have bath/WC • €85, breakfast included • No table d'hôte • Park, car park. Credit cards not accepted, no dogs admitted

 Basking in the sunshine filtering through the leaves of the hundred-year-old trees.

The quiet park, filled with the peaceful gurgle of the waters of the Vouge, is the setting for this 17C home, beautifully decorated with paintings by the lady of the house, almost giving the impression of an art gallery. The four rooms, set around the workshop, are cosily comfortable and equipped with private bathrooms. If the fancy takes you, why not try your hand at a little drawing? Others less inclined will prefer a walk round the park and the fish farm pond.

Access : *12km northeast bound on the D 116 and D 109c*

GILLY-LÈS-CÎTEAUX - 21640

LEVERNOIS - 21200

LA CLOSERIE DE GILLY
Mme Lanaud

Au Bourg
21640 Gilly-lès-Cîteaux
Tel. 03 80 62 87 74
contact@closerie-gilly.com
www.closerie-gilly.com
Languages : Eng., Sp.

Closed 1 week at Christmas and 1 week in Feb
• 5 rooms with bath/WC • €70 to €85, breakfast
included • No table d'hôte • Terrace, park, car
park. No dogs admitted • Outdoor swimming
pool

PARC
M. et Mme Oudot

13 rue du Golf
21200 Levernois
Tel. 03 80 24 63 00
hotel.le.parc@wanadoo.fr
www.hotelleparc.fr
Languages : Eng.

Closed from 26 Nov to 26 Jan • 25 rooms, all of
which have bath/WC or shower/WC and television • €44 to €94; breakfast €8 • No restaurant
• Car park, park. Dogs not admitted

 **Take the time to savour some fine local
vintages and regional munchies.**

This handsome late 18C abode surrounded by
vineyards and forest opens onto a park planted
with hundred-year-old trees. It is home to four
pretty rooms, tastefully decorated and furnished with antiques, and one small gîte in an
outhouse, which is less spacious but just as
snug. Delightful swimming pool and charming
walks in the region. The lady of the house takes
great pleasure in explaining the finer points of
wine-tasting so that you are able to fully appreciate the region's many treasures...

*Discovering wine. 1 and 2hr oenology
lessons with tasting of 3 to 4 wines*

Access : *11km northeast bound on the D 116 and
D 109c*

  **Listening to the wind rustling the leaves of
the hundred-year-old trees in the park.**

A lovely flowered courtyard separates these
two buildings, whose distinctive Burgundy-
style façades are covered in Virginia creeper.
The eye is drawn to the tall trees standing in the
pleasant grounds. A cosy family atmosphere
reigns throughout the rooms decorated with
old furniture, retro lamps and flowered drapes.
All are equally impeccably looked after and
those in the second building are slightly larger.
Most attentive family welcome.

Access : *5km south-east of Beaune on the
Verdun-sur-le-Doubs road, D 970 and D 111*

MEURSAULT - 21190

LUSIGNY-SUR-OUCHE - 21360

DOMAINE DU MOULIN AUX MOINES
M. Hanique

Auxey-Duresses
21190 Meursault
Tel. 03 80 21 60 79
contact@laterrasse.fr
www.laterrasse.fr

Open all year • 3 rooms and 1 gîte at the mill, 3 rooms 500m away at Meursault, all have bathrooms • €76 to €125; breakfast €7 • No restaurant • Garden, car park

LA SAURA
M. et Mme Berthaud

Route de Beaune
21360 Lusigny-sur-Ouche
Tel. 03 80 20 17 46
la-saura@wanadoo.fr
www.douix.com/la-saura

Open all year • 6 rooms with shower/WC • €70 to €90, breakfast included • No table d'hôte • Garden, car park. Credit cards not accepted • Outdoor swimming pool, horse-riding, tennis, golf and boating on the canal nearby

 We most liked Its unique location in the heart of the prestigious Meursault vineyard.

This handsome property surrounded by vineyards once belonged to the Abbey of Cluny. Stone walls, beams, tiled floors and a fireplace add a great deal of cachet to the tastefully-appointed rooms; ask for the one in the mill. The inner courtyard, right on a riverbank, is also very pleasant. A wealth of activities awaits guests, including tastings of the estate's wine and visits to the dovecote and to the small wine-growing museum with an interesting 15C wine press.

We most liked The fine collection of contemporary art.

The owner, a painter in his spare time, has acquired a fine collection of contemporary works, including several abstracts which blend in beautifully with the original fireplace, beams and stone floors. The rooms are decorated in a variety of eclectic styles, marrying parquet floor and antiques in one and a wrought-iron bed, terracotta tiles and painted furniture in another; all overlook the terraced garden. An art gallery and a swimming pool have recently been built in the outbuildings.

Access : *In the middle of the estate's vineyards*

Access : *2km southbound from Bligny-sur-Ouche on the D 970*

NOLAY - 21340

AU TEMPS D'AUTREFOIS
M. Pocheron

Place Monge
21340 Nolay
Tel. 03 80 21 76 37
noellepocheron@wanadoo.fr
www.terroirs-b.com/gite
Languages : Eng.

Open all year • 4 rooms, one of which is an apartment, with bath/WC or shower/WC • €63, breakfast included • No table d'hôte • Credit cards not accepted

 The well-preserved charm of yesteryear.

A deliciously faded atmosphere emanates from this attractive 14C half-timbered house, standing on a little square opposite a fountain. The warm, welcoming interior features exposed beams, antique furniture, chequered curtains and tiled floors. The quiet, pretty rooms are adorned with old black and white photos of Nolay. In the summer, breakfast is served on the terrace of the inn, on the opposite side of the square.

Access : *In the village*

ROUGEMONT - 21500

CHAMBRE D'HÔTE MME BACCHIERI
Mme Bacchieri

La Forge, bord du Canal de Bourgogne
21500 Rougemont
Tel. 03 80 92 35 99

 Languages : Eng., Sp.

Closed from 1 Dec to 1 Jan • 3 rooms with bath/WC • €50, breakfast included • No table d'hôte • Car park. Credit cards not accepted • Boating

 Boating on the untroubled waters of the Burgundy Canal.

This delightful little house on the banks of the Burgundy Canal in the Armançon Valley lives up to its promise of peace and quiet. The welcoming, well-kept rooms are full of character and above all very peaceful; all have a fireplace. The manicured garden near the lock and the bicycle towpath along the banks of the canal further enhance its charm. Lavish breakfasts and gracious welcome.

Access : *10km to the north-west of Montbard on the D 905*

VILLEFERRY - 21350

VANDENESSE-EN-AUXOIS - 21320

« AU FIL DE L'EAU »
M. Greneu

Canal de Bourgogne
21320 Vandenesse-en-Auxois
Tel. 06 72 51 62 91
jacques.greneu@wanadoo.fr
www.penichevoyage.fr

Open all year • 4 rooms with bathrooms • €73, breakfast included • No table d'hôte • Credit cards not accepted, no dogs admitted

LE VERGER SOUS LES VIGNES
M. Mersky

Le Haut du Village
21350 Villeferry
Tel. 03 80 49 60 04
info@bourgogne-en-douce.com
www.bourgogne-en-douce.com
Languages : Eng., Ger.

Open all year • 8 rooms, all with bath/WC • €60 to €80, breakfast included • Table d'hôte €22 • Garden, car park • Sauna, Jacuzzi

Treat yourself to a night in a floating bedroom.

Climb on board this fully renovated old trading barge, ideally located for enjoying sunny breakfasts overlooking the church and town. Inside admire the small sitting room and the painted frescoes on the doors that lead to the bedrooms. The latter are understandably a little cramped and offer limited comfort, but this is largely compensated for by the overall charm of the place. Small river tours can be organised if you decide to stay for a few nights.

The charm of this unusual cluster of houses.

This group of 18 chambres d'hôte laid out in several houses in the upper reaches of the small village has been carefully designed to preserve the independence and privacy of guests, whilst offering them the chance to meet in the communal areas (library, reading room and fitness room with sauna and Jacuzzi). Large windows and flower-decked terraces command a peaceful view of the surrounding countryside.

Beginners' wine-tasting course, tourist excursions with commentary, discovering music

Access : *11km northbound from Alise-Ste-Reine on the D905 and D 103*

Access : *7km southeast bound from Pouilly-en-Auxoix*

CHAULGNES - 58400

17

BEAUMONDE
Mme Trinquard

Le Margat
58400 Chaulgnes
Tel. 03 86 37 86 16
cheryl.jj.trinquard@wanadoo.fr
Languages : Eng.

Open all year (reservations only in winter) • 4 non-smoking rooms with bathrooms, 2 have power showers, all have television • €60 to €75, breakfast included • Table d'hôte €22, drinks included • Park, private car park. Credit cards not accepted, dogs not admitted • Outdoor swimming pool, fitness room, fishing in pond

We most liked
The discreet but friendly welcome.

This handsome characterful house (1960), set in 7ha of grounds in the heart of the Burgundy countryside, invites guests to enjoy the overflow swimming pool, fitness room or fireside, depending on the season. The tastefully decorated and pleasantly understated rooms, are very well equipped. Meals are a happy blend of French and Australian influences, birthplace of the welcoming owner.

Access : *7km north of Pougues-les-Eaux, by the D 138 and D 267*

CORVOL-D'EMBERNARD - 58210

18

LE COLOMBIER DE CORVOL
M. et Mme Collet

58210 Corvol-d'Embernard
Tel. 03 86 29 79 60
robert.collet1@wanadoo.fr
www.lecolombierdecorvol.com
Languages : Eng., Du.

Closed 15 Oct to late Nov • 5 non-smoking rooms; all have bath/WC or shower/WC • €95 to €105, breakfast included • Table d'hôte €30 to €40 • Park, car park. Dogs welcome by request • Outdoor heated swimming pool, badminton court, bicycles

We most liked
Admiring the works of art on display in each room.

Belgian-born Robert Collet assuages his two passions in this farmhouse (1812) nestling in the Nivernais countryside: art and cooking. The dining room, sitting room and bedrooms are crammed with paintings, sculpture, photos, etc, which are either his own work or that of artists chosen by him. Contemporary furniture adorns the rooms decorated on an animal theme (cockerel, pheasant, boar). There is no lack of outdoor activities either, including a heated swimming pool, badminton, bicycles, walking.

Access : *By the D 977 towards Nevers, between Varzy and Prémery*

LA CHARITÉ-SUR-LOIRE - 58400

LA GRANDE SAUVE
M. et Mme Derangere

Route de Limanton
58290 Moulins-Engilbert
Tel. 03 86 84 36 40
derangeredom@club-internet.fr

Open from Easter to Nov • 3 non-smoking rooms, all with shower/WC or bath/WC • €50, breakfast included • No table d'hôte • Park, car park. Credit cards not accepted, no dogs admitted • Petanque, table football, badminton and angling

LE BON LABOUREUR
M. Boulin

Quai Romain Mollot
58400 La Charité-sur-Loire
Tel. 03 86 70 22 85
lebonlaboureur@wanadoo.fr
www.lebonlaboureur.com
Languages : Eng.

Open all year • 16 rooms with bath/WC or shower/WC, all with television • €45 to €55; breakfast €6.50 • Menus €18 to €26 (closed 3 weeks late Jan early Feb and 2 weeks in Nov) • Garden. Dogs not admitted in rooms • Reading room

 The tasteful blend of sophistication and simplicity.

Very near to a sprawling Burgundy farm, amid trees and greenery, this generously proportioned house invites guests to take their time. You will immediately feel at home in the tastefully decorated rooms adorned with lovely antique furniture. Breakfast is served in the large sitting room, or in fine weather, on the terrace that is shaded from the sun by trees – an excellent way to start the day. Stabling for horses available.

 Killing time in the peaceful garden on a summer's day.

This former coaching inn, complete with a barn formerly used by bargees, is located on an island on the Loire. The gracious proprietors take great pleasure in welcoming their guests in style. All the rooms are renovated, light and airy and perfectly kept. The breakfast room with a veranda section overlooking a charming garden is another high spot of this address.

Access : *2km southwest bound from Moulins-Engilbert, on Limanton road*

Access : *Near the town centre on the Loire, on the D 955 towards Sancerre*

NEVERS - 58000

CLOS SAINTE-MARIE
M. et Mme F. Vincent

25 rue du Petit Mouësse
58000 Nevers
Tel. 03 86 71 94 50
clos.ste.marie@wanadoo.fr
www.clos-sainte-marie.fr
Languages : Eng., It.

Closed 24 Dec to 2 Jan • 17 rooms with bath/WC or shower/WC, all with television; 8 are non-smoking • €70 to €78; breakfast €9 • No restaurant • Garden, car park. No dogs admitted

Relaxing to the sound of the pools in the hotel's inner courtyard.

Some of the rooms of this hotel near a busy street overlook the road but are well sound-proofed to ensure a good night's sleep; most are however laid out around a lush green, peaceful patio whose ornamental pools are home to goldfish. The bedrooms, most of which are spacious, are all excellently looked after and furnished with antiques picked up in local markets; some have been recently renovated.

Access : *2km from the town centre on the N 81 towards Dijon*

SAINT-PÈRE - 58200

L'ORÉE DES VIGNES
Mme Kandin

Croquant
58200 Saint-Père
Tel. 03 86 28 12 50
loreedesvignes@wanadoo.fr
www.loreedesvignes.com
Languages : Eng.

Open all year • 5 non-smoking rooms, all have bathrooms. Smoking area available in house • €54 to €56, breakfast included; half-board available • Table d'hôte €24 (by reservation only) • Terrace, garden, car park. Credit cards not accepted, no dogs admitted

The well-stocked information corner in the hall.

This pretty stone-walled farmhouse topped with a traditional tiled roof has a number of assets. First and foremost, its spacious, taste-fully decorated rooms with sloping ceilings. Next, the pleasure of eating in the handsome dining room complete with Burgundy and Spanish Renaissance furniture. Finally the sitting room with its old bread oven and the terrace where you can sit back and contemplate the beautiful garden.

Foie gras course, first three weekends of December and by request from November to March

Access : *3.2km eastbound from Cosne-Cours-sur-Loire on the D 33 and the D 168*

SAUVIGNY-LES-BOIS - 58160

CHÂTEAU DE MARIGNY
Mme Belz-Hensoldt

58160 Sauvigny-les-Bois
Tel. 03 86 90 98 49
belz.marigny@wanadoo.fr
http://perso.wanadoo.fr/marigny
Languages : Eng., Ger.

Open all year • 3 non-smoking rooms upstairs all with bath/WC or shower/WC • €95 to €105, breakfast included • No table d'hôte • Terrace, park, car park, television room with piano. Credit cards not accepted, dogs not admitted

 Admiring the view of the Loire Valley.

Guests must first show their credentials by announcing themselves at the electric gate before they can venture into this handsome Napoleon III castle which belonged to Alain Prost at one time. Its current owners, of German origins, are delightful. He is a keen gardener and tends the grounds, while she takes excellent care of guests. After a restful night's sleep in one of the characterful rooms, guests are treated to a hearty breakfast of cold meats, cheese, cereals, etc.

Access : *8km from Nevers by the N 81*

AUTUN - 71400

MAISON SAINTE-BARBE
M. et Mme Lequime

7 place Sainte-Barbe
71400 Autun
Tel. 03 85 86 24 77
maison.sainte.barbe.autun@wanadoo.fr
www.maisonsaintebarbe.fr.st

Open all year • 3 rooms upstairs, all with bath/WC • €58, breakfast included • No table d'hôte • Garden, car park. Credit cards not accepted

 The exhibitions of work by local artists.

This 18C house (whose foundations date back to the 15C) overlooks a small square in the old town. After passing under a porch, you will go up a spiral staircase to reach the sitting room pleasantly decorated with old furniture. The three generously proportioned bedrooms are all individually decorated and also adorned with lovely antiques. Outdoors, a small chapel adjacent to the garden is home to carved figurines dating from the 12C.

Access : *A few minutes from Saint Lazare Cathedral*

BOURBON-LANCY - 71140

LE GRAND HOTEL
M. Monssus

1 parc Thermal
71140 Bourbon-Lancy
Tel. 03 85 89 08 87
ghthermal@stbl.fr
www.grand-hotel-thermal.com
Languages : Eng., Sp., It.

Open 2 Apr to 27 Oct • 27 rooms with bath/WC or shower/WC, all have television and 8 have a kitchenette • €58 to €76; breakfast €6; half-board available • Menus €13 (weekdays) to €35 • Terrace, inner courtyard, park, car park

A leisurely stroll along the ramparts of this spa town.

This hotel, a former convent, lies on the edge of the spa centre's woody park. The gradually renovated and spacious rooms feature a variety of functional or more old-fashioned furniture and all benefit from the pervading restful atmosphere. Light floods in through the dining room's large bay windows but on fine days many guests prefer the terrace in the cloisters.

Work and keep-fit seminars

Access : *In the town centre, next to the spa and park*

BOURGVILAIN - 71520

LE MOULIN DES ARBILLONS
M. et Mme Dubois-Favre

71520 Bourgvilain
Tel. 03 85 50 82 83
arbillon@club-internet.fr
www.club-internet.fr/perso/arbillon

Open 15 Apr to 15 Oct • 5 rooms with shower/WC • €58 to €79, breakfast included • No table d'hôte • Terrace, garden, park. Credit cards not accepted, no dogs admitted • Wine cellar, tasting and sales

The rural setting of this group of 18C, 19C and 20C buildings.

The 18C mill is flanked by a handsome 19C country house and set in a park which boasts a river and a pond. Beautiful period wardrobes grace the generally well-proportioned rooms, all of which overlook the valley and village. A bold blue and white colour scheme and vaulted ceiling make the smallest room our favourite. Breakfast is served in the 20C orangery which features frescoes, iron furniture and a porcelain stove.

Access : *8km southbound from Cluny on the D 980 then the D 22*

CHARDONNAY - 71700

LE TINAILLER DU MANOIR DE CHAMPVENT
Mme Rullière

Lieu-dit Champvent
71700 Chardonnay
Tel. 03 85 40 50 23
theatredechampvent@wanadoo.fr
Languages : Eng., It.

Closed from 1 Nov to 1 Apr • 5 rooms with shower/WC • €54 to €58, breakfast included • No table d'hôte • Garden, park, car park. Credit cards not accepted, no dogs admitted • Art gallery

 The regular drama performances.

Venture past the porch and you will discover a lovely stone manor house. The rooms are in the outbuildings and furnished with antiques, still-lifes and abstract works by a family ancestor. A room is set aside for regular drama performances and exhibitions of sculpture. The gardens are equally attractive and children generally love romping through the meadow. Flowered courtyard.

> *Theatre (arts and techniques)*

Access : *11km to the south-west of Tournus on the D 56 then the D 463*

CHAROLLES - 71120

LA POSTE
M. et Mme Doucet

2 avenue de la Libération
71120 Charolles
Tel. 03 85 24 11 32
hotel-de-la-liberation-doucet@wanadoo.fr
www.la-poste-hotel.com
Languages : Eng.

Closed fortnight late Nov and fortnight beginning of the year, Sun evening and Mon • 15 rooms, 3 of which have a terrace, all have bath/WC and television • €48 to €130; breakfast €10; half-board available • Menus €23 to €70 • Terrace, garage

 The festive atmosphere of the cattle markets.

The comfortable bedrooms of this traditional well-kept Burgundian house are equally classical with their chocolate box patterns. Alcove statues, ornaments, period furniture and Charolles porcelain tableware abound in the refined bourgeois décor of the dining room. Burgundy's legendary generosity and hospitality are done full justice in the delicious menu, where the local Charolais beef, of course, has pride of place. Meals are served in the flowered courtyard in fine weather.

Access : *On a street corner, opposite the church in the town centre*

CLUNY - 71250

LA MAISON DES GARDES
M. Beaulieu

18 avenue Charles-de-Gaulle
71250 Cluny
Tel. 03 85 59 19 46
philippebeaulieu@club-internet.fr

Open all year • 5 rooms with bathrooms • €60, breakfast included • No table d'hôte • Garden. Credit cards not accepted, no dogs admitted

 Two magnificent old cedar trees stand guard over the park.

This former guard house in the heart of the town has been in the same family for over 300 years. There are three rooms in the main building and two others, one of which is a family apartment, in a separate wing. The overall atmosphere is one of simplicity enhanced by a choice of antiques and old rustic beams. If the weather prevents you from enjoying the lovely garden, breakfast is served in the sitting room by the fireplace. A charming place just two minutes from the abbey.

Access : *In the town*

LA COMELLE - 71990

MAISON DE BOURGOGNE
Mme Virginie Joos

Maison de Bourgogne
71990 La Comelle
Tel. 03 85 82 56 09

Closed from 1 Nov to 15 Mar • 3 rooms with bath/WC or shower/WC • €45 to €48, breakfast included • No table d'hôte • Terrace, garden, car park. Credit cards not accepted, dogs not admitted

Feast your eyes on the vast expanses of greenery.

This recently restored farmhouse commands a splendid view of the lovely Morvan countryside. The rooms (light wall coverings and parquet floors) are simple and comfortable and the two large rooms on the ground floor lead directly onto the terrace where breakfast is served as soon as the weather turns fine. Pleasant friendly welcome.

Access : *On the D 114*

LE BREUIL - 71670

LAIZY - 71190

LE DOMAINE DE MONTVALTIN
M. et Mme Delorme

71670 Le Breuil
Tel. 03 85 55 87 12
domainedemontvaltin@hotmail.com
www.domainedemontvaltin.com

Closed in Feb • 5 non-smoking rooms, one with disabled access, all with bath/WC and modem • €50 to €85, breakfast included • No table d'hôte • Garden, car park • Indoor swimming pool, pétanque, tennis court, horse riding, angling

FERME DE LA CHASSAGNE
Mme Gorlier

Les 4 Vents
71190 Laizy
Tel. 03 85 82 39 47
francoise.gorlier@wanadoo.fr

Closed 11 Nov to 15 Feb • 4 rooms with bathrooms • €45, breakfast included • Table d'hôte (except Sun) €17 • Garden, car park. Credit cards not accepted, no dogs admitted

 An isolated country retreat, just a few minutes from town.

Five minutes from Le Creusot, this mid-20C fully renovated farmhouse in the countryside is home to comfortable, individually decorated rooms that combine warmth and sophistication. Old furniture adorns the sitting room. Facilities for leisure activities include a tennis court, indoor swimming pool, pretty garden and a pond full of carp. Gîtes and a chalet also available. Visits can be organised on request to a wine producer, followed by wine tasting.

 The warm welcome extended by the owners of this delightful house.

Built on the doorstep of the Morvan Nature Park, this rustic old farmhouse has been restored and has kept all its character. The rooms are simply decorated but very comfortable and pleasant. A large square table is set by the fireplace at mealtimes (farm grown produce, garden vegetables and homemade desserts). Children adore visiting the farm animals.

Access : *Head for the riding school (centre équestre), avenue de Montvaltin, then take a left turn along a private lane (white fencing)*

Access : *14km southwest bound from Autun on the N 81 then lane on the right*

LOUHANS - 71500

MOULIN DE BOURGCHÂTEAU
M. Donatelli

Rue du Guidon
71500 Louhans
Tel. 03 85 75 37 12
bourgchateau@netcourrier.com
www.bourgchateau.com
Languages : Eng., It.

Open all year • 19 rooms with bath/WC or shower/WC, all have television • €54 to €85; breakfast €9; half-board available • Restaurant closed Mon out of season, menus €24 (weekdays) to €60 • Park, car park • 2 pedalos available, local wines sold

Relaxing amidst the cogs and gears of the old mill's machinery.

This enchanting 1778 mill spanning the Seille River was in use up until 1973. The modern, immaculate rooms on the upper floors enjoy a wonderful view of the woodland and river. A millstone and its hopper, leftovers from the mill's working days, lend the dining room a great deal of character. Local wines are on sale in one of the outbuildings. Two pedalos are available for the use of guests who fancy a spin on the river.

Access : *Leave Louhans towards Chalon on Rue du 11-Nov-1918, then Rue du Guidon, turn right into the lane towards Bourgchâteau*

MARCIGNY - 71110

LES RÉCOLLETS
M. Cottin

4 place du Champ-de-Foire
71110 Marcigny
Tel. 03 85 25 05 16
contact@lesrecollets.com
lesrecollets.com

Open all year • 5 rooms with bath/WC and television • €72, breakfast included • Table d'hôte €20 to €22 • Garden, car park • Outdoor swimming pool

The tranquillity of a spiritual retreat on the route of the Romanesque churches.

The owners of this former 17C convent have gradually set about renovating the enormous building. While they have yet to finish their task, they have nonetheless managed to create a swimming pool and a spacious gîte. The charm of yesteryear prevails in the kitchen and dining room and all the generously proportioned bedrooms are pleasantly decorated. Theme weekends organised: wine, walking or cooking.

Access : *In the village*

POISSON - 71600

CHAMBRE D'HÔTE M. MATHIEU
M. et Mme Mathieu

Sermaize
71600 Poisson
Tel. 03 85 81 06 10
mp.mathieu@laposte.net

Closed from 1 Nov to 15 Mar • 5 rooms with shower/WC • €50 to €60, breakfast included • No table d'hôte • Garden, parking. Credit cards not accepted

 The library's excellent collection of works about the region.

This former 14C hunting lodge with its impressive circular tower and flower-filled courtyard forms a very pleasing picture. An original spiral staircase winds up to a few personalised rooms, two of them have bathrooms in the tower. The suite boasts immense beams, cosy armchairs and walls lined with prints of 19C paintings and old photos by Doisneau. The garden overlooking the open countryside is very pleasant in the summer.

Access : *12.5km south-east of Paray-le-Monial on the D 34 then the D 458, towards Saint-Julien-de-Civry*

SAINT-MAURICE-LÈS-CHÂTEAUNEUF - 71740

LA VIOLETTERIE
Mme Chartier

71740 Saint-Maurice-lès-Châteauneuf
Tel. 03 85 26 26 60
madeleinechartier@yahoo.fr

Closed from 11 Nov to 15 Mar • 3 rooms, one of which is under the eaves, all have bath/WC • €55, breakfast included • Table d'hôte €18 (evenings only and by reservation only) • Garden, car park. Credit cards not accepted, no dogs admitted

 The sophisticated 19C ambience.

A wrought-iron gate takes you into the courtyard and garden and a flight of steps leads into this 19C mansion. The former holiday home of architect Roux-Spitz, it is now a hotel with light, airy rooms. Those in the attic with painted furniture have retained their original tiled floors and beams. The elegant wood panelling and the fireplace in the sitting and dining room further add to the establishment's appeal.

Access : *10km to the north-east of Charlieu on the D 487, then the D 987 towards La Clayette*

THIL-SUR-ARROUX - 71190

37

LA BRUYÈRE DU BOIS DROIT
M. Develay

Route de Saint-Didier-sur-Arroux
71190 Thil-sur-Arroux
Tel. 03 85 54 26 32

Open all year • 3 rooms, 2 of which are upstairs, all have shower/WC • €40 to €44, breakfast included, half-board available • Table d'hôte €15 • Garden, car park. Credit cards not accepted, no dogs admitted

Forget your diet just for a meal...

The three bedrooms in the converted stone stables are more than pleasant, but we still preferred those upstairs, which are more spacious with comfortable well-equipped bathrooms. Take a seat at the large dining table for breakfast or to try the tasty recipes made from farm produce and delicious garden vegetables.

Access : *15km eastbound from Luzy on the D 228*

VARENNES-SOUS-DUN - 71800

38

À LA FERME MME DESMURS
M. et Mme Desmurs

La Saigne
71800 Varennes-sous-Dun
Tel. 03 85 28 12 79
michelealaindesmurs@wanadoo.fr

Open all year • 3 rooms with bath/WC • €45, breakfast included • Table d'hôte €19 • Garden, car park. Credit cards not accepted, no dogs admitted

The friendly atmosphere of this working farm.

The simple comfortable rooms of this cattle-breeding farm (Charolais of course) are located in the house next to the barn. While they might not be the lap of luxury, you will quickly appreciate their generous proportions. An immense room downstairs is furnished with a long table and fireplace. Upstairs there is a dining room with a small kitchen for the use of guests.

Access : *4km eastbound from La Clayette on D 987, then take a minor road*

ANCY-LE-FRANC - 89160

AU MOULIN D'ANCY LE FRANC
M. et Mme Guiennot

Chemin de Halage
89160 Ancy-le-Franc
Tel. 03 86 75 02 65
info@moulin-ancy.com
www.moulin-ancy.com
Languages : Eng.

Open from Apr to Oct, rest of the year by reservation • 5 non-smoking rooms, including 4 apartments upstairs, all have bath or shower/WC • €65 to €76, breakfast included • No table d'hôte • Park, private car park. Credit cards not accepted, dogs not admitted • Mountain bike rentals

The idyllic setting.

The Guiennot couple renovated this most impressive (5 floors and over 400m^2) 17C mill. Today one room and four apartments are available for guests. Marie-Pierre, an artist, has turned one floor into a painter's studio, while Jean-Louis has converted an old sawmill into an art gallery for local artists. The bucolic site - a 2ha-island poised between canal and river - cannot fail but appeal!

Access : *On the way out of Ancy-le-Franc, head towards Montbard, over the Bourgogne canal and turn left before the Armançon bridge*

APPOIGNY - 89380

LE PUITS D'ATHIE
Mme Siad et M. Fèvre

1 rue de l'Abreuvoir
89380 Appoigny
Tel. 03 86 53 10 59
bnbpuitsd'athie@wanadoo.fr
www.appoigny.com
Languages : Eng., Ger., Sp.

Open all year • 4 rooms, including 3 non-smoking apartments, all have bathrooms • €69 to €160, breakfast included • Table d'hôte €45 • Park. Credit cards not accepted • Outhouse with games room with billiards and pinball machine

The happy marriage of old and new.

This handsome Burgundian property should not be missed. Two rooms are located in the main wing, while the others, including the "Porte d'Orient" apartment, a magnificent room with king size bed, balneo bathtub and dressing-room, are reached via the orangery, in an independent wing. At breakfast time, dig in to homemade jams made from a variety of creative recipes; at dinner time, guests are invited to taste up-to-date recipes served with regional wines.

Modelling, sculpture course

Access : *In the village 50m from the Yonne*

CHEVANNES - 89240

41

CHÂTEAU DE RIBOURDIN
M. et Mme Brodard

89240 Chevannes
Tel. 03 86 41 23 16
château.de.ribourdin@wanadoo.fr
www.chateauderibourdin.com
Languages : Eng.

Open all year • 5 rooms, one of which is on the ground floor and has disabled access • €70 to €80, breakfast included • No table d'hôte • Garden. Credit cards not accepted, no dogs admitted • Outdoor swimming pool

We most liked
The select atmosphere of this wonderful little castle.

The 16C dovecote and castle stand at the foot of the village in the midst of wheat fields. Patience and care lavished over the years have resulted in the beautiful restoration visible today. The 18C barn now houses the bedrooms, each of which is named after a local castle and the spacious breakfast room has a fireplace. The overall look is rustic, mirroring the countryside views from the windows.

Access : *9km to the south-west of Auxerre on the N 151 then the D 1, then a minor road*

COLLAN - 89700

42

LA MARMOTTE
M. et Mme Lecolle

2 rue de l'École
89700 Collan
Tel. 03 86 55 26 44
lamarmotte.glecolle@wanadoo.fr
www.bonadresse.com/bourgogne/collan.htm
Languages : Eng.

Open all year • 3 non-smoking rooms with bathrooms • €45, breakfast included • No table d'hôte • Garden, car park. Credit cards not accepted, no dogs admitted • Nearby: horse-drawn carriage rides, boating on the Burgundy canal and angling

We most liked
The footpaths through the Chablis vineyards.

This beautiful old stone house lies in the heart of one of the Yonne's picturesque little villages. All the personalised rooms are named after a colour chosen for the interior decoration. The "Blue" room has cane furniture, while open beams and a wrought-iron four-poster bed grace the "Pink" room. Breakfast is served in the winter garden to the tinkling sound of the fountain.

Access : *7.5km to the north-east of Chablis on the D 150 then the D 35*

ESCOLIVES-SAINTE-CAMILLE - 89290

DOMAINE BORGNAT LE COLOMBIER
Mme Borgnat

1 rue de l'Église
89290 Escolives-Sainte-Camille
Tel. 03 86 53 35 28
regine@domaineborgnat.com
www.domaineborgnat.com
Languages : Eng., Ger., Sp.

Open all year • 5 rooms, 3 of which have shower/WC, the other 2 have bath/WC • €52, breakfast included; half-board available • Table d'hôte €24 • Garden, car park • Outdoor swimming pool, tours of the wine cellars

 Visiting the superb cellars.

This fortified 17C farmhouse presides over a superb wine-growing estate. On the accommodation side, guests can choose between the simple comfort of B&B rooms or the self-catering cottage in the former dovecote. Bistro tables, a piano and a terrace around the swimming pool set the scene for breakfasts. Meals are invariably served with a choice of "homegrown" wines. Don't miss the chance to visit the splendid 12C and 17C cellars for further tasting sessions.

Wine tasting courses

Access : *9.5km southbound from Auxerre on the D 239*

LÉZINNES - 89160

CHAMBRE D'HÔTE M. PIEDALLU
M. et Mme Piedallu

5 avenue de la Gare
89160 Lézinnes
Tel. 03 86 75 68 23

Open all year • 3 rooms with shower/WC • €44, breakfast included • No table d'hôte • Garden, car park. Credit cards not accepted, no dogs admitted

 The immaculate upkeep of this contemporary house.

This brand-new house has been built in keeping with local styles and even has a square stone tower. The interior is equally pleasing and the spacious, well-appointed rooms with sloping ceilings are furnished with antiques. The breakfast room leads onto a pleasant veranda and guests have the run of a private sitting room for a quiet read.

Access : *11km to the south-east of Tonnerre on the D 905*

L'ISLE-SUR-SEREIN - 89440

45

AUBERGE LE POT D'ÉTAIN
M. et Mme Pechery

24 rue Bouchardat
89440 L'Isle-sur-Serein
Tel. 03 86 33 88 10
potdetain@ipoint.fr
www.potdetain.com

Closed in Feb, the last fortnight of Oct, Sun evening, Tue lunchtime and Mon (in Jul and Aug) • 9 rooms, all rooms have bath/WC or shower/WC and television • €56 to €75; breakfast €8; half-board available • Menus €25 (weekdays) to €49.90 • Terrace, garage

 Meals are served in the flowered inner courtyard in the summer.

Who could possibly want to remain stuck to the boiling tarmac of the A6 when the enchanting valley of Serein is so close at hand? Particularly as we've found "the" place that will capture your heart for ever. Nothing quite matches the unparalleled desire to please as that of this 18C coaching inn. Choose your room from the inn's web-site. All display the same faultless style and character as that present in the tasty Burgundian dishes and the fine selection of Chablis vintages.

Access : *In the village, on the D 86: leave Avallon north-east bound on the D 957 then left 2km after Montréal*

MOLAY - 89310

46

LE CALOUNIER
M. et Mme Collin

5 rue de la Fontaine
Hameau de Arton
89310 Molay
Tel. 03 86 82 67 81
info@lecalounier.fr
www.lecalounier.fr
Languages : Eng.

Closed Jan and Feb • 4 non-smoking rooms and 1 apartment, 2 of which are on the ground floor and have disabled access. All rooms have bathrooms with WC • €61, breakfast included; half-board available • Table d'hôte €17 to €24 • Library, garden, car park. Credit cards not accepted, no dogs admitted

 The cookery courses run by the owner, a cordon-bleu chef.

It is impossible to resist the charm of this lavishly restored Burgundian farm, named after the walnut trees on the estate. The rooms are situated in two wings and are decorated in a hybrid mixture of "colonial" and rustic styles, with bold colour schemes, old furniture picked up in local antique shops and works by local artists. The barn, graced with two large windows, is home to the dining and sitting rooms. Local produce has pride of place on the dining table.

Regional cooking

Access : *8km northbound from Noyers on the D 86, and then a minor road*

NEUVY-SAUTOUR - 89570

LA GRANGE DE BOULAY
M. et Mme Gron

Lieu-dit Boulay
89570 Neuvy-Sautour
Tel. 03 86 56 43 52
christiane-laurent@wanadoo.fr
www.lagrangedeboulay.com

Open all year • 5 non-smoking rooms on two floors with bath/WC or shower/WC, one has a jacuzzi • €70 to €90, breakfast included • Table d'hôte €20 • Terrace, park, car park, barbecues, kitchenette. Credit cards not accepted, dogs not admitted • 2 outdoor swimming pools, bicycle and mountain bike rentals, petanque, table tennis and billiards

 The variety of types of accommodation available.

This recently restored old house can accommodate up to 42 people in three gîtes and 5 guestrooms. The latter are located in a building known as the "Palombière" (wood-pigeon), and each is in a different style. The "Colonial" for example exhibits a distinctly exotic flavour with an Indonesian-type bed. Also worthy of mention is the "Forge" gîte which boasts a large medieval style room and a mezzanine with billiards table. Swimming pools, table tennis and mountain bikes also available on site.

Access : *At Neuvy-Sautour, take the D 12 for 2km towards Chailley then Boulay*

SACY - 89270

LES VIEILLES FONTAINES
M. et Mme Moine

89270 Sacy
Tel. 03 86 81 51 62
vf.cm@free.fr
http://lesvieillesfontaines.free.fr
Languages : Eng., Sp.

Closed in Jan and Feb • 3 rooms and 1 apartment with shower/WC • €58, breakfast included • Table d'hôte €27 (evenings only) • Garden, car park. Credit cards not accepted, no dogs admitted

 Putting your feet up with a good book in the magnificent vaulted cellar-sitting room.

This delightful stone house in the heart of an old Burgundy village used to belong to a local wine-grower. The simple but comfortable rooms have parquet floors. The sitting room and kitchen, fitted out in the old vaulted wine cellar, are definitely worth a look. Meals are served in the owners' dining room, graced with a fireplace and a beautiful wrought-iron light, or on the covered terrace, weather permitting.

Access : *In the town near the church*

TANNERRE-EN-PUISAYE - 89350

49

LE MOULIN DE LA FORGE
M. et Mme Gagnot

89350 Tannerre-en-Puisaye
Tel. 03 86 45 40 25
renegagnot@aol.com

Open all year • 5 rooms, 3 of which are on the ground floor, all have bath/WC • €52, breakfast included • No table d'hôte • Terrace, garden, car park. Credit cards not accepted • Outdoor swimming pool

 Fishing in the estate's river.

It is impossible not to admire the careful restoration of this 14C mill. The wheel has been rebuilt and the old sawmill turned into a pleasing rustic room with a kitchenette for the sole use of guests. Bare beams and 1930s furniture grace the comfortable rooms. Venture out into the landscaped parkland and explore the river, waterfall and pond teeming with fish.

Access : *11km to the northeast of Saint-Fargeau on the D 18 then the D 160*

VERMENTON - 89270

50

LE MOULINOT
M. et Mme Wootton

Route d'Auxerre - RN 6
89270 Vermenton
Tel. 03 86 81 60 42
lemoulinot@aol.com
www.moulinot.com
Languages : Eng., Du.

Closed 20 Dec to 10 Jan • 6 rooms with bathrooms • €55 to €80, breakfast included • No table d'hôte • Garden, park, car park. Credit cards not accepted, no dogs admitted • Outdoor swimming pool

 The wealth of water activities.

Guests have to cross a narrow bridge over the rapid waters of the Cure to reach the idyllic site of this 18C mill. A fine wood staircase leads up to pretty, spacious rooms each of which is individually decorated. Cane furniture, beams, fireplaces and reproduction Impressionist paintings adorn the dining and sitting rooms overlooking the pond. Swimming, fishing, canoeing and mountain biking are just a few of the countless outdoor activities close at hand and the port is just five minutes away.

Access : *Take the small private bridge spanning the Cure*

VÉZELAY - 89450

VERMENTON - 89270

PLACE VOLTAIRE
M. Kimber

15 place Voltaire
89270 Vermenton
Tel. 03 86 81 59 63
richardandlyn @ wanadoo.fr
 www.15placevoltaire.com

Closed Jan • 4 rooms with bath/WC • €50 to €70,
breakfast included • Table d'hôte €15 • Garden.
Credit cards not accepted

LES AQUARELLES
Mme Basseporte

 Fontette, 6 ruelle des Grands Prés
89450 Vézelay
Tel. 03 86 33 34 35
Languages : Eng., It.

Closed from 19 Dec to 15 Mar, 12 Nov to 5 Dec,
Tue and Wed out of season • 10 rooms, one of
which has disabled access, each has bath/WC
• €46 to €52; breakfast €6.50; half-board available • Menu à la carte €11.50 to €35 • Terrace,
car park. Dogs not admitted in restaurant

 The smiling welcome of the British owners.

 The path winding its way through the fields to Vézelay.

Comprised of two corner buildings laid out
around a delightful small garden, this pretty
stone house features four carefully decorated
rooms adorned with antiques. It is said that the
King's room was thus baptised after Louis-
Philippe passed through the establishment
when he came to inaugurate the canal. The
other three rooms are slightly smaller and all
are conveniently equipped with a fridge.
English breakfasts served in the large dining
room. Pleasant veranda.

When this old farmstead was turned into a
hotel, the owners were determined to preserve
its original character and cachet. The stables
now house a sitting room, while the oak furnished bedrooms have been installed in the
former hayloft. Meals are served on two enormous farm tables. In the summertime, Mrs
Basseporte insists that dinner be taken outside
to benefit from the warmth of the beautiful old
limestone walls.

Access : *In the town*

Access : *5km eastbound from Vézelay on the
D 957 (Avallon road)*

VÉZELAY - 89450

53

VÉZELAY - 89450

54

CRISPOL
Mme Schori

Fontette
89450 Vézelay
Tel. 03 86 33 26 25
crispol@wanadoo.fr
www.crispol.com
Languages : Eng., Ger.

Closed Jan and Feb, Tue lunchtime and Mon
• 12 rooms in a separate wing, one of which has
disabled access. All rooms have bath/WC and
television • €72; breakfast €9; half-board available • Menus €21 • Terrace, garden, car park

LA PALOMBIÈRE
Mme Danguy-Pandel

Place du Champ-de-Foire
89450 Vézelay
Tel. 03 86 33 28 50
lapalombiere-host@wanadoo.fr
www.lapalombierevezelay.com
Languages : Eng., Ger.

Closed from Jan to Feb • 10 rooms with bathrooms • €55 to €79; breakfast €9 • No table
d'hôte • Garden, car park

**The impeccable upkeep of this
establishment.**

A number of surprises await visitors inside the
thick stone walls of this building in the heart of
a hamlet. Firstly, the unexpected contemporary style of the rooms' decoration with sharp
corners, lacquered ceilings and works by the
owner-artist. Next, the peaceful garden sheltered from the hairpin bend in the road.
Finally, the elegant restaurant which surveys
the Cure Valley, with the hilltop basilica in the
background.

The pleasant blend of styles and periods.

Situated in the lower part of town, this elegant
18C mansion swamped in Virginia creeper is not
lacking in character. The spacious, snug rooms
feature an eclectic mixture of styles and periods ranging from Louis XIII, Louis XIV and
Empire to satin bedspreads and "retro" bathrooms. Breakfasts, which are lavishly accompanied with home-made jams, are served on
the veranda which opens onto the surrounding
countryside. The flowered garden is at its best
in full bloom in early summer.

Discovering wild plants course

Access : *In the lower part of town*

Access : *Leave Vézelay on the D 957 towards
Avallon and drive 5km; the hotel is on the
roadside*

VOUTENAY-SUR-CURE - 89270

55

AUBERGE LE VOUTENAY
M. et Mme Poirier

89270 Voutenay-sur-Cure
Tel. 03 86 33 51 92
auberge.voutenay@wanadoo.fr
www.monsite.wanadoo.fr/auberge.voutenay

Closed 1-21 Jan, 18-24 Jun, 19-25 Nov, Sun eve, Mon and Tue • 8 rooms with bath/WC, and an apartment opening onto the garden • €45 to €65; breakfast €8; half-board available • Menus €25 to €43 (limited seating so it is necessary to book) • Garden, car park. No dogs admitted

> The mountain bikes and canoes available for use by guests.

The inn's canine mascot happily does the honours of this handsome 18C mansion which is little by little undergoing a facelift. The bedrooms are being renovated, a spacious 45sq metre flat has just been installed and the restaurant boasts a handsome fireplace with a carved wooden mantelpiece. The slightly unruly walled garden planted with hundred-year-old trees and extending down as far as the River Cure, is sheer bliss. A hiking path runs alongside the establishment.

Access : *On the N 6 from Auxerre to Avallon*

Brittany – Breizh to its inhabitants – is a region of harsh granite coastlines, dense, mysterious forests and pretty ports tightly packed with brightly painted fishing boats. Its charm lies in its brisk sea breeze, its incredibly varied landscapes, its countless legends and the people themselves, born, so they say, with a drop of salt water in their blood. Proud of the customs and language handed down from distant Celtic ancestors, today's Bretons nurture their identity throughout the year with a calendar of events, in which modern-day bards and minstrels exalt their folklore and traditions. Of course, such devotion to culture requires plenty of good, wholesome nourishment: sweet and savoury pancakes, thick slices of *kouign-aman* (pronounced "queen-aman") dripping in caramelised sugar and salted butter and mugs of cold cider. However, Brittany's gastronomic reputation extends far beyond such tasty titbits and gourmets can feast on the oysters, lobster, crab and other seafood delicacies for which this rocky peninsula is renowned.

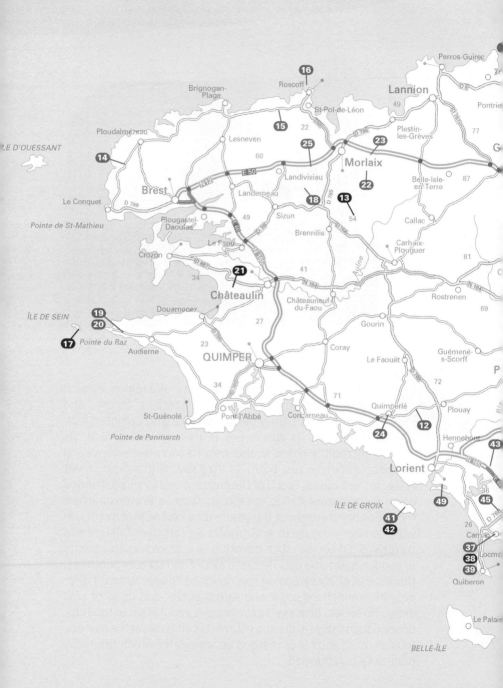

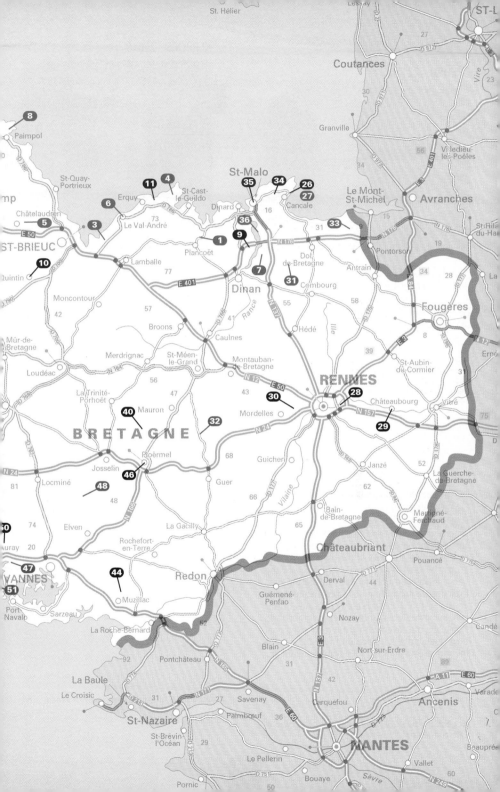

KERBORS - 22610

CRÉHEN - 22130

MANOIR DE TROÉZEL VRAS
M. et Mme Maynier

22610 Kerbors
Tel. 02 96 22 89 68
troezel.vras@free.fr
http://troezel.vras.free.fr
Languages : Eng., Sp.

Closed 20 Oct to 1 Apr • 5 rooms with shower/WC • €68 (€61 low season), breakfast included • Table d'hôte €20 (except Sun) • Garden, car park. Credit cards not accepted, no dogs admitted

LA BELLE NOË
Mme Chantal Bigot

22130 Créhen
Tel. 02 96 84 08 47
belle.noe@wanadoo.fr
www.crehen.com

Open all year • 4 non-smoking rooms, including one duplex, all with shower/WC • €56, breakfast included • Table d'hôte €23 • Garden, car park. Credit cards not accepted, no dogs admitted

The numerous walking and biking opportunities.

This pretty 17C manor house surrounded by rambling peaceful countryside has everything the travel-weary visitor could wish for. Terracotta tiled floors, apricot painted walls, antique wardrobes and prints of local landscapes adorn the bedrooms. The equally agreeable dining room features white-painted beams and a stone fireplace. Depending on the season, meals are served in the garden or near a log fire: seafood is a speciality all year round.

Impossible not to fall in love with this establishment!

Among the shrubs and flowers that surround this old farmhouse grows a selection of rare roses that are the envy of the region's florists. Enjoy the view of meadows and fields, and the peace disturbed only by the whispering of a lazy breeze from time to time. The magnificently restored house is home to curios, furniture and other knick-knacks picked up here and there and displayed with great taste. Regional fare takes pride of place on the table d'hôte menu; reservations for four people minimum.

Access : *9km to the north-east of Tréguier on the Paimpol road towards Pleumeur-Gautier, then Kerbors*

Access : *1.5km from Créhen on the D 768 then a lane to the left*

MORIEUX - 22400

LE MANOIR DE LA VILLE GOURIO
M. et Mme Guihot

22400 Morieux
Tel. 02 96 32 72 60
golf@lacriniere.fr
www.lacriniere.fr

Closed Oct to late Mar • 5 rooms with bath/WC and television • €58 to €107; breakfast €9 • Table d'hôte €11 • Terrace, garden, park, car park. No dogs admitted

 Taking a golf lesson with a pro.

This 17C Brittany manor house overlooks a 9-hole golf course surrounded by trees which are almost as old as the house. The rustic rooms upstairs all overlook the garden, fairways and ponds. On the ground floor, guests have the run of a reading room, a billiards table and a breakfast room where a fire takes the chill out of those brisk autumn mornings. The former stables house a bar, restaurant, night club and the clubhouse – ask here for expert tips and private coaching.

Access : *11km southbound from Val-André on the D 786 and the D 34*

PLÉLO - 22170

AU CHAR À BANCS
M. et Mme Lamour

22170 Plélo
Tel. 02 96 74 13 63
charabanc@wanadoo.fr
www.aucharabanc.com

Open all year • 5 rooms with bath/WC • €64 to €89, breakfast included • Table d'hôte €25 (closed weekdays Sep to Jun and Tue in Jul and Aug) • Terrace, garden. Dogs not admitted

 The country appeal of this 17C mill and its outhouses that simply ooze with charm!

The whole family has a role to play on this estate. One of the daughters, an interior decorator, chose the cosy decoration of the rooms under the eaves in the old farmhouse: antiques, lovely old-fashioned-style bathrooms, ancient beams and floorboards. The master of the house is in charge of meals which he concocts from home-grown vegetables and pork raised on the farm (which is run by his son), while another daughter makes delicious pancakes.

Access : *1km northbound from Plélo on the D 84*

PLÉNEUF-VAL-ANDRÉ - 22370

VILLA MARGUERITE
M. et Mme Campion-Levive

34 rue des Garennes
22370 Pléneuf-Val-André
Tel. 02 96 72 85 88

Open Apr to Sep (by reservation in low season) • 4 rooms on 2 floors, 3 with balcony and sea view, all with bath/WC • €58 to €63, breakfast included • No table d'hôte • Garden. Credit cards not accepted, no dogs admitted

 Strolling along the pedestrian coast path alongside Val-André beach.

This pretty villa, quite in keeping with the architectural style of this quaint 19C seaside resort, enjoys a fine view over the Bay of St-Brieuc. Sea-lovers will adore the rooms, most of which have sea-facing balconies. All are decorated in a sober yet fetching style with floorboards, colourful walls and two have four-poster beds. Peaceful nights guaranteed thanks to the large garden surrounding the house. Note the interesting antique furniture which adorns the breakfast room.

Access : *300m from the town centre, on the sea front*

PLEUDIHEN-SUR-RANCE - 22690

MAISON DE LA VALLÉE
M. et Mme Chenu

Lieu-dit Le Val Hervelin
22690 Pleudihen-sur-Rance
Tel. 02 96 83 35 61
chenu.francis@22.cernet.fr
www.maisondelavallee.com

Open all year • 3 rooms and 2 apartments with bath/WC and television • €72, breakfast included • No table d'hôte • Garden, car park. Credit cards not accepted, no dogs admitted

 Being greeted with an aperitif!

This lovely blue granite house built in 1894 is typical of the more opulent homes of St Malo. On either side of the hallway are a rustic-inspired sitting room and a contemporary-style veranda overlooking the valley below. Upstairs are three rooms and two apartments with comfortable bedding and sophisticated decor featuring a pleasant blend of cherry wood furniture and stained beams. Two gîtes available in a separate wing. Deliciously generous breakfasts.

Access : *3km south-east bound of Pleudihen-sur-Rance, near the D 795*

PLÉVENON- 22240

LE RELAIS DE FRÉHEL
M. et Mme Billet

22240 Plévenon
Tel. 02 96 41 43 02
www.relaiscapfrehel.fr

Closed late Oct to late Feb • 5 rooms and 2 gîtes, all with bath/WC • €55, breakfast included • Table d'hôte €22 • Park, garden, car park. Credit cards not accepted, no dogs admitted • Library

 Peace and quiet amid old stones and greenery.

This pink sandstone 19C farmhouse is typical of the houses of Brittany and inside guests are treated to the vision of a happy mixture of furnishings. Regionally made wardrobes and shelves rub shoulders with exotic armchairs and tables, all of which are set against a backdrop of bare stone and beams. The place also has a rum distillery and a cellar, offering a fine selection of rums and other spirits. The rooms and gîtes are all comfortable and well kept. Attractive wooded park.

Access : *1.5km from Plevenon on the Cap-Fréhel road*

PLOUBAZLANEC - 22620

LA MAISON DES ÎLES
Mme Yveline Le Roux

29 route de la Vieille Côte,
à la pointe de l'Arcouest
22620 Ploubazlanec
Tel. 02 96 55 87 01

Open all year • 4 rooms with shower/WC or bath/WC • €70, breakfast included • Table d'hôte €22 • Garden, car park

 The delightful sight of the islands of Bréhat in the distance.

This comfortable family home built in 1906 is ideally located, just two minutes from the landing stage at the pointe de l'Arcouest. The fully renovated interior is an interesting combination of contemporary and older decoration. The bedrooms upstairs are decorated according to themes: the sea, England or exotic. All boast faultless bedding and beautifully polished old family furniture. The ocean-inspired menu, by reservation only, is the work of a real cordon bleu chef.

Access : *3km from Ploubazlanec on the D 789*

QUINTIN - 22800

PLOUËR-SUR-RANCE - 22490

MANOIR DE RIGOURDAINE
M. Van Valenberg

Route de Langrolay
22490 Plouër-sur-Rance
Tel. 02 96 86 89 96
hotel.rigourdaine@wanadoo.fr
www.hotel-rigourdaine.fr
Languages : Eng., Ger.

Closed from 13 Nov to 31 Mar • 19 rooms, 5 of
which are split-level, 2 have disabled access.
Rooms have bath/WC or shower/WC and television • €70 to €82 (€62 to €74 low season);
breakfast €7 • No restaurant • Park, private car
park. No dogs admitted • Games room with
billiards, private fishing

 We most liked
**The countless paths around the Rance
estuary.**

A narrow lane leads up to this picturesque
farmstead, which is almost as old as the River
Rance itself. Its secluded position overlooking
the estuary ensures guests a peaceful night's
sleep, awakened only by the calls of the
seagulls overhead. Good old country furniture
and brightly coloured fabrics grace the bedrooms, while old beams, bare stone walls and
a gigantic family table adorn the breakfast
room. Full of character.

Access : *3km northbound from Plouer-sur-Rance
on the D 12 towards Langrolay, then right at a
private road*

COMMERCE
M. Gourdin

2 rue Rochonen
22800 Quintin
Tel. 02 96 74 94 67
hotelducommerce@cegetel.net
http://www.hotelducommerce.fr.cc
Languages : Eng., It.

Closed from 23 Dec to 7 Jan, fortnight in Mar or
Apr, 25 Aug to 2 Sep and on Mon, Fri eve and Sun
eve (except by reservation) • 11 rooms, all have
shower/WC and television; non-smokers only
• €55 to €66 (€50 to €60 low season); breakfast
€7; half-board available • Menus €14 (weekdays
except evenings in season) to €42

 We most liked
Walking along the banks of the Gouët.

The origins of this impressive granite house
covered in Virginia creeper have been traced
back to the 18C. The modern, personalised
rooms have been recently renovated and each
is named after an appetising spice or condi-
ment, such as Fleur de sel, paprika or cinnamon. A beautiful period fireplace with a carved
wooden mantelpiece is the centrepiece of the
rustic wainscoted dining room.

Access : *In the centre of the village, on the
D 790 between Saint-Brieuc and Rostrenen*

SABLES-D'OR-LES-PINS - 22240

MANOIR SAINT-MICHEL
M. et Mme Fournel-Besnier

La Carquois
22240 Sables-d'Or-les-Pins
Tel. 02 96 41 48 87
manoir-st-michel@fournel.de
www.fournel.de
Languages : Eng., Ger.

Closed 5 Nov to 30 Mar • 20 rooms on 2 floors, all have bath/WC or shower/WC and television • €47 to €110; breakfast €6 • No restaurant • Car park, garden. Dogs not admitted • Fishing in the lake, internet access

In fine weather, breakfast overlooking the garden with the ocean in the background.

What better spot for a romantic stay than this 16C and 17C manor? The little lane leading up to the property is quickly forgotten as you are greeted by the lovely stone walls of the building and the immense garden and pond. You may even catch a glimpse of the breathtaking Sables-d'Or-les-Pins beach. An old-fashioned charm pervades the rooms which are appointed with splendid old wardrobes and furnished in a variety of styles ranging from rustic to Louis XIII and Louis XV. Attentive staff.

Access : *1.5km eastbound on the D 34*

ARZANO - 29300

CHÂTEAU DE KERLAREC
M. et Mme Bellin

Kerlarec
29300 Arzano
Tel. 02 98 71 75 06
château-de-kerlarec@wanadoo.fr
www.chateau-de-kerlarec.com
Languages : Eng., It.

Open all year • 6 rooms with bath/WC • €78 to €110, breakfast included; half-board available • Table d'hôte €20 to €50 • Park, car park. Credit cards not accepted, no dogs allowed • Outdoor swimming pool, tennis, exhibitions. 18-hole golf course and horse-riding nearby

The well-preserved Second Empire style.

It is easy to see why the current owners fell in love with this 1830 mansion set in a park complete with ornamental pool. The Second Empire reigns supreme amid the period frescoes, antique furniture and objets d'art gleaned from local antique shops and flea markets or brought back from voyages overseas. Relax in the peace and quiet of the spacious, individually decorated bedrooms. Don't leave without a look at the Jeanne d'Arc room.

Access : *6km eastbound from Quimperlé on the D 765 Lorient road, and left onto the Arzano road (D 22)*

BERRIEN - 29690

LA FERME DE PORZ KLOZ
M. et Mme Berthou

Trédudon-le-Moine
29690 Berrien
Tel. 02 98 99 61 65
yvberthou@orange.fr

http://monsite.orange.fr/porzkloz
Languages : Eng.

Open Mar to Nov • 6 rooms and 1 apartment with bath/WC • €45 to €90 (€39 to €80 low season); breakfast €7 • No table d'hôte • Car park. Credit cards not accepted, no dogs admitted • Horse-riding, swimming pool, tennis and golf nearby

 Finding out more about Brittany's less well-known hinterland.

Time seems to have stood still in this cluster of 17C farmhouses, formerly outbuildings of the Abbey of Releq, where only the best locally-grown produce is good enough for the dinner table. The bedrooms, decorated with family heirlooms, are particularly delightful and most are large enough to sleep entire families. Admire the photos relating aspects of daily life in 19C Brittany in the reception.

Access : *11km to north-west of Huelgoat on the D 14, take the Berrien road and the D 42 on the left*

BRÉLÈS - 29810

LE MOULIN DE BEL AIR
M. Mony

Route de l'Aber Ildut
29810 Brélès
Tel. 02 98 04 36 01
info.belair@aumoulindebelair.com
www.aumoulindebelair.com
Languages : Eng.

Open all year • 3 non-smoking rooms all with bath/WC, 1 has a balneotherapy bath tub • €60 to €70, breakfast included • Table d'hôte €18 to €45 drinks included (evenings only) • Car park. Credit cards not accepted, no dogs admitted in restaurant • Hiking

 The unforgettable view of Aber Ildut.

It was no easy task to endow this abode, initially in ruins, with all its former splendour. Tastefully renovated using authentic materials and methods, this lovely granite house surrounded by greenery today offers superbly fitted out bedrooms whose welcoming decor features a mixture of wood, antique furniture, paintings and curios. At mealtimes, settle down to enjoy the delicious dishes concocted by a genuine chef. Cooking courses organised depending on the season.

Visit to manors and castles, cooking and oenology weekend

Access : *West of Brélèes on the D 25 Lanildut road*

CLÉDER - 29233

15

COS-MILIN
Mme Moysan

29233 Cléder
Tel. 02 98 69 42 16
www.gites-finistere.com/gites/cozmilin

Open all year • 3 non-smoking rooms, all have bathrooms • €50, breakfast included • No table d'hôte • Sitting room, garden, car park. Credit cards not accepted, no dogs admitted

 Traditional Breton favourites at breakfast.

The seaside and coastal footpaths are not far from this stone-built house with slate roof. Individually decorated bedrooms combine old and new in an imaginative blend and, on the ground floor, the elegant sitting and breakfast rooms are furnished in the same eclectic style. Tuck into a delicious spread of pancakes, "far", a local rum and raisin flan and other traditional Breton delicacies at breakfast, before relaxing on a deck chair in the flowered garden.

Access : *10km westbound from Saint-Pol, take the D 10 and at Lléder follow signs to "les plages"*

ÎLE-DE-BATZ - 29253

16

TI VA ZADOU
M. et Mme Prigent

Le bourg
29253 Île-de-Batz
Tel. 02 98 61 76 91

Closed from 15 Nov to 1 Feb • 4 rooms on 2 floors, all have bathrooms, except for one family room with a bathroom on the landing • €60, breakfast included • No table d'hôte • Credit cards not accepted, no dogs admitted

 Cycling around on the lanes of this tiny island village.

A sense of humour and a love of life set the tone in this blue-shuttered residence, whose name means "house of my fathers" in Breton. Old and new mingle happily in the cosy, welcoming bedrooms and all have a splendid view of the port, the cluster of islets and the mainland. Family heirlooms take pride of place in the sitting and breakfast rooms, both with fireplace. Bicycles can be rented nearby.

Access : *Near the harbour*

ÎLE-DE-SEIN - 29990

AR-MEN
Mme Fouquet

Route du Phare
29990 Île-de-Sein
Tel. 02 98 70 90 77
hotel.armen@wanadoo.fr
www.hotel-armen.com

Closed 7 to 30 Jan and 1 to 24 Oct • 10 rooms with sea view, all have shower/WC • €53 to €68; breakfast €7; half-board available • Restaurant closed Sun evening and Wed (in season); menus from €19 • Sitting room-library

 Tasting the charm of island life.

Forget the hurly-burly of urban life for a few days and head for the island of Sein! After a short crossing, pass through the village and head towards the lighthouse to reach the imposing pink façade of this house. The modestly-sized, relatively simple rooms are painted bright colours and all enjoy a sea view. The meals are equally simple and rich in sea flavours; try the island's speciality, lobster stew. Sitting room-cum-library with fireplace and friendly welcome.

Access : *On the way out of the village towards the lighthouse*

LOC-EGUINER-ST-THÉGONNEC - 29410

TY-DREUX
Mme Martin

29410 Loc-Eguiner-St-Thégonnec
Tel. 02 98 78 08 21
ty-dreux@club-internet.fr
gites-peche-saint-thegonnec.com
Languages : Eng.

Open all year • 7 rooms with shower/WC and 3 gîtes • €47 to €57, breakfast included • Table d'hôte €20 • Garden. Credit cards not accepted, no dogs admitted

 It is worthwhile remembering that home-made cider is pretty potent!

The name of this dairy farm, more than worth a trip, in the heart of the countryside means "weaver's house" in testimony to its textile heritage. Period furniture, a huge 18C granite fireplace and a permanent exhibition of costumes belonging to former generations set the scene for this establishment which upholds local traditions. Modern canopied beds add character to the renovated rooms. Meals are a chance to sample the succulently prepared farm-grown produce.

Access : *3.5km to the south-east of Guimiliau on the Plouneour-Menez road (D 111)*

PLOGOFF - 29770

AN TIEZ BIHAN
M. et Mme Ganne

Kerhuret
29770 Plogoff
Tel. 02 98 70 34 85
www.fumoir-delapointeduraz.com
Languages : Ger.

Closed 15 Nov to 1 Jan • 5 rooms and 1gîte all with shower/WC • €43, breakfast included • Table d'hôte €20 by reservation (except Wed and Sun) • Car park, garden. Credit cards not accepted

 Tucking into homemade pancakes and jams at breakfast time.

A recent restoration has breathed a new lease of life into this old farmhouse, whose new owners wisely chose to retain the original proportions and materials. Several little houses, formerly stables and barns, are now home to simply furnished rooms and a gîte is also available. The main building houses the dining room where you can sample delicious local seafood. Hikers will enjoy the chance to set off along the coast path as far as the Pointe du Raz.

Access : *2.5km along the D 784 towards the Pointe du Raz*

PLOGOFF - 29770

DE LESCOFF
M. et Mme Le Corre

29 rue des Hirondelles - Lieu-dit "Lescoff"
29770 Plogoff
Tel. 02 98 70 38 24

Open all year • 3 rooms with bath/WC • €40, breakfast included • No table d'hôte • Car park, garden, terrace. Credit cards not accepted

 A bracing walk along the cliffs to the Pointe du Raz during rough weather.

The little town of Lescoff is home to the last cluster of houses before you reach the unspoilt, windswept site of the Pointe du Raz. Laid out around a little courtyard, the buildings of this former working farm offer a highly inviting picture. The rooms make up in charm what they may lack in size with rustic furniture and bare stone or white roughcast walls. Guests have the use of a practical kitchenette in the breakfast room with a sloping ceiling on the first floor.

Access : *300m from the Pointe du Raz car park*

PLOMODIERN - 29550

PORZ-MORVAN
M. Nicolas

Route de Lescuz
29550 Plomodiern
Tel. 02 98 81 53 23
christian.nicolas19@wanadoo.fr
Languages : Eng.

Closed 10 Jan to late Feb • 12 rooms, 4 upstairs, 8 are in a separate wing. All have bath/WC or shower/WC and television • €48 to €50; breakfast €6 • Crêperie in an old barn • Terrace, garden, car park • Tennis

 Feasting on pancakes!

Those in search of peace and quiet will adore this delightful stone farmhouse built in 1830 just next door – as the seagull flies – from the famous viewpoint of Ménez-Hom (330 m), which overlooks the region. Most of the gradually-renovated rooms are on the garden level in the former cow-shed. The barn has been converted into a friendly crêperie where the old rafters and timbers have been preserved. Large garden with pond and warm welcome guaranteed.

Access : *3km eastbound from Plomodiern on a minor road*

PLOUGONVEN - 29640

LA GRANGE DE COATÉLAN
M. et Mme Ternay

Coatélan
29640 Plougonven
Tel. 02 98 72 60 16
la-grange-de-coatelan@wanadoo.fr
www.lagrangedecoatelan.com

Closed during Christmas and Feb half-term holidays • 5 rooms with bath/WC • €48 to €68, breakfast included • Table d'hôte €20 (closed Mon and Tue from 16 Nov to 31 Mar and Wednesdays) • Terrace, garden, car park. Dogs not admitted

 The friendly atmosphere.

An ideal country retreat awaits you in this old Brittany farmhouse. All of the individually decorated rooms are full of charm with old furniture, painted exposed beams and enchanting bathrooms. Those hoping for an early night should avoid the Green and the Pink rooms that are just above the restaurant, and ask for the Blue room, in a small independent house. Local dishes served by the fireside or on the terrace depending on the season.

Access : *4km westbound from Plougonven on the D 109 at Coatélan*

PLOUIGNEAU - 29610

23

MANOIR DE LANLEYA
M. Marrec

Au bourg de Lanleya
29610 Plouigneau
Tel. 02 98 79 94 15
manoir.lanleya@wanadoo.fr
www.manoir-lanleya.com
Languages : Eng.

Open all year • 5 non-smoking rooms with shower/WC • €66, breakfast included • No table d'hôte • Garden, car park. Credit cards not accepted, no dogs admitted

The manor's legend, related by the lord of the house.

The quality of the restoration is such that it is difficult to believe that this 16C manor house and its adjoining 18C malouinière were saved from ruin in the nick of time. The stunning interior features Breton furniture, old beams, slate floors, exposed stone walls, a beautiful spiral staircase, pink granite fireplace and rich fabrics. The Louis XV room is particularly splendid, but the others, which are smaller, display the same exquisite taste. Lovely riverside garden.

Access : *5km to the north-east of Morlaix on the D 712, then take the D 64 towards Lanmeur*

QUIMPERLÉ - 29300

24

LA MAISON D'HIPPOLYTE
Mme Lescoat

2 quai Surcouf
29300 Quimperlé
Tel. 02 98 39 09 11
Languages : Eng.

Open all year • 4 non-smoking soundproofed rooms, all with shower/WC • €50, breakfast included • No table d'hôte • Car park, terrace. Credit cards not accepted

Admiring the Laïta, the saltwater river that runs beside the house.

Formerly the home of the greatest salmon fisherman of the town, the house now reveals the owners' daughter's artistic talents. Charmingly decorated, the interior combines elegant family heirlooms and the original old floorboards made from the same wood used to build boats. The day starts with a selection of fruit (or vegetable) juices, served with homemade jams and bread. Themed poetry evenings.

Access : *On the river bank, 50m from the tourist office*

SAINT-THÉGONNEC - 29410

LE CHATELLIER
Mme Lescarmure

Route de Saint-Malo
35260 Cancale
Tel. 02 99 89 81 84
hotelchatel@aol.com
www.hotellechatellier.com

Open all year • 13 rooms, one of which has disabled access, with bath/WC or shower/WC and television • €56 to €74; breakfast €8 • No restaurant • Garden, car park

AR PRESBITAL KOZ
Mme Prigent

18 rue Lividic
29410 Saint-Thégonnec
Tel. 02 98 79 45 62
andre.prigent@wanadoo.fr

Languages : Eng.

Open all year • 6 rooms on 2 floors, 4 of which have bath/WC, the other 2 have shower/WC • €50, breakfast included • Table d'hôte €20 (evenings only, closed Sun) • Garden, car park. Credit cards not accepted, no dogs admitted

The untamed landscape of the rocky Pointe du Grouin just a stone's throw away.

This comfortable stone house, a former farm turned into a hotel, makes an ideal base camp to explore the region in fine weather and get away from the bustling seaside resort. The spacious rooms are decorated in a rustic style and spotlessly clean. A log fire heats the sitting room during the cold winter nights. At the bottom of the garden the 1618 Manor is home to three snug guest rooms.

The nearby "enclos paroissiaux".

This former 18C presbytery, hidden by a curtain of cypress trees, is home to comfortable, well-dimensioned rooms, each of which is decorated in a different colour and furnished with antiques. The largest has a fireplace. Admire the collection of ducks from all over the world in the smoking and sitting rooms. In the summer, wander round the garden and vegetable plot or rent a bicycle (from the hotel) and venture further afield.

Access : *2km westbound on the D 355 towards Saint-Malo*

Access : *Near the Saint Bernadette Retirement Home*

CANCALE - 35260

27

CESSON-SÉVIGNÉ - 35510

28

LE MANOIR DES DOUETS FLEURIS
Mme Myriam Cérasy

35260 Cancale
Tel. 02 23 15 13 81
manoirdesdouetsfleuris@wanadoo.fr
www.manoirdesdouetsfleuris.com

Open all year • 5 rooms and 3 apartments with shower/WC or bath/WC • €79 to €90, breakfast included • No table d'hôte • Garden, car park. No dogs admitted • Pond

GERMINAL
M. et Mme Goualin

9 cours de la Vilaine
35510 Cesson-Sévigné
Tel. 02 99 83 11 01
le-germinal@wanadoo.fr
www.legerminal.com
Languages : Eng.

Closed during the Christmas school holidays • 20 rooms on 3 floors, all have bath/WC and television • €70 to €110; breakfast €9.50 • Restaurant closed Sun; menus €17 to €40 • Terrace, car park.

 Going for a walk along the customs path down to the seafront.

Built in the 17C, this manor seems to retain some of the region's history within its thick stonewalls. The sitting room is full of character with its Celtic fireplace, and is also elegantly comfortable with its cosy leather armchairs. The prettily decorated spacious rooms are light and faultlessly kept; the apartments have their own private sitting room. Immense flower-decked garden overlooking a pond. Brittany-style breakfasts.

 The terrace overlooking the river.

An unusual spot, to say the least: this 19C mill stands on an islet of the River Vilaine. Another little island has a car park and guests reach the hotel over a footbridge. The new owners are determined to add a new lease of life to their establishment and both the restaurant and the rooms are being renovated. The views and idyllic location are gradually re-establishing this unique building as one of the unexpected delights of the Rennes area.

Access : *1.8km north-west of Cancale on the D 336, St-Malo road then a lane on the right*

Access : *6km eastbound from Rennes, on a small island in the Vilaine*

CHÂTEAUBOURG - 35220

AR MILIN'
M. Burel

30 rue de Paris
35220 Châteaubourg
Tel. 02 99 00 30 91
resa.armilin@wanadoo.fr
www.armilin.com
Languages : Eng., Sp., It.

Closed 1 to 8 Jan • 32 rooms in the Moulin and Résidence du Parc, with bath/WC or shower/WC and television • €86 to €146 (€80 to €124 low season); breakfast €12; half-board available • Menus €27 to €45 • Park and arboretum, terrace, car park • Tennis court

 The superb 12.5-acre park complete with arboretum and sculptures.

Welcome to Ar Milin', an inviting flour mill built in the 19C on the banks of the Vilaine. The building is home to two restaurants: a comfortable dining room with exposed rafters and a veranda overlooking the river and a pleasantly contemporary-style bistro. A few rooms full of character are available in the mill, but the majority of the accommodation is located in a pavilion surrounded by greenery which is calmer and more modern in spirit.

Cooking lessons with 2 chefs. Tasting weekends. Sculpture exhibition in the park from May to Sep

Access : *16km west of Rennes on the N 157, Châteaubourg exit, 900m from the exit in the heart of the village*

LE RHEU - 35650

MANOIR DU PLESSIS
M. Desmots

Route de Lorient
35650 Le Rheu
Tel. 02 99 14 79 79
info@manoirduplessis.fr
www.manoirduplessis.fr
Languages : Eng.

Closed 26 Jan to 2 Feb and 12 to 26 Feb • 5 rooms with bath/WC and television • €95; breakfast €9 • Menus €16 to €38 • Terrace, park, car park. No dogs allowed in rooms • Billiard room

 Indulge in a game of billiards before sitting down to the chef's tasty cooking.

A six-acre park protects this lovely old manor house from the busy Lorient road. The manor is well known for its excellent up-to-date cooking, stylish dining rooms, with parquet floors, wainscoting, fireplaces and Louis XVI-style furniture and its lush green terrace. The spacious bedrooms, all of which overlook the park, are equally worthy of praise and equipped with all the modern comforts in a pleasantly old-fashioned style.

Access : *6km westbound of Rennes on the Lorient road*

LE TRONCHET - 35540

31

LE BAILLAGE
Mme Scalart

Le Baillage
35540 Le Tronchet
Tel. 02 99 58 17 98
info@lebaillage.com
www.lebaillage.com

Open all year • 4 rooms upstairs, all with bath/WC and television • €65 to €75, breakfast included • No table d'hôte • Garden, sitting room, private car park. Credit cards not accepted, no dogs admitted • Golf nearby

 we most liked **Taking the time to daydream between two outings on the Emerald Coast.**

The garden and immense wooded park of the estate are not enclosed, which adds to the impression of wilderness created by this welcoming environment. The handsome abode has a fine-looking interior enhanced by bare stone walls and original old beams. The rooms are comfortable and equipped with elegant bathrooms; there is one family apartment under the eaves with its own sitting room and private hall. Scrumptious breakfasts.

Access : *In the town, near the golf course*

PAIMPONT - 35380

32

LA CORNE DE CERF
Mme Morvan

Le Cannée
35380 Paimpont
Tel. 02 99 07 84 19

Closed in Jan • 3 rooms with bathroom • €55, breakfast included • No table d'hôte • Library, garden. Credit cards not accepted, no dogs admitted

 we most liked **The epitome of sophistication.**

This lovely old home is hidden deep in the heart of the forest of Brocéliande, a land steeped in legends of wizards and magic. A profusion of paintings, tapestries and painted furniture set the tone for the tasteful, elegant interior decoration. The light, airy rooms open onto a delightful, well cared-for garden. There is absolutely no shortage of leisure activities in the vicinity including many footpaths, and water sports on the village lake.

Access : *2km southbound from Paimpont on the D 71*

SAINT-COULOMB - 35350

ROZ-SUR-COUESNON - 35610

LA BERGERIE
M. et Mme Piel

La Poultière
35610 Roz-sur-Couesnon
Tel. 02 99 80 29 68
www.la-bergerie-mont-saint-michel.com

Open all year • 5 rooms upstairs with bath/WC • €45 to €55, breakfast included • No table d'hôte • Garden, car park

AUBERGE DE LA MOTTE JEAN
Mme Simon

La Motte-Jean
35350 Saint-Coulomb
Tel. 02 99 89 41 99
hotel-pointe-du-grouin@wanadoo.fr
www.hotelpointedugrouin.com
Languages : Eng.

Open all year • 12 rooms located in 2 modern buildings. Rooms have bath/WC or shower/WC, all have television • €78 to €130 (€65 to €110 low season); breakfast €7; half-board available • Menus €20 to €61 • Garden, car park. Dogs not admitted in rooms • Duck pond

Breakfasts are served by the fireside in winter and opposite the garden in summer.

The headlands, bluffs and capes carved by the ocean and the island of Guesclin, whose fort belongs to singer-songwriter Léo Ferré, are just two minutes away from this secluded farmhouse which dates from 1707. The good taste of the lady of the house can be seen in the cosy style and old furniture in the rooms, particularly those in the former stables. Gardeners will adore the rose bushes in the beautiful garden "à la française".

Ideally located close to the bay of Mont-Saint-Michel.

The owners of this flower-decked 17C long-cottage extend a warm welcome to guests as they endeavour to make them feel fully at home. Upstairs the well-soundproofed rooms under the eaves are faultlessly kept. They are furnished with regional-style family heirlooms. A dining room with a kitchen area is available to guests who wish to prepare their own meals. Anglers will enjoy the attractive pond, home to ducks and swans, set in a park where donkeys and sheep graze peacefully.

Access : *On leaving Cancale, take the D 355 towards Saint-Malo*

Access : *2km north-west of Roz-sur-Couesnon on the D 797*

SAINT-MALO - 35400

QUIC-EN-GROIGNE
Mme Roualec

8 rue d'Estrées
35400 Saint-Malo
Tel. 02 99 20 22 20
rozenn.roualec@wanadoo.fr
www.quic-en-groigne.com
Languages : Eng.

Closed 10 to 24 Jan and 23 to 26 Dec • 15 non-smoking rooms on 2 levels, all have bath/WC or shower/WC and television • €61 to €67 (€57 to €62 low season); breakfast €7.30 • No restaurant • Garage. No dogs admitted

 The peace and quiet of this hotel located in the heart of St Malo.

The name, taken from the tower next to the castle, is a reminder of Anne of Brittany's haughty reply to the townspeople of St Malo who took a very poor view of the ramparts erected round their town. The duchess dismissed them with the words: "Grumble as you will ('qui qu'en groigne'), so I decide". The hotel is in an old stone house near the beaches. The rooms are modern and gradually being redone. Breakfasts can be taken in the cane-furnished veranda or the pleasant garden.

Access : *In the old town, take Rue de Toulouse from Porte Saint-Louis, at the end turn right twice*

SAINT-SULIAC - 35430

LES MOUETTES
Mme Rouvrais

17 Grande-Rue
35430 Saint-Suliac
Tel. 02 99 58 30 41
contact@les-mouettes-saint-suliac.com
http://www.les-mouettes-saint-suliac.com
Languages : Eng.

Open all year • 5 rooms, one of which has disabled access, all have bathrooms • €49 (€45 low season), breakfast included • No table d'hôte • Garden. Credit cards not accepted, no dogs admitted

 The sincerity of the warm welcome.

Formerly the village grocery store and pork butchers, this stone house built in 1870 stands on the main road leading to the banks of the River Rance. Today it features snug rooms painted in pastel colours and decorated with old paintings and furniture picked up in second-hand antique shops. One of the rooms is equipped for disabled guests. The breakfast room, complete with library, as well as the small garden in the rear, are both very pleasant.

Access : *In the heart of the village*

CARNAC - 56340

L'ALCYONE
Mme Balsan

Impasse de Beaumer - Carnac-plage
56340 Carnac
Tel. 02 97 52 78 11

Closed fortnight in Jan and fortnight in Nov • 5 rooms with bathrooms • €62 (€59 low season), breakfast included • No table d'hôte • Garden, car park. Credit cards not accepted, dogs admitted on request

 Scrumptious breakfasts.

Whitewashed walls, parquet floors and tasteful fabrics await behind the creeper-clad façade of this 1870 farmhouse. The soft, inviting sofas in the sitting room and the deck chairs in the garden overlooking the fields make it impossible not to take things easy. The sea and menhirs are within easy reach, as is one of the most beautiful beaches of the bay of Carnac.

Access : *On leaving Carnac Plage drive towards Trinité-sur-Mer*

CARNAC - 56340

AUBERGE LE RÂTELIER
M. Bouvart

 4 chemin du Douet
56340 Carnac
Tel. 02 97 52 05 04
contact @ le-ratelier.com
 www.le-ratelier.com

Closed from 13 to 30 Nov, Tue and Wed out of season • 8 rooms, some have shower/WC and television • €46 to €55 (€38 to €50 low season); breakfast €8; half-board available • Menus €18 to €43 • Courtyard, car park

 The superb view of Carnac's famous menhirs without risking wrack and ruin!

This stone farmhouse on a quiet side street of the old village was built by a soldier returning from Napoleon's Grande Armée, or so the story goes. Its granite façade, swamped by Virginia creeper, hides a welcoming, country interior: the unfussy rustic charm of the bedrooms makes up for their small size. The beams and manger in the former cow-shed, converted into a dining room, are original and the pretty flowered fabrics add a cheerful touch.

Access : *In the old village, a short distance from the church*

CARNAC - 56340

TY ME MAMM
Mme Daniel

Quelvezin
56340 Carnac
Tel. 02 97 52 45 87
tymemam @ wanadoo.fr
www.tymemam.com
Languages : Eng.

Open all year • 4 rooms, one of which is on the ground floor, with shower/WC • €50, breakfast included • No table d'hôte • Garden, car park. Credit cards not accepted

Your hosts' hospitality and spontaneity.

Off the beaten track, this handsome farmhouse, built in 1900 and entirely restored, stands in a large garden, bordered by a pond on one side. Each of the immaculate rooms, named after one of Carnac's beaches, is decorated in a mixture of rustic and modern styles. Breakfast time by the side of the huge granite fireplace is always pleasant. Guests have the use of a fridge and a microwave.

Access : *5km northbound from Carnac on the D 768 and then the Quelvezin road (C 202)*

GUILLIERS - 56490

RELAIS DU PORHOËT
M. et Mme Courtel

11 place de l'Église
56490 Guilliers
Tel. 02 97 74 40 17
aurelaisduporhoet @ wanadoo.fr
www.aurelaisduporhoet.com
Languages : Eng.

Closed 1 week in Oct, 1 week in Jul, Sun evening and Mon (out of season) • 12 rooms with bath/WC or shower/WC and television • €43 to €56; breakfast €8; half-board available • Menus €13.50 (weekdays) to €38 • Garden, private car park. No dogs admitted

 The delightful young owners so in love with their region.

Let's not beat about the bush: this handsome country inn, adorned with flowers in the summer, is a very special place. Peaceful nights of refreshing sleep in rustic-style bedrooms more than large enough to swing a cat and delicious, generous helpings of good local recipes served in a pretty dining room complete with a huge fireplace. Children can romp to their heart's content in the garden.

Access : *In the centre of the village, opposite the church*

ÎLE DE GROIX - 56590

ILE DE GROIX - 56590

LA GREK
M. et Mme Le Touze

3 place du Leurhé
56590 Île de Groix
Tel. 02 97 86 89 85
groe@infonie.fr
www.groix.com
Languages : Eng.

Closed in Jan • 4 non-smoking rooms, with bath/WC • €60 (€40 low season), breakfast included • No table d'hôte • Garden, car park. Credit cards not accepted, no dogs admitted

 Hoping a storm would blow up and cut us off for days.

The name of this Art Deco-style property, formerly the home of a tuna boat owner, is the nickname given to the inhabitants of this wind-swept island. Restored in 1993 and 1997, the hotel has retained its appealing insular charm. One of the best things about the elegant, comfortable bedrooms is the enormous bath-rooms. Antique furniture adorns the sitting rooms, one of which has a fine collection of old coffee pots. Laze about in the large walled garden.

Access : *In the village*

LA MARINE
Mme Hubert

7 rue du Général-de-Gaulle
56590 Île de Groix
Tel. 02 97 86 80 05
hotel.dela.marine@wanadoo.fr
www.hoteldelamarine.com

Closed in Jan, 1 week in Dec, Sun evening and Mon out of season except in the school holidays • 22 rooms with bath/WC or shower with or without WC • €45 to €95 (€40 to €82 low season); breakfast €8.50; half-board available • Menus €17 to €25 • Terrace, garden

 Sailing round the island on an old pirate ship.

The short walk from the landing stage to the main town is enough to work up a healthy appetite and ensure you do full justice to the hearty, varied dishes rustled up in the kitchen of this plush bourgeois 19C home. Don't worry about the calories, the best way to explore the Island of Groix is on foot or by bicycle! Simple, spotless rooms, a terrace shaded by tall pine trees and a walled garden will make you wish you had planned to stay longer...

Access : *In the town, 5min walk from the port*

LANDÉVANT - 56690

43

TALVERN
M. et Mme Gillot

Talvern
56690 Landévant
Tel. 02 97 56 99 80
talvern@chambre-morbihan.com
www.chambre-morbihan.com
Languages : Eng., Sp.

Open all year • 3 rooms and 2 apartments, 1 with disabled access, all have bath/WC • €55, breakfast included • Table d'hôte €20 (evenings only) • Garden, car park. Credit cards not accepted, no dogs admitted • Walking

 You may be lucky enough to meet a deer or stag on one of your walks.

Who would have believed in the rebirth of this building that was practically in ruins just a few years ago! It has however been fully, and admirably, renovated and has comfortable and elegant bedrooms decorated on the theme of spices. The bathrooms are a pleasing blend of bare stone walls and modern fittings. Epicureans will appreciate the table d'hôte meals, organised by a genuine chef who shares his passion for cooking and his secrets during cooking courses.

Cookery courses from November to March

Access : *North exit, Baud road, 1.3km along a road on the right*

NOYAL-MUZILLAC - 56190

44

MANOIR DE BODREVAN
M. et Mme Rüfenacht

56190 Noyal-Muzillac
Tel. 02 97 45 62 26
www.tourisme-muzillac.com
Languages : Eng., Ger.

Closed 10 to 30 Jan and 15 Nov to 15 Dec • 6 rooms, 1 of which has disabled access; all have bath/WC or shower/WC and television • €85 to €120 (€75 to €105 low season); breakfast €12; half-board available • Menus €21 (evenings only for guests) • Private car park, garden. No dogs admitted in restaurant

 The delightful flower garden noted for its roses.

If in need from a break from the stress of urban life, this former 16C hunting lodge set in the heart of Brittany's peaceful countryside, will suit you to a T. The "prestige boarding house" atmosphere announced on the sign outside the manor is more than amply justified. An eclectic taste in interior decoration, bordering on the baroque at times, sets the tone for the spacious rooms. Only house guests are invited to partake of the appetising set menu.

Access : *2km north-east on the D 153 and a minor road*

PLOEMEL - 56400

M. MALHERBE
M. et Mme Malherbe

Kerimel
56400 Ploemel
Tel. 02 97 56 83 53
chaumieres.kerimel@wanadoo.fr
http://kerimel.free.fr
Languages : Eng.

Closed 14 Nov to 3 Feb • 4 non-smoking rooms, with bathrooms and television • €70, breakfast included • No table d'hôte • Garden, car park. Credit cards not accepted, no dogs admitted

The enveloping warmth of the wood stove after a day in the open air.

This cluster of 17C cottages laid out around a large lawn complete with flower-beds is definitely worth a photo or two. Inside, the stylish renovation of the attic rooms with period furniture, comfortable bedding and well-fitted bathrooms leaves nothing to be desired. Tuck into the profusion of Breton delicacies at breakfast time (croissants, "far", pancakes, home-made jams), served in front of the huge granite fireplace in winter. Guests also have the run of a pleasant sitting room and library.

Access : *8km northbound from Carnac on the D 119, go through the town towards Erdeven, after 1.5km turn right towards Kerimel*

PLOËRMEL - 56800

LE THY
M. et Mme Dinael

19 rue de la Gare
56800 Ploërmel
Tel. 02 97 74 05 21
info@lethy.com
www.le-thy.com
Languages : Eng., Sp.

Open all year • 7 rooms with bath/WC or shower/WC and television • €50 to €60; breakfast €5 • No restaurant but the bar serves sandwiches • Small car park. No dogs admitted • Concerts and theatre at weekends

The path lined with 220 species of hydrangea on the banks of the lac au Duc.

This unusual hotel has absolutely nothing in common with your run-of-the-mill establishment. The contemporary-style rooms are named after and in homage to artists from all periods: Tapies, Hooper, Bonnard, Hugo Pratt, Klimt, Van Gogh and a Flemish artist's studio. A cabaret room, decorated with old golf clubs, organises concerts at the weekends. Trendy, personalised and immaculate – definitely worth a visit!

Access : *In the town centre*

PLOUGOUMELEN - 56400

FERME DE GUERLAN
M. Le Douaran

À Guerlan
56400 Plougoumelen
Tel. 02 97 57 65 50
ledouaran @ aol.com
www.bedbreak.com/guerlan
Languages : Eng., Sp.

Closed from 15 Nov to 15 Mar • 5 rooms, one of which is a family room and one has disabled access • €38 to €50, breakfast included • No table d'hôte • Garden, car park. Credit cards not accepted

> **The rapturous smiles of toddlers visiting the farm.**

This impressive 18C country seat makes an ideal base for exploring the Gulf of Morbihan. The spotless rooms are a happy marriage of old and new. One is designed for families and another for disabled guests. A fireplace graces the enormous dining room and guests have the use of a kitchen and a shaded garden. The owners are very happy to show you round the farm.

Access : *Westbound from Vannes on the N 165, Plougoumelen exit, towards Meriadec*

PLUMELEC - 56420

AUBERGE LE MOULIN DE CALLAC
M. et Mme Theroine

56420 Plumelec
Tel. 02 97 67 12 65
moulindecallac @ wanadoo.fr

Open Mar to late Dec • 5 non-smoking rooms, all with bath/WC or shower/WC • €50, breakfast included • Table d'hôte €15 including drinks • Terrace, garden, car park. Dogs not admitted • City-mountain biking

> **The leafy green setting.**

Allow yourself to be won over by the appeal of this blue-shuttered Brittany cottage and its 3ha park. The delightful rooms awaiting guests are simple and modestly proportioned but the bedding is excellent. Bare stone walls and exposed beams enhance the fine Brittany furniture in the restaurant. Pancakes and local recipes are served on Quimper chinaware, opposite a log fire burning in a handsome granite fireplace or on the terrace overlooking a pond. Fine collection of teapots.

Access : *8km southeast of Plumelec on the D 10 then a minor road*

SAINTE-ANNE-D'AURAY - 56400

RIANTEC - 56670

L'AUBERGE
M. et Mme Larvoir

56 route de Vannes
56400 Sainte-Anne-d'Auray
Tel. 02 97 57 61 55
auberge-jl-larvoir@wanadoo.fr
www.auberge-larvoir.com
Languages : Eng.

Closed in Jan • 17 rooms with bath/WC or shower/WC, all have television • €60 to €100 (€50 to €90 low season); breakfast €9; half-board available • Air-conditioned restaurant; menus from €20 (weekdays) to €85 • Car park

LA CHAUMIÈRE DE KERVASSAL
M. et Mme Watine

Lieu-dit Kervassal
56670 Riantec
Tel. 02 97 33 58 66
gonzague.watine@wanadoo.fr
http://pro.wanadoo.fr/chaumiere.kervassal
Languages : Eng., Sp., Port.

Open May to Oct • 3 non-smoking rooms under the eaves with bathrooms • €69, breakfast included • No table d'hôte • Sitting room, garden, car park. Credit cards not accepted, no dogs admitted • Beach nearby

 The faultless taste of this delightful home.

It is difficult not to fall head over heels in love with this beautifully restored 17C cottage. It has everything from an impeccable thatched roof, exposed beams and stone walls, period furniture and tasteful fabrics down to abundant bouquets of flowers. Inside and out it is a delight for the eyes. The tranquil bedrooms have high ceilings and ultra-modern bathrooms. Exquisite breakfasts are served in the garden in the summer.

 The pilgrimages or "pardons" of Saint Ann are a sight to behold.

The impressive basilica, the house of Nicolazic and the pilgrimages in honour of Saint Ann, the patron saint of Brittany, offer an authentic insight into Breton tradition at is most fervent and picturesque. This spruce, flower-decked inn offers modern rooms in bright fabrics, decorated with regional or Art Deco-style furniture. Admire the elegant Quimper tableware as you eat in the traditionally-furnished Breton dining room, which is clearly, and justifiably, proud of its local produce.

Access : *At the entrance to the village, on the main street*

Access : *8km eastbound from Port-Louis on the D 781, then the D 33, Merlevenez road*

SAINT-PHILIBERT - 56470

51

CHAMBRE D'HÔTE MME GOUZER
Mme Gouzer

17 route de Quéhan (C 203)
56470 Saint-Philibert
Tel. 02 97 55 17 78
fgouzer@club-internet.fr
www.residence-mer.com
Languages : Eng., Ger., Sp.

Open all year • 3 rooms with shower/WC • €65 to €75, breakfast included • No table d'hôte • Garden, car park. Credit cards not accepted, no dogs allowed

The sweeping view over the River Crach and the oyster beds.

Lovers of seafood, oysters in particular, and Brittany in general will adore this place. This charming oyster farmhouse enjoys an exceptional situation, in the midst of pine trees, overlooking the River Crach and opposite the busy port of Trinité sur Mer. Guests are always welcomed warmly. The light, airy rooms all command a view of this fascinating coastal scenery. Two rooms are equipped with a kitchenette and the largest also boasts a balcony.

Access : *2km on the Auray road, turn left at the first set of traffic lights (after Kérisper bridge)*

Sleeping Beauty is said to slumber still within the thick walls of one of the Loire's fairy-tale castles, like Chambord, Azay-le-Rideau or Chenonceau. A list of the region's architectural wonders and glorious gardens would be endless; but its treasures are shown to full effect in a season of 'son et lumière' shows depicting the fabled deeds of brave and courtly knights and the thwarted love of fair demoiselles. The landscape has inspired any number of writers, from Pierre de Ronsard, "the Prince of Poets", to Balzac and Georges Sand. All succumbed to the charm of this valley of kings, without forgetting to give the game-rich woodlands their due. To savour the region's two-fold talent for storytelling and culinary arts, first tuck into a delicious chicken stew, then curl up by the fireside to hear your hosts' age-old local legends.

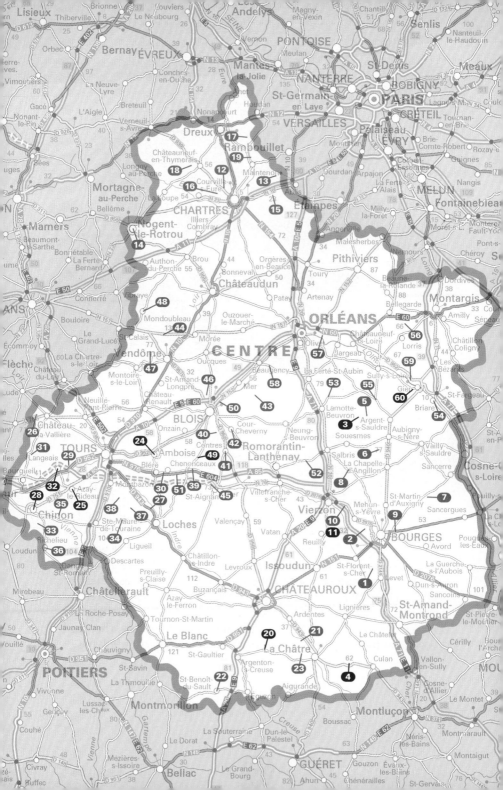

ARCAY - 18340

BERRY-BOUY - 18500

CHÂTEAU DE BEL AIR
M. et Mme Maginiau

Lieu-dit le Grand-Chemin
18340 Arcay
Tel. 02 48 25 36 72
Languages : Eng., Sp.

Open all year • 6 rooms with bath/WC • €45, breakfast included • No table d'hôte • Park, car park. Credit cards not accepted

DOMAINE DE L'ERMITAGE
M. et Mme De La Farge

L'Ermitage
18500 Berry-Bouy
Tel. 02 48 26 87 46
domaine-ermitage@wanadoo.fr

Closed 20 to 31 Dec • 5 rooms with bathrooms • €58 to €61, breakfast included • No table d'hôte • Car park. Credit cards not accepted, no dogs admitted

Unbeatable value for money.

This 19C castle stands in a 10-acre parkland whose trees and grounds afford calm and comfort. Most of the large rooms are furnished in a Louis XVI style. One also features a private sitting room with fireplace, while another connects with a room which can accommodate two child-sized beds. The stately dining room, complete with monumental fireplace, is equally characterful. Bicycle rentals and golf practice in the grounds.

The tranquillity of the park disturbed only by the twittering of birds.

This handsome property, formerly the priory of the Abbey of Saint Sulpice of Bourges, owes its name to a hermit who stayed here for a while. The nearby paper mill dates back to 1495. Nowadays, the well-proportioned, tastefully decorated rooms are situated in two buildings, each as quiet as the next. Take a pleasant stroll through the grounds and admire the ancient trees, venturing perhaps into the wine cellars to taste the estate's own production of Menetou-Salon.

Access : *11km northbound from Châteauneuf on the D 73*

Access : *6km to the north-west of Bourges on the D 60*

BRINON-SUR-SAULDRE - 18410

CHÂTEAUMEILLANT - 18370

LA SOLOGNOTE
M. et Mme De Passos

34 Grande-Rue
18410 Brinon-sur-Sauldre
Tel. 02 48 58 50 29
lasolognote@wanadoo.fr
www.lasolognote.com
Languages : Eng., Sp.

Closed from 6 to 23 Mar • 13 rooms with bath/WC or shower/WC and television • €58 to €92; breakfast €10; half-board available • Air-conditioned restaurant; menus €22 to €68 (closed Tue and Wed from 11 Nov to 1 Apr) • Garden, car park

 A glimpse of village life in France.

Anyone who has read Alain-Fournier will instantly recognise the inimitable soul of this old country village full of French character and charm. The unpretentious hotel stands in the main street where it blends in perfectly with the other redbrick houses. Cosy or more contemporary rooms are laid out around a delightful courtyard-garden. The red floor tiles, stained-glass and period furniture are all synonymous with local styles and the fine porcelain bears the hallmark of Gien.

Access : *Leave the N 20 at Lamotte-Beuvron onto the D 923*

AUBERGE DU PIET À TERRE
M. Finet et Mme Piet

21 rue du Château
18370 Châteaumeillant
Tel. 02 48 61 41 74
tfinet@wanadoo.fr
http://le.piet.a.terre.free.fr
Languages : Eng.

Open from Mar to Dec • 5 rooms with bath/WC or shower/WC, all have television • €74 to €79; breakfast €15.50 • Air-conditioned restaurant; menus €43.50 (weekdays) to €120; limited seating • Dogs not admitted

 The parents' suite with a proper child's room.

Hear ye, hear ye, good folk! Here is a pleasant inn where every weary traveller should rest awhile! Entrust your faithful steed to the groom, have no fear, the stables, sorry the car park, is next door to the mounted constabulary, and rest your tired feet in this country haven. The rooms are as pretty as a picture and the tavern replete with good victuals to tickle even the finest palate. The chef's devotion has won the establishment a well-earned Michelin star.

Access : *Next to the gendarmerie (police station)*

CLÉMONT - 18410

LE DOMAINE DES GIVRYS
M. et Mme Daudé

Les Givrys
18410 Clémont
Tel. 02 48 58 80 74
givrys@wanadoo.fr
www.domainedesgivrys.com

Open all year • 5 non-smoking rooms, 3 of which are upstairs, all with bath/WC or shower/WC • €65, breakfast included • Table d'hôte €30 including drinks • Park, car park. Credit cards not accepted, dogs not admitted • Trout and black bass fishing

> We most liked
> **Something almost magical seems to reign over the site.**

This old Sologne farmhouse, on the banks of a river and a pond full of fish, seems endowed with the same peace and quiet that can be felt in the forest. The building is home to five rooms, three of which are under the eaves upstairs, which attractively combine rustic charm with a contemporary design. Tiled floors and exposed beams. The large dining room provides a pleasant setting at mealtimes and in winter a welcoming fire is lit in the sitting room.

Access : *At Clémont, take the D79 towards Ste-Montaine, then drive for 4km and turn left onto a forest lane*

ENNORDRES - 18380

LES CHATELAINS
M. et Mme Geneviève

18380 Ennordres
Tel. 02 48 58 40 37
contact@leschatelains.com
www.leschatelains.com

Open all year • 5 non-smoking rooms, including 2 apartments, all with bath/WC or shower/WC • €68 to €100, breakfast included • Table d'hôte €28 including drinks • Park, car park • Outdoor swimming pool

> We most liked
> **The beauty of this site saved from neglect.**

This fully restored old family farmhouse comes as a delightful surprise. While the outer wall and roof were the work of local craftsmen, the interior decoration is entirely the work of the lady of the house. A tasteful choice of colours reigns throughout, including in the rooms which range from romantic and cosy to Spanish in flavour. Finally, the table d'hôte meals have reached the summit of refinement and gastronomy, without however leaving you penniless at the end of the day.

Access : *6km eastbound from Ennordres on the D171. Cross over the D940 at "La Surprise", after 2km take lane on the right*

MONTIGNY - 18250

NANÇAY - 18330

DOMAINE DE LA RECULÉE
Mme Gressin

18250 Montigny
Tel. 02 48 69 59 18
e.gressin@wanadoo.fr
www.domainedelareculee.fr

Closed from 15 Nov to 1 Apr • 5 non-smoking rooms, 3 of which are upstairs, all with bath/WC or shower/WC • €56, breakfast included • Table d'hôte €22 drinks included • Park, car park, kitchenette. Credit cards not accepted • Outdoor swimming pool

LES CROCUS
Mme Gueru

7 rue du Grand-Maulnes
18330 Nançay
Tel. 02 48 51 88 28
lescrocus@cario.fr
www.lescrocus.com

Open all year • 5 non-smoking rooms, all with shower/WC • €54, breakfast included • Table d'hôte €23 drinks included • Park, car park • Outdoor swimming pool

 The kind welcome and peaceful countryside.

Even though this Sancerre farm is no longer a working farm, it is enjoying a second youth since the former stables have been turned into chambres d'hôte. All the rooms are immaculately kept, but we did particularly like the one in the dovecote and the aptly named Cabane, lined in wood from ceiling to floor. Local specialities take pride of place on the table d'hôte menu supplied by local producers. Delicious!

 Rumour has it that every inhabitant of Nançay is an antique dealer.

When they bought this house in the heart of the village, the owners decided to install three chambres d'hôte in the main house (among which the romantic Louis XV room) and another in a separate wing, all of which are decorated along different themes. The result is highly pleasant, overlooking a pretty flowered park, dotted with little fountains. In summer, breakfast is served under a canopy and afterwards guests can dive into the swimming pool or admire the owners' collection of 1 200 records.

> *Theme weekends: philosophy, gastronomy and art*

Access : *In the village*

Access : *5km from Montigny on the D44. In the village follow the signs marked Chambres d'hôte*

SAINT-GERMAIN-DU-PUY - 18390

VIGNOUX-SUR-BARANGEON - 18500

DOMAINE DE JACQUELIN
M. Jolly

18390 Saint-Germain-du-Puy
Tel. 02 48 30 84 97
chambresjolly@wanadoo.fr
http://monsite.wanadoo.fr/jollychambres

Open all year • 5 non-smoking rooms, 2 of which are upstairs, all with bath/WC or shower/WC • €60, breakfast included • No table d'hôte • Park, car park

VILLEMENARD
M. et Mme Gréaud

18500 Vignoux-sur-Barangeon
Tel. 02 48 51 53 40
villemenard@wanadoo.fr
www.villemenard.com

Open all year • 6 rooms with shower/WC • €50 to €55, breakfast included • No table d'hôte • Park, terrace, car park. Credit cards not accepted, dogs not admitted • River and pond on the property. Billiards room

The lovely wooded park and the river.

On the doorstep of Bourges, in an unspoilt haven, stands an authentic 15C farmhouse that formerly belonged to the Château de Villemenard. A family-run affair since 1860, this sprawling house is home to five rooms whose decoration pays homage to the surrounding countryside. Proud of their abode and fully bent on ensuring it remains in the family for many years to come, the owners enjoy welcoming guests whom they never fail to make feel at home.

An afternoon stroll through ancient woodland.

The lane, lined with ponds, crosses a river before reaching this wonderful 19C country house which is still the hub of a thriving agricultural business. The interior decoration is particularly worthy of note: beautiful azulejos tiles grace the entrance and dining room, weapons and prints adorn the staircase and a superb varnished wooden bar stands in the billiards room. All the well-dimensioned, quiet rooms overlook the peaceful Berry countryside.

Access : *4km eastbound from Bourges on the N 151*

Access : *6km northbound from Méhun on the D 79 towards Vouzeron*

VIGNOUX-SUR-BARANGEON - 18500

LE PRIEURÉ
Famille Ribail

2 rue Jean-Graczyk
18500 Vignoux-sur-Barangeon
Tel. 02 48 51 58 80
prieurehotel@wanadoo.fr
www.leprieurehotel.com
Languages : Eng.

Open Jun to Sep • 7 rooms upstairs with shower/WC and television • €54 to €65.50 (€49 to €60 low season); breakfast €6.50; half-board available • Menus €20 (weekdays) to €37.50. Restaurant closed Tue and Wed • Terrace, garden, car park • Outdoor swimming pool

 A religious devotion to guests' welfare.

Built in 1860 for the village priest, the ogival windows immediately evoke this priory's religious roots. The establishment's former spiritual vocation has given way to a more down-to-earth, but equally committed desire for hospitality. The intimate, bright rooms are named after flowers. Traditional dishes and flavourful Berry wines are consumed with gusto on the pleasant terrace. Connoisseurs will immediately recognise the beautiful tableware as Foëcy porcelain!

Cooking lessons in autumn

Access : *Set back from the lane, on the D 30 (towards Neuvy-sur-Barangeon), near the church*

BAILLEAU-L'ÉVÊQUE - 28300

LA FERME DU CHÂTEAU
M. et Mme Vasseur

À Lévesville
28300 Bailleau-l'Évêque
Tel. 02 37 22 97 02
Languages : Eng.

Closed 1 Jan and 25 Dec • 3 rooms with shower/WC • €55 to €60, breakfast included • Table d'hôte €17.50 • Garden, car park. Credit cards not accepted, dogs not admitted

 The overwhelming peace and quiet of this country spot.

A pretty manor farm laid out around a spacious inner courtyard next door to a small castle. The good-sized rooms are cheerful, well equipped and all are peaceful. The simple, unaffected welcome, reasonable prices, pretty garden and its location only 15km from Chartres are among the most noteworthy of this establishment's many charms.

Access : *8km to the north-west of Chartres on the N 154 then the D 134*

ÉCROSNES - 28320

CHÂTEAU DE JONVILLIERS
M. et Mme Thompson

17 rue Lucien-Petit
28320 Écrosnes
Tel. 02 37 31 41 26
info@chateaudejonvilliers.com
www.chateaudejonvilliers.com
Languages : Eng.

Open all year • 5 non-smoking rooms with shower/WC • €65 to €85, breakfast included • No table d'hôte • Garden, car park. Dogs not admitted

The sheer elegance of this majestic property.

A pleasant drive leads up to this elegant 18C castle which stands in private grounds next to thick woodland. Peace and quiet reign in all the spacious, tastefully decorated rooms. Delicious and generous helpings of breakfast fare are served in a huge antique furnished dining room. Note that the establishment is entirely non-smoking.

Access : *4km to the north-east of Gallardon on the D 32*

NOGENT-LE-ROTROU - 28400

L'AULNAYE
M. et Mme Dumas

Route d'Alençon
28400 Nogent-le-Rotrou
Tel. 02 37 52 02 11
http://laulnaye-accueil-France.com
Languages : Eng.

Open all year • 3 rooms with bath/shower and WC • €68 to €70, breakfast included • No table d'hôte • Park, car park. Credit cards not accepted, no dogs admitted

The tranquillity of the park so close to the town centre.

The main appeal of this almost Victorian-looking 19C mansion is its priceless position in the heart of a park full of countless species of trees and plants. The plush interior decoration is also worthy of note: a handsome wooden staircase leads up to the rooms, all of which boast parquet floors, period furniture and marble fireplaces. Delicious breakfasts are served in the wainscoted dining room in winter and in the delightful wrought-iron conservatory in the summer.

Access : *3.5km westbound from Nogent-le Rotrou towards Alençon*

OINVILLE-SOUS-AUNEAU - 28700

CAROLINE LETHUILLIER
Mme Lethuillier

2 rue des Prunus - Cherville
28700 Oinville-sous-Auneau
Tel. 02 37 31 72 80
info@cherville.com
www.cherville.com
Languages : Eng., Ger.

Open all year • 4 non-smoking rooms, all have bath/WC or shower/WC • €55 to €59, breakfast included • No table d'hôte • Garden, car park, kitchenette. Credit cards not accepted, no dogs allowed

 The authenticity of this old farmhouse.

The owners of this country estate, still a working farm, have tastefully renovated one of the old outhouses to create four refreshing and charming bedrooms (three have sloping ceilings). Breakfasts, served in a room which sports bare stone walls and the original manger, are an opportunity to taste specialities from the garden and pancakes stuffed with home-made jams made by the lady of the house.

Access : *N 10 towards Chartres, 13km from the roundabout, head towards Umpeau, go through the village, on the right at Cherville*

SAINT-AUBIN-DES-BOIS - 28300

L'ERABLAIS
M. et Mme Guinard

38 rue Jean-Moulin à Chazay
28300 Saint-Aubin-des-Bois
Tel. 02 37 32 80 53
jmguinard@aol.com
www.erablais.com
Languages : Eng.

Open all year • 3 non-smoking rooms, all have shower/WC • €47, breakfast included • No table d'hôte • Garden, private car park, kitchenette, library. Credit cards not accepted, dogs not admitted • Bicycles rented

 The peace and quiet of the countryside.

The 19C farmhouse, tucked away in a hamlet near Chartres, is made up of five buildings built from traditional materials. The former stables are now home to three attractive guest rooms (two of which have sloping ceilings) individually decorated on a flower theme. Home-made jams are served at breakfast which is taken on the terrace or in a room overlooking the fields of crops. Bicycles available on request; water-skiing and angling nearby.

Access : *D 24 towards Senonches, at Saint-Aubin-des-Bois, left towards Chazay. On rue Jean Moulin, on the right.*

SAINT-LAURENT-LA-GÂTINE - 28210

CLOS SAINT-LAURENT
M. et Mme James

6 rue de l'Église
28210 Saint-Laurent-la-Gâtine
Tel. 02 37 38 24 02
james@clos-saint-laurent.com
www.clos-saint-laurent.com
Languages : Eng.

Closed 23 Dec to 2 Jan • 4 non-smoking rooms, all have bath/WC or shower/WC • €68 to €85, breakfast included • No table d'hôte • Garden, private car park. Credit cards not accepted, dogs not admitted

 The tranquil location of this old farmhouse.

The Clos is a fine example of a successful conversion. The owners of this old farmhouse have created three spacious airy bedrooms, tastefully decorating them in a smart country style with bare beams, white walls and tiled floors. The bathrooms are equally praiseworthy. If you then add the delightful breakfast room complete with fireplace and the garden-terrace, you will agree that it is excellent value for money.

Access : *By the N 154 head towards Dreux, Nogent-le-Roi exit by the D 26, then D 21 towards Anet. House opposite the church.*

SAINT-MAIXME-HAUTERIVE - 28170

LA RONDELLIÈRE
M. et Mme Langlois

11 rue de la Mairie
28170 Saint-Maixme-Hauterive
Tel. 02 37 51 68 26
jeanpaul.langlois@wanadoo.fr
www.ferme-rondelliere.com

Open all year • 4 non-smoking rooms upstairs, all have bath/WC • €40, breakfast included • Table d'hôte €15 drinks included • Car park. Credit cards not accepted • Tennis court

 Set in a typical village, among fields of cereal crops and woods.

This farmhouse, which lies hidden in the heart of a peaceful country town, opens onto a spacious courtyard surrounded by buildings with flint walls and small tiled roofs. The former outhouses are today home to a reception room with kitchen and four bedrooms. The latter, under the eaves, are spacious and colourful and all have fully equipped bathrooms. Garden produce takes pride of place on the table d'hôte menu. Garden and private pond.

Access : *12km east of Senonches on the D 140*

VILLIERS-LE-MORHIER - 28130

LES CHANDELLES
M. et Mme Simon

19 rue des Sablons, village les Chandelles
28130 Villiers-le-Morhier
Tel. 02 37 82 71 59
info@chandelles-golf.com
www.chandelles-golf.com
Languages : Eng., Sp.

Open all year • 5 non-smoking rooms with bath/WC and television • €60, breakfast included • No table d'hôte • Garden, car park. No dogs admitted • Wifi internet access

 A wealth of leisure activities so close at hand.

An impressive wooden porch leads into this renovated 1840 farmhouse set in grounds where horses graze peacefully. The barn has been converted into a guest wing which features bold colour schemes and excellent bathrooms. Interesting old furniture picked up from antique dealers and flea markets adds character to the breakfast room. On the leisure side, you can choose between golf and horse-riding (the owner's twin passions – he is a golf pro) or try your hand at fishing.

> *Golf courses*

Access : *8km northbound from Maintenon on the D 116, towards Coulomb*

BOUESSE - 36200

CHÂTEAU DE BOUESSE
M. et Mme Lorry

36200 Bouesse
Tel. 02 54 25 12 20
château.bouesse@wanadoo.frf
www.chateaubouesse.com
Languages : Eng.

Closed Jan-Mar, Mon and Tue from Apr 1 to May 15 and from Oct 1 to end Dec • 12 rooms, all with WC/bath, 6 with television • €85 to €110, breakfast €13; half-board available • Menus €32 (weekdays) to €40 • Terrace, park, car park

 The bedroom in the dungeon and raftered ceiling.

Joan of Arc, Charles VII, Louis XI and Charles VIII are just a few of the famous names to have stayed in this small fortified 13C castle. Today the charm of yesteryear can still be felt in the spacious bedrooms, some medieval-style with four-poster beds and fireplaces, others with a more intimate appeal, and in the elegant restaurant which boasts a 15C fresco on the ceiling and a lovely terrace overlooking the garden à la française. Wouldn't it be easy to get used to a life of luxury?

Access : *In the centre of the village, 11km from Argenton-sur-Creuse by N 20*

MONTIPOURET - 36230

MAISON VOILÀ
M. Pluylaar

La Brande
36230 Montipouret
Tel. 02 54 31 17 91
maisonvoila@yahoo.com
www.maisonvoila.com

Open all year • 3 non-smoking rooms, all with bath/WC • €70 to €80, breakfast included • Table d'hôte €25 • Terrace, garden, car park. Credit cards not accepted, dogs not admitted • Outdoor swimming pool, tennis court

 A quiet country setting ideal for a break away from it all.

This 19C country farmhouse is comprised of two buildings surrounded by a beautifully tended garden planted with fruit trees. The interior is warm and welcoming, from the rustic dining room with beams and fireplace, to the cosy rooms, located in the sheepfold, all of which are on the ground floor and mostly furnished with antiques. Pleasant terrace with a grill, splendid summer pool, tennis court and Jacuzzi.

Access : *5km northeast of La Brande on the D49 and minor road*

SAINT-BENOÎT-DU-SAULT - 36170

LE PORTAIL
Mme Boyer

Rue Émile-Surun
36170 Saint-Benoît-du-Sault
Tel. 02 54 47 57 20

Open all year • 3 rooms, one of which is a studio, with shower/WC • €43 to €58, breakfast included • No table d'hôte • Credit cards not accepted, dogs admitted on request

 Wandering around the historic medieval city.

A fortified gate, carved stone cross and spiral staircase bear witness to the venerable age of this beautiful 14C-15C former property of the Knights Templar. Character and authenticity emanate from the old beams and medieval or Renaissance inspired furniture in the bedrooms and apartment. The breakfast room is equally appealing and the lady of the house's gracious welcome is quite faultless.

Access : *In the medieval city*

SARZAY - 36230

MONTGARNI
M. et Mme Labaurie

23 Montgarni
36230 Sarzay
Tel. 02 54 31 31 05
mic.lab@wanadoo.fr
www.sarzay-hotes.com
Languages : Eng.

Open all year • 5 non-smoking rooms with shower/WC • €44, breakfast included; half-board available • Table d'hôte €18 • Park, car park. Dogs not admitted • Outdoor swimming pool. Farm-grown produce

 The gourmet owner-chef's inspired culinary talents.

This farming couple have been extending their friendly hospitality to guests in search of tranquillity and the good things in life for over 15 years. The rooms in the 19C mansion, half-hidden by greenery, are extremely comfortable. Only 100% local produce crosses the threshold of the kitchen to become healthy, mouth-watering dishes. If you feel like some gentle exercise, the immense parkland which extends into the unspoilt Berry countryside offers some great walks.

> *October to late March: duck cookery course weekends (carving and preserving)*

Access : *1.5km southbound from Sarzay on the D 41 towards Chassignolles*

AMBOISE - 37400

LE BLASON
M. Yung

11 place Richelieu
37400 Amboise
Tel. 02 47 23 22 41
hotel@leblason.fr
www.leblason.fr
Languages : Eng., Ger.

Closed from 10 Jan to 10 Feb • 25 rooms, 2 of which have disabled access, all have shower/WC and television • €49 to €57; breakfast €6.50 • Menus €18 to €43 • Terrace, garage

 The easy-going atmosphere.

Leonardo da Vinci ended his days in this town, also home to this 15C house with a half-timbered façade. The renovated rooms, some of which are under the eaves, sport pastel colours and a rustic charm (period beams). Those in need of a little boost to the morale might like to know that the rooms on the front overlook "Rue Joyeuse".

Access : *On a square in the town centre*

AZAY-LE-RIDEAU - 37190

DE BIENCOURT
M. Marioton

7 rue Balzac
37190 Azay-le-Rideau
Tel. 02 47 45 20 75
biencourt @ infonie.fr
www.hotelbiencourt.com
Languages : Eng., Sp.

Open from mid-Mar to mid-Nov • 15 rooms located in the main building and the old school, with bath/WC or shower/WC, some have television • €47 to €53; breakfast €7 • No restaurant • Inner courtyard. No dogs admitted

The nearby castle surrounded by water and parkland.

This elegant 18C property is tucked away in a semi-pedestrian street that leads to one of France's most beautiful Renaissance castles. Space and rustic furniture characterise the rooms, which have sloping ceilings on the top floor. A number of rooms decorated in Directoire style are also available in a former school in the rear of the courtyard. Breakfast is served in a pleasant conservatory.

Access : *In the town centre (near the post office), on the semi-pedestrian street leading to the castle*

BRAYE-SUR-MAULNE - 37330

LE DOMAINE DE LA BERGERIE
Famille Defond

37330 Braye-sur-Maulne
Tel. 02 47 24 90 88
clairedefond @ gmx.net
www.people.freenet.de/bergerie/

Open from mid-Feb to late Dec • 3 non-smoking rooms on the 2nd floor, all with bath/WC • €75, breakfast included • Table d'hôte €30 • Park, car park. Credit cards not accepted

Watching a deer cavort down by the pond from the terrace.

Despite its impressive stature, this early 19C chateau seems almost lost in the vast expanse of greenery surrounding it. A landscaped park, decked in multi-coloured blooms and a large vegetable garden that boasts nearly 50 varieties of tomatoes. The table d'hôte meals, prepared essentially from produce from the estate are a mouth-watering festival of flavour. Flawless rooms and gîtes in keeping with the style of the rest of the abode – smart and simple at the same time.

Access : *3km northbound of Château La Vallière, towards Laval*

CHAMBOURG-SUR-INDRE - 37310

LE CLOS DU PETIT MARRAY
M. et Mme Plantin

37310 Chambourg-sur-Indre
Tel. 02 47 92 50 67
serge.plantin@wanadoo.fr
http://petit.marray.free.fr
Languages : Eng.

Open all year • 4 rooms with bathrooms • €52 to €62, breakfast included • Table d'hôte €26 (evenings only and by reservation) • Garden, car park. Credit cards not accepted, no dogs admitted • Play area and fishing for children

 Walking along the banks of the Indre.

Children will enjoy fishing in the pond in the grounds of this handsome 19C farmhouse in the heart of the countryside. Names evocative of well-being and freedom have been given to each of the generously-sized and tastefully decorated rooms. A library and the nearby forest will keep you busy throughout your stay.

Access : *5km northbound from Loches on the N 143, towards Tours*

CHINON - 37500

DIDEROT
M. et Mme Dutheil

4 rue Buffon - 7 rue Diderot
37500 Chinon
Tel. 02 47 93 18 87
hoteldiderot@hoteldiderot.com
www.hoteldiderot.com
Languages : Eng., Ger., Sp.

Closed fortnight early Jan • 27 rooms, 1 with disabled access, all have bath/WC or shower/WC, some have television • €52 to €73; breakfast €7 • No restaurant • Inner courtyard, private car park. No dogs admitted

 Homemade lavender jam made with home grown lavender!

Olive, banana, lemon, mandarin and medlar trees form a spectacularly exotic curtain of greenery to this 18C abode. A classical accent is being given to the gradually renovated rooms, the quietest overlooking the courtyard. Homemade jams figure prominently on the breakfast table, served next to a crackling log fire in winter or out on the terrace whenever the weather permits.

Access : *A short distance from the town centre, on a quiet street between Place Jeanne d'Arc and Rue Diderot*

CINQ-MARS-LA-PILE - 37130

LA MEULIÈRE
M. et Mme Manier

10 rue de la Gare
37130 Cinq-Mars-la-Pile
Tel. 02 47 96 53 63
cgmanier-lameuliere@wanadoo.fr
http://lameuliere.free.fr
Languages : Eng.

Open all year • 3 rooms with bathrooms • €45 to €53, breakfast included • No table d'hôte • Garden, car park. Credit cards not accepted, no dogs admitted

 The tranquillity of this establishment within walking distance of the station.

The uncontested bonus of this handsome 19C mansion is its situation close to the station without any of the noise or fuss you might expect. A fine wooden staircase takes you up to colourful, well-soundproofed rooms furnished with antiques. A comfortable dining room provides the backdrop to breakfasts. In the summer, deck chairs can be found in the garden for a quiet afternoon nap.

Access : *Near the railway station*

CIVRAY-DE-TOURAINE - 37150

CHAMBRE D'HÔTE LA MARMITTIÈRE
M. et Mme Boblet

22 Vallée-de-Mesvres
37150 Civray-de-Touraine
Tel. 02 47 23 51 04
marmittiere@libertysurf.fr
http://perso.libertysurf.fr/marmittiere
Languages : Eng.

Open from 16 Mar to 14 Nov • 3 non-smoking rooms with shower/WC • €56, breakfast included • Table d'hôte €23 (closed Sat-Sun and by reservation only) • Terrace, garden, car park. Credit cards not accepted, no dogs admitted

 Breakfasts and dinners are prepared with 100% organic produce.

The breakfast room and table d'hôte are located in a 17C wine-growers home, while the rooms have been fitted out in an early 20C stone villa. The interior decoration, although contemporary and highly colourful, blends in wonderfully with the old walls. To wind up this enticing picture, take a stroll round the garden and be ready to encounter some of its residents – the estate's donkeys and chickens – roaming freely.

Access : *4km westbound of Chenonceaux on the D 40 then a minor road*

CONTINVOIR - 37340

LA BUTTE DE L'ÉPINE
M. Bodet

37340 Continvoir
Tel. 02 47 96 62 25
mibodet@wanadoo.fr
www.labutte-de-lepine.com
Languages : Eng.

Closed from Nov to end Feb • 3 non-smoking rooms, one of which is upstairs, all with shower/WC • €60, breakfast included • No table d'hôte • Park. Credit cards not accepted, no dogs admitted

The amazing care taken to restore this period house to its former glory.

The owners have spent years faithfully restoring this delightful residence of 16C-17C origins using only authentic materials. The sitting-breakfast room is imaginatively strewn with period furniture and features a huge fireplace. The spotless rooms are genuine boudoirs, the most romantic of which is upstairs. Well-tended flower-beds grace the park behind the house.

Access : *2km eastbound from Gizeux on the D 15*

LANGEAIS - 37130

MAISON ERRARD
M. et Mme Errard

2 rue Gambetta
37130 Langeais
Tel. 02 47 96 82 12
info@errard.com
www.errard.com
Languages : Eng.

Closed Dec, Jan, lunchtimes from Mon to Fri (except public holidays) and Sun and Mon evenings from Oct to Apr • 10 rooms with bath/WC and television • €68 to €95; breakfast €12 • Air-conditioned restaurant; menus €29 to €51 • Terrace, garage

The gargantuan hospitality of this provincial inn.

This hostelry is surrounded by some of Touraine's most beautiful castles and within walking distance of Langeais. Guests can choose between plush 19C or contemporary rooms, but those overlooking the street are noisier, even though the traffic can hardly be called "busy" after nightfall. Any doubts you may still have that you are in the birthplace of Rabelais' Gargantua, epic trencherman, will immediately vanish at the sight of the Brobdingnagian dishes liberally washed down with Loire wines.

Access : *In the town centre, opposite the tourist office*

LIGRÉ - 37500

MANTHELAN - 37240

LA MILAUDIÈRE
M. Marolleau

5 rue St-Martin
37500 Ligré
Tel. 02 47 98 37 53
milaudiere@club-internet.fr
www.milaudiere.com
Languages : Eng., Sp.

Open all year • 7 rooms, one of which is on the ground floor and 3 are upstairs, all with shower/WC • €45 to €60, breakfast included • No table d'hôte • Car park. Credit cards not accepted, no dogs admitted

LE VIEUX TILLEUL
Mme Lootvoet-Van Havere

8 rue Nationale
37240 Manthelan
Tel. 02 47 92 24 32
le-vieux-tilleul@wanadoo.fr
www.le-vieux-tilleul.net

Open all year • 4 non-smoking rooms and 2 apartments, all with bath/WC or shower/WC • €65 to €80, breakfast included • Table d'hôte €20 including drinks, by reservation in the evening • Garden, terrace, car park. Credit cards not accepted, dogs not admitted

 The owners' exquisite charm and hospitality.

The walls of this original old 18C house are built out of "tuffeau", a soft local chalk. The owners dug in and undertook the majority of the restoration work themselves and can rightly be proud of the result. The rooms under the eaves are extremely pleasant and those on the ground floor with their old tiled floors, net curtains and rustic furniture are full of character. The breakfast room which boasts an old bread oven is also something of an eye-opener.

 Admiring the splendid old lime tree.

Formerly abandoned after being a post house then a hotel, this home has regained its charm of yesteryear and is now ready to continue to add to its rich heritage. The restoration and decoration were masterfully supervised with the idea of retaining the site's original appeal whilst creating a refined setting. Well-kept, cosy rooms and apartments and an equally comfortable sitting room, more contemporary in style. Table d'hôte menu in keeping with current taste.

Access : *8km to the south-east of Chinon, towards Île-Bouchard on the D 749, then take the D 29*

Access : *In the town*

PANZOULT - 37220

DOMAINE DE BEAUSÉJOUR
M. et Mme Chauveau

37220 Panzoult
Tel. 02 47 58 64 64
info@domainedebeausejour.com
www.domaine.de.beausejour.com
Languages : Eng.

Open all year • 3 rooms with shower/WC • €77 to €85 (€67 to €77 low season), breakfast included • No table d'hôte • Car park. Credit cards not accepted • Outdoor swimming pool

 Relaxing on a genuine wine-growing estate in Gargantua's homeland: in vino veritas!

This delightful house was built in 1978 from old materials gleaned in the region, some said to be three centuries old! The slate floors of the carefully decorated rooms contrast beautifully with the choice antique furniture. The superb view over Rabelais' beloved Chinon vineyards bodes well for a pleasant stay; those who so desire can taste some of the estate's best vintages in the company of the proprietress.

Visits to wine cellars and tasting

Access : *5km north-west of Bouchard on the D 757, then drive towards Chinon on the D 21*

RICHELIEU - 37120

LA MAISON
Mme Couvrat-Desvergnes

6 rue Henri-Proust
37120 Richelieu
Tel. 02 47 58 29 40
lamaisondemichele@yahou.com
www.lamaisondemichele.com

Open 15 Apr to late Sep • 4 rooms upstairs with bath/WC • €90, breakfast included • No table d'hôte • Terrace, garden, car park. Credit cards not accepted

 The pleasant garden and bamboo grove.

One of the quiet side streets of this town created in 1631 by Richelieu as an "ideal city" is home to an opulent stone house with a welcoming façade. There are two immense sittings rooms and upstairs, via a handsome staircase, spacious, comfortable and tastefully furnished rooms. The wallpaper matches the fully fitted bathrooms. Warm welcome.

Access : *Next to Sacré Coeur school and the library*

SAINT-BAULD - 37310

LE MOULIN DU COUDRAY
Mme Péria

37310 Saint-Bauld
Tel. 02 47 92 82 64
sylvie.peria@free.fr
www.lemoulinducoudray.fr.st

Open all year • 4 non-smoking rooms, including one family room, with bath/WC • €58 to €62, breakfast included • Table d'hôte €23 by reservation only weekends and public holidays • Park, pond, car park. Credit cards not accepted • Fitness facilities

The pleasantly quiet site.

This delightful faultlessly restored 16C mill lies just beneath the town. The bay windows in the dining room overlook an immense tree-lined park with pond and stream. One relatively spacious independent family apartment and three pretty rooms, decorated in homage to the writers after whom they are named. Traditional appetising table d'hôte and fitness facilities for those who wish to work off the calories put on during meals!

Access : *On the way into the town*

SAINT-BRANCHS - 37320

LE LOGIS DE LA PAQUERAIE
M. et Mme Binet

La Paqueraie
37320 Saint-Branchs
Tel. 02 47 26 31 51
monique.binet@wanadoo.fr
http://perso.wanadoo.fr/lapaqueraie/

Open all year • 4 rooms with bathrooms and one gîte • €90, breakfast included • Table d'hôte €30 (beverages included) • Garden, car park. Credit cards not accepted, no dogs allowed in rooms • Outdoor swimming pool. Fishing, hiking, tennis, 18-hole golf course and riding nearby

The delightful landscaped garden and swimming pool.

The traditional regional architectural style, rampant curtain of Virginia creeper and the venerable old oaks in the park all combine to lend this recently built house a much older feel! The rooms display an excellent blend of practicality, comfort and sophistication. Mirrors, antiques and an original fireplace grace the sitting room. At mealtimes, you will sample classic French cooking made with local produce. If still not convinced, the peace and quiet of the grounds are bound to win you over.

Cooking, flower arranging, watercolour courses and bicycling excursions

Access : *On leaving Cormery (coming from Tours) take the D 32 and turn right after the level-crossing*

BOURRÉ - 41400

MANOIR DE LA SALLE DU ROC
M. et Mme Boussard

69 route de Vierzon
41400 Bourré
Tel. 02 54 32 73 54
boussard.patricia@wanadoo.fr
www.manoirdelasalleduroc.monsite.wanadoo.fr
Languages : Eng.

Open all year • 4 rooms with shower/WC • €70 to €110, (€60 to €100 low season), breakfast included • No table d'hôte • Park, car park. American Express cards not accepted, no dogs admitted

 Luxury, calm and voluptuousness, a stone's throw from the troglodyte village of Bourré.

A handsome tree-lined drive leads up to this pretty manor built against a rock face. The eye is naturally drawn to the welcoming façade, but also to the lovely park surrounding it, whose features include pools, old stone stair-cases, clipped boxwood hedges, statues, flow-erbeds and over 500 rosebushes. The charm of the interior also greets the eye, whether in the ground-floor sitting rooms and the lovely library or upstairs in the comfortably fur-nished, plush bedrooms.

Access : *2km northbound of Montrichard on the D 62*

CHITENAY - 41120

LE CLOS BIGOT
M. et Mme Bravo-Meret

41120 Chitenay
Tel. 02 54 44 21 28
clos.bigot@wanadoo.fr
www.gites-cheverny.com

Open all year (by reservation in winter) • 3 rooms and 1 apartment with shower/WC • €60 to €88, breakfast included • No table d'hôte • Garden, car park. Credit cards not accepted, no dogs allowed

 A tranquil invitation to take things easy.

A deafening calm reigns throughout this 17C farmstead surrounded by forest and fields. The rooms under the eaves are very pleasant and an apartment has been built next to the dovecote, which is now a bathroom. Comfy old furniture and a warm, welcoming stove in the sitting room are all the invitation you'll need to while away an hour or two. An 18-hole golf course, tennis court, riding stables, and, of course, the world-famous Loire châteaux are within easy reach.

Access : *2km to the south-east of Chitenay towards Contres, then a lane*

CONTRES - 41700

LA RABOUILLÈRE
Mme Thimonnier

Chemin de Marçon
41700 Contres
Tel. 02 54 79 05 14
rabouillere@wanadoo.fr
www.larabouillere.com

Open all year • 5 rooms, one of which is upstairs, with bath/WC • €65 to €95, breakfast included • No table d'hôte • Park, car park. No dogs admitted

 The sophisticated decorative flair.

The half-timbered walls of this Sologne farmhouse look so authentic it is hard to believe they were entirely built from materials found in neighbouring farms. The sumptuously furnished rooms all have exposed beams. Breakfasts are served by the fireside in winter and in the garden in summer. The gentle countryside is perfect for long country rambles.

Access : *10km southbound from Cheverny on the D 102, then a minor road*

COUR-CHEVERNY - 41700

LE BÉGUINAGE
M. et Mme Deloison

41700 Cour-Cheverny
Tel. 02 54 79 29 92
le.beguinage@wanadoo.fr
www.lebeguinage.fr.st
Languages : Eng.

Closed 5 to 22 Jan • 6 rooms, all with shower/WC • €52 to €75, breakfast included • No table d'hôte • Park, car park. No dogs allowed • Hot-air ballooning, golf, hiking

 Flying over the Loire châteaux in a hot-air balloon.

The manicured park and pond are not the only treasures of this stone property covered in Virginia creeper. Parquet or tiled floors, exposed beams, fireplaces, king-size beds and generous dimensions all grace the sophisticated bedrooms: with the smallest measuring 20sq m, this is truly "the great indoors". For a quite matchless view of some of France's architectural gems, forget the cost and treat yourself to a flight over the Loire châteaux in a hot-air balloon piloted by the proprietor.

Access : *Near town centre and château*

DANZÉ - 41160

CROUY-SUR-COSSON - 41220

CHAMBRE D'HÔTE LA BORDE
M. et Mme Kamette

41160 Danzé
Tel. 02 54 80 68 42
michelkamette@minitel.net
Languages : Eng., Ger., Sp.

Open all year • 3 non-smoking rooms and 2 apartments upstairs, all with bath/WC or shower/WC • €49 to €64, breakfast included • No table d'hôte • Park, car park • Heated indoor swimming pool

LE MOULIN DE CROUY
M. et Mme Harrault

3 route de Cordellerie
41220 Crouy-sur-Cosson
Tel. 02 54 87 56 19
lemoulindecrouy@wanadoo.fr
www.lemoulindecrouy.com

Open all year • 4 non-smoking rooms and 2 apartments upstairs, all with bath/WC or shower/WC • €65, breakfast included • Table d'hôte €24 drinks included • Park, car park • Outdoor swimming pool with sun deck, games room, mountain and city bikes for rent

 Strolling along the banks of the Boulon, a trout river that runs through the estate.

After leaving the main road for a small forest lane, you will reach a green clearing. In front of you stands a white manor house, rebuilt in the late 19C and surrounded by a 10ha park. Each of the three rooms and two apartments is simply decorated with comfortable bathrooms. If the rumble of the trains in the distance disturbs your peace and quiet, head for the indoor swimming pool heated by solar panels.

Pinching home decoration ideas in the lovely shop.

Two minutes from the village but in the heart of the countryside, this old mill and its adjacent farmhouse are set in 14ha of wooded parkland, reached along a handsome drive lined with hundred-year-old trees. The owners, upholsterers and decorators, have endowed each room with its own special charm. Outdoors, guests can enjoy the swimming pool, sun deck and summer sitting room in fine weather. Seasonal produce and game during the hunting season take pride of place on the table d'hôte menu.

Access : *2km northbound from Danzé on the D 24*

Access : *On the way out of the village, behind the campsite*

MAREUIL-SUR-CHER - 41110

LES AULNAIES
M. Bodic

2 rue des Aulnaies
41110 Mareuil-sur-Cher
Tel. 02 54 75 43 89
lesaulnaies@aol.com

Open all year • 5 non-smoking rooms upstairs, all have bath/WC, hair-dryers and television • €72 to €95, breakfast included • Table d'hôte €25 • Terrace, park, car park. Credit cards not accepted, dogs not admitted • Outdoor swimming pool, angling, hiking

 Leaving with a terrine of foie gras you have prepared yourself.

Amidst vineyards and forest, this vast sheepfold has been masterfully restored and has retained its authentic cachet. Admire the rustic character of the immense living area, comprising a dining room and a small lounge area with fireplace. The setting however pales in comparison to the incomparable flavours of the table d'hôte meals, in which local cooking takes pride of place with game and fresh local produce in prominent position. Two- or three-day cooking courses organised (half-board).

Access : *6km westbound from Saint-Aignan on the D90 towards Orbigny*

MAROLLES - 41330

LE CHANT DES MUSES
Mme Alaimo

5 rue de la Mairie
41330 Marolles
Tel. 02 54 20 09 46
alaimo.danielle@wanadoo.fr
www.le-chant-des-muses.com

Open all year • 4 non-smoking rooms upstairs, all with bath/WC or shower/WC • €75 to €90, breakfast included • Table d'hôte €38 drinks included • Garden, car park, sitting room with internet and fax • Outdoor swimming pool

 Giving in to the charm of the muses, who are said to have inspired Ronsard.

Built in 1860, this village house is home to four magnificent tastefully decorated rooms, each of which is endowed with its own special appeal. Bright colours and floral prints for Rêveries (dreams), and exposed beams for Conte de fées (fairy tales). Breakfast is served on a splendid veranda, and outdoors, guests can take a dip in the refreshing swimming pool on sunny days. Faultless table d'hôte menu.

Gastronomic weekend in Dec with restaurant owner and à la carte weekend by request

Access : *In the village*

MAZANGÉ - 41100

LE MOULIN D'ÉCHOISEAU
M. et Mme Lautman

Le Gué du Loir
41100 Mazangé
Tel. 02 54 72 19 34
moulin-echoiseau@wanadoo.fr
http://perso.wanadoo.fr/moulin-echoiseau
Languages : Eng., Sp.

Open all year • 4 non-smoking rooms, all with bath/WC or shower/WC • €55 to €70, breakfast included • Table d'hôte €30 drinks included • Park, garden, library, car park. Credit cards not accepted • Outdoor swimming pool

 The magnificent flower-decked park, the owner's pride and joy.

Formerly the summer residence of young Alfred de Musset, this old mill is endowed with a rare quality of peacefulness, interrupted only by the little stream that runs alongside. You will enjoy whiling away the hours in the billiards room and well-stocked library. The rooms and apartments are equally full of character, among which the aptly named Amadeus, furnished with Austrian pieces. Delicious table d'hôte meals where traditional, carefully prepared dishes take pride of place.

> *Theme weekend: discovering the Val de Loir*

Access : *1km southbound from Mazangé on the D24 at the Gué du Loir. Go past the Manoir de Bonaventure and continue for 100m to the Moulin d'Echoiseau*

MONDOUBLEAU - 41170

PEYRON-GAUBERT
M. et Mme Peyron-Gaubert

Carrefour de l'Ormeau
41170 Mondoubleau
Tel. 02 54 80 93 76
i.peyron1@tiscali.fr
 www.carrefour-de-lormeau.com
Languages : Eng.

Open all year • 5 rooms with bathrooms • €43 to €48, breakfast included • Table d'hôte €22 (evening only, by reservation only from Apr to Oct) • Garden, car park. Credit cards not accepted, no dogs admitted in restaurant • Exhibition and concert room

This one-off address, also a cabinetmaker's workshop.

The least you can say about this 17C redbrick house is that it is unusual, home to both a B&B establishment and exhibition hall for the cabinetmaker-owner's imaginative furniture. The rooms, of varying sizes, house some of the finished articles; simple, elegant waxed furniture made out of elm, ash and acacia wood. Concerts are sometimes held on the top floor. The garden to the rear is also very pleasant.

> *Cooking courses*

Access : *In the town, opposite the Ford garage*

PONTLEVOY - 41400

SAINT-DENIS-SUR-LOIRE - 41000

HÔTEL DE L'ÉCOLE
M. et Mme Preteseille

12 route de Montrichard
41400 Pontlevoy
Tel. 02 54 32 50 30
Languages : Eng.

Closed from 19 Feb to 23 Mar, from 13 Nov to 7 Dec, Sun evening and Mon (except Jul-Aug) • 11 rooms with bath/WC or shower/WC, some have television • €57; breakfast €11; half-board available • Menus €21.50 to €52 • Terrace, garden, private car park. No dogs admitted

LA VILLA MÉDICIS
M. et Mme Cabin-Saint-Marcel

1 rue Médicis, Macé
41000 Saint-Denis-sur-Loire
Tel. 02 54 74 46 38
medicis.bienvenue@wanadoo.fr
www.lavillamedicis.fr

Open all year (reservations only in winter) • 6 non-smoking rooms and 1 apartment, with bath/WC or shower/WC • €68 to €98, breakfast included • Table d'hôte €32 (evenings only by reservation) • Park, car park. Credit cards not accepted, no dogs allowed

The delightful flowered garden and murmuring fountain.

You'll immediately reach for your camera when you catch sight of this adorable house covered in variegated vine and surrounded by masses of brightly coloured geraniums. A distinctly old-fashioned feel in the rooms is compensated for by their size and spotless upkeep. Tables are prettily laid out in one of two rustic dining rooms or on the pleasing shaded terrace. What better invitation to enjoy finely judged dishes which make the most of local produce!

The exuberant foliage all around.

Once a spa hotel, this 1852 building is named after Marie de Médici who used to take the waters in the park. Some of the beautifully laid-out rooms command a view of the park. Tea and coffee making facilities can be used by guests in the pretty sitting room. If the sun is shining, take breakfast outside, then set out on a stroll or try your hand at kayaking, golf, riding or hiking nearby.

Access : *In the town centre, on the D 764 between Montrichard and Blois*

Access : *4km to the north-east of Blois on the N 152, towards Orléans*

SELLES-SAINT-DENIS - 41300

SAINT-GEORGES-SUR-CHER - 41400

LES ATELLERIES
Mme Quintin

41300 Selles-Saint-Denis
Tel. 02 54 96 13 84
emmanuel.quintin@wanadoo.fr
www.lesatelleries.com

Languages : Eng.

Closed Feb and Mar • 3 rooms with bath/WC
• €50, breakfast included • No table d'hôte
• Sitting room, park. Credit cards not accepted,
no dogs admitted

LE PRIEURÉ DE LA CHAISE
Mme Duret-Therizols

8 rue du Prieuré - Lieu-dit la Chaise
41400 Saint-Georges-sur-Cher
Tel. 02 54 32 59 77
prieuredelachaise@yahoo.fr
http://www.prieuredelachaise.com
Languages : Eng.

Open all year • 6 non-smoking rooms with
shower/WC • €60 to €120, breakfast included
• No table d'hôte • Garden, car park, park. No
dogs admitted • Outdoor swimming pool

**The beautiful Sologne countryside
surrounding this farm.**

Set in a 150-acre estate of woodland, moors
and ponds, this old Sologne farm is sure to
appeal to small-game hunters. Dog kennels are
available and guests can go out hunting for the
day with locals who know all the best coverts.
As for the accommodation, the rooms are
soberly decorated and well kept, two are
installed in the former bakery where the old
bread oven is still visible. Bicycles can be
rented from the estate.

Tasting the estate's wines.

A chance to stay in this former priory built in
the heart of a wine-growing estate should not
be missed. Next door to a magnificent 13C
chapel (Mass is still celebrated here once a
year), the 16C manor and its rooms are all
equally elegant: soft stone walls, red-brick
tiles, beams, fireplace and antique furniture
and tapestries. The 17C outhouses have been
converted into a wine-growing museum which
you will come upon as you stroll around the
tree-lined grounds.

> *Small game hunting weekends*

Access : *16km to the north-east of
Romorantin-Lanthenay on the D 123 between
Selles-Saint-Denis and Marcilly*

Access : *2km southbound of St-Georges-sur-Cher
on the D 27A*

VOUZON - 41600

BRIARE - 45250

CHÂTEAU DU CORVIER
Mme de Henin

41600 Vouzon
Tel. 02 54 83 04 93
chateaulecorvier@hotmail.com
www.chateaulecorvier.com

Open all year • 6 non-smoking rooms, one of which has disabled access, all have bath/WC • €82, breakfast included • No table d'hôte • Park, car park. Credit cards not accepted, dogs not admitted • Outdoor swimming pool

DOMAINE DE LA THIAU
Mme Bénédicte François Ducluzeau

Route de Gien
45250 Briare
Tel. 02 38 38 20 92
lathiau@club-internet.fr

 http://lathiau.club.fr
Languages : Eng., Ger., Sp.

Open all year • 4 non-smoking rooms upstairs with shower/WC • €47 to €60, breakfast included; half-board available • No table d'hôte • Garden, car park • Fitness room, tennis court, bicycle rentals

 Losing track of time as you wander around the park.

This Louis XIII-style castle (built in 1908), in the heart of a 40ha-estate, features spacious rooms with high ceilings, such as the dining room with its immense table. The sumptuous sitting room decorated with matching furniture is worthy of a king, while the elegant, well-kept rooms (including one apartment) are a credit to the flowers after which they are named. One of the rooms on the ground floor has been designed for disabled guests.

The private lane through the estate that leads down to the banks of the Loire.

It is impossible not to miss the ancient old trees, one of which is over two hundred years old, that have taken root in the extensive grounds around this graceful 18C house. The rooms have a pleasantly old-fashioned appeal with flowered wallpaper and period-style patterns on the walls and family heirlooms and antiques picked up in the region. Tennis courts, table tennis and bicycle rentals on the estate.

Access : *5km westbound from Vouzon on the D153 towards Yvoy-le-Marron*

Access : *300m from the Loire*

CERDON - 45620

LES VIEUX GUAYS
M. et Mme Martinez

45620 Cerdon
Tel. 02 38 36 03 76
alyotrine@aol.com

Open all year • 5 non-smoking rooms, including 1 family room, all with shower/WC • €60 to €75, breakfast included • No table d'hôte • Park, car park. Credit cards not accepted • Outdoor swimming pool, tennis court and angling

 Getting your ear attuned to the local dialect: "guay" means happy.

A 1km drive leads to this family estate in the heart of the forest. Three ground floor and two more recent rooms upstairs are a picture of rusticity with bare beams, brickwork and tiled floors. Tennis court and swimming pool available. At nightfall, from the terrace, guests can catch glimpses of the deer as they come to drink from the pond. The absence of table d'hôte meals is largely compensated for by the quality of the welcome.

Access : 2km southbound from Cerdon on the D65 then left onto a lane

CHAILLY-EN-GÂTINAIS - 45260

LA FERME DU GRAND CHESNOY
M. Chevalier

45260 Chailly-en-Gâtinais
Tel. 02 38 96 27 67
bclechesnoy@yahoo.fr
Languages : Eng.

Closed from 1 Dec to 31 Mar • 4 non-smoking rooms with bathrooms • €65, breakfast included • No table d'hôte • Sitting room, garden, car park. Credit cards not accepted, no dogs admitted • Tennis, billiards

 The country spirit of the decoration.

This immense two-hundred-acre estate of woodland, fields and ponds surrounds an immense property built on the banks of the Orléans Canal. Luckily, the owners retained the original parquet floors, family heirlooms, antiques and tapestries in the rooms installed in the 1896 tower. The extremely generously-sized bathrooms are very well fitted-out. A charming dovecote, tennis courts and countless footpaths into the immense forest complete the picture.

Access : 8.5km northbound from Lorris on the D 44, take the Bellegarde road and then the minor road on the right

CHÉCY - 45430

57

LES COURTILS
Mme Monthel

Rue de l'Avé
45430 Chécy
Tel. 02 38 91 32 02
infos@les-courtils.com
www.les-courtils.com
Languages : Eng.

Open all year • 4 rooms with bathrooms • €52, breakfast included • No table d'hôte • Garden. Credit cards not accepted, no dogs admitted

 The owners' loving care and attention is visible in every tiniest detail.

The moment you cross the threshold, you begin to feel at home! The view of the Loire is quite exceptional and the interior decoration rises to the challenge. Flowered fabrics, a tasteful blend of beiges and creams, antique and modern furniture, tiled floors. Each room is named after a local plant – let's see whether you can match the English to the French: "Bitter Apple", "Morning Glory", "Honeysuckle" and "Nasturtium". The friezes in the bathrooms were hand-stencilled.

Access : *10km eastbound from Orléans on the N 460*

LAILLY-EN-VAL - 45740

58

DOMAINE DE MONTIZEAU
Mme Abeille

Monçay
45740 Lailly-en-Val
Tel. 02 38 45 34 74
abeille@domaine-montizeau.com

Open all year • 4 non-smoking rooms, including one apartment, all with bath/WC or shower/WC and broadband internet access • €65 to €95, breakfast included • Table d'hôte €27 • Park, car park, kitchenette. Credit cards not accepted, dogs not admitted

 The cry of the stag during rutting season.

In the heart of a former hunting estate, this regional-style Sologne house was formerly used to accommodate the whips in charge of the hounds. Today three rooms and one apartment are located in the former stables, kennels, and upstairs in the main house. Broadband Internet access in each room creates a perfect blend of tradition and modernity. Generous breakfasts and gastronomic table d'hôte menu with game in season.

Access : *4.5km southeast from Lailly-en-Val on the D19, then narrow road on the right*

NEVOY - 45500

LE DOMAINE DE SAINTE-BARBE
Mme Le Lay

45500 Nevoy
Tel. 02 38 67 59 53
annielelay@aol.com
www.sainte-barbe.net

Closed from 20 Dec to 6 Jan and 10 to 28 Aug • 4 rooms, 3 of which have bathrooms, and one gîte 25m from the house • €65, breakfast included • No table d'hôte • Garden, car park. Credit cards not accepted, no dogs admitted • Outdoor swimming pool, jacuzzi, tennis court

 The easy-going personality of the hospitable lady of the house.

This house is imbued with the charm of homes which have belonged to the same family for generations. A few decorative touches from the lady of the house have lent the interior chintz fabrics, tiled floors, ornaments and old furniture. The rooms, some of which have a canopied bed, overlook the garden. Breakfast is served on the terrace overlooking fields and woods in the summer. For those who can't tear themselves away, there's also an independent self-catering holiday cottage.

Access : *4km north-west of Gien towards Lorris, after the level-crossing take the second road on the left and follow the signs*

POILLY-LEZ-GIEN - 45500

VILLA HÔTEL
M. et Mme Petit

Z. A. Le Clair Ruisseau
45500 Poilly-lez-Gien
Tel. 02 38 27 03 30
Languages : Eng.

Open all year • 24 rooms with shower/WC and television, 2 rooms have disabled access, 10 rooms are non-smoking • €34, breakfast €6; half-board available • Restaurant closed Fri, Sat and Sun, day before national holidays and national holidays, evenings only; menus €11 to €14 • Car park

 A visit to the delightful museums of Gien, one devoted to porcelain, the other to hunting.

Book your room well in advance because this hotel is often full. Its success can be explained by its quiet neighbourhood location, friendly welcome, modern comforts and immaculate upkeep, though the delightful rooms are not exactly enormous. In the kitchen, the lady of the house rustles up a different main dish every evening and starters and desserts are available from a buffet. Gien porcelain plates adorn the restaurant walls.

Access : *2km south-west of Gien on the D 940 towards Bourges*

CHAMPAGNE ARDENNE

It is easy to spot visitors bound for Champagne-Ardenne by the sparkle in their eyes and a sudden, irrepressible delight when they finally come face to face with mile upon mile of vineyards: in their minds' eye, they are already uncorking a bottle of the famous delicacy which was known as "devil's wine" before a monk discovered the secret of Champagne's divine bubbles. As they continue their voyage, the beautiful cathedral of Reims rises up before them and they remember the delicious taste of its sweet pink biscuits delicately dipped in a glass of demi-sec. At Troyes, their eyes drink in the sight of tiny lanes lined with half-timbered houses while their palate thrills to the flavour of andouillettes, the local chitterling sausages. After such indulgence, our pilgrims welcome the sanctuary of the dense Ardennes forests, bordered by the meandering Meuse. But far from fasting and penitence, this woodland retreat offers a host of undreamt-of delights: the graceful flight of the crane over an unruffled lake or the prospect of sampling the famous Ardennes wild boar.

CHÂTEL-CHÉHÉRY - 08250

CHÂTEAU DE CHÂTEL
M. et Mme Huet

08250 Châtel-Chéhéry
Tel. 03 24 30 78 54
jacques.huet9@wanadoo.fr
perso.wanadoo.fr/chateaudechatel

Closed Sun evenings • 3 rooms with shower/WC • €80 (€60 to €70 low season), breakfast included; half-board available • Table d'hôte €22 (evening only) • Park, car park. Credit cards not accepted, dogs not admitted • Outdoor swimming pool

 A glass of champagne is offered to guests on the "Gastronomic" package.

This 18C hillside castle and park dominating the Aire Valley has charm in abundance. Despite major renovation work, numerous traces of the apartments' former glorious days are still visible, including a superb staircase, huge fireplaces and period furniture. All the well-dimensioned rooms have excellent bathrooms. A wide choice of leisure activities is also available with swimming pool, tennis courts on request and walking or cycling trails.

Access : *9km to the north-west of Varennes-en-Argonne on the D 38A and then the D 42*

RUMIGNY - 08290

LA COUR DES PRÉS
M. Avril

08290 Rumigny
Tel. 03 24 35 52 66
la-cour-des-pres@laposte.net

Closed from Nov to Apr • 2 rooms with shower/WC • €65 to €75, breakfast included • No table d'hôte • Park, car park. Credit cards not accepted, dogs not admitted • Castle visits (except Tue), dinner-concerts in the summer

 The lady of the house's spontaneity and warmth.

It would be difficult to find somewhere more authentic than this moated stronghold, built in 1546 by the provost of Rumigny. The present owner, a direct descendant, is clearly proud of her roots and only too happy to relate her family's history. The wood panelling and period furniture in the rooms are original, as is the magnificent dining room in what was formerly the guard room. Stroll round the park and admire the ancestral beeches.

Access : *On the D 877, entering the village from the east, on the corner of the D 27*

COURTERON - 10250

FERME DE LA GLOIRE DIEU
M. Ruelle

10250 Courteron
Tel. 03 25 38 20 67

Closed in Jan and Feb • 3 rooms with shower/WC • €40, breakfast included • Table d'hôte €18 • Park, terrace, car park. Credit cards not accepted

The delicious farm-grown produce which can be tasted there and/or taken home.

The sign "Farm to the Glory of God" rather gives the game away, even before you've had a chance to glimpse the fascinating architectural remains of the 13C monastery. This immense 16C fortified farm nestles at the foot of a valley; its pretty, well-kept rooms still have their original exposed stone walls. The profusion of patés, cooked meats and poultry, fresh from the farm, will entice even the most delicate of palates. Warm, friendly and very reasonably priced.

Access : *10km eastbound from Riceys on the D 70 then the N 71*

ESTISSAC - 10190

DOMAINE DU VOIRLOUP
M. et Mme Hulo

3 place Betty-Dié
10190 Estissac
Tel. 03 25 43 14 27
le.voirloup@free.fr
www.vrlp.com
Languages : Eng.

Open all year • 3 non-smoking rooms, all have bathrooms, television and telephone • €60 to €80, breakfast included • Table d'hôte €25 • Terrace, garden, car park. Credit cards not accepted, dogs not admitted • Internet available

The decoration of this immense bourgeois home built in 1904.

This comfortable bourgeois home, built in the early 20C in the middle of 8000m^2 of grounds, sports a smart tasteful interior. The simply decorated rooms are functional, furnished in a contemporary style and equipped with Wifi internet access, etc. Homemade cakes, bread and jams take pride of place on the breakfast table. The table d'hôte for its part offers family and regional dishes and when the weather is fine, meals are served out of doors beneath an arbour.

Access : *In the centre of the village*

ESTISSAC - 10190

LE MOULIN D'EGUEBAUDE
M. Mesley

36 rue Pierre-Brossolette
10190 Estissac
Tel. 03 25 40 42 18
eguebaude@aol.com
Languages : Eng., Sp.

Closed 24 to 25 Dec and 31 Dec to 1 Jan
• 8 non-smoking rooms, 3 of which in a separate
wing, all have bath/WC and television • €49 to
€71, breakfast included • Table d'hôte €21
(evenings only) • Terrace, garden, car park,
small kitchen. Credit cards not accepted, dogs
not admitted • Sauna, fish farm

 Tasting the specialities of the Aubois region.

This old mill welcomes guests for a peaceful
relaxing stay between woodlands and fish-
farming ponds. In a regional Champagne-style
building, three impeccably fitted and warmly
decorated rooms have recently been added to
the five already located in the mill itself. When
she is not rustling up a local speciality or two
(fillet of salmon with herb sauce), the owner
can be found in her shop which specialises in
regional delicacies.

Access : *In the town*

LAUBRESSEL - 10270

LES COLOMBAGES CHAMPENOIS
Mme Jeanne

33 rue du Haut
10270 Laubressel
Tel. 03 25 80 27 37
aux.colombages.champenois@wanadoo.fr

Open all year • 6 rooms with shower/WC • €42,
breakfast included • No table d'hôte • Garden,
car park. Credit cards not accepted, dogs not
admitted • Outdoor swimming pool

Gazing over the meadows stretching over the horizon.

Although built only 10 years ago from old
materials gleaned from neighbouring ruins,
these two enchanting half-timbered houses
look as if they've always been here. The inge-
nious owner has even managed to rebuild a
dovecote! The stylish rooms are a tasteful
mixture of old beams and modern furniture.
The kitchen serves mainly farm-grown produce.

Access : *7km to the north-east of
Lusigny-sur-Barse on the N 19 and then the D 186*

BOURSAULT - 51480

LA BOURSAULTIÈRE
Mme De Coninck

44 rue de la Duchesse-d'Uzès
51480 Boursault
Tel. 03 26 58 47 76

Open all year • 4 rooms with shower/WC • €60, breakfast included • No table d'hôte • Garden, car park. Credit cards not accepted

 The mammoth breakfasts, liberally served with smiles.

Bordered by Champagne vineyards on all sides, this attractive stone house provides enchanting rooms lined with medieval or Renaissance-style printed fabrics. The luxurious bathrooms are lightened by beautiful Italian tiles. As soon as the sun shines, you will appreciate the refreshing cool of the paved courtyard, strewn with succulent green plants. Exemplary welcome.

Access : *9km westbound from Épernay on the N 3 and then the D 222*

BOUZY - 51150

LES BARBOTINES
M. Bonnaire

1 place Tritant
51150 Bouzy
Tel. 03 26 57 07 31
contact@lesbarbotines.com
www.lesbarbotines.com

Closed 15 Dec to 15 Jan and 1 to 14 Aug • 5 non-smoking rooms on two storeys, one of which has disabled access, all have bath/WC • €78, breakfast included • No table d'hôte • Garden, car park. Dogs not admitted

The country ambience invites you to wind down.

The Champagne tourist road wends its way past this handsome winegrower's house built in the 19C. A corridor leads into two sitting rooms, decorated in a style that combines classical with modern, a breakfast room and the former storeroom, now a large multi-purpose room. Upstairs the rooms are graced with old furniture and well-designed bathrooms. Outdoors, take the time to admire the well-tended flower garden.

Access : *16km eastbound from Epernay on the D 201 and D 9*

CRUGNY - 51170

LA MAISON BLEUE
M. de Bohan

46 rue Haute
51170 Crugny
Tel. 03 26 50 84 63
maisonbleue@aol.com
www.la-maison-bleue.com

Closed from 20 Dec to 31 Jan • 6 non-smoking rooms, all with bathrooms • €74 to €88, breakfast €5.50 • Table d'hôte €25 drinks included and €35 • Park, car park. Dogs not admitted in restaurant • Outdoor swimming pool, sauna, Jacuzzi

 Savouring the peace and quiet of this welcoming house and park.

This faultlessly kept house, extended by a walled courtyard is home to spacious, individually decorated rooms: Chinese, bamboo or period. The room on the top floor under the eaves overlooks the village rooftops and the surrounding countryside. The large sitting room is strewn with ancient artefacts of African origin. Tasty classical dishes on the menu. On the leisure side guests can choose between the shade of the park, lazing by the pond or a dip in the heated swimming pool.

Access : *Southeast of Fisme on the RD 386*

MAREUIL-SUR-AY - 51160

LA FAMILLE GUY CHARBAUT
M. et Mme Charbaut

12 rue du Pont
51160 Mareuil-sur-Ay
Tel. 03 26 52 60 59
champagne.guy.charbaut@wanadoo.fr
www.champagne-guy-charbaut.com
Languages : Eng., Ger.

Open all year except Christmas and New Year's Day • 6 rooms with bath/WC • €68, breakfast included • Table d'hôte €40 (evening only) • Car park. No dogs admitted in restaurant • Visits to the family's vineyards and the wine cellars

 The tour of the family estate's vineyard, cellars and grape presses.

Wine growers from father to son since 1930, the Charbauts bend over backwards to make your stay as pleasant as possible in their beautiful old house. They relish taking guests round the grape presses and cellars and introducing them to some of the best white and rosé vintage champagnes. All the airy, spacious rooms have their own sitting room and are decorated with period furniture. In the evenings, dinner is served in the superb wine cellar where the champagne, of course, flows freely!

Access : *In the wine estate*

MATOUGUES - 51510

MUTIGNY - 51160

LA GROSSE HAIE
M. et Mme Songy

Chemin de Saint-Pierre
51510 Matougues
Tel. 03 26 70 97 12
songy.chambre@wanadoo.fr
Languages : Eng., Ger.

Closed 24 and 25 Dec • 3 non-smoking rooms upstairs with shower/WC • €45, breakfast included • Table d'hôte €18 to €27 (closed Sun) • Garden, park, car park. Credit cards not accepted, no dogs admitted • Farm visits

MANOIR DE MONTFLAMBERT
M. et Mme Lheureux Plékhoff

51160 Mutigny
Tel. 03 26 52 33 21
manoir-de-montflambert@wanadoo.fr

Open all year • 6 non-smoking rooms, all with bath/WC • €86, breakfast included • No table d'hôte • Park, car park. Dogs not admitted

Breathing in the rich, evocative scents of the orchard.

A stone's throw from a farm which rears splendid Charolais cattle, this hospitable house knows how to tempt its guests into the out-of-doors. The children can romp unfettered in the orchard and the strawberries, artichokes and other cottage-garden delights are just waiting to be plucked, and, it comes as no surprise to discover, figure prominently on the menu. Pink, white and blue adorn the simply decorated rooms and the traffic on the nearby road will have almost disappeared by nightfall.

The site in the heart of Champagne's vineyards.

This magnificent 17C manor house, said to have been the scene of Henry IV's amorous escapades with Countess Montflambert, stands in the midst of an immense park extended by a handsome stretch of water. A splendid wooden fireplace and grand piano grace the sitting room that is both warm and intimate. Upstairs all the spacious rooms are individually decorated and furnished and all are equally comfortable. Very friendly welcome.

Access : *7km northeast from Epernay on the D201*

Access : *12km westbound from Châlons-en-Champagne on the D 3, towards Épernay*

REIMS - 51100

CRYSTAL
Mme Jantet

86 place Drouet-d'Erlon
51100 Reims
Tel. 03 26 88 44 44
hotelcrystal@wanadoo.fr
www.hotel-crystal.fr
Languages : Eng., Ger.

Closed 24 Dec to 3 Jan • 31 rooms, 23 of which have shower/WC, 8 have bath/WC, all have television • €50 to €72; breakfast €9.50 • No restaurant • Garden

 The fully original lift shaft.

This 1920s house provides a welcome and unexpected haven of greenery and calm in the heart of busy Reims, sheltered from the bustle of Place Drouet-d'Erlon by a curtain of buildings. The rooms have recently been treated to good quality furniture and new bedding and the bathrooms are spruce and practical. In the summer, breakfast is served in the charming flowered courtyard-garden.

Access : *In the town centre near the railway station*

REIMS - 51100

UNIVERS
M. Bombaron

41 boulevard Foch
51100 Reims
Tel. 03 26 88 68 08
contact@hotel-univers-reims.com
www.hotel-univers-reims.com

Open all year • 42 rooms, 36 of which have bath/WC, 6 have shower/WC, all have television • €71 to €97 (€62 to €87 low season); breakfast €11 • Menus €35 to €48.50 • Public car park nearby

 Sipping a glass of champagne at the hotel bar.

The Art Deco origins of this corner building built in 1932 opposite Colbert Square are betrayed by a number of architectural features. Excellent soundproofing, king size beds, wifi internet access, burr walnut furniture and beautiful bathrooms: the comfortable rooms are regularly spruced up. The stylish lounge-bar is snug and cosy and the restaurant is panelled in dark wood.

Access : *Near the railway station, opposite Colbert Gardens*

SAINT-RÉMY-EN-BOUZEMONT - 51290

SAINT-EUPHRAISE-ET-CLAIRIZET - 51390

CHAMBRE D'HÔTE DELONG
M. et Mme Delong

24 rue des Tilleuls
51390 Saint-Euphraise-et-Clairizet
Tel. 03 26 49 20 86
jdscom@wanadoo.fr
www.domainedelong.com
Languages : Eng.

Open all year • 4 rooms, with bath/WC • €58, breakfast included • No table d'hôte • Car park. Dogs not admitted • Visits to the wine cellar and press. Hiking, mountain biking

AU BROCHET DU LAC
M. Gringuillard

15-17 Grande-Rue
51290 Saint-Rémy-en-Bouzemont
Tel. 03 26 72 51 06
info@au-brochet-du-lac.com
 www.au-brochet-du-lac.com
Languages : Eng.

Closed from Christmas to New Year • 5 rooms with shower/WC • €45, breakfast included; half-board available • Table d'hôte €19 (evening only) • Sitting room, terrace, car park. Dogs not admitted in restaurant • Mountain bike rental and canoeing

Awaiting the arrival of the migratory birds over the nearby Lake Der.

This enchanting wood-framed house is the ideal spot to explore Lake Der-Chantecoq and try some of its countless leisure activities – boating, water-skiing, fishing, swimming. The house is very well-equipped and rents out mountain bikes and canoes. Pristine bedrooms are decorated with good country furnishings and wood features prominently in the red-tiled living room where a roaring fire is most welcome in winter.

Fishing and canoeing weekend

Access : *6km westbound from Arrigny on the D 57 and the D 58, in the centre of the village and not far from the lake*

Opening a bottle of champagne after visiting the estate's cellars.

This former cowshed has stylishly been given a new lease of life in the heart of a thriving family wine business. Exposed stone walls, beams and rafters add character while good quality bedding and furniture and pleasant bathrooms add comfort to the rooms. The equally attractive breakfast room boasts brick walls and a huge country dining table. The owner, a descendant of a long line of "vignerons", happily does the honours of his cellar and grape press.

Access : *In the heart of the village*

TOULON-LA-MONTAGNE - 51130

LES CORETTES
M. Salmon

Chemin du Pâti
51130 Toulon-la-Montagne
Tel. 03 26 59 06 92

Closed 31 Jan to 1 Mar • 5 rooms with bath/WC
• €57, breakfast included • Table d'hôte €28 to
34 (drinks included) (evenings only for guests)
• Garden, car park. Credit cards not accepted,
no dogs admitted

Discovering the champagne vineyards during a theme weekend.

In the heart of a winegrowing village stands this graceful and welcoming abode. After passing through the flower-decked garden you enter the elegant sitting room; the dining room features a handsome stone fireplace. All the individually decorated rooms are generously proportioned and comfortable. Upstairs is a splendid French billiards table. The traditional cuisine is prepared by the lady of the house and served with champagne or house wines that the owner will be happy to have you try.

Access : *18km north-east bound from Sézanne on the D 39, Vert-Toulon road and then the D 18*

CHAMOUILLEY - 52100

LE MOULIN
M. et Mme Forêt

52100 Chamouilley
Tel. 03 25 55 81 93
lemoulinchamouilley@wanadoo.fr
Languages : Eng.

Open all year • 5 non-smoking rooms, all have bath/WC, power shower, satellite television • €56 to €60, breakfast included • Table d'hôte €29 (evenings only by reservation) • Garden, park, car park. Credit cards not accepted • Outdoor swimming pool, children's play area

The owner's warm welcome.

Close your eyes and imagine yourself transported to a haven of peace and quiet on an island between the tail race of this former mill and the River Marne, just a few steps from the town. A park and swimming pool await you outside, while indoors is a lovely sitting-cum-reading room. The rooms, furnished in a contemporary style, are tasteful and welcomingly understated; all boast faultless facilities (bathrooms with balneo showers, bath robes, etc). What's more, the owner's delightful smile and unaffected welcome cannot fail but appeal.

Access : *Near the town centre, take small lane for 500m between Marne canal and river*

LANGRES - 52200

LE CHEVAL BLANC
M. et Mme Chevalier

4 rue de l'Estres
52200 Langres
Tel. 03 25 87 07 00
info@hotel-langres.com
www.hotel-langres.com
Languages : Eng.

Closed from 5 to 30 Nov • 22 rooms, 11 of which
are in a separate wing and one has disabled
access. All have bath/WC or shower/WC and
television • €65 to €89; breakfast €9; half-board
available • Restaurant closed Wed lunchtime;
menus €26 to €68 • Garage

 A past which dates back to 834.

First an abbey, then a parish church, the White
Horse became an inn during the Revolution and
its walls could date from any time between the
9C to the 16C. One thing is sure though, they
provide excellent natural soundproofing! The
rooms in the "Diderot pavilion", a stone house
opposite the main hotel, have been recently
renovated and their vaulted ceilings and arches
are full of character. Paintings and contemporary light fittings set the scene for the restaurant.

Access : *In the town centre*

PRANGEY - 52190

L'ORANGERIE
M. et Mme Trinquesse

8 place Adrien-Guillaume
52190 Prangey
Tel. 03 25 87 54 85
Languages : Eng.

Open all year, by reservation out of season
• 3 rooms with shower/WC • €60 to €65, breakfast included • No table d'hôte • Credit cards
not accepted, dogs not admitted

 The graceful feminine touch.

Gentility and the romantic reign supreme in
this ivy-covered house, next door to the castle
and church in a pleasantly secluded village, set
in Champagne's unspoilt countryside. Charm
fills the bright, cosy rooms, one of which,
decorated in shades of blue, commands a view
of the stately abode and its 12C tower. Best of
all, though, is the lady of the house's exquisite
welcome.

Access : *16km southbound from Langres on the
N 74 and then the D 26*

CORSICA

Corse-du-Sud - 2A
Haute-Corse - 2B

Corsica catches the eye like a jewel glinting in the bright Mediterranean sun. Its citadels perched up high on the island's rocky flanks will amply reward you for your perseverance and courage as you embark upon the twisting mountain roads. Enjoy spectacular views and breathe in the fragrance of wild rosemary as you slowly make your way up the rugged, maquis-covered mountains. The sudden sight of a secluded chapel, the discovery of a timeless village or an encounter with a herd of mountain sheep are just a few of the prizes that travellers to the Île de Beauté take home in their memories. Corsicans are as proud of their natural heritage as they are of their history and traditions. Years of experience have taught them how to revive the weary traveller with platters piled high with cooked meats, cheese and home-made pastries. After exploring the island's wild interior, you will probably be ready to plunge into the clear turquoise waters and recharge your solar batteries as you bask on the warm sand of a deserted bay.

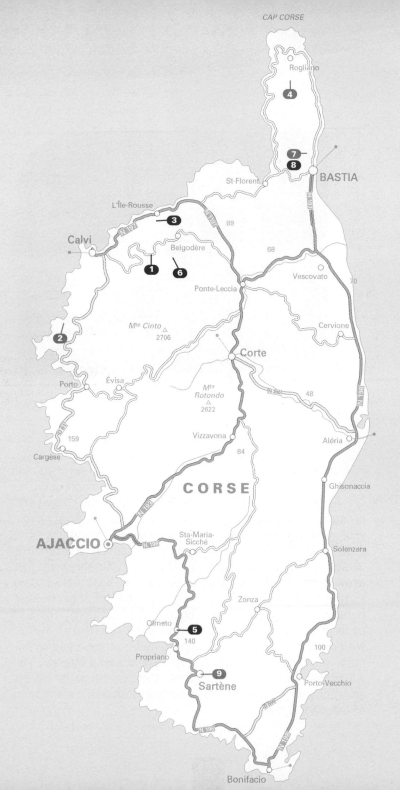

FELICETO - 20225

MARE E MONTI
M. et Mme Renucci

20225 Feliceto
Tel. 04 95 63 02 00
mare-e-monti@wanadoo.fr
www.maremonti.c.la
Languages : Eng., It.

Closed from 1 Nov to 30 Mar • 18 air-conditioned rooms with bath/WC or shower/WC • €97 to €124 (€70 to €97 low season); breakfast €7 • No restaurant • Car park. No dogs admitted • Swimming pool

The sweet scent of Corsica's wild flowers wafting over the sun-drenched terrace.

Exquisitely set between sea and mountains ("mare e monti" in Corsican), this is one of the rare "American palaces" of Balagne, of which there are many more around the coast of Cap Corse. After striking it rich in sugar cane, this family's ancestors returned from Puerto Rico in the 19C to build this elegant blue-shuttered white house. Character overflows from the slightly monastic rooms offset with brass beds, red floor tiles, fireplaces, etc. Delightful little chapel and exuberant garden.

Access : *20km southbound from Île-Rousse*

GALÉRIA - 20245

A MARTINELLA
Mme Corteggiani

Route du Port
20245 Galéria
Tel. 04 95 62 00 44

Closed from late Sep to 1 Apr • 5 rooms on the first floor with private terraces, all with shower/WC • €55 (€43 low season), breakfast €5.50 • No table d'hôte • Garden, car park. Credit cards not accepted, dogs not admitted • Beach and the Scandola Nature Reserve nearby

Exploring the under-water treasures of the Nature Reserve of Scandola.

An unpretentious, excellently kept place, to which you should add the priceless location just 150m from a large pebble beach and the nature reserve of Scandola. It is easy to see why the place is so popular. The simple rooms all have their own private terrace, while the tranquillity of the garden and the owner's genuinely warm welcome all contribute to its charm.

Access : *150m from the beach*

L'ÎLE-ROUSSE - 20220

FUNTANA MARINA
M. et Mme Khaldi

Route de Monticello
20220 L'Île-Rousse
Tel. 04 95 60 16 12
hotel-funtana-marina@wanadoo.fr
www.hotel-funtana.com
Languages : Eng., It.

Open all year • 29 rooms with bath or shower • €86 to €95 (€50 to €65 low season); breakfast €8.60 • No restaurant • Car park. No dogs admitted • Outdoor swimming pool

The site dominating the harbour of Île Rousse.

The narrow mountain lane that leads up to this recent house hidden by luxuriant vegetation is worth taking, if only to enjoy the super view of the sea and the harbour of Île Rousse. Comfortable renovated rooms all have matching bathrooms, but it's the panoramic swimming pool and your hosts' wonderful welcome that make this place so memorable.

Access : *In the upper part of Île-Rousse, 1km drive*

LURI - 20228

LI FUNDALI
M. et Mme Gabelle-Crescioni

Spergane
20228 Luri
Tel. 04 95 35 06 15
Languages : Eng., Sp., It.

Closed from Nov to Mar • 16 rooms with shower/WC • €40 to €45, breakfast included; half-board available • Table d'hôte €14 • Terrace, garden, car park. Credit cards not accepted, dogs not admitted

The owners' boundless hospitality.

This charming house, drenched in sunshine and encircled by foliage, nestles in a hollow (fundali) of the lush green valley of Luri. After trekking along the countless paths around the estate, you will happily return to a simple, yet immaculate room for a well-earned rest. Afterwards you can sit down around the large communal table and sample the delicious family recipes, under your host's attentive eye.

Access : *In the valley*

OLMETO - 20113

SANTA MARIA
M. et Mme Ettori

Place de l'Église
20113 Olmeto
Tel. 04 95 74 65 59
ettorinathalie@aol.com
www.hotel-restaurant-santa-maria.com
Languages : Eng., It.

Closed in Nov and Dec • 12 air-conditioned rooms with shower/WC and television • €55; breakfast €7; half-board available • Menus €16 to €24 • Terrace

Realising how out of place the word "stress" seems on the Island of Beauty.

This old granite house which stands opposite the church has been gazing down on the Gulf of Valinco for over a century. A steep staircase leads up to practical, well-kept rooms, rather lacking in charm however. The vaulted dining room, the only remains of an old oil mill, is pleasant enough, but the highlight of the establishment has got to be the wonderful flowered terrace where you can sample Mimi's delicious cooking.

Access : *In the centre of the village, 8km northbound from Propriano on the N 196*

PIOGGIOLA - 20259

A TRAMULA
M. Giovanetti

20259 Pioggiola
Tel. 04 95 61 93 54

Open all year • 7 rooms with shower/WC • €60 to €70; breakfast €5 • No restaurant • Park, car park. Credit cards not accepted

The warm welcome from the native Corsican owner who loves to talk about his country.

The bedrooms on the first floor of this handsome stone-built house all display the same tasteful blend of salmon-coloured walls, terracotta floor tiles, new furniture and modern bathrooms. The bar and sitting room, heated by a stove and fireplace, are most welcoming. Pull on your walking boots and hike round the grounds on the slopes of the mountainside. The honey, lavishly served at breakfast time, is made by the owner himself.

Access : *1.9km westbound from Olmi-Cappella towards Tartagine forest*

SAN-MARTINO-DI-LOTA - 20200

CHÂTEAU CAGNINACCI
Famille Cagninacci

20200 San-Martino-di-Lota
Tel. 06 78 29 03 94
www.chateaucagninacci.com
Languages : Eng., It.

Closed from 1 Oct to 14 May • 4 rooms, 2 of which air-conditioned, overlooking the island of Elba, with shower/WC • €110 (€85 low season), breakfast included • No table d'hôte • Terrace. Credit cards not accepted, dogs not admitted • Wifi internet access

The utter peace and quiet of this spot hidden in greenery.

This lovely 17C Capuchin convent, remodelled in the 19C style of a Tuscan villa, is built on a steep mountain hillside. Tastefully renovated, it offers spacious rooms furnished with antiques, and immaculate bathrooms. Wherever you look, you are met with the superb view of the island of Elba and the sea. Taking breakfast on the terrace surrounded by greenery and warmed by the sun's first rays is a moment of sheer bliss.

Access : *10km to the north-west of Bastia on the D 80 (towards Cap Corse), then the D 131 at Pietranera*

LA CORNICHE
M. Anziani

20200 San-Martino-di-Lota
Tel. 04 95 31 40 98
info@hotel-lacorniche.com
www.hotel-lacorniche.com
Languages : Eng., It.

Closed in Jan • 19 rooms with bath/WC and television • €70 to €99 (€48 to €62 low season); breakfast €8.50; half-board available • Restaurant closed Mon and Tue lunchtime; menus €27 • Terrace, car park • Outdoor swimming pool

The swimming pool on the flanks of the mountain, sheltered by a chestnut grove.

The shaded terrace of this establishment perched up high above Bastia is a feast for the eyes. Look out and savour the view of the two-storey bell tower and the houses of the old village cut into the rock face in sharp contrast with the deep blue water stretching out in the background. The practical rooms are gradually being individualised with terracotta tiles and hand-painted walls; they too command a view of the sea. The restaurant is known and appreciated for its excellent Corsican menu.

Access : *13km northbound from Bastia on the D 80, then turn left on the D 131*

SARTÈNE - 20100

9

DOMAINE DE CROCCANO
M. et Mme Perrier

Route de Granace
20100 Sartène
Tel. 04 95 77 11 37
christian.perrier@wanadoo.fr
www.corsenature.com
Languages : Eng., Sp., It.

Closed in Dec • 3 non-smoking rooms with bath/WC • €90 (€70 low season), breakfast included; half-board available • Non-smoking restaurant for half-board guests only • Terrace, park, car park. Dogs not admitted • Horse-riding on the estate

Waking up to the sight of horses cantering through the maquis.

Travellers in search of nature, silence and peace and quiet will fall in love with this solid granite house peeping out from behind a wilderness of cork oaks and olive trees. Beautiful old stone walls and vitrified cork floor tiles add style to the snug, cosy rooms. The lovely owners organise horse-rides through the fragrant Corsican shrub, or for those otherwise inclined, walking and botanic trails.

Horse-riding and walking excursions, horse trekking

Access : *3.5km to the north-east of Sartène on the D 148*

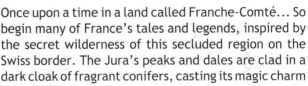

Once upon a time in a land called Franche-Comté... So begin many of France's tales and legends, inspired by the secret wilderness of this secluded region on the Swiss border. The Jura's peaks and dales are clad in a dark cloak of fragrant conifers, casting its magic charm over unwitting explorers of the range's grottoes and gorges. The spell is also woven by a multitude of torrents, waterfalls and deep, mysterious lakes, their dark blue waters reflecting the surrounding hills. The nimble fingers of local woodworkers transform its wood into clocks, toys and pipes which will delight anyone with a love of fine craftsmanship. Hungry travellers will be only too happy to give in to temptation and savour the rich hazelnut tang of Comté cheese, made to a recipe passed down through the generations. But beware, the delicate aroma of smoked and salted meats, in which you can almost taste the pine and juniper, together with the tempting bouquet of the region's subtle, fruity wines may well lure you back for more.

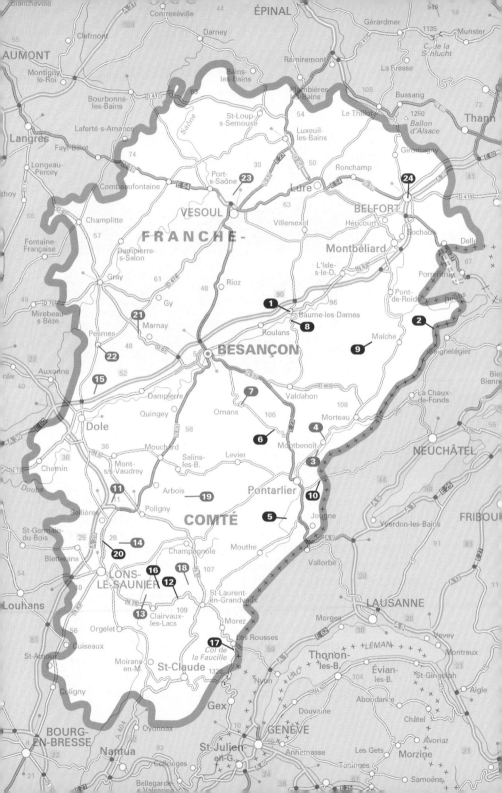

BAUME-LES-DAMES - 25110

HOSTELLERIE DU CHÂTEAU D'AS
MM. Patrick et Laurent Cachot

24 rue du Château-Gaillard
25110 Baume-les-Dames
Tel. 03 81 84 00 66
chateau.das@wanadoo.com
www.château-das.com

Closed from 22 Jan to 4 Feb, from 24 Sep to 14 Oct, Sun evening, Mon and Tue lunchtime • 6 rooms with bath/WC or shower/WC and television • €59 to €76; breakfast €10; half-board available • Menus €19 to €69 • Terrace, car park

You either love or hate the local cheese speciality: Cancoillotte!

This comfortable house, which would blend in perfectly in any number of German or Swiss towns, was built on the heights of this little town in the 1930s. The light, airy and well-equipped rooms have recently been treated to a facelift. The dining room has however retained the grandeur of its bygone days with original light fixtures and grandfather clock. Classic cuisine.

Access : *In the upper part of town, on the outskirts*

GOUMOIS - 25470

TAILLARD
M. Taillard

3 route de la Corniche
25470 Goumois
Tel. 03 81 44 20 75
hotel.taillard@wanadoo.fr
www.hoteltaillard.com
Languages : Eng., It.

Open from mid-Mar to mid-Nov • 21 rooms, 1 with disabled access, all have bath/WC or shower/WC and television • €65 to €90; breakfast €11.50; half-board available • Menus €22 to €70 • Terrace, garden, car park • Reading room, outdoor swimming pool, fitness room

An enchanting traditional hostelry nestled in greenery.

The Taillard family has been perfecting the art of hospitality since 1874 within the walls of this lovely hotel overlooking the Doubs Valley. The rooms in the annex, larger and more comfortable, are often preferred to those in the main wing which are due for a spot of sprucing up. In the predominantly warm wood finishings of the restaurant, classical dishes are spiced up with regional accents and accompanied by a fine wine list. Look out for the paintings by the master of the house.

"Fly fishing" with guide weekend, hunting and gastronomy weekend

Access : *Overlooking the village*

HAUTERIVE-LA-FRESSE - 25650

CHEZ LES COLIN
Mme Colin

25650 Hauterive-la-Fresse
Tel. 03 81 46 51 63
chezlescolin @ wanadoo.fr
www.chezlescolin.fr

Open all year • 6 rooms with washbasins • €80, full board • Car park. Credit cards not accepted, dogs not admitted

 The sumptuous setting between meadows and fir trees.

This former customs house perched on a ridge of the Franco-Swiss Jura range is ideal for those in search of a 100% nature and country stay. Each of the six rooms, furnished with regional pine, has its own wash-basin and shared showers and toilets on the landing. The mistress of the house takes great pleasure in whipping up tasty regionally-inspired dishes. Courses organised: yoga, watercolour painting, golf, cross-country skiing, etc.

Yoga, watercolour, cross-country skiing

Access : *10km southeast of Pontarlier, follow the D 47 between Pontarlier and Les Gras*

LA LONGEVILLE - 25650

LE CRÊT L'AGNEAU
M. et Mme Jacquet-Pierroulet

Les auberges
25650 La Longeville
Tel. 03 81 38 12 51
lecret.lagneau @ wanadoo.fr
www.lecret-lagneau.com
Languages : Eng., Sp.

Open all year • 6 rooms with shower / WC • €75 to €96, breakfast included • Table d'hôte €22 to €25 • Car park. Credit cards not accepted, no dogs admitted • Snowshoe trekking and cross-country skiing

The countless excursions organised by the owner, a cross-country ski instructor.

This superb 17C farmhouse, tucked away between fir trees and meadows has been offering accommodation and sustenance to all those "in the know" for over twenty years. Wood prevails in the cosy bedrooms. However the main reason for its lasting success is two-fold: first the generous helpings of locally-sourced food cooked by the lady of the house, and second the variety of outings on foot, mountain bikes, snowshoes or skis organised by the owner.

Access : *5.5km northbound from Montbenoît on the D 131 as far as La Longeville-Auberge*

MALBUISSON - 25160

MOUTHIER-HAUTE-PIERRE - 25920

LE BON ACCUEIL
M. et Mme Faivre

Rue de la Source
25160 Malbuisson
Tel. 03 81 69 30 58
lebonaccueilfaivre@wanadoo.fr
Languages : Eng.

Closed 16 to 25 Apr, 29 Oct to 7 Nov, 17 Dec to 16 Jan • 12 rooms, most of which have shower/WC, some have bath/WC, all have television • €66 to €96; breakfast €9; half-board available • Menus €29 to €55 • Garden, garage, car park. No dogs admitted

LA CASCADE
M. et Mme Savonet

4 route des Gorges-de-Noailles
25920 Mouthier-Haute-Pierre
Tel. 03 81 60 95 30
hotellacascade@wanadoo.fr
Languages : Eng., Ger.

Closed from 1 Jan to 13 Mar • 16 rooms, one of which has disabled access, most have bath/WC, some have shower/WC, all have television • €52 to €67; breakfast €8; half-board available • Restaurant non-smoking only; menus €20 to €48 • Car park. No dogs admitted • Trout fishing and canoeing on the Loue

The breakfast table laden with brioche, jams, home-made yoghurt and fresh fruit juice.

On the edge of a forest of fir trees, this manicured, hospitable village inn is the sort of place you want to tell your friends about. Immaculate, modern, spacious rooms. Beautiful spruce wood rafters, brightly coloured blinds and large windows overlooking the forest set the scene for the recently extended dining room. The cherry on the cake is without doubt the deliciously inventive cooking.

Canoeing down the beautiful gorges of the River Loue.

The valley of the Loue is what you will see when you throw open the windows of the recently spruced-up rooms of this traditional old hostelry. Excellent family cooking is served in a non-smoking atmosphere, while huge bay windows provide guests with a restful view of the green landscape.

Access : *In the village, on a bend by the side of the road*

Access : *On the main road, in the centre of the village*

ORNANS - 25290

LE JARDIN DE GUSTAVE
M. Rigoulot

28 rue Édouard-Bastide
25290 Ornans
Tel. 03 81 62 21 47
www.louelison.com
Languages : Ger.

Open all year • 3 rooms, all with bath/WC or shower/WC • €60 to €78, breakfast included • Table d'hôte €25, drinks included • Terrace, television room, garage. Credit cards not accepted

 The owner's kind welcome.

This town house stands on the main street of Ornans alongside of which runs the Loue. Two of the rooms overlook the garden and river, while the third overlooks the street but is well sound-proofed. The personalised pleasant rooms were decorated by the owner herself; the "Jungle" room, for example, sports a distinctly exotic African inspiration... At mealtimes you will be treated to regional specialities in winter and lighter dishes, served in the garden, in the summer.

> *Furniture ageing and fabric painting courses*

Access : *In the town*

PONT-LES-MOULINS - 25110

L'AUBERGE DES MOULINS
M. et Mme Porru

Route de Pontarlier
25110 Pont-les-Moulins
Tel. 03 81 84 09 99
auberge.desmoulins@wanadoo.fr
http://perso.wanadoo.fr/auberge.desmoulins/
Languages : Ger., Eng., It.

Closed from 22 Dec to 20 Jan, Fri, Sun evenings from Sep to Jun (except holidays), Sat lunchtime and Fri • 14 rooms with bath/WC or shower/WC, all have television • €51; breakfast €6.50; half-board available • Menus €16.80 (weekdays) to €19.20 • Park, car park • Private fishing

 The wealth of magnificent natural sites: grottoes, nature reserves and unforgettable views.

Jura is renowned for its excellent trout and this place is bound to appeal to those bitten by the fishing bug: the country house stands in a park which boasts its very own private stream. Back at the hotel, relax in rooms of varying sizes and styles and dream of the one that got away. A cosy restaurant serves tasty regional dishes.

Access : *Southbound from Baume-les-Dames, drive for 6km on the D 50*

VAUCLUSE - 25380

VERRIÈRES-DE-JOUX - 25300

LE MOULIN
M. et Mme Malavaux

Le Moulin du Milieu, Route de Consolation
25380 Vaucluse
Tel. 03 81 44 35 18

Closed from 15 Oct to 1 Mar and Wed • 6 rooms, some with terrace, all have bath/WC or shower/WC and television • €45 to €68; breakfast €6.50; half-board available • Menus €20 to €30.50 • Garden, car park. Dogs not admitted in restaurant • Private fishing

 The spectacular natural site of the Cirque de Consolation.

This unusual 1930s villa, complete with turret and a colonnaded terrace, was built by a miller from the valley. The piously preserved Art Deco/old-fashioned decoration – including a Le Corbusier chaise longue in the hall, certainly adds charm to the establishment. Some of the bedrooms have terraces. The windows of the dining room open onto a shaded garden that leads down to the banks of the Dessoubre.

Access : *From Montbéliard leave the D 437 at St-Hippolyte, take the D 39 and at Pont Neuf turn left towards Consolation*

AUBERGE LE TILLAU
M. Parent

Le Mont-des-Verrières
25300 Verrières-de-Joux
Tel. 03 81 69 46 72
luc.parent@wanadoo.fr
www.letillau.com

Closed from 15 Nov to 15 Dec, April school holidays, Sun evening and Mon • 11 rooms with shower/WC • €52; breakfast €7; half-board available • Menus €12 (weekdays) to €33 • Terrace • Sauna, games room, hiking and mountain biking

 Toast your toes in front of a roaring log fire after a day in the open air.

This enchanting mountain inn, 1200m up, is ideal to clear your lungs of urban pollution as you breathe in the crisp, fresh scent of meadows and fir trees. The rooms are appealingly decorated in an alpine style and you can relax in the reading room or soothe your muscles in the Jacuzzi and sauna. The mountain air is guaranteed to work up a healthy appetite for the profusion of local delicacies, including cooked meats and cheeses, sometimes accompanied by more eclectic creations.

Access : *7km eastbound from La Cluse-et-Mijoux on the D 67bis and a minor road*

BONLIEU - 39130

BERSAILLIN - 39800

LA FERME DU CHÂTEAU
Association E. de Villeneuve-Bargemont

Rue de la Poste
39800 Bersaillin
Tel. 03 84 25 91 31

Closed in Jan • 3 rooms and 3 apartments, one of which has disabled access, all with shower/WC • €74 to €76; breakfast included • No table d'hôte • Car park • Painting exhibitions, concerts in the summer

L'ALPAGE
M. Lerch

1 chemin de la Madone
39130 Bonlieu
Tel. 03 84 25 57 53
reservation@alpage-hotel.com
www.alpage-hotel.com

Closed from 15 Nov to 15 Dec, Mon and Tue lunchtime except during the school holidays • 9 rooms with shower/WC • €60; breakfast €8.50; half-board available • Menus €24 to €36 • Terrace, car park. No dogs admitted in rooms

 Just two minutes from Jura's vineyards and the "Route du Comté".

Many of the original features of this admirably restored 18C farmhouse have been preserved, including the wonderful vaults and columns of the main chamber, where exhibitions and concerts are held in the summer. The sober, yet elegant bedrooms command a view of the countryside and one has been specially equipped for disabled guests. Guests also have the use of a well-equipped kitchen.

 The sweeping view over the entire valley of lakes.

A narrow road winds up to this delightful chalet built in the upper reaches of Bonlieu. The valley of lakes and its wooded hillsides are visible from almost all the comfortable bedrooms. Plants and immense bay windows bathe the dining room in dappled light and the sheltered terrace also commands the same sweeping view. Tasty local dishes.

Access : *On the N 78 drive towards Saint-Laurent-en-Grandvaux*

Access : *9km westbound from Poligny on the N 83 and then the D 22*

CHAREZIER - 39130

13

CHAMBRE D'HÔTE MME DEVENAT
Mme Devenat

17 rue du Vieux-Lavoir
39130 Charezier
Tel. 03 84 48 35 79

Open all year • 4 rooms with shower/WC • €40, breakfast included; half-board available • Table d'hôte €11 (closed 1 May to 15 Sep) • Garden, car park. Credit cards not accepted, no dogs admitted in restaurant

The wide range of regional delicacies on offer.

Guests immediately feel at home in this large, welcoming family house cradled in a tiny village halfway between Clairvaux les Lacs and Lake Chalain. The rooms in the little house near the thicket are more independent and a handsome wooden staircase leads up to the others in the main house. The memory of the delicious local specialities, a different one each day, will have you planning your return trip the moment you arrive home.

Access : *13km to the south-west of Lake Chalain on the D 27*

CHÂTEAU-CHALON - 39210

14

LE RELAIS DES ABBESSES
M. Vidal

Rue de la Roche
39210 Château-Chalon
Tel. 03 84 44 98 56
relaisdesabbesses@wanadoo.fr
www.chambres-hotes-jura.com

Closed Feb, Nov and by reservation • 4 non-smoking rooms, all with shower/WC • €61 to €63, breakfast included, half-board available • Table d'hôte €22 to €29, drinks included • Garden, car park. Credit cards not accepted, no dogs allowed

Breakfasts served on the terrace overlooking the valley in summer.

This village house located in a superb medieval city is home to tastefully decorated and furnished rooms, all of which enjoy lovely views of the Côtes de Beaune and Voiteur. The table d'hôte, whose reputation is more than well established, features a fine menu of classical French cuisine made with fresh produce (terrine of boar, tenderloin of pork in pastry). In summer, breakfast is served in the garden and terrace which overlook the valley.

Access : *In the town*

CHÂTENOIS - 39700

À LA THUILERIE DES FONTAINES
M. et Mme Meunier

2 rue des Fontaines
39700 Châtenois
Tel. 03 84 70 51 79
michel.meunier2@wanadoo.fr
http://perso.orange.fr/hotes-
michel.meunier/michel.htm
Languages : Ger., Eng.

Open all year • 4 rooms with shower/WC • €50, breakfast included • No table d'hôte • Terrace, park, car park. Credit cards not accepted, dogs not admitted • Outdoor swimming pool

 Pick your owners' brains about their beloved region.

Hospitality and attention to detail are the hallmarks of this 18C country house located between the extensive Serre forest and the lower Doubs valley. A flight of stone stairs leads up to well-cared for, very "comfy" and totally peaceful rooms. Stroll round the attractive park or laze on the deck chairs round the swimming pool near the old stables.

Horse riding, heritage courses

Access : *7.5km to the north-east of Dole on the N73 towards Besançon, then take the D 10 and the D 79 to Châtenois*

DOUCIER - 39130

LE COMTOIS
M. Menozzi

 806 route des 3 lacs
39130 Doucier
Tel. 03 84 25 71 21
restaurant.comtois@wanadoo.fr

Closed from 19 Dec to 11 Feb, Tue evening, Wed and Sun evening • 8 rooms with showers, some have WC • €50; breakfast €7; half-board available • Menus €20 to €30 • Terrace

The wonderful footpath to Hérisson Falls just a few kilometres away.

Le Comtois offers an ideal introduction to this fascinating region. The heart of a remote Jura village is home to this spruce auberge offering a few rooms and above all a menu worthy of the most demanding traveller. A warm neo-rustic setting provides the backdrop to delicious recipes with a modern slant prepared with a strong focus on local products. The owner, who is also President of Jura's Association of Wine Waiters, will wax lyrical about wine and food for as long as you'll listen...

Access : *In the centre of the village, opposite the post office*

LA CURE - 39220

17

ARBEZ FRANCO-SUISSE
M. Arbez

39220 La Cure
Tel. 03 84 60 02 20
hotelarbez@netgdi.com
www.hotelarbez.fr.st
Languages : Eng., Sp.

Open all year • 10 rooms, half of which are in France and half are in Switzerland, with bath/WC or shower/WC, all have television • €59; breakfast €7; half-board available • Menus €15 to €33 • Car park. Dogs not admitted in restaurant

 Testing your balance on the "commando course" at nearby Fort Rousses!

Make sure you take your passport when you go to the bathroom and also remember to decide which half of you will sleep in Switzerland and which in France! This Swiss-French inn, quite literally on the border, offers modern rooms lined in pine and has a choice of classic restaurant fare or quick brasserie snacks and dishes, all within easy reach of alpine ski slopes, cross-country ski trails, snowshoe paths and Rousses Lake. Is there anything else to declare?

Access : *On the Swiss border, to the south-east of Rousses, drive 2.5km on the N 5 (towards Geneva)*

LE FRASNOIS - 39130

18

LES CINQ LACS
M. et Mme Colombato

66 route des Lacs
39130 Le Frasnois
Tel. 03 84 25 51 32
pcolomba@wanadoo.fr
http://auberge.5.lacs.free.fr
Languages : Eng., Sp.

Open all year (by reservation) • 5 non-smoking rooms, one of which has disabled access, all have bath/WC • €52, breakfast included; half-board available • Table d'hôte €17 • Terrace. Credit cards not accepted, no dogs admitted • Excursions around the lakes

 The owners' useful tips about the area.

Hikers have held this old Jura farmstead in great esteem ever since it opened; it nestles in the heart of a lush green landscape of lakes, waterfalls and forest. The comfortable rooms were individually decorated by the lady of the house and each is named after one of the region's innumerable lakes. Don't miss the opportunity to taste the many local specialities on the dining table, served before a roaring fire in winter or on the sheltered terrace in the summer.

Access : *3.5km northbound from Illay on the D 75*

PONT-D'HÉRY - 39110

MOULIN CHANTEPIERRE
M. et Mme Godin

Route du Val-Cercennes, Moutaine
39110 Pont-d'Héry
Tel. 03 84 73 29 90
chante-pierre@tele2.fr
www.chantepierre.com
Languages : Eng.

Closed Jan • 3 non-smoking rooms, all with shower/WC • €60, breakfast included • No table d'hôte • Garden, car park. Credit cards not accepted, dogs not admitted

 The owners' graceful hospitality.

In this former 19C watermill on the banks of the Furieuse stream, the owners offer three exquisite guestrooms: "Ingrid" in white and blue, "Ornella", wrought-iron furniture and "Romy" furnished with lovely little armchairs. Depending on the weather, the breakfasts, comprised of home-made products – pastries, bread, yoghurts, and fruit in summer, are served in a pleasant breakfast room or teak furnished terrace.

Access : *7km south of Salins-les-Bains on the D 467 towards a place known as "Moutaine"*

SAINT-GERMAIN-LES-ARLAY - 39210

HOSTELLERIE SAINT-GERMAIN
M. et Mme Tupin

Grande-Rue
39210 Saint-Germain-les-Arlay
Tel. 03 84 44 60 91
hoststgermain@.fr
www.hostelleriesaintgermain.com
Languages : Eng., Ger., Sp., Port., Russ.

Closed early Nov and Mondays • 6 rooms, most have bath/WC, some have shower/WC, all have television • €52 to €72; breakfast €7; half-board available • Menus €17 to €59 • Terrace, car park

 The homemade foie gras with morels and vin jaune!

Should you want to find out more about this region's rich store of traditions and legends, the Hostellerie St Germain, right in the heart of Jura's vineyards, is the ideal place to start. A refreshing night's sleep in the spotless rooms will leave you eager to begin exploring, and after a hard day's touring, you will be able to tuck into the delicious traditional recipes served in one of two vaulted dining rooms, complete with exposed beams and stonework.

Access : *At the crossroads in the centre of the village, opposite the church*

CULT - 70150

PESMES - 70140

CHAMBRE D'HÔTE LES ÉGRIGNES
M. et Mme Lego

Le Château - Route d'Hugier
70150 Cult
Tel. 03 84 31 92 06
lesegrignes@wanadoo.fr
www.les-egrignes.com
Languages : Eng., Ger.

Open all year • 3 non-smoking rooms, all with bath/WC • €80, breakfast included • Table d'hôte €25 (evenings only by reservation) • Sitting room, park, car park. Credit cards not accepted, no dogs admitted

Forget about your diet and do justice to the lady of the house's delicious cooking.

This 19C mansion stands proudly in grounds lined with trees and flowers. A tasteful, well-thought out interior restoration has enhanced the original moulded ceilings, stucco work, staircase and trompe-l'oeil marble. Louis-Philippe, Directoire and Napoleon III furniture graces the elegant rooms all of which enjoy the same pastoral view. In the dining room, note the lovely old porcelain stove which dates from 1805.

Access : *4km north-east of Marnay*

LA MAISON ROYALE
M. Hoyet

Rue de la Maison Royale
70140 Pesmes
Tel. 03 84 31 23 23
Languages : Ger., Eng., It., Sp.

Closed from 15 Oct to 31 Mar • 5 rooms with shower/WC • €70, breakfast included • No table d'hôte • Garden, car park. Credit cards not accepted, dogs not admitted • Library, billiards, organ, art exhibitions and cultural events

Living like royalty without blowing the family fortune!

The quality of the restoration and the sheer beauty of this superb 15C stronghold always draw gasps of admiration. The hospitable owners have filled this aptly named establishment with objects from their countless trips around the world. Most of the highly individualised rooms enjoy an exceptional view over the village rooftops and the countryside. Relax in style with a game of billiards, play a few notes on the organ and if the weather is fine, take time to enjoy the pretty flowered garden.

Access : *In the town centre, near a service station*

PUSY-ET-ÉPENOUX - 70000

CHÂTEAU D'ÉPENOUX
M. Cerletti

5 rue Ruffier
70000 Pusy-et-Épenoux
Tel. 03 84 75 19 60
château.epenoux@orange.fr
www.chateau-epenoux.com
Languages : Eng., Ger., Port.

Open all year • 5 non-smoking rooms, all have bath/WC or shower/WC • €80 to €90, breakfast included • Table d'hôte €23, drinks included • Park, car park. No dogs allowed

 Walking through the park and admiring the ancient trees.

This handsome 18C château, surrounded by a wooded park, welcomes guests into an elegant setting. At mealtimes, the friendly owner invites her guests to taste traditional dishes, prepared only for castle guests, served on a beautifully laid table complete with fine china, silverware and crystal glasses. Upstairs, four spacious rooms furnished with antiques and tastefully decorated, are the epitome of comfort.

Access : *At Vesoul, take the N 19, then the D 10 towards Saint-Loup-sur-Vesoul*

BELFORT - 90000

VAUBAN
M. Lorange

4 rue du Magasin
90000 Belfort
Tel. 03 84 21 59 37
hotel.vauban@wanadoo.fr
www.hotel-vauban.com
Languages : Eng., Ger.

Closed from Christmas to New Year, Feb holidays and Sun • 14 rooms with bath/WC or shower/WC, all have television • €80 to €84; breakfast €9 • No restaurant • Garden. Dogs not admitted

 The easy-going family atmosphere.

You will feel more like a friend of the family than a paying guest behind the colourful façade of this inviting hotel where hundreds of paintings by the owner and his artist friends adorn the walls. The rooms, gradually being renovated, are pretty and well soundproofed; ask for one in the rear from which you will enjoy a view of the pretty flowered garden stretching down to the banks of the Savoureuse.

Access : *Near the tourist office, on the street running alongside the Savoureuse*

ILE DE FRANCE AND PARIS

Historic Paris, the City of Light, is the first name to spring to mind at the mention of the île de France. The slender outline of the Eiffel Tower dominates France's chic and cosmopolitan capital, where former royal palaces are brazenly adorned with glass pyramids, railway stations become museums and close-set alleyways of bohemian houses lead off broad, plane-planted boulevards. Paris is a never-ending kaleidoscope of contrasts: the sleepy village side street decked in flowers and the bustle of the big department stores; the artists' studios of Montmartre and the crowded cafés where screen celebrities sit side by side with star-struck fans; a view of Paris by night from a bateau-mouche and the whirlwind glitz of a cabaret. But the fertile land along the Seine is not content to stay in the shadows of France's illustrious first city; the region is also home to secluded châteaux set in formal gardens, the magic of Disneyland and the turn-of-the-century gaiety of the summer cafés along the banks of the Marne. And who could forget the sheer splendour of Versailles, home to the 'most beautiful palace in the world'?

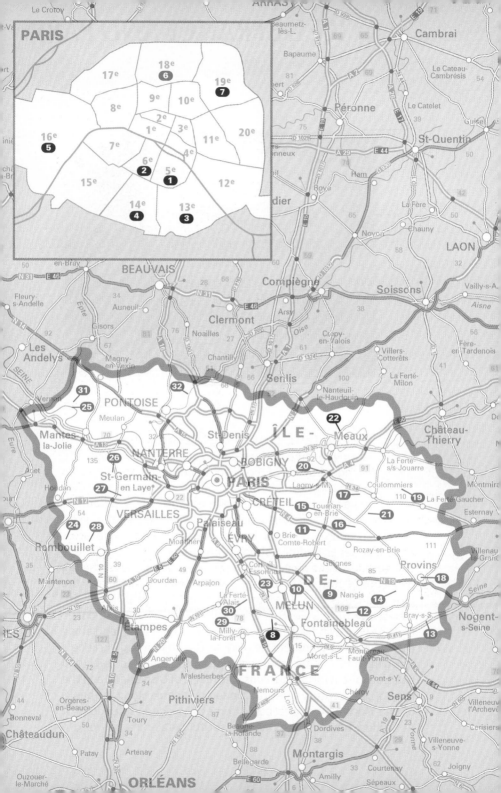

PARIS - 75005

PIERRE NICOLE
M. Dayot

39 rue Pierre-Nicole
75005 Paris
Tel. 01 43 54 76 86
hotelpierre-nicole@voila.fr
Languages : Eng., Ger.

Closed 1 to 21 Aug • 33 rooms, most have bath/WC or shower/WC, all have television • €80 to €100; breakfast €7 • No restaurant • No dogs admitted

 Ambling round the deliciously romantic Jardin de Luxembourg.

This hotel, in a handsome Haussmann building, pays homage to a controversial 17C theologian of Paris's Port-Royal Abbey. Many more recent celebrities, such as novelist Gabriel García Márquez and Patrick Modiano have stayed in these compact, practical and well-kept rooms, which maybe lack a little Parisian chic. The comparative calm of this side street, close to the busy restaurants of the Boulevard Montparnasse, should ensure a good night's sleep.

Access : *Coming from Bd du Montparnasse, continue onto Bd de Port-Royal and take the third street on the left*

PARIS - 75006

HÔTEL DE SÈVRES
M. Baguès

22 rue de l'Abbé-Grégoire
75006 Paris
Tel. 01 45 48 84 07
info@hoteldesevres.com
www.hoteldesevres.com
Languages : Eng.

Open all year • 31 rooms with bath/WC or shower/WC and television • €105 to €130; breakfast €10 • No restaurant • No dogs allowed

 The unusual chapel of the Miraculous Medal on Rue du Bac.

A 19C stone building near the upmarket Bon Marché department store. The modern rooms, some of which have brass beds, sport colourful fabrics. Plants adorn the light breakfast room overlooking a flower-decked courtyard. The preferential rates in the nearby car park for hotel guests are a definite bonus.

Access : *Go up Rue de Vaugirard and take the second left past Bd du Montparnasse*

PARIS - 75013

RESIDENCE VERT GALANT
M. et Mme Laborde

43 rue Croulebarbe
75013 Paris
Tel. 01 44 08 83 50
www.vertgalant.com
Languages : Eng., Ger.

Open all year • 15 rooms, 11 of which have bath/WC, 4 have shower/WC, all have television • €90 to €100; breakfast €7 • Restaurant closed 6 to 21 Aug; menus €26 to €32.50 • No dogs admitted in rooms

The village ambience, just two minutes from the Place d'Italie.

This hotel in the Gobelins area is welcome proof that it is still possible to find quiet accommodation in the heart of Paris at a reasonable price. All the functional, neatly kept rooms are sheltered by a restful curtain of greenery. Depending on the weather, breakfast is served in the small garden lined by vines or in a winter-garden dining room. The owners of the Vert Galant also run the cheerful Basque restaurant next door.

Access : *From Place d'Italie, go along Avenue des Gobelins and turn left*

PARIS - 75014

APOLLON MONTPARNASSE
M. Prigent

91 rue de l'Ouest
75014 Paris
Tel. 01 43 95 62 00
apollonm@wanadoo.fr
www.apollon-montparnasse.com
Languages : Ger., Eng., Sp.

Open all year • 33 rooms, 22 of which have shower/WC, 11 have bath/WC, all have television • €88 to €98 breakfast €9 • No restaurant • Nearby car park. No dogs allowed • Near Montparnasse railway station

A pleasant welcome in the heart of Montparnasse.

This small hotel is ideally placed for those intending to spend a few days in the French capital, close to the Montparnasse railway station and Air France's shuttle buses, the Rue de la Gaîté and cinemas for evenings out and Ricardo Bofill's amazing architectural feats. The bedrooms, in fairness, are more practical than charming, but look all the better for their recent makeover. Vaulted breakfast room.

Access : *From Place de Catalogne go along Rue du Château and turn right*

PARIS - 75016

BOILEAU
M. Fabrice Royer

81 rue Boileau
75016 Paris
Tel. 01 42 88 83 74
info@hotel-boileau.com
www.hotel-boileau.com
Languages : Eng., Ger., Sp.

Open all year • 31 rooms with bath/WC or shower/WC and television, 1 of which has disabled access • €72 to €92 (€63 to €75 low season); breakfast €8.50 • No restaurant

 The oriental inspiration in some of the rooms.

Situated in a smart street of what used to be the "village of Auteuil" close to the private Boileau hamlet, a distinctly un-Parisian atmosphere continues to reign in this hotel. Paintings and ornaments picked up in antique shops relate tales from Brittany and North Africa. The statues in alcoves and wainscoting in the lobby lend it a resolutely classical air. The rooms are discreetly personalized in style. Breakfast is served in a room flooded with sunlight overlooking a flowered mini-patio.

Access : *From Place de la Porte de Saint-Cloud take Rue Michel-Ange, then first right and second left*

PARIS - 75018

CHAMBRE D'HÔTE PARIS-OASIS
Mme Bignon

14 rue André del Sarte
75018 Paris
Tel. 01 42 55 95 16
helene-bignon@wanadoo.fr
www.paris-oasis.com

Closed 1 week in Aug and 1 week late Dec • 3 non-smoking rooms, one of which has a small kitchen, 1 apartment and 1 studio, all with shower/WC • €90, breakfast €15 • No table d'hôte • Terrace, garden. Credit cards not accepted, dogs not admitted • Indoor swimming pool

 The brunches, served in the small garden in summertime.

Two minutes from Montmartre, this group of buildings is home to three chambres d'hôte, a studio, an apartment and even an indoor swimming pool. As is often the case in Paris, the dimensions are on the modest side but the rooms are nonetheless arranged carefully and fitted out with good quality materials. Attractive tiled floors, colourful murals and superb statuettes made by the lady of the house. A successful combination of comfort and careful attention.

Access : *At the foot of the Butte Montmartre*

PARIS - 75019

HOTEL LAUMIÈRE
Mme Desprat

4 rue Petit
75019 Paris
Tel. 01 42 06 10 77
lelaumiere@wanadoo.fr
www.hotel-lelaumiere.com
Languages : Eng., Sp.

Open all year • 54 rooms with bath/WC or shower/WC and television • €54 to €76; breakfast €7.60 • No restaurant

 A (well-needed) breath of fresh air in the picturesque Buttes Chaumont Park.

This charming small hotel, run by the same family since 1931, makes up for its distance from Paris' main monuments with a whole host of other advantages: the attractive modern style of the renovated interior, a leafy corner where breakfast is served on sunny days and the nearby Laumière métro station. If you prefer more space and calm, book one of the four rooms overlooking the cheerful garden.

Access : *From Place de Stalingrad take Av J Jaurès, turn right into Rue A Carrel, take the second on the left and the second on the right*

BARBIZON - 77630

HOSTELLERIE LA CLÉ D'OR
M. Gayer

73 Grande-Rue
77630 Barbizon
Tel. 01 60 66 40 96
cle.dor@wanadoo.fr
www.hotelcledor.com
Languages : Eng.

Open all year • 15 rooms, all with bathrooms • €56 to €133; breakfast €11; half-board available • Restaurant closed Sun evenings Nov to Mar; menus €29 to €39, drinks included • Terrace, garden, car park, meeting room

 The canvases hanging in the bedrooms.

This former post house, whose façade is a riot of flowering wisteria in springtime, is located just opposite the Auberge Ganne, much favoured by the artists of the Barbizon School in the 19C. The personalised bedrooms of the "Golden Key" overlook the garden-terrace. The delicious up-to-date cuisine made from seasonal produce is served in a plush dining room (parquet floor, beams and fireplace).

Access : *In the centre of the village on the main street*

BRÉAU - 77720

LA FERME DU COUVENT
M. et Mme Legrand

Rue de la Chapelle-Gauthier
77720 Bréau
Tel. 01 64 38 75 15
ferme.couvent@wanadoo.fr
www.lafermeducouvent.fr

Open all year • 13 rooms with shower/WC • €57, breakfast included • Table d'hôte €20 (week-days, by reservation only) • Garden, park. Credit cards not accepted • Tennis court

Flying over the Brie region in a hot-air balloon.

What better place to relax than this handsome 18C farmhouse planted in the middle of nearly 20 acres of parkland in the countryside. Attractive modern furniture graces the bedrooms, freshly painted in shades of cream with sloping ceilings. If you fancy something different, climb aboard the experienced owners' multi-coloured hot-air balloon for a proper bird's eye view of the Brie region.

Access : *14.5km eastbound from Vaux-le-Vicomte on the Provins road (D 408) and then the D 227 on the left*

CHARTRETTES - 77590

CHÂTEAU DE ROUILLON
Mme Morize-Thévenin

41 avenue Charles-de-Gaulle
77590 Chartrettes
Tel. 01 60 69 64 40
château.de.rouillon@club-internet.fr
www.chateauderouillon.net
Languages : Eng.

Open all year • 5 non-smoking rooms, including 1 apartment, all with bathrooms • €82 to €104, breakfast included • No table d'hôte • Terrace, park, private car park. Credit cards not accepted, no dogs allowed • Table tennis, mountain bike rentals

The choice of leisure activities (angling, water skiing, mountain bikes, etc).

A gracious French-style park extending down to the banks of the Seine and a sophisticated interior, in which every chair and object seems to tell a story, set the scene for your stay in this 17C castle. Each bedroom overlooks the river and is decorated individually and equipped with spacious, light bathrooms. Breakfasts are served in an elegant dining room or on the terrace.

Access : *In the centre of the village on the banks of the Seine*

CHÂTRES - 77610

LE PORTAIL BLEU
M. et Mme Laurent

 2 route de Fontenay
77610 Châtres
Tel. 01 64 25 84 94
leportailbleu@voila.fr
www.leportailbleu.com
Languages : Eng.

Open all year • 4 rooms, including 3 apartments, all with shower/WC and television • €59, breakfast included • Table d'hôte €20 • Terrace, garden, car park. Credit cards not accepted, dogs not admitted • Library

 Ideal for a relaxing country retreat.

The owners of this restored farmhouse never fail to treat their guests to a warm welcome. The rooms, located in two buildings surrounded by an attractive garden, are a picture of cosy comfort. The welcoming dining room features a large communal table, handsome wooden fireplace and countless paintings on the wall: quiches, pies and other house specialities often made from home-grown produce.

Access : *In the village centre*

ÉCHOUBOULAINS - 77830

FERME DE LA RECETTE
Famille Dufour

 Au hameau d'Échou
77830 Échouboulains
Tel. 01 64 31 81 09
info@fermedelarecette.com
www.fermedelarecette.com

Closed during the Feb holidays • 7 rooms with bath/WC and television • €54, breakfast included • Table d'hôte €23 (weekdays) to €31 • Dogs not admitted in rooms

The farmer-owner's friendly, genuine welcome.

The origins of this farm, formerly the property of the Cistercian abbey of Preuilly, have been traced back to the 12C. It now houses cosy rooms with snug, inviting duvets. Meals are served in a dining room where stone and wood feature prominently. Remember to reserve one of the tables near the windows so that you can enjoy the view of the pond, meadows and contented grazing cows.

Access : *11km to the north of Montereau-Fault-Yonne on the N 105 Melun road then on the D 107 at Valence-en-Brie*

GRISY-SUR-SEINE - 77480

LA FERME DE TOUSSACQ
Mme Colas

Hameau de Toussacq
77480 Grisy-sur-Seine
Tel. 01 64 01 82 90
toussacq@wanadoo.fr
www.hameau-de-toussacq.com

Open all year • 5 non-smoking rooms with bathrooms • €48, breakfast included • Table d'hôte €15 (only by reservation) • Garden, park, car park. No dogs admitted in restaurant • Chapel and dovecote visits

 The country atmosphere on the banks of the Seine.

Don't be put off by the somewhat forbidding aspect of this 17C farmhouse: you will, in any case, be sleeping in the castle outbuildings, whose loving restoration has taken more than 25 years. Bedrooms are simply styled with sloping ceilings and the breakfast room is a pleasant blend of rustic and modern. A fountain, chapel and dovecote together with a few sheep can be seen in the park. Appetising home cooking with a sprinkling of home-grown produce.

Access : *20km southbound from Provins on the Nogent-sur-Seine road (N 19), then the D 78 and the D 411*

LIZINES - 77650

CHAMBRE D'HÔTE M. DORMION
M. et Mme Dormion

2 rue des Glycines
77650 Lizines
Tel. 01 60 67 32 56

Open all year • 5 non-smoking rooms, all are in the attic with kitchenettes, all with shower/WC • €45, breakfast included • No table d'hôte • Garden, park. Credit cards not accepted, no dogs admitted

The immaculate bedrooms.

This three-century-old building, still a working farm, has offered accommodation and sustenance to visitors for over a decade. The spotless rooms with sloping ceilings are decorated with rustic furniture and each one has its own kitchenette. An old barn has been converted into a light, airy breakfast room with an enormous bay window. Venture out of doors and admire the lawn and orchard in the garden.

Access : *15km to the south-west of Provins on the N 19 and the D 209*

ORMEAUX - 77540

NEUFMOUTIERS-EN-BRIE - 77610

LA FERME DU VIEUX CHÂTEAU
Mme Maegerlein

Chemin du Pont-Levis
77540 Ormeaux
Tel. 06 78 02 25 17
BandB77@wanadoo.fr
www.chambres-table-hotes.com
Languages : Eng., Ger.

BELLEVUE
M. et Mme Galpin

77610 Neufmoutiers-en-Brie
Tel. 01 64 07 11 05
bellevue@fr.st
www.bellevue.fr.st

Open all year • 7 rooms, 5 of which are in a separate wing, all have bath/WC and television • €57 to €76, breakfast included • No table d'hôte • Garden, car park

Open all year by reservation • 4 non-smoking rooms, all have television, all with shower/WC • €48 to €65, breakfast included • Table d'hôte €13 to €55 • Garden, car park. Credit cards not accepted, no dogs admitted in rooms

Guests and their horses are received warmly.

The "old castle" is no longer visible, but the exquisitely restored 18C farmhouse is guaranteed to satisfy even the most demanding visitor. The owners' decorative flair has combined rich materials and period furniture with collections of old tools and popular arts. The bathrooms of the cosy rooms are all fitted with power showers. The high ceilinged lounge is graced with a huge Louis XIII fireplace. You are welcome to try your hand at carriage riding in the company of the farm's mare, Ivoire.

The elegant setting of this 19C manor house.

Don't be put off by the sight of the surrounding residential suburbia, because the garden of this fine 19C manor house commands a view of open fields which stretch as far as the eye can see. All the split-level bedrooms have a few personal touches. Two lodges with private garden and deck chairs are the most pleasant. A superb dining room with beams, old flagstones and a beautiful wood table set an elegant tone for mealtimes.

Access : *In the town*

Access : *10km south of Disneyland-Paris, on the A 4 take exit no 13, the D 231 then the D 96*

POMMEUSE - 77515

PROVINS - 77160

LE MOULIN DE POMMEUSE
M. et Mme Thomas

32 avenue du Général-Huerne
77515 Pommeuse
Tel. 01 64 75 29 45
info@le-moulin-de-pommeuse.com
www.le-moulin-de-pommeuse.com
Languages : Eng.

Open all year • 5 non-smoking rooms with shower/WC • €62, breakfast included • Table d'hôte €16 to €30 • Park, car park. Dogs not admitted • Hammam, sauna, 14C water mill

FERME DU CHATEL
M. Lebel

5 rue de la Chapelle-Saint-Jean
77160 Provins
Tel. 01 64 00 10 73
fermeduchatel@wanadoo.fr
Languages : Eng.

Open all year • 5 non-smoking rooms, all have bathrooms • €44 to €46 • No table d'hôte • Garden, car park. Credit cards not accepted, no dogs admitted

 As soon as you've crossed the threshold, you'll start to feel at home.

The lady of the house certainly knows how to receive her guests in style, offering them a drink on arrival, the traditional sprig of lily of the valley on May 1 and gifts at Christmas. The setting of the 14C water mill is quite delightful, as are the rooms, which have suitably agricultural names such as Sowing, Harvesting, Threshing. Relax in the small sitting room in the old machine room or in the park which hides its very own island!

 "Wasting" time in the orchard garden.

This old house, built and rebuilt from the 12C to the 18C, enjoys a superb position in the heart of the medieval town. The bedrooms, under exposed rafters, are peaceful and spotless with well-equipped bathrooms. Breakfast is served in a rustic dining room full of character; afterwards head for the huge garden and wander between the fruit trees.

Access : *5km westbound from Coulommiers on the N 34, then a minor road*

Access : *In the medieval city*

SAINT-GERMAIN-SUR-MORIN - 77860

SAINT-DENIS-LÈS-REBAIS - 77510

BRIE CHAMPAGNE
M. et Mme Bodin

22 Chantareine
77510 Saint-Denis-lès-Rebais
Tel. 01 64 65 46 45
contact@chambres-brie-champagne.com
www.chambres-brie-champagne.com
Languages : Eng.

Open all year • 3 non-smoking rooms, 1 has a kitchenette, all have bath/WC or shower/WC • €62, breakfast included • No table d'hôte • Terrace, park, private car park. Credit cards not accepted, no dogs admitted

LES HAUTS DE MONTGUILLON
Mme Legendre

22 rue de Saint-Quentin, Hameau de Montguillon
77860 Saint-Germain-sur-Morin
Tel. 01 60 04 45 53
chantal.legendre@wanadoo.fr

Open all year • 3 rooms, 2 of which are upstairs, all have bathrooms • €65, breakfast included • Garden, car park. Credit cards not accepted, no dogs admitted • Disneyland Paris nearby

 The cheerful decoration.

This lovingly restored farmhouse is conveniently located near Disneyland-Paris. A tasteful contrast of pastel shades and dark timbered beams prevails in the bedrooms which have large beds, old wardrobes and chest of drawers picked up in second-hand shops and brand new bathrooms. This creative mixture of old and new continues in the rest of the establishment, particularly in the hall with its old bread oven. The shaded, well-manicured garden is the place to be on sunny days.

 Breakfasting under the arbour.

This old farmhouse covered in Virginia creeper and wisteria extends a warm country welcome to guests. The half-timbered walls and family heirlooms in the dining room are just a foretaste of the authentic character of this guesthouse whose cosy bedrooms are located in a converted corn loft. Generously served meals are served in the shady garden or by a roaring fire indoors depending on the season.

Access : *Southbound from St-Germain sur Morin, in the upper part of Montguillon*

Access : *Take exit 16 off the A 4, then the N 34 towards Coulommiers and D 222 towards Rebais. Beyond Mazagran, left onto the D 19 towards "Chantareine" on the D 22*

SAINTS - 77120

LA BASTIDE DE L'AUBETIN
M. et Mme Pyla

3 rue du Chardon
77120 Saints
Tel. 01 64 03 27 86
evelyne.pyla@free.fr
http://evelyne.pyla.free.fr

Open all year • 2 rooms, all with bath/WC or shower/WC • €80 to €100, breakfast included • Table d'hôte €25, drinks included • Terrace, park, car park. Credit cards not accepted, dogs not admitted

 The faultless decoration of this Parisian "bastide".

A lane then a dirt track lead to this delightful country house tucked away in a flower-decked garden lined in trees. The owners have three guestrooms, one of which on the ground-floor, all of which are decorated in bright Spanish tiles and colours. At mealtimes, savour the mouth-watering dishes made with home-grown vegetables and produce from local farms.

Access : *From Saints, exit eastbound on the D 15*

VARREDDES - 77910

AUBERGE DU CHEVAL BLANC
Mme Cousin

55 rue Victor-Clairet
77910 Varreddes
Tel. 01 64 33 18 03
r.cousin2@libertysurf.fr
www.auberge-cheval-blanc.fr
Languages : Eng., Sp.

Closed from 1 to 24 Aug, Sun evening, Mon and Tue lunchtime • 8 rooms with bath/WC and television • €77 to €96; breakfast €10 • Menus €34 to €50 • Garden, private car park

 The terrace decked in flowers and shaded by trees.

This former staging inn houses recently redone "chocolate-box" bedrooms featuring designer fabrics, pine and wrought-iron furniture and teak-floored bathrooms. In the plush dining room hung with still-lifes, the accent is on creativity and healthy local produce. Don't even think about leaving without tasting the inimitable Brie de Meaux cheese!

Access : *On the main road in the village*

VOSVES - 77190

LA FERME DE VOSVES
Mme Lemarchand

155 rue de Boissise
77190 Vosves
Tel. 01 64 39 22 28
contact@fermedevosves.com
www.fermedevosves.com
Languages : Eng.

Closed from 21 Dec to 3 Jan • 2 rooms • €60 to €65, breakfast included • No table d'hôte • Garden, car park. Credit cards not accepted, no dogs admitted

 The simple, unpretentious welcome and setting.

This green-shuttered old farmhouse is bordered by two attractive gardens full of fruit trees and flowers and complete with a well. The unostentatious, tranquil bedrooms, spread throughout the buildings and the warm, unaffected welcome from the lady of the house are reason enough to stay, but the sitting room with piano and dining room with fireplace and watercolours by the owner are also delightful.

I am a watercolour artist and many people come here because they are interested in painting

Access : *10km northbound from Barbizon on the N 7 and the D 372, then take Rue de la Gare*

LA BOISSIÈRE-ÉCOLE - 78125

LA GÂTINE
M. Chauzy

15 route de Faverolles
78125 La Boissière-École
Tel. 01 34 94 32 79
marion.gatine@wanadoo.fr
www.lagatine.com

Closed from 15 Jan to 15 Feb • 6 non-smoking rooms, 1 with disabled access, all have bathrooms • €72 to €95, breakfast included • Table d'hôte €32 (by reservation) • Terrace, park, car park. Credit cards not accepted, no dogs admitted • Possibility of access to Country Spa facilities

 Winding down in a spa resort in the heart of the countryside just one hour from Paris.

This estate on the edge of the Rambouillet forest boasts a country spa resort with a host of beauty treatments, massages and keep-fit programmes to boost the spirits flagging urbanites. Each of the bedrooms, located in a thatched cottage, is decorated differently on a travel theme. The lobby is the scene of temporary art exhibitions which change each month. In season, don't miss the chance to sample the local game.

Access : *From Faverolles, turn left on the D 152 towards la Boissière-École. 3km further on, La Gâtine is on your left*

MOISSON - 78840

MONTAINVILLE - 78124

LE PRIEURÉ MAÏALEN
M. et Mme Lévi

4 allée du Jamboree
78840 Moisson
Tel. 01 34 79 37 20
blc.blevi@orange.fr
Languages : Eng., Sp.

Open all year • 4 rooms with bathrooms • €69, breakfast included, half-board available • Table d'hôte €22 (only by reservation) • Garden, car park. Credit cards not accepted, no dogs admitted • Outdoor swimming pool. Golf, horse-riding, tennis and leisure park nearby

LA FAUCONNERIE DU ROY
M. et Mme Oger

1 rue de l'Ormoir
78124 Montainville
Tel. 01 34 75 17 24
oger@lafauconnerie.com
www.lafauconnerie.com
Languages : Eng., Sp.

Closed 22 Dec to 2 Jan • 2 rooms with shower/WC and one gîte • €80, breakfast included • No table d'hôte • Car park. Credit cards not accepted, no dogs admitted • Outdoor swimming pool

 A spin in one of the owner's vintage cars.

A former 16C priory is an excellent place to spend a night in the heart of this village so dear to Monet. Time and care have clearly been lavished on the interior and each room is a delight to behold. The "Boat" room contains an 18C model sailing boat, "Scheherazade" is steeped in mystery and "Provence" bathed in bright, cheerful colours. Antique furniture, ornaments and a collection of LPs add a personal touch to the sitting room and the flowered garden is perfect to relax in.

Special "table d'hôte" cooking course

Access : *3km to the south-east of Roche-Guyon*

 The history behind these beautifully preserved buildings.

History and character meet your eye wherever you turn in this falconry built in 1680 for Louis XIV. Everything is authentic from the original wooden carved staircase and doors, tiled floors and period furniture down to the piano in the breakfast room. Excellent mattresses, canopy and four-poster beds and good quality bathrooms have been chosen for the bedrooms. Swimming pool, children's play area in the park and bicycle rental available.

Access : *6km eastbound from Thoiry on the D 45, take the Maule road and turn right*

NEAUPHLE-LE-CHÂTEAU - 78640

LE CLOS SAINT-NICOLAS
Mme Drouelle

33 rue Saint-Nicolas
78640 Neauphle-le-Château
Tel. 01 34 89 76 10
mariefrance.drouelle@wanadoo.fr
www.clos-saint-nicolas.com

Open all year • 3 rooms with shower/WC and television • €85, breakfast included • No table d'hôte • Garden, car park

 Discovering this haven of peace and quiet.

Not far from the town centre stands this handsome 19C home, surrounded by a walled garden and recently renovated for the comfort of guests. On the first floor are three eminently comfortable rooms whose parquet floors, colourful fabrics and period furniture add to the warm welcome. Relax in the Napoleon sitting room. Delicious breakfasts and homemade jams are served amid the orange and lemon trees on the veranda-cum-winter garden.

Access : *21km eastbound from Versailles*

POIGNY-LA-FORÊT - 78125

LE CHÂTEAU
M. Meley

2 rue de l'Église
78125 Poigny-la-Forêt
Tel. 01 34 84 73 42
le-château-de-depoigny@wanadoo.fr

Open from 4 Jan to 23 Dec • 5 rooms, one of which is a family room, all with bathrooms • €65 to €75, breakfast included • No table d'hôte • Garden, car park. No dogs allowed

The quiet park and its two-hundred-year-old trees.

Not far from Rambouillet, this sumptuous abode, built in 1830 and laden with family heirlooms, is a treat for the eye. On the second floor, each of the rooms is styled on a different theme: Morocco, India, China, Syria, rustic, etc. Copious breakfasts. The garden full of ducks, ganders, dogs and horses has a distinctly Noah's Ark air about it. Definitely worth making a beeline for!

Access : *8km to the north-west of Rambouillet on the D 936 then the D 107*

MOIGNY-SUR-ÉCOLE - 91490

29

CLOS DE LA CROIX BLANCHE
M. Lenoir

9 rue du Souvenir
91490 Moigny-sur-École
Tel. 01 64 98 47 84
lenoir@aol.com
www.compagnie-des-clos.com

Open all year • 4 rooms, one of which is on the ground floor , all with shower/WC • €57 to €62, breakfast included • Table d'hôte €17 • Garden. Credit cards not accepted

We most liked
The sheltered landscaped garden.

High walls protect this handsome stone house and its beautifully laid-out garden from prying eyes. The tastefully decorated rooms are totally tranquil and the one on split-levels is very practical for families. If you listen quietly you may still hear the clucking of the former inhabitants of the breakfast room, where the chicken roosts can still be seen. A pleasant stay and cordial welcome assured.

Access : *3.5km northbound from Milly-la-Forêt*

NAINVILLE-LES-ROCHES - 91750

30

LE CLOS DES FONTAINES
Mme Soton

3 rue de l'Église
91750 Nainville-les-Roches
Tel. 01 64 98 40 56
soton@closdesfontaines.com
www.closdesfontaines.com
Languages : Eng.

Open all year • 5 non-smoking rooms, 1 with disabled access, all have bath/WC or shower/WC, television and Internet access • €105 (€88 low season); breakfast included • No table d'hôte • Park, car park. No dogs admitted • Outdoor swimming pool, tennis, petanque

We most liked
The timeless peace and quiet.

Nestling between the tiny church and town houses, this former presbytery is set in pleasant park planted with trees. The attractive contemporary rooms are tastefully decorated on the theme of spices after which they are named (Saffron, Cinnamon, Nutmeg, etc.). Home-made pastries and jams are served at breakfast time in a modern room which leads into the veranda-sitting room. Tennis, pétanque, fitness room and sauna on site.

> *Oenology course, watercolour and drawing course*

Access : *In the heart of the village*

PARMAIN - 95620

CHÉRENCE - 95510

MONSIEUR DELALEU
M. Delaleu

131 rue du Maréchal-Foch
95620 Parmain
Tel. 01 34 73 02 92
chambresdhotes.parmain@wanadoo.fr

Open all year • 4 rooms • €52, breakfast included • No table d'hôte • Garden, car park. Credit cards not accepted, no dogs admitted

LE SAINT-DENIS
Mme Pernelle

1 rue des Cabarets
95510 Chérence
Tel. 01 34 78 15 02

Open all year (by reservation) • 5 rooms with bathrooms • €62 to €65, breakfast included • No table d'hôte • Garden, car park. Credit cards not accepted, no dogs admitted

The unusual bathrooms.

By the time you have opened your suitcase, you will feel that you have come home. Each of the spacious, colourful rooms is named after a playing card; Spade, Heart, Diamond and Club. However the highly unusual bathrooms, all are different, are what guests always rave about. Children are in heaven over the vaulted cellar turned into a games room, the mini football pitch and the visit to the working farm.

The lavish breakfasts.

This appealing stone house in the lovely medieval village of Chérence was formerly a traditional hotel-restaurant. It was turned into a B&B establishment in 1996, offering simple, compact rooms in all shapes and sizes. The ground floor, full of nooks and crannies, houses the dining and sitting room complete with fireplace. Spending or wasting time in the delightful garden is definitely a high point. Faultless welcome.

Access : *1km westbound from Isle-Adam on the D 64*

Access : *4km to the north-east of Roche-Guyon on the D 100*

LANGUEDOC ROUSSILLON

Languedoc-Roussillon is home to a diverse collage of landscape and culture: the feverish rhythm of its festivals, the dizzying beauty of the Tarn Gorges, the haughty splendour of the Pyrenees, the bewitching spell of its caves and stone statues, the seclusion of its clifftop Cathar citadels which witnessed one of the bloodiest chapters of France's history, the heady perfumes of its sun-burnt garrigue, the nonchalance of the pink flamingos on its long salt flats, the splendour of Carcassonne's ramparts, the ornamental exuberance of Catalan altarpieces, the quietly flowing waters of the Midi Canal and the harsh majesty of the Cévennes mountains. Taking in so many contrasts is likely to exhaust more than a few explorers, but effective remedies are close at hand: a steaming plate of *aligot* – mashed potato, garlic and cheese – and a simmering cassoulet, the famously rich combination of duck, sausage, beans and herbs, all washed down with a glass of ruby-red wine.

ARGELIERS - 11120

LA BAÏSA
Mme Françoise Vidard-Geoffroy

Au Port
11120 Argeliers
Tel. 06 07 88 18 30
francoisegv19@hotmail.com
www.peniche-chambres-hotes.com
Languages : Eng., It.

Open all year • 3 rooms with bath/WC • €65 to €75, breakfast included • Table d'hôte €20 to €25 • Park. Credit cards not accepted, no dogs admitted

 The unusual accommodation in "cabines d'hôte".

Welcome aboard the Baïsa, an attractive barge moored alongside the Midi canal. All the cabins have private bathrooms and are very comfortable. On the breakfast table are homemade pastries and jams and the table d'hôte meal (evenings only) is served in a snug sitting-dining room. Two-day excursions along the canal are organised, offering guests the chance to enjoy the sun deck as they watch the countryside roll gently by.

Access : *100m from the village of Argeliers*

BIZANET - 11200

DOMAINE DE SAINT-JEAN
M. et Mme Delbourg

11200 Bizanet
Tel. 04 68 45 17 31
didierdelbourgbizanet@yahoo.fr
Languages : Sp.

Open all year • 4 upstairs rooms, all have bathrooms • €55 to €70, breakfast included • No table d'hôte • Garden. Credit cards not accepted, dogs not admitted

Whiling away time in the former wine cellar converted into a sitting room.

This rambling 19C wine-growing property stands amid vineyards and pine trees, ready to welcome travellers in search of quiet authenticity. Hand-stencilled furniture and walls adorn the accommodation in the converted vat house: each room is named after one of the family's ancestors; the one with a private terrace enjoys a particularly lovely view of the Fontfroide massif. The well-tended garden is Mr Delbourg's pride and joy.

Access : *2.5km to the north-west of the abbey on the D 613 towards Lagrasse, then on a minor road*

CARCASSONNE - 11000

LA MAISON SUR LA COLLINE
Mme Galinier

Lieu-dit Sainte-Croix
11000 Carcassonne
Tel. 04 68 47 57 94
contact@lamaisonsurlacolline.com
www.lamaisonsurlacolline.com
Languages : Eng., Sp.

Closed from 20 Dec to 14 Feb • 6 rooms with bathrooms and television • €65 to €90, breakfast included • Table d'hôte €30 (evenings only by reservation) • Garden, car park. Credit cards not accepted, no dogs allowed in restaurant • Outdoor swimming pool

As soon as you hear the chirping of the cicadas you know you're in the south.

Broom, cypress trees, thyme and wild mint lend a wonderfully relaxing atmosphere to this hillside farmstead overlooking the historic city of Carcassonne. Old red floor tiles, antiques and knick-knacks adorn the spacious rooms. Each has its own colour scheme, beige, blue, yellow – the "white" room has a private garden. Breakfast is served by the pool in the summer.

Access : *1km southbound from the historic town on the Sainte-Croix road*

CASTELNAUDARY - 11400

HÔTEL DU CANAL
Mme Geli-Devolle

2 ter avenue Arnaut-Vidal
11400 Castelnaudary
Tel. 04 68 94 05 05
hotelducanal@wanadoo.fr
www.hotelducanal.com
Languages : Eng.

Open all year • 38 rooms, 2 have disabled access. All have bath/WC, television (and broadband internet access for €5/night) • €55 to €61; breakfast €6 • No restaurant • Garden, car park • Billiards room

 Stepping out of the hotel onto the banks of the Canal du Midi.

These handsome ochre walls housed a quick-lime factory back in the 19C. The quiet if ordinary rooms overlook the garden or the canal and in the summer, you will want to linger over breakfast for hours as you gaze at the canal's quietly flowing waters. It would be a crime to leave town without sampling its world-renowned cassoulet!

Access : *Towards Pamiers on the banks of the Midi canal*

DOUZENS - 11700

CUCUGNAN - 11350

L'ÉCURIE DE CUCUGNAN
M. et Mme Gauch

10 rue Achille-Mir
11350 Cucugnan
Tel. 04 68 33 37 42
ecurie.cucugnan @ wanadoo.fr
www.queribus.fr
Languages : Eng., Sp.

Open all year • 5 rooms with shower/WC, air-conditioning and modem • €58 (€54 low season), breakfast included • No table d'hôte • Car park. Credit cards not accepted • Outdoor swimming pool

LE DOMAINE DU PARC
Mme Patricia Deniaux

3 rue du Barri
11700 Douzens
Tel. 06 77 88 48 53
domaineduparc @ free.fr
www.ledomaineduparc.com

Open all year • 6 rooms with bath/WC, air-conditioning • €65 to €80, breakfast included • Table d'hôte €20 • Park, car park. Credit cards not accepted • Outdoor swimming pool

The bucolic charm of the park with its profusion of plant species.

This former winegrowers' property has been carefully restored so as to preserve the charm and soul of yesteryear. The eminently comfortable rooms are tastefully decorated with a choice of harmonious colours. Don't miss the delicious breakfasts served in a room, perhaps the prettiest of the house, adorned with romantic 19C paintings. In fine weather, relax in a lounger or hammock or enjoy a game of petanque.

We most liked The luxury of not having to choose between quality and price.

Recently created in the old stables, these rooms full of character offer a high quality of comfort: elegantly decorated bathrooms, wifi Internet access and air-conditioning. Depending on the weather, meals are served in the spacious dining room with fireplace and wrought-iron furniture, or on the peaceful terrace overlooking the Padern Valley. In summer, the owners organise wine tasting sessions of regional wines.

Access : *In the village*

Access : *In the upper part of the village*

FANJEAUX - 11270

MOUSSOULENS - 11170

LE RELAIS ST-DOMINIQUE
M. et Mme Micouleau

11270 Fanjeaux
Tel. 04 68 24 68 17
norbert.micouleau@wanadoo.fr
www.lerelaissaintdominique.com
Languages : Eng., Sp.

Open all year • 6 rooms, 1 with disabled access, all with shower/WC • €60 to €70, breakfast included • No table d'hôte • Park, car park. No dogs admitted • Outdoor swimming pool

LA ROUGEANNE
M. et Mme Glorieux

8 allée du Parc
11170 Moussoulens
Tel. 04 68 24 46 30
info@larougeanne.com
www.larougeanne.com

Open all year • 4 rooms with bath/WC • €75 to €80, breakfast included • No table d'hôte • Park, car park. Credit cards not accepted, dogs not admitted • Outdoor swimming pool

 What a difficult choice: a doze in the sun or in the shade?

The rustic interior of this delightful country home is all the more appealing because of the choice of simple decoration in perfect keeping with the setting. The extremely comfortable bedrooms (private bathrooms) are faultlessly kept. On sunny mornings breakfast is served on the patio, after which you can take a dip in the pool surrounded by greenery. Regional specialities and produce from the estate on sale in an adjacent shop.

 The refreshing tranquillity of the Scandinavian-inspired sitting room.

This former winegrower's house nestling in a park planted with many different trees commands a splendid view of the Pyrenean mountains in the distance. The mezzanine rooms, called "Verveine" and "Tommette" are designed for families while "Romarin" and "Olivier" are smaller but equally comfortable and perfect for couples. Guests have the run of a splendid swimming pool surrounded by trees and the dovecote converted into a children's library will delight younger visitors.

Access : *North of Fanjeaux on the D 802*

Access : *In the village*

NARBONNE - 11100

DOMAINE DE GLEIZES
M. et Mme Martel

11100 Narbonne
Tel. 04 68 32 94 48
domainedegleizes@wanadoo.fr
www.domaine-de-gleizes.com

Open all year • 4 rooms with shower/WC and television • €59, breakfast included • Table d'hôte €28 • Garden, car park

 Sipping a glass of the estate's excellent wine.

The buildings of this winegrowing estate enjoy a magnificently calm setting amid vineyards and orchards. Located in the outhouses, the four ground-floor rooms all have an independent access. Guests like the modern furniture, tasteful decoration and pleasant bathrooms. Depending on the weather, breakfast is served in the courtyard or on one of the small terraces. Regional recipes and produce take pride of place on the table d'hôte menu, and in summer festive paella evenings are organised.

Access : *Near the centre of Narbonne*

PEYRIAC-DE-MER - 11440

LA MILHAUQUE
M. et Mme Barbouteau

11440 Peyriac-de-Mer
Tel. 04 68 41 69 76

Open all year • 3 rooms with shower/WC • €52 to €70, breakfast included • No table d'hôte • Park, garden. Credit cards not accepted, no dogs admitted • Outdoor swimming pool

 Walking along the sign-posted paths through the fragrant gorse to Bages pond.

An uneven narrow lane leads to this house surrounded by flowers with a beautifully laid-out garden and a small patio. The fully restored former sheepfold is now home to three characterful rooms, two of which have low ceilings and picture windows. The third, more conventional, in the main building, boasts a Polish bed and an immense bathroom. Fish alone is served on the table d'hôte menu, and the house speciality is eel.

Access : *2km north-west from Peyriac-sur-Mer on the N 9 then a lane left*

PORTEL-DES-CORBIERES - 11490

DOMAINE DE LA PIERRE CHAUDE
M. et Mme Pasternak

Les Campets
11490 Portel-des-Corbières
Tel. 04 68 48 89 79
lescampets@aol.com
www.lapierrechaude.com
Languages : Eng.

Closed from 1 Jan to 15 Feb • 4 rooms with bath/WC • €75 to €85, breakfast included • No table d'hôte • Terrace, garden, car park. Credit cards not accepted, no dogs admitted

 Everything!

This 18C former wine and spirit house nestled in a hamlet amid vineyards and pinewoods, was beautifully restored in 1960 by a pupil of the architect Gaudi. Since then, constant improvements have turned the estate into a pleasant getaway with splendid bedrooms (terracotta tiles, wrought iron, worn wooden furniture, warm fabrics, etc.), a lovely Andalusian-style patio-cum-sitting room, a terrace shaded by fig trees and a garden rich with the sweet scents of southern France. Unforgettable!

Access : *In a place known as Les Campets, 6km from the Wildlife Park on the D 611A towards Durban-Corbières*

PUIVERT - 11230

LA COCAGNIÈRE
Mme Sylviane Guérin et M. Gilbert Courtade

3 place du Pijol, hameau de Campsylvestre
11230 Puivert
Tel. 04 68 20 81 90
lacocagniere@wanadoo.fr
www.lacocagniere.com
Languages : Ger., Eng., It., Sp.

Open all year • 4 rooms with shower/WC • €45 to €55, breakfast included • Table d'hôte €18 • Car park. Credit cards not accepted, no dogs admitted

 It is impossible not to full in love with this property.

How could you remain insensitive to the appeal of this faultlessly renovated former sheepfold? It has everything: an atmosphere full of authenticity, cosy comfort and a warm friendly welcome. What's more, if you're lucky in the evenings at the end of the summer, after an excellent meal of succulent sophisticated dishes, you may hear the cries of a stag mingle with the chant of the crickets. A moment of pure joy that it is difficult to tear oneself away from.

Access : *6km eastbound from Puivert on the D 117, then small lane to the right*

SAINT-MARTIN-LE-VIEIL - 11170

ABBAYE DE VILLELONGUE
M. Jean Eloffe

11170 Saint-Martin-le-Vieil
Tel. 04 68 76 92 58

Closed 10 days in Nov and 10 days at Christmas • 4 rooms with shower/WC • €60, breakfast included • No table d'hôte • Car park, park, garden. Credit cards not accepted, no dogs admitted • Guided and non-guided visits of the abbey daily

 Quietly meditating in the abbey gardens, before or after the throngs of daily visitors.

Stand still and drink in the silence and solemnity of the former Cistercian abbey built in the 12C. Be reassured, however, the comfort on offer is far from monastic and old furniture, canopy beds and private bathrooms now set the scene in the rooms. All the rooms gaze down on the lovely cloisters and garden, where breakfast is served in the summer. In the winter, they are served in the monks' storeroom, restored in 1998.

Access : *5km to the north-west on the D 64*

THÉZAN-DES-CORBIÈRES - 11200

LA BASTIDE DE DONOS
M. Alain Chardigny

11200 Thézan-des-Corbières
Tel. 04 68 43 32 11
www.chateaudonos.com
Languages : Eng., It.

Closed 22 Dec to 7 Jan • 4 rooms and 2 apartments, all with bath/WC or shower/WC • €85, breakfast included • No table d'hôte • Park, car park. No dogs admitted • Private pond 300m away

 A voyage back in time.

This fully restored 17C country house is now home to four rooms and two apartments noted for the pleasing blend of sophisticated comfort and tasteful decoration: bare stone walls and old beams enhanced by light colours and matching fabrics. Splendid view of the old washhouse and castle. Swimming and canoeing on the private lake. Tasting of wines from the estate.

Access : *4km past the exit to Thézan*

AIGUES-MORTES - 30220

15

HERMITAGE DE SAINT-ANTOINE
Mme Dejavel

9 boulevard Intérieur Nord
30220 Aigues-Mortes
Tel. 06 03 04 34 05
ryhermit@club-internet.fr
www.hermitagesa.com
Languages : Eng.

Open all year • 3 rooms, all with shower/WC or
bath/WC • €74, breakfast included • No table
d'hôte • Credit cards not accepted, no dogs
admitted • Air-conditioning

The cosy atmosphere protected by the ramparts.

Like many of the homes of Aigues-Mortes, this
house in the historic town is limited in space
but compensates with the charm of a doll's
house. The three simply furnished small bedrooms (one of which has a balcony overlooking
the courtyard) with coconut matting on the
floors and bright colours are truly delightful.
When the weather permits, breakfast is served
in the summer garden. Warm welcome.

Access : *Opposite porte Saint-Antoine*

AUBUSSARGUES - 30190

16

MAS CONIL
M. Schurmann

Chemin de Collorgues
30190 Aubussargues
Tel. 04 66 63 97 00
hotes@masconil.com
www.masconil.com
Languages : Eng., Ger.

Closed for 10 days at Christmas • 4 rooms and
1 apartment, all with bath/WC • €90 to €100,
breakfast included • Table d'hôte €28 (evenings
by reservation) • Garden. No dogs admitted in
restaurant • Outdoor swimming pool, vegetable
garden

**Throwing open the lavender-coloured
shutters in the morning to the Provençal
sunshine.**

This fully renovated superb drystone mas is
home to four double rooms and a family apartment, dotted with old furniture; some rooms
have lovely old tiled floors. The excellent
bedding adds to the cosy comfort and the
soothing choice of colours invites guests to
enjoy a refreshing night's sleep. The table
d'hôte menu varies with the seasons, offering
a Provençal based cuisine served in the shade
of an old tree. A few Swiss specialities are
served by the immense fireplace.

*January: truffles, Spring: bicycling week,
Autumn: bedspread week*

Access : *Near the Château d'Aubussargues*

BARJAC - 30430

LA SÉRÉNITÉ
Mme L'Helgoualch

Place de la Mairie
30430 Barjac
Tel. 04 66 24 54 63
catherine@la-serenite.fr
www.la-serenite.fr
Languages : Eng.

Closed from 1 Nov to 16 Mar • 3 non-smoking rooms with bath/WC or shower/WC • €80 to €135, breakfast included • No table d'hôte • Terrace. Credit cards not accepted, no dogs admitted

 Snuggling up in the book-lined bedroom or in front of the fire.

Fragrant lavender and beeswax greet you as you cross the threshold of this 17C country home. Afterwards, feast your eyes on the sophisticated good taste of the ochre-coloured walls, hand-stencilled friezes, rich fabrics, antiques and ornaments picked up by the antique dealer-owner and on the personalised rooms decorated with fine linen and lace. Settle down and relax as you savour the delicious breakfasts served by the fireside or on the flowered terrace in the summer.

Access : *6km westbound from Aven d'Orgnac on the D 317 and then the D 176*

BEAUCAIRE - 30300

MAS DE LAFONT
Mme Niquet

30300 Beaucaire
Tel. 04 66 59 29 59
www.masdelafont.com

Open from 1 May to 1 Oct • 3 non-smoking rooms, all with bath/WC • €85 to €90, breakfast included • No table d'hôte • Garden. Credit cards not accepted, dogs not admitted • Outdoor swimming pool

 The soothing calm of the site.

This Provençal mas dating from the 17C, located on an agricultural estate amidst vineyards and apricot trees, opens its doors to guests in summertime. The main room is equipped with a fitted kitchen. The rooms, with bare stonewalls and beams, are generously proportioned and attractively furnished with family heirlooms. All overlook the garden and the arbour where a swimming pool enables guests to cool down on sunny afternoons. Extremely well looked after, just two minutes from the Midi Canal.

Access : *6km southwest from Beaucaire, Saint-Gilles road, then left at Nouriguier lock (écluse)*

BELLEGARDE - 30127

PÉNICHE FARNIENTE
M. Laurent Michel

Port de Plaisance
30127 Bellegarde
Tel. 04 66 01 45 52
http://penichefarniente.free.fr

Closed during Christmas half-term holidays • 3 air-conditioned cabins, with shower/WC • €50 to €60, breakfast included • No table d'hôte • Terrace. Credit cards not accepted, dogs not admitted

The gentle lapping of the canal waters against the hull.

After having wound its way round the centre of France since its construction in 1923, this barge has found a berth and a second youth in the Bellegarde marina. Pleasantly restored with wood-lined interiors, it now houses three relatively spacious and comfortable cabins. Breakfasts are served on the deck transformed into a terrace or in the dining room when the sun is less forthcoming. Friendly welcome guaranteed in this unusual form of accommodation.

Access : *12km northwest from Arles*

CASTILLON-DU-GARD - 30210

VIC
M. Vic

Mas de Raffin
30210 Castillon-du-Gard
Tel. 04 66 37 13 28
viccastillon4@aol.com
www.chambresdhotes-vic.com
Languages : Eng.

Open all year • 5 rooms with shower/WC or bath/WC • €70 to €90, breakfast included • No table d'hôte • Garden, car park. Credit cards not accepted • Outdoor swimming pool, spa, hammam

The happy marriage of old and new.

It would be difficult to find a more idyllic spot for this former wine-growing farm set amidst the unspoilt landscape of fragrant scrub, vines and hundred-year-old olive trees. Red and yellow features predominantly in the bright rooms where modern amenities blend in wonderfully with old stones and antique furniture; some are vaulted while others are split-level. Savour breakfast served under the refreshing shade of a mulberry tree.

Access : *4km to the north-east of Pont-du-Gard on the D 19 and then the D 228*

LA ROQUE-SUR-CÈZE - 30200

LA TONNELLE
M. et Mme Rigaud

Place des Marronniers
30200 La Roque-sur-Cèze
Tel. 04 66 82 79 37
latonnelle30@aol.com

Open all year • 6 rooms with shower/WC • €72, breakfast included • No table d'hôte • Car park. No dogs admitted

 Row, row, row your boat, gently down the Cèze!

Merrily, merrily, merrily, merrily, life is but a dream! The infectious good humour of the owner is impossible to resist as she guides you round her lovely country house that can't be missed on the way into the village. Each of the sober, immaculate rooms is named after a flower. In the summer, treat yourself to breakfast in the shade of an arbour while you gaze down on the village and its girdle of cypress trees.

Access : *17km to the north-west of Bagnols-sur-Cèze on the N 86 then the D 298 towards Barjac, and the D 166*

LE VIGAN - 30570

CHÂTEAU DU REY
Mme Cazalis de Fondouce

Le Rey
30570 Le Vigan
Tel. 04 67 82 40 06
abeura@club-internet.fr
www.château-du-rey.com
Languages : Eng., It.

Closed 30 Sep to 1 Apr • 12 rooms and 1 apartment, all have bath/WC and television • €70 to €97; breakfast €8; half-board available • Restaurant closed on Sun evening and Mon except in Jul and Aug; menus €22 to €32 • Terrace, riverside park, car park • Outdoor swimming pool, private fishing

 Eight centuries of family history.

This lovely 13C fortress, remodelled by the tireless Viollet-le-Duc, Napoleon's architect, has been in the same family for over eight centuries! The rooms, some with fireplace, are furnished with elegant period furniture. The former sheep pen is now the dining room and its vaulted ceiling makes it pleasantly cool in summer. The view from the terrace extends over the immense parkland and river, much prized by anglers.

Access : *5km eastbound on the D 999 (towards Ganges), turn left just before Pont d'Hérault*

MONTCLUS - 30630

LA MAGNANERIE DE BERNAS
M. et Mme Keller

Le Hameau de Bernas
30630 Montclus
Tel. 04 66 82 37 36
lamagnanerie@wanadoo.fr
www.magnanerie-de-bernas.com
Languages : Eng., Ger., It.

Open from 1 Apr to late Oct • 15 rooms, two are split-level, one has disabled access, all have bath/WC and television • €65 to €120; breakfast €12; half-board available • Restaurant closed Tue, Wed in Mar, Apr and Oct; menus €20 to €45 • Terrace, garden, car park • Outdoor swimming pool

 Treasure hunting in this 13C Knights Templar stronghold.

Patrick and Katrin, a young Swiss couple with energy to spare, have recently finished their patient, flawless restoration of this medieval former command post. Beautiful stone walls, exposed beams and rich, warm fabrics adorn the tasteful rooms, most of which look down over the Cèze valley. Character abounds in the vaulted dining room, but the highlight is perhaps the shaded courtyard-terrace and south-facing garden, designed by a professional landscape gardener, none other than Patrick himself.

Access : *Between Barjac and Bagnols-sur-Cèze, then 2km eastbound from Monclus*

MUS - 30121

LA PAILLÈRE
Mme Blanche

26 rue du Puit-Vieux
30121 Mus
Tel. 04 66 35 55 93
welcome@paillere.com
www.paillere.com

Closed in Feb • 6 rooms upstairs with bathrooms and television • €65 to €85, breakfast included • Table d'hôte €25 drinks included • Terrace, sitting room

 Guests are greeted with a drink on arrival.

Come and enjoy the charm and tranquillity of this elegant 17C abode. Each of the rooms has been individually decorated with either Colonial-style or Provençal-style furniture. The rooms are laid out around a shaded patio-terrace overrun with Virginia creeper, where generous breakfasts are served. Several attractive sitting rooms, one of which is adorned with an impressive fireplace that is most welcome in winter. Mediterranean-style cuisine on the table d'hôte menu.

Access : *18km southwest on the A9, N°26 exit*

PORT-CAMARGUE - 30240

REMOULINS - 30120

LA TERRE DES LAURIERS
M. Langlois

Pont du Gard, rive droite
30120 Remoulins
Tel. 04 66 37 19 45
langlois@laterredeslauriers.com
www.laterredeslauriers.com
Languages : Eng., Sp.

Closed Feb school holidays and fortnight in Dec
• 5 rooms and 2 gîtes, all with bath/WC, air-conditioning • €99, breakfast included • No table d'hôte • Park, car park. Credit cards not accepted, no dogs admitted • Outdoor swimming pool and private beach

 Strolling past the poplar and olive trees in the park down to the river.

While it may lack the appeal of an old house, this "youthful" 30-year-old house covered in greenery boasts a magnificent park of over 10 acres. The five air-conditioned rooms combine space and comfort, but you may prefer the privacy of the 18C sheepfold or the lovely chalet, both of which are immaculately kept. Hidden by a hedge of laurels, the heated secure swimming pool will afford many hours of relaxation.

Country weekends, musical weekends

Access : *800m from the Pont du Gard*

RELAIS DE L'OUSTAU CAMARGUEN
M. Daweritz

3 route des Marines
30240 Port-Camargue
Tel. 04 66 51 51 65
oustaucamarguen@wanadoo.fr
www.oustaucamarguen.com
Languages : Eng., Ger.

Open from 23 Mar to 4 Nov • 39 air-conditioned rooms, most on ground-floor, with bath/WC or shower/WC and television • €99; breakfast €11; half-board available • Air-conditioned restaurant; menus €27 (evenings only) • Terrace, garden, private car park • Outdoor swimming pool

 Winding down in the peaceful atmosphere of this small mas.

This recently-built hotel has adopted a traditional Camargue style as its name suggests. All the rooms are spacious and on the ground-floor and some have small, flower-decked terraces overlooking the pleasant garden. The tasteful interior decoration was clearly inspired by neighbouring Provence. A country style with exposed beams in the restaurant, a pleasant pool-side terrace and a select traditional menu comprise the establishment's other appeals.

Access : *On Route des Marines*

SAINT-LAURENT-D'AIGOUZE - 30220

27

MAS DE LA MONTILLE
M. Panier

Route des Saintes-Maries-de-la-Mer
30220 Saint-Laurent-d'Aigouze
Tel. 04 66 35 59 43
http://masdelamontille.free.fr
Languages : Eng.

Closed in Jan • 5 rooms and 1 apartment, all
with shower/WC or bath/WC • €110, breakfast
included • Table d'hôte €20 to €25 • Park,
terrace. Credit cards not accepted, no dogs
admitted • Air-conditioning, outdoor swimming
pool, Jacuzzi

 **The charm of the East in the soft southern
sunshine.**

Originally from Syria, the owner of this Cama-
rgues mas decided to enrich the decoration of
her home with a few touches from the east; the
furnishings and fabrics are perfectly at home in
this fully renovated abode and in the rooms in
a separate wing. Guests are enchanted by the
warm welcome and the quality of the table
d'hôte meals (by reservation at lunchtime and
in the evenings) served on the patio or under
the pergola. Swimming pool with sun deck and
Jacuzzi.

Access : *5km from Aigues-Mortes, towards Arles*

SAINT-MAMERT-DU-GARD - 30730

28

LA MAZADE
Mme Couston

Rue Mazade
30730 Saint-Mamert-du-Gard
Tel. 04 66 81 17 56
www.bbfrance.com/couston.html

Open all year • 3 rooms with bathrooms • €55 to
€60, breakfast included • Table d'hôte €25 (by
reservation) • Garden, car park. Credit cards
not accepted, no dogs admitted

 **Mrs Couston's highly personal approach
to interior decoration.**

This beautiful country mas, set in the heart of
a sleepy village, reveals the talents of its
owner's flair for interior decoration. An almost
staggering collection of antique and contemporary furniture, rugs and modern and folk art
blends surprisingly well in the plant-filled
rooms: the result is truly unique. All the rooms
overlook the garden and arbour, where dinner
is served in the long summer evenings.

Access : *17km westbound from Nîmes on the
D 999 and then the D 1*

SAINT-VICTOR-DE-MALCAP - 30500

SAINT-QUENTIN-LA-POTERIE - 30700

LE MAS DU CAROUBIER
Mme Charpentier

684 route de Vallabrix
30700 Saint-Quentin-la-Poterie
Tel. 04 66 22 12 72
contact@mas-caroubier.com
www.mas-caroubier.com

Closed in Dec • 4 rooms and 1 gîte with bath/shower and WC • €70 to €90, breakfast included • No table d'hôte • Garden. Credit cards not accepted, no dogs admitted • Outdoor swimming pool

LA BASTIDE DES SENTEURS
M. Subileau

30500 Saint-Victor-de-Malcap
Tel. 04 66 60 24 45
subileau@bastide-senteurs.com
www.bastide-senteurs.com
Languages : Eng.

Open from Mar to Oct • 14 rooms, one of which has disabled access, all have bath/WC and television • €65 to €140 (€65 to €120 low season) ; breakfast €10; half-board available • Menus €35 to €75 • Private car park, terrace • Swimming pool

Choosing which local wine to drink with the chef's cuisine.

This 19C stronghold is built against the walls of a delightful village dominated by the shadow of a medieval castle. The fully renovated abode offers pleasant, colourful rooms decked out in antique and wrought iron furniture. Some enjoy a fine view of the Cèze Valley and all are equally tranquil. Gourmets will love sitting down in the stylish Southern-flavoured dining room or on the terrace opening onto the over-flow swimming pool.

Initiation and discovery of wine

Access : *In the village*

Relaxing in the peace and quiet.

The ochre walls and green shutters of this 18C mas suddenly greet you at the end of a country lane. Inside, the guests' welfare is clearly the only thing that counts, from the gracious wel-come and rooms filled with old furniture to the delicious homemade jams at breakfast time. Outside, the turquoise water of the swimming pool and quiet garden encourage you to idle away long summer afternoons, unless of course you would prefer to do a pottery, painting or cookery course.

Cookery, painting and pottery courses.

Access : *5km to the north-east of Saint-Quentin-la-Poterie on the D 982 and then the D 5*

SOMMIÈRES - 30250

MAS FONTCLAIRE
Mme Labbé

8 rue Émile-Jamais
30250 Sommières
Tel. 04 66 77 78 69
http://masfontclare.free.fr
Languages : Eng.

Open all year • 3 rooms with shower/WC and television • €68 to €80, breakfast included • No table d'hôte • Garden, car park. Credit cards not accepted • Outdoor swimming pool

Speech may be silver, but silence is golden!

Imagine waking up to blue, cloudless skies and tucking into delicious home-made jams and freshly squeezed orange juice, served on the patio in the summer or by the fireside in winter. You only need to put one foot over the threshold of this former wine-grower's house to know you're in for a treat. The three rooms in the converted outbuildings are decorated in different styles: Provençal, modern and Louis XVI. The quality of the silence is such that you may even find yourself whispering!

Access : *In the village*

TAVEL - 30126

LE PONT DU ROY
M. Schorgeré

Route de Nîmes - D 976
30126 Tavel
Tel. 04 66 50 22 03
contact@hotelpontduroy.fr
www.hotelpontduroy.fr

Open from 6 Apr to 30 Sep • 14 air-conditioned rooms with bath/WC or shower/WC and television • €73 to €93 (€61 to €83 low season); breakfast €7.50; half-board available • Menus €26 to €47 (evenings only for hotel guests) • Terrace, garden, private car park • Outdoor swimming pool, petanque, play area

Never make the mistake of thinking that pétanque is "just a game"!

You can always dive into the swimming pool for a refreshing dip if things get too hot on the pétanque ground! Built in the style of a Provençal mas, this house was turned into a hotel in 1986. The pastel coloured rooms overlook either the shaded garden or the legendary vineyards of Tavel. A fresh country look prevails in the restaurant and in the summer tables are laid outside on the terrace. The self-taught owner-chef rustles up regional dishes depending on what he finds in the market.

Access : *3km to the south-east of Tavel, on the D 4 then the D 976 (Roquemaure-Remoulins road)*

GIGNAC - 34150

MAS CAMBOUNET
Mme Perret

34150 Gignac
Tel. 04 67 57 55 03
perretcambounet@wanadoo.fr
www.mas-cambounet.com
Languages : Eng.

Closed in Nov • 6 rooms with shower/WC • €64 to €70, breakfast €8 • Table d'hôte €15 (week-days) to €40 • Park, terrace, car park. No dogs admitted

VILLENEUVE-LÈS-AVIGNON - 30400

HÔTEL DE L'ATELIER
M. Burret

5 rue de la Foire
30400 Villeneuve-lès-Avignon
Tel. 04 90 25 01 84
hotel-latelier@libertysurf.fr
www.hoteldelatelier.com
Languages : Eng.

Closed in Jan • 23 rooms, all have bath/WC or shower/WC and television • €61 to €101 (€52 to €84 low season); breakfast €9 • No restaurant • Garden, garage • Exhibition of painting and sculpture, tea room

The view of Avignon from the patio and tiny terrace.

This 16C "workshop" in the heart of a pictur-esque town has just been creatively redesigned by a film set decorator. Tasteful ornaments, antique furniture, rush matting, elegant bath-rooms, exposed beams, fireplaces and a lovely staircase are combined in this masterful reno-vation which has retained the character of the abode's ancestral walls. Mediterranean-style breakfast room, exhibitions of painting and sculpture.

Basking in the peace among vineyards, olive groves and sweet gorse.

The owners of this splendid mas are also farm-ers, which explains the faultless quality of the table d'hôte menus in which home-grown pro-duce features prominently. To keep pace with the demand, they have even opened a table gourmande which functions like a restaurant. On the accommodation side, four rooms full of character and comfort are available, each with its own independent entrance. The "La Buège" room, in the former barn with mezzanine and fireplace, is an absolute must.

> *Cooking workshop weekend*

Access : *4km south-east from Gignac on the N 109, then a lane right*

Access : *In the old town*

JONQUIÈRES - 34725

35

CHÂTEAU DE JONQUIÈRES
M. et Mme De Cabissole

34725 Jonquières
Tel. 04 67 96 62 58
contact@chateau-jonquieres.com
www.chateau-jonquieres.com
Languages : Eng.

Open from Apr to Nov • 4 rooms with shower/WC
or bath/WC • €85 to €90, breakfast included
• No table d'hôte • Park, car park. Credit cards
not accepted, no dogs admitted • Outdoor
swimming pool

 Enjoying fine art and music over a glass of wine at festival time.

The origins of this splendid castle may still be
clouded in mystery, but it is evident that the
passing of time has done little to alter its
original appeal or style. The four chambres
d'hôte within command a peaceful view of the
park with its hundred-year-old box trees and
majestic bamboos. Tasting of the estate's
wines (of great repute) organised in the cellar.
A royal welcome awaits you in this site full of
history and character.

Access : *In the village*

LE CAYLAR - 34520

36

LE BARRY DU GRAND CHEMIN
M. et Mme Vandenbroucke

88 faubourg Saint-Martin
34520 Le Caylar
Tel. 04 67 44 50 19
lebarry34@aol.com
www.le-barry.fr
Languages : Eng., Du., Ger., Sp., Port.

Open all year • 5 rooms with shower/WC • €52 to
€55, breakfast included; half-board available
• Table d'hôte €23 to €26 • Car park. Credit
cards not accepted, dogs not admitted

 The secretive, silent countryside – the "causse" – surrounding this stone farmstead.

Built in 1850, the immaculate stone walls of
this house stand at the foot of the strange,
tormented Roc Castel in the heart of the
unspoilt Larzac limestone plateau. The ground
floor rooms are quiet and very well-maintained
if not vast. Tuck into the delicious chargrilled
fare cooked over an open fire in the delightful
vaulted dining room, which remains refreshingly cool in the height of summer.

Access : *In the village*

MONTPELLIER - 34090

PARC
Mme Jacquin

 8 rue Achille-Bège
34090 Montpellier
Tel. 04 67 41 16 49
hotelduparcmtp@wanadoo.fr
www.hotelduparc-montpellier.com
Languages : Eng., It.

Open all year • 19 rooms, most have shower/WC, some have bath/WC or shower without WC, all have air-conditioning and television • €49 to €78; breakfast €9.50 • No restaurant • Car park. Dogs not admitted

---

MONTAGNAC - 34530

MONSIEUR GENER
M. et Mme Gener

 34 avenue Pierre-Sirven
34530 Montagnac
Tel. 04 67 24 03 21
valexboyer@aol.com
 Languages : Eng.

Open all year • 4 rooms with shower/WC, all air-conditioned • €48, breakfast included • No table d'hôte • Terrace, garden, car park. Credit cards not accepted

---

 Pézenas and its wealth of craft stalls within easy reach.

In 1750, the buildings laid out around the well-sheltered, spacious inner courtyard belonged to the mounted constabulary. Nowadays, the stables have been converted into large, calm, well-appointed rooms, in some of which the old oak partitions between the loose-boxes can still be seen. In the summer, breakfast is served on a pleasant upstairs terrace.

Being treated like a regular.

Despite the fact that the park has been sold off, the noble walls of this 18C mansion are as smart as ever and the plush bourgeois rooms are being gradually and tastefully renovated. The regulars of this establishment, located in a quiet side street, appreciate its calm just two minutes away from the town centre and the nearest tram stop; they generally leave their cars in the private car park in the courtyard. In the summer, breakfast is sometimes served on the terrace.

Access : *Drive up Rue Proudhon (towards the zoo), and at the ECAT, take a left at Rue Turgot*

Access : *6.5km to the north-west of Pézenas on the N 9 then the N 113*

MOULÈS-ET-BAUCELS - 34190

39

DOMAINE DE BLANCARDY
Mme Laure Martial

34190 Moulès-et-Baucels
Tel. 04 67 73 94 94
blancardy@blancardy.com
www.blancardy.com
Languages : Eng., Sp.

Closed mid-Jan to early Mar • 12 rooms and 1 apartment, all with bath/WC and television • €50 to €80, breakfast included • Table d'hôte €13 to €48 • Park, car park. Dogs admitted in rooms by request

Taking this old fortified farmhouse by storm.

Set between vines and sweet-smelling gorse, this robust 12C country house is home to a generous welcoming inn. The rooms, laid out in the mas and its outhouses combine simplicity and luxury. However there is no doubt that the table d'hôte meals will leave the greatest impression. In a fine vaulted dining room you will be treated to specialities made from produce from the estate; duck takes pride of place (foies gras, confits, terrines and fillets), washed down by wines produced by the owner.

Access : *On the way out of the village, turn right towards Blancardy and l'Eglisette*

NISSAN-LEZ-ENSÉRUNE - 34440

40

LE PLÔ
M. et Mme Patry

7 avenue de la Gare
34440 Nissan-Lez-Ensérune
Tel. 04 67 37 38 21
patry.c@wanadoo.fr
www.bedbreakfast-nissan.com

Open from Apr to late Dec • 4 non-smoking rooms upstairs, all with bath/WC • €40 to €75, breakfast €7.50 • No table d'hôte • Terrace, garden, car park. Credit cards not accepted, dogs not admitted

The minimalist Zen ambience throughout the house.

This superb 18C abode of character in the heart of the village is bathed in light: white walls and windows everywhere that light up the immense rooms. Upstairs, the bedrooms are soberly decorated: simple modern furniture, lovely original tiled floors, black or grey marble fireplaces, colourful bedspreads. Two large apartments with loggia on the 2nd floor reached by a stone staircase. The buffet breakfast is served in the dining room overlooking the garden.

Access : *7km southwest from Béziers on the N9*

LA CANOURGUE - 48500

SAINT-ANDRÉ-DE-BUÈGES - 34190

MAS DE BOMBÉQUIOLS
M. et Mme Dann

Route de Brissac
34190 Saint-André-de-Buèges
Tel. 04 67 73 72 67
bombequiols@wanadoo.fr
http://masdebombequiols.free.fr

Open all year by reservation only • 6 rooms and 3 apartments, all with shower/WC or bath/WC • €90, breakfast included • Table d'hôte €30, drinks included • Park, car park. Credit cards not accepted, no dogs admitted • Outdoor swimming pool

 Enjoying the immense vista of the unhampered horizon.

Surrounded by an estate of over 70 ha, this country house dating from the 10C is home to a maze of staircases and inner courtyards that extend over some 800 square metres. Each bedroom possesses an individual and authentic charm with bare stone walls and warm wood fires. The table d'hôte meals, by reservation, are served in the splendid vaulted dining room. Outdoors there is a large swimming pool, and further on three ponds, all of which are a refreshing addition to the estate's peace and quiet.

Private concerts or opera singing course

Access : *2km north-east of St-André-de-Buèges on the D 1*

MME FAGES « CHEZ ANNE-MARIE »
M. et Mme Fages

La Vialette
48500 La Canourgue
Tel. 04 66 32 83 00
www.gite-sauveterre.com

Open all year • 5 rooms, all with shower/WC • €48, breakfast included • Table d'hôte €16 • Car park. Credit cards not accepted

 Enjoying the family atmosphere while retaining your independence.

This old 14C Causses farmhouse has been superbly restored with a mixture of old stone and comfortable modern fittings. The five rooms are delightfully decorated with crocheted lace. The vaulted ceilings and exposed beams lend the establishment a cosy country ambience. Generous table d'hôte meals are served in a dining room with wood furnishings.

Access : *9km south-east from La Canourgue on the D 998, then small road to the right*

LA GARDE-GUÉRIN - 48800

AUBERGE RÉGORDANE
M. Nogier

48800 La Garde-Guérin
Tel. 04 66 46 82 88
pierre.nogier@free.fr
www.regordane.com
Languages : Eng.

Closed from 15 Oct to 14 Apr • 15 rooms with bath/WC or shower/WC, some have television • €54 to €65; breakfast €8; half-board available • Menus €19 to €36 • Terrace in an inner courtyard

> **The head-spinning view of the gorges of Chassezac from the village.**

This fortified village was founded by the bishops of Mende along the old Roman road linking Auvergne with the Languedoc in an effort to eradicate highway robbery. An order of knights from La Garde Guérin were entrusted with the task of escorting voyagers. The stronghold of one of these knights is now a characterful inn with small rooms and mullioned windows, a restaurant with vaulted ceiling and a beautiful terrace-courtyard of granite flagstones.

Access : *In the heart of the village*

ARBOUSSOLS - 66320

LES FENÊTRES DU SOLEIL
M. et Mme Cholot-Deville

Rue de la Fontaine
66320 Arboussols
Tel. 04 68 05 56 25
lesfenetresdusoleil@wanadoo.fr

Open all year • 4 rooms with bath/WC • €72.50, breakfast included • No table d'hôte • Garden. Credit cards not accepted, no dogs admitted

> **Relaxing in the bath tub of the Grenat room and admiring Canigou.**

The entrance to this old but entirely restored village house is through a wooden gate and a flower-decked garden. The blocks of solid rock in the dining room are proof that the house was built into the hill face. The bright pleasant rooms have been beautifully finished with special attention to the bedding (electric slatted bed bases). Exhibitions of work by local artists.

Access : *In the village*

ELNE - 66200

CAN OLIBA
M. Boisard et Mme Le Corre

24 rue de la Paix
66200 Elne
Tel. 04 68 22 11 09
elna@club-internet.fr
www.can-oliba.com
Languages : Eng.

Open all year • 6 non-smoking rooms with bath/WC • €70, breakfast included • Table d'hôte €22 (by reservation and evenings only) • Garden. Credit cards not accepted, no dogs admitted • Swimming pool

 The owner's experience as interior decorator can be seen everywhere.

Visitors inevitably fall head over heels in love with this attractive 17C Catalan abode not far from the cathedral. A fine stone staircase and delightful sitting room strewn with antique furniture immediately set the tone and visitors cannot help but be spellbound. In the unusual rooms, the colours, furniture, curios and paintings vie with each other to incite guests to return and try them all... Don't miss the tiny walled garden complete with swimming pool. Irresistible!

Access : *In the historic centre of the town, near Sainte-Eulalie Cathedral*

LAS-ILLAS - 66480

HOSTAL DELS TRABUCAYRES
M. Davesne

66480 Las Illas
Tel. 04 68 83 07 56
Languages : Ger.

Closed from 6 Jan to 15 Mar, from 25 to 30 Oct, Tue and Wed out of season • 5 rooms upstairs, 3 of which have a terrace, with shower/WC • €30 to €34; breakfast €5.10; half-board available • Menus €12 to €45 • Terrace, car park. Dogs not admitted in the rooms • Hiking

 Long walks in the silent forest of cork oaks surrounding the hotel.

Don't give up! The winding hairpin bends of this tiny mountain road may seem endless but your efforts will be repaid tenfold. This tiny hamlet in the middle of nowhere is home to an old inn which provided accommodation to the exiled officers of Spain's Republican Army in 1936. Admire the view from the simple but pleasant rooms. The restaurant in a converted barn serves typically Catalan dishes.

Access : *Take the D 618 between Céret and Le Boulou; at Maureillas take the D 13 and drive south-west for 11km*

LATOUR-DE-CAROL - 66760

47

PERPIGNAN - 66100

48

AUBERGE CATALANE
Mme Ernst

10 avenue du Puymorens
66760 Latour-de-Carol
Tel. 04 68 04 80 66
auberge-catalane@club-internet.fr
www.auberge-catalane.fr
Languages : Eng., Sp.

Closed 15 to 23 Apr, 11 Nov to 26 Dec, Sun
evening and Mon except during school holidays
• 10 rooms with shower/WC and television • €52
(€48 low season); breakfast €6; half-board
available • Menus €14.90 to €32.40 • Terrace,
car park

 **Taking a ride on the little canary-yellow
train through the picturesque Cerdagne
region.**

This inn, built in 1929, returned to the family
when the original owner's grandchildren
bought it back a few years ago and today the
great-grandson, Benoît, presides over the
kitchens. The rooms have been renovated and
modernised, but the original Art Deco-inspired
furniture has been retained; some bedrooms
have balconies overlooking the village rooftops. Dining room-veranda.

Access : *On the main road of the village (N 20)
between Bourg-Madame and the Puymorens Pass*

DOMAINE DU MAS BOLUIX
M. et Mme Ceilles

chemin du Pou de les Colobres
66100 Perpignan
Tel. 04 68 08 17 70
www.domaine-de-boluix.com
Languages : Sp.

Open all year • 6 rooms with bath/WC • €82,
breakfast included • No table d'hôte • Terrace,
garden, car park. Credit cards not accepted,
dogs not admitted • Swimming pool and tennis
nearby

 **The secluded situation on the doorstep of
Perpignan.**

An easy-going atmosphere reigns throughout
this 18C mas set in the midst of Cabestany's
vineyards and orchards. Restored in 1998, the
interior is comfortable, roomy and spotlessly
clean. Each of the personalised rooms, whose
immaculate walls are hung with bright regional
fabrics, is named after a famous Catalan: Dali,
Rigaud, Maillol, Picasso, Casals. The sweeping
view over Roussillon, the coast and that
emblem of Catalonia, the mighty Canigou
mountain, is definitely worth a trip.

Access : *5km southbound from Perpignan
towards Argelès, then Cabestany, Midipole and
Mas Guivido*

PRUGNANES - 66220

DOMAINE DE COUSSÈRES
Joo et Ann Maes

66220 Prugnanes
Tel. 04 68 59 23 55
www.cousseres.com
Languages : Ger., Eng., Du.

Open from 15 Mar to 15 Oct • 6 rooms with shower/WC • €78, breakfast included • Table d'hôte €25 (evenings only) • Car park, park. Credit cards not accepted, no dogs admitted • Swimming pool

 Basking in the silence disturbed only by the twittering of birds.

The setting will take your breath away: perched on a hillock surrounded by vineyards, this superb fortified house dominates the impressive landscape of mountains and sweet-scented scrub. The spacious, tastefully and individually decorated rooms and the welcoming dining room and massive table within all live up to expectations. A lovely garden, swimming pool and maze of terraces around the house enhance the matchless calm and tranquillity of this spot.

Access : *5km to the north-west of Saint-Paul-de-Fenouillet on the D 117 and D 20*

THUIR - 66300

CASA DEL ARTE
Mme Toubert

Mas Petit
66300 Thuir
Tel. 04 68 53 44 78
casadelarte@wanadoo.fr
www.casadelarte.fr.fm
Languages : Eng., Sp.

Open all year • 6 rooms with shower/WC • €85 to €105, breakfast included • Meals €25 • Garden, car park • Outdoor swimming pool, sun deck

 The arty feel to the individually decorated rooms.

The owner-painter has converted this 11C and 14C mas into a real art gallery. The walls of the often well proportioned rooms and bathrooms are covered in colourful paintings; the one devoted to ancient Rome is particularly lovely. Works by local artists adorn the walls of the sitting room, whose centrepiece is a medieval fireplace. The sun deck overlooking the swimming pool, the hundred-year-old oaks in the park and the small bamboo grove invite guests to take life easy.

Access : *17km westbound from Perpignan, towards Thuir and Ille-sur-Têt*

TRESSERRE - 66300

LA MAJUCECAVE
Mme Valérie Bessou

Hameau des Nidoleres
66300 Tresserre
Tel. 04 68 83 92 57
lamajucecave@tiscali.fr
http://lamajucecave.chez.tiscali.fr
Languages : Eng.

Open from Easter to Oct • 5 rooms, all with shower/WC • €65, breakfast included • No table d'hôte • Park. Credit cards not accepted, no dogs admitted • Outdoor swimming pool

The charm of the rooms and the beauty of the site are breathtaking.

Given the winegrowing context, it is understandable that the rooms of this former wine cellar bear the names of the different vines grown in the region. All display a tasteful mixture of old and modern and those overlooking the swimming pool are particularly delightful. The largest, "Carignan" is big enough for an entire family. Homemade pastries, cakes and jams feature prominently on the breakfast table, served on the terrace or in the lovely dining room.

Access : *4km north-east of Boulou on the N 9, then a lane to the left*

VALCEBOLLÈRE - 66340

AUBERGE LES ÉCUREUILS
M. et Mme Laffitte

66340 Valcebollère
Tel. 04 68 04 52 03
auberge-ecureuils@wanadoo.fr
www.aubergeecureuils.com
Languages : Eng., Ger.

Closed from 5 to 20 May and 3 Nov to 4 Dec • 15 rooms with bath/WC, some have television • €70 to €95; breakfast €9 to €11; half-board available • Menus €20 (weekdays) to €50 • Terrace, fitness room • Indoor swimming pool, balneo, hammam, cross-country skiing, snowshoe trekking

Whether it be smuggler's footpaths or secluded fishing spots, the owner is a treasure-trove of tips.

Only twenty-or-so souls still live in this half-abandoned village, perched at an altitude of 1 500m on a dead-end road in the remote Pyrenees. Should you decide to join them for a day or so, you won't regret it! The genuine warmth and solicitude of the owners of this former 18C sheep-fold, full of character, are quite captivating. Comfortable rooms, with bathrooms done out in Spanish marble, and an elegant rustic dining room complete the picture.

Ethological approach to horses, Alpine and cross-country skiing

Access : *9km to the south-east of Bourg-Madame on the D 70, then the D 30*

Corrèze - 19
Creuse - 23
Haute-Vienne - 87

Life in Limousin is lived as it should be: tired Parisians in need of greenery flock here to taste the simple joys of country life, breathe in the bracing air of its high plateaux, stroll along the banks of rivers alive with fish and wander through its woodlands in search of mushrooms and chestnuts. The sight of peaceful cattle grazing in utter contentment or lambs frolicking in the meadows in spring is enough to rejuvenate even the most jaded city-dweller. By late October, the forests are swathed in a cloak of autumn colours and the ground becomes a soft carpet of russet leaves. A perfect backdrop to the granite walls and soft sandstone façades of sleepy hamlets and peaceful cities, where ancestral crafts, such as Limoges porcelain and Aubusson tapestries, combine a love of tradition with a whole-hearted desire to embrace the best in contemporary art. The food is as wholesome as the region: savoury bacon soup, steaming Limousin stew and, as any proud local will tell you, the most tender, succulent beef in the world.

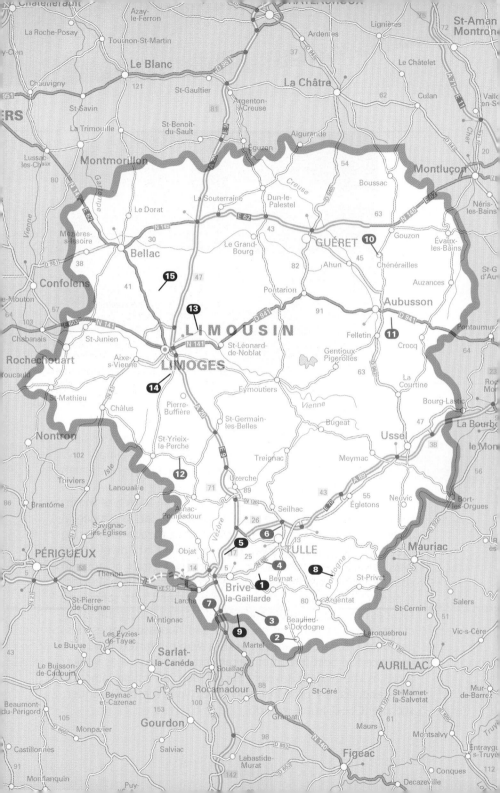

AUBAZINE - 19190

LA TOUR
M. Lachaud

Place de l'Église
19190 Aubazine
Tel. 05 55 25 71 17
Languages : Eng., Sp.

Closed 8 to 29 Jan • 18 rooms with bath/WC or shower/WC and television • €48 to €50; breakfast €7; half-board available • Menus €18 (weekdays) to €38

We most liked | Amble alongside the pretty Canal des Moines dug in the 12C.

On the village square, opposite the Cistercian Abbey stand two characterful houses, the older one flanked by the tower from which the hotel takes its name. Bright wallpaper livens up the bedrooms, while the main dining room and smaller rooms for families or business lunches feature a rustic flavour in keeping with the array of regional delicacies on the menu. Apéritifs and after-dinner coffee are served on the terrace.

Access : *On the main square in the village, opposite the abbey*

BEAULIEU-SUR-DORDOGNE - 19120

LA MAISON
M. Henriet

11 rue de la Gendarmerie
19120 Beaulieu-sur-Dordogne
Tel. 05 55 91 24 97
lamaison19@wanadoo.fr
http://lamaison19.chez-alice.fr

Closed from Oct to Mar • 6 rooms, 4 overlooking a patio, all have bath/WC • €57 to €68, breakfast included • No table d'hôte • Credit cards not accepted, no dogs admitted • Terraced garden, outdoor swimming pool

We most liked | More hacienda than country farmhouse.

The arcades, ruddy ochre walls and profusion of hydrangeas, rose bushes and lemon trees in the patio are more reminiscent of an exotic hacienda than a French country farmhouse: all becomes clear when you learn that this astonishing 19C house was built by one of Napoelon's generals, homesick for Mexico. The adorable, unusually named rooms – "The Bride", "The Indians", "The Caricatures" - are quite unique; two overlook the sumptuous hanging garden and swimming pool.

Access : *In the village*

CORNIL - 19150

COLLONGES-LA-ROUGE - 19500

JEANNE MAISON D'HÔTES
M. Monteil

Le Bourg
19500 Collonges-la-Rouge
Tel. 05 55 25 42 31
info@jeannemaisondhotes.com
www.jeannemaisondhotes.com

Open all year • 5 non-smoking rooms with bath/WC • €80, breakfast included • Table d'hôte €32 drinks included • Terrace, garden, car park. Dogs not admitted

LA LUPRONNE
Mme Lesieur

Le Mons
19150 Cornil
Tel. 05 55 27 26 47
lalupronne@free.fr
http://lalupronne.free.fr
Languages : Eng.

Open all year • 3 non-smoking rooms and 2 apartments upstairs, all with bath/WC or shower/WC • €55 to €67, breakfast included • Table d'hôte €19 to €21 including drinks • Garden, car park, board games. Credit cards not accepted, dogs not admitted • Table tennis, table football, children's games in the garden

 The "Cheminée" room, named after the splendid fireplace and bench it contains.

This handsome red sandstone house, built in the 15C-17C nestles in the heart of one of the most beautiful villages of France. To reach the house, you go through a small interior garden hidden behind a high wall and an old door. A tower leads up to the five guest rooms. Rustic-style decoration with stone, beams, handsome antique furniture: each of the individually decorated rooms is equally inviting. At mealtimes, enjoy the set menu in the company of the owners who are friendly and welcoming.

 The "lupronne" is said to be the partner of the imp.

This family home, dating from the Napoleonic era, was first designed to allow the residents to live totally autonomously. All the original facilities (well, chestnut drying device, etc.) still exist and what's more, still work. On request, the owners will light the wood oven to add to the authentic character of the dining room where tasty local dishes are served. Upstairs, the bright rooms are adorned with antique furniture and superb wooden floors, combining comfort and immaculate home keeping.

Access : *On the A 20, N°52 Noailles/Collonges-la-Rouge exit. Sign-posted in the village*

Access : *8km along the N89 towards Tulle, leave at Cornil. In Cornil follow the chambres d'hôte signposts*

DONZENAC - 19270

LE RELAIS DU BAS LIMOUSIN
M. et Mme Delavier

Sadroc
19270 Donzenac
Tel. 05 55 84 52 06
relais-du-bas-limousin@wanadoo.fr
www.relaisbaslimousin.fr
Languages : Eng.

Closed during Feb and Nov school holidays • 22 rooms with bath/WC or shower/WC and television • €43 to €76; breakfast €7; half-board available • Restaurant closed Sun evening except Jul-Aug and Mon lunchtime; menus €16 (weekdays) to €48 • Terrace, garden, garage, car park • Outdoor swimming pool

A visit to the disused slate quarries – if you're not afraid of heights!

This solid construction inspired by regional styles dates from the 1960s and was clearly built to last a few centuries. The stylish personalised rooms have matching fabrics, bedspreads and lampshades and those facing the rear look out over a peaceful Limousin landscape. Welcoming family dining rooms, a veranda flooded with light and a terrace opening onto the garden complete with swimming pool and play area.

Access : *6km on the D 920 towards Uzerche*

NAVES - 19460

CHEZ M. ET MME PERROT
M. et Mme Perrot

Gourdinot
19460 Naves
Tel. 05 55 27 08 93
brunhild.perrot@wanadoo.fr
www.hotes-naves-correze.com
Languages : Eng.

Open all year • 3 rooms upstairs, one of which has a loggia, with shower/WC • €38 to €41, breakfast included; half-board available • Table d'hôte €15 • Car park. Credit cards not accepted, dogs not admitted

The sense of being right in the middle of nowhere.

This old Corrèze farmhouse built out of rough-hewn stone and nestling in a wooded valley is ideal for touring the region: Millevaches – literally "Thousand cows" plateau, Lake Seilhac and Uzerche. Soak up the peaceful atmosphere of the cosy bedrooms and relax by the fireside in the company of your lively young hosts. In the morning, you will awake to the enticing smell of fresh-baked bread, steaming coffee and a breakfast table piled high with a profusion of home-made gingerbreads and preserves.

Access : *5km northbound from Naves on the N 20, then take a minor road*

NESPOULS - 19600

À LA TABLE DE LA BERGÈRE
Mme Verlhac

Belveyre
19600 Nespouls
Tel. 05 55 85 82 58

Open all year • 5 rooms with bathrooms • €40, breakfast included; half-board available • No table d'hôte • Garden, car park. Credit cards not accepted, no dogs admitted

 If this farm wins any more awards, it may well run out of space to display them.

This sturdily built farmstead in the midst of oaks, meadows and dry stone huts is very well placed to explore the region's wealth of tourist sights. The rooms, furnished with family heirlooms, are very inviting, particularly those on the second floor, while the flavourful regional cooking, friendly atmosphere and Madame's ability to make you feel at home are unparalleled.

Access : *Nespouls exit no 53, at the roundabout, turn right, then 1st right and 1st left*

SAINT-MARTIN-LA-MÉANNE - 19320

LES VOYAGEURS
M. et Mme Chaumeil

Place de la Mairie
19320 Saint-Martin-la-Méanne
Tel. 05 55 29 11 53
info@hotellesvoyageurs.com
www.hotellesvoyageurs.com
Languages : Eng.

Open mid-Mar to mid-Nov; closed Sun evening and Mon out of season • 8 rooms upstairs with bath/WC or shower/WC, some have television • €43 to €53; breakfast €6; half-board available • Menus €16 to €35 • Terrace, garden, car park • Private pond for anglers

 The lady of the house's warm greeting.

This establishment, which has been run by the same family for five generations, is ideal to get away from it all and take things easy. Within its solid stone walls, built in 1853, you'll find simple, but well cared-for bedrooms. Admire the wood carving in the rustic dining room, if you can tear yourself away from the traditional cuisine prepared by the chef-owner for a minute. After lunch or dinner, venture out into the garden as far as the pond and watch the carp and pike.

Access : *On a square in the centre of the village*

TURENNE - 19500

LA MAISON DES CHANOINES
M. et Mme Cheyroux

Chemin de l'Église
19500 Turenne
Tel. 05 55 85 93 43
www.maison-des-chanoines.com

Open from Easter to mid-Oct • 6 rooms located in 2 buildings, with bath/WC or shower/WC • €70 to €90; breakfast €9; half-board available • Menus €30 to €40 (evenings only by reservation) • Terrace. Dogs not admitted in rooms

The terrace overlooking a manicured herb garden.

It is well worth venturing past the late-Gothic door and into this lovely 16C house set in the heart of a picturesque village. There is as much character inside as out from the vaulted dining room, fireplace to the spiral staircase up to the rooms, which are furnished with the results of forays to local antiques dealers. At mealtimes, roll up your sleeves and dig into the chef's creative recipes prepared with the best local produce (including Périgord truffles). Limited seating only.

Access : *In the centre of the village*

CHÉNÉRAILLES - 23130

LA MAISON BLEUE
M. Grazielle

Au hameau Montignat
23130 Chénérailles
Tel. 05 55 81 88 80
lamaisonbleue2002@yahoo.fr
www.la-maison-bleue-en-creuse.com

Open all year • 3 non-smoking rooms, all with bath/WC • €65 to €70, breakfast included • Table d'hôte €21 including drinks • Garden, terrace, car park. Credit cards not accepted

The memory of this little piece of paradise will linger on for many a year.

It is difficult not to be won over by this lovingly restored old stone farmhouse. The television-sitting room is located in the barn complete with rustic floorboards. The rooms, an invitation to escape to distant lands, are decorated with objects from all over the world, from the aptly named "Indian" room upstairs, to the "Pearl" in a small outhouse. In summertime, breakfast is served on the terrace. The delicious table d'hôte meals are full of the flavour of local produce.

Access : *At the end of the hamlet of Montignat*

COUSSAC-BONNEVAL - 87500

SAINT-PARDOUX-LE-NEUF- 23200

CHAMBRE D'HÔTE M. DUMONTANT
M. et Mme Dumontant

 Les Vergnes
23200 Saint-Pardoux-le-Neuf
Tel. 05 55 66 23 74
sylvie.dumontant@freesbee.fr
www.lesvergnes.com

Closed from late Sep to early May • 6 rooms with bathrooms and separate WC • €57, breakfast included • Table d'hôte €16 to €25 • Terrace, car park. Credit cards not accepted • Fishing

 Fishing in the nearby pond.

If in desperate need of a break from city life, your prayers will be answered in this 18C farmhouse, set in the heart of the countryside and surrounded by a prosperous working farm, only 7km from the tapestry capital of France. All the spacious, fully renovated rooms overlook the pond and nearby woodland. Original exposed stone walls and a huge fireplace add character to the dining room.

Access : *7km eastbound from Aubusson on the N 141*

LE MOULIN DE MARSAGUET
M. Gizardin

 87500 Coussac-Bonneval
Tel. 05 55 75 28 29
gizardin.renaud@akeonet.com
www.tourismorama-moulindemarsaguet.com
Languages : Eng.

Closed from late Sep to mid-Apr • 3 rooms with shower/WC • €45, breakfast included • Table d'hôte €20 • Garden, terrace, car park. Credit cards not accepted, dogs admitted by request • Cookery courses. Fishing, boating and swimming

 Finding out how tasty farm delicacies are made.

The hospitality of this farming family will make you want to return to their rambling 18C farmstead and its immense 30-acre fishpond. Anglers will love catching pike while the others can go swimming or boating. The light, airy rooms are simply decorated and every evening brings an excellent opportunity to wine and dine on the succulent home-made delicacies in lively company.

Access : *3.6km northbound from Coussac on the D 17 towards La Roche-l'Abeille, then take the D 57*

SAINT-PRIEST-TAURION - 87480

LE RELAIS DU TAURION
M. Roger

2 chemin des Contamines
87480 Saint-Priest-Taurion
Tel. 05 55 39 70 14
Languages : Eng.

Closed from 15 Dec to 15 Jan • 8 rooms with bath/WC or shower/WC, almost all have television • €50 to €72; breakfast €9 • Restaurant closed Sun evening and Mon; menus €20 (weekdays) to €35 • Terrace, garden, car park. No dogs admitted • Swimming, fishing, canoeing nearby

 The delightful owners.

This grand hundred-year-old mansion covered in Virginia creeper is home to immaculate little rooms, some of which have old marble fireplaces. Old beams and rustic furniture add charm to the sitting room. In the fine weather, tables are laid amid the luxuriant foliage of the flowered garden. Traditional cuisine.

Access : *11km to the north-east of Limoges on the D 29*

SOLIGNAC - 87110

SAINT-ÉLOI
Mme Ashton

66 avenue Saint-Éloi
87110 Solignac
Tel. 05 55 00 44 52
lesaint.eloi@wanadoo.fr
www.lesainteloi.eu

Closed 3 weeks in Jan, 1 week in Jun, fortnight in Sep, Mon, Sat lunchtime and Sun evening • 15 rooms with bath/WC and television, one room has disabled access • €50 to €75; breakfast €9; half-board available • Menus €21 (weekdays) to €45 • Terrace. No dogs admitted • Tea room with painting and sculpture exhibitions

 The blessed union of medieval and modern.

Opposite the abbey founded by St Éloi, this half-timbered house in local stone welcomes guests in a spirit of peace and quiet. Spacious, well-soundproofed rooms are adorned with bright sunny fabrics and paintings. From his stained-glass window, good King Dagobert's treasurer, the patron saint of goldsmiths, gazes benignly down on diners as they savour the owner's flavourful cooking in a 12C dining room complete with granite fireplace.

Access : *10km southbound from Limoges on the D 704 (towards St-Yrieix), then right on the D 32*

THOURON - 87140

15

LA POMME DE PIN
M. Mounier

Étang de Tricherie
87140 Thouron
Tel. 05 55 53 43 43

Closed 20 Jan to 12 Feb and 1 to 25 Sep • 7 rooms with bath/WC and television • €59 to €69; breakfast €7; half-board available • Menus €28 to €42 • Terrace, garden. No dogs admitted in rooms

 Feast your eyes on a landscape of ponds, lakes and forest.

All the quiet, spacious rooms in the former spinning mill enjoy a view of the river, while the old mill on the banks of the millpond houses three dining rooms. The first offers an authentically rustic setting with rough stonewalls and a huge fireplace where meat is roasted; another is airier and overlooks the wonderful Limousin countryside. The sound of running water accompanies the meals served on the pleasant terrace.

Access : *Northbound from Limoges on the A 20, take exit no 26, then take the D 5 towards Nantiat*

If you are planning a trip to Lorraine and want to do justice to the region's wealth of wonderful sights, make sure you pack your walking boots. However, before you set off for the distant reaches of its lofty slopes, pause for a moment in Nancy and take in its splendid artistic heritage, without forgetting to admire the lights of Metz. You can then move on through a string of tiny spa resorts, renowned for the slimming properties of their water, and the famous centres of craftsmanship which produce the legendary Baccarat crystal, enamels of Longwy and porcelain of Lunéville, before you reach the poignant silence of the dormant mines and quarries at Domrémy and Colombey. The deep lakes, thick forests and wild animals of the Vosges Regional Park will keep you entranced as you make your way down through the gentle hillsides, dotted with plum-laden orchards. Stop for a little 'light' refreshment in a *marcairerie*, one of the region's old farm-inns, and sample the famous quiches and tarts, before finishing with a slab of pungent Munster cheese or a kirsch-flavoured dessert for the sweet-toothed among us.

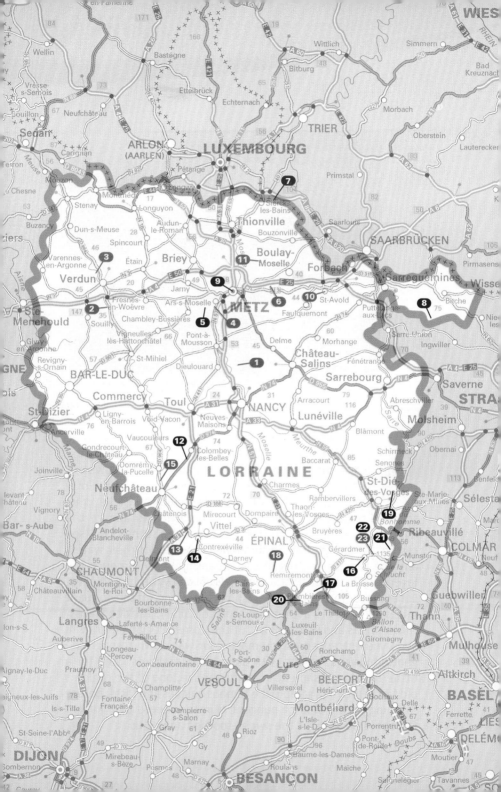

BELLEAU - 54610

ANCEMONT - 55320

CHÂTEAU DE MOREY
M. et Mme Karst

D 44A
54610 Belleau
Tel. 03 83 31 50 98
chateaudemorey@wanadoo.fr
www.chateaudemorey.com

Open all year • 5 non-smoking rooms, all with bathrooms • €65, breakfast included • Table d'hôte €25 including drinks • Garden, car park. Dogs not admitted • Fitness facilities, indoor swimming pool

 The panoramic view of the valley is matchless.

In the heart of the countryside, this magnificent 16C chateau is surrounded by a huge park planted with century-old trees. Well restored after a fire, it is home to four spacious rooms with bare stonewalls and modern comforts including a small lounge area and TV. Guests can make use of a kitchen, games room, library, stabling for horses, indoor swimming pool and mountain bikes. Everything you could wish for in an unspoilt site. Table d'hôte meals by reservation.

Access : *Southeast of Pont-à-Mousson on the D 57 and D 10*

CHÂTEAU DE LABESSIÈRE
M. Eichenauer

9 rue du Four
55320 Ancemont
Tel. 03 29 85 70 21
rene.eichenauer@wanadoo.fr
www.labessiere.com
Languages : Eng., Ger.

Open all year except Christmas holidays • 4 rooms with shower/WC • €74, breakfast included; half-board available • Table d'hôte €28 (including drinks) • Garden, car park. Credit cards not accepted, dogs welcome by request • Indoor swimming pool

 A mite outdated but full of charm.

Midway between Argonne and the Côtes de Meuse, this unassuming 18C castle makes an ideal base camp to explore the region. Pastel wallpaper, canopied beds and old furniture all add to rather than detract from the rooms' appeal. The same pleasantly outmoded atmosphere prevails in the sitting room, remarkably well stocked with guides, brochures and works on the Meuse. The table d'hôte, shaded garden and attractive outdoor swimming pool further enhance the establishment's allure.

> *Visit to battle fields of Argonne with maps, CD and audio-guide*

Access : *15km southbound from Verdun on the D 34 (Saint-Mihiel road)*

CHARNY-SUR-MEUSE - 55100

LES CHARMILLES
Mme Valérie Godard

12 rue de la Gare
55100 Charny-sur-Meuse
Tel. 03 29 86 93 49
valerie@les-charmilles.com

Closed from 10 to 26 Feb • 3 rooms with bathrooms • €55, breakfast included • Table d'hôte €20 including drinks

Relaxing in the garden.

First a café, then a hotel, this early 20C house is now home to attractive rooms with a tasteful blend of old and modern. Those on the second floor are bright, spacious and well equipped. Seasonal, local produce features prominently on the table d'hôte menu served on the lovely veranda overlooking a lush green garden (reservations only), which is also where breakfast is served. A sitting room with a library and board games is available for use by guests.

Access : *8km northbound from Charny-sur-Meuse on the D 38*

ANCY-SUR-MOSELLE - 57130

HAUMALET
M. et Mme Haumalet

2 rue des Quarrés
57130 Ancy-sur-Moselle
Tel. 03 87 30 91 54
haumalet@wanadoo.fr

Open all year • 3 non-smoking rooms upstairs, with bathrooms and television • €50 to €55, breakfast included • No table d'hôte • Garden, car park. Dogs not admitted

The gracious welcome of the owners for whom nothing is too much trouble!

In a little wine-growing village, this old house, formerly the property of the Prince Bishop of Metz, is home to spacious, fully independent rooms. The individualised decoration combines modern touches and lovely old well-polished furniture. Sitting room-library upstairs. Small garden and terrace. Visits and wine-tasting of Ancy wine organised.

Access : *13km southeast of Metz on the N57 and D6*

GORZE - 57680

HOSTELLERIE DU LION D'OR
M. Erman

105 rue du Commerce
57680 Gorze
Tel. 03 87 52 00 90
Languages : Ger.

Closed Sun evening and Mon • 15 rooms located in 2 buildings, with bath/WC or shower/WC, all have television • €55 to €60; breakfast €8; half-board available • Menus €28 to €40 • Terrace, garden, car park • Children's play area

 The dense foliage shading the terrace.

Run by the same family for over fifty years, this 19C coaching inn has moved with the times without losing sight of its roots. The rooms have been gradually updated and we recommend those opening onto the lovely patio with a trout aquarium and splendid rafters. Back in the restaurant, a huge stone fireplace, fine enough to grace any castle banquet hall, holds its own among the distinctly contemporary-style furniture.

Access : *To the south-west of Metz, on the D 6*

LANDONVILLERS - 57530

LE MOULIN
M. et Mme Weber

Allée du Moulin
57530 Landonvillers
Tel. 03 87 64 24 81
weber.c2@wanadoo.fr
www.studio-synchro.fr/weber

Open all year • 4 non-smoking rooms with bathrooms • €53 to €63, breakfast included • Table d'hôte €20 including drinks • Park, car park. Dogs not admitted

 The unspoilt environment, perfect to observe birds and wild flowers.

Guests are treated to a friendly welcome in this impressive mill-cum-manor house, tucked away in 4ha of parkland. Unusual bedrooms where rustic and modern are combined to create a pleasant country ambience. The nature theme pervades the overall design from exposed beams and wooden floors to dried flowers. Breakfast is served in a room which doubles as a leisure and reading room (well stocked in books) where guests can relax to the background murmur of the nearby river.

Access : *3km northwest of Courcelles-Chaussy on the D71*

MANDEREN - 57480

AU RELAIS DU CHÂTEAU DE MENSBERG
M. Schneider

15 rue du Château
57480 Manderen
Tel. 03 82 83 73 16

aurelaismensberg@aol.com
www.relais-mensberg.com

Closed 1 to 26 Jan • 13 rooms, one of which has disabled access, almost all have shower/WC (2 have bath/WC), all have television • €50 to €60 (€37.50 to €45 low season); breakfast €7.50; half-board available • Restaurant closed Mon from 27 Jan to 31 Mar and Tue; menus €18 to €46 • Terrace, garden, car park

 The castle forms a handsome backdrop to a wide variety of performances.

"Malbrouck" was the name the French soldiers gave to one of their most redoutable enemies, the Duke of Marlborough. The duke set up his HQ here at Mensberg (also called Marlborough) Castle in 1705 but was unable to do battle, giving rise to a nursery rhyme still sung today. Three rooms overlook the beautifully restored castle. In addition to a rustic dining room graced by a huge stone fireplace, the inn has two split-level sitting rooms and a quiet terrace in the rear.

Access : *From Sierck-les-Bains take the N 153 northbound for 2km, then at Apach turn right on the D 64*

MEISENTHAL - 57960

AUBERGE DES MÉSANGES
M. et Mme Walter

2 rue du Tiseur
57960 Meisenthal
Tel. 03 87 96 92 28

hotel-restaurant.auberge-mesanges@wanadoo.fr
www.aubergedesmesanges.com
Languages : Eng., Ger.

Closed from 10 to 26 Feb and from 24 Dec to 2 Jan • 20 rooms with shower/WC, half of the rooms have television • €45 to €51 (€39 to €44 low season); breakfast €6; half-board available • Restaurant closed Sun evening and Mon; menus €9.50 (weekdays) to €17 • Terrace, car park

 Need to get back in touch with the things that really matter?

This inn, on the edge of the Nature Reserve of the Northern Vosges, is ideally located in calm surroundings and close to a whole range of leisure pursuits, including walking, golf, museums and castles. Good-sized, practically-equipped rooms in excellent order. Meals are served in a dining room whose uncluttered rustic style perfectly complements the simple, regional fare.

Access : *Near the centre of the village*

METZ - 57000

SAINT-AVOLD - 57500

LA CATHÉDRALE
M. Hocine

25 place de la Chambre
57000 Metz
Tel. 03 87 75 00 02
hotelcathedrale-metz@wanadoo.fr
www.hotelcathedrale-metz.fr
Languages : Eng., Ger., It.

Open all year • 30 rooms and 1 apartment on 3 floors, most have bath/WC, some have shower/WC, all have television • €68 to €95; breakfast €11 • No restaurant

DOMAINE DU MOULIN
M. Muller

13 rue de la Vallée
57500 Saint-Avold
Tel. 03 87 92 55 15
gitesdefrance@fr.st

Open all year • 5 rooms with bath/WC, modem access • €70, breakfast included • No table d'hôte • Sitting room, garden, car park. No dogs admitted • Fitness room

 The splendid view of St Étienne Cathedral from most of the rooms.

The passing of time seems to have left no traces on the fine façade of this former coaching inn, which first opened its doors in 1627. Inside, however, the owners have really gone to town: individually styled rooms are adorned with wrought-iron furniture, bright fabrics or old pieces of furniture picked up in auctions and antique shops. The timber frames, fireplaces and parquet all bear witness to the establishment's four-hundred-year commitment to hostelry.

 The friendly welcome and hospitality.

This old mill was formerly part of the estate of the abbey of Longeville. Rebuilt with care using lovely old materials, it has retained all its character and now houses five pretty rooms, furnished with country pieces, new bedding and fully equipped bathrooms. Generous breakfasts that vary with the seasons are served in a pleasant living room. Garden and shaded terrace. Honey is produced on the estate.

Access : *In the town centre, near Saint-Étienne Cathedral*

Access : *2km westbound from Saint-Avold on the N 3 then the D 103p*

SAINT-HUBERT - 57640

LA FERME DE GODCHURE
M. Flahaut

57640 Saint-Hubert
Tel. 03 87 77 03 96
dominiqueflahaut@aol.com
www.lafermedegodchure.fr

Open all year • 4 non-smoking rooms, all with shower/WC or bath/WC • €65 to €82, breakfast included • No table d'hôte • Car park, garden. No dogs admitted

LE RELAIS ROSE
M. Loëffler

24 rue de Neufchâteau
88300 Autreville
Tel. 03 83 52 04 98
catherine.loeffler@wanadoo.fr

 Languages : Eng., Ger.

Open all year • 16 rooms located in 3 buildings, most have bath/WC or shower/WC, all have television, some are non-smoking • €48 to €80; breakfast €8.50; half-board available • Menus €20 to €30 • Terrace, garden, garage, car park

 The whole family bends over backwards to please its guests.

A prayer-stool, a handsome wardrobe, a well-worn leather armchair, an unusual patchwork of wallpapers from every age and era, some adorned with wonderfully garish flowers: the list is endless and the result a higgledy-piggledy mixture which proudly refuses to toe the line to any theme or age, and will strike a chord with your secret nonconformist side! For all their casually eclectic style, the renovated rooms are most appealing and the restaurant tables are laid with elegant china from Limoges.

 Nothing is too much trouble to make guests feel at home.

Right out in the countryside, this listed farm building in a flower-decked courtyard of a former Cistercian farmstead is now home to a gîte. The old barn has been turned into a guesthouse with brand new comfortable rooms equipped with splendid modern bathrooms. Each of the rooms is personalised with names such as Orchidée, Okoumé, Opaline, but if you fancy a four-poster bed, ask for Olympe.

Access : *In the village, on the N 74 between Colombey-les-Belles and Neufchâteau*

Access : *12km eastbound from Metz on the D 3, towards Bouzonville, then the D 57 and the D 52*

BULGNÉVILLE - 88140

13

CHAMBRES D'HÔTES M. BRETON
M. Breton

74 rue des Récollets
88140 Bulgnéville
Tel. 03 29 09 21 72
benoit.breton@wanadoo.fr
Languages : Eng., Ger.

Open all year, in winter by reservation only
• 4 rooms with shower/WC • €68, breakfast
included • No table d'hôte • Garden, car park.
Credit cards not accepted

A faultlessly decorated country home.

This unostentatious country house dating from
1720 was entirely redecorated by the owner-
antique dealer. The result invites the admiration of everyone who sees it: spacious, comfortable rooms decorated with a tasteful blend
of period furniture and modern décor. The
sandstone bathrooms are particularly lovely
and the garden behind the house is also worthy
of note.

Access : *7.5km westbound from Contrexéville
on the D 164*

CONTREXÉVILLE - 88140

14

LA SOUVERAINE
M. Paris

Parc Thermal
88140 Contrexéville
Tel. 03 29 08 09 59
contact@hotel-souveraine.com
www.hotel-souveraine.com

Closed 24 Sep to early Apr • 31 rooms, half
overlook the park, all have bath/WC or
shower/WC and television • €85; breakfast €9;
half-board available • Menus €26 to €34 • Car
park. No dogs admitted in restaurant

**The branches laden with crows do have a
slightly Hitchcockian air to them.**

Contrexéville was "the" place to take the
waters at the height of the Belle Époque. The
glass awning and friezes which embellish the
graceful pink and white façade of this elegant
home, leave one in no doubt about its allegiance to a former illustrious guest, the Grand
Duchess Vladimir, aunt of Czar Nicholas II.
Marble fireplaces, moulded ceilings and brass
beds continue to grace the recently renovated
bedrooms, some of which overlook the resort
park.

Access : *In the spa resort*

GÉRARDMER - 88400

COUSSEY - 88630

LE CHALET DU LAC
M. Bernier

97 chemin de la Droite du Lac
88400 Gérardmer
Tel. 03 29 63 38 76
Languages : Eng., Ger.

Closed from 1 to 31 Oct • 11 rooms, 4 of which are in a separate chalet, with shower/WC and television • €59; breakfast €9; half-board available • Menus €21 to €42 • Garden, car park • Table-tennis

LA DEMEURE DU GARDIEN DU TEMPS QUI PASSE
M. et Mme Ramsamy

47 Grand'Rue
88630 Coussey
Tel. 03 29 06 99 83
ch.hotescoussey88@easyconnect.fr
www.lademeure88.com

Open all year • 5 non-smoking rooms with bathrooms • €60 to €65, breakfast included • Table d'hôte €25 • Garden, car park

 Time seems to stand still on the shores of the lake.

This trim, traditional Vosges chalet built in 1866 is one of the few holiday homes of this sort, so popular round Lake Gérardmer in the 19C, to have made it through to the present day. The sober, immaculate rooms, sometimes furnished with family heirlooms, are delightfully old-fashioned. Alsace tableware and cut-crystal glasses adorn the tables in the "winstub"-style restaurant with a sweeping view. The garden tumbles down to the lake and it is a real pleasure to wander round its paths.

 The warm family welcome.

This former post house, whose oldest section dates back to the 18C, oozes with discreet refined charm. The sitting room, complete with a handsome Lorraine fireplace, and the splendid library are full of character. The spacious rooms are adorned with lovely old furniture picked up in antique shops. The exotic cuisine further adds to the overall appeal. Lovely garden with barbecue.

Access : *On the Épinal road, 1km to the west, opposite the lake*

Access : *6km northbound from Neuchateau*

GIRMONT-VAL-D'AJOL - 88340

AUBERGE DE LA VIGOTTE
M. et Mme Bouguerne

88340 Girmont-Val-d'Ajol
Tel. 03 29 61 06 32
courrier @ lavigotte.com
www.lavigotte.com
Languages : Eng.

Closed from 2 Nov to 20 Dec • 18 rooms and 1 apartment, most have bath/WC, some have shower/WC • €55 to €65; breakfast €7; half-board available • Restaurant closed Tue and Wed; menus €18 to €38 • Terrace, garden, car park. No dogs admitted in restaurant • Tennis, fishing and swimming in private ponds, play area, hiking, cross-country skiing

 It is impossible to find a fault with this Vosgian inn.

A quick glimpse at the web site of the "via gotta" – "way of springs" – will give you an idea of the new owners' energetic, up-to-date approach since buying the inn in 2000. In no time at all, this old farmhouse, perched at a height of 700m in a forest of fir trees and ponds, has become a very pleasant and popular hostelry thanks to its delightful rooms and "country chic" restaurant. The chef's inventive recipes are a feast for the eyes as well as the mouth.

Access : *Between the Ajol Valley and Remiremont (D 23), at Faymon take the D 83 for 5km*

LA CHAPELLE-AUX-BOIS - 88240

LES GRANDS PRÉS
Mme Chassard

9 les Grands-Prés
88240 La Chapelle-aux-Bois
Tel. 03 29 36 31 00

Open all year • 3 rooms and 2 gîtes with shower/WC • €40, breakfast included; half-board available • Table d'hôte €15 • Garden, car park. Credit cards not accepted, dogs not admitted in restaurant

Fishing in the garden.

This immense 19C house encircled by lush green countryside lies just a few minutes from the spa resort of Bains-les-Bains. Spotless, soberly styled rooms overlook a garden through which a fishing stream gurgles and babbles. Home-grown vegetables from the cottage garden and fresh poultry and rabbit reared on the premises are among the specialities on the dinner table.

Access : *3.5km to the south-east of Bains-les-Bains towards Saint-Loup, then take a minor road*

LA PETITE-FOSSE - 88490

19

AUBERGE DU SPITZEMBERG
M. et Mme Calba

88490 La Petite-Fosse
Tel. 03 29 51 20 46
Languages : Eng., Ger.

Open all year • 10 rooms upstairs with bath/WC or shower/WC, some have television • €48 to €61; breakfast €7; half-board available • Restaurant closed Mon evening and Tue evening from 15 Oct to 15 Mar; menus €17 (weekdays) to €25 • Garden, garage, car park • Mini-golf and walks in the forest

We most liked Swathed in a curtain of greenery.

Step inside this haven of tranquillity in the remote forest of the Vosges and forget your troubles for a while. The comfortable rooms are pleasantly homely and welcoming and the tasty, unfussy cooking, made with rigorously selected regional produce, is served in a rustic dining room. All you have to decide now is which direction to head off for your long walk in the country. No need to leave that trail of breadcrumbs, though; all the paths are well signposted.

Access : *3.5km from Provenchères-sur-Fave on the D 45, then take a forest road*

LE VAL-D'AJOL - 88340

20

LA RÉSIDENCE
Mme Bongeot

5 rue des Mousses
88340 Le Val-d'Ajol
Tel. 03 29 30 68 52
contact@la-residence.com
www.la-residence.com
Languages : Eng., Ger.

Closed from 11 to 25 Mar and 26 Nov to 26 Dec • 49 rooms located in 3 buildings with bath/WC or shower/WC and television • €65 to €90; breakfast €10; half-board available • Menus €13 (weekdays) to €42 • Park, car park • Swimming pool with a retractable roof, tennis

We most liked Waking up to the dawn chorus.

Contemporary and Louis XV rooms are spread over three buildings backing onto the forest which make up the Residence: a mid-19C country house linked to an "orangery" by a glass-covered gallery and a former coaching inn, 50m away. A fireplace and an aquarium adorn the light, airy dining room. Shop selling regional produce. Swimming pool with removable roof, tennis court and a mature wooded park comprise the leisure facilities.

Access : *On leaving the village take the lane leading to Hamanxard*

LE VALTIN - 88230

21

LE VAL JOLI
M. et Mme Laruelle

12 bis Le Village
88230 Le Valtin
Tel. 03 29 60 91 37
le-val-joli@wanadoo.fr
www.levaljoli.com
Languages : Ger.

Closed from 12 Nov to 7 Dec, Sun evening, Mon evening and Tue lunchtime (except school holidays and public holidays) • 7 rooms and 3 apartments, with bath or shower/WC • €79 to €82; breakfast €12; half-board available • Restaurant closed Mon lunchtime; menus €18 (weekdays) to €70 • Terrace, garden, car park • Tennis, hiking

That sound, unlike anything else you have ever heard, is that of a rutting buck!

This appealing country inn almost on the doorstep of the superb Route des Crêtes (Peak Road) has a number of renovated rooms; and all the accommodation overlooks the dense pine forests and mountains. A strong emphasis is given to local produce on the menu and meals are served in the rustic dining room – yes, the 19C carved wooden ceiling is original – or in the more modern veranda. The owner-mayor is a mine of helpful tips about the "panoramic path" around the village, dotted with viewpoints.

Access : *In the village, drive along the D 23 from Fraize to the Schlucht Pass*

XONRUPT-LONGEMER - 88400

22

LE COLLET
M. et Mme Lapôtre

Col de la Schlucht
88400 Xonrupt-Longemer
Tel. 03 29 60 09 57
hotcollet@aol.com
www.chalethotel-lecollet.com
Languages : Eng., Ger.

Closed from 4 Nov to 4 Dec • 25 rooms, all have bath/WC or shower/WC and television • €72 to €92; breakfast €10; half-board available • Menus €23 to €26 • Terrace, car park. No dogs admitted in restaurant • Skiing and hiking trails nearby

A perfect base camp to explore the breathtaking Route des Crêtes (Peak Route).

The walls of this hotel chalet, lost in a forest of fir trees, make it impossible to guess what is inside. For the hospitable owners, entertaining guests does not simply mean providing a cheerful mountain décor with pretty fabrics and painted furniture or a deliciously tempting regional menu: it is above all, a state of mind. Their attention to detail can be felt in the smell of warm brioche in the morning, the wealth of useful tips for walkers or the magic shows for children.

Access : *2km from the Schlucht Pass on the Gérardmer road, by the D 417*

XONRUPT-LONGEMER - 88400

23

LA DEVINIÈRE
M. et Mme Feltz

318 montée des Broches
88400 Xonrupt-Longemer
Tel. 03 29 63 23 89
feltzsylvie@hotmail.com
www.chambredhote-deviniere.com

Closed from 2 to 19 Oct • 5 rooms upstairs, all with shower/WC or bath/WC and television • €55 to €62, breakfast included • No table d'hôte • Garage • Outdoor swimming pool, sauna

This splendid quiet site commands a sumptuous view of the surrounding forest.

Allow yourself to be won over by this fully restored old farmhouse and its welcoming façade decked in a profusion of flowers. Inside are six handsome bedrooms decorated with splendid Austrian furniture. Buffet breakfasts of homemade produce are served in the dining room or, in fine weather, on the welcoming terrace. The daughter of the house, a beautician, offers body treatments and massages in the beauty parlour.

Access : *4km north-eastbound from Gérardmer on the D 417*

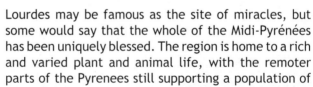

Lourdes may be famous as the site of miracles, but some would say that the whole of the Midi-Pyrénées has been uniquely blessed. The region is home to a rich and varied plant and animal life, with the remoter parts of the Pyrenees still supporting a population of brown bears. A great rampart guarding the border with Spain, these breathtaking mountains are riven by spectacularly deep clefts and are drained by rushing torrents. At sunset, the towers of medieval cities and fortresses glow in the evening light; forbidding Cathar castles are stained a bloody red, Albi and its famous fortified cathedral turn crimson while Toulouse is veiled in dusty pink. Deep beneath the surface of the earth at Lascaux and elsewhere are equally extraordinary sights, the vivid cave-paintings of our gifted prehistoric ancestors. To this list of regional marvels must be added the bounteous lands along the River Garonne, a fertile land famous for its cereal crops, vegetables fruit and wine, which has given rise to a host of culinary traditions; it would be a crime to leave without sampling a sumptuous cassoulet, confit de canard or foie gras.

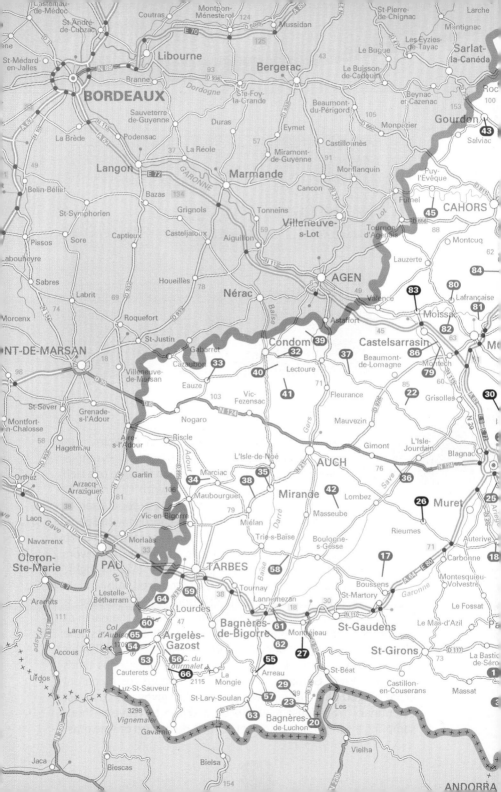

LÉRAN - 09600

BENAC - 09000

CHÂTEAU DE BENAC
M. et Mme Doumenc

09000 Benac
Tel. 05 61 02 65 20
www.haute-ariege.com

Open all year • 6 non-smoking rooms with shower/WC • €60, breakfast included • Table d'hôte €20 • Park, terrace, car park. Credit cards not accepted, dogs not admitted

L'IMPASSE DU TEMPLE
M. et Mme Furness

1 impasse du Temple
09600 Léran
Tel. 05 61 01 50 02
john.furness@wanadoo.fr
www.chezroo.com

Open all year • 5 rooms on 2 floors, all with bath/WC • €65 to €70, breakfast included, half-board available • Table d'hôte €22 • Terrace, garden. No dogs admitted • Outdoor swimming pool

 The tranquillity of this Ariège village.

 Watching the two llamas as they "ecologically" keep the grass down.

In the centre of the town, behind the unassuming façade of this 18C mansion are recently decorated, spacious, comfortable rooms with antique furniture. Those on the second floor under the eaves are the prettiest. To the rear of the house is a delightful shaded garden where you can relax and take a refreshing dip in the pool when the weather is hot. Traditional regional and also Australian cuisine.

In the valley of the Barguillière and in the middle of an immense 11ha estate set amid forest and meadows, stands this handsome 17C home. On the ground floor, two sumptuous sitting rooms directly overlook the wooded, flower-decked park. Upstairs, each of the six rooms has been named after its decoration theme. The mainly vegetarian menu is occasionally supplemented by poultry or fish. Homemade ice cream.

Access : *At Aigues-Vives take the D 28 towards Léran*

Access : *7km westbound from Foix on the D 17*

RABAT-LES-TROIS-SEIGNEURS - 09400

LES FORGES D'ENFALITS
M. et Mme Pellerin

Chemin d'Enfalits
09400 Rabat-les-Trois-Seigneurs
Tel. 05 61 03 83 45
www.forgesdenfalits.com

Open all year • 5 non-smoking rooms with shower/WC • €54, breakfast included • Park, terrace, car park. Credit cards not accepted • Swimming pool, tennis court

The immense open spaces.

As you venture onto this former forge site, complete with a 7ha park, ponds and waterfalls, one wonders how it could have remained neglected for over a century. Inside the single storey house, you will find a magnificent 110 square-metre room furnished with an immense country dining table, a lounge area by the fireside and a billiards table next to the bar. The uncluttered decoration of the five superb rooms only adds to their charm.

Access : *At Rabat les Trois Seigneurs, take the first lane on the left (chemin d'Enfalits) right to the end*

RIEUCROS - 09500

DOMAINE DE MARLAS
Mme Magali Bagros

09500 Rieucros
Tel. 05 61 02 30 80
www.france-bonjour.com/domaine-de-marlas/

Open all year • 5 non-smoking rooms with bathrooms • €65 to €68, breakfast included • Table d'hôte €20 • Park, car park. Credit cards not accepted, dogs not admitted • Outdoor swimming pool

The fixtures and fittings are as pleasant as they are unexpected.

This former manor and farmyard are set on an immense estate bordered by a river. The building itself is nothing to write home about, but the interior is a genuine treat for the eye, particularly the five rooms. The "Cowshed" with its cream-coloured romanticism and the "Pond" are among the most spacious and on two levels. The sitting room is contemporary in style, while the dining room is more countrified. Southern-flavoured table d'hôte menu.

Access : *1.5km eastbound from Rieucros on the D119 towards Mirepoix, then narrow lane on the left*

BOZOULS - 12340

BELCASTEL - 12390

HÔTEL DU VIEUX PONT
Mmes Fagegaltier

12390 Belcastel
Tel. 05 65 64 52 29
hotel-du-vieux-pont@wanadoo.fr
www.hotelbelcastel.com
Languages : Eng.

Closed from 1 Jan to 15 Mar, Sun evening, Mon and Tue lunchtime • 7 rooms in a converted barn, one of which has disabled access, all have bath/WC and television • €76 to €92; breakfast €12; half-board available • Menus €27 (week-days) to €80 • Car park

 The village of Belcastel, voted one of the most beautiful in Aveyron.

Two old stone houses stand on either side of the beautiful 15C arched bridge which spans the River Aveyron. The hotel, on the left bank, is home to small rooms with parquet floors, most of which overlook the river. In the summer, breakfast is served in the garden. The restaurant, on the right bank, is an elegant blend of rustic and modern styles; its gourmet dishes do full justice to the excellent local produce and have earned the house "star" status in the Michelin Red Guide since 1991.

Access : *In the heart of the village, opposite the old bridge*

LES BRUNES
Mme Philipponnat-David

12340 Bozouls
Tel. 05 65 48 50 11
lesbrunes@wanadoo.fr
www.lesbrunes.com

Open all year • 5 rooms with bath/WC • €80, breakfast included • No table d'hôte • Garden, car park. Credit cards not accepted, no dogs admitted

 Enjoy the pleasant surprise of discovering that authenticity can rhyme with modernity.

You will first be bowled over by the country appeal of this stunning property in the heart of a hamlet, before being captivated by the high standard of the interior. The work of master cabinet makers, the furniture is beautifully displayed in the various rooms. While the "Paumes" room offers the comfort of a Jacuzzi bath tub and a power shower, the "Clos" is probably the most appealing when the sunshine lights up the woodwork. Don't miss the lovely grandfather clock in the small sitting room...

Access : *4km from Bozouls on the D 988 then turn right and drive for 1km*

BOZOULS - 12340

À LA ROUTE D'ARGENT
M. Catusse

La Rotonde
12340 Bozouls
Tel. 05 65 44 92 27
yves.catusse@wanadoo.fr

Closed in Jan, Feb, Sun evening and Mon except evenings in Jul-Aug • 21 rooms with bath/WC or shower/WC and television, 6 in a separate wing, 1 with disabled access • €40 to €58; breakfast €6; half-board available • Air-conditioned restaurant; menus €16 (weekdays) to €38 • Car park, garage • Outdoor swimming pool

 Tasty traditional fare lovingly prepared by the owner-chef.

The unassuming façade of this family hostelry hides a contemporary interior. Unpolished metal, modern light fixtures, warm woodwork and light fabrics set the scene in the lobby and restaurant. The bar-sitting room lit by a veranda window is equally unusual in style with a fresco and map of the region engraved on a sheet of glass. The rooms are cheerful and comfortable; those in the annex are more spacious with balconies overlooking a small garden.

Access : *On the way into Bozouls, at the crossroads between the D 988 and the D 920*

CONQUES - 12320

CHEZ CHARLES ET ALICE
M. et Mme Gaillac

Rue du Chanoine André-Bénazech
12320 Conques
Tel. 05 65 72 82 10

Open from 25 Mar to mid-Nov • 4 rooms with private entrance, all with shower/WC • €52 to €64, breakfast included • No table d'hôte • Credit cards not accepted, no dogs admitted

 The cachet of this enchanting listed village.

This little stone house with a slate roof is perfectly at home in the lovely village. Each room has its own independent access and commands a matchless view of the magnificent abbey church of Ste Foy. The furniture, the work of a well-known cabinet maker, adds an attractive note to the establishment's comfort. Breakfast is served in a warm vaulted room full of character. High quality leather goods on sale in a shop.

Access : *In the village*

ENTRAYGUES-SUR-TRUYÈRE - 12140

AUBERGE DU FEL
Mme Albespy

Le Fel
12140 Entraygues-sur-Truyère
Tel. 05 65 44 52 30
info@auberge-du-fel.com
http://auberge-du-fel.com
Languages : Eng.

Open from 1 Apr to 4 Nov • 10 rooms with bath/WC or shower/WC and television, 1 with disabled access • €58 to €63; breakfast €8; half-board available • Restaurant closed lunchtimes except Sat, Sun, national and school holidays; menus €20 (weekdays) to €40 • Terrace, garden

 This hamlet overlooking the Lot Valley feels like the middle of nowhere.

This stone house, veiled in Virginia creeper and nestling in a peaceful hamlet, is perfect for those in search of ultimate quietude. The owner however takes nothing for granted and is devoted to the upkeep of her inn, from the pretty personalised bedrooms, each named after a vine, to the delicious dining room, part of which overlooks the Lot Valley. Pounti, charcuterie, truffade and other local dishes are just a few of the delicacies you can taste, all washed down with a Fel wine perhaps.

Grape picking and gastronomic weekends, chestnuts and mushrooms, discovering the land

Access : *10km westbound of Entraygues-sur-Truyère, take the D 107, turn right on the D 573*

ESTAING - 12190

AUBERGE SAINT-FLEURET
Mme Moreau

19 rue François d'Estaing
12190 Estaing
Tel. 05 65 44 01 44
info@auberge-st-fleuret.com

www.auberge-st-fleuret.com
Languages : Eng.

Open from 15 Mar to 15 Nov, closed Sun evening and Mon out of season • 14 rooms with shower/WC, some have television • €49 to €53; breakfast €8; half-board available • Menus €17 (weekdays) to €55 • Garden, garage

 Savouring the full-flavoured cuisine in front of the fire or overlooking the garden depending on the season.

"A good meal and a good night's sleep" is the self-declared motto of this welcoming inn, a staging post in its former life. The rooms may not be enormous, but are renovated, colourful and well soundproofed, with a view either of the village or the garden. Don't forget to book a table in the restaurant. The chef gets up before dawn to select the best produce of the season which he skilfully assembles into a host of tasty regional dishes.

Cooking lessons and discovery of local wines

Access : *In the heart of the village*

MILLAU - 12100

CHÂTEAU DE CREISSELS
M. et Mme Austruy

Route de Saint-Affrique - Creissels
12100 Millau
Tel. 05 65 60 16 59
www.château-de-creissels.com
Languages : Eng.

Closed Jan and Feb • 30 rooms, 2 of which have disabled access, 12 are in the old castle. Most rooms have bath/WC, some have shower/WC, all have television • €49 to €92; breakfast €8.50; half-board available • Restaurant closed Sun evening and Mon lunchtime; menus €24 to €52 • Terrace, garden, car park

 View of the village and valley.

Chequered parquet floors, wainscoting, a marble fireplace and period furniture: the "Bishop's Room" in the medieval castle can hardly be said to lack character. The others, more everyday, are located in the 1970s wing and have balconies. A vaulted 12C hall houses the restaurant. On fine days, tables are laid outdoors under the arcades of a gallery overlooking the village rooftops.

Access : *In a small village above Millau, on the road to Albi*

NANT - 12230

L'HERMITAGE SAINT-PIERRE
M. et Mme Macq

Lieu-dit Saint-Pierre-de-Revens
12230 Nant
Tel. 05 65 62 27 99
madeleine.macq@wanadoo.fr
http://hermitage.st.pierre.site.voila.fr

Open all year • 5 rooms with shower/WC • €79, breakfast included • Table d'hôte €25 (by reservation from 15 Oct to 15 Apr) • Credit cards not accepted, dogs not admitted • Swimming in the river nearby

 The laughter of the children swimming in the crystal-clear waters of the Dourbie.

You can't blame the owners for falling head over heels with this spot steeped in history which was originally a chapel (10C and 11C), then a Knights Templar post and a parish church. Now a B&B establishment, it offers beautifully decorated rooms whose heritage can still be seen in any number of details, such as the stone vaults, period furniture, four-poster beds or a 17C altarpiece. The garden at the foothills of the Causse Noir and on the banks of the Dourbie is equally delightful.

Access : *11km to the north-west of Nant towards Millau on the D 991*

SAINT-GEORGES-DE-LUZENÇON - 12100

LA SAISONNERAIE
M. et Mme Vales

 Luzençon
12100 Saint-Georges-de-Luzençon
Tel. 05 65 62 58 86
www.lasaisonneraie.com

Open all year • 4 rooms with bath/WC • €63, breakfast included • Table d'hôte €21 • Garden, car park. Credit cards not accepted, no dogs admitted

 The breathtaking view, wherever you look.

This 11C building, set in a small high-perched village, is home to four beautifully decorated rooms. Three of them, including the "Moroccan" which is particularly attractive, have an independent access. The Blanche and Soleil rooms, rustic in style, have whitewashed walls and exposed beams. Traditional Aveyron family cuisine on the menu, with a few excursions into North Africa's tajines.

Access : *In the village*

SAINT-JEAN-DU-BRUEL - 12230

MIDI-PAPILLON
M. et Mme Papillon

 12230 Saint-Jean-du-Bruel
Tel. 05 65 62 26 04
Languages : Eng., Sp.

Open from Palm Sunday to 11 Nov • 18 rooms with bath/WC, some have shower/WC • €33.60 to €60.50; breakfast €5; half-board available • Menus €13.70 (weekdays) to €38 • Garden, car park, garage • Outdoor swimming pool

 A hotel committed to upholding country traditions.

Ten pigs fatted up each year by a local farmer, a full-time gardener supplying fresh fruit and vegetables to the kitchen table, a farmyard full of barn animals and mushrooms picked by shepherds: since 1850 the Papillon family has been a perfect illustration of the fierce local desire to remain close to its roots. Personalised bedrooms, without the modern distraction of television, and a pleasant restaurant whose bay windows overlook the Dourbie and its lovely 15C arched bridge.

Access : *In the village, on the D 999, next to the stone bridge*

SAINT-SERNIN-SUR-RANCE - 12380

CARAYON
M. Carayon

Place du Fort
12380 Saint-Sernin-sur-Rance
Tel. 05 65 98 19 19
carayon.hotel@wanadoo.fr
www.hotel-carayon.com
Languages : Eng., Ger., Sp.

Closed Sun evening, Mon and Tue lunchtime (except Jul-Aug) • 74 rooms, 4 of which with disabled access, with bath/WC or shower/WC and television • €41 to €89; breakfast €8; half-board available • Menus €15 to €54 • Garage, private car park, park, terrace • Tennis, mini-golf, keep-fit rooms, sauna, swimming pools

The countless leisure activities dotted around the tree-lined park.

Since 1876, this coaching inn has been the hub of this peaceful Aveyron village standing on the banks of the Rance. The Carayon family has been perfecting the art of receiving guests here for four generations. You will sleep either in the original building, a more recent wing or in one of the little houses in the park. The rooms are comfortable and practically fitted out; we recommend those opening onto the woodland. The spacious dining room leads onto a terrace overlooking the open fields.

Access : *In the heart of the village*

SONNAC - 12700

LA MELESSENS
M. Pesso

Tournhac
12700 Sonnac
Tel. 05 65 80 86 59
bienvenue@la-melessens.fr
www.la-melessens.fr

Closed Jan and Feb • 3 rooms with shower/WC • €60, breakfast included • Table d'hôte €15 • Park, car park. Credit cards not accepted, no dogs admitted • Outdoor swimming pool, sitting room-library

The skilful blend of character and sophistication.

It is sometimes difficult to believe that you're in a farmhouse, such is the high standard of the interior decoration. From the three large rooms with their spacious mezzanines to the sitting room and library (over 6 000 books), guests are invariably impressed by the faultless care taken with the upkeep. You may even want to take a yoga course to enhance the restorative virtues of your stay. Generous vegetarian meals served in the evenings; a barbecue is also available for meat lovers.

Access : *12km north of Peyrusse-le-Roc on the D 87 then the D 40*

ALAN - 31420

LE POUPAT
Mme Marnay

Route de Bachas
31420 Alan
Tel. 05 61 98 98 14
michelle.bechard@wanadoo.fr
Languages : Eng., Sp.

Open all year • 3 rooms with bath/WC • €52, breakfast included • Table d'hôte €17 • Play area, park, garden, car park • Outdoor swimming pool, horses

 Riding round the countryside on one of the three horses available to guests.

This sprawling 16C building, nestling within extensive parkland lost in the countryside, is ideal for weary travellers in need of a peaceful night's rest. On the ground-floor, the sitting and dining rooms boast impressive period fireplaces and are furnished with Louis XV-style pieces. Upstairs, bare beams, rustic furniture, colourful walls and knickknacks adorn the sober rooms. Guests appreciate the pleasant homely atmosphere.

Access : *1km from Alan on the Bachas road*

AUTERIVE - 31190

LA MANUFACTURE
Mme Balansa

2 rue des Docteurs-Basset
31190 Auterive
Tel. 05 61 50 08 50
manufacture@manufacture-royale.net
www.manufacture-royale.net
Languages : Eng., Sp.

Closed Nov to Mar • 5 non-smoking rooms and 1 gîte, all with bath/WC or shower/WC and internet access • €75 to €80, breakfast included • No table d'hôte • Park, terrace, car park. Credit cards not accepted, dogs not admitted • Outdoor swimming pool, table tennis, bicycles

 Admire the period furniture and objects.

This royal bed-linen factory (18C), converted into living accommodation around 1880 by Dr Jules Basset, has retained many traces of its rich past: the swimming pool is located in the former rinsing pool, family portraits adorn the staircase and the spacious bedrooms are furnished with family heirlooms. An ideal chance to take a step back in time while continuing to enjoy modern comforts and a pleasantly relaxed youthful welcome.

Access : *In the village on the banks of the Ariège*

AYGUESVIVES - 31450

BAGNÈRES-DE-LUCHON - 31110

LA PRADASSE
M. et Mme Antoine

39 chemin de Toulouse
31450 Ayguesvives
Tel. 05 61 81 55 96
contact@lapradasse.com
www.lapradasse.com
Languages : Eng., Sp.

Open all year • 5 rooms with bath/WC or shower/WC, 1 with disabled access • €80, breakfast included; half-board available • Table d'hôte €25 • Park, car park. No dogs admitted • Outdoor swimming pool

PAVILLON SÉVIGNÉ
Mme Seiter

2 avenue Jacques-Barrau
31110 Bagnères-de-Luchon
Tel. 05 61 79 31 50
seiter@pavillonsevigne.com
http://www.pavillonsevigne.com

Open all year • 5 non-smoking rooms on 2 floors, all with bath/WC or shower/WC and modem access • €80 to €90, breakfast included; half-board available • Table d'hôte €22.50 • Credit cards not accepted, dogs not admitted

 The exquisite interior decoration is worthy of the cover of any Home and Garden magazine.

The brochure of La Pradasse mentions "characterful rooms set in a haven of peace and quiet". Which is totally misleading, because the reality is much better! The superbly restored, early-19C barn has rooms that are each more charming than the last, so much so that you will want to try them all. The large sitting room has been extended by a veranda, and outside are an extensive park, flower garden, vegetable plot and swimming pool just waiting to be discovered.

 Exquisite antique furniture.

This 19C manor house is home to pleasant airy rooms decorated with carefully selected fabrics and furnished with some quite remarkable antiques. At weekends, meals are served in the dining room overlooking the garden and in a neighbouring restaurant the rest of the week (half-board). Lovely sitting room-library with piano. Antique lovers will make a beeline for this address, particularly as it is equally well appointed in modern comforts.

Access : *15km south-east of Toulouse on the N 113, then the D 16 for 1.1km*

Access : *In the town centre*

CABANAC-SÉGUENVILLE - 31480

BALMA - 31130

LE MANOIR SAINT-CLAIR
M. Bourdoncle

20 chemin de Sironis
31130 Balma
Tel. 05 61 24 36 98
manoirsaintclair@cegetel.net
www.manoirsaintclair.com
Languages : Eng., Sp.

Open all year • 3 non-smoking rooms upstairs, all with bath/WC or shower/WC, air-conditioning and television • €75 to €85, breakfast included • No table d'hôte • Terrace, garden, car park. Credit cards not accepted, no dogs admitted

Savouring the calm of the countryside just two minutes from Toulouse.

An immaculately groomed park with well-tended paths and lovely roses surrounds this authentic 17C pink brick manor house. Breakfasts are served on the veranda, which leads up to the personalised simple but well-cared for rooms, whose names evoke local historic events: "Cathare", "Pastel" and "Aeropostale", the latter is the most spacious and overlooks Saint-Clair Lake. Delightfully welcoming owners.

Access : *4km east of Toulouse on the D 50*

CHÂTEAU DE SÉGUENVILLE
M. Lareng

Séguenville
31480 Cabanac-Séguenville
Tel. 05 62 13 42 67
info@chateau-de-seguenville.com
www.chateau-de-seguenville.com
Languages : Eng.

Closed from 15 Dec to 15 Jan • 5 rooms with bath/WC or shower/WC • €95 to €110, breakfast included • Table d'hôte €22 • Park, car park. Credit cards not accepted, no dogs admitted • Outdoor swimming pool

Exploring the park and its hundred-year-old trees with the Pyrenees in the background.

The origins of this château, set in a secluded park, date back to 1271, but its current architecture bears more resemblance to the 19C because it was rebuilt after the French Revolution. The guestrooms, reached by a lovely staircase, are full of charm with old parquet floors or tiles, handsome fireplaces, antique furniture, bright colours, curios and immaculate bathrooms. On the ground-floor, two inviting sitting rooms add to the establishment's appeal.

Beginners' wine-tasting course

Access : *5km from Cox on the D 1 north-west of l'Isle-Jourdain*

JUZET-DE-LUCHON - 31110

LE POUJASTOU
M. Cottereau

Rue du Sabotier
31110 Juzet-de-Luchon
Tel. 05 61 94 32 88
info@lepoujastou.com
www.lepoujastou.com
Languages : Eng., Russ.

Closed in Nov • 5 rooms upstairs, all have bath/WC or shower/WC • €48, breakfast included; half-board available • Table d'hôte €8 to €17 • Terrace, garden, car park. Credit cards not accepted, no dogs admitted

 Your host, an alpine guide, organises snowshoe excursions in winter and mountain biking in summer.

This large south-facing house, which commands fine views of the Luchonnais peaks, began life as the village's concert hall in the 18C. Stylishly renovated, it now offers brand new ochre-coloured bedrooms, some sizeable, others more compact. A warm sitting room lined with works on the region's fauna and flora and a Pyrenean-style dining room are on the ground floor. A terrace, garden and finely-flavoured home cooking round off the picture of an excellent establishment.

Sport and leisure weekends

Access : *Near the church*

MONTESQUIEU-LAURAGAIS - 31450

CHAMBRE D'HÔTE BIGOT
M. Pinel

Lieu-dit Bigot
31450 Montesquieu-Lauragais
Tel. 05 61 27 02 83
joseph.pinel@libertysurf.fr
hotelbigot.chez.tiscali.fr

Closed for a fortnight in Feb • 5 rooms, one of which has a Jacuzzi • €50 to €68, breakfast included; half board available • Table d'hôte €15 (weekdays) to €25 • Sitting room, terrace, car park. Credit cards not accepted, no dogs allowed in rooms • Outdoor swimming pool

 The marriage of old and new.

You won't be disappointed by the comfort of this fully renovated 17C farmhouse. Beautiful old furniture, in the family for donkey's years or picked up in local antique shops, graces the rooms, one of which has a Jacuzzi bathtub. The old beams, brick walls and original mangers of the former stables add character to the breakfast room. The huge covered terrace is very pleasant in fine weather.

Access : *5km to the north-east on the D 11, take the lane on the left after the A 61, towards Villenouvelle*

RAMONVILLE-SAINT-AGNE - 31250

25

LA PÉNICHE SOLEÏADO
Mme Roussel

Pont-de-Mange-Pomme
31250 Ramonville-Saint-Agne
Tel. 06 86 27 83 19

Open all year • 3 non-smoking rooms, all with bathrooms • €80, breakfast included; half-board available • Table d'hôte €30 • Terrace. Credit cards not accepted, dogs not admitted

The irresistible charm of this barge on the Midi canal.

There is of course no point in expecting to enjoy the same space you would find in castles or manor houses, but this barge moored along the Midi canal shaded by plane trees is nonetheless full of character. The wooden interior is both warm and simple with a pleasant sitting-dining room area and pretty bedrooms with private bathrooms. The friendly welcome and the meals served on deck also add to the appeal of this unusual form of accommodation.

Access : *At the roundabout at the south port (Port Sud), take the road behind the pharmacy, towards "Ferme Cinquante"*

RIEUMES - 31370

26

AUBERGE LES PALMIERS
M. Vallès

13 place du Foirail
31370 Rieumes
Tel. 05 61 91 81 01
auberge_lespalmiers@yahoo.fr
www.auberge-lespalmiers.com
Languages : Eng., Sp.

Closed one week in Jan and late Aug to early Sep • 12 rooms, one of which has disabled access, with bath/WC or shower/WC and television • €58 to €75; breakfast €7; half-board available • Restaurant closed Sun evening and Mon; menus €11 (weekdays) to €30 • Garden, terrace. Dogs not admitted in rooms • Outdoor swimming pool

The friendly, down-to-earth owners.

Several palm trees adorn the garden behind this picturesque inn. Built in the 19C, it was recently extended, and borders the pretty village square. The spacious, comfortable rooms feature a happy marriage of rustic furniture, parquet floors and contemporary touches. Fancy a snack or a full three-course meal? Sit down under the beams in the dining room and build up your strength with generous helpings of traditional cuisine.

Access : *In the heart of the village*

SAINT-BERTRAND-DE-COMMINGES - 31510

27

HÔTEL DU COMMINGES
Mme Alaphilippe

Place de la Basilique
31510 Saint-Bertrand-de-Comminges
Tel. 05 61 88 31 43

Open from 1 Apr to 31 Oct • 14 rooms, most have bath/WC or showers, with or without WC • €31 to €53; breakfast €6.50 • No restaurant • Small car park. No dogs admitted

 The peace and quiet of a convent.

Overlooking the forecourt of the fascinating Cathédrale Ste-Marie, this hotel was once a convent and it cannot be faulted for its peace and quiet, particularly in the summer, when the square is entirely free of cars. The guests' quarters and rooms are all fitted with handsome country furniture. During the long summer months, a pleasant terrace is laid under an arbour behind the main building. Run by the same family for three generations, it is a place you will remember.

Access : *In the centre of the village, opposite the cathedral*

SAINT-FÉLIX-LAURAGAIS - 31540

28

AUBERGE DU POIDS PUBLIC
M. Taffarello

Rue St-Roch
31540 Saint-Félix-Lauragais
Tel. 05 62 18 85 00
poidspublic@wanadoo.fr
www.auberge-du-poidspublic.com
Languages : Eng., Ger., Sp.

Closed Jan and 1 week in Nov • 11 rooms and 1 apartment with bath/WC or shower/WC and television, 4 are air-conditioned • €63 to €98; breakfast €11; half-board available • Menus €28 to €68 • Terrace, garage

 The unusual and historic public weighing-scales next door to this charming inn.

This inn is the talk of the town and the region! Some vaunt the quality of the cooking which is a creative blend of classical cuisine and local produce, while others sing the praises of the country-style restaurant with its pleasant terrace overlooking the countryside. Finally, the comfortable, low-key rooms have been gradually renovated and are immaculately cared for. All in all, this attractive village inn is a treat, as much for the eye as for the palate.

Access : *In the village*

VACQUIERS - 31340

SAINT-PAUL-D'OUEIL - 31110

VILLA LES PINS
Mme Daigre

Route de Bouloc
31340 Vacquiers
Tel. 05 61 84 96 04
www.villa-les-pins.com
Languages : Eng., Sp.

Open all year (by reservation only) • 15 rooms with bath/WC or shower/WC and television • €65 to €86; breakfast €7 • Menus €16 to €35 (evenings only) • Car park, terrace, garden

MAISON JEANNE
Mme Guerre

Au bourg
31110 Saint-Paul-d'Oueil
Tel. 05 61 79 81 63
www.maison-jeanne-luchon.com
Languages : Sp.

Open all year • 4 non-smoking rooms, all with bath/WC or shower/WC • €73, breakfast included • No table d'hôte • Garden. Credit cards not accepted, dogs not admitted

 Summer evenings on the charming terrace overlooking the park.

To the north of busy Toulouse, this pleasant halt is beautifully quiet. A pine forest surrounds this extensive villa with a pleasant guesthouse atmosphere. The rooms, more spacious on the first floor, have a plush bourgeois flavour created by antique furniture, chandeliers and thick curtains. The same ambience extends to the dining room and its impressive fireplace.

 Getting back to grass roots.

The shingled terrace, stone walls and marble floors of this handsome sun-drenched house are typical of the Oueil valley. Guests appreciate the comfortable and stylish bedrooms furnished with antiques and pretty fabrics, all of which command fine views of the Pyrenean peaks. The lady of the house did the delicate stencil-work on the walls and floors herself. Home from home!

Access : *2km westbound on the D 30*

Access : *8km northwest of Bagnères-de-Luchon on the D 51 and D 618*

VARENNES - 31450

CHÂTEAU DES VARENNES
M. et Mme Mericq

31450 Varennes
Tel. 05 61 81 69 24
j.mericq@wanadoo.fr

Open all year • 5 rooms with bath/WC • €100, breakfast included • Table d'hôte €35 • Terrace, garden, park, car park • Outdoor swimming pool. Tennis court and horse-riding nearby

 The view of the slopes of Lauragais from the swimming pool.

The magic begins from the moment you set foot in the park of this 16C castle next to the church. Push open the iron gate, venture into the wonderful courtyard and through a heavy wooden door into the main pink brick building, where you will find yourself gazing up at a double flight of stairs. Superbly exotic colours adorn the "Bédouin" room on the ground floor and those upstairs are equally elegant and opulent. The sitting rooms and vaulted cellars add the finishing touch.

Access : *15km westbound from Saint-Félix on the Toulouse road (D 2)*

CAUSSENS - 32100

AU VIEUX PRESSOIR
M. Martin

Saint-Fort
32100 Caussens
Tel. 05 62 68 21 32
auvieuxpressoir@wanadoo.fr
http://perso.wanadoo.fr/vieuxpressoir

Closed for a fortnight in February • 4 rooms and 1 family room with shower/WC • €51, breakfast included; half-board available • Meals at l'Auberge: €17 to €26 • Terrace, garden, park, car park. No dogs admitted in rooms • Outdoor swimming pool, jacuzzi

 The lively atmosphere at the weekends.

This lovely old 17C stone house commands a fine view over the vineyards, countryside and the flocks of ducks reared on the property. The rooms, furnished with old pieces, are comfortable and well looked after. The family suite in the attic has been thoughtfully equipped with a games room and a VHS recorder. Farm produce takes pride of place on the dinner table and connoisseurs in search of fine foie gras will not be disappointed.

Access : *11km from Caussens on the D 7 and take a lane on the right*

EAUZE - 32800

CHAMBRE D'HÔTE HOURCAZET
Mme Lejeunne

Hourcazet
32800 Eauze
Tel. 05 62 09 99 53
claude.lejeunne@wanadoo.fr
site.voila.fr/hourcazet
Languages : Eng., It.

Open all year • 4 rooms with shower/WC • €60 to €65, breakfast included • No table d'hôte • Terrace, park, car park. Credit cards not accepted

Soaking up the vineyard ambience.

An air of tranquillity reigns in these two houses standing side by side in the midst of Armagnac's vineyards. The rooms are tastefully decorated with beautiful fabrics and furniture and equipped with fine bathrooms. The largest are under the massive beams up in the converted attic, the other two open directly onto the garden. Meals are served in a traditionally decorated dining room or on one of two terraces. Forty winks can be had in the garden complete with pond.

Access : *7km westbound from Eauze on the D 626, then the N 524 towards Cazaubon, and a lane "chemin Espajos" 500m on the right*

JUILLAC - 32230

AU CHÂTEAU
M. et Mme de Rességuier

32230 Juillac
Tel. 05 62 09 37 93
deresseguier@marciac.net
auchateaujuillac.com

Closed for one week Sep-Oct • 4 rooms with bathrooms • €50, breakfast included • Table d'hôte €20 • Terrace, garden, park, car park. Credit cards not accepted, no dogs admitted • Fishing

Lie on your back and gaze up into the branches of the ancient trees.

Fie, fair visitor! What you see is no castle, but an 18C charterhouse, now the headquarters of a thriving farming business. The rooms, in a separate wing, are vast and tastefully decorated and the bathrooms boast all the modern comforts. As you would expect, a generously spread table d'hôte showcases the wealth of produce grown and reared on the farm. Bicycling, walking and fishing feature among the possible leisure activities, and the owner and mayor of Juillac is a wonderful source of advice.

Access : *5km westbound from Marciac, towards Juillac on the D 255*

MIRANDE - 32300

35

AU PRÉSIDENT
M. Piquemil

Route d'Auch
32300 Mirande
Tel. 05 62 66 64 06 ou 06 10 37 28
jacques.piquemil@wanadoo.fr
www.chez.com/aupresident
Languages : Eng., Sp.

Open all year • 4 rooms, 2 of which are on garden level, with bathrooms • €50, breakfast included • No table d'hôte • Terrace, garden, car park. Credit cards not accepted, no dogs admitted • Billiards, children's play area

Trying your luck on the billiards table in the elegant sitting room.

This lovely abode flanked with turrets belonged to the president of Mirande's law courts during the first half of the 20C, hence its name. The bedrooms with sloping ceilings all have brand new bathrooms. Those on the ground floor are enormous and adorned with family heirlooms. In the winter, breakfast is served by the fireside in the huge dining room and in a sheltered courtyard in the summer. Pretty garden.

Access : *3km northbound from Mirande on the N 21 route d'Auch*

MONFERRAN-SAVÈS - 32490

36

LE MEILLON
M. et Mme Lannes

32490 Monferran-Savès
Tel. 05 62 07 83 34

Open all year • 4 rooms with shower/WC or bath/WC • €70, breakfast included • Table d'hôte €30 • Car park. No dogs admitted • Outdoor swimming pool, Jacuzzi

The view of the Pyrenees and Canigou.

This characterful 16C abode has retained its authentic identity with the addition of the comfort of modern fixtures and fittings. Once past the entrance, where you can still see the family coat of arms, guests can relax in the Jacuzzi and work out in a brand new fitness room. Each of the prettily decorated rooms features a different colour scheme. A shaded terrace overlooks the generously proportioned swimming pool and dominates the surrounding countryside.

Access : *8km westbound from Isle-Jourdain on the D 161 then the D 253*

SAINT-MAUR - 32300

SAINT-CLAR - 32380

DOMAINE DE LORAN
M. et Mme Nédellec

32300 Saint-Maur
Tel. 05 62 66 51 55

Open from Apr to Oct (by reservation the rest of the year) • 2 rooms and 2 apartments with bathrooms • €50 to €55, breakfast included • No table d'hôte • Park, car park. Credit cards not accepted • Billiards

LA GARLANDE
M. et Mme Cournot

12 place de la Mairie
32380 Saint-Clar
Tel. 05 62 66 47 31
nicole.cournot@wanadoo.fr
www.lagarlande.com
Languages : Eng.

Closed from 6 Nov to 23 Mar • 3 rooms with bathrooms • €54 to €65, breakfast included • No table d'hôte • Garden. Credit cards not accepted, no dogs admitted

 Harmony abounds in all the rooms.

Standing firmly four-square on its arcades, this beautiful, rambling house with an ochre façade is in the heart of the village opposite a 16C hall. The rooms, decorated with tapestries and well-polished antiques, have retained their original parquet or tiled floors. The bathrooms have been renovated. The reading room and walled herb garden are perfect places to relax. Guests have the use of a summer kitchen.

Photography courses

Access : *Opposite the covered market*

Fishing in the lake hidden in the park.

Two towers, a long colonnade of plane trees and parkland graced with age-old trees make this old Gascony farmhouse look more like a castle. A lovely wooden staircase will take you up to the spacious rooms furnished with antiques. The immense dining room on the ground floor with dark wainscoting boasts period furniture. Fishing, billiards and table tennis will keep you amused for hours. Charolais cattle reared (meat sold on order).

Access : *From the N 21 take the long lane that leads to the Domaine de Loran*

SAINT-MÉZARD - 32700

CHAMBRES D'HÔTES LE SABATHÉ
M. et Mme Barreteau

Le Sabathé
32700 Saint-Mézard
Tel. 05 62 28 84 26
barreteau.sabathe@wanadoo.fr
http://perso.wanadoo.fr/barreteau.sabathe
Languages : Eng.

Open all year • 4 rooms with shower/WC • €40 to €44, breakfast included; half-board available • Table d'hôte €13 to €17 • Terrace, car park. Credit cards not accepted

 Take refuge in this sanctuary of meditation.

Tai Chi sessions are organised every morning in this unaffected, almost monastic abode. The old farm on the doorstep of the town aims to provide sanctuary to those in search of a place for meditation. The rooms, spread throughout the outbuildings, are all fully independent. Depending on the weather, meals are served by the fireside in the dining room or on a tiny walled terrace in front of the main hall, overlooking the chapel of Notre-Dame-d'Esclaux.

Tai chi and Qi Gong courses

Access : *12km northbound on the D 36*

SAINT-ORENS-POUY-PETIT - 32100

LE TUCO
Mme Sarhan

32100 Saint-Orens-Pouy-Petit
Tel. 05 62 28 39 50
http://letuco.free.fr

Open from 1 Apr to 2 Nov • 5 rooms with bath/WC • €95, breakfast included • Table d'hôte €30 • Park, car park. Credit cards not accepted, dogs not admitted • Outdoor swimming pool

 The 12ha park and hill that commands a magnificent view.

The sight of this reassuring house with lavender-coloured shutters rising up in the distance is instantly appealing, but it is difficult to imagine the treasures it contains within. Spacious stone-walled rooms, some half-timbered, furnished with a mixture of pieces, perhaps a little over-the-top but not without charm. The individual theme decoration of the rooms is most successful. Delightful inner courtyard with wrought-iron furniture and fountain. Gastronomic table d'hôte.

Access : *7km southeast from Condom on the D654 then small lane to the right*

SIMORRE - 32420

SAINT-PUY - 32310

LA FERME DE MARIE BARRAILH
Mme Barrailh

 Le Peydousset
32420 Simorre
Tel. 05 62 65 36 48
contact@lafermedemariebarrailh.com
www.lafermedemariebarrailh.com

Open all year • 3 rooms with bath/WC • €70, breakfast included • Table d'hôte €20 • Garden, car park. Credit cards not accepted, no dogs admitted • Outdoor swimming pool

LA LUMIANE
M. Eman

 Grande Rue
32310 Saint-Puy
Tel. 05 62 28 95 95
info@lalumiane.com
www.lalumiane.com

Open all year • 5 non-smoking rooms upstairs, all with shower/WC or bath/WC • €55 to €59, breakfast included • Table d'hôte €19 • Terrace, garden. No dogs admitted • Outdoor swimming pool

 The kindness of the lady of the house.

You cannot fail to be impressed by this pleasant old farmhouse with its earthen-coloured walls and generous dimensions from the entrance to the equally spacious colourful bedrooms. However it is the faultless courtesy of the owners who have raised the art of hospitality to a genuine science, that guests remember most. The table d'hôte menu features a selection of the best of Gers gastronomy. Courses in fine art or cooking depending on your fancy.

 Bathing in the swimming pool overlooking the peaceful Gèle valley.

This 17C nobleman's house, which rises in the heart of the village near a handsome church, has retained the majority of its original interior fittings: tiled floor in the corridor, handsome staircase, sitting room with wooden floor and fireplace, etc. The rooms, in the former barn, are equally charming: roughcast walls, antique furniture, colourful fabrics, etc. Dining outdoors is a genuine pleasure, as a visit to this establishment will confirm.

Access : *North exit out of town on the D 12 towards Saramon*

Access : *Behind the church*

GOURDON - 46300

GRAMAT - 46500

DOMAINE DU BERTHIOL
Famille Dubreuil

Route de Cahors
46300 Gourdon
Tel. 05 65 41 33 33
domaine-du-berthiol@wanadoo.fr
www.hotelperigord.com
Languages : Eng.

Open from Apr to mid-Dec • 29 rooms with bath/WC or shower/WC and television • €77 to €84 (€67 to €75 low season); breakfast €11; half-board available • Air-conditioned restaurant; menus €24 to €48 • Park, car park. No dogs admitted • Outdoor swimming pool, tennis

 Lush green countryside.

On the outskirts of the town in the middle of a beautifully maintained park, this impressive country house offers identical rooms with fully equipped bathrooms. Tennis courts, swimming pool and children's play area. The contemporary dining room opens onto the pleasant greenery. The menu shows a marked preference for local produce. Immense banquet hall in another wing.

Access : *1km eastbound from Gourdon on the D 704*

MOULIN DE FRESQUET
M. et Mme Ramelot

46500 Gramat
Tel. 05 65 38 70 60
info@moulindefresquet.com
www.moulindefresquet.com

Closed from 1 Nov to 1 Apr • 5 non-smoking rooms with bathrooms • €62 to €95, breakfast included; half-board available • Table d'hôte €24 including beverages (evenings only) • Park, car park. Credit cards not accepted, no dogs admitted

 Wining and dining by candlelight on Périgord's succulent fare.

The good life at its best! This authentic 17C water mill stands in an idyllic rural spot, just 800m from the centre of Gramat. Lovely furniture and tapestries, exposed stonework and beams and a profusion of good books set the scene for the interior. The comfortable, elegant rooms have been recently restored and most enjoy a view of the enchanting shaded garden and the stream, much prized by fishermen. Gracious hosts and wonderful food.

Access : *On the way into Gramat*

GRÉZELS - 46700

CHÂTEAU DE LA COSTE
M. Coppé

46700 Grézels
Tel. 05 65 21 38 28
gervais.coppe@wanadoo.fr
Languages : Eng., Ger.

Open in Jul and Aug • 4 rooms with shower/WC • €80 to €115, breakfast included • No table d'hôte • Credit cards not accepted, no dogs admitted

The Cahors Wine Museum within the walls of this fortified castle.

If you're passing through, this medieval fortress dominating the Lot Valley is definitely worth a visit. Character abounds in the rooms which have been given evocative names such as "Study of the setting sun", "Lookout tower" and "Squire's abode" – all are furnished with lovely period pieces. In addition, the striking dining room commands an exceptional view. Don't leave without visiting the Wine Museum.

Access : *16km westbound from Luzech on the D 8*

LALBENQUE - 46230

LA VAYSSADE
M. Baysse

46230 Lalbenque
Tel. 05 65 24 31 51
jpbaysse@lavayssade.com
www.lavayssade.com

Closed Mar and Oct to Nov • 5 non-smoking rooms, with shower/WC • €66 to €75, breakfast included • Table d'hôte €24 including drinks • Garden, car park. Dogs not admitted • Outdoor swimming pool, mountain bikes for rent, table tennis

An almost magical spot, two minutes from the capital of the black diamond.

This estate has been in the same family for four generations and the barn has been faultlessly transformed into accommodation. Flooded in sunlight thanks to large windows, the spacious ground floor room with mezzanine is a tasteful blend of old and new, with the modern sofa perfectly at home against the original walls and rafters. This happy combination is echoed in the rooms, equipped with excellent bedding.

Watercolour courses. Truffle weekends in January, February and December

Access : *In the town, behind the school*

LOUBRESSAC - 46130

CHÂTEAU DE GAMOT
M. et Mme Belières

46130 Loubressac
Tel. 05 65 10 92 03
annie-belieres@wanadoo.fr
www.domaine-de-gamot.com

Closed from 1 Oct and 1 May • 5 rooms, some have bathrooms • €45 to €65, breakfast included • No table d'hôte • Garden, car park. Credit cards not accepted, no dogs admitted

 Conveniently located near Quercy's main tourist attractions.

The allure of this rambling 17C stately home and its pastoral setting opposite the castle of Castelnau never fails to weave its magic spell. The comfortable rooms are well proportioned. Guests who visit in June and September enjoy the run of the owners' private swimming pool. Other leisure activities in the vicinity include a 9-hole golf course, tennis courts and horse-riding.

Access : *5km westbound from St-Céré on the D 673 and the D 30*

MARCILHAC-SUR-CÉLÉ - 46160

LES TILLEULS
Mme Ménassol

Le Bourg
46160 Marcilhac-sur-Célé
Tel. 05 65 40 62 68
michelle.menassol@wanadoo.fr
www.les-tilleuls.fr.st

Closed from 16 Nov to 16 Dec • 4 rooms with shower/WC • €40 to €42, breakfast included • No table d'hôte • Park, car park. Credit cards not accepted

 Meeting the enchanting owner.

Cradled in the heart of the village, this 19C stately home owes its success to the lady of the house's efforts to make guests feel truly welcome: she is always well informed about life in the region and is happy to suggest local activities. The rooms are comfortable and unfussy and the breakfasts copious to say the least: prepare to delve into a memorable array of up to 50 home-made jams. The garden, complete with barbecue and hammock, is slightly unruly and instantly likeable.

Access : *In the village*

MARTEL - 46600

LA COUR AU TILLEUL
Mme Jouvet

Avenue du Capitani
46600 Martel
Tel. 05 65 37 34 08
www.la-cour-au-tilleul.com

Open all year • 3 rooms with shower/WC • €60 (€50 low season), breakfast included • No table d'hôte • Credit cards not accepted

 A bright, well cared-for interior behind very old walls.

The walls of this enchanting stone house bedecked in flowers date back to the 12C no less! A great deal of time has clearly been lavished on the decoration of the tranquil, spacious rooms which are located to the rear of the house. Depending on the season, breakfast is served in the brightly coloured blue and orange dining room or in the inner courtyard under the shade of a linden tree. The welcome is as friendly as you could wish.

Access : *In the village*

ROCAMADOUR - 46500

LE TROUBADOUR
M. Menot

Route de Brive
46500 Rocamadour
Tel. 05 65 33 70 27
troubadour@rocamadour.com
www.hotel-troubadour.com
Languages : Eng.

Open from 15 Feb to 15 Nov • 10 rooms and 2 apartments with bath/WC or shower/WC and television • €65 to €79 (€55 to €70 low season); breakfast €10; half-board available • Air-conditioned restaurant; menus €26 to €36 • Car park, garden, terrace. • Swimming pool, billiards

 Lazing around the swimming pool after a hard day's sightseeing.

A handsome flowered and tree-lined garden protects the peace and quiet of this tastefully renovated old farmhouse. Forget the size of the rooms and admire the rustic furniture and floorboards of the pristine bedrooms. Some enjoy a view of the swimming pool with the countryside in the distance. The restaurant, which is open only to guests, doesn't believe in fussy, elaborate cuisine. Friendly, family welcome.

Access : *2.5km to the north-east on the D 673*

ROCAMADOUR - 46500

LES VIEILLES TOURS
M. Tayebi et Mme Delpech

Lieu-dit Lafage
46500 Rocamadour
Tel. 05 65 33 68 01
les.vieillestours@wanadoo.fr
www.vieilles-rocamadour.com
Languages : Eng., Sp.

Closed from 4 Nov to Apr • 17 rooms located in 2 buildings, almost all are on garden level, with bath/WC and television • €72 to €115; breakfast €12; half-board available • Menus €29 to €39 • Terrace, garden, car park • Outdoor swimming pool

Sleeping in a 13C falconry!

The construction of this secluded hunting lodge took place over several centuries from the 13C to the 17C. Most of the rooms in the outhouses open directly onto the garden and enjoy a splendid view of the countryside. Diners can choose between a welcoming country-style restaurant or a quiet, shaded terrace to sample an up-dated repertoire.

Access : *4km westbound from Rocamadour on the D 673 towards Payrac, then take a minor road*

SAINT-SIMON - 46320

LES MOYNES
Mme Arets

Les Moynes de Saint-Simon
46320 Saint-Simon
Tel. 05 65 40 48 90
les.moynes@free.fr
http://les.moynes.free.fr
Languages : Eng.

Open from 15 Apr to 14 Nov • 5 rooms, one of which has disabled access, with bath/WC or shower/WC and television • €50 to €60, breakfast included; half-board available • Table d'hôte €19 • Terrace, car park, park. Credit cards not accepted, no dogs allowed in restaurant • Outdoor swimming pool, table-tennis, mountain biking

A guided tour of the duck farm in the company of the owner.

This recently renovated Quercy house, which dates back to 1885, is located in a nearly 30-acre working farm. Bright colours, timber beams and stone walls, new parquet flooring and well-fitted bathrooms depict the snug rooms, all with names which reflect the region. Breakfasts and dinners are served in a delightful dining room complete with old mangers and a fireplace big enough to sit in.

Access : *7km north-west of Assier on the D 11 and D 25, towards Flaujac*

ARCIZANS-AVANT - 65400

CHAMBRE D'HÔTE MME VERMEIL
Mme Vermeil

3 rue du Château
65400 Arcizans-Avant
Tel. 05 62 97 55 96

Open all year • 3 rooms with valley or mountain view with shower/WC • €43, breakfast included • No table d'hôte • Credit cards not accepted, dogs not admitted

 A panoramic wide-screen view of the valley.

This handsome 19C house boasts a wealth of attractions. Wood prevails in the attic rooms – walls, floors and furniture – which afford a fine view of the valley or the mountains. Guests have the run of a kitchen, a pleasant garden and a dining room with a relief map of the Pyrenees: plan your next expedition over a coffee and feel free to ask for advice from the owner, a mountain guide who speaks from experience.

Access : *5km southbound from Argèles on the D10, then on the D13.*

ARRAS-EN-LAVEDAN - 65400

LES GERBES
M. Didier Theil

65400 Arras-en-Lavedan
Tel. 05 62 97 93 94
www.pyrenees-chambres-hotes.com

Open all year • 5 non-smoking rooms all with bath/WC or shower/WC • €60, breakfast included • Table d'hôte €20 • Garden, car park. Credit cards not accepted, dogs not admitted

 Hunting down the ideal refuge on the way up the Soulor and the Aubisque.

Since its restoration this traditional 17C country house is home to five personalised rooms full of character and decorated with a particularly successful blend of old and new. "Ancolie" with its fireplace is perhaps the most appealing room. The table d'hôte menu features regional family dishes served in a cosy dining room adorned with old rafters. A roaring fire is lit in the sitting room to warm up those caught out in the snow. Splendid view of the mountains.

Access : *On the way out of town on a narrow road*

ARREAU - 65240

55

ANGLETERRE
Mme Aubiban

Route de Luchon
65240 Arreau
Tel. 05 62 98 63 30
contact@hotel-angleterre-arreau.com
www.hotel-angleterre-arreau.com
Languages : Eng., Sp.

In winter open Sat-Sun and school holidays; closed 1 Apr to 15 May and 10 Oct to 25 Dec • 17 rooms with bath/WC or shower/WC and television • €64 to €94; breakfast €8.50; half-board available • Restaurant closed Mon and Tue lunchtime; menus €19 to €35 • Car park, garden. No dogs admitted • Heated swimming pool

 The friendly welcome and the family atmosphere.

A little village typical of the Aure Valley is the site of this former coaching inn. All the rooms have been recently renovated. The stylish dining room sports country furniture, old utensils dotted about here and there and bright, contemporary colours. Meals are also served in the veranda facing the garden where a swimming pool and play area will keep the children busy.

Access : *On leaving Arreau, take the D 618 towards Luchon*

BEAUCENS - 65400

56

ETH BÉRYÈ PETIT
M. et Mme Vielle

15 route de Vielle
65400 Beaucens
Tel. 05 62 97 90 02
contact@beryepetit.com
www.beryepetit.com
Languages : Eng., Sp.

Open all year • 3 rooms with bathrooms • €53 to €62, breakfast included • Table d'hôte €18, including beverages (evenings only from 1 Nov to 30 Apr) • Terrace, garden, car park. Credit cards not accepted, dogs not admitted

 The lady of the house's gracious welcome.

This country house, whose name means "little orchard" in Occitan, was built in 1790 in the purest traditions of regional architecture. Tastefully decorated rooms overlook the Lavedan and the Pyrenean peaks, the one upstairs is the most spacious and leads out onto a balcony which runs along the entire length of the façade. There are two others under the eaves. Breakfast is always a delight by the fireside or on the terrace.

Access : *8.5km to the south-east of Argelès on the D 100, then take a minor road*

CAMPARAN - 65170

LA COUETTE DE BIÉOU
Mme Moreilhon

65170 Camparan
Tel. 05 62 39 41 10
Languages : Sp.

Open all year • 3 rooms with shower/WC • €42 to €45, breakfast included • No table d'hôte • Car park. Credit cards not accepted, no dogs admitted

Stupendous view of the valley and the Pyrenean peaks.

Right in the heart of town, this attractive stone farm with flower-decked balconies commands a matchless view of the valley and the Pyrenees. Wood sets the tone in the cosy rooms which enjoy exceptional views, one of which overlooks Saint-Lary-Soulan. The hospitable owners are both genial souls and if you're lucky, you'll be able to see how the local "gâteau à la broche" is made, even lending a welcome helping hand in the four hours of spit-roasting in front of the fire.

Access : *4km northbound, on the Arreau road and then turn right*

CASTELNAU-MAGNOAC - 65230

LE MOULIN D'ARIES
M. Dorit Weimer

À Aries-Espenan
65230 Castelnau-Magnoac
Tel. 05 62 39 81 85
moulindaries@aol.com
www.poterie.fr
Languages : Eng., Ger.

Open from 15 May to end Oct • 5 rooms with bathrooms and separate WC • €60, breakfast included • Table d'hôte €20 (evenings) • Reading room. No dogs admitted in restaurant

Open the door and breathe in the perfume of yesteryear.

Time and care have clearly been lavished over the restoration of this 14C mill next door to an attractive manor whose stylish interior reveals original wood floors, an ancient staircase and latched doors. White prevails in the spacious rooms with king-size beds and well-equipped bathrooms. In the mill are a reading and television room and a small bar, all set against the backdrop of the old millstones. Forget about your diet and treat yourself to Gascony's delicacies!

Access : *4km to the south-east of Castelnau-Magnoac on the D 623 towards Boulogne, then turn right towards Aries-Espenan*

MONTGAILLARD - 65200

59

MAISON BURRET
M. Cazaux

67 le Cap-de-la-Vielle
65200 Montgaillard
Tel. 05 62 91 54 29
joetjl.cazaux@wanadoo.fr
www.maisonburret.com
Languages : Eng., Sp.

Open all year • 3 rooms, one of which is an apartment, with shower/WC • €45 to €55, breakfast included • Table d'hôte €18 • Garden, car park. Credit cards not accepted, dogs not admitted

 Authentic and delightfully anachronistic.

Countless original architectural features are still visible in this lovely farmhouse, dating from 1791, such as the dovecote, bakery, stables, cowshed, handsome carved staircase and collection of old agricultural machinery. The comfortable rooms have been decorated with some fine antique pieces and in the winter a fire is lit in the one on the ground floor. Meals are served in a friendly dining room.

Access : *5km northbound from Pouzac on the D 935*

OMEX - 65100

60

LES ROCAILLES
M. Fanlou

65100 Omex
Tel. 05 62 94 46 19
muriellefanlou@aol.com
www.lesrocailles.com
Languages : Eng.

Closed from 1 Nov to Easter • 3 rooms with shower/WC • €68, breakfast included • No table d'hôte • Garden, car park. Credit cards not accepted, dogs not admitted • Outdoor swimming pool

 The discreet luxury of this snug little nest.

It is impossible not to be won over by the charm of this small stone house with comfortably modern rooms. One of the rooms, named "The Seamstress" by the owner and former wardrobe mistress of the Paris Opera House, is home to an old sewing machine and a mannequin; it also has a private terrace. Those under the eaves are air-conditioned and command a fine view of the valley. A fireplace and old furniture set the scene in the dining room and the flowered garden and swimming pool are most welcome.

Access : *4.5km to the south-west of Lourdes on the D 13 then the D 213*

SAINT-ARROMAN - 65250

PINAS - 65300

DOMAINE VÉGA
M. et Mme Mun

65250 Saint-Arroman
Tel. 05 62 98 96 77

Open from Jun to Sep • 5 rooms with bath/WC or shower/WC • €58, breakfast included; half-board available • Table d'hôte €18 (weekdays) to €25 • Park, car park. Credit cards not accepted, dogs not admitted • Landscaped swimming pool

DOMAINE DE JEAN-PIERRE
Mme Colombier

20 route de Villeneuve
65300 Pinas
Tel. 05 62 98 15 08

marie@domainedejeanpierre.com
www.domainedejeanpierre.com
Languages : Eng., Sp.

Open all year • 3 rooms upstairs with shower/WC • €50, breakfast included • No table d'hôte • Park. Credit cards not accepted • Tennis and golf nearby

 Lovely landscaped garden and grounds.

Originally built in the 16C, this manor house was the property of a Russian prince in the Belle Époque and a Buddhist centre in the 1970s. Now a B&B, it offers pleasant rooms named after flowers, with unusual carved headboards. All overlook the cedars, giant thuja and linden trees in the park and the countryside beyond. In the kitchen, the chef prepares imaginative recipes based on regional produce.

 Long walks in the country.

This handsome house covered in Virginia creeper stands at an altitude of 600m on the plateau of Lannemezan, looking south towards the Pyrenees. Old furniture and pretty fabrics adorn the spacious, quiet rooms, all of which overlook the beautifully cared-for grounds. The distant notes of a piano being played in the sitting room can sometimes be heard. In the summer, breakfast is served on the terrace. Simple, cordial welcome.

Access : *At Lannemezan, take the D 929 and at La Barthe-de-Neste the D 142*

Access : *200m eastbound from the town on the D 158*

SAINT-LARY-SOULAN - 65170

LA FERME DE SOULAN
M. et Mme Amelot

Soulan
65170 Saint-Lary-Soulan
Tel. 05 62 98 43 21
fermedesoulan@tiscali.fr
http://fermedesoulan.free.fr
Languages : Eng.

Closed 15 Apr to 15 May and in Nov • 4 rooms with bathrooms and television • €85 to €88 (€82 to €85 low season), breakfast included; half-board available • Menus €22 (evenings only, including beverages) • Garden. Credit cards not accepted, dogs not admitted • Sauna, hammam

The superb view overlooking the Aure Valley from this mountain village at an altitude of 1280m.

Peace and quiet and pure mountain air pervade this old farmhouse located in the heart of a high-perched village whose name means sun in the local dialect. The buildings, set around a paved courtyard, are home to a ground floor countrified dining room with a fireplace and two comfortable bedrooms with exposed beams and wainscoting. Upstairs are two other rooms with sloping ceilings and a panoramic sitting room with a south-facing picture window. On the leisure side, sauna and blue tiled hammam.

Access : *North-west of St-Lary-Soulan; go to Vieille-Aure, then turn left onto the D 123*

SAINT-PÉ-DE-BIGORRE - 65270

LE GRAND CÈDRE
M. et Mme Peters

6 rue du Barry
65270 Saint-Pé-de-Bigorre
Tel. 05 62 41 82 04
christian@grandcedre.com
www.grandcedre.com
Languages : Eng., Ger.

Open all year • 4 rooms with bathrooms • €70, breakfast included • Table d'hôte €25 including beverages (by reservation) • Terrace, park, car park. Internet access. Credit cards not accepted • Sauna, spa

Botanical walks in the park.

This 17C country seat owes its name to the three-hundred-year-old cedar planted in the centre of the park, which casts a welcome shade over a few deckchairs. Each of the personalised rooms, linked by an outdoor gallery, is in a different style: Art Deco, Louis-Philippe, Henry II and Louis XV. The music room and piano, classical dining room, greenhouse with orchids, geraniums and cacti, pergola of roses and delightful cottage garden are a feast for the eye.

Access : *In the village*

SALLES - 65400

65

LE BELVÉDÈRE
Mme Crampe

6 rue de l'Église
65400 Salles
Tel. 05 62 97 23 68
www.argeles-pyrenees.com
Languages : Sp.

Closed in Nov • 3 rooms with shower/WC • €60, breakfast included; half-board available • Table d'hôte (evenings for half-board guests only except Sun) • Park, car park. Credit cards not accepted, no dogs admitted • Excursions to the mountains, swimming pool

The enchanting perspective from this 18C abode.

The sweeping view of the valleys of Luz, Cauterets and Arrens with the Pyrenean peaks in the distance from this handsome manor house does full justice to its name. The rooms under the eaves are modern in flavour while those on the first floor are decorated with lovely old furniture and a fireplace; all enjoy the same view. In the winter, meals are served by the fireside and in the summer under an arbour.

Access : *12.5km southbound from Lourdes on the N 21 then the D 102*

VISCOS - 65120

66

LA GRANGE AUX MARMOTTES
M. et Mme Senac

Au village
65120 Viscos
Tel. 05 62 92 91 13
hotel@grangeauxmarmottes.com
www.grangeauxmarmottes.com
Languages : Eng., Sp.

Closed from 5 Nov to 15 Dec • 6 rooms with bath/WC or shower/WC and television • €73 to €85 (€65 to €79 low season); breakfast €10; half-board available • Menus €19 to €43 • Terrace, garden • Outdoor swimming pool

Heaven for sleepyheads and marmots.

The region is so untamed and rich in spectacular natural sights that you will spend all your days out exploring until the mountain cows come home! This old stone barn, with its cosy rooms and perfect peace and quiet are just what you need when your head finally does touch the pillow. The sun will already be high in the sky before you're ready to get up and feast your eyes on the sumptuous view of the valley, hemmed in all sides by peaks and summits.

> *In partnership with the Vallée de Luz, we organise skiing/snowshoe/dog sleigh excursions in winter*

Access : *To the north-west of Luz-Saint-Sauveur towards Pierrefitte-Nestalas*

ALBI - 81000

BOUT-DU-PONT-DE-LARN - 81660

GEORGE V
Mme Selles

29 avenue du Maréchal-Joffre
81000 Albi
Tel. 05 63 54 24 16
info@hotelgeorgev.com
www.hotelgeorgev.com
Languages : Eng., Sp.

Open all year • 9 rooms, all have showers with or without WC, television, some have fireplaces • €33 to €44; breakfast €5.50 • No restaurant • Inner courtyard

LA MÉTAIRIE NEUVE
M. Tournier

81660 Pont-de-Larn
Tel. 05 63 97 73 50
metairieneuve@wanadoo.fr
www.metairieneuve.com
Languages : Eng.

Closed from 15 Dec to 22 Jan • 14 rooms, most have bath/WC, some have shower/WC, all have television • €76 to €89; breakfast €10; half-board available • Restaurant closed Sun evening and Mon (Oct to Easter) and Sat lunchtime; menus €26 (weekdays) to €35 • Terrace, garden, car park • Outdoor swimming pool

Basking in the first rays of morning sunshine.

Although not as luxurious as its famous Parisian namesake, this establishment is fully worthy of notice and most definitely less expensive than your average palace! The recently spruced up, spacious rooms are quiet despite the nearby railway station and decorated in pastel shades with good quality furniture; some have fireplaces. In the rear, a small shaded courtyard is perfect for open-air breakfasts.

Access : *On one of the roads to the railway station*

After a refreshing night's sleep, dig into a delicious breakfast.

We recommend booking one of the rooms recently renovated in a "country chic" style, which are not without character, overlooking the garden of this 18C family farmhouse converted into an inn in the 1980s. There are two pleasantly decorated rustic indoor dining rooms, but most guests prefer the rafters of the old barn which is now a delightful summer terrace.

Access : *2km eastbound from Mazamet: leave on the N 112 towards Saint-Pons and turn left at La Richarde*

CASTRES - 81100

LE CASTELET
M. et Mme Dubois

St-Hippolyte
81100 Castres
Tel. 05 63 35 96 27
contact@lecastelet.fr
www.lecastelet.fr

Open all year • 5 rooms with shower/WC or bath/WC • €90, breakfast included • No table d'hôte • Park, car park. Credit cards not accepted, no dogs admitted • Billiards, outdoor swimming pool

> *We most liked* The impressive and protective presence of the ancient oak trees.

In just a few minutes you are out of the town centre and in the heart of the countryside, the site of this 19C mansion tucked away among valleys and meadows. From the billiards room to the splendid swimming pool, guests are enchanted by the peace that pervades the site. All the more so as the rooms feature a happy blend of sophisticated decoration and modern bathrooms equipped with power showers or balneo bubble baths. Delicious family dishes. A little expensive, but excellent value for money.

Access : *5km westbound from Castres on the D622 then small road to the right*

BURLATS - 81100

LE CASTEL DE BURLATS
M. et Mme Dauphin

8 place du 8-Mai-1945
81100 Burlats
Tel. 05 63 35 29 20
le.castel.de-burlats@wanadoo.fr
www.lecasteldeburlats.fr.st
Languages : Eng.

Closed Feb school holidays • 10 non-smoking rooms, all have bath/WC or shower/WC and television • €61 to €100; breakfast €10 • Menus €23 to €55 (evenings only) • Park, garden, private car park • Billiards room, reading room, hiking trails nearby

> *We most liked* Savouring a whisky in the Renaissance salon.

You cannot miss this lovely 14C and 16C "castel" at the entrance to this medieval village in the gorges of the Agout. Spacious rooms, individually decorated with furniture picked up in antique shops, overlook a park where Mother Nature appears to have been given a free rein. Try your hand at billiards or catch up on the region's art and history in the Renaissance room complete with fireplace, wainscoting and beams. Even if it's your first stay, you will be greeted like a friend of the family.

Access : *9km north-east of Castres on the D 89, then take the D 58 that runs alongside the Agout*

CORDES-SUR-CIEL - 81170

AURIFAT
Mme Wanklyn

81170 Cordes-sur-Ciel
Tel. 05 63 56 07 03
aurifat@wanadoo.fr
www.aurifat.com
Languages : Eng.

Closed from mid-Dec to mid-Feb • 4 non-smoking rooms with shower/WC • €74 (€66 low season), breakfast included • No table d'hôte • Garden, car park. Credit cards not accepted, dogs not admitted • Outdoor swimming pool

 A magical place steeped in history.

The superb restoration of this 13C half-timbered brick watchtower is most impressive. Its name, which means "path of gold" was inspired by the Aurosse stream which runs down below. All the cane-furnished rooms have a balcony overlooking the fields and valley. Make sure you have a peep in the suite in the 17C dovecote. The terraced gardens are also worth exploring. The tower's situation, just a few minutes walk from the medieval heart of Cordes, is one of its greatest assets.

Access : *600m from the city on the St-Jean road*

CORDES-SUR-CIEL - 81170

HOSTELLERIE DU VIEUX CORDES
M. et Mme Thuriès

Haut de la Cité
81170 Cordes-sur-Ciel
Tel. 05 63 53 79 20
vieux.cordes@thuries.fr
 www.thuries.fr
Languages : Eng., Sp.

Closed in Jan • 18 rooms at the Hostellerie, 8 are in a separate wing: La Cité. All rooms have bath/WC or shower/WC and television • €49 to €120; breakfast €9; half-board available • Restaurant closed Sun eve, Tue lunchtime and Mon out of season, menus €17.50 to €36 (no restaurant in separate wing) • Terrace

Exploring the countless secrets of the medieval city of Cordes.

The tasteful bedrooms might lack the character of the main building, an old monastery with an original spiral staircase, but they do allow visitors to explore and enjoy the heart of this medieval Gothic town, "the city of a hundred arches". The windows overlook the valley of Cérou and command picturesque views of the tiny paved streets or of the old wisteria whose perfume lingers on the exquisite patio terrace. Salmon and duck take pride of place on the menu.

Access : *In the town centre, between the covered market and the church*

CORDES-SUR-CIEL - 81170

MAISON BAKEA
M. et Mme Aguirre

26 Le Planol
81170 Cordes-sur-Ciel
Tel. 05 63 56 29 54
lamaison.bakea@alice.fr
www.maisonbakea.chez-alice.fr
Languages : Eng., Sp.

Closed 5 Nov to 1 Apr • 5 non-smoking rooms with shower/WC • €55 to €78, breakfast included • No table d'hôte • Credit cards accepted in high season, no dogs admitted

A serene atmosphere reigns throughout this establishment run by two opera singers.

This beautiful 13C house blends perfectly into the picturesque medieval town. A delightfully restored inner courtyard enhances the appeal of the covered passages, brickwork and timbers. Bright colours, antique furniture, stained-glass windows, bare flagstones and beams set the tone for the personalised bedrooms, each of which has a modern bathroom. The terrace overlooking the hilly countryside is impossible to resist. A dream come true!

> *Singing and sculpture courses, stone cutting courses*

Access : *800m from Cordes on the Planol in the medieval city*

LACABARÈDE - 81240

DEMEURE DE FLORE
M. Di Bari

106 route Nationale
81240 Lacabarède
Tel. 05 63 98 32 32
contact@demeuredeflore.com
www.demeuredeflore.com

Closed from 2 to 30 Jan and Mon out of season • 10 rooms (3 in a detached house) and one apartment, one of which has disabled access, with bath/WC and television • €89 to €100; breakfast €10; half-board available • Menus €26 to €34 • Terrace, garden, private car park. Dogs not admitted in restaurant • Outdoor swimming pool

Wandering around the delightfully unruly garden.

From the moment you set foot (or wheel) on the drive lined by majestic linden trees, you will fall under the spell of this charming manor-villa, built back in 1882. The rooms are decorated with elegant Louis XVI furniture and three open directly onto the swimming pool with the Montagne Noire in the background. The meals demonstrate a distinctly Italian-Provençal influence but the establishment also serves an excellent cup of tea – even by British standards!

Access : *In Lacabarède, leave the N 112 and drive along a lane bordered with lime trees*

ROUAIROUX - 81240

LA RANQUIÈRE
M. et Mme Lecoutre

 Domaine de la Ranquière
81240 Rouairoux
Tel. 05 63 98 87 50
ranquiere@aol.com
Languages : Eng.

Closed Dec to Mar • 4 rooms with bath/WC or shower/WC • €60 to €70 (€50 to €60 low season), breakfast included • Table d'hôte €20 to €40 (evenings only by reservation) • Terrace, garden, park, car park. Credit cards not accepted, dogs not admitted • Swimming pool

🙂 **This smart trim farmhouse would be at home in any interior decorating magazine.**

Blue, yellow, green or pink - which room of this splendid 17C farmhouse set on a 5-acre estate will you be lucky enough to sleep in? Whatever the colour, they are all brimming with charm and delightfully appointed with bare beams, polished red tiles, worn wooden doors, colourful fabrics and antique furniture. The warm welcome, inviting garden and orchard, handsome pool and terrace overlooking the Montagne Noire all add to the appeal of this maison d'hôte.

Access : *At Lacabarède take the D 52 towards Rouairoux, 800m further on turn left towards La Ranquière*

SAINT-AMANS-SOULT - 81240

CHEZ FRANÇOISE
Mme Zaffuto

 En Rosières
81240 Saint-Amans-Soult
Tel. 05 63 97 90 68
fzaf@tiscali.fr
www.chez-françoise.com

Open all year • 3 rooms with shower/WC or bath/WC • €64, breakfast included • Table d'hôte €18 • Park, car park. Credit cards not accepted, no dogs admitted • Outdoor swimming pool

🙂 **The profusion of greenery with the mountains in the distance.**

Climbing plants smother the walls of this early 20C building that is home to three rooms, of which two are apartments, decorated along themes which vary between understated elegance and reckless romanticism. A leisure room on the ground floor leads directly onto the sunny terrace where breakfasts of cold meats and cheese are served. In the park is a lovely swimming pool surrounded by a wooden deck. The table d'hôte, twice a week by reservation, alternates between regional and Swiss specialities.

Access : *In the upper part of town*

SAINTE-GEMME - 81190

LE PEYRUGAL
M. Forest

81190 Sainte-Gemme
Tel. 05 63 76 59 86
lepeyrugal@wanadoo.fr

Open all year • 3 rooms with shower/WC • €58, breakfast included • Table d'hôte €20 • Park, car park. Credit cards not accepted • Outdoor swimming pool

 Taking the small path to picnic by the waterside.

Discover the bucolic charm of this 18C mas set among fields and woodland. Entirely renovated by a couple of enthusiasts, the building has now regained its former youth and character. Each of the three immense bedrooms (the smallest is 42 square metres) has its own private entrance and all modern comforts. The lady of the house, who adores cooking, loves introducing guests to regional specialities and savours. Swimming pool in a lovely green setting.

Access : *5km north-eastbound from Carmaux on the N 88 then right turn towards Vers*

VIVIERS-LES-MONTAGNES - 81290

LE PASTEILLÉ
M. et Mme Limes

La Ferme
81290 Viviers-les-Montagnes
Tel. 05 63 72 15 64
j.limes@wanadoo.fr

Open all year • 4 non-smoking rooms with shower/WC or bath/WC • €48, breakfast included • No table d'hôte • Park, car park. Credit cards not accepted, no dogs admitted

 The owners' welcome and kindness.

This fully restored old family farmhouse, located in the heart of a 5ha estate, is a picture of tranquillity. The spacious sitting room, furnished with sofas and armchairs around the fireplace, offers hours of pleasant relaxation. An elm staircase leads up to the rooms whose comfort is enhanced by pretty pastel colours. Homemade breakfasts are served on an immense country table. No table d'hôte meals but lots of good ideas and advice for the best places in the vicinity.

Access : *1km outside the town on the D 621 towards Toulouse*

ESCATALENS - 82700

79

MAISON DES CHEVALIERS
M. et Mme Choux

Place de la Mairie
82700 Escatalens
Tel. 05 63 68 71 23
claude.choux@wanadoo.fr
www.maisondeschevaliers.com
Languages : Eng., Sp., Port.

Open all year • 6 rooms with bathrooms • €75, breakfast included; half-board available • Table d'hôte €22 • Terrace, garden, park, car park. Credit cards not accepted • Outdoor swimming pool

The imaginative cooking of the lady of the house, originally from southern Portugal.

Good taste and a certain daring distinguish the restoration of this lovely 18C manor house. Warm, sunny colours adorn the immense bedrooms complete with four-poster beds and period furniture, while the bathrooms boast lovely old bathtubs and washbasins in Portuguese marble. A games room and a music room have been installed in the outbuildings. Delightful courtyard and a swimming pool set in the middle of a meadow.

Access : *14km westbound from Montauban on the N 113*

LAFRANÇAISE - 82130

80

LE PLATANE
Mme Horf

Coques-Lunel
82130 Lafrançaise
Tel. 05 63 65 92 18
le.platane@wanadoo.fr
www.leplatane.fr.tt
Languages : Ger.

Open all year • 4 rooms with shower/WC • €70, breakfast included; half-board available • Table d'hôte €20 • Garden, car park. Credit cards not accepted • Outdoor swimming pool, horse-riding

The quintessence of comfort.

This lovely brick country house, flanked by stables and a dovecote, dates from 1904. Comfort was clearly high on the priority list of the restoration and the rooms are spacious and decorated in a modern or Neo-rustic style. Sunbathe around the oval swimming pool or head for the shade of the park's magnificent old planes, lindens and weeping willows. Horse-riding and bicycling available for those in need of more exercise.

Access : *10km eastbound from Moissac on the D 927, the D 2 and then the D 68*

MEAUZAC - 82290

LAMOTHE-CAPDEVILLE - 82130

LA MAISON DE MANON
M. et Mme Pico

122 chemin Antoine-Cadillac
82130 Lamothe-Capdeville
Tel. 05 63 31 36 29
manon.pico@wanadoo.fr
http://www.lamaisondemanon.com
Languages : Eng.

Closed Nov • 3 rooms and 1 apartment, all with bath/WC or shower/WC • €70 to €75 (€65 to €70 low season), breakfast included • No table d'hôte • Terrace, garden, car park. Credit cards not accepted, dogs not admitted • Outdoor swimming pool

The faultless welcome.

From this secluded house on a small hill, the view stretches over the hilly countryside, the rooftops of Montauban, and on a fine day, as far as the Pyrenean mountains. The understated decoration of the well-groomed bedrooms was inspired by the evocative towns whose names they bear (Madras, Venice, Asmara); all open onto the partially covered terrace, which over-looks the park and swimming pool.

Access : *1.5km north-east of Lamothe-Capdeville on the D 78 and D 69 Mirabel road then a lane to the left*

MANOIR DES CHANTERELLES
M. et Mme Brard

Bernon-Boutonnelle
82290 Meauzac
Tel. 05 63 24 60 70
nathalie@manoirdeschanterelles.com
www.manoirdeschanterelles.com
Languages : Eng.

Open all year • 5 non-smoking rooms on 2 floors, all with bathrooms, air-conditioning and modem access • €70 to €120, breakfast included • Table d'hôte €25 to €30 • Terrace, park, car park. Credit cards not accepted • Outdoor swimming pool, billiards

The unusual decoration of the rooms.

This delightful manor is home to personalised rooms decorated in a variety of themes: "Louis XVI" has period furniture, "Savane" is African in spirit and the "Orientale" apartment of North African inspiration. Countless leisure activities available including a billiards table, swimming pool, tennis court and pleasant grounds complete with apple orchard. The owners' warm welcome adds the finishing touch to this delightful establishment.

Hot air balloon and micro-light weekends

Access : *2.5km north-west from Meauzac on the D 45 to Bernon-Boutounelle*

MOISSAC - 82200

83

LE MOULIN DE MOISSAC
M. Barthélémy

Esplanade du Moulin
82200 Moissac
Tel. 05 63 32 88 99
hotel@lemoulindemoissac.com
www.lemoulindemoissac.com
Languages : Eng., Ger., Sp.

Open all year • 35 air-conditioned rooms with bath/WC and television, lift, 2 with disabled access, 26 non-smoking rooms • €46 to €100; breakfast €9; half-board available • Air-conditioned restaurant closed Sat lunchtime and Sun; menus €19 to €34 • Private car park. No dogs allowed in restaurant • In the heart of the historic centre

Gazing at the Tarn from the windows of this lovely mill before visiting the former abbey of Moissac.

After a former vocation as a flour mill, this establishment is now devoted to the well-being of its guests. The origins of the mill, anchored on the right bank of the Tarn, date back to 1474. Countless transformations and several fortunes later, a serious rejuvenation programme has endowed the impressive building with great charm, from the comfortable theme rooms (country, alpine or seafaring) to the cosy piano-bar and delightful restaurant with a contemporary bistro atmosphere.

Access : *From the A 62 motorway, take exit 9 towards Moissac Centre, turn right after Napoléon Bridge*

MONTPEZAT-DE-QUERCY - 82270

84

DOMAINE DE LAFON
M. et Mme Perrone

Pech de Lafon
82270 Montpezat-de-Quercy
Tel. 05 63 02 05 09
micheline.perrone@domainedelafon.com
www.domainedelafon.com

Closed 15 Feb to 15 Mar and a fortnight in Nov • 3 rooms with bathrooms • €76 (€68 low season), breakfast included; half-board available • Table d'hôte €23 (evenings by reservation) • Terrace, garden, car park. Credit cards not accepted, no dogs admitted in dining room

Taking a course in trompe l'œil painting.

Perched on a green hillside, this 19C square manor house enjoys a sweeping view of the surrounding countryside. Admire the immense rooms decorated by the owner, an artist and a former theatre set designer. The "Indian" is cloaked in oriental fabrics, marble and architectural trompe-l'œil scenes, azulejos tiles adorn the "Parrots" and "Baldaquin" features a pretty yellow and grey foliage pattern. Not to be missed!

Access : *2km on the D 20 towards Molières, then turn left towards Mirabel for 2km*

SAINT-PORQUIER - 82700

SAINT-ANTONIN-NOBLE-VAL - 82140

LA RÉSIDENCE
M. et Mme Weijers

37 rue Droite
82140 Saint-Antonin-Noble-Val
Tel. 05 63 67 37 56
info@laresidence-france.com
www.laresidence-France.com
Languages : Eng., Ger., Du.

Closed fortnight in Feb and fortnight in Nov
• 5 non-smoking rooms overlooking the garden
or the terrace, all have bath/WC • €70 to €85,
breakfast included; half-board available
• Table d'hôte €23 (evening only) • Garden.
Credit cards not accepted, dogs not admitted

 The idyllic location in the heart of the medieval village.

Contemporary furniture and pastel colours
combine happily in this 18C manor house run by
a German-Dutch couple. Most of the spacious
tastefully decorated rooms overlook the Roc
d'Anglars; book the one with a private terrace
if possible. In summer, linger in the walled
garden, unless of course you would prefer the
more energetic appeal of the nearby climbing
centre.

Hiking weekends

Access : *In the heart of the medieval village*

LES HORTENSIAS
M. et Mme Barthe

82700 Saint-Porquier
Tel. 05 63 68 73 62
Languages : Sp.

Open all year • 3 non-smoking rooms, all with
bath/WC or shower/WC and modem access
• €60, breakfast included • No table d'hôte
• Garden, car park. Credit cards not accepted,
dogs not admitted • Outdoor swimming pool

 The unaffected friendly welcome.

This typical pink brick house simply overflows
with charm. The three attractive bedrooms,
recently renovated and named after flowers,
are furnished with family heirlooms. The old
wine house is now home to the dining room and
an exquisite covered terrace overlooking the
vegetable and flower gardens. The enticing
swimming pool offers guests the chance of a
refreshing dip after basking in the hot southern
sun.

Access : *In the town*

NORD PAS DE CALAIS

This region of northern France has everything to warm the soul. According to a local saying, "the hearts of the men of the north are warm enough to thaw the coldest climate." Just watch these northerners as they throw themselves body and soul into the traditional 'Dance of the Giants', re-enacted everywhere in countless fairs, fêtes and carnivals. Several tons of chips and mussels – and who knows how many litres of beer! – are needed to sustain thousands of stall-holders and over one million visitors to Lille's annual Grande Braderie, just one of many huge street markets. The influence of Flanders can be seen not only in the names of many of the towns and inhabitants and the wealth of Gothic architectural treasures, but also in filling local dishes such as *carbonade* of beef, braised in amber beer, and *potjevleesch*, a chicken or rabbit stew with potatoes. Slender belfries, neat rows of former miners' houses and the distant outline of windmills further remind visitors that they are on the border of Belgium, or, as a glance over the Channel on a sunny day will prove, just a pebble's throw from the white cliffs of Dover!

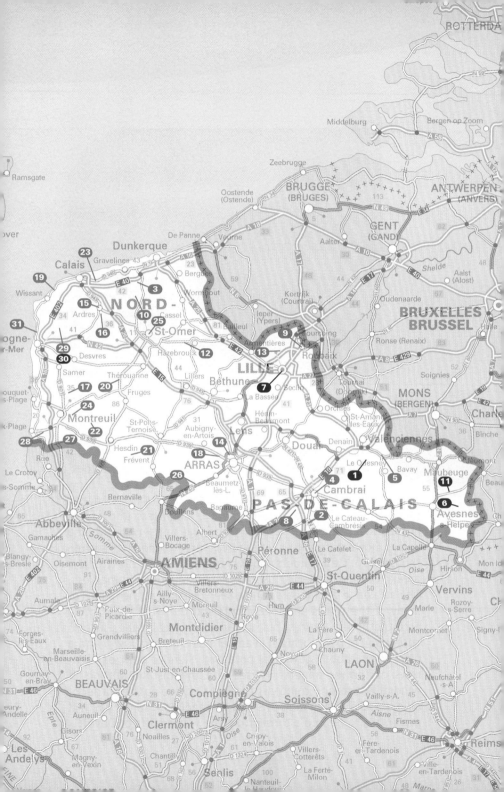

ARTRES - 59269

LA GENTILHOMMIÈRE
Mme Fournier

2 place de l'Église
59269 Artres
Tel. 03 27 28 18 80
la.gentilhommiere@wanadoo.fr
www.hotel-lagentilhommiere.com
Languages : Eng., Ger.

Closed from 2 to 25 Aug, Sun evenings • 10 rooms with bath/WC and television • €80; breakfast €10 • Menus €32 to €49 • Garden, private car park • Horse-riding treks (by reservation), hiking, mountain biking, horse-drawn carriage rides

The Fine Arts Museum of Valenciennes – the "Athens of the North".

This redbrick farmstead on the doorstep of Valenciennes was built in 1746: its surprisingly airy, well-proportioned rooms overlook a quiet inner courtyard or the manicured garden. Sample delicious regional dishes in the light restaurant installed in the converted cowshed, complete with vaulted ceiling and old mangers. The hotel can arrange horse-riding excursions and outings in a horse-drawn carriage if you book ahead.

Gastronomic weekend

Access : *Southbound from Valenciennes on the D 958 (towards Le Cateau), take a left on the D 400 after Famars*

BANTEUX - 59266

FERME DE BONAVIS
Mme Delcambre

59266 Banteux
Tel. 03 27 78 55 08
contact@bonavis.fr
www.bonavis.fr

Languages : Eng.

Open all year • 5 rooms with bathrooms • €47 to €56, breakfast included • No table d'hôte • Credit cards not accepted, no dogs admitted

Children adore exploring the ins and outs of this working farm.

You can't help but be impressed by the handsome scale of this former coaching inn, turned into a farm at the end of the Second World War. High ceilings and parquet floors set the scene for the well-decorated and well-soundproofed rooms. Countless leisure activities on the farm or nearby, including boules, table-tennis, table-football, cycling and walking trails; gliding and aerodrome 9km away.

Access : *11km southbound from Cambrai on the N 44*

BOURBOURG - 59630

LE WITHOF
Mme Battais

Chemin du Château
59630 Bourbourg
Tel. 03 28 22 16 17

Closed fortnight in Aug • 5 non-smoking rooms with bathrooms • €52, breakfast included • No table d'hôte • Garden, car park. No dogs admitted

The magnificent architecture of this 16C farm.

This fortified 16C farmhouse seems to float on its moat which, combined with its turrets and an imposing entrance reminiscent of a drawbridge, gives it the allure of a full-blown castle. This stately atmosphere extends through handsome doors into spacious bedrooms, all with immense bathrooms. On sunny days, breakfast is served in the courtyard. Excellent value for money.

Access : *14km to the south-west of Dunkerque on the A 16 towards Calais (exit no 23)*

CAMBRAI - 59400

LE CLOS SAINT-JACQUES
M. et Mme Quéro

9 rue Saint-Jacques
59400 Cambrai
Tel. 03 27 74 37 61
rquero@wanadoo.fr
www.leclosstjacques.com

Open all year • 5 non-smoking rooms and 1 apartment, all with bathrooms • €72 to €85, breakfast €8.50 • Table d'hôte €20 to €35 • Car park. Dogs not admitted

Pluck up your courage and venture down to the hospital's former crypts.

The owner, who knows absolutely everything about his lovely house in the town centre, is more than happy to share some of the more unusual episodes with guests. Each room is a picture of sophistication and discernment, enhanced by moulded ceilings, mosaics and woodwork. The five bedrooms and one apartment are no exception and sport antiques or family heirlooms and attractive fabrics. The regional-inspired menu, made from high quality produce, is the work of a genuine cordon bleu chef.

Access : *In the town*

JENLAIN - 59144

CHÂTEAU D'EN HAUT
M. Demarcq

59144 Jenlain
Tel. 03 27 49 71 80
chateaudenhaut@fr.st
www.chateaudenhaut.fr.st
Languages : Eng.

Open all year • 5 rooms with bathrooms • €55 to €80, breakfast included • No table d'hôte • Park, car park. Credit cards not accepted, no dogs admitted

 A castle literally crammed with antiques.

A long paved drive leads up to this magnificent 18C château and dovecote, set in the middle of pleasant parkland. The remarkable interior, rich in marquetry, antiques and period paintings is certainly worthy of the grand approach and is beautifully cared for by the charming hosts. Four-poster beds adorn the comfortable bedrooms and guests have the run of a light, airy breakfast room, library and even a small chapel.

Access : *6km to the south-east of Valenciennes on the D 934 and the D 59*

LIESSIES - 59740

CHÂTEAU DE LA MOTTE
M. Plateau

59740 Liessies
Tel. 03 27 61 81 94
contact@chateaudelamotte.fr
www.chateaudelamotte.fr
Languages : Eng.

Closed from 18 Dec to 9 Feb and Sun evening and Mon lunchtime out of season • 9 rooms in 2 wings, most have bath/WC, some have shower/WC, all have television • €65; breakfast €8.30; half-board available • Menus €21 (weekdays) to €65 • Park, car park • Mountain-bike rentals

 Sampling a little slice of the very, er,... "robust" local Boulette d'Avesnes cheese.

This delightful pink-brick edifice was built in the 18C on the edge of the forest of l'Abbé Val Joly for the Benedictine brotherhood of Liessies; the monks may have gone, but the peace and quiet remains. The wide bay windows of the restaurant, reminiscent of an orangery, overlook a leafy park and the rooms, furnished with rustic or period pieces, and the bathrooms have just been treated to a new lease of life. Guests can look forward to exploring the paths of the Avesnes Nature Reserve.

Access : *Leave Liessies southbound on the D 133 or the D 963 and take the minor road to Motte*

RIBÉCOURT-LA-TOUR - 59159

LILLE - 59000

BRUEGHEL
Mme Lhermie

3-5 parvis Saint-Maurice
59000 Lille
Tel. 03 20 06 06 69
hotel.brueghel@wanadoo.fr
www.hotel-brueghel.com
Languages : Eng., Sp.

Open all year • 65 rooms with bath/WC or shower/WC, all have television • €80 to €90 (€75 low season); breakfast €8 • No restaurant • Public car park nearby

LE CLOS XAVIANNE
M. et Mme Leriche

20 rue de Marcoing
59159 Ribécourt-la-Tour
Tel. 03 27 37 52 61
http://ferme.leriche.free.fr

Open all year • 3 rooms, including one apartment under the eaves, all with bathrooms • €50 to €63, breakfast included • No table d'hôte • Garden, car park. Credit cards not accepted, dogs not admitted

 The lively historic centre of Lille and its convivial atmosphere.

This unpretentious establishment is rarely empty and it's not hard to see why. There's the typically Flemish first impression of its redbrick and chalk-white façade, then its pleasing old-fashioned interior with dark wainscoting and a period lift shaft in wood and wrought-iron, not to mention the fresh, pastel-coloured rooms, most of which overlook the Gothic church of St Maurice. Best of all is its practical location in the heart of Lille, just two minutes from the Grand'Place.

 The collection of old watering cans at the foot of the dovecote.

This working cereal farm is home to three rooms, located in the old cowshed off the main house. Elegance depicts the two rooms, upstairs, while the attic apartment is enhanced by the appeal of original beams. The large walled courtyard leads into an English-style garden that boasts over 300 species of plants. A collection of old agricultural tools is displayed in an impressive barn that borders on a museum.

Access : *Opposite St Maurice Church*

Access : *11km southwest of Cambrai on the D29*

ROUBAIX - 59100

SAINT-PIERRE-BROUCK - 59630

ABRI DU PASSANT
M. Renart

14 rue Vauban
59100 Roubaix
Tel. 03 20 11 07 62
jfrenart@caramail.com
http://abri-du-passant.ifrance.com/
Languages : Eng.

Closed in Aug • 4 rooms with bathrooms • €34; breakfast €5; half-board available • Table d'hôte €11 (evening only during the week, by reservation) • Garden. Credit cards not accepted

 Contemporary works of art adorn the whole house.

You will not be disappointed by the restful mood of this late-19C property next door to Barbieux park. Many original architectural features, such as the tiled mosaic floor in the hall, impressive high ceilings and lovely light wood staircase, still reveal an almost Victorian love of discreet home comforts. The bedrooms and bathrooms are all generously proportioned. The sitting and dining room provide the setting for an exhibition of works of art by a young local painter.

Access : *To the south-west of the town, near the park*

CHÂTEAU DE SAINT-PIERRE-BROUCK
M. et Mme Duvivier-Alba

287 route de la Bistade
59630 Saint-Pierre-Brouck
Tel. 03 28 27 50 05
contact@lechateau.net
www.lechateau.net
Languages : Eng., It.

Open all year by reservation • 5 non-smoking rooms with bathrooms • €70 to €75, breakfast included • Table d'hôte €25 (by reservation only) • Park, car park. Credit cards not accepted, no dogs admitted

 Cosily comfortable.

Nestling in a five-acre park, this impressive château built in 1905 is home to richly furnished rooms complete with moulded ceilings and marble fireplaces, and named after flowers. Make sure you taste the mistress of the house's tasty Flemish-flavoured cooking, served in the plush dining room or in the lovely winter garden-cum-conservatory overlooking the countryside.

Access : *8km northbound from Éperlecques National Forest, on the D 1*

SARS-POTERIES - 59216

HÔTEL DU MARQUAIS
Mmes Carrié et Guinot

65 rue du Général-de-Gaulle
59216 Sars-Poteries
Tel. 03 27 61 62 72
hoteldumarquais@aol.com

www.hoteldumarquais.com

Closed from 1 to 15 Feb • 11 non-smoking rooms with bath/WC or shower/WC • €50; breakfast €7 • No restaurant • Garden, car park • Tennis

Picking out a treasure in the stone pottery workshops of Sars, still in working order.

Painted brick walls and old furniture grace the bedrooms of this former farmhouse, converted into a hotel. Depending on the weather, breakfast is served on the large communal table in the hall or on the terrace overlooking the garden. Guests can choose between tennis or a visit to the Museum-Workshop of Glass in the rambling house of the former director of the glassworks.

Access : *On the main road through town, on the outskirts*

WALLON-CAPPEL - 59190

LA FERME DES LONGS-CHAMPS
M. Mentasti-Boniec

98 rue des Longs Champs
59190 Wallon-Cappel
Tel. 03 28 40 09 07
leslongschamps@aol.com
www.fermedeslongschamps.com

Open all year • 3 non-smoking rooms, two of which are upstairs, with modern bathrooms, television and modem • €70 to €80, breakfast included • No table d'hôte • Terrace, garden, car park. Credit cards not accepted, dogs not admitted

Walking in the garden and around the estate.

Surrounded by fields as far as the eye can see, this 18C farmhouse has lost nothing of its original authenticity. Once past the small porch, you enter an inner courtyard dotted with duck ponds and extended by a garden. The three tastefully decorated rooms with wooden floorboards and antique furniture and a cosy sitting room with Flemish fireplace and comfortable leather armchairs are located in a separate wing. Tasty generous breakfasts.

Access : *9km southbound from Cassel*

WAMBRECHIES - 59118

13

FANTASIA
M. Defaut et Mme Lecocq

Au Port de Plaisance
59118 Wambrechies
Tel. 06 16 44 09 82
contact@peniche-fantasia.com
www.peniche-fantasia.com

Open all year • 3 non-smoking air-conditioned rooms with bathrooms • €80, breakfast included • Table d'hôte €32 (by reservation 48hr in advance) • Terrace. Credit cards not accepted, dogs not admitted

A floating maison d'hôte!

Maybe we should invent a new term for this floating establishment run by a welcoming couple who are crazy about boats. This barge built in 1951 has lost none of its original charm. After being received in the wheelhouse, you will descend to the main room, decorated in the spirit of yachts of yesteryear. Three air-conditioned wood-panelled cabins, of modest proportions but more than amply comfortable, await guests. Table d'hôte meals must be reserved 48hr in advance.

Access : *At the marina*

ANZIN-SAINT-AUBIN - 62223

14

LES VOLETS BLEUS
M. et Mme Rousseau

47 rue Briquet Taillandier
62223 Anzin-Saint-Aubin
Tel. 03 21 23 39 90
rousseau_philippe@yahoo.fr
www.voletsbleus.com

Open all year • 3 rooms, one of which is upstairs, with bath/WC, bathrobes, slippers, television and modem • €74, breakfast included • Table d'hôte €19 to €35 • Terrace, car park. Credit cards not accepted, dogs not admitted

The enthusiastic owner bends over backwards to make guests feel welcome.

The white façade and blue shutters of this house surrounded by a flower-decked wooded garden are full of promise. While the general upkeep of the house cannot be faulted, the creativity of the cuisine will definitely be the highlight of your sojourn. Gargantuan buffet breakfasts of sweet and savoury delights, including homemade flans and jams, terrine of duck fillets, smoked trout and a cheese platter. The gastronomic table d'hôte menu is the work of a genuine cordon bleu.

Access : *Opposite Arras golf course*

AUTINGUES - 62610

ARDRES - 62610

AU PETIT TAMBOUR D'AUTINGUES
M. et Mme de St-Just

288 rue de Louches
62610 Autingues
Tel. 03 21 36 25 38
www.petit-tambour.com

Open all year • 5 non-smoking rooms, two on ground floor, one of which has disabled access, all with bath/WC or shower/WC • €58, breakfast included • No table d'hôte • Park, garden, car park. Credit cards not accepted, dogs not admitted

LES DRAPS D'OR
M. et Mme Borel

152 rue Lambert d'Ardres
62610 Ardres
Tel. 03 21 82 20 44
christine@drapsdor.com
www.drapsdor.com

Open all year • 3 non-smoking rooms with bath/WC • €52, breakfast included • No table d'hôte • Garden, locked car park. Credit cards not accepted

We most liked The owners' pleasant welcome.

This simple modern-looking house, independent from the main wing, hides its old age behind a white façade and blue shutters. A handsome period bread oven stands in one of the two ground floor rooms. The other three rooms, upstairs (including a chalet-style apartment under the eaves), are equally full of charm with their exposed beams. The 6ha-park is comprised of woodland and meadows, including stabling for horses.

We most liked Strolling down to the lake.

This large somewhat unassuming yellow-walled house in the centre of the town has in fact enjoyed a rich and varied history since its construction in 1630. In turn, post house, hotel and boarding school for young ladies, its devotion to hospitality is nothing new. Golden yellow tones adorn the sitting room set off by predominantly blue furniture; the rooms for their part are more restrained in style. The flower-decked wooded garden affords many hours of relaxation.

Access : In the town, Louches road

Access : Next to the church

BEUSSENT - 62170

17

LA HAUTE CHAMBRE
M. Barsby

124 route d'Hucqueliers, hameau le Ménage
62170 Beussent
Tel. 03 21 90 91 92

Closed from 1 to 15 Sep and from 15 Dec to 15 Jan • 5 rooms upstairs with shower / WC • €90, breakfast included • No table d'hôte • Garden, park, car park. Credit cards not accepted, dogs admitted by request • Visit to the owner's sculpture studio

A delightful 19C manor nestling behind a curtain of greenery.

Sumptuous! If we only had one word to describe this mid-19C country house and its idyllic park, that would be it. A collection of the sculptor-owner's works is dotted around the grounds. The comfortable, exquisitely furnished rooms are a feast for the eyes and the breakfasts generous enough to satisfy the most demanding appetites. Exploring the park, home to some 300 animals, is always a hit with children.

Access : *10km northbound from Montreuil on the N 1 then the D 127*

DUISANS - 62161

18

LE CLOS GRINCOURT
Mme Annie Senlis

18 rue du Château
62161 Duisans
Tel. 03 21 48 68 33
contact @ leclosgrincourt.com

 www.leclosgrincourt.com

Open all year • 2 non-smoking rooms and 1 apartment • €50, breakfast included • No table d'hôte • Park, car park. Credit cards not accepted, no dogs admitted

The Clos believes in pampering its guests.

As you drive up the paved lane to this delightful manor house, get ready to be coddled and indulged. A lovely white spiral staircase leads up to rooms, more akin to suites, all of which overlook the park, which becomes a carpet of daffodils in the spring. Family photos adorn the walls of this lovely building begun in the reign of Louis XIV but only finished in the Second Empire.

Access : *9km westbound from Arras on the N 39*

FAUQUEMBERGUES - 62560

ESCALLES - 62179

LA RÊVERIE
Mme Blancquaert

19 rue Jonnart
62560 Fauquembergues
Tel. 03 21 12 12 38
Bblareverie@wanadoo.fr

Open all year • 3 non-smoking rooms with bath/WC and television • €58, breakfast included • Table d'hôte €30 • Terrace, garden, car park. Credit cards not accepted

LA GRAND'MAISON
M. Boutroy

Hameau de la Haute-Escalles
62179 Escalles
Tel. 03 21 85 27 75
lagrandmaison@infonie.fr

 www.lagrandmaison.chez.tiscali.fr
Languages : Eng.

Open all year • 6 rooms, all have bath/WC or shower/WC and television • €50 to €60, breakfast included • No table d'hôte • Garden, car park. Credit cards not accepted, dogs admitted on request

 Daydreaming on the terrace shaded by lime trees.

This late 19C manor house within the town has remained authentic. The plush sitting room with its large mirrors and inviting sofas still boasts a period marble fireplace and woodwork. The conservatory opens onto the immense garden divided into two parts. A spiral staircase leads up to three discreetly decorated rooms, in which the owners have endeavoured to maintain the house's original cachet. Varied table d'hôte menu by reservation.

 Poised between land and sea.

Wedged between two headlands and almost in sight of the white cliffs of Dover, this lovely 18C flower-decked farm has a spacious inner courtyard whose centrepiece is a dovecote. The spacious rooms overflow with antiques, the "prestige" rooms are the most comfortable. Children can romp to their heart's content in their very own play area and in the garden, which is home to a few animals. Walking, mountain biking and windsurfing less than 2km away.

Access : *In the town centre*

Access : *2km eastbound from Cap-Blanc-Nez on the D 243*

FILLIÈVRES - 62770

LE MOULIN
M. et Mme Legrand

16 rue de Saint-Pol
62770 Fillièvres
Tel. 03 21 41 13 20
aufildeleau@free.fr
http://aufildeleau.free.fr

Open all year • 5 non-smoking rooms with bathrooms • €49 to €53, breakfast included • Table d'hôte €20 (evenings) • Garden, park, car park. Credit cards not accepted, dogs admitted by request • Fishing, canoeing, mountain bike rental

The idyllic country setting of this mill.

This 18C mill, which boasts its original wheel and mechanism, lies on the road of the Field of the Cloth of Gold, where François I and Henry VIII's diplomatic summit once indulged their shared passion for power politics and full-blown pageantry. The well-restored mill is home to spacious rooms furnished with old pieces, where only the murmur of the Canche flowing beneath the windows will disturb the quiet. Magnificent park with two ponds, one for fishing.

Access : *7km to the south-east of Vieil-Hesdin on the D 340*

LOISON-SUR-CRÉQUOISE - 62990

LA COMMANDERIE
Mme Flament

Allée des Templiers
62990 Loison-sur-Créquoise
Tel. 03 21 86 49 87
www.lacommanderieloison.com
Languages : Eng.

Closed in Feb • 3 non-smoking rooms with shower/WC • €62 to €70, breakfast included • No table d'hôte • Garden, car park. Credit cards not accepted, no dogs admitted

The atmosphere, dripping with character and history.

The wonderful architecture of this former Knights' Templar command post, said to date back to the 12C, has been beautifully restored. Each of the refined rooms is named after one of the family's ancestors: Alice, Maria, Mancienne and Tantise. An agreeable clutter of old objects adorns the ground floor including pewter pots, a classically-French zinc bar and a set of forge bellows turned into a coffee table. The gurgling waters of the Créquoise add to the appeal of the park.

Access : *Take the long drive near the river*

MARLES-SUR-CANCHE - 62170

MARCK - 62730

LE MANOIR DU MELDICK
M. et Mme Houzet

2528 avenue du Général-de-Gaulle - Le Fort-Vert
62730 Marck
Tel. 03 21 85 74 34
jeandaniele.houzet@free.fr
www.manoir-du-meldick.com

Closed 24 Dec to 6 Jan • 4 rooms with shower/WC • €60, breakfast included • No table d'hôte • Car park. Credit cards not accepted, no dogs admitted

MANOIR FRANCIS
Mme Leroy

1 rue de l'Église
62170 Marles-sur-Canche
Tel. 03 21 81 38 80
manoir.francis@wanadoo.fr
Languages : Eng.

Open all year • 3 rooms with bath/WC • €60, breakfast included • No table d'hôte • Garden. Credit cards not accepted, dogs not admitted

 The owners' attentive care.

So close to the port of Calais and yet so far, this lovingly restored manor house is a little gem of a find. Each of the spacious, individually decorated rooms is named after a flower: "Daisy", "Cornflower", "Rose" and "Poppy" – "Hyacinth" has a king-sized bed. All are equipped with coffee and tea making facilities and biscuits. Even better than home!

 The lady of the house's attention to detail.

You have to go under the immense porch and through the garden, home to a host of farmyard animals, to reach this 17C fortified farmhouse. We loved the interior, particularly the ground floor with its lovely chalk vaults upheld by diagonal beams. Old furniture, a private sitting room and unusual bathrooms complement the spacious rooms. The terrace under the shade of an apple tree is enchanting.

Access : *5.5km to the south-east of Montreuil-sur-Mer on the D 113*

Access : *6km eastbound from Calais on the D 940 and the D 119*

SAINT-OMER - 62500

25

CAPS ET MARAIS D'OPALE
M. et Mme Bogaert

11 quai du Commerce
62500 Saint-Omer
Tel. 03 21 93 89 82
mariec.bogaert@wanadoo.fr
www.bb-opale.fr.st

Open all year • 2 rooms and 1 apartment, with bath/WC or shower/WC, all with television • €53, breakfast included • No table d'hôte • Garden, car park. Credit cards not accepted, dogs not admitted

We most liked **The unaltered cachet of this manor house.**

This late 19C manor house, on the banks of the canal, has undergone much restoration work, which far from detracting from its charm has added to it. In the sitting room a marble fireplace is enhanced by period woodwork and moulded ceilings. The veranda, with its pretty mosaic of tiles, opens onto the deliciously peaceful walled garden. Upstairs two individually and tastefully decorated rooms and one apartment are both spacious and comfortable. Theme workshops organised: embroidery, cooking, etc.

Access : *150m from the railway station, near the marshes, shops and town centre, 500m from the auditorium*

SAULTY - 62158

26

CHÂTEAU DE SAULTY
Mme Dalle

82 rue de la Gare
62158 Saulty
Tel. 03 21 48 24 76
chateaudesaulty@nordnet.fr
Languages : Eng.

Closed in Jan • 4 rooms with bathrooms • €55, breakfast included • No table d'hôte • Park, car park. Credit cards not accepted, no dogs admitted

We most liked **A glass of home-grown apple or pear juice at breakfast time.**

This splendid castle, built in 1835, lies opposite a superb park and a fruit orchard. The rooms, of varying sizes, have parquet floors and are decorated with old or pine furniture; all have a decorative marble fireplace. An assortment of home-made jams and fruit juices are served at breakfast in the ancestral dining room. Library and table-tennis.

Access : *19km to the south-west of Arras towards Doullens on the N 25*

TIGNY-NOYELLE - 62180

VERTON - 62180

LE PRIEURÉ
M. Delbecque

Impasse de l'Église
62180 Tigny-Noyelle
Tel. 03 21 86 04 38
r.delbecque@wanadoo.fr
www.leprieure-tigny.com
Languages : Eng., Ger., Greek

Open all year • 5 rooms with bath/WC and television • €70 to €98, breakfast included • Table d'hôte €28 (evenings only) • Garden, park

LA CHAUMIÈRE
Mme Terrien

19 rue du Bihen
62180 Verton
Tel. 03 21 84 27 10
genevieve.terrien@free.fr
www.alachaumiere.com

Open all year • 4 non-smoking rooms • €59; breakfast included • No table d'hôte • Garden, car park. Credit cards not accepted, no dogs admitted

 Stylish interior decoration.

The owner-antique dealer has lovingly restored his pretty turquoise-shuttered house, set in a small park. The rooms are stylish and feature exposed beams and antiques; the split-level room is most praiseworthy, as is the suite with sitting room and fireplace. The breakfast room and the superb regional fireplace are also worth a look. Golfers will adore the prospect of trying out the 36-hole golf course of Nampont, only 3km away.

 The charm of a doll's house.

This quaint cottage with its thatched roof and flowered garden is just 4km from the sea. An atmosphere of refined elegance and warmth pervades the place. Each of the non-smoking rooms has its own individual personality. Stay for a few days and you'll notice that breakfast is served on different tableware each morning, thanks to the lady of the house's wonderful collection. Golf nearby.

Access : *Behind the church*

Access : *4km eastbound from Berck on the D 303*

WIERRE-EFFROY - 62720

LE BEAUCAMP
M. et Mme Bernard

62720 Wierre-Effroy
Tel. 03 21 30 56 13
contact@lebeaucamp.com
www.lebeaucamp.com

Closed 20 Dec to 20 Jan • 5 non-smoking rooms with bath/WC or shower/WC and television • €90 to €100, breakfast included • No table d'hôte • Park, garden, car park. Dogs not admitted • Sauna

 We most liked **Beginning the day with a generous flavourful breakfast.**

This impressive manor house, built in 1860 by the current owner's great grandfather, stands in the heart of a 10ha-estate. An independent gîte can sleep six people in a tastefully decorated interior with Indian furniture. However the most attractive rooms are those upstairs, reached by the original wooden staircase. They offer a pleasant combination of elegance and comfort including polished wooden floors, marble fireplaces and modern bathrooms. Sauna available.

Access : *1km southwest from Wierre-Effroy on the D 238, Marquise road and left onto the Wimille road*

WIERRE-EFFROY - 62720

LA FERME DU VERT
M. Bernard

Rue du Vert
62720 Wierre-Effroy
Tel. 03 21 87 67 00
ferme.du.vert@wanadoo.fr
www.fermeduvert.com
Languages : Eng.

Closed from 15 Dec to 20 Jan and Sun from Nov to Mar • 16 rooms with shower/WC • €60 to €85; breakfast €9; half-board available • Menus €22 to €39 • Garden, park, car park. Dogs not admitted in restaurant

 We most liked **Visiting the cheese-workshop, also run by your hosts.**

A perfect invitation to get back to grass roots. You won't be disappointed by the comfortable, quiet rooms, decorated simply and tastefully; the largest are full of amusing nooks and crannies. Sample the delicious home cooking made with local produce. Before leaving, make sure you stop by the next door cheese-makers and stock up on fresh and matured cheeses.

Access : *10km to the north-east of Boulogne on the N 42 and the D 234*

WIMEREUX - 62930

31

LA GOÉLETTE
Mme Avot

13 digue de Mer
62930 Wimereux
Tel. 03 21 32 62 44
mary@lagoelette.com
www.lagoelette.com
Languages : Ger., Eng., Flemish

Open all year • 4 rooms with bath/WC and television • €80 to €130, breakfast included • No table d'hôte • Credit cards not accepted, no dogs admitted

Gulping down the fresh sea air when you open your shutters in the morning.

Who could resist the charm of this 1900 villa so well located on the dyke-promenade of Wimereux? The perfectly restored interior has remained authentic and the rooms now reveal their original harmonious shades, moulded ceilings and warm sea-faring pine furniture. The Blue and Yellow rooms offer a wonderful view of the sea, while the others overlook the inner garden. Ask your hosts for walking tips.

Access : *On the seafront*

NORMANDY

Hormandy, the muse of poets and artists from the world over, offers an ever-changing vision of rural pleasures. Take a bracing walk along the miles of coastline and admire her string of elegant seaside resorts. You will be left breathless when you first catch sight of Mont Saint-Michel rising from the sands or look down over Étretat's chalky cliffs into the sea crashing on the rocks below. It is impossible not to be moved by the memory of the men who died on Normandy's beaches in June 1944 or to be captivated by the cottage-garden charm of Guernsey and Jersey. Further inland, acres of neat'hedge-lined fields meet the eye, home to thoroughbred horses and herds of dairy cows. Breathe in the scent of the apple orchards in spring and admire the half-timbered cottages and smart manor houses, before wandering down to the Seine, following its meanders past medieval cities, daunting castles and venerable abbeys. No description would be complete, however, without Normandy's culinary classics: fresh fish and seafood, creamy, ivory-white Camembert, cider and, last but not least, the famous oak-aged apple brandy, Calvados.

BANVILLE - 14480

ARROMANCHES-LES-BAINS - 14117

FERME LE PETIT VAL
M. Gérard Lesage

24 rue du Camp-Romain
14480 Banville
Tel. 02 31 37 92 18
fermelepetitval@wanadoo.fr
Languages : Eng.

Open all year • 5 rooms, 2 of which are on the ground floor and 3 are upstairs, all have bathrooms • €52 to €60, breakfast included • No table d'hôte • Garden, car park. Credit cards not accepted, no dogs admitted

LA MARINE
M. Durand

1 quai du Canada
14117 Arromanches-les-Bains
Tel. 02 31 22 34 19
hotel.de.la.marine@wanadoo.fr
www.hotel-de-la-marine.fr
Languages : Ger., Eng., It.

Closed from 27 Nov to 15 Feb • 28 rooms with bath/WC or shower/WC and television • €61 to €87; breakfast €9; half-board available • Menus €22 to €35 • Car park

Watch the cows grazing in the meadows.

Imagine the Allied Forces landing on D-Day.

The discreet, practical rooms of this rambling white hotel resemble the cabins of a luxury liner. Taking pride of place on the menu are lobster – choose your own in the tank – fish and shellfish, served in the turquoise dining room and bar-brasserie. All the windows overlook the Channel and the horizon out of which the Allied forces emerged, before landing at dawn on "the longest day", 6th June 1944.

This characteristic farmhouse, thought to date from the 17C, is ideal to get back to grass roots. Its snug, quietly elegant rooms are spread over two wings around a central courtyard. Family heirlooms adorn the pleasant breakfast room. In the summer, the flowered garden is particularly inviting.

Access : *In the town*

Access : *At the port*

BAYEUX - 14400

D'ARGOUGES
M. et Mme Ropartz

21 rue Saint-Patrice
14400 Bayeux
Tel. 02 31 92 88 86
dargouges@aol.com
www.hotel-dargouges.com
Languages : Eng.

Closed 24 and 25 Dec • 28 rooms, most have bath/WC, some have shower/WC, all have television • €68 to €100 (€52 to €84 low season); breakfast €8 • No restaurant • Garden, garage, car park. No dogs admitted

A quiet garden in the heart of the town.

It is more than worthwhile venturing past the rather austere façade of this 18C house to catch a glimpse of the lovely garden in the rear. The house's glorious past can still be seen in the intricate patterns of the parquet floors, old doors and worn beams in some of the rooms. A number of the most spacious bedrooms are perfect for families: new bedding, fabrics and wallpaper are on the agenda for the bedrooms.

Access : *On the road from the town centre to the N 13, Cherbourg road*

CAMBREMER - 14340

MANOIR DE CANTEPIE
Mme Gherrak

Le Cadran
14340 Cambremer
Tel. 02 31 62 87 27
Languages : Eng., Ger., Sw.

Closed from 15 Nov to 1 Mar • 3 rooms upstairs, with bathrooms • €70, breakfast included • No table d'hôte • Garden, park, car park. Credit cards not accepted, no dogs admitted

Normandy at its best!

This splendid early 17C manor house will weave its magic spell the minute you set foot within its elegant, tasteful walls. A superb oak staircase takes you up to immense, well-appointed rooms; the old-fashioned bathrooms are particularly stunning. Family heirlooms grace the sitting room and the flowered grounds are clearly the work of a devoted gardener. Not to be missed!

Access : *11km westbound from Lisieux on the N 13 then the D 50*

CAMBREMER - 14340

LES MARRONNIERS
M. et Mme Darondel

Les Marronniers
14340 Cambremer
Tel. 02 31 63 08 28
chantal.darondel@wanadoo.fr

www.les-marronniers.com
Languages : Eng.

Open all year • 5 rooms with shower/WC • €50 to €58, breakfast included • No table d'hôte • Park. Credit cards not accepted, no dogs admitted

 Time and care have clearly been lavished over the rooms.

This pleasant 17C edifice set in the middle of a flowered park enjoys a lovely view over the Dive Valley, with the sea in the distance. Each of the personalised rooms has been named after a goddess: "Venus", is full of light, "Diane" is smaller but much more romantic. Tuck into the ample breakfasts served on a pretty patio.

Access : *5km on a by-road*

CRÉPON - 14480

LA FERME DE LA RANÇONNIÈRE
Famille Sileghem et Vereecke

Route d'Arromanches-les-Bains
14480 Crépon
Tel. 02 31 22 21 73
ranconniere@wanadoo.fr

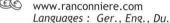
www.ranconniere.com
Languages : Ger., Eng., Du.

Open all year • 35 rooms, 1 of which has disabled access, with bath/WC or shower/WC and television • €50 to €135; breakfast €11; half-board available • Menus €20 (weekdays) to €40 • Garden, car park

 A stay in these farms is like reading a page of a history book.

High ceilings upheld by worn beams, vaults, monumental fireplaces, exposed stone walls and flagstones are just some of the original decorative features of this 13C fortified farmhouse. The furniture and ornaments showcased in the rooms were found in local second-hand and antique shops. For a few euros extra, treat yourself to the luxury of added space and calm in the 18C Ferme de Mathan just 800m away.

1944 Jeep with visits to historic sites of the Second World War

Access : *Westbound from Bayeux, take the D 12 towards Douvres-la-Délivrande for 12km, turn left onto the D 65*

CRÉPON - 14480

DAMPIERRE - 14350

LE MANOIR DE CRÉPON
Mme Poisson

14480 Crépon
Tel. 02 31 22 21 27
manoirdecrepon@wanadoo.fr
www.manoirdecrepon.com
Languages : Eng.

Closed from 10 Jan to 10 Feb • 4 rooms with bath/WC • €75, breakfast included • No table d'hôte • Garden, car park • Mountain biking

CHÂTEAU DE DAMPIERRE
MM. Cherrier et Jouvin

Le Château
14350 Dampierre
Tel. 02 31 67 31 81
www.chateau-de-dampierre.com

Open all year • 5 rooms overlooking the dovecote with shower/WC • €60 to €90, breakfast €3 • No table d'hôte • Credit cards not accepted, dogs not admitted • Receptions organised

A faultlessly decorated home.

Towering trees grace an immense park surrounding this 18C manor house whose blood-red façade is characteristic of the region. Once inside the well-dimensioned, comfortable rooms, the owner-antique dealer's flair is visible in the beautiful choice of furniture. On cold winter days, a log fire burns in the breakfast room, formerly the kitchen. Bicycles rented on the estate.

Access : *In the village*

The sight of the impressive corner watchtowers at the end of the drive invariably takes one's breath away.

In the heart of the Normandy countryside on the borders of Calvados and Manche, this splendid 16C manor house, is the work of François Gabriel who also built the château of Carrouges. The rooms are more functional than you might expect in a castle, and are comfortably equipped and well cared for. They look down onto the deep moat, former Henry IV-style gatehouse and superbly restored pigeon coop, whose 2200 nesting alcoves bear witness to the prestige of the lords of Dampierre.

Access : *9km from Thorigny-sur-Vire on the D 13, then right on the D 53*

FORMIGNY - 14710

LA FERME DU MOUCHEL
Mme Lenourichel

Lieu-dit Le Mouchel
14710 Formigny
Tel. 02 31 22 53 79

odile.lenourichel@wanadoo.fr
www.ferme-du-mouchel.com

Open all year • 4 non-smoking rooms with bathrooms • €47 to €50, breakfast included • No table d'hôte • Garden, car park. Credit cards not accepted, dogs not admitted • Near the D-Day Landing Beaches

 The spontaneity and quality of Odile's welcome.

This inviting manor farmhouse which dates back to the 16C stands at the end of a tiny country lane. Three delightful rooms are located upstairs in the main wing, while another room complete with an adjoining small room, is situated in the wing next door, on the ground-floor of which breakfast is served. The welcoming owners, who also raise dairy cows, might even introduce you to the pleasures of milking if you're lucky!

Access : *Leave the Carentan-Bayeux N 13 road at Formigny on the D 517, turn right, then left onto a minor road*

GÉFOSSE-FONTENAY - 14230

MANOIR DE L'HERMEREL
M. et Mme Lemarié

14230 Géfosse-Fontenay
Tel. 02 31 22 64 12
lemariehermerel@aol.com
www.manoir-hermerel.com
Languages : Eng.

Closed from 15 Nov to 15 Feb • 4 rooms with bathrooms • €70, breakfast included • No table d'hôte • Car park. No dogs admitted

 A guided visit of the manor and the farm.

Surrounded by meadows, this 17C fortified manor-farm with its proud aspect, handsome porch, regular lines and elegant dovecote could easily pass for a castle. The rooms in the manor are a subtle blend of comfort and charm. The sitting room in a 15C Gothic chapel is supremely restful and your hosts' unaffected welcome quite captivating.

Access : *8km northbound from Isigny on the D 514 then take the D 200 to Osmanville*

GONNEVILLE-SUR-MER - 14510

FERME DES GLYCINES
M. et Mme Exmelin

Carrefour Malernes
14510 Gonneville-sur-Mer
Tel. 02 31 28 01 15
Languages : Eng.

Closed from Jan to Mar, Nov to late Dec and Mon to Thu in low season • 3 rooms with shower/WC • €52, breakfast included • No table d'hôte • Garden, car park. Credit cards not accepted, no dogs admitted

"Old Macdonald had a farm!"

Children love the horses, sheep, hens and ducks who live in the grounds of this timber-framed farm which dates from 1780 and is surrounded by over 40 acres of orchards and park. The colour schemes render the rooms most pleasant and one has a private terrace. Farm produce features prominently on the breakfast table, served by the fireside in winter. Delightful garden.

Access : *At Houlgate take the D 24 for 4km, turn left at the crossroads between the D 24 and D 142*

GRANDCAMP-MAISY - 14450

LA FAISANDERIE
Mme Le Devin

14450 Grandcamp-Maisy
Tel. 02 31 22 70 06

Open all year • 3 rooms with bathrooms • €50 to €90, breakfast included • No table d'hôte • Garden, car park. Credit cards not accepted, dogs not admitted • Swimming pool

A magical site set amidst parkland, meadows and forests.

If you dream of finding out more about the life of a stud farm, head for this welcoming manor house covered in Virginia creeper, just outside the town centre. The estate raises thoroughbreds. The pretty sitting room is warmed by a splendid period fireplace. All the different rooms are furnished with rustic or painted cane pieces. Breakfasts are served in a delightful dining room whose walls sport Liberty print-style wallpaper.

Discovering the life of a stud farm

Access : *In the town*

HONFLEUR - 14600

LA COUR SAINTE CATHERINE
M. et Mme Giaglis

74 rue du Puits
14600 Honfleur
Tel. 02 31 89 42 40
giaglis@wanadoo.fr
www.giaglis.com

5 rooms under the eaves with bath/WC and television • €85, breakfast included • No table d'hôte • Garden, car park. Credit cards not accepted, dogs not admitted

 The owners' unaffected warm welcome.

Right in the heart of the historic town, this maison d'hôte located in a former 17C convent has two rooms and three apartments, all of which are decorated with great talent. The sitting room is graced by an original fireplace, embellished with wood carvings. The pleasant inner flower-decked courtyard, laid out like a parish garden, adds a splash of colour to the bare stonewalls and half-timbered façade. Breakfast is served in the old press house.

Access : *Eastbound from the church of Ste-Catherine along the rue du Puits*

LA CAMBE - 14230

FERME DE SAVIGNY
Mme Ledevin

14230 La Cambe
Tel. 02 31 21 12 33
re.ledevin@libertysurf.fr
http://perso.wanadoo.fr/ferme-savigny/

Open all year • 4 rooms with bathrooms • €40 to €45, breakfast included • No table d'hôte • Garden, car park. Dogs not admitted

 An impressive weeping willow takes pride of place in the huge courtyard

This old farmhouse, flanked by a small tower with a pretty spiral staircase, offers four attractive comfortable rooms, all of which are tastefully and individually decorated. White walls and beams, Liberty-print bed canopies, handsome Normandy wardrobes or 1920s period furniture. Breakfast is served in the sitting room with a black stone floor, or, when the weather permits, under the arbour. Attractive garden.

Access : *2.5km from La Cambe on the D 613 and D 113*

LONGVILLERS - 14310

LA NOUVELLE FRANCE
Mme Godey

Lieu-dit La Nouvelle France
14310 Longvillers
Tel. 02 31 77 63 36
courrier@la-nouvelle-france.com
www.la-nouvelle-france.com

Open all year • 3 rooms on ground-floor and 2 in another wing, with bath/WC • €43, breakfast included • No table d'hôte on Sat-Sun; menu €17 • Terrace, garden. Credit cards not accepted, no dogs admitted • Swings, table-tennis.

This little gem is Normandy through and through - but keep it to yourself.

On the edge of a country lane in a little grove stands a delightful stone farmhouse behind a former barn, now home to three bright, cheery rooms and a sitting room. Sober, tasteful interior decoration, a restful garden, a drive lined with birch trees and superb country views from the moment you wake up. Delicious breakfasts and a 100% Norman table d'hôte served in the owners' home.

Access : *4km northbound of Aunay-sur-Odon on the D 6, then D 216 towards Longvillers*

LONGVILLERS - 14310

MANOIR DE MATHAN
M. et Mme de Mathan

14310 Longvillers
Tel. 02 31 77 10 37
mathan.normandie@caramail.com
Langues : Eng.

Open from late Mar to 15 Nov • 4 rooms on 3 levels with bathrooms, non-smokers only • €43 to €50, breakfast included • No table d'hôte • Garden-orchard, car park. Credit cards not accepted, no dogs admitted • Horse riding 500m away.

The owners' faultless hospitality.

Half-way between Aunay-sur-Odon and Villers-Bocage, surrounded by fields and orchards, an imposing manor farmhouse founded in the 15C but reworked several times. A spiral staircase with its own entrance leads up to a sitting room, a small kitchen and three fine rooms all of which are most comfortable. A courtyard shaded by a chestnut tree is lined with barns and outhouses for farm equipment. The former bakery now houses a delightful gîte. Riding centre nearby.

Access : *3km northbound of Aunay-sur-Odon on the D 6, half-way from Longvillers*

MANVIEUX - 14117

LA GENTILHOMMIÈRE
M. et Mme Rottier

4 route de Port
14117 Manvieux
Tel. 02 31 51 97 91
lagentilhommiere4@wanadoo.fr
http://monsite.wanadoo.fr/lagentilhommiere4

Open all year • 5 rooms with bath/WC • €60, breakfast included • No table d'hôte • Garden, car park. Credit cards not accepted, dogs not admitted

The lush green site so close to the sea.

You are guaranteed a good night's sleep in this sturdy stone-built 18C house, two minutes from Arromanches beach. Each room, with its own private sitting room, is decorated along an individual colour theme. The lady of the house makes her own bread and yoghurt for the tasty generous breakfasts served on an enormous wooden table in the Normandy-style dining room with exposed rafters.

Access : *At L'Eglise, 2km from Arromanches, not far from the D-Day landing beaches*

MEUVAINES - 14960

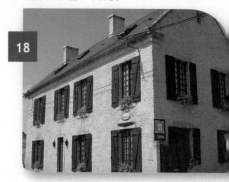

L'ANCIENNE ÉCOLE
M. Darthenay

Route d'Arromanches
14960 Meuvaines
Tel. 02 31 22 39 59
françoise.georges@ancienne-ecole.net
www.ancienne-ecole.net
Langues : Ger., Eng., Du.

Closed late Dec • 3 rooms with bath/WC • €48, breakfast included; half-board available • Table d'hôte €22 (evenings only) • Terrace, car park. No dogs admitted

Betwixt land and sea.

As the name suggests, this building which dates from 1741 was formerly the village school. Now a B&B establishment, it offers rustic rooms under the eaves, all of which overlook the countryside. Regional specialities feature prominently on the table, set by the fireside in the pleasant dining room. Nearby are the D-Day Landing beaches and the delightful inland villages of Bessin.

Access : *8km to the south-east of Arromanches on the D 65*

ORBEC - 14290

LE MANOIR DE L'ENGAGISTE
Mme Dubois

15 rue Saint-Rémy
14290 Orbec
Tel. 02 31 32 57 22
engagiste@wanadoo.fr
www.engagiste.com
Langues : Eng.

Open all year • 4 rooms, all with disabled access
• €85, breakfast included • No table d'hôte
• Garden

 An immaculately decorated half-timbered manor house.

Right in the heart of town, this beautifully restored 16C mansion is definitely worth staying a day or two. You will want to snuggle up in the thoughtfully decorated bedrooms with terracotta tiled floors, wood panelling and old tapestries. In the winter, a huge fire burns in the exquisite sitting room whose centrepiece is a mezzanine with exhibitions of paintings and sculpture. An old carriage takes pride of place in the vast inner courtyard. Not to be missed!

Access : *In the heart of the town*

SAINT-MARTIN-AUX-CHARTRAINS - 14130

MANOIR LE MESNIL
M. et Mme Hom

Route de Trouville
14130 Saint-Martin-aux-Chartrains
Tel. 02 31 64 71 01
manoirlemesnil@aol.com
www.manoirlemesnil.com

Closed for 1 week in Jan and 1 week in Nov
• 3 non-smoking rooms on two storeys, all with bath/WC • €60 to €70, breakfast included • No table d'hôte • Park, car park. Dogs not admitted

 Treat yourself to this haven of tranquillity so close to Deauville.

This mansion with character, built in 1880, stands in a splendid 7 000 square-metre wooded park. It is home to four relatively spacious rooms, each of which is decorated on an individual theme with its own palette of colours. On the leisure side, there is a reading room, well stocked with tourist brochures and guides, which is also where the lady of the house serves delicious breakfasts. A pretty half-timbered independent house is home to a gîte with two studios.

Access : *3km northbound from Pont-l'Évêque on the N 177 towards Deauville*

VOUILLY - 14230

SUBLES - 14400

LE MOULIN DE HARD
Mme Fichot

Lieu-dit Le Moulin-de-Hard
14400 Subles
Tel. 02 31 21 37 17
www.gites-de-france-calvados.fr
Langues : Eng., Ger.

Open all year • 3 non-smoking rooms with shower/WC • €85 to €100, breakfast included • No table d'hôte • Garden, car park. Credit cards not accepted, no dogs admitted • Fishing in the Drôme

 The care taken with the indoor and outdoor fittings.

This handsome 18C watermill stands deep in the country in a landscaped garden through which runs the Drôme, a little river where anglers can savour the pleasure of catching gudgeon in the private fishing waters. Modern fittings add comfort to the rooms which combine old and new decorative elements in the same style found in the communal rooms. Snug sitting room with fireplace and generous breakfasts served in a bright, panoramic kitchen-cum-dining-room.

Access : *6km south-west of Bayeux on the D 572, then D 99 left after Subles*

CHÂTEAU DE VOUILLY
M. et Mme Hamel

14230 Vouilly
Tel. 02 31 22 08 59
château.vouilly@wanadoo.fr
www.chateau-vouilly.com
Langues : Eng.

Closed from Dec to Feb • 5 rooms with bathrooms • €70 to €90, breakfast included • No table d'hôte • Garden, car park. No dogs admitted

 A step back in time.

This 18C château surrounded by a moat and carefully tended gardens was commandeered as the American press HQ during the landings in June 1944. Beautifully restored by the owner himself, the rooms are spacious and comfortable and some have old furniture. On the ground floor, guests have the run of a string of impressive sitting rooms, one of which doubles as a breakfast room, with lovely old two-tone tiled floors.

Access : *8km to the south-east of Isigny on the D 5*

AIZIER - 27500

23

LES SOURCES BLEUES
M. et Mme Laurent

Route du Vieux-Port
27500 Aizier
Tel. 02 32 57 26 68
www.les-sources-bleues.com

Open all year • 4 non-smoking rooms on 2 floors, with baths, showers and separate WC • €55 to €68, breakfast included • Table d'hôte €20 (evening only) • Garden, car park

 Exploring the wooded park on the banks of the Seine.

Nestled in a delightfully untrammelled park, this lovely Norman house built in 1854 enjoys a wonderful view over the Seine and the boats plying their course to and from Le Havre. Wood, old tiles and parquet floors prevail in the welcoming interior. The rooms are comfortably uncluttered and the most pleasant have sloping ceilings. On the leisure side, you can choose from tennis, horse-riding and canoeing.

Access : *5km northbound from Bourneville on the D 139*

CONTEVILLE - 27210

24

LE VIEUX PRESSOIR
Mme Anfrey

Hameau le Clos-Potier
27210 Conteville
Tel. 02 32 57 60 79
www.la-ferme-du-pressoir.com

Open all year • 7 rooms with bathrooms • €60, breakfast included • Table d'hôte €25 by reservation (closed Sun) • Car park. Credit cards not accepted, no dogs admitted

 Delightfully old-fashioned.

Lovers of calm and authenticity will immediately fall head over heels for this attractive 18C timber-framed farm set in the midst of Normandy's green fields. The picture-perfect interior features a wealth of 19C and 20C objects and furniture picked up in second-hand and antique shops. Rooms which make up in charm what they lack in size, a garden that can hardly be seen for flowers, ducks paddling on the pond and a three-hundred-year-old press add the finishing touches to this rural landscape.

Access : *13.5km from Honfleur on the Pont-Audemer road (D 580), then take the D 312 on the left*

FOULBEC - 27210

LA CROIX-SAINT-LEUFROY - 27490

L'EAU-ASIS
M. Ratiskol

La Vallée Guillemard
27210 Foulbec
Tel. 02 32 56 59 92
alain-ratiskol@wanadoo.fr

Open from 1 Mar to 30 Sep • 3 rooms, two of which are upstairs, with bath/WC and small kitchens • €53, breakfast €6 • No table d'hôte • Terrace, park, garage. Credit cards not accepted, dogs not admitted

MANOIR DE LA BOISSIÈRE
M. et Mme Sénecal

Hameau de la Boissaye
27490 La Croix-Saint-Leufroy
Tel. 02 32 67 70 85
chambreslaboissiere@wanadoo.fr

www.chambres-la-boissiere.com

Open all year • 5 rooms, 3 of which under the eaves, all with bathrooms • €46, breakfast included • Table d'hôte €21 • Garden, car park. Credit cards not accepted, dogs not admitted

The magnificent water sports complex close by.

This pleasant house, built in a regional style in the heart of an attractive wooded park, overlooks the quiet countryside. The living room with its comfortable lounge and fireplace invites guests to relax and wind down. Alternatively you may want to try your hand at billiards in the specially fitted out room. Each of the bedrooms is individually decorated and equipped with a functional bathroom.

The peaceful charm of this 15C house.

Hidden away in the midst of fields of cereal crops, this working farm seems to have been built around the dining room. Fireplaces, Normandy wardrobes, timber beams and pretty restored tiled floors. Each room is individually decorated in either a romantic or cosy spirit. Family heirlooms adorn all the rooms. Outdoors the old porch and duck pond make your stay even more irresistible. Normandy-inspired table d'hôte meals by reservation.

Access : *4km southeast of Conteville on the D312*

Access : *2km northeast on the D10*

LES PRÉAUX - 27500

LE PRIEURÉ DES FONTAINES
M. et Mme Decarsin

Route de Lisieux
27500 Les Préaux
Tel. 02 32 56 07 78
jacques.decarsin@wanadoo.fr
www.prieure-des-fontaines.fr
Langues : Eng., Sp.

Open all year • 5 non-smoking rooms, with bathrooms and telephone • €95, breakfast included • No table d'hôte • Garden, car park. Credit cards not accepted, no dogs admitted • Outdoor swimming pool, mountain biking, table-tennis

Bicycling in the nearby forest.

This 17C priory cradled in the valley of La Risles has been so well restored, you would be forgiven for thinking that it's new. The well-dimensioned, comfortable rooms are graced with old furniture, beams and tiled floors; all are non-smoking and equipped with telephones. A sitting room with fireplace, hall with piano and lovely garden are perfect to relax in.

Access : *5km to the south-west of Pont-Audemer on the D 139*

LA CHARTERIE
M. de Morchoven et Mme François

La Charterie
27230 Saint-Aubin-de-Scellon
Tel. 02 32 45 46 52
la.charterie@wanadoo.fr
http://monsite.wanadoo.fr/la.charterie

Open all year • 4 rooms upstairs, all with bath/WC • €55, breakfast included • Table d'hôte €20 drinks included • Garden, car park. Credit cards not accepted, no dogs admitted

Making the most of the peace and quiet as you listen to the birds and wander around the countryside.

This brick-built mansion topped by a bell tower and flanked by half-timbered 18C outhouses stands at the end of a drive in a park. The four spacious rooms decorated with Liberty prints have wonderful high ceilings. Breakfast is served in the large ground-floor living room. In winter, a roaring fire warms the sitting room. Outside you can enjoy the English-style garden, orchard and vegetable plot which surround this handsome property.

Access : *1km south-east of Saint-Aubin-de-Scellon on the D 41*

SAINT-SYLVESTRE-DE-CORMEILLES - 27260

LA MAISON POMMEROSE
Mme Van Hove

Saint-Sylvestre-l'Église
27260 Saint-Sylvestre-de-Cormeilles
Tel. 02 32 57 13 05
genevieve.vanhose@wanadoo.fr
www.pommerose.com

Open all year • 3 non-smoking rooms under the eaves, all with bath/WC or shower/WC • €56 to €58, breakfast included • Table d'hôte €17 including drinks (by reservation) • Garden, terrace, car park. Credit cards not accepted

 All of Normandy wrapped up in a house.

Be prepared to fall under the spell of this lovely half-timbered house, nestling in a haven of greenery and tranquillity. In addition to its preserved authentic character, it offers all the comforts of modern facilities which admirably blend in with the tiled floors and wood panelling. A handsome limestone fireplace takes pride of place in the dining room. Outside, the sloping garden planted with apple trees is the departure point for walks along the many country paths in the vicinity.

Access : *2km from the centre of Cormeilles, towards Lieurey, Bernay by the D810 and left after the sign to St-Pierre-de-Cormeilles*

VERNEUIL-SUR-AVRE - 27130

CHÂTEAU DE LA PUISAYE
Mme Diana Costes

27130 Verneuil-sur-Avre
Tel. 02 32 58 65 35
info@chateaudelapuisaye.com
www.chateaudelapuisaye.com

Open all year • 4 rooms and 1 apartment, with bath/WC • €98, breakfast included • Table d'hôte €14 to €37 • Park, garden, car park. Credit cards not accepted, dogs not admitted

The immense park, pond and bridle paths.

This château which dates back to Napoleon III can hardly be said to lack authenticity, from the parquet floors and wood panelling to the marble fireplaces. What's more it has been treated to a masterful restoration. The rooms and bathrooms have all been entirely renovated in an old-fashioned spirit with antique furniture and elegant bathtubs and taps. Fine views of the park. Two plush sitting rooms with armchairs and sofas. Homemade jams and cakes served with the English-style breakfast.

Access : *3.2km from the centre of Verneuil-sur-Avre on the C19*

AVRANCHES - 50300

LA CROIX D'OR
M. Bertheaume

83 rue de la Constitution
50300 Avranches
Tel. 02 33 58 04 88
hotelcroixdor@wanadoo.fr
www.hoteldelacroixdor.fr
Langues : Eng.

Closed in Jan and Sun evenings from 15 Oct to 1 Apr • 27 rooms located in several buildings around a courtyard. Rooms have bath/WC or shower/WC and television • €60 to €95; breakfast €8.40; half-board available • Menus €17 (weekdays) to €55 • Garden, private car park

 Daydreaming in the delightful garden.

This 17C coaching inn stands near the Patton Memorial which commemorates the "Avranches Breakthrough". Its half-timbered façade borders a pretty garden planted with apple trees and hydrangeas. Quiet rooms, some of which have been renovated. A countrified dining room whose collections of gleaming clocks, well-worn wardrobes, porcelain and copper pots, exposed beams and stonework would almost be worthy of a museum.

Access : *From the Mont-Saint-Michel, at Place du Général Patton, turn left onto Rue de la Constitution towards the town centre*

BARFLEUR - 50760

LE CONQUÉRANT
M. et Mme Delomenède

16/18 rue Saint-Thomas-Becket
50760 Barfleur
Tel. 02 33 54 00 82
Langues : Eng., Ger.

Open from 15 Mar to 15 Nov • 10 rooms, most with bath/WC or shower/WC, and television • €62 to €103; breakfast €6.50 to €10.60 • No restaurant, but there is a crêperie open in the evening for hotel guests; menus €15 to €25.40 • Garden, small private car park. No dogs admitted

 Drinking in the atmosphere of this tiny fishing harbour in a quayside café.

This handsome 17C granite house is just two minutes from the port: back in 1066, its shipyard built the vessel which carried William the Conqueror to the shores of England and victory. Twisting corridors, proof of the house's long past, lead to rustic, immaculate rooms, some of which boast beautiful Norman wardrobes. Breakfasts and supper banquets of sweet and savoury pancakes are served outdoors in the garden.

Access : *In the street at right-angles to the seaside, between the harbour and Rue de la Poste*

BARNEVILLE-CARTERET - 50270

LES ISLES
M. de Mello

9 boulevard Maritime
50270 Barneville-Carteret
Tel. 02 33 04 90 76
hotel-des-isles@wanadoo.fr
www.hoteldesisles.fr

Closed in Feb • 31 rooms with television, some are non-smoking • €79 (€59 low season); breakfast €10; half-board available • Menus €15 to €33 • Terrace, garden, patio • Heated swimming pool, jacuzzi, reading room

 In fine weather, the eye can see as far as Alderney, Guernsey, Herm, Sark and Jersey.

This seaside villa, opposite the Channel Islands, is perfect for a bracing holiday break. There are plans to give the rooms, already spruced up in 2004, something of a makeover, and to add a patio, while the communal parts of the house will retain their nautical flavour. Pleasant bar, reading room and panoramic breakfast room where a superb buffet is served. A number of paintings by Brazilian artists dotted about the place add a touch of exoticism.

Cooking, golf and sand yachting courses

Access : *Overlooking the beach*

VILLAGE GROUCHY
M. Sebire

11 rue du Vieux-Lavoir
50560 Blainville-sur-Mer
Tel. 02 33 47 20 31
jr.sebire@free.fr
jr.sebire.free.fr

Closed from Jan to Mar • 5 rooms with shower/WC • €40, breakfast included • No table d'hôte • Garden, car park. Credit cards not accepted, no dogs admitted

 The rustic modern flavour of this fishermen's house.

Village Grouchy is the name of an old fishing village that formerly stood here. Nowadays the granite walls of this old fishermen's house offer spacious rooms lined in wood from floor to ceiling. In the morning, take a seat on the wooden benches around a large table and toast yourself by the fireside. Summer kitchen in the immense garden in the rear. Warm and welcoming.

Access : *2km northbound from Blainville-sur-Mer on the D 72*

FLAMANVILLE - 50340

BEL AIR
M. et Mme Morel

2 rue du Château
50340 Flamanville
Tel. 02 33 04 48 00
hotelbelair@aol.com
www.hotelbelair-normandie.com
Langues : Eng., Sp.

Closed from 1 Dec to 31 Jan • 11 rooms, 6 of which are non-smoking, all have bath/WC or shower/WC and television • €65 to €110 (€59 to €75 low season); breakfast €10 • No restaurant • Garden, car park. No dogs admitted • Piano bar

 The excisemen's cliff path.

The windows of the cosy rooms overlook the neat fields of the Cotentin ("little coast") region of north-western Normandy. The breakfast room is set in a light, airy conservatory, the old-fashioned lounge-bar has a marble fireplace and piano; palm trees adorn the lovely garden. All this awaits you in the thick granite walls of this house, formerly the home of the steward of the castle farms, just a few fields from the beaches overlooking the Atlantic.

Cooking lessons

Access : *By the D 4 that goes through the village, near the château*

HUISNES-SUR-MER - 50170

LE MOULIN DE LA BUTTE
Mme Rabasté

11 rue du Moulin-de-la-Butte
50170 Huisnes-sur-Mer
Tel. 02 33 58 52 62
beatrice.rabaste@club-internet.fr
 www.bedandbreakfastineurope.com/
lemoulindelabutte

Open all year • 5 rooms on 2 levels, with bath/WC and television, 1 with disabled access • €35, breakfast included • No table d'hôte • Terrace. Credit cards not accepted, no dogs admitted • Bicycles available

 Recharging your batteries in this splendid landscape.

Located at the gates of this traditional village in the bay of Mont-Saint-Michel, this recent villa offers quiet accommodation in spacious rooms decorated in a personalised, low-key style; all enjoy the stunning prospect of the famous abbey and rocky island. Breakfast is served in the panoramic sitting room. The owners and staff extend a warm welcome and tourist tips to guests, when they aren't caring for their immaculate and very functional establishment. Guests can borrow bicycles.

Access : *Between Avranches and Mont-St-Michel (D 275), head towards Huisnes-sur-Mer, then towards the German Military Cemetery, then turn left on a minor road*

JUVIGNY-LE-TERTRE - 50520

LE LOGIS
M. et Mme Fillâtre

50520 Juvigny-le-Tertre
Tel. 02 33 59 38 20
fillatre.claude@wanadoo.fr
http://gitefillatre.free.fr

 Langues : Eng.

Closed from 15 Nov to 15 Mar • 3 rooms with shower/WC • €38 to €42, breakfast included; half-board available • No table d'hôte • Car park. Credit cards not accepted

 What is so wonderful about France is that you can taste everything!

Old stones and good local produce are the hallmark of this 17C farm. The rooms in the former dovecote are contemporary in style while the one in the main wing, with granite fireplace and beams carved with the royal fleur-de-lys insignia, has more character. Tennis courts and water sports nearby. The farm organises visits and tasting sessions, so save space in the boot to stock up on farm produce, cider and home-made preserves.

> *Jam-making courses*

Access : *12km westbound from Mortain on the D 977 and the D 5, then take the D 55 towards Saint-Hilaire*

MONTCHATON - 50660

LE QUESNOT
M. Germanicus

3 rue du Mont-César
50660 Montchaton
Tel. 02 33 45 05 88

Closed from 15 Nov to Easter • 3 rooms with shower/WC • €45, breakfast included • No table d'hôte • Garden, car park. Credit cards not accepted, no dogs admitted

 Cradled in a leafy nest of flowers.

Built out of local stone, this 18C house is surrounded by a curtain of foliage and flowers. All the stylish, well-kept rooms are upstairs. On the ground floor is a vast country living-room for the sole use of guests. From the terrace and small garden, you will be able to see the village church perched on an outcrop. Extremely friendly and welcoming.

Access : *6.5km to the south-west of Coutances on the D 20 then the D 72*

MONTVIRON - 50530

39

MANOIR DE LA CROIX
M. et Mme Wagner

La Croix du Gros Chêne
50530 Montviron
Tel. 02 33 60 68 30
contact@manoirdelacroix.com
www.manoirdelacroix.com

Open all year (by reservation) • 2 rooms and 2 apartments (non-smoking only) with bath/WC • €64 (room), €82 (apartment), breakfast included • No table d'hôte • Garden, car park. Credit cards not accepted, no dogs admitted

 We most liked **Gulp down the fresh air – inside and out of this non-smoking establishment.**

If your lungs have had enough of urban pollution, head for this bubble of atmospheric purity. This 19C Anglo-Norman-style manor house overlooks a lovely garden, home to palms and other rare trees. The Empire and Louis-Philippe suites are immense and adorned with antiques, the other rooms and bathrooms are invariably spotless. The breakfast table is laden with cooked meats, cheeses and home-made jams and preserves.

Access : *8km to the north-west of Avranches towards Granville (D 973), then the D 41 (1km after Montviron)*

OMONVILLE-LA-PETITE - 50440

40

LA FOSSARDIÈRE
M. Fossard G.

Hameau de la Fosse
50440 Omonville-la-Petite
Tel. 02 33 52 19 83
Langues : Eng.

Closed from 15 Nov to 15 Mar • 10 rooms dotted around a hamlet, 9 have bath/WC, one has shower/WC • €41 to €64; breakfast €9 • No restaurant • Car park • Sauna, thalassotherapy, pond with picnic terrace

 We most liked **Nothing could be more pastoral than this hamlet.**

This hamlet-cum-hotel is on the doorstep of Omonville, the last resting place of Jacques Prévert, poet-screenwriter and counter-cultural icon. The rooms, which vary in size and comfort, are spread over several sandstone houses. Breakfast is served in the hamlet's former bakery. Young and old always find plenty to do in or around the private pond, 300m away, whether rowing, picnicking or simply making daisy chains.

Access : *Near Cap de la Hague, between Saint-Germain-des-Vaux and Omonville-la-Rogue, opposite Anse Saint-Martin*

RÉVILLE - 50760

LE MANOIR DE CABOURG
Mme Marie

10 route du Martinet
50760 Réville
Tel. 02 33 54 48 42

Open all year • 3 rooms with shower/WC • €47 to €52, breakfast included • No table d'hôte • Garden, car park. Credit cards not accepted, no dogs admitted

 Perfectly located, just 150m from the beach.

A lovely drive lined in poplar trees leads up to this 15C fortified farm just two minutes from the Saire Valley and the seaside. The white walls of the rooms are dotted with the occasional block of granite and mullioned windows, loopholes and arrow slits, now glazed, you'll be glad to hear. Toast your toes in front of the roaring log fire lit in the sitting room in winter after trekking round the region's countless marvels of Romanesque architecture. Charming welcome.

Access : *3.5km northbound from Saint-Vaast on the D 1, 150m from the seashore*

SAINTE-GENEVIÈVE - 50760

MANOIR DE LA FÉVRERIE
Mme Caillet

4 route d'Arville
50760 Sainte-Geneviève
Tel. 02 33 54 33 53
caillet.manoirlafevrerie@wanadoo.fr

Open all year • 3 rooms with shower/WC • €62 to €70, breakfast included • No table d'hôte • Car park. Credit cards not accepted, no dogs admitted

 A matchless attention to detail.

The sea and Barfleur's picturesque harbour are only three kilometres from this charming 16C and 17C manor house. The snug bedrooms, reached by a granite staircase, were undoubtedly the work of a romantic at heart, as the pastel wallpaper, old furniture and striped or floral fabrics confirm. Breakfasts, served by the fireside in winter, are a feast for the eyes and the palate. We defy you to resist the temptation to curl up in the soft, inviting sofas and deep armchairs in the sitting room.

Access : *3km westbound from Barfleur on the D 25 and the D 525 Sainte-Geneviève road*

TAMERVILLE - 50700

TOURLAVILLE - 50110

MANOIR DE BELLAUNEY
Mme Allix-Desfauteaux

11 route de Quettehou
50700 Tamerville
Tel. 02 33 40 10 62
bellauney@wanadoo.fr
www.bellauney.com
Langues : Eng.

Closed from 1 Nov to Easter • 3 rooms upstairs with shower/WC • €55 to €75, breakfast included • No table d'hôte • Garden, car park. Credit cards not accepted, no dogs admitted

MANOIR SAINT-JEAN
M. et Mme Guérard

Le hameau Saint-Jean
50110 Tourlaville
Tel. 02 33 22 00 86

Open all year • 3 non-smoking rooms with shower/WC • €50 to €55, breakfast included • No table d'hôte • Car park. Credit cards not accepted, no dogs admitted

History oozes from every crevice of this old manor house.

This 16C manor house, flanked by a tower and three handsome Romanesque arches is set in a lovely, tended mature garden. An impressive staircase leads up to the individually decorated rooms, each of which evokes a significant period in the domain's history. "Medieval" on the ground floor, "Louis XV" and "19C Norman" upstairs. The original wainscoting in the breakfast room adds the final touch to this historic abode.

Access : *3km to the north-east of Valognes towards Quettehou*

It would be difficult to find a more amiable ambassador for the region.

This warm, welcoming 18C manor lies on the edge of the park of the Château des Ravalets. The view from the windows over Trottebec, Cherbourg and the coast is quite superb. The immaculate rooms are adorned with family heirlooms, as are the sitting rooms. Your graceful hostess could talk until the cows come home about her region's immense natural and cultural heritage.

Access : *1km past the castle on the D 322, then head for the "centre aéré" (play centre) and the Brix road*

ALENÇON - 61000

LE GRAND CERF
M. Bouvet

21 rue Saint-Blaise
61000 Alençon
Tel. 02 33 26 00 51
legrandcerf-alencon@wanadoo.fr
www.hotelgrandcerf-61.com
Langues : Eng.

Closed 20 Dec to 6 Jan • 22 rooms, all have bath/WC or shower/WC and television • €55 to €78; breakfast €7; half-board available • Restaurant closed Sun; menus €14 to €27 • Terrace

 Whether made out of wrought-iron or threads as fine as human hair, lace is everywhere.

The ornate wrought-iron adorning the façade of this hotel, built in 1843, has withstood the passing of time and lives up to Alençon's reputation as the capital of lace. The hotel has recently been treated to a facelift, but the hall is still adorned with the establishment's namesake, a stag's head and the restaurant and most of the rooms have retained their original dimensions and moulded ceilings. In the summer, meals are served in a delightful inner walled courtyard.

Access : *From Place du Général de Gaulle, drive towards the town centre, the hotel is on the right past the préfecture*

LONGNY-AU-PERCHE - 61290

L'ORANGERIE
M. et Mme Desailly

9 rue du Docteur-Vivares
61290 Longny-au-Perche
Tel. 02 33 25 11 78
desailly-fondeur@tele2.fr
http://lorangerie.free.fr
Langues : Eng., Sp.

Open all year • 3 rooms with bath/WC • €48, breakfast included • Table d'hôte (only by reservation) €14 • Garden. Credit cards not accepted, no dogs admitted

 Settle down for a quiet evening in front of the fire after a day in the open air.

This attractive former orangery is now home to three lovely rooms, each of which is named after a wild flower: honeysuckle, buttercup and bluebell; the last of these is perfect for families. A large sitting room is ideal for long autumn evenings, grilling chestnuts or sizzling mushrooms over a crackling log fire. Ducks and fish have taken up residence in an old wash house hidden in the garden.

Access : *In the village*

RÂNES - 61150

SAINT-PIERRE
M. et Mme Delaunay

6 rue de la Libération
61150 Rânes
Tel. 02 33 39 75 14
info@hotelsaintpierreranes.com
www.hotelsaintpierreranes.com
Langues : Eng.

Open all year • 12 rooms with bath/WC or shower/WC and television • €52 to €68; breakfast €8; half-board available • Restaurant closed Fri evening; menus €15 to €42 • Terrace

 The pleasant family welcome of this village inn.

Two minutes from an old castle now a gendarmerie, this stone-built house stands in the centre of the village, a stone's throw from the old castle. Parquet flooring, stylish wallpaper, exquisite wardrobes and rustic furniture adorn the appealing little rooms which are exceedingly reasonably priced. You will also appreciate the warm dining room; as well as the traditional recipes (frog's legs) made with local produce; make sure you sample the chef's speciality: tripe.

Access : *In the centre of the village near the main square*

CRIQUETOT-L'ESNEVAL - 76280

LE MANOIR
M. et Mme Quevilly

5 place des Anciens-Élèves
76280 Criquetot-l'Esneval
Tel. 02 35 29 31 90
serge.quevilly@wanadoo.fr

Open all year • 5 rooms on 2 floors, non-smokers only, all with bath/WC and television • €56 to €60, breakfast included, half-board available • Table d'hôte €15 (by reservation) • Park, car park. Credit cards not accepted, no dogs admitted

 The "house in the country" atmosphere.

This brick and stone manor house in the centre of a tiny Normandy village was formerly the residence of the lords of Esneval. Today it houses five spacious rooms full of character furnished with antiques including some splendid Normandy wardrobes. The wooded, flowered park invites guests to relax and wind down. Breakfast is served on the large communal table. The lady of the house, ever eager to please her guests, extends a warm welcome.

Access : *8km south-east of Etretat on the D 139*

DERCHIGNY-GRAINCOURT - 76370

LE MANOIR DE GRAINCOURT
M. et Mme Baron

10 place Ludovic-Panel
76370 Derchigny-Graincourt
Tel. 02 35 84 12 88
contact@manoir-de-graincourt.fr
www.manoir-de-graincourt.fr

Open all year • 5 non-smoking rooms upstairs, all with bath/WC • €80 to €95, breakfast included • Table d'hôte €30 • Garden, car park. No dogs admitted

Relaxing under the park's cedar trees.

The graceful welcome to this 19C Normandy manor house, which comes with a half-timbered façade and is flanked by a wing that was formerly a convent, cannot be faulted. The convent is now home to pretty rooms furnished with antiques that open onto the garden. On the leisure side, guests have the run of a sitting room-library and a billiards room. Depending on the season, breakfast is either served in the roomy kitchen heated by a stove or outdoors.

Access : *9km eastbound from Dieppe on the D 925*

DIEPPE - 76200

LA VILLA FLORIDA
M. et Mme Noël

24 chemin du Golf
76200 Dieppe
Tel. 02 35 84 40 37
villa-florida@wanadoo.fr
www.lavillaflorida.com
Langues : Eng.

Open all year • 4 rooms, one with mezzanine, with bath/WC or shower/WC • €70, breakfast included • No table d'hôte • Garden, car park. Credit cards not accepted, dogs not admitted

The faultlessly kind welcome.

This imaginatively designed slate covered house nestles in a delightful garden that opens onto the Dieppe golf course. Serenity and light fill the handsome interior proportions. Sober, contemporary rooms, each with a small private terrace, ensure total peace and quiet for all. Breakfasts are taken in the sitting room or garden, depending on the weather.

Golf, yoga

Access : *2km eastbound of Dieppe, towards Pourville on the D 75, before the golf course*

DIEPPE - 76200

51

VILLA DES CAPUCINS
M. Boré

11 rue des Capucins
76200 Dieppe
Tel. 02 35 82 16 52
villa.des.capucins@wanadoo.fr
www.villa-des-capucins.fr

Open all year • 5 rooms with bathrooms • €62 to €65, breakfast included • No table d'hôte • Garden

 The pleasant welcome of the owners who adore receiving guests.

This brick-built abode in the outhouses of an old priory is located near the port in the Pollet district. The rooms, most of which are on two levels, are all independent and open onto a stunning flower garden. Personalised decoration, antiques and a muted atmosphere characterise the rooms. The stylish, welcoming breakfast room is located in the former kitchens.

Access : *Two minutes from the port in the historic district known as "du Pollet"*

EU - 76260

52

MANOIR DE BEAUMONT
Mme Demarquet

Route de Beaumont
76260 Eu
Tel. 02 35 50 91 91
catherine@demarquet.com

 www.demarquet.com
Langues : Eng.

Open all year • 3 rooms with shower / WC • €47 to €55, breakfast included • No table d'hôte • Garden, car park. Credit cards not accepted, no dogs admitted

Guests are offered a welcome drink on arrival.

On the edge of the forest, this former hunting lodge of the château of Eu enjoys a matchless view of the valley. The comfortable, tastefully decorated rooms overlook the park and the countryside; the family room has been thoughtfully equipped with a kitchenette. Relax in the sitting room and library and delve into the numerous books – in French and English – on the area. Bicycles and horse loose-boxes are also available for guests and their four-legged companions.

Access : *2km eastbound from Eu on the D 49 towards the forest*

FORGES-LES-EAUX - 76440

AUBERGE DU BEAU LIEU
M. et Mme Ramelet

Route de Paris - Le Fossé
76440 Forges-les-Eaux
Tel. 02 35 90 50 36
aubeaulieu@aol.com
www.auberge-du-beau-lieu.com
Langues : Eng.

Closed from 8 Jan to 8 Feb • 2 rooms, with bath/WC and television • €56 to €76; breakfast €12 • Menus €18 (weekdays) to €57 • Terrace, garden, car park

 What could be more symbolic of Normandy than apple trees and dairy cows?

Two minutes from the tiny spa-resort of Forges, this attractive country inn is home to cosy rooms which open directly onto the garden and a snug rustic restaurant complete with beams and a stone fireplace. The tableware is a reminder of the town's illustrious porcelain industry. The warmth of your hosts' welcome is such that you will even forget you're in a hotel.

Access : *2km on the D 915, towards Gournay*

ISNEAUVILLE - 76230

LA MUETTE
M. et Mme Auffret

1057 rue des Bosquets
76230 Isneauville
Tel. 02 35 60 57 69
jdftm.auffret@wanadoo.fr
www.charmance-lamuette.com

Open from mid-Mar to mid-Dec • 5 rooms, 4 of which are under the eaves, all with bath/WC • €75, breakfast included • No table d'hôte • Park, garden, car park. Credit cards not accepted, dogs not admitted

 The tranquillity of the spot, troubled only by bird song.

Snug welcoming rooms await you inside this old 18C press house. Half-timbered façades, tiled floors and exposed beams endow the interior with a strong Norman character, all of which is enhanced by the warm refined decoration. Outdoors, the orchard, vegetable plot and flower garden overlook a delightful wooded park, an ideal departure point for walks in the neighbouring forest. The delicious breakfasts are prepared with homemade produce.

Access : *By the centre of Isneauville, route de la Muette then 1km on rue des Bosquets on the left*

JUMIÈGES - 76480

LE RELAIS DE L'ABBAYE
M. et Mme Chatel

798 rue du Quesney
76480 Jumièges
Tel. 02 35 37 24 98

Open all year • 4 rooms with shower/WC • €42, breakfast included • No table d'hôte • Garden, car park. Credit cards not accepted

Roman Polanski's "Tess" could well have been shot near here!

Nestling in the shadow of the famous abbey, this pretty Norman slate-roofed house has everything you could wish for in a B&B establishment. A sophisticated rustic interior with beams, timbers, enormous fireplace, ornaments and antique plates. The rooms under the eaves upstairs are the most pleasant and the bathrooms merit a special prize. In the summer, breakfast is served in the garden.

Access : *Near the abbey*

LANDES-VIEILLES-ET-NEUVES - 76390

CHÂTEAU DES LANDES
M. et Mme Lemettre

76390 Landes-Vieilles-et-Neuves
Tel. 02 35 94 03 79
jgsimon@chateaudeslandes.com
www.chateaudeslandes.com

Open all year • 5 rooms including 1 apartment, on two storeys, all with bathrooms • €52 to €58, breakfast included • No table d'hôte • Park, garden, car park. Credit cards not accepted, dogs not admitted

Living like a king without going bankrupt.

Nothing is too much trouble for the owners in their efforts to make you feel at home in their pretty early 19C château, surrounded by a garden and park of two-hundred-year-old sequoias. On either side of the hall are the dining room and two sitting rooms panelled in wood with period fireplaces and chandeliers. At the rear is the large veranda where breakfast is served in summertime. Upstairs the spacious, pastel-coloured rooms are most comfortable.

Access : *15km northeast of Neufchâteau-en-Bray on the N 29-E 44 then the D 7*

LE TRÉPORT - 76470

LE HAVRE - 76600

VENT D'OUEST
M. Lassarat

4 rue Caligny
76600 Le Havre
Tel. 02 35 42 50 69
contact@ventdouest.fr
www.ventdouest.fr
Langues : Eng.

Open all year • 38 rooms, all have bath/WC or shower/WC and television • €88 to €115; breakfast €12 • No restaurant (room service available) • No dogs allowed • Tea room

GOLF HÔTEL
Evergreen SARL

102 route de Dieppe
76470 Le Tréport
Tel. 02 27 28 01 52
evergreen2@wanadoo.fr
 www.treport-hotels.com
Langues : Eng., Ger.

Closed Christmas weekend • 10 non-smoking rooms, all have television • €47 to €70; breakfast €7.20 • No restaurant • Park, car park. No dogs admitted

Extremely well-equipped rooms.

In front of the entrance to Tréport's campsite, turn left onto the tree-lined drive which will take you up to this lovely late-19C half-timbered property set in the grounds of an immense park. All the non-smoking rooms are generously sized, well-equipped and personalised; all have a fridge. Friendly and excellent value for money.

Visiting the port of Le Havre in a launch.

Betwixt land and sea, the "Westerly" is a haven of charm in the heart of Le Havre's Modern Quarter designed by 20C architect Auguste Perret. A stone's throw from the harbour, the interior decoration has a distinctly briny flavour. The guest-rooms, on the other hand, are more adventurous and guests can choose between "country", "meditation" or "mountain" rooms, among others. Knick-knacks, snug quilts and a host of tiny details make all the difference.

Access : *Near Tréport campsite*

Access : *Drive along Quai Colbert past Vauban docks, turn right at Quai George V (Commerce docks) and continue straight on as far as St Joseph's Church*

LE TRÉPORT - 76470

59

LE PRIEURÉ SAINTE-CROIX
M. et Mme Carton

76470 Le Tréport
Tel. 02 35 86 14 77
carton.nicole@wanadoo.fr
http://prieuresaintecroix.free.fr
Langues : Eng.

Open all year • 5 rooms (including 1 apartment) with bathrooms • €48 to €60, breakfast included • No table d'hôte • Garden, car park. Credit cards not accepted, no dogs admitted

Listening to the silence all around.

This farmhouse built in the reign of Louis-Philippe was formerly part of the castle of Eu's estate and is still a working cattle-farm. All the rooms, located in a separate wing, have been decorated in the same spirit with parquet floors, period furniture and recent bathrooms. The breakfast area, although entirely revamped, has retained its rustic appeal. Take a seat under the hundred-year-old flowering cherry trees in the garden.

Access : *2km eastbound from Tréport on the D 925 (Abbeville-Dieppe road)*

MARTAINVILLE-ÉPREVILLE - 76116

60

SWEET HOME
M. et Mme Aucreterre

534 rue des Marronniers
76116 Martainville-Épreville
Tel. 02 35 23 76 05
jean-yves.aucreterre@libertysurf.fr
http://www.jy.aucreterre.free.fr

Open all year • 4 non-smoking rooms upstairs, all with shower/WC or bath/WC and television • €49 to €70, breakfast included • Table d'hôte €12.50 • Garden, car park. Credit cards not accepted, no dogs admitted • Angling

Difficult to find a more romantic establishment.

This opulent Normandy home, tucked away in a haven of greenery and flowers, has four tastefully decorated rooms. Bright, light colours, cushions and bouquets of flowers further enhanced by distinctly modern bathrooms. The owners, who are justly enthusiastic about their home, are particularly proud of the "Green room". Sumptuous breakfasts that change every day. Tasty snacks in the evening by request.

Access : *By Impasse du Coquetier*

MAUQUENCHY - 76440

LE CLOS DU QUESNAY
M. et Mme Morisse

651 route de Rouen
76440 Mauquenchy
Tel. 02 35 90 00 97
info@leclosduquesnay.fr
www.leclosduquesnay.fr

Open all year • 4 non-smoking rooms, one of which has disabled access and 1 apartment, all with bathrooms • €50, breakfast included • Table d'hôte €19 • Park, garden, car park. Credit cards not accepted, dogs not admitted

The orchard of apple trees.

It's difficult to imagine that this early 19C farmhouse was in ruins not so long ago. It took three years to restore it to its present splendour. It is a delight to discover the tasteful mixture of authenticity and modernity, as in the sitting room where contemporary armchairs rub shoulders with family heirlooms. The handsome rooms (one of which has access for the disabled) offer an understated cosy comfort. Scrumptious Normandy-inspired table d'hôte meals.

Access : *1km eastbound on the D919, Forges-les-Eaux road*

ROUEN - 76000

LE CLOS JOUVENET
Mme de Witte

42 rue Hyacinthe-Langlois
76000 Rouen
Tel. 02 35 89 80 66
cdewitte@club-internet.fr
www.leclosjouvenet.com
Langues : Eng.

Closed Christmas holidays and Jan • 4 non-smoking rooms, all with bath/WC or shower/WC • €80 to €100, breakfast included • No table d'hôte • Terrace, library, private car park. Credit cards not accepted, no dogs allowed

The delightful view of the town and its steeples.

This enchanting 19C manor house perched on the hillside overlooking the town from the quiet of its immense garden is within wonderfully easy reach of Rouen. The energetic lady of the house enthusiastically welcomes guests to her cosy, elegant, immaculately kept rooms, which survey either the orchard or the town's steeples. In the morning, she prepares the excellent breakfasts herself, which are served in the kitchen, plush dining room or garden, depending on the season.

Access : *In the town centre*

ROUEN - 76000

HÔTEL DE LA CATHÉDRALE
M. Delaunay

12 rue Saint-Romain
76000 Rouen
Tel. 02 35 71 57 95
contact@hotel-de-la-cathedrale.fr
www.hotel-de-la-cathedrale.fr
Langues : Eng.

Open all year • 26 rooms with bath/WC or shower/WC, all have television • €62 to €89; breakfast €7.50 • No restaurant

 Breakfasting on the delightful patio which doubles as a tearoom in the afternoons.

This enchanting 17C establishment, located on one of Rouen's most beautiful old streets just a two minute walk from the cathedral, is proof that it is still possible to find good, well-priced accommodation in the heart of a tourist neigh-bourhood. Period furniture of varying styles, half-timbered walls, brightly coloured wallpaper and knick-knacks set the scene of this pleasantly old-fashioned hotel. An immense fireplace takes pride of place in the breakfast room with its raftered ceiling.

Access : *In the heart of the old town*

ROUEN - 76000

LE VIEUX CARRÉ
M. Beaumont

34 rue Ganterie
76000 Rouen
Tel. 02 35 71 67 70
vieux-carre@mcom.fr
www.vieux-carre.fr
Langues : Eng., It.

Open all year • 13 rooms, one of which has disabled access, with bath/WC or shower/WC and television • €55 to €60; breakfast €7 • Menus €13 (lunchtime only)

 There was nothing we didn't love!

The handsome walls of this house built in 1715, in the company of other august façades of the same vintage, line a street which is typical of Rouen and makes an ideal base camp from which to explore this "museum town". The interior is equally faultless and the rooms are decorated with frescoes and old wardrobes straight out of a boarding school dorm. The sitting room is snug and welcoming and the hotel boasts a courtyard terrace where mouth-watering pastries and a few choice dishes are served.

Access : *In the heart of the old town, between the Palais de Justice and the Musée des Beaux Arts*

SAINT-SAËNS - 76680

LE LOGIS D'EAWY
Mme Benkousky

1 rue du 31-Août-1944
76680 Saint-Saëns
Tel. 06 19 15 52 04
flocokousky@freesbee.fr
www.logisdeawy.com

Open all year • 2 rooms, one of which has disabled access and 2 apartments, all with bathrooms • €50 to €70, breakfast included • No table d'hôte • Garden, credit cards not accepted, dogs not admitted

A delightful stopover in the heart of a characterful town.

You cannot miss the half-timbered front of this old post house built in 1821. After passing under a porch, you will reach a paved courtyard extended by a flower garden. Inside, the original woodwork, fireplace, tiles and wooden floors combine to maintain the house's authenticity. A spiral staircase leads up to the rooms. High quality breakfasts. A delightful place at a reasonable price.

Access : In the town centre, opposite the tourist office and the church

SOMMERY - 76440

FERME DE BRAY
M. et Mme Perrier

76440 Sommery
Tel. 02 35 90 57 27
www.ferme.de.bray.free.fr
Langues : Eng.

Open all year • 5 rooms with bathrooms • €46, breakfast included • No table d'hôte • Garden, car park. Credit cards not accepted, no dogs admitted • Farm visits, fishing

The farm continues to uphold local rural traditions.

The land has been farmed by the same family for 18 generations and their 17C and 18C farmhouse, which doubles as a museum and a B&B, is simply astounding. Rural through and through, the furniture and the simplicity of the interior decoration echo this country spirit: each of the rooms, lightened by striped wallpaper, has its own fireplace. Activities abound on the farm, including a visit to the press, mill, dairy parlour, dovecote, not to mention exhibitions and fishing in the pond.

Access : 10km to the north-east of Forges-les-Eaux on the D 915

VALMONT - 76540

LE CLOS DU VIVIER
Mme Cachera

4 chemin du Vivier
76540 Valmont
Tel. 02 35 29 90 95
le.clos.du.vivier@wanadoo.fr
www.leclosduvivier.com
Langues : Eng., Sp.

Open all year • 2 rooms and 1 apartment with bath/WC • €90 to €100, breakfast included • No table d'hôte • Garden, car park. Credit cards not accepted

Breakfasting by the garden where ducks, swans, chickens and peacocks roam free.

This large 17C cottage, hidden deep in the countryside, was formerly an outbuilding of the Château de Valmont. Over the years, the current owners have tirelessly transformed it into a pleasant getaway where they take great pleasure in welcoming guests. Exposed beams, bare stonework and fireplaces make interesting architectural features in the sitting rooms. The appealing "cottage" atmosphere of the rooms has been wisely preserved.

Access : *2km eastbound of Valmont on the D 150 towards Ourville*

VARENGEVILLE-SUR-MER - 76119

LA TERRASSE
M. et Mme Delafontaine

Route de Vasterival
76119 Varengeville-sur-Mer
Tel. 02 35 85 12 54
francois.delafontaine@wanadoo.fr
www.hotel-restaurant-la-terrasse.com
Langues : Eng.

Open from 16 Mar to 14 Oct • 22 rooms with bath/WC or shower/WC • €50 to €57; breakfast €7.50; half-board available • Menus €20 to €35 • Garden, car park. No dogs admitted in restaurant • Tennis

The family donkey grazing in the meadow alongside the path leading down to the beach.

At the end of a pretty little lane flanked by fir trees, stands an early-20C brick house, which is the family home of the current owners. Nothing opulent or ostentatious deflects from the establishment's quiet charm: the TV has been thankfully banned from the calm rooms, enhanced by colourful fabrics and tartan carpets. Half of the bedrooms enjoy a sea view. Panoramic restaurant and a shaded garden.

Access : *3km to the north-west on the D 75, then take the small minor road lined by fir trees*

VILLERS-ÉCALLES - 76360

LES FLORIMANES
Mme Lerevert

850 rue Gadeau
76360 Villers-Écalles
Tel. 02 35 91 98 59
florimanes@free.fr
www.florimanes.net

Open all year • 3 non-smoking rooms upstairs all with bath/WC or shower/WC • €72 to €76, breakfast included • No table d'hôte • Park, garden, credit cards not accepted, dogs not admitted

 The refined palette of colours.

This 17C manor tucked away in a landscaped park will delight all country lovers. The lady of the house's artistic talents can be felt in every nook and cranny, from the sophisticated interior decoration to the paintings on the walls. The handsome rooms, all of which are upstairs, are equipped with excellent bedding, parquet floors and original fireplaces. Breakfasts are served in the garden whenever the weather permits. Picture-framing courses organised.

Framing and binding courses

Access : *1km southbound on the D88, route de Duclair and lane on the right after the tennis courts*

YVETOT - 76190

AUBERGE DU VAL AU CESNE
M. Carel

Val au Cesne
76190 Yvetot
Tel. 02 35 56 63 06
valaucesne@hotmail.com
www.valaucesne.fr
Langues : Eng.

Closed 8 to 28 Jan, 20 Aug to 2 Sep, 19 Nov to 2 Dec • 5 rooms, all with bath/WC, television and telephone • €90; breakfast €9 • Menus €25 to €50, drinks included • Terrace, garden, car park, function room

 The enchanting dining rooms.

A lush green garden complete with aviary surrounds this three-hundred-year-old Normandy inn made up of two delightful half-timbered houses. One sports a "bijou" style decoration with exquisitely kept bedrooms, each of which has its own private terrace. The other cottage is home to the country-style dining rooms, furnished with antiques and handsome fireplaces. A feast of traditional country cooking and a fine selection of wines.

Cooking lessons

Access : *On the D 5 between Duclair and Yvetot*

First there is the peaceful valley of the Loire, the "Garden of France", renowned for its peaceful ambience, enchanting views, sumptuous manor houses and castles, magnificent floral gardens, lavish orchards, fields of vegetables and acre upon acre of vineyards. Tuck into a slab of rillettes pâté liberally spread on a crunchy baguette, a steaming platter of eels or a slice of goat's cheese while you savour a glass of light Loire wine. Continue westwards towards the sea to Nantes, once a port of entrance for enticing spices brought back from the New World: this is the home of the famous dry Muscadet. Further south, the Vendée still echoes to the cries of the Royalists' tragic last stand. Explore the secrets of its salt marshes, relax in its seaside resorts or head for the spectacular attractions of the Puy du Fou amusement park. Simple, country fare is not lacking, so make sure you taste a delicious dish of *mojettes* (white beans), a piping-hot plate of *chaudrée* (fish stew) or a mouth-watering slice of fresh brioche.

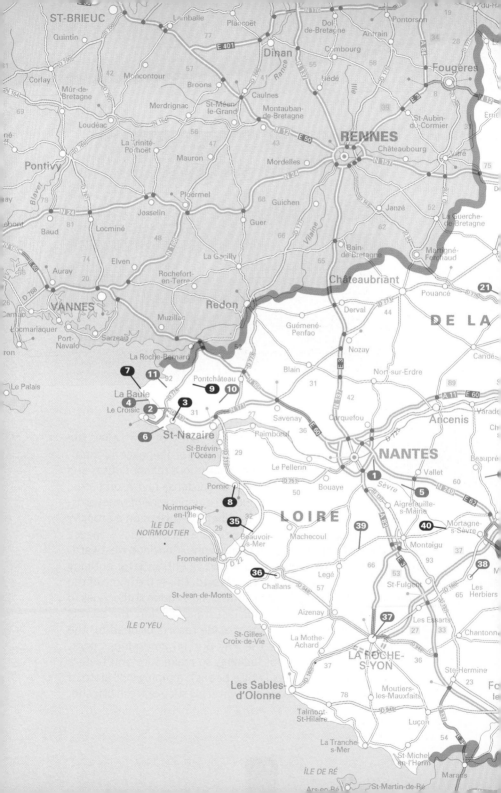

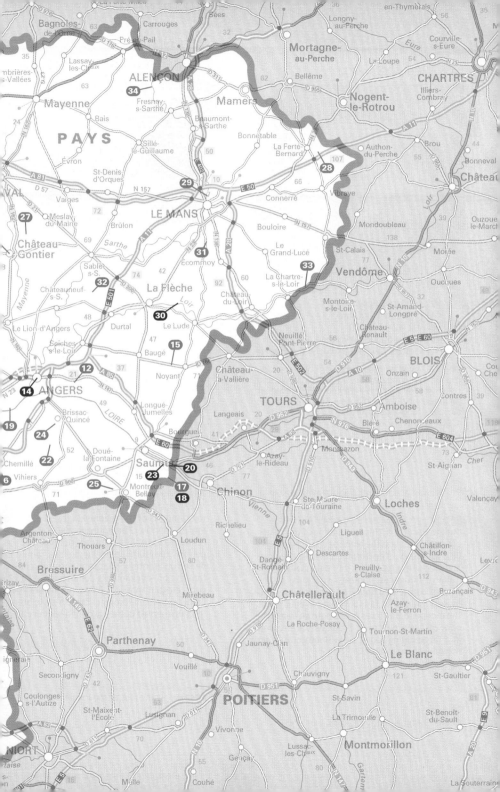

BASSE-GOULAINE - 44115

L'ORANGERIE DU PARC
M. Métro

195 rue du Grignon
44115 Basse-Goulaine
Tel. 02 40 54 91 30
lorangerieduparc@voila.fr
www.gites-de-France-44.fr/lorangerie

Open all year by reservation • 5 non-smoking rooms, 4 with mezzanine, all with bath/WC and television by request • €69 to €75, breakfast included • No table d'hôte • Terrace, private car park, dogs not admitted

Nantes and its vineyards are within easy reach.

Built in the 1850s, this outbuilding of the castle of Grézillières was the home of one of Napoleon III's ministers. The former orangery, whose architecture is typical of the region with a few Italian influences, houses spacious rooms whose charm (tiled floors, beams, antiques and tapestries) cannot fail to win you over. Each of the independent rooms opens onto an immense park with age-old trees. Breakfasts are served in a large dining room, or in summertime, on the handsome terrace.

Access : *On the south ring-road, exit N°45*

GUÉRANDE - 44350

LA GUÉRANDIÈRE
Mme Lauvray

5 rue Vannetaise
44350 Guérande
Tel. 02 40 62 17 15
contact@guerandiere.com
www.guerandiere.com
Langues : Eng.

Open all year (by reservation out of season) • 6 non-smoking rooms on two floors, all with bathrooms • €75 to €85 (€55 to €75 low season); breakfast €10 • No table d'hôte • Walled garden, car park. Dogs admitted on request • Bicycle rentals

The cosy, timeless atmosphere of this handsome property.

This imposing 19C mansion, partly built against the ramparts of the medieval city, is not lacking in charms. The interior decoration has remained faithful to the spirit of houses of this period: furniture belonging to the family or picked up in antique shops and carefully chosen fabrics and knick-knacks combine to create a cosy, elegant interior. A fine period staircase leads up to the bedrooms. English-style breakfasts are served in the garden in summertime.

Access : *At the foot of the ramparts in the medieval town*

LA BAULE - 44500

HOSTELLERIE DU BOIS
M. et Mme Lethuillier

65 avenue Lajarrige
44500 La Baule
Tel. 02 40 60 24 78
hostellerie-du-bois@wanadoo.fr
www.hostellerie-du-bois.com
Langues : Eng., Sp., It.

Closed from 15 Nov to 15 Mar • 15 non-smoking rooms on 2 floors, overlooking the garden or the street, all have bath/WC or shower/WC and television • €70 to €73 (€60 to €63 low season); breakfast €7; half-board available • Restaurant closed Sat, menus €22 (evenings only) • Terrace, garden

 La Baule les Pins provides a welcome break from the concrete jungle along the coast.

Poised between the ocean and Parc des Dryades, this 1920s seaside hotel has a distinctive green and white half-timbered façade. The well-travelled owners have carefully preserved its pleasantly old-fashioned flavour as a showcase for the countless ornaments and pieces of furniture brought back from their travels in the Far East. The small garden in the back is simply delightful.

Access : *At Place des Palmiers head for the railway station*

LA TURBALLE - 44420

LE MANOIR DES QUATRE SAISONS
M. et Mme Meyran

744 boulevard de Lauvergnac
44420 La Turballe
Tel. 02 40 11 76 16
www.manoir-des-quatre-saisons.com

Open all year • 5 rooms including 1 apartment and 1 studio, all with shower/WC or bath/WC and television • €65 to €84 (€58 to €79 low season), breakfast included • No table d'hôte • Terrace, private car park, kitchenette in studio. Credit cards not accepted, dogs welcome by request • Outdoor swimming pool

 The graceful and enthusiastic welcome by the owners.

Who would believe that this lovely home is only 40 years old? Entirely built out of old materials, stone, beams and slate picked up here and there, it offers a surprisingly convincing picture of authenticity. The interior decoration is a combination of various styles of furniture enhanced by the splendid beams that adorn all the ceilings. Most of the rooms (all under the eaves except one) have a small sitting room. Delicious breakfasts.

Access : *1.5km northbound from Turballe on the D 333*

LE PALLET - 44330

CHÂTEAU DE LA SÉBINIÈRE
Mme Cannaférina

44330 Le Pallet
Tel. 02 40 80 49 25
info@chateausebiniere.com
www.chateausebiniere.com
Langues : Eng.

Open all year • 3 non-smoking rooms, all have bathrooms; television by request • €80 to €100, breakfast included • Table d'hôte €30 • Terrace, park, private car park. Dogs admitted on request • Outdoor swimming pool, billiards room

 Long riverside walks on the banks of the Sèvre.

Clinging to the hills surrounding the village of Le Pallet, this fully restored castle, protected by woodlands and 13 hectares of vineyards, invites guests to take things easy. The enchanting bedrooms, decorated in an old-fashioned style and the sitting rooms (whitewashed walls, tiled floors and comfy furniture) are filled with a timeless aura of peace and quiet. Muscadet wine tasting on the estate.

Access : *At Pallet, the castle is past the vine museum. Two-thirds of the way up the hill, take the first private drive on the right*

LE POULIGUEN - 44510

CHALET LAKMÉ
M. et Mme Coyon

9 rue Pierre-1er-de-Serbie
44510 Le Pouliguen
Tel. 02 40 00 95 04
contact@chaletlakme.com
www.chaletlakme.com
Langues : Eng.

Open all year • 2 rooms and 2 apartments with bath/WC, television and modem • €75 to €80, breakfast included • No table d'hôte • Garden. Credit cards not accepted, no dogs admitted

 Staying in this lively house on the edge of a small wood.

In this old family guesthouse just 200m from the beach, a variety of trends and styles combine harmoniously in a pleasant picture. The colourful decoration cannot fail to catch the eye, without however tiring the onlooker. Two rooms and two apartments offer charm, cosy comfort and high-tech facilities (wifi Internet access and a DVD library to keep old and young busy). The south-facing terrace (for breakfast in fine weather) is flooded in sunshine in summertime.

Access : *8km eastbound from Le Croisic on the N 171*

PIRIAC-SUR-MER - 44420

POSTE ET RESTAURANT LA TERRASSE FLEURIE
Mme Myriam Malnoé

26 rue de la Plage
44420 Piriac-sur-Mer
Tel. 02 40 23 50 90
hoteldelaposte.piriac@wanadoo.fr
Langues : Eng.

Open from 10 Feb to 5 Nov • 14 rooms on 2 floors with bath/WC or showers with or without WC, some have television • €44 to €69; breakfast €8; half-board available • Restaurant closed Mon; menus €15 (weekdays) to €37 • No dogs admitted

 The delightful footpath to the Pointe du Castelli.

This appealing 1930s villa lies in the heart of a tiny fishing port surrounded by picturesque 17C houses. Its spacious, well-appointed rooms are being progressively renovated! The family dining room is lit by immense arcades and in the summer, tables are laid outdoors.

Access : *In the centre of the village, on the main road opposite the chemist*

PORNIC - 44210

RELAIS SAINT-GILLES
M. et Mme Robineau

7 rue Fernand-de-Mun
44210 Pornic
Tel. 02 40 82 02 25
www.relaissaintgilles.com
Langues : Eng., Sp.

Closed 30 Sep to 1 Apr • 25 rooms, including 1 apartment, with bath/WC and television • €61 to €70 (€50 to €57 low season); breakfast €7.10 • No restaurant • Terrace

 A castle set in foliage, sandy beaches and a picture-postcard harbour: what more could you wish for?

This mid-19C coaching inn can be found on a quiet side street of this seaside resort. Two wings stand on either side of a terrace shaded by an arbour of climbing vines. Inside are regularly spruced up rooms with fresh wallpaper and paintwork, some with old furniture, and a plush bourgeois dining room. Your host, a former merchant navy officer, can point you towards a whole host of beautiful footpaths.

Access : *In the upper part of town, on a quiet street above the castle*

SAINT-LYPHARD - 44110

LES CHAUMIÈRES DU LAC
M. Logodin

Route d'Herbignac
44110 Saint-Lyphard
Tel. 02 40 91 32 32
jclogodin@leschaumieresdulac.com
www.leschaumieresdulac.com
Langues : Eng.

Closed from 23 Dec to 11 Feb • 20 rooms, 2 of which have disabled access, all have bath/WC and television • €74 to €95 (€64 to €79 low season); breakfast €10; half-board available • Auberge Les Typhas; menus €19.90 (weekdays) to €28.80 • Garden, car park • Swimming in a small lake

We most liked
France's best chefs and gourmets only use Guérande's "fleur de sel" – find out why.

This recently built hamlet of cottages right in the heart of the Brière Nature Reserve may not be the epitome of authenticity, but it is definitely an excellent way of finding out more about the region's salt marshes. The appeal is further enhanced by the tasteful yellow and white restaurant, pretty terrace and stylish bedrooms with canopy beds. All the more so once you've caught a glimpse of what the inside of a local cottage really looked like, at the reconstructed cottages in Kerhinet.

Access : *Outside the village, by the minor road, opposite the lake*

SAINT-MALO-DE-GUERSAC - 44550

TY GWENN
M. Collard

25 Île-d'Errand
44550 Saint-Malo-de-Guersac
Tel. 02 40 91 15 04

Closed from 1 Oct to 1 Apr • 3 non-smoking rooms, all have shower/WC, television and a small fridge • €56, breakfast included • Table d'hôte €20 (evening only) • Sitting room, garden, car park. Credit cards not accepted, no dogs admitted • Outdoor swimming pool, billiards. Sailing, golf course, horse-riding and angling nearby

We most liked
Barge excursions along the canals of the Brière (on request).

The whitewashed walls, thatched roof and the leaded windows framed with curtains of this adorable cottage may well find you hunting for your camera. Inside, the romantic, snug rooms are equally appealing. In the sitting room you will be met with a sophisticated picture of exposed beams, a fireplace, lovely fabrics and a billiards table. Guests – non-smokers only – have the run of a delightful garden and swimming pool.

Access : *3km from Saint-Malo*

SAINT-MOLF - 44350

KERVENEL
M. Brasselet

D 252 - Le Pigeon-Blanc
44350 Saint-Molf
Tel. 02 40 42 50 38
ybrasselet@aol.com
www.loire-atlantique-tourisme.com

Open from Apr to Sep • 3 rooms with bath/WC
• €60, breakfast included • No table d'hôte • Car
park, sitting room. Credit cards not accepted,
no dogs admitted • Bicycle rentals.

Lounging in the garden in fine weather.

This former farmhouse restored in the 1970s
borders on the Brière Regional Park. A lovely
granite façade hides spacious rooms named
after the style in which they are furnished:
Louis XVI, Louis XVIII and contemporary. Tasteful bed linen, comfortable bathrooms and the
tranquillity of the site all contribute to making
your stay a pleasant one.

Access : 2.5km on the D 33 towards La Turballe

ANDARD - 49800

LE GRAND TALON
Mme Guervilly

3 route des Chapelles
49800 Andard
Tel. 02 41 80 42 85

Open all year • 3 rooms with shower/WC • €57 to
€65, breakfast included • No table d'hôte
• Park, car park. Credit cards not accepted

 **Mrs Guervilly does her utmost to make
your stay as pleasant as possible.**

The graceful façade of this elegant 18C abode,
covered in russet-red leaves in autumn, overlooks a square courtyard just two minutes from
Angers. The peaceful bedrooms are tastefully
decorated. If you're lucky with the weather,
you can breakfast and picnic in the garden
under a parasol.

Access : 11km eastbound from Angers on the
N 147, towards Saumur then take the D 113

ANDREZÉ - 49600

CHÂTEAU DE LA MORINIÈRE
M. et Mme Pringarbé

49600 Andrezé
Tel. 02 41 75 40 30
PRINGARBE.Pascal@wanadoo.fr

Closed from 25 Dec to 1 Jan • 5 rooms with bathrooms • €71 to €77, breakfast included • Table d'hôte €28 • Park. Credit cards not accepted, dogs not admitted

 Discovering the legends that have marked the history of this site.

Formerly one of Napoleon III's country homes, this superb chateau overlooking the Beuvron Valley has retained an air of mystery. Each of the rooms, decorated on a specific theme, is named after a fairy. The Fire fairy, romantically draped in velvet or the Earth fairy, in honour of Chemillé, the capital of medicinal plants. The owner, a former restaurant owner, carries out marvels at mealtimes, combining fresh produce with regional flavours.

Access : *On the D 246*

ANGERS - 49100

HÔTEL DU MAIL
M. Le-Calvez

8 rue des Ursules
49100 Angers
Tel. 02 41 25 05 25
contact@hotel-du-mail.com
www.hotel-du-mail.com
Langues : Eng.

• 29 rooms on 2 floors, most have bath/WC, the others have shower/WC, all have television • €60 to €70; breakfast €8 • No restaurant • Private car park in the inner courtyard

 Angers is famed for its mild climate and a tradition of gracious living.

This discreet hotel standing in a side street of the historic town was an Ursuline convent in the 17C, before becoming a guesthouse and now boutique hotel. It takes a bit of finding but your efforts will be amply rewarded by the personalised, beautifully decorated rooms awaiting you. The breakfast room is decorated in a classic bourgeois style and guests can also venture onto a lovely mini-terrace in the inner courtyard. Definitely worth mailing home about!

Access : *In a quiet street behind the town hall*

AUVERSE - 49490

DOMAINE DE LA BRÉGELLERIE
M. et Mme Sohn

Route de Chigne
49490 Auverse
Tel. 02 41 82 11 69
isabelle.sohn@wanadoo.fr
http://la.bregellerie.free.fr
Langues : Eng.

Open all year • 5 non-smoking rooms, 4 of which are upstairs, all have bathrooms • €55 to €70, breakfast included • No table d'hôte • Garden, car park. Credit cards not accepted • Outdoor swimming pool, fishing in the pond

most liked "The Loire" bedroom.

After a full-scale renovation this old farmstead has been elevated to the rank of inn. The names of the individually decorated rooms located in a recent wing reveal their one-off themes: "Forest", "Vines", "Fields", "Pond" and "The Loire", whose curious boat-shaped bathtub is worth a special mention. A breakfast room, elegantly understated, a pool table, a large summer swimming pool in the garden and a pond – fishing possible – add the finishing touches.

Access : *14.5km to the south-west on the D 767, Noyant road and the D 79 on the right*

CHEMILLÉ - 49120

LE CLOS DU MARAIS
Mme Poireau

6 chemin du Marais
49120 Chemillé
Tel. 02 41 30 08 04
poireauhelene@aol.com

Open all year • 5 non-smoking rooms, all with shower/WC • €48, breakfast included • No table d'hôte • Car park, credit cards not accepted, dogs not admitted • Angling

 most liked The gurgling of the water garden in its lush green setting.

Even though the appeal of this large house set on the upper reaches is undeniable, the elegant decoration and generous interior volumes remain its finest qualities. The huge sitting room features a tasteful blend of old and new and each of the five rooms on the mezzanine (named after medicinal plants in honour of the region) possesses its own inimitable charm. We however preferred the "Sage" room. Exceptional value for money.

Access : *Leave the town towards Saint-Lézin*

DOMAINE DE MESTRÉ
M. et Mme Dauge-de Courcy

49590 Fontevraud-l'Abbaye
Tel. 02 41 51 72 32
domaine-de-mestre@wanadoo.fr
www.dauge-fontevraud.com

Closed from 20 Dec to 1 Apr • 12 rooms with
bathrooms • €70; breakfast €8 • Table d'hôte
€24 (evenings only) • Park, car park. Credit
cards not accepted, no dogs admitted

PRIEURÉ-SAINT-LAZARE
M. Deslandres-Bouf

Abbaye Royale de Fontevraud, rue
Saint-Jean-de-l'Habit
49590 Fontevraud-L'Abbaye
Tel. 02 41 51 73 16
contact@hotelfp-fontevraud.com
www.hotelfp-fontevraud.com
Langues : Eng., Ger.

Open from 1 Apr to 12 Nov • 52 rooms, 6 are for
non-smokers, with bath/WC or shower/WC, all
have television • €67 to €112 (€60 to €107 low
season); breakfast €11; half-board available
• Restaurant closed Tue and Wed lunchtime;
menus €18 (weekdays) to €49 • Garden, private
car park. Dogs not admitted

**Lavender, vetiver, olive oil, thyme,
cinnamon, nutmeg and rose-scented
soaps.**

This farm and its old tithe barn, dating back to
the 13C, once belonged to the Royal Abbey of
Fontevraud: nowadays, it is home to attractive, individually decorated rooms in which it is
easy to feel at home. Breakfast and dinner,
made with home-grown ingredients, are served
in the former chapel. The estate's woods and
gardens are home to ancient cedar and lime-
trees and a visit to the estate's craft soap
factory is always a pleasure.

**Find sanctuary within the walls of the
abbey gardens.**

The building was indeed a priory and a lazaret
before being turned into a hotel. Although rich
in history, its ancient walls have an eternal
quality that appears to withstand the wear and
tear of time: the almost monastical bedroom-
cells provide a haven of peace and quiet for
busy urban dwellers and the vaulted breakfast
room and restaurant tables around the cloisters further extend this invitation to meditate
and take stock.

Access : *In the abbey grounds*

Access : *1km northbound from Fontevraud on
the D 947, towards Montsoreau*

LA POSSONNIERE - 49170

19

LA ROUSSELIÈRE
M. de Béru

49170 La Possonnière
Tel. 02 41 39 13 21
larousseliere@unimedia.fr
www.anjou-et-loire.com/rousseliere

Open all year • 5 rooms with bath/WC • €75, breakfast included • Meals €23 • Park. Credit cards not accepted, dogs not admitted • Outdoor swimming pool, billiards, pétanque, table tennis

 The welcome, the site and the price.

This eminently bourgeois property full of charm is flanked by outhouses and stands on a vast 4ha estate. The ground floor is comprised of a series of rooms, including a billiards room for enthusiasts. Among the five bedrooms, each of which is decorated on a different theme, the voluntarily outdated style of the "Rose", in an outhouse, is particularly attractive. Tasty table d'hôte meals served by an enthusiastic cordon bleu chef.

Access : *On the outskirts of town*

MONTSOREAU - 49730

20

LE BUSSY
Mme Roi

4 rue Jeanne-d'Arc
49730 Montsoreau
Tel. 02 41 38 11 11
hotel.lebussy@wanadoo.fr
www.hotel-lebussy.fr
Langues : Eng.

Closed Jan-Dec and on Tue and Wed in Feb, Mar, Nov and Dec • 12 rooms, all have bath/WC or shower/WC and television • €55 to €70; breakfast €9 • No restaurant • Private car park

 What better place to curl up with one of Alexander Dumas' novels of romance and action?

The sign outside this 18C house at the top of the village pays homage to one of Dumas' famous heroes, Bussy d'Amboise, sweetheart of the Dame de Monsoreau. Most of the rooms, furnished in a Louis Philippe style and equipped with brand new bathrooms, survey the castle and the Loire. In the summer, breakfast is served in the flower-decked garden and throughout the rest of the year, in a delightful troglodyte room. Friendly and welcoming.

Access : *In the upper part of town behind the castle*

NYOISEAU - 49500

LES HAUTS DE BRÈGES
M. et Mme Pellier

Brèges
49500 Nyoiseau
Tel. 02 41 61 39 07
b.pellier@wanadoo.fr

www.hauts-de-breges.com

Open all year • 3 rooms with bath/WC • €41, breakfast included • Table d'hôte €15 • Park, car park. Credit cards not accepted, dogs not admitted • Angling

 Watching the fish dart about in the pond.

Once the property of the late 15C Nyoiseau Abbey, this fully restored old farmhouse in the heart of a 3ha-estate also dates from the same period. The dining-sitting room with exposed beams and stonework and the three simply but pleasantly decorated rooms are located in the former stables. The tasty table d'hôte meals are lovingly prepared with produce grown in the garden (or from small local growers) and homemade recipes.

Access : *3km northwest from Segré on the D 775 and the D 71*

THOUARCÉ - 49380

LE CLOS DES 3 ROIS
M. et Mme Duseaux

13 rue Jacques-du-Bellay
49380 Thouarcé
Tel. 02 41 66 34 04
infos@closdes3rois.fr
www.closdes3rois.fr

Open all year • 5 non-smoking rooms with bath/WC or shower/WC, air-conditioning • €58 to €73, breakfast included • No table d'hôte • Garden. Dogs not admitted • Outdoor swimming pool

Following in the footsteps of the great kings of France through the Angers region.

A glowing success is the most appropriate term for this former solicitor's home. Each room is not only totally independent but also endowed with a style all its own. The blue room and its contemporary bathroom, the parrot room on two levels and three others, equally tastefully decorated. The owners organise tasting evenings in the presence of winegrowers, including a vin nouveau evening during the last weekend of November. Heated swimming pool.

Access : *In the village*

TURQUANT - 49730

DEMEURE DE LA VIGNOLE
Mme Bartholeyns

3 impasse Marguerite-d'Anjou
49730 Turquant
Tel. 02 41 53 67 00
demeure@demeure-vignole.com
www.demeure-vignole.com
Langues : Eng.

Open from 15 Mar to 15 Nov • 8 rooms, one of which has disabled access, all have bath/WC and television • €75.50 to €116.50; breakfast €8.50; half-board available • Menus €26 (evenings only by reservation) • Terrace, garden, car park. Dogs not admitted in restaurant

The troglodyte chamber where the villagers met in the 12C.

This exquisite estate only opened its doors as a hotel in 2000 following several years of major restoration work under the supervision of the architects of France's Listed Monuments. The 15C manor house and 17C outbuildings perched on the cliff have been turned into individually decorated rooms, where every effort has been taken to retain their historic decorative features such as beams, fireplace and bread oven. A terraced garden commands a wonderful view of the valley. Admirable.

Access : *10km from Saumur on the D 947, in the heart of the village*

VAUCHRÉTIEN - 49320

LE MOULIN DE CLABEAU
M. Daviau

Clabeau
49320 Vauchrétien
Tel. 02 41 91 22 09

• 3 non-smoking rooms, with bath/WC or shower/WC • €58, breakfast included • No table d'hôte • Car park. Credit cards not accepted, dogs not admitted

The warm welcome around a glass of wine from the estate.

Surrounded by lush green countryside, this old watermill on the banks of the Aubance has been in the same family since 1537! It is home to three rooms full of character and simplicity, named after the owners' daughters. The family room, in particular, boasts a splendid bathroom. The superb rustic sitting room, adorned with its original timber beams, seems to have retained an unchanging quality of authenticity. In season, local produce and crafts on sale in a small shop.

Access : *3km northwest of Brissac-Quincié on the D 123, to "La Frémonière"*

VAUDELNAY - 49260

LES LOGES DE VIGNES
M. et Mme Albert

205 rue du Château d'Oiré à Oiré
49260 Vaudelnay
Tel. 02 41 52 21 78
vieuxpressoir@wanadoo.fr

Open all year • 4 non-smoking rooms, one of which has disabled access, all with shower/WC • €54, breakfast included • No table d'hôte • Garden, car park. Dogs not admitted

 The owners' kindness and friendly welcome.

Welcome to this winegrowing estate of 25ha. Recently fitted out in a building independent from the main house, the rooms (one of which has access for the disabled) cannot be faulted. An immense living room with a lounge area on the ground floor is perfect for winding down and relaxing. Introduction to the house wines (Saumur A.O.C.) in the estate's cellar.

Access : *4km westbound from Vaudelnay-bourg, on the D 87 towards "Oiré"*

CHÂTEAU-GONTIER - 53200

LE CHÊNE VERT
Mme Heron

Route de Nantes
53200 Château-Gontier
Tel. 02 43 07 90 48
www.chateau-chene-vert.com

Open all year • 5 rooms with bath/WC or shower/WC • €65, breakfast included • Table d'hôte €23 including drinks • Park, car park

 The lady of the house's communicative gaiety as she welcomes you.

Never has a castle seemed more hospitable! Behind the walls of this sumptuous abode lie treasures of decorative talent and flair. Among the five rooms that take you on a whirlwind tour around the world, the Queen Elisabeth (furnished with pieces from a former hotel of the same name) and the romantic Rose are masterpieces of taste and refinement. Meals are washed down with wine from the family vineyard in Bordeaux. Exceptional value for money at this end of the market.

Access : *2km from the town centre on the D20*

RUILLÉ-FROID-FONDS - 53170

CORMES - 72400

LOGIS VILLEPROUVÉE
M. et Mme Davenel

53170 Ruillé-Froid-Fonds
Tel. 02 43 07 71 62
christ.davenel@wanadoo.fr
http://perso.wanadoo.fr/villeprouve/bb

Open all year • 4 non-smoking rooms with bath/WC • €42 to €47, breakfast included • Table d'hôte €13 (evenings only) • Terrace, park, private car park. Credit cards not accepted, dogs not admitted

MANOIR DE PLANCHETTE
M. et Mme Cherrier

72400 Cormes
Tel. 02 43 93 24 75
manoir.de.planchette@wanadoo.fr

Open all year • 3 non-smoking rooms all with bathrooms • €50 to €66, breakfast included • No table d'hôte • Park, car park. Credit cards not accepted • Billiards, children's play area

> **More than a guest, you are a friend of the family.**

While you may at first glance think you have reached a farm just like any other, everything changes as soon as you venture across the threshold of this old 14C priory. The owner, a true history enthusiast, has endeavoured to create a delightful medieval atmosphere with a cosy snug feel to boot. A total success from the chalkstone fireplaces and the four-poster beds to the immense tapestry of the Dukes of Anjou to the old Spanish furniture. Delicious home cooking.

> **The gentle tick-tock of the grandfather clock in the dining room.**

The oldest section of this manor dates from the 13C. After careful restoration work, it is now devoted to ensuring guests' well-being. The park, which overlooks the surrounding countryside, boasts a delightful summerhouse where breakfast is served in season, as well as a children's play area. The bright spacious rooms are a pretty blend of antique furniture and natural coloured walls. Finally the pleasant sitting room with armchairs and a billiards table offers many hours of relaxation.

Access : *1km northbound from Ruillé-Froid-Fonds on the Bignon-du-Maine road*

Access : *5km southbound from la Ferté-Bernard on the D1, then the D261, then lane right for 1km*

COULAINES - 72190

LUCHÉ-PRINGÉ - 72800

MADAME BORDEAU
Mme Bordeau

Le Monet
72190 Coulaines
Tel. 02 43 82 25 50

Open all year • 4 rooms with shower/WC • €50, breakfast included • No table d'hôte • Garden, car park. Credit cards not accepted, no dogs admitted

L'AUBERGE DU PORT DES ROCHES
M. et Mme Lesiourd

Le Port des Roches
72800 Luché-Pringé
Tel. 02 43 45 44 48
Langues : Eng.

Closed in Feb, Sun evening, Mon and Tue lunchtime • 12 rooms with bath/WC or shower/WC, half of them have television • €45 to €55; breakfast €7; half-board available • Menus €23 to €46 • Terrace and riverside garden, private car park

We most liked **A country atmosphere on the doorstep of Le Mans.**

Saved from ruin in the nick of time, this small country house has made a spectacular recovery. Madame clearly spends many hours in her garden. Inside, the original character has been preserved and enhanced by a generous sprinkling of modern comforts. The rooms are not enormous but beautifully furnished; those on the ground floor have exposed beams and the others are under the eaves. A log fire is lit in the winter to take the chill off the morning in the breakfast room.

Access : 5km northbound from Le Mans, towards Mamers then Ballon on the D 300

 We most liked **Strolling along the banks of the river Loir.**

This smart country inn on the banks of the Loir now enjoys a supremely quiet location: it's hard to imagine, that not so long ago, soft local stone was quarried from the surrounding hillsides and loaded onto boats which would be moored in front of the hotel. Light, airy, colourful rooms, a comfortable dining room with a homely feel and a riverside garden-terrace await guests in search of peace and quiet.

Access : 2.5km eastbound on the D 13 towards Mancigné, then take the D 214

MONCÉ-EN-BELIN - 72230

31

LE PETIT PONT
Mme Brou

3 rue du Petit-Pont
72230 Moncé-en-Belin
Tel. 02 43 42 03 32

Open all year • One room in the house and 5 others in a separate wing, all with shower/WC • €50 to €60, breakfast included • Table d'hôte €15 to €20 • Garden, car park. No dogs admitted • Outdoor swimming pool

 Your tireless hostess did much of the restoration herself.

Over the years, your energetic hostess has painstakingly restored her lovely house, covered in variegated vine and part of a former working farm. Her efforts have resulted in beautifully appointed, individually decorated rooms (non-smokers only). One of the rooms and a self-catering cottage are in the main building, while the others are in an independent wing. Friendly and welcoming.

Access : *11km southbound from Le Mans on the D 147 towards Arnage, then take the D 307*

NOTRE-DAME-DU-PÉ - 72300

32

LA REBOURSIÈRE
M. Chappuy

72300 Notre-Dame-du-Pé
Tel. 02 43 92 92 41
gilles-chappuy@wanadoo.fr
www.lareboursiere.fr.st

Open all year • 3 non-smoking rooms, one of which has disabled access, all with shower/WC • €60, breakfast included, half-board available • Table d'hôte €23 including drinks • Terrace, park, car park. Dogs not admitted • Outdoor swimming pool

 Making the most of the quiet Sarthe countryside.

To reach this authentic 19C farmhouse in perfect condition in the heart of a park you venture along a tree-lined drive. The former stables now house three spacious rooms, each of which is individually decorated and furnished with antiques. Home grown produce from the vegetable garden and orchard takes pride of place on the table; meals are served in a rustic-style dining room or on the terrace. Pleasant view of the valley from the swimming pool. There is also a gîte with a private garden.

Access : *1km southbound on the D134 then a minor road*

PONCÉ-SUR-LE-LOIR - 72340

CHÂTEAU DE LA VOLONIÈRE
M. Becquelin

49 rue Principale
72340 Poncé-sur-le-Loir
Tel. 02 43 79 68 16
chateau-de-la-voloniere @ wanadoo.fr
http://chateaudelavoloniere.free.fr

Closed in Feb (except by reservation) • 5 rooms
with bath/WC • €60 to €80, breakfast included
• No table d'hôte • Park, car park • Visits to the
Loire chateaux

 Bohemian and easy-going.

Guests can depend on a perfect welcome when
they arrive in this château, next door to the
birthplace of the 16C poet, Pierre Ronsard. A
bold colour scheme and antiques set the scene
for the bedrooms, each of which is decorated
on a the theme of a well-known tale: "Blue-
beard", "Arabian Nights", "Merlin" and
"Romeo and Juliet". The 15C chapel has been
turned into the dining room and exhibitions are
held in the former troglodyte kitchen.

Access : *In the village*

SAINT-LÉONARD-DES-BOIS - 72130

LE MOULIN DE LINTHE
M. et Mme Rollini

Route de Sougé-le-Ganelon
72130 Saint-Léonard-des-Bois
Tel. 02 43 33 79 22
www.moulindelinthe.net

Closed Jan to Apr • 5 rooms with bath/WC • €60,
breakfast included • No table d'hôte • Terrace,
garden, car park. Credit cards not accepted, no
dogs admitted • Fishing in the River Sarthe

 **Savour the refreshing peace and quiet of
this riverside location.**

Get back to grass roots in this three-hundred-
year-old mill surrounded by fields. Anglers can
try their luck tempting the pike in the Sarthe at
the bottom of the garden, others may prefer to
go for long bike rides round the countryside or
simply relax in the garden. Each of the spacious, airy rooms is furnished in a different
style: Norman, Louis XVI, 1930s. The sitting
room commands a lovely view of the millwheel.

Access : *400m south of the village towards
Sougé-le-Ganelon*

BOUIN - 85230

CHALLANS - 85300

HÔTEL DU MARTINET
Mme Huchet

1 bis place de la Croix-Blanche
85230 Bouin
Tel. 02 51 49 08 94
hotel.martinet@wanadoo.fr
www.lemartinet.com
Langues : Eng.

Open all year • 30 rooms, 7 of which are on the ground floor, with bath/WC or shower/WC and television • €54 to €65; breakfast €7; half-board available • Menus €23 to €36 • Garden, car park. No dogs admitted in restaurant • Outdoor swimming pool, fitness room

Breathe in the scent of fresh flowers and beeswax.

The discreet walls of this 18C house hide a whole host of assets including a quiet garden, a swimming pool and spotless rooms – those on the ground floor with tiled floors and cane furniture are the most pleasant. Come the evening, take your places in the delightful dining room with its painted woodwork, parquet floor and marble fireplace. The owner, ever-active and unfailingly friendly, will often present you with the catch of the day, brought home by one of her sons and cooked by the other!

Access : *In the centre of the village*

L'ANTIQUITÉ
M. et Mme Belleville

14 rue Galliéni
85300 Challans
Tel. 02 51 68 02 84
hotelantiquite@wanadoo.fr
www.hotelantiquite.com
Langues : Eng.

Open all year • 16 rooms with bath/WC or shower/WC and television • €60 to €80 (€52 to €74 low season); breakfast €6.50 • No restaurant • Private car park. No dogs admitted • Swimming pool

The breakfast room which leads into a lovely veranda.

Given the establishment's name, you will not be surprised to learn that this family-run establishment is strewn with antiques picked up in local second-hand shops. Most of the rooms, housed in an imposing white-fronted building, are graced with red-brick tiles, period furniture and old engravings and paintings. A recent wing, with four rather more spacious rooms fitted with brand new bathrooms, has been laid out around the outdoor swimming pool.

Access : *Near the exhibition hall*

LES HERBIERS - 85500

LA ROCHE-SUR-YON - 85000

LA MÉTAIRIE DU BOURG
M. et Mme Retailleau

85500 Les Herbiers
Tel. 02 51 67 23 97

Open all year • 3 rooms with bath/WC • €50 to €55, breakfast included • No table d'hôte • Garden, car park. Credit cards not accepted, no dogs admitted • Working farm (cattle breeding)

LOGIS DE LA COUPERIE
Mme Oliveau

85000 La Roche-sur-Yon
Tel. 02 51 24 10 18

Open all year • 3 rooms and 1 apartment, all have bath/WC or shower/WC and television • €86 to €110 (€84 to €106 low season); breakfast €9 • No table d'hôte • Park with cottage garden and pond, car park. Credit cards not accepted, no dogs admitted • Library-sitting room, fishing, bicycling

 Your hostess' faultless attention to detail.

As soon as your foot crosses the threshold of this delightful country seat, rebuilt after the Revolution, you know you'll never want to leave. Perhaps it is because the lady of the house is so clearly determined to pamper her guests? Perhaps it is the romantic rooms named after fragrant flowers? Or is it the well-tended garden, vegetable plot or pond where swans and ducks paddle? An unforgettable experience.

Two minutes from the Puy du Fou Theme Park.

This fine old secluded farmhouse is typical of the region with its stone walls and round tiled roof. Still a working cattle farm, it also offers spotless B&B rooms whose generous dimensions include high raftered ceilings. In the sitting room, a conscious effort has been made to maintain a stylish rustic character with tiled floor, exposed beams, old furniture and a fireplace. Copious breakfasts served by the friendly hosts.

Access : *5km to the north-east of Herbiers on the D 755, then the D 11 and a minor road*

Access : *5km eastbound, leave on the D 948 towards Niort, then take a left on the D 80*

ROCHESERVIERE - 85620

39

LE CHÂTEAU DU PAVILLON
M. et Mme Rio

Rue du Gué-Baron
85620 Rocheserviere
Tel. 02 51 06 55 99
ggilann@aol.com
www.le-chateau-du-pavillon.com

Closed 14 Oct to 14 Apr • 4 non-smoking rooms on two floors, all with bathrooms and television • €80 to €120; breakfast €9 • No table d'hôte • Nursery, terrace, park. Credit cards not accepted, dogs not admitted • Outdoor swimming pool

Charm, elegance and comfort are the motto of this house.

Eight hectares of grounds with a small lake and swimming pool flank this château, dating from 1885, which radiates charm and elegance: spacious Louis XIV dining room, Louis XV sitting room, marble fireplace and grand piano. A lovely wooden staircase leads up to inviting romantic bedrooms. Also available are two gîtes and an extremely well appointed nursery for under 10 year olds. Table d'hôte available at weekends, by reservation.

Access : *North of the town*

TIFFAUGES - 85130

40

LE MANOIR DE LA BARBACANE
M. et Mme Baume

2 place de l'Église
85130 Tiffauges
Tel. 02 51 65 75 59
manoir@hotel-barbacane.com
www.hotel-barbacane.com
Langues : Eng.

Closed last week in Dec and Sun from Oct to Apr • 19 rooms with bath/WC or shower/WC and television • Menus €75 to €120 (€63 to €100 low season); breakfast €10 • No restaurant • Garden, garage. No dogs admitted • Outdoor swimming pool, billiards

The aura of living history.

A visit to Barbacane Castle is like stepping back in time to the Middle Ages, but the hotel itself, installed in a 19C property, bears a rather striking resemblance to an English manor house! A countrified atmosphere and numerous knick-knacks set the scene inside. Plans are afoot to renovate the rather threadbare rooms, some of which survey the castle of the sinister Gilles de Rais, former Lord of Tiffauges, but better known as Blue Beard...

Access : *Half-way between Montaigu and Cholet on the D 753 in the centre of the village*

Aisne - 02
Oise - 60
Somme - 80

Ready for an action-packed ride over Picardy's fair and historic lands? The birthplace of France itself – the first French king, Clovis, was born in Soissons – Picardy is renowned for its wealthy Cistercian abbeys, splendid Gothic cathedrals, flamboyant town halls, marvellous castles, as well as its poignant reminders of the two World Wars. Those who prefer the pleasures of the countryside can take a boat trip through the floating gardens of Amiens, explore the botanical reserve of Marais de Cessière or observe the thousands of birds in the estuary of the Somme and at the Marquenterre bird sanctuary. Acre upon acre of unspoilt hills, woodland, plateaux, copses, pastures and vineyards welcome you with open arms. Picardy's rich culinary talents have been refined over the centuries and it would be unthinkable to leave without tasting the famous *pré-salé* – lamb fattened on the salt marshes – some smoked eel, duck pâté or a dessert laced with Chantilly cream.

AMBLENY - 02290

BRUYÈRES-SUR-FÈRE - 02130

DOMAINE DE MONTAIGU
M. Philippe de Reyer

Hameau « Le Soulier »
02290 Ambleny
Tel. 03 23 74 06 62
info@domainedemontaigu.com
www.domainedemontaigu.com

Open all year • 5 non-smoking rooms with bath/WC and television • €75, breakfast included • Table d'hôte €25 • Terrace, park, garden, car park. Credit cards not accepted, dogs not admitted • Outdoor swimming pool

VAL-CHRÉTIEN
M. et Mme Sion

Ancienne abbaye du Val Chrétien
02130 Bruyères-sur-Fère
Tel. 03 23 71 66 71
val.chretien@wanadoo.fr
http://perso.wanadoo.fr/valchretien/
Langues : Eng., Sp., Japanese

Open all year • 5 rooms upstairs with shower/WC • €54 to €64, breakfast included; half-board available • Table d'hôte €20 • Park. Credit cards not accepted, no dogs admitted • Tennis

The entire site is a masterful success.

When they took over this handsome 18C estate full of character, the two associates created a superb dining room in the former barn. Complete with a large window, beams and limestone walls, it boasts table d'hôte meals worthy of many a star restaurant. Ultra smart rooms, an equally stately sitting room, and in the vaulted period cellars, a sauna and a small keep-fit area. Outdoors, a fountain plays in the large courtyard. Pleasant wooded area.

Exceptional location in the heart of the legendary site of the Tardenois.

This building on the banks of the Ourcq and in the heart of the 12C ruins of the Abbey of Val Chrétien is quite remarkable. The rooms are soberly decorated with one striking exception, which is lined in red velvet and complete with a four-poster bed. On the ground floor are a breakfast room with exposed beams and a library where a fire is lit in winter. The covered tennis court is in an outbuilding.

Access : *2km eastbound from Ambleny*

Access : *8km westbound from Fère-en-Tardenois on the D 310, towards Bruyères-sur-Fère, on a by-road*

CONNIGIS - 02330

CHAUNY - 02300

CHAMBRE D'HÔTE M. LECLÈRE
M. et Mme Leclère

1 rue de Launay
02330 Connigis
Tel. 03 23 71 90 51

Closed from 20 to 31 Dec • 5 rooms with shower/WC • €46 to €55, breakfast included • Table d'hôte €16 • Park, car park. Dogs not admitted • Bicycle rentals, hiking trails, trout fishing 200m away

LA TOQUE BLANCHE
M. et Mme Lequeux

24 avenue Victor-Hugo
02300 Chauny
Tel. 03 23 39 98 98
info@toque.blanche.fr
www.toque-blanche.fr
Langues : Eng.

Closed from 2 to 8 Jan, 16 to 25 Feb, 7 to 26 Aug, Sat lunchtime, Sun evening and Mon • 6 rooms on 2 floors with bath/WC or shower/WC, 3 have television, 2 are for non-smokers • €74 to €89; breakfast €12; half-board available • Air-conditioned restaurant; menus €34 to €72 • Terrace, park, private car park. No dogs allowed in rooms • Tennis

 Duck foie gras is the house speciality.

The Toque Blanche (Chef's hat), a lovely 1920s bourgeois house, not only provides comfortable personalised rooms but also offers cooking renowned for its subtle blends of flavours in either an Art Deco or a more classically-inspired dining room. Don't worry if your waistline seems to have expanded during the meal, you can walk off the extra calories in the immense shaded park.

 Walking or bicycling through vineyards.

This husband and wife team of Champagne producers has been painstakingly restoring this 16C farmhouse, once part of the Château de Connigis estate, for over ten years now. Thanks to their efforts, guests are now welcomed into spacious rooms with original parquet floors overlooking a magnificent park alongside the vineyards; the room in the tower, slightly removed from the main wing and decorated in an attractive Flemish style, is the quietest. Children's play area and bicycle rentals.

Access : *12km eastbound from Château-Thierry on the N 3 and the D 4*

Access : *Near the town centre*

ÉTRÉAUPONT - 02580

5

AUBERGE DU VAL DE L'OISE
M. et Mme Trokay

8 rue Albert-Ledent
02580 Étréaupont
Tel. 03 23 97 91 10
contact@clos-du-montvinage.fr
www.clos-du-montvinage.fr
Langues : Eng.

Closed 1 week in Jan, 1 week in Aug, Christmas week, Sun evening, Mon and Tue lunchtimes • 20 rooms, one has disabled access, with bath/WC or shower/WC and television • €65 to €109; breakfast €9.50; half-board available • Menus €14 to €40 • Terrace, garden, private car park. No dogs admitted in rooms • Billiards room

 The honeymoon suite and its four-poster bed!

Driving through the village, the eye is drawn to the intricate pattern of the brick walls of this delightful late-19C mansion. A pleasantly old-fashioned atmosphere extends to the well-dimensioned rooms furnished in a Louis-Philippe style, while a recently opened wing is home to the establishment's brand new restaurant, pleasantly decorated and serving traditional French favourites.

Access : *On the N 2, between Vervins and La Capelle, in the village*

L'ÉPINE-AUX-BOIS - 02540

6

DOMAINE DES PATRUS
Mme Manning-Royol

la Haute Épine
02540 L'Épine-aux-Bois
Tel. 03 23 69 85 85
contact@domainedespatrus.com
www.domainedespatrus.com
Langues : Eng., Ger.

Closed from Dec to Feb • 5 rooms, 2 of which are under the eaves, with shower/WC • €70 to €95, breakfast included • Table d'hôte €30 (including wine) (evening by reservation) • Sitting room-library, park, car park. Dogs not admitted • Gallery devoted to La Fontaine. Wine and champagne tasting

 The collection of paintings devoted to La Fontaine's fables.

In addition to the comfort it offers, another reason to stop at this handsome farmhouse is the pleasure of waking up in the morning and gazing out onto the peaceful countryside. The individually decorated rooms are furnished in traditional style; those with sloping ceilings have a little private sitting room. The mezzanine in the library is most attractive. Ask to see the owner's collection of works inspired by La Fontaine's fables; she is a fan and is only too happy to explain them.

Access : *8km westbound from Montmirail on the D 933, towards Meaux*

RESSONS-LE-LONG - 02290

FERME DE LA MONTAGNE
M. Ferté

02290 Ressons-le-Long
Tel. 03 23 74 23 71
lafermedelamontagne@free.fr
http://lafermedelamontagne.free.fr

Langues : Eng., Ger.

Closed Jan and Feb • 5 rooms with bathrooms • €50, breakfast included • No table d'hôte • Garden, car park. Credit cards not accepted, no dogs admitted • Billiards and piano

The sweeping view of the Aisne Valley.

Built on the edge of the plateau, this old farm of the Abbey of Notre-Dame de Soissons whose foundations date back to the 13C, enjoys a superb view of the Aisne Valley. All the generously-sized rooms have independent access and well-equipped bathrooms. A billiards table and piano adorn the sitting room, which also commands a splendid view of the countryside. Warm and welcoming.

Painting, music, yoga, etc. courses

Access : *8km westbound from Soissons on the N 31 and the D 1160*

REUILLY-SAUVIGNY - 02850

AUBERGE LE RELAIS
M. et Mme Berthuit

2 rue de Paris
02850 Reuilly-Sauvigny
Tel. 03 23 70 35 36
auberge.relais.de.reuilly@wanadoo.fr
www.relaisreuilly.com
Langues : Eng.

Closed from 28 Jan to 1 Mar, from 19 Aug to 6 Sep • 7 rooms with bath/WC or shower/WC, all are air-conditioned and have television • €74 to €92; breakfast €13; half-board available • Air-conditioned restaurant; menus €30 (weekdays) to €78 • Garden, car park. Dogs not admitted in rooms

Limousin veal served with green asparagus in truffle sauce.

The flower-decked walls of this welcoming roadside-inn invite travellers to pause and stay for a while. The interior decoration reveals a masterful grasp of colour and light: the Provençal or contemporary rooms enjoy a superb view over the Champagne vineyards and the Marne Valley. Not to be outdone, the menu is appetising and up-to-date and served on a veranda or in the plush dining room.

Access : *In the village by the N 3, between Château-Thierry and Dormans*

SAINT-QUENTIN - 02100

HÔTEL DES CANONNIERS
Mme Michel

15 rue des Canonniers
02100 Saint-Quentin
Tel. 03 23 62 87 87
lescanonniers@aol.com
www.hotel-canonniers.com
Langues : Eng.

Closed from 1 to 15 Aug and Sun evening (except by reservation) • 7 rooms, all of which have equipped kitchenettes, with bath/WC or shower/WC and television • €60 to €115; breakfast €10 • No restaurant • Terrace, garden, private car park • Billiards

 Drop by the Lecuyer Museum and admire the portraits by Quentin de La Tour.

Whether you stay for a night or for two weeks, the Canonniers offers superb personalised suites with a kitchenette at wonderfully reasonable prices. This handsome house, built in 1754, provides the service of a hotel and the charm of a maison d'hôte: guests can play billiards or lounge on the terrace opposite the lush green garden. The establishment also caters to businesses and meetings are held in its handsome old reception rooms.

Access : *Drive past the town hall, take a left on Rue de la Comédie, past the theatre, turn right*

VILLERS-AGRON-AIGUIZY - 02130

MANOIR DE LA SEMOIGNE
M. et Mme Ferry

Chemin de la Ferme
02130 Villers-Agron-Aiguizy
Tel. 03 23 71 60 67
manoir.semoigne@clubt.fr
http://manoirdelasemoigne.online.fr
Langues : Eng., Ger.

Open all year • 4 rooms with bathrooms with bath/WC • €70 to €90, breakfast included • No table d'hôte • Park. No dogs admitted • Golf nearby

 The luxury of an 18-hole golf course right in the grounds.

Golfers will, of course, not be able to resist the prospect of spending a few days in this 18C mansion, whose park and river are home to an attractive golf course. Each of the spacious, quiet bedrooms is named after and decorated in a different colour: beige, blue, yellow, etc. The bathrooms are large and well-equipped. The table d'hôte has laid the accent on wholesome farm produce. If a round of golf doesn't appeal, perhaps tennis or trout fishing will take your fancy.

Access : *15km to the south-east of Fère-en-Tardenois*

VILLERS-COTTERETS - 02600

LE RÉGENT
M. Brunet

26 rue du Général-Mangin
02600 Villers-Cotterets
Tel. 03 23 96 01 46
info@hotel-leregent.com
www.hotel-leregent.com
Langues : Eng., Ger., Sp.

Closed 25 to 31 Dec • 28 rooms at the front or the back, with bath/WC or shower/WC, all have television • €70 to €80; breakfast €8 • No restaurant • Car park

Remember to bring a copy of The Three Musketeers, written by local boy, Alexander Dumas.

This elegant 18C mansion, just two minutes from the town, is so smart and spruce it could almost be new. Venture past the porch and into the romantic paved courtyard. Inside, classically decorated rooms in keeping with the architecture await you; some are listed by the Fine Arts, others have been renovated in a contemporary style.

Access : *Drive into Villers-Cotterets, the hotel is not far from the town centre, near the post office*

BARON - 60305

LE DOMAINE DE CYCLONE
Mme Petitot

2 rue de la Gonesse
60305 Baron
Tel. 06 08 98 05 50
domainedecyclone@wanadoo.fr
www.chambres-hotes.org

Open all year • 5 non-smoking rooms, all with bath/WC • €80 to €90, breakfast included • No table d'hôte • Park, terrace, car park. Credit cards not accepted, dogs not admitted • Riding lessons and outings

The façades covered in wisteria and Virginia creeper.

This lovely abode and its 10ha-estate cannot be missed in the village. The tower, where Joan of Arc slept, dates from the 15C but the majority of the building was added in the 17C. A splendid Dutch chandelier catches the eye immediately you venture indoors. Most of the bedrooms, decorated in keeping with the spirit of the premises, overlook the park. The owners, enthusiastic riders, own 45 horses which guests can make use of.

Access : *In the town*

BERNEUIL-SUR-AISNE - 60350

LE MANOIR DE ROCHEFORT
Mme Abadie

60350 Berneuil-sur-Aisne
Tel. 03 44 85 81 78

Closed Jan and Feb • 4 rooms with bath/WC or shower/WC • €79, breakfast included • No table d'hôte • Park, private car park. Credit cards not accepted

 An enchanting stay in an old fortified manor.

The owners above all sought to preserve its authentic character when they restored this 17C manor house. The former chapel is now home to four soberly elegant rooms, whose thick walls (80cm) ensure perfect soundproofing. When the weather is fine, generous breakfasts are served on the terrace; otherwise guests are invited into a breakfast room graced with antique furniture including a splendid Renaissance buffet. Hiking trails start in the nearby forest.

Access : *In the upper reaches of the village along rue de Guinant*

CHELLES - 60350

RELAIS BRUNEHAUT
M. et Mme Frenel

3 rue de l'Église
60350 Chelles
Tel. 03 44 42 85 05

Open all year • 11 rooms, one of which has a kitchenette, all have bath/WC or shower/WC and television • €50 to €70; breakfast €8; half-board available • Restaurant closed 15 Jan to 13 Feb, Mon and Tue lunchtime; menus €24 (weekdays) to €38 • Inner courtyard, garden, private car park. No dogs admitted in restaurant

 Disneyland's Sleeping Beauty Castle was partly inspired by that of Pierrefonds.

A stay in this delightful coaching inn, actually two buildings set round a flowered courtyard, is the perfect opportunity to discover Pierrefonds, home to a splendid reconstruction of a medieval Gothic castle masterminded by Napoleon's talented architect, Viollet-le-Duc. The inn's mill, still in working order, houses most of the appealing, rustic rooms, filled with the sound of the gurgling stream nearby. The restaurant serves tasty, traditional cooking.

Access : *In the centre of the village, 5km eastbound from Pierrefonds on the D 85*

CREIL - 60100

LA FERME DE VAUX
M. et Mme Joly

11 et 19 route de Vaux
60100 Creil
Tel. 03 44 64 77 00
joly.eveline@wanadoo.fr
lafermedevaux.com
Langues : Eng.

Open all year except Sat lunchtime and Sun evening • 28 rooms, 10 of which are upstairs, the others are on garden level, all have bath/WC and television • €70; breakfast €7.50; half-board available • Menus €17 to €36 • Car park • Wifi internet access

The porcelain of Creil is sought after by collectors from all over the world.

The owners of this old farm take great pleasure in sharing their "art de vivre" with guests. Each of the bedrooms is individually decorated, but the medieval chapel and its far-reaching gastronomic reputation are what attracts gourmets from all over the region. Savour the traditional French cuisine served in a Gothic dining room complete with arched windows and tapestries, or in the other more classical but equally sophisticated dining room. Some temptations are definitely worth giving in to!

Access : *On leaving Creil after the N 16/D 120 crossroads, drive towards Verneuil, on the way into the Vaux Industrial Zone*

GOUVIEUX - 60270

HOST. DU PAVILLON SAINT-HUBERT
Mme Luck-Bocquet

Avenue de Toutevoie
60270 Gouvieux
Tel. 03 44 57 07 04
pavillon.sthubert@wanadoo.fr
www.pavillon-sainthubert.com
Langues : Eng.

Closed 15 Jan to 13 Feb, Sun evening and Mon • 18 rooms, all have bath/WC or shower/WC and television • €55 to €75; breakfast €8; half-board available • Menus €32 (weekdays) to €40 • Riverside terrace, garden, car park

Chocolate lovers should not miss the chance to taste a "Crottin de Chantilly"!

This little gem is hidden at the end of a cul-de-sac, on the banks of the Oise surrounded by acres of peaceful countryside; ask for one of the renovated rooms overlooking the river. In fine weather, let the kids loose in the garden while you linger under the shade of plane trees on the terrace and watch the barges glide gently past. Appetising traditional cuisine.

Access : *Leave Chantilly on the D 909 as far as Gouvieux, turn right and at Chaumont take a left into the dead-end road towards the Oise*

LONGUEIL-ANNEL - 60150

M. ET MME BENATTAR
M. et Mme Benattar

3 rue de la Mairie
60150 Longueil-Annel
Tel. 03 44 76 16 28
A-B-andre@wanadoo.fr
www.gites-de-france.fr

Open all year • 2 rooms and 1 apartment, with bathrooms • €70, breakfast included • No table d'hôte • Garden, car park. Credit cards not accepted, dogs not admitted

 The Japanese garden which is fully at home on the patio.

The owner is bound to communicate her genuine passion for her home, a fully restored 18C farmhouse. The superb landscaped garden, through which a stream runs, serves as a playground to ducks that seem to be as in love with the site as the owner herself. Upstairs are two rooms and one apartment with a small sitting room, which overlooks the opulent dining room furnished with period pieces and enhanced by a solid stone fireplace.

Access : *In the town*

PIERREFONDS - 60350

DOMAINE DU BOIS D'AUCOURT
M. Clément-Bayard

60350 Pierrefonds
Tel. 03 44 42 80 34
bois.d.aucourt@wanadoo.fr
www.boisdaucourt.com
Langues : Eng.

Closed Jan • 11 rooms with bath/WC • €77 to €119, breakfast €10 • No restaurant • Car park. No dogs admitted • Tennis, walking, mountain biking, horse-riding

 A handsome family property surrounded by foliage.

The peaceful silence of the forest of Compiègne has crept into the walls of this large 19C half-timbered manor house. The rooms, all non-smoking, are decorated individually and all have faultless bathrooms. The only problem is deciding between the "Scottish", "Sevillan", "Tuscan", "Zen" or "Tropical" rooms. Breakfast is served in your hosts' warm, welcoming kitchen.

Access : *1.6km westbound from Pierrefonds on the D 85*

PIERREFONDS - 60350

L'ERMITAGE
Mme Elizabeth Dandoy

74 rue de l'Impératrice-Eugénie
60350 Pierrefonds
Tel. 03 44 42 85 64
elizabeth.dandoy@wanadoo.fr
www.oisermitage.com

Open all year • 4 rooms with bath/WC or shower/WC • €60 to €80, breakfast included • No table d'hôte • Park, garden, car park. Credit cards not accepted, dogs not admitted

 The peace and quiet of the site is interrupted only by birdsong.

When they recently purchased this old house built in 1860, the current owners wanted to ensure that the extensive restoration work would not detract from the original understated elegance. They accomplished their task, from the reception hall and its period slate floor, to the rooms upstairs whose walls are either whitewashed or hung with fabric and boast their original parquet floors. Outdoors, a dovecote stands in the park that remains pleasantly shaded by century-old beech and oak trees.

Access : *Northeast of Pierrefonds on the D335 Soissons road*

PUITS-LA-VALLÉE - 60480

LA FAISANDERIE
M. et Mme Dumetz

8 rue du Château
60480 Puits-la-Vallée
Tel. 03 44 80 70 29
catherine.dumetz@business.fr

Open all year • 4 rooms, all with bath/WC and television • €45 to €70, breakfast included • Table d'hôte €16 • Terrace, garden, private car park. Credit cards not accepted, dogs not admitted • Library, bicycles, table tennis

The lady of the house's faultless welcome.

A gravelled drive leads to this handsome property separated from the rest of the village by wooded parklands. The comfortable "Blue", "Rose", Green" rooms and "Gold" apartment are attractively decorated in a clever mixture of styles. Home-made jams and cakes feature prominently on the breakfast table. Dinner time is a chance to savour tasty dishes in which pheasant, unsurprisingly enough given the property's name, takes pride of place.

Access : *In the town centre*

DURY - 80480

LE PETIT CHÂTEAU
M. Saguez

2 rue Grimaux
80480 Dury
Tel. 03 22 95 29 52
a.saguez@wanadoo.fr
http://perso.wanadoo.fr/am.saguez
Langues : Eng.

Open all year • 5 non-smoking rooms, one of which is on ground level, all have bathrooms • €70 to €75, breakfast included • No table d'hôte • Garden, park, car park. Credit cards not accepted, no dogs admitted • Horse-drawn carriage rides

 The appeal of a countryside setting, just a ten-minute drive from the centre of Amiens.

You will soon forget the nearby road when you see the wonderful country setting of this 19C house and are warmly greeted by the convivial owners. The rooms, non-smoking only, are located in a separate wing and are for the most part spacious, but the smallest of them is also the cosiest. The substantial breakfast, taken in the company of your discreet hosts, will set you up for the day.

Access : *6km southbound from Amiens on the N 1 towards Beauvais*

GAPENNES - 80150

LA NICOULETTE
Mme Solange Nicolle

7 rue de Saint-Riquier
80150 Gapennes
Tel. 03 22 28 92 77
nicoulette@wanadoo.fr
http://monsite.wanadoo.fr/nicoulette

Open all year • 5 rooms including 1 family room and 1 apartment, all with bath/WC • €76, breakfast included • No table d'hôte • Garden, private car park. Credit cards not accepted, dogs not admitted • Jacuzzi, bicycles lent

 The delightful welcome.

After having learnt the trade in a hotel chain, Mme Nicolle decided to open her own establishment. Although the rooms are a recent addition, throughout you will appreciate the owner's obvious experience, pleasantly combined with a weakness for old furniture. New, comfortable bedding, attractive bathrooms equipped with thick towels and bathrobes, and a Jacuzzi room to relax in style.

Access : *Leave the village southbound*

PORT-LE-GRAND - 80132

LE CROTOY - 80550

LES TOURELLES
M. et Mme Ferreira Da Silva

2 rue Pierre-Guerlain
80550 Le Crotoy
Tel. 03 22 27 16 33
lestourelles@nhgroupe.com
www.lestourelles.com
Langues : Eng.

Closed from 7 to 31 Jan • 33 rooms, most have shower/WC, the others have bath/WC, some have television • €60 to €85; (€57 to €76 low season); breakfast €8; half-board available • Menus €21 to €31 • Children's dormitory

 The children's "dorm".

The fairy-tale twin turrets of this 19C red and white brick mansion dominate the tiny seaside resort and the "only south-facing beach of the North" (Pierre Guerlain). Most of the rooms, on a contemporary seafaring theme or in a delightfully clean-lined Swedish style, overlook the bay of the Somme. Delicious mounds of fresh fish and seafood will restore the disconsolate spirits of unlucky "shrimpers".

Theme weekends on art, literature, sport. Painting and sculpture exhibition

Access : *Overlooking the bay, on the beach road*

LE BOIS DE BONANCE
M. et Mme Maillard

Bois-de-Bonance
80132 Port-le-Grand
Tel. 03 22 24 11 97
maillard.chambrehote@bonance.com
www.bonance.com
Langues : Eng., Ger.

Closed from Nov to Feb • 4 rooms, 2 of which are in a separate wing, with bath/WC • €76, breakfast included • No table d'hôte • Garden • Swimming pool, keep-fit track, table-tennis, children's play area

 The charm of a country garden.

You may be amused to learn that the pink walls and narrow Gothic-style windows of this 19C holiday home, in a secluded spot far from the bustle of traffic, are sometimes described as "English"! Whatever, the antique furnished rooms have been decorated with infinite taste; those in the former servants' quarters open directly onto the beautiful garden, brimming with flowers in the summer. In the winter, a cheerful fire adds warmth to the pleasant breakfast room.

Access : *11km eastbound from Saint-Valery-sur-Somme on the D 940, then the D 40 and a minor road*

QUEND - 80120

AUBERGE LE FIACRE
M. et Mme Masmonteil

6 rue des Pommiers - hameau de
Routhiauville
80120 Quend
Tel. 03 22 23 47 30
lefiacre@wanadoo.fr
www.aufiacre.fr
Langues : Eng., Ger.

Closed mid-Jan to mid-Feb • 11 rooms, one of
which has disabled access, most have bath/WC,
some have shower/WC and television • €76 to
€80; breakfast €11; half-board available • Restaurant closed Tue and Wed lunchtimes; menus
€19.50 (weekdays) to €40 • Garden, car park.
Dogs not admitted in rooms • Golf course

 Fancy a short "two-kilometre-run" in the dunes?

This old farmstead has been converted into an
appealing inn surrounded in foliage, whose
restful, welcoming rooms open onto a lovely
garden. In addition, three more modern apartments have recently been created. The restaurant, for its part, has retained a resolutely
country style with exposed beams and tiled
floors, a perfect setting for its classic repertoire. Character and quality: what more could
you want!

Access : *Leave the D 940 at Quend, between
Berck-sur-Mer and Rue, and take the
D 32 towards Fort-Mahon-Plage*

SAINT-VALERY-SUR-SOMME - 80230

LA GRIBANE
M. et Mme Douchet

297 quai Jeanne-d'Arc
80230 Saint-Valery-sur-Somme
Tel. 03 22 60 97 55
Langues : Eng.

Closed 15 Dec to 15 Feb • 4 rooms with
shower/WC • €70 to €85, breakfast included
• No table d'hôte • Park, car park. Credit cards
not accepted, no dogs admitted

 The garden has been created in a polder opposite the ramparts.

This 1930 house takes its name from the 18C
merchant vessel used to navigate the rivers.
The rooms of the main wing, painted in tones of
blue, white and beige, overlook the bay; the
others are in a pavilion in the middle of the
garden. The large bay windows of the breakfast
room look out onto the wonderful garden,
wedged between the land reclaimed from the
sea and the old city walls.

Access : *In the historic town, near the beach*

SAINT-VALERY-SUR-SOMME - 80230

27

LE RELAIS GUILLAUME DE NORMANDY
MM. Crimet et Dupré

Quai du Romerel
80230 Saint-Valery-sur-Somme
Tel. 03 22 60 82 36
relais-guillaume@wanadoo.fr
www.guillaumedenormandy.com
Langues : Eng.

Closed from 19 Dec to 10 Jan and Tue
• 14 rooms, all have bath/WC or shower/WC and television • €61 to €71; breakfast €7.80; half-board available • Air-conditioned restaurant; menus €18 to €40 • Terrace, car park. No dogs admitted in restaurant

 A trip across the bay of the Somme aboard a real steam train.

Take in the lovely Picardy coast from the windows of this elegant manor house facing the bay and on the outskirts of St-Valery-sur-Somme. None of the rooms are enormous, but half face the Channel, where you will sometimes be able to catch a glimpse of seals. The soberly decorated panoramic dining room also enables diners to enjoy the view while sampling the delicious traditional fare rustled up by the chef.

Access : *On the dike, opposite the bay of the Somme*

POITOU CHARENTES

Illustrious names such as Cognac, Angoulême or La Rochelle all echo through France's history, but there is just as much to appreciate in the here and now. Start your journey lazing on the sandy beaches of its unspoilt coastline where the scent of pine trees mingles with the fresh sea air. A stay in a thalassotherapy resort will revive your flagging spirits, further boosted by a platter of oysters and lightly buttered bread. A bicycle is the best way to discover the region's delightfully unhilly coastal islands as you pedal along quaint little country lanes, lined with tiny blue and white cottages and multicoloured hollyhocks. Back on the mainland, embark on a barge and explore the thousand and one canals of the marshy, and mercifully mosquito-free, "Green Venice". You will have earned yourself a taste of vintage Cognac, or perhaps a glass of the less heady local apéritif, the fruity, ice-cold Pineau. If all this seems just too restful, head for Futuroscope, a theme park devoted to the moving image, and enjoy an action-packed day or two of life in the future.

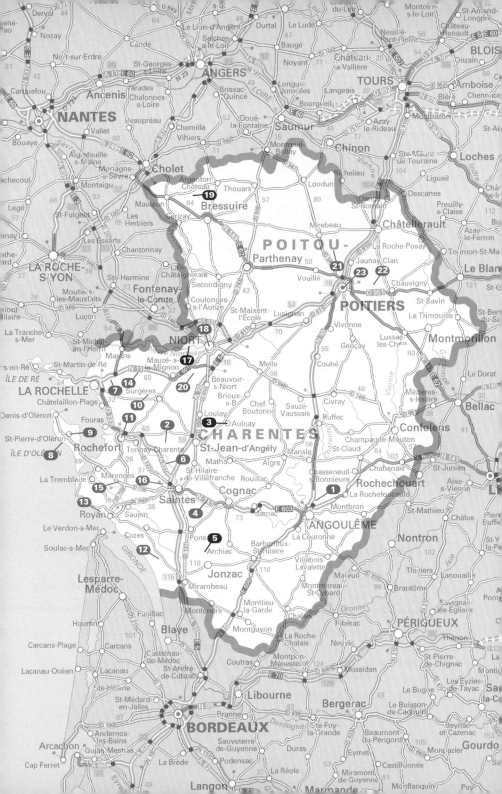

CHAMPNIERS - 16430

LA TEMPLERIE
M. et Mme Richon

Denat
16430 Champniers
Tel. 05 45 68 49 00
Langues : Eng., Sp.

Open all year • 5 rooms, 2 of which are on the ground floor with disabled access and 1 family room, all have bath/WC • €45, breakfast included • No table d'hôte • Garden, car park. No dogs admitted • Outdoor swimming pool

> **The windows of this farm have enjoyed the same pastoral view for two hundred years.**

Guests are always assured of a warm welcome within this typically regional farmhouse. The rooms, located in the former outbuildings, are colourful and some are furnished with antiques; two open directly onto the garden and the swimming pool. In the winter, a cheerful fire is lit in the immense dining room. The sitting room with a lovely library on a mezzanine particularly caught our fancy.

Access : *9.5km northbound from Angoulême towards Poitiers on the N 10, then Balzac on the D 105*

ARCHINGEAY - 17380

LES HORTENSIAS
M. et Mme Jacques

16 rue des Sablières
17380 Archingeay
Tel. 05 46 97 85 70
jpmt.jacques@wanadoo.fr
www.gite-prop.com/17/5114/
Langues : Eng.

Open all year • 3 non-smoking rooms, 1 with disabled access, all with bathrooms • €52 to €58, breakfast included • Table d'hôte €22, drinks included, (Mon, Tue and Fri by reservation) • Garden, private car park. Credit cards not accepted, no dogs allowed

> **The tranquillity.**

This entirely rebuilt former wine-growers' farmhouse is home to two exquisitely decorated bedrooms and a gîte fitted with regional cherry-wood furniture. The mistress of the house serves breakfast and three times a week, also offers delicious family-style dishes made with local and garden produce.

Access : *At Tonnay-Boutonne, take the D 114 towards Archingeay. In the town, head for Les Nouillers and follow the signposts*

CHÉRAC - 17610

AULNAY - 17470

LA PANTOUFLE
M. Djahidé Paksoy

5 impasse des Dimiers
17610 Chérac
Tel. 05 46 95 37 10
lapantoufle@free.fr
www.lapantoufle.free.fr

Open all year • 3 rooms, all with bathrooms • €45, breakfast included • Table d'hôte €17 including drinks (by reservation) • Garden, car park. Credit cards not accepted, dogs not admitted

LE DONJON
M. et Mme Imbach

4 rue des Hivers
17470 Aulnay
Tel. 05 46 33 67 67
hoteldudonjon@wanadoo.fr
www.hoteldudonjon.com
Langues : Eng.

Closed fortnight in Jan and Feb • 10 rooms, one of which has disabled access, all have bath/WC or shower/WC and television • €65 to €75 (€54 to €61 low season); breakfast €6.50 • No restaurant

 The charm of this quaint little village.

This home with its limestone façade typical of the Charentes region dates from 1694. The reception hall leads into a dining room and a cosy sitting room. The three pleasant rooms are located upstairs. The lady of the house, a genuine cordon bleu, makes her own smoked ham, duck breast, rillettes of duck, and orange and nut wine. The vegetables come from the garden. Simply delicious. Outdoors, the walled garden is ideal for sunbathing.

 Long chats around the fire in the sitting room.

The green shuttered façade of this house stands near the Church of St Pierre, a master-piece of regional Romanesque architecture. The interior of the house has been carefully restored in order to preserve the lovely old beams and gold-coloured limestone walls. Old furniture graces all the rooms and the bed-rooms are further brightened by colourful bed-spreads and matching curtains; all have mod-ern bathrooms.

Access : *10km westbound from Cognac on the N141, towards Saintes*

Access : *In the heart of the village, near the main square*

CLAM - 17500

LE VIEUX LOGIS
Mme Brard

3 rue du 8-Mai-1945
17500 Clam
Tel. 05 46 70 20 13
info@vieuxlogis.com
www.vieuxlogis.com
Langues : Eng.

Open all year • 10 ground-floor rooms with bath/WC or shower/WC and television • €52 to €62 breakfast €8; half-board available • Air-conditioned restaurant; menus €15 to €38 • Terrace, garden, car park. No dogs admitted in rooms • Outdoor swimming pool

 The owners' warm welcome and infectious good nature.

This 'Old Abode' was formerly home to the village's café-grocer's shop. The tiny cup of piping hot espresso on the bar and the shelves laden with tins and jars have since made way for two country-style dining rooms, the walls of which are adorned by photos taken by the master of the house. His cheerful spouse rustles up tasty local dishes. The modern ground-floor building opens onto the garden and the comfortable, pleasant rooms are equipped with terraces.

Access : *6km northbound of Jonzac on the D 142*

CRAZANNES - 17350

CHÂTEAU DE CRAZANNES
M. et Mme de Rochefort

24 rue du Château
17350 Crazannes
Tel. 06 80 65 40 96
crazannes@worldonline.fr
www.crazannes.com
Langues : Eng.

Open all year • 6 rooms, 2 of which are apartments on 2 floors, all with bathrooms • €90 to €160, breakfast included • Snacks available • Terrace, garden, car park. Dogs not admitted • Outdoor swimming pool

 The sheer luxury of this listed château.

Eight hectares of grounds surround this superb listed 14C château which has been treated to a lavish restoration. It boasts six splendid bedrooms, three of which in the 16C keep noted for their light interior and enormous bathrooms. The regionally inspired cuisine is prepared with fresh market produce and served in the former sheepfold, decorated with old farm tools.

Access : *Take Saintes exit no 35, follow RN 137 towards Rochefort, turn right towards Plassay on RN 119 and follow signs to Château de Crazanne*

DOMPIERRE-SUR-MER - 17139

LOGIS SAINT-LÉONARD
M. et Mme Schwartz

6 rue des Chaumes-l'Abbaye
17139 Dompierre-sur-Mer
Tel. 05 46 35 14 65
logis-st-leonard@wanadoo.fr
Langues : Eng.

Open all year • 4 rooms upstairs, all have bath/WC or shower/WC • €68, breakfast included • No table d'hôte • Park, car park, sitting room-library. Credit cards not accepted • Outdoor swimming pool, billiards, table tennis, jacuzzi, fishing

 A haven of peace and quiet just ten minutes from the lively bustle of La Rochelle.

A magnificent tree-lined park surrounds this spacious restored house which offers three personalised guest-rooms. The owners have decorated each room personally with objects and furniture brought back from their travels in Polynesia and Africa. The breakfast table is piled high with mouth-watering home-made cakes and jams. On the leisure side, you can choose between table-tennis, a soak in the Jacuzzi or a dip in the swimming pool set amidst trees. Very welcoming and friendly.

Access : *In the town centre*

ILE D'OLERON - 17310

LES TRÉMIÈRES
Mme Frat

5 route de Saint-Pierre
17310 La Cotinière
Tel. 05 46 47 44 25
lestremieres@hotmail.fr
www.oleron.org

Open all year • 5 rooms, 2 of which are apartments, with shower/WC • €56 to €64 (€50 to €58 low season); breakfast included • No table d'hôte • Garden, car park. Credit cards not accepted, no dogs admitted

 Just two minutes from the port and its brightly-coloured fishing boats.

This early 20C house with sandy-coloured walls and blue shutters is only a short walk from the port of La Cotinière and its shops. All the rooms and suites are personalised and immaculately cared for. Take things easy in the comfortable leather sofas and armchairs by the fireside in the sitting room. In the summertime, breakfast is served under the chestnut tree.

Access : *600m from the entrance to the village coming from Maisonneuve*

ILE D'OLÉRON - 17310

9

MADAME MICHELINE DENIEAU
Mme Denieau

20 rue de la Legère, la Menounière
17310 Saint-Pierre-d'Oléron
Tel. 05 46 47 14 34
denieau.jean-pierre@wanadoo.fr
Langues : Eng., Sp.

Open all year • 5 rooms with shower/WC • €52,
breakfast included • No table d'hôte • Garden,
car park. Credit cards not accepted

**Bicycling round the island as you explore
its oyster beds and farms.**

Oléron wines and the famous Pineau - a fortified aperitif - are still produced on the estate
of this stone farmhouse which is a fine example
of island architecture. The neat and simple
rooms are in the outbuildings; the most recent
have old furniture and gaily painted green or
blue beams; those with a mezzanine are very
popular with families. Guests have the run of a
kitchen, complete with an old kneading trough
and a fireplace.

Access : *3km westbound from
Saint-Pierre-d'Oléron*

PUYRAVAULT - 17700

10

LE CLOS DE LA GARENNE
M. et Mme François

9 rue de la Garenne
17700 Puyravault
Tel. 05 46 35 47 71
info@closdelagarenne.com
www.closdelagarenne.com
Langues : Ger., Eng., It., Sp.

Open all year • 4 non-smoking rooms, including
one studio with disabled access, all with
bath/WC or shower/WC • €65, breakfast
included • Table d'hôte €25 • Terrace, park, car
park. No dogs allowed • Billiards, library, board
games, children's play area

**The authenticity of this regional manor
house.**

The owners extend a warm welcome to guests
to their handsome manor house steeped in
history. On the ground-floor, the 17C dining
room and 18C sitting room with Louis XV fireplace, etc, overlook the terraces and grounds.
The spacious elegant bedrooms are all furnished with antiques, either in the family for
years or picked up in antique shops. A cottage
and one-room flat are also available. Excellent
value for money.

Access : *In the town*

ROCHEFORT - 17300

11

PALMIER SUR COUR
M. et Mme Blasselle

55 rue de la République
17300 Rochefort
Tel. 05 46 99 55 54
palmiersurcour@wanadoo.fr
www.palmiersurcour.com
Langues : Eng., Sp.

Closed 15 Dec to Feb school holidays • 3 rooms with bath/WC or shower/WC • €58 to €64 (€52.20 to €57.60 low season), breakfast included • No table d'hôte • Patio, sitting-room, library with television and Internet access, kitchenette. Credit cards not accepted, no dogs admitted • Bicycle rentals

 A Mediterranean atmosphere in the heart of the Charentes.

This small 19C mansion in the heart of the historic district is now home to enchanting personalised bedrooms. The "Corderie" pays homage to the famous Rochefort monument, "Aziyadé" is a reference to a local boy and writer, Pierre Loti, while "Marine" is tastefully decorated in blue and white. The patio and palm trees invite you to linger over the tasty breakfasts... A genuinely friendly house which sports a distinctly Southern fragrance.

Access : *In the town centre*

SAINT-FORT-SUR-GIRONDE - 17240

12

LE CHÂTEAU DES SALLES
Mme Couillaud

Carrefour D 125 et D 730
17240 Saint-Fort-sur-Gironde
Tel. 05 46 49 95 10
chateaudessalles@wanadoo.fr
www.chateaudessalles.com
Langues : Eng., Ger.

Closed 1 Nov to Easter • 5 rooms with shower/WC • €80 to €110; breakfast €9; half-board available • Table d'hôte €35 • Park, garden, car park. No dogs admitted • Cognac and Pineau de Charentes on sale

 The delicious fare on the table d'hôte lit by candles in the evenings.

The owners of the 15C castle, entirely renovated in the 19C, produce their own Pineau, a delicious aperitif, as well as wines and cognac, which can be bought from the estate. The tastefully furnished, south-facing rooms open onto the garden and its sumptuous magnolia tree; the largest room, under the eaves, displays a happy blend of old and contemporary styles. Lovely old furniture, a piano and a games table grace the sitting room. Candle-lit dining in the evenings.

Access : *7.5km south-east of Mortagne by D 145 then at the D 125 and D 730 crossroads*

SAINT-PALAIS-SUR-MER - 17420

MA MAISON DE MER
Mme Hutchinson

21 avenue du Platin
17420 Saint-Palais-sur-Mer
Tel. 05 46 23 64 86
reservations@mamaisondemer.com
www.mamaisondemer.com
Langues : Eng.

Open all year • 6 non-smoking rooms, all have bath/WC • €80 to €140 (€60 to €95 low season), breakfast included • Table d'hôte, evenings only in Jul and Aug; €35 • Terrace, garden, car park, television room. No dogs allowed • 200m from the beach

The cosy atmosphere of this house right on the waterfront.

A row of pine trees along the beach hides this handsome 1920's home from view. It has been recently renovated in a delightful seaside style with cane furniture, a white and grey colour theme and rush mats in the bedrooms. A timeless, slightly "British" atmosphere reigns throughout this English-owned property... On the ground floor are a dining room and bar; Franco-British cuisine.

Access : *200m from the town centre*

SAINT-SAUVEUR-D'AUNIS - 17540

LE LOGIS DE L'AUNIS
Mme Ecarot

8 rue de Ligoure
17540 Saint-Sauveur-d'Aunis
Tel. 05 46 09 02 14
jocelyne.ecarot@wanadoo.fr
www.logisdelaunis.com
Langues : Eng.

Open all year • 3 non-smoking rooms, all with bath/WC or shower/WC, television and safe • €85, breakfast included • Table d'hôte €28 • Terrace, garden, car park. Credit cards not accepted, no dogs allowed • Outdoor swimming pool

The delightful walled courtyard complete with flower-decked garden and swimming pool.

This traditional regional property set in the heart of a quiet village has been tastefully restored. It is home to three attractive rooms, one of which on the ground-floor, two sitting rooms (one with fireplace and another opening onto the garden and pool), as well as a dining room in which wood, stone and wrought iron feature prominently. Home-made cakes and jams on the breakfast table, while local produce takes pride of place on the table d'hôte, evenings only.

Access : *In the town centre*

ST-GEORGES-DES-COTEAUX - 17810

SAINT-SORNIN - 17600

LA CAUSSOLIÈRE
M. Gates

10 rue du Petit-Moulin
17600 Saint-Sornin
Tel. 05 46 85 44 62
reservations@caussoliere.com
www.caussoliere.com
Langues : Eng., Ger.

Closed 15 Nov to 15 Mar • 4 non-smoking rooms;
all have bathrooms • €65 to €85, breakfast
included • Table d'hôte €15 to €30 • Terrace,
garden, television and library room, private car
park. Credit cards not accepted, no dogs
allowed • Outdoor swimming pool

 **The splendid location of this house poised
between ocean and countryside.**

Only birdsong interrupts the peace and quiet of
this masterfully restored farmhouse set in an
immense garden planted with a riot of fragrant
plants. The interior is equally inviting with
personalised bedrooms (antique or painted furniture, pastel colour themes, bare stone and
timbers) and the breakfast room-veranda facing the greenery is also delightful.

Access : *12.5km southeast of Marennes on the
D 728, Saintes road*

CHAMBRE D'HÔTE M. TROUVÉ
M. et Mme Trouvé

5 rue de l'Église
17810 Saint-Georges-des-Coteaux
Tel. 05 46 92 96 66
adtrouve@yahoo.fr
 Langues : Eng.

Closed from 15 Nov to 1 Apr • 4 rooms with
shower/WC • €49, breakfast included • No table
d'hôte • Garden, car park. Credit cards not
accepted, no dogs admitted • Tennis and horse-
riding centre in the village

 **Each bedroom pays light-hearted tribute to
a famous author.**

You will not be disappointed should you decide
to spend a night or two in this 18C farmstead,
surrounded by a large garden. The cow-shed
and barn have been turned into an immense
room which serves as a combined lobby, sitting
room, library and billiards room. Country furniture adorns the bedrooms, each named after
a favourite author – Agatha Christie and Tin-
tin's creator, Hergé are among them. Make
sure you take a look at the old wash house or
"bujor".

Access : *9km to the north-west of Saintes
towards Rochefort on the N 137 then the D 127*

COULON - 79510

NIORT - 79000

AU MARAIS
Mme Nerrière

46 quai Louis-Hardy
79510 Coulon
Tel. 05 49 35 90 43
information@hotel-aumarais.com
www.hotel-aumarais.com

Closed from 15 Dec to 5 Feb • 18 rooms located in 2 houses, one has disabled access. Rooms have bath/WC or shower/WC, all have television • €70 to €75; breakfast €12 to €14 • No restaurant

LA MAGNOLIÈRE
M. et Mme Marchadier

16 impasse de l'Abbaye
79000 Niort
Tel. 05 49 35 36 06
a.marchadier@libertysurf.fr
www.marais-poitevin.com/heberg-ch/magnoliere/magnoliere.htm

Closed 15 to 31 Dec • 3 non-smoking rooms, all with bath/WC or shower/WC and television • €79, breakfast included • No table d'hôte • Garden, car park. Credit cards not accepted, dogs not admitted • Library, outdoor swimming pool

Glide over the waters of "Green Venice".

A perfect place to begin exploring the aquatic maze of what is known as "Green Venice". The pale stone walls and blue shutters of this pair of 19C boatmen's houses face the marsh's landing stage. The modern, cheerful rooms are decorated with bold Provençal fabrics and most give onto the toing-and-froing of the boats. In summer, the area is busy during the day but after nightfall, all becomes peaceful and car-free!

The tranquillity and atmosphere which reigns throughout this establishment.

This comfortable bourgeois home, built in the 19C on the site of a former abbey, a few traces of which remain, stands on the threshold of the Marais poitevin. The rooms are named after women artists - Marie Laurencin, Suzanne Valadon, Berthe Morisot, and furnished with lovely antique pieces. All overlook the garden, home to a magnificent several hundred-year-old magnolia tree, which extends down to the river. On the leisure side: sitting room-library, swimming pool, angling, boating, etc.

Access : *Near the landing stage where boat trips leave*

Access : *4km from Coulon on the D 9*

VALLANS - 79270

NUEIL-LES-AUBIERS - 79250

LE MOULIN DE LA SORINIÈRE
M. et Mme Froger et M. et Mme Brard

79250 Nueil-les-Aubiers
Tel. 05 49 72 39 20
moulin-soriniere@wanadoo.fr
www.moulin-soriniere.com

Closed Easter and Nov half-term holidays • 8 rooms, 2 with disabled access, all with bathrooms and television • €46 to €47; breakfast €7 • Menus €14 (weekdays) to €30 • Terrace, garden, car park. No dogs allowed in restaurant

LE LOGIS D'ANTAN
Mme Ragouilliaux et M. Di Battista

140 rue Saint-Louis
79270 Vallans
Tel. 05 49 04 86 75
info@logisdantan.com
www.logisdantan.com
Langues : Ger., Eng., It., Sp.

Open all year • 5 non-smoking rooms, all with bathrooms and television • €64, breakfast included • Table d'hôte €24, drinks included (evenings only) • Terrace, park, private car park. Credit cards not accepted, no dogs allowed in restaurant

We most liked The well-preserved authenticity of this old property.

A well-tended flowered walled park and woodland encircle this immense stone manor house, which dates from 1850 and is located just a stone's throw from Green Venice. It offers five spacious bedrooms decorated in a style which mixes country and bourgeois styles. At mealtimes you will be invited to taste regional dishes with a modern flavour such as magret of duck with garden figs, chocolate cake, etc. In summertime, dinner is served on the veranda.

We most liked The calm of this old country mill.

This 19C property, perched on the banks of the Argent, has been given a new lease of life since its conversion into a hotel-restaurant. The reception is located in the former machine room, the dining room sports original timber beams and an old fireplace and the four bedrooms sport a rustic style. Four more spacious rooms are available in a separate wing. In the kitchen, the chef rustles up tasty dishes with a modern slant.

Access : *In the town centre*

Access : *2km southwest of Nueil-les-Aubiers on the D 33 and C 3, Cerizay road*

CHENECHÉ - 86380

CHÂTEAU DE LABAROM
M. et Mme Le Gallais

86380 Cheneché
Tel. 05 49 51 24 22
chateau.de.labarom@wanadoo.fr
Langues : Eng.

Closed from 1 Nov to 30 Mar • 3 rooms with shower/WC • €69 to €75, breakfast included • No table d'hôte • Dovecote, park, car park. Credit cards not accepted, no dogs admitted • Outdoor swimming pool

 Oh la la! Row upon row of books about the region and all in French!

This 16C and 17C château was built in three hundred acres of parkland. It makes an ideal base camp to explore the region. We loved the well-worn aristocratic feel of the creaky floor boards and old furniture. The spacious rooms are lined in fabric and graced with beautiful antiques: the monumental period fireplace in the breakfast room cannot fail to catch the eye. The owner, who dabbles in art in his spare time, will happily talk you through the rudiments of painting on porcelain.

Access : *15km to the north-west of the Futuroscope, towards Neuville and Lencloître then the D 15*

LAVOUX - 86800

LOGIS DU CHÂTEAU DU BOIS DOUCET
M. et Mme de Villoutreys

86800 Lavoux
Tel. 05 49 44 20 26

Open all year by reservation • 3 rooms including 1 apartment, all with bath/WC • €70 to €80, breakfast included • Table d'hôte €30 • Park, garden, car park. Credit cards not accepted

 The owners' enthusiasm for their home.

In the heart of the family estate of 400 ha, this 17C home, which is a listed historic monument, as are the castle and the French-style garden, has lost nothing of its authenticity. Antique family heirlooms and tapestries set the scene for the dining room while the vaulted sitting room is Louis XIII in spirit. Upstairs, the apartment with its immense fireplace commands a view of the garden, while two other comfortable rooms are located in a restored wing. Regional specialities (by reservation).

Access : *6km from Lavoux on the D139 then a lane*

POITIERS - 86000

23

CHÂTEAU DE VAUMORET
M. Johnson

Rue du Breuil-Mingot
86000 Poitiers
Tel. 05 49 61 32 11
chateau-vaumoret@wanadoo.fr

Closed 3 to 25 Feb • 5 rooms with bath/WC
• €59 to €69, breakfast included • No table
d'hôte • Park, car park. No dogs admitted

A countryside setting on the doorstep of Poitiers.

Nearly 45 acres of green meadows and woodland encircle this beautifully restored 17C mansion. The rooms, in the right wing, boast some fine old furniture, prints and paintings and all have immaculate bathrooms. Enjoy breakfast in a light, airy room, then borrow a bike and start exploring.

Access : *10km north-east of Poitiers towards La Roche-Posay on the D 3, then Sèvres-Anxaumont on the D 18*

PROVENCE, ALPS and the FRENCH RIVIERA

As you listen to the fishmongers hawking their wares under its sunny blue skies, you cannot help but fall in love with the infectious, happy-go-lucky spirit of Marseilles. Elsewhere, the steady chirring of the cicadas is interrupted only by the sheep-bells ringing in the hills as the shepherds bring their flocks home at night. The sun rises early over the ochre walls of hilltop villages which keep a careful watch over the fields of lavender below. Venture into the multitude of tiny hinterland villages and slow down to the gentle pace of the villagers as they leave the shade of the lime trees for the refreshingly cool walls of the café. However, come 2pm, you will soon begin to wonder where everyone is. On hot summer afternoons, everyone exercises their God-given right to a nap, from the fashionable beaches of Saint Tropez and seaside cabins of the Camargue to medieval walled cities surrounded by cypresses or a tiny fishing boat off the coast of Toulon. As the sun begins to set, life starts up again and the players of pétanque emerge; join them as they down a glass of pastis, then feast on bubbling *bouillabaisse*.

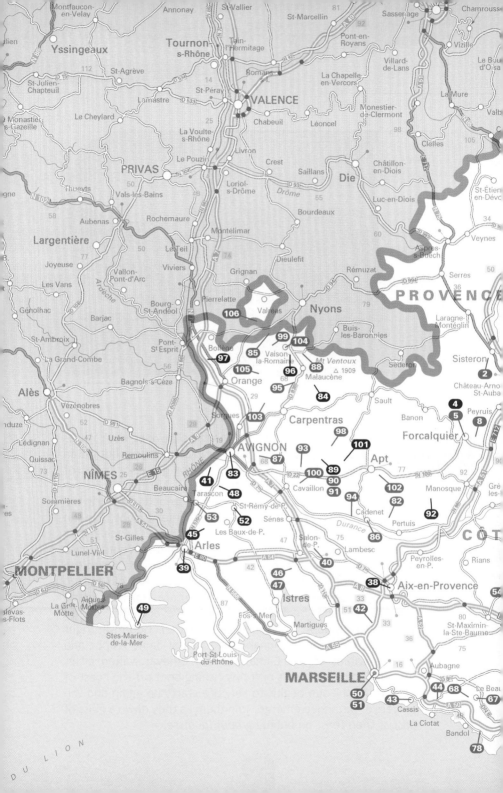

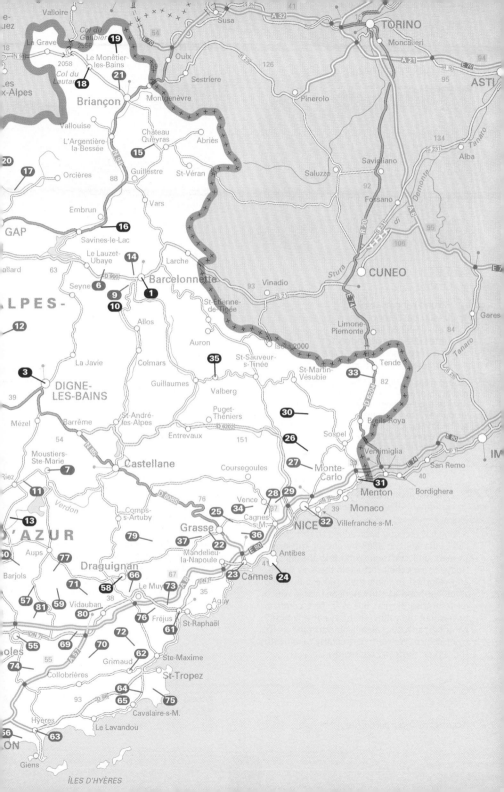

BEVONS - 04200

BARCELONNETTE - 04400

AZTECA
M. Chabre

3 rue François-Arnaud
04400 Barcelonnette
Tel. 04 92 81 46 36
hotelazteca@wanadoo.fr
http://perso.orange.fr/hotel-azteca
Langues : Ger., Eng., It.

Closed from 13 Nov to 5 Dec • 27 non-smoking rooms, 5 of which are split-level and one has disabled access. Rooms have bath/WC and television • €72 to €107; breakfast €9 • No restaurant • Private car park, private shuttle bus to the ski resorts • Nearby: swimming pool, tennis, golf, horse-riding, climbing

> **The fascinating link between this tiny mountain village and Mexico.**

A wing has recently been added to this "Mexican" villa built in 1888 by one of the many farmers and craftsmen who left the hills of Ubaye to seek their fortune in the New World, and returned to mark their success in grand style. The hotel's Latin American theme, which may surprise at first but is in fact common throughout the valley, features naive "mural" paintings, an Aztec calendar and arts and crafts from Mexico. We were particularly taken with the three "Mexican" bedrooms.

Access : *Near the post office*

MAS DU FIGUIER
M. Levrault

La Fontaine
04200 Bevons
Tel. 04 92 62 81 28
mas.du.figuier@wanadoo.fr
www.guideprovence.com/gites/masdufiguier
Langues : Eng.

Closed Nov to Jan • 4 rooms with bathrooms • €55, breakfast included; half-board available • Table d'hôte €20 • Park, car park. Credit cards not accepted, dogs not admitted

> **Trekking up to the ridge of the Lure – on donkey-back!**

A field of lavender stretches in front of this remote 17C mas – or Provençal farm – which stands at an altitude of 650m opposite the Lure Mountain. A proudly southern flavour prevails in the welcoming rooms, decorated in warm colours with tiled ceilings and exposed beams. We particularly liked the large bathrooms and their Moorish influence. In the winter, the fireside in the sitting room is definitely the cosiest spot in the house.

Access : *8km westbound from Sisteron on the N 85, the D 946 and the D 553*

DIGNE-LES-BAINS - 04000

VILLA GAÏA
M. et Mme Martin

24 route de Nice
04000 Digne-les-Bains
Tel. 04 92 31 21 60
hotel.gaia@wanadoo.fr
www.hotelvilla.gaia.fr
Langues : Ger., Eng., It.

Closed 1 week in Jul and from Nov to mid-Apr • 12 rooms with bath/WC or shower/WC • €70 to €99; breakfast €9; half-board available • Restaurant closed 1 to 10 Jul, Wed out of season; menus (guests only) €26 • Library, terrace, park, car park. No dogs admitted

Listen to the wind rustling through the leaves of the ancient trees in the park as you fall asleep.

A relaxed family atmosphere reigns throughout this villa built in 1730, reworked in the early 20C and finally turned into a hotel in 1993. The period furniture, knick-knacks, tiles and well-preserved woodwork visible throughout the comfortable rooms, library and sitting rooms bear witness to the villa's past. In the evening, guests of the Villa Gaïa gather in the attractive plush dining room to sample an enticingly simple set menu.

Access : *Take the N 85 towards Nice for 2km*

FORCALQUIER - 04300

AUBERGE CHAREMBEAU
M. Berger

Route de Niozelles
04300 Forcalquier
Tel. 04 92 70 91 70
contact@charembeau.com
www.charembeau.com
Langues : Ger., Eng., Du.

Open from 1 Mar to 15 Nov • 24 rooms, one of which has disabled access, with bath/WC or shower/WC, all have television, some have a balcony or terrace • €61 to €92 (€52 to €79 low season); breakfast €8.50 • No restaurant • Park, car park • Swimming pool, tennis, bicycles, horse-riding, mountain-bike rentals

What better way to explore the region than by bicycle or on horse-back (on request)!

This lovely 18C farmhouse, which lies in a secluded landscape of hill and dale, enjoys the patronage of regular, satisfied customers. The lady of the house chose the Provençal fittings and fixtures in the well-proportioned bedrooms herself. The house doesn't have a restaurant but guests are welcome to picnic in the shaded park and perhaps taste the famous local goat's-cheese, known as banon.

Access : *Eastbound from Forcalquier, on the N 100 towards Niozelles for 2.5km, then right on a minor road*

FORCALQUIER - 04300

CAMPAGNE « LE PARADIS »
M. Pourcin

04300 Forcalquier
Tel. 04 92 75 37 33
campagneleparadis@wanadoo.fr
www.campagneleparadis.com

Open all year • 4 rooms with shower/WC • €55, breakfast included • No table d'hôte • Garden, terrace, car park. Credit cards not accepted, no dogs admitted

 Horses everywhere – the riding stables are only a horseshoe's throw away!

The old horse mangers and photos on the walls of the vaulted breakfast room bear witness to the establishment's long-standing relations with our four-legged friends. The old farmhouse nestles at the foot of a citadel, overlooking the quiet countryside. The immaculate bare walls of the bedrooms in the old barn add a monastical flavour; two have a mezzanine.

Access : *Villeneuve road on the D 16 and the D 216*

MÉOLANS-REVEL - 04340

MAISON D'HÔTE DES MÉANS
Mme Millet

Les Méans
04340 Méolans-Revel
Tel. 04 92 81 03 91
elisabeth@les-means.com
www.les-means.com
Langues : Eng., Sp., It.

Closed 30 Nov to 30 Apr • 3 rooms and 2 apartments, all have bath/WC, some have a balcony • €55 to €78, breakfast included • Table d'hôte €25 to €30, beverages included • Terrace, garden, car park. No dogs admitted in dining room • Scandinavian bath tub, wifi internet access

 A glimpse of the typical interior of houses in the valley.

Built when this secluded mountain region still swore allegiance to the counts of Savoy, this 16C farmhouse at an altitude of 1 000m is just the place to get away from it all and catch up on your beauty sleep. The spacious, well-appointed rooms all have lovely bathrooms with earthenware tiles; some also have a balcony. In the winter, a roaring log fire takes the chill off the large vaulted room on the ground floor. In the summertime, meals are often served in the garden, near the old bread oven.

Access : *4km from Martinet on the D 900, Gap road*

MOUSTIERS-SAINTE-MARIE - 04360

MONASTÈRE DE SEGRIÈS
M. et Mme Allègre

04360 Moustiers-Sainte-Marie
Tel. 04 92 74 64 32
segries@free.fr

Closed from late Oct to Easter • 5 rooms with bathrooms • €55, breakfast included; half-board available • Table d'hôte €18 • Terrace, park, car park. Credit cards not accepted, dogs not admitted

Only tell special friends about this enchanting monastery.

The fragrance of lavender and rosemary is all around you as you make your way up the winding lane to this superb monastery surrounded by oak trees. The spacious rooms, which overlook the cloisters and pool or the valley, are so quiet, you may well wonder if the monastery is still cloaked in its vow of silence. Deep sofas and a billiards table set the scene in the sitting room. It's the sort of place you want to tell everyone about and then worry that it might get overcrowded!

Access : *6km to the north-west of Moustiers on the D 952*

PIERRERUE - 04300

JAS DES NEVIÈRES
M. Duermael

Route de Saint-Pierre
04300 Pierrerue
Tel. 04 92 75 24 99
duermael@wanadoo.fr
http://jas-des-nevieres.com
Langues : Eng., It.

Closed from 1 Nov to 31 Mar • 4 rooms, 2 of which are on the ground floor with shower/WC, the 2 upstairs have bath/WC • €70 (€65 low season), breakfast included • No table d'hôte • Terrace, car park. Credit cards not accepted • Outdoor swimming pool

"Baa, baa, black sheep have you any wool?"

The thick stone walls of this former sheepfold in the heart of the hamlet hide an undreamt-of haven of style and sophistication. We were unable to find fault with the refined good taste of the lovely bedrooms. Breakfast is served on a delightful inner patio, which echoes to the chirping of cicadas in the summertime. From the pool, you will be able to enjoy an uninterrupted view of mile upon mile of open fields.

Access : *6km eastbound from Forcalquier on the D 12 then the D 212*

PRA-LOUP - 04400

LA FERME DU COUVENT
M. Riehl

Les Molanes
04400 Pra-Loup
Tel. 04 92 84 05 05
info@ferme-du-couvent.fr
www.ferme-du-couvent.com
Langues : Eng., Sp.

Closed 1 week in May and 1 week in Jun • 5 rooms, each with its own entrance and private terrace, bath/WC • €48 to €80, breakfast included; half-board available • Table d'hôte €25 • Garden. No dogs admitted in restaurant • Tennis

 A 100% authentic Ubaye farmhouse.

In the heart of the resort, this 14C farm is a welcome surprise among the string of modern chalets. The farm's venerable age is still visible inside, in its low door-frames, floor made out of larch logs, narrow windows and cool rooms. Each of the simple bedrooms has its own terrace overlooking the valley, Barcelonette and the peaks. We particularly liked the fireside dinners.

Skiing, snowshoe and relaxation weekends

Access : *In the resort*

PRA-LOUP - 04400

LE PRIEURÉ
M. Paradis

Les Molanes
04400 Pra-Loup
Tel. 04 92 84 11 43
hotel.leprieure@wanadoo.fr
www.prieure-praloup.com
Langues : Eng.

Closed from 22 Apr to 9 Jun and 17 Sep to 14 Dec • 14 rooms on 2 floors, with bath/WC or shower/WC, all have television • €65 to €78 (€55 to €68 low season); breakfast €8.50; half-board available • Menus €13.85 to €18.50 • Terrace, garden, car park. No dogs admitted in restaurant • Summer swimming pool

 Did you notice the owner's name? What more shall we say?

May the devil take you if don't find happiness in this 17C priory! All the more so, as the chairlift of this alpine resort overlooking the lovely valley of Ubaye is on the doorstep of a superb skiing domain which unabashedly claims to be "a top resort for top people"! If the thrill of swooping down a powdery slope doesn't appeal, slap on the sun cream and relax on the south-facing terrace! A cheerful fire burns in the restaurant where you can sample a wide range of tasty dishes.

Access : *8.5km to the south-west of Barcelonnette, on the D 902, then the D 908 and right on the D 109*

ROUMOULES - 04500

LE VIEUX CASTEL
M. et Mme Léonardi

1 route des Châteaux
04500 Roumoules
Tel. 04 92 77 75 42
vieuxcastel@free.fr
http://vieuxcastel.free.fr

Closed Dec to Feb • 5 non-smoking rooms, all have bath/WC • €60, breakfast included; half-board available • Table d'hôte €20, beverages included • Garden, sitting room. Credit cards not accepted, dogs not admitted

 The authenticity of this elegant Provençal property with lavender-coloured shutters.

Planted over three hundred years ago, mature chestnut trees still stand guard over this 17C house, formerly the property of the Clérissy family, inventors of Moustiers porcelain. The bedrooms have coffered ceilings and are decorated with hand-painted stencils; all are non-smoking. Arches, a fireplace and period furniture in the dining-room set off the ornate stone patterned floor.

Access : *4km to the north-east of Riez, Moustiers-Ste-Marie road (D 952), on the way into the village of Roumoules*

SAINT-GENIEZ - 04200

DOMAINE DES RAYES
M. Masure

04200 Saint-Geniez
Tel. 04 92 61 22 76
les.rayes@wanadoo.fr
www.lesrayes.fr
Langues : Eng., Du.

Open all year • 5 rooms with shower/WC • €65 to €79, breakfast included • Table d'hôte €19 • Car park. Dogs not admitted • Outdoor swimming pool, children's play area

 Blessed with silence.

Exceptional is the only word to describe the location of this 17C sheepfold perched at an altitude of 1 300m and surrounded by open heath. Quiet, often immense bedrooms are decorated in a bold local palette. Wining and dining in the inviting dining room, reading in the superb vaulted sitting rooms or daydreaming on the terrace which commands a stunning view of the Durance Valley; all offer their own particular pleasure.

Access : *17km to the north-east of Sisteron, Saint-Geniez road on the D 3*

SAINT-PONS - 04400

SAINT-LAURENT-DU-VERDON - 04500

MOULIN DU CHÂTEAU
M. et Mme Staempfli-Faoro

Le Village
04500 Saint-Laurent-du-Verdon
Tel. 04 92 74 02 47
info@moulin-du-chateau.com
www.moulin-du-chateau.com
Langues : Ger., Eng., It., Sp.

Closed early Nov to late Feb • 10 rooms, one with disabled access, with shower/WC, half have television • €87 to €99 (€78 to €92 low season); breakfast €9; half-board available • Restaurant closed Mon, Thu and lunchtime; menus (guests only) €32 • Terrace, garden. Dogs not admitted in the restaurant • Library, billiards

 The friendly guesthouse atmosphere.

The former oil mill, built in the 17C and nestled in an extensive wooded garden, adjoins the castle of this town located in the heart of the Verdon regional nature reserve. The press and millstone continue to take pride of place in the middle of the spacious sitting room. Immaculate walls, wrought-iron beds, brightly-coloured fabrics and small cane armchairs preside over the deliberately unfussy bedrooms. The set menu is served in a rustic dining room or on the delicious terrace.

Access : *Behind the château*

DOMAINE DE LARA
Mme Signoret

RD 609
04400 Saint-Pons
Tel. 04 92 81 52 81
arlette.signoret@wanadoo.fr
www.domainedelara.com

Closed from 20 to 28 Jun and 13 Nov to 20 Dec • 5 non-smoking rooms with bathrooms • €69 to €74, breakfast included • No table d'hôte • Park, car park. Credit cards not accepted, dogs not admitted

 Relaxing in the park with the Pain de Sucre mountain in the background.

The valley of the "Mexicans" is the home of this old Provençal home surrounded by greenery and now converted into chambres d'hôte full of character. Beams, tiled floors, old stones, well-polished carved furniture and old-fashioned quilts on the beds all blend together to create a warm authentic setting. Superb Provençal staircase and amazing sitting room. Copious breakfasts with Mexican-style hot chocolate, Russian tea, raspberry jelly, golden jam, local honey, pies...

Access : *2km northwest from Barcelonnette on the D900 and the D9*

ARVIEUX - 05350

LA GIRANDOLE
M. Morel

Brunissard
05350 Arvieux
Tel. 04 92 46 84 12
lagirandole@tiscali.fr
lagirandole.info
Langues : Eng.

Closed from 15 Sep to 15 Dec • 6 non-smoking rooms with shower/WC and bath/WC and 2 gîtes, wifi internet access • €75, breakfast included • No table d'hôte • Garden, car park. Credit cards not accepted, no dogs admitted • Outdoor swimming pool

Well-situated on the "Sundial Route" – a themed tour of the villages of Haute-Provence.

Both the architecture and the sundial which adorns the façade of this old farmhouse are typical of the valley of Arvieux. The interior has been tastefully refurbished with old furniture and objects, colourful prints and fabrics, a piano and soft sofas in the sitting room. The rooms display a more uncluttered style with plain white walls and have balconies with a variety of views over the pleasant hilly landscape. Guests have the use of a kitchen.

Access : *3km northbound on the D 902*

BARATIER - 05200

LES PEUPLIERS
M. Bellot

Chemin de Lesdier
05200 Baratier
Tel. 04 92 43 03 47
info@hotel-les-peupliers.com
www.hotel-les-peupliers.com
Langues : Ger., Eng., It., Sp.

Closed from 18 mar to 6 Apr, 23 Sep to 26 Oct and Tue and Fri lunchtimes • 24 rooms, 6 of which are non-smoking, with bath/WC or shower/WC and television • €50 to €60; breakfast €6.50; half-board available • Menus €12.50 to €37 • Terrace, car park • Outdoor swimming pool, petanque

As welcoming in winter as in summer.

This alpine chalet enjoys a wonderful position surrounded by mountains and overlooking the lake of Serre Ponçon. The rooms are a cheerful mixture of sturdy, hand-painted furniture and bold regional fabrics; those on the second floor with a lake-view balcony were our favourite. Stone and wood feature prominently in the alpine dining room. Put your feet up on the shaded, south-facing terrace after a couple of hours energetic hiking, mountain biking or cross-country skiing, depending on the season!

Access : *Leave the N 94 towards Les Orres, then Baratier, in the village, take the second turning on the right*

LE MONÊTIER-LES-BAINS - 05220

BUISSARD - 05500

LES CHEMINS VERTS
Mme Dubois

05500 Buissard
Tel. 04 92 50 57 57
lescheminsverts@free.fr
www.lescheminsverts.com
Languages : It.

Open all year • 4 rooms and one gîte, with shower/WC • €46, breakfast included; half-board available • Table d'hôte €13.50 • Terrace, car park. Credit cards not accepted, dogs not admitted

 Fill your lungs with fresh mountain air.

At an altitude of 1 200m, this pretty 18C farmhouse, run by amiable, helpful hosts, surveys the Drac valley and the rocky bastion of Dévoluy massif. The tasteful rooms are comfortable; the one called "Fleurette" has the best view. A brand new apartment is also available and the sitting room and panoramic terrace are worthy of note.

Access : *1km eastbound from Saint-Julien-en-Champsaur on the D 15*

L'ALLIEY
M. et Mme Buisson

11 rue des Écoles
05220 Le Monêtier-les-Bains
Tel. 04 92 24 40 20
hotel@alliey.com
www.alliey.com
Languages : Eng., Ger., It.

Closed mid-Apr to mid-Jun and mid-Sep to mid-Dec • 22 rooms, all with bath/WC and television • €82 to €102 (€82 to €99 low season); breakfast €11; half-board available in season • Table d'hôte €29 • Terrace, park. Dogs not admitted in restaurant • Indoor swimming pool

 The warm mountain atmosphere.

Tucked away in a village, this house is full of charm. Wood is the prevailing feature of the warm atmosphere whether in the lobby area, sitting rooms, dining room or the alpine-style bedrooms, all of which are decorated with handsome larch wood furniture. After a day's skiing or hiking, relax in the balneo centre before heading for the restaurant to sample the tasty regional dishes and make your choice from the fine wine list, which boasts a number of excellent vintages.

Access : *In the centre of the village*

NÉVACHE - 05100

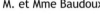

LE CHALET D'EN HÔ
M. et Mme Baudoux

Hameau des Chazals - Le Roubion
05100 Névache
Tel. 04 92 20 12 29
chaletdenho@aol.com
www.chaletdenho.com
Langues : Eng.

Closed from 15 Apr to 1 Jun, 16 Sep to 26 Oct and 4 Nov to 21 Dec • 14 non-smoking rooms with bath/WC or shower/WC and television, most have a balcony • €99 to €124 (€51 to €71 low season); breakfast €10; half-board available • Menu €25 (evenings only) • Car park. No dogs admitted in restaurant • Cross-country skiing, hiking, sauna

 Breakfast on the terrace overlooking the valley's multitude of wild flowers.

The climb up to this larchwood chalet will reward you with lovely bedrooms named after the mountains and lakes you can see from the balconies. A tasteful marriage of walls lined in pine and local draperies and the dining room is adorned with tools which recall the local tradition of woodworking. The nature-loving owners are always happy to pass on tips and expert advice on exploring the lovely Clarée Valley.

Watercolour week, sophrology week, cross-country skiing week, snowshoe week

Access : *Northbound from Briançon, leave the N 94 for the D 994G that follows the Clarée, turn right at Roubion*

POLIGNY - 05500

LE CHALET DES ALPAGES
M. et Mme Potut

Les Forestons
05500 Poligny
Tel. 04 92 23 08 95
www.le-chalet-des-alpages.com
Langues : Eng.

Open all year • 5 non-smoking rooms, all with bath/WC • €86 to €110, breakfast included • Table d'hôte €20 • Garage. Credit cards not accepted, no dogs admitted • Fitness facilities, sauna, Jacuzzi, hot outdoor tub

 Taking a dip in the Norwegian bathtub in the heart of winter.

It is easy to see why the owners chose this location for their maison d'hôte. The chalet, set on an immense meadow close to the forest, commands a priceless view of the Noyer pass, the Fararud, Cuchon and Vieux Chaillol mountains. The Alpine spirit of the cosy interior decoration is equally appealing. Each of the attractive well-equipped bedrooms boasts either a balcony or a small garden for those on the ground floor. Regional and Provençal flavoured cuisine.

Access : *From Poligny, head towards the Col du Noyer for 2km to the place known as Les Forestons, and turn left onto the small lane*

CABRIS - 06530

SAINT-CHAFFREY - 05330

LES MARMOTTES
M. Lucas

22 rue du Centre - village de Chantemerle
05330 Saint-Chaffrey
Tel. 04 92 24 11 17
lucas.marmottes@wanadoo.fr
perso.wanadoo.fr/chalet.marmottes
Langues : Eng., It.

Open all year • 5 non-smoking rooms, all with bath/WC and television • €86 to €124, breakfast included • Table d'hôte €21, drinks included • Dogs not admitted

MADAME FARAUT
Mme Faraut

14 rue de l'Agachon
06530 Cabris
Tel. 04 93 60 52 36
Langues : Eng., Ger., Sp.

Closed from 1 Oct to 31 Mar • 5 rooms with shower/WC • €60, breakfast included • No table d'hôte • Credit cards not accepted

We most liked Wandering around the lanes of this old village so popular with contemporary artists.

The yellow walls of this tiny village house are bound to catch your eye. The restful rooms are painted a spotless white; some of them enjoy a view of the Esterel massif and St-Cassien Lake, as does the sitting room. A light-hearted atmosphere also prevails in the beams and fireplace in the breakfast room and the countryside almost seems to creep in through the large bay window.

We most liked Relaxing around the lovely fireplace in the sitting room.

This former barn converted into a guesthouse and set in the heart of the historic village of Chantemerle has retained all its charm of yesteryear. Wood prevails in the spacious personalised bedrooms, sitting room and dining room. An immense oak table, which can seat up to twelve guests, invites the visitor to sit down in the company of other guests and partake of the lady of the house's copious family cooking.

> *Walking excursions on a heritage theme*

Access : *In the village centre*

Access : *In a lane in the village*

CANNES - 06400

VILLA L'ÉGLANTIER
M. et Mme Daran

14 rue Campestra
06400 Cannes
Tel. 04 93 68 22 43
www.bnbnet.com
Langues : Eng.

Open all year • 4 rooms with bath/WC • €75 to
€100, breakfast included • No table d'hôte
• Terrace, garden. Credit cards not accepted

 A haven of peace and quiet within walking distance of the Croisette.

This large white villa hidden away on the
heights of Cannes is set in a lovely garden
planted with palm, orange and other exotic
trees. Built in the 1920s, its original Art Deco
soul can still be felt. The guestrooms, spacious,
quiet and tastefully decorated, all have large
bathrooms. The White, Green and Blue rooms
upstairs have a balcony or a terrace, while the
Red room, on the ground-floor, opens onto the
garden.

Access : *On the heights of Cannes*

CAP-D'ANTIBES - 06160

LA JABOTTE
M. April et M. Mora

13 avenue Max-Maurey
06160 Cap-d'Antibes
Tel. 04 93 61 45 89
info@jabotte.com
www.jabotte.com
Langues : Eng., Du.

Closed 3 weeks in Nov and 1 week at Christmas
• 10 non-smoking rooms with shower/WC
• €82 to €88 (€59 to €64 low season); breakfast
€8 • No restaurant • Terrace, garden, car park.
No dogs admitted

 Superbly located just a stone's throw from a lovely sandy beach.

This establishment, well located in a quiet side
street at right angles to Salis Beach, is home to
tastefully decorated trim bedrooms. Their tiny
terraces all overlook a pleasant gravelled patio
adorned with plants. The work of one of the
owners, a calligraphist in his spare time, can be
seen in some of the rooms and in the smart
sitting room where delicious breakfasts are
served. Warm, friendly welcome.

Access : *100m from Salis Beach*

CHÂTEAUNEUF-DE-GRASSE - 06740

BASTIDE LA ROUVEIRADO
Mme Coppel

22 chemin des Colles
06740 Châteauneuf-de-Grasse
Tel. 04 93 77 78 49
info@larouveirado.com
www.larouveirado.com

Closed Jan • 5 rooms, 4 of which with shower/WC and 1 with bath/WC • €70 to €110, breakfast included • No table d'hôte • Park, car park • Outdoor swimming pool

 Take the time to explore the little country roads around Grasse.

It may take a little time to find this recently built house because it is well hidden in the hinterland. The owners live in the main wing and have installed five rooms in other wings, whose French windows open directly outdoors and onto the swimming pool. Simply decorated in good taste with black wrought iron beds and pretty earthenware tiles in the bathrooms. Small copse of holm oaks at the rear of the park.

Access : *Southeast from Grasse, near the Club Med resort*

COARAZE - 06390

L'AUBERGE DU SOLEIL
Mme Jacquet

5 chemin de la Bégude
06390 Coaraze
Tel. 04 93 79 08 11
auberge.du.soleil@wanadoo.fr
www.notreaubergedusoleil.com
Langues : Eng.

Closed from 1 to 15 Jan, open weekends from 1 Nov to 15 Apr • 8 rooms with bath/WC • €62 to €84; breakfast €8; half-board available • Menus €24 • Garden • Outdoor swimming pool

 Delicious little Provençal dishes cooked by the lady of the house.

This lovely mansion was built in 1863 and its atmosphere of quiet serenity can only be reached on foot. The immaculate rooms are a happy combination of old and new; four enjoy a view of the valley and the terraced fields. The immense dining room and conservatory also command an impressive vista. Madame uses only fresh produce in her cooking, whose reputation extends throughout the region. As for relaxation, look no further than the billiard table, garden, orchard and pool.

Access : *A 8 motorway, Nice-Est exit, then highway towards La Trinité-Drap-Sospel; at La Pointe de Contes, turn left towards Contes-Coaraze*

CONTES - 06390

LES CYPRÈS
Mme Djordjian

289 route de Chateauneuf
06390 Contes
Tel. 04 93 62 58 77
info@lescypres.fr
www.lescypres.fr

Open all year • 3 non-smoking rooms with shower/WC • €68 to €75, breakfast included • No table d'hôte • Terrace, garden, car park. Credit cards not accepted, dogs not admitted

The breakfasts that often turn into brunches.

This 1920s house in Nice has recently been treated to a complete makeover before reopening to guests. The three ground floor rooms all have direct access outdoors. The attractive tiled bathrooms are a pleasant combination of good taste and understatement, as are the old red tiles on the floors of the other rooms. The day starts under the pergola or under the trellis covered in a rare grape that is used to make mouth-watering jams.

Access : *At Contes, cross over the second bridge on the left, opposite the service station, take the D815*

LA COLLE-SUR-LOUP - 06480

LA BASTIDE DE SAINT-DONAT
M. Rosso

Route du Pont-de-Pierre, parc Saint-Donat
06480 La Colle-sur-Loup
Tel. 04 93 32 93 41
www.bastide-saint-donat.com
Langues : Eng., It.

Open all year • 5 rooms with shower/WC or bath/WC • €65 to €95, breakfast included • No table d'hôte • Terrace, garden. Credit cards not accepted

Dawdling on the terrace overlooking the river.

The stone walls of this sheepfold built in 1850 hide a wealth of ornate interior decoration. The ground floor has been beautifully restored in keeping with local traditions, including arcades, columns, fireplace and terracotta floor tiles. The pastel shades of the bedrooms are a perfect contrast to the old beams and furniture; some have a balcony. As you sit on the terrace, you will be able to listen to the river babbling gently below.

Access : *2km southbound from Saint-Paul on the D 6*

LA GAUDE - 06610

L'ORANGERAIE
M. Lallemand

 66 chemin du Maoupas quartier de la Baronne
06610 La Gaude
Tel. 04 92 12 13 69
lorangeraie@gmail.com
www.orangeraie.fr

Open all year • 4 rooms and 3 apartments with bath/WC or shower/WC and air-conditioning • €85 to €95, breakfast included • Table d'hôte €24 including drinks • Terrace, park, car park • Outdoor swimming pool

 The simple unpretentious but warm welcome.

This working farm is specialised in fruit: clementines, oranges, figs and olives. The house, set in the heart of the 2ha-estate, commands a matchless view of the Var Valley. The four rooms, located in a recently built wing, have direct access to the terrace and swimming pool. The rooms are simply furnished but nonetheless comfortable. Organic menu featuring vegetables from the garden and farm-raised poultry.

Access : *10km northbound from Cagnes-sur-Mer on the D118 towards Saint-Laurent-du-Var*

LE SUQUET - 06450

AUBERGE DU BON PUITS
M. et Mme Corniglion

 06450 Le Suquet
Tel. 04 93 03 17 65
lebonpuits@wanadoo.fr
http://www.logis06.com
Langues : Ger., Eng., It.

Closed from 1 Dec to 15 Apr and Tue except from 15 Jul to 30 Aug • 8 rooms, 2 of which are non-smoking, with bath/WC, air-conditioning and television • €60 to €65; breakfast €9; half-board available • Menus €22 to €32 • Terrace, park, car park. Credit cards not accepted • Animal park, play area, white-water sports and fishing, scenic walks

 The joyful shouts of the pony riders in the small animal park.

Children are welcomed with open arms in this old stone coaching inn complete with a play area and a lovely animal park on the banks of the Vésubie. Since 1890, the rooms have been constantly smartened up and embellished by the owners and their forebears. The kitchen is also a family affair and the delicious recipes have been handed down from mother to daughter for generations. Meals are served under the well-polished beams of the gleaming dining room.

White-water sports weekend. Pony riding

Access : *On the D 2565, between Plan-du-Var and Bollène-Vésubie*

MENTON - 06500

PIERROT-PIERRETTE
M. Mitolo

Place de l'Église - Monti
06500 Menton
Tel. 04 93 35 79 76
pierrotpierrette@aol.com
Langues : Ger., Eng., It.

Closed from 4 Dec to 11 Jan • 7 rooms, 4 of which are in a separate wing, all have shower/WC, no television • €68 to €77; breakfast €8; half-board available • Menus €28 to €39 • Garden • Swimming pool

Your northern pallor will soon turn a lovely golden brown under Menton's bright sun.

This delightful little inn perched in the upper reaches of a peaceful hamlet lies just outside Menton. Most of the family-sized simply-furnished rooms have balconies. The charm of the rustic dining room is further enhanced by delicious homemade specialities (duck foie gras, bouillabaisse), but guests also come back for the luxurious garden, full of exotic southern plants and sweet-scented roses, and the swimming pool overlooking the valley of Carei.

Access : *5km northbound from Menton, on the D 2566 towards Sospel*

NICE - 06000

LE CASTEL ENCHANTÉ
M. Ferrary

61 route de Saint-Pierre-de-Féric
06000 Nice
Tel. 04 93 97 02 08
contact@castel-enchante.com
www.castel-enchante.com

Open all year • 3 non-smoking rooms upstairs and 1 apartment, all with bath/WC or shower/WC • €100, breakfast included • No table d'hôte • Terrace, garden, car park. Credit cards not accepted • Outdoor swimming pool

The palm and the orange trees and the view of the sea.

Built in the mid-19C in the upper reaches of Nice, this impressive abode of Italian inspiration is little by little being treated to a second youth. While antique furniture graces the various rooms, guests are delighted to discover that the bedding is brand new and that parts of the house have recently been redecorated. There's a small swimming pool in the pretty garden surrounded by peaceful greenery. Breakfast is served on the terrace.

Access : *West Nice, Saint-Philippe district*

SAINT-DALMAS-DE-TENDE - 06430

LE MOUTON DORT
M. Schlesser

28 avenue des
Martyrs-de-la-Résistance
06430 Saint-Dalmas-de-Tende
Tel. 04 93 79 18 08
www.lemoutondort.com

Open all year • 5 non-smoking rooms with shower/WC • €80, breakfast included • Table d'hôte €20 including drinks • Terrace, garden, car park. Credit cards not accepted, dogs not admitted • Outdoor swimming pool

 The spirit of Italy can be felt all around.

All of the identical five rooms in this house, perched on a steep slope, are simply but tastefully decorated with made-to-measure wooden furniture. Two however also boast a vaulted stone ceiling. Fitted out in the same style, the bathrooms have lovely tiled walls and floors. Each room has its own private, covered terrace overlooking the valley. Table d'hôte meals in the small restaurant next door.

Access : *4km southbound on the N204, above the railway station*

TOURRETTES-SUR-LOUP - 06140

MAS DES CIGALES
M. Prieur-Gelis

1673 route des Quenières
06140 Tourrettes-sur-Loup
Tel. 04 93 59 25 73
lemasdescigales@free.fr
www.lemasdescigales.com
Langues : Eng., Ger.

Open all year • 5 air-conditioned rooms with bath/WC and television • €92 to €97 (€72 to €77 low season), breakfast included • Table d'hôte €20 except Tue and Thu • Garden, car park. No dogs admitted • Outdoor swimming pool, tennis, mountain bikes, wifi internet access

 The surrounding countryside, perfect for taking a stroll.

This pleasant villa perched on a hillside of pine trees commands a wonderful view of the Riviera coast. Hand-painted furniture adorns the personalised rooms named after local fauna and flora: Nasturtium, Peony, Butterfly, Violet and Olive. You can choose between a covered veranda overlooking the garden or (in summer) a poolside table for breakfast. If you lean slightly over the terrace, you will catch sight of a small waterfall and the property's tennis courts.

Access : *1.5km westbound from Tourrettes on the D 22110 towards Pont-du-Loup*

VALBERG - 06470

BLANCHE NEIGE
M. et Mme Kretchmann

10 avenue de Valbery
06470 Valberg
Tel. 04 93 02 50 04
contact@hotelblancheneige.fr
www.hotelblancheneige.fr
Langues : Eng.

Closed in Nov, Mon evening and Tue in low season • 17 rooms with shower/WC, some have bath/WC, all have television • €90 (€76 low season); breakfast €8 to €10; half-board available • Menus €24 • Terrace, garage, car park. No dogs admitted • Skiing, hiking

Hey Ho, Hey Ho, it's out to play we go!

Once upon a time there was a chalet whose green and yellow shutters looked onto a forest of larch trees. Legend has it that these small rooms decorated with hand-quilted bedspreads and painted furniture were formerly the home of seven cheerful dwarves and their guest, Snow White – the hotel's namesake. Nowadays the region's white gold – 50km of slopes between 1 500 and 2 000m – has stolen the limelight from the princesses of yesteryear. Snug restaurant and spacious terrace overlooking the road.

Access : *At the entrance to the resort*

VALBONNE - 06560

LE CHENEAU
M. et Mme Ringenbach

205 route d'Antibes
06560 Valbonne
Tel. 04 93 12 13 94
ringbach@club-internet.fr
www.ibbp.com

Open all year • 3 non-smoking rooms with bath/WC • €70 to €80, breakfast included • No table d'hôte • Terrace, garden, car park. Credit cards not accepted, dogs not admitted

It's so difficult to choose between the sea, the mountain and the river!

Your first impression of the imposing owner may be dubious, but don't be put off, he couldn't be more charming. His large home, located in a residential district, has three comfortable unpretentious rooms that are carefully decorated and well looked after. Immense bathroom and fitted kitchen available to guests. In the garden, take the time to relax on the large terrace, part of which is shaded.

Access : *10km southeast from Grasse*

AIX-EN-PROVENCE - 13100

VAL-DU-TIGNET - 06530

MAS DE CLAIREFONTAINE
M. et Mme Lapostat

3196 route de Draguignan
06530 Val- du-Tignet
Tel. 04 93 66 39 69
andre.lapostat@wanadoo.fr
http://masdeclairefontaine.online.fr
Langues : Eng.

Open all year • 2 rooms and 1 apartment with bathrooms and television • €99 and €110, breakfast included • No table d'hôte • Terrace, park, car park. Credit cards not accepted, no dogs admitted • Outdoor swimming pool. Fishing and sailing on the lake nearby

 As you drive up to the mas, wind down your window and listen to the cicadas chirping!

The picture of the stone mas and its terraced garden dotted with umbrella pines and clumps of reeds will make you reach for your camera. The Provençal-style bedrooms and bathrooms are strewn with delightful details such as delicately scented Fragonard soaps, postcards and sweets, that make you feel you were expected. The Iris room has its own private terrace. In the summer months, guests are invited to eat outside in the welcome shade of the oak tree.

> *Cooking courses*

Access : *10km to the south-east of Grasse, Draguignan road*

QUATRE DAUPHINS
M. et Mme Lafont

54 rue Roux-Alphéran
13100 Aix-en-Provence
Tel. 04 42 38 16 39
lesquatredauphins@wanadoo.fr
Langues : Eng., It.

Open all year • 13 air-conditioned rooms with bath/WC or shower/WC, all have television and internet access • €70 to €100 (€65 to €90 low season); breakfast €9 • No restaurant

 You won't regret opting for the romantic rooms under the eaves, however stifling in summer!

The tiny lanes lined with lovely old 17C and 18C mansions, the busy café terraces of the Cours Mirabeau, a multitude of tiny restaurants and colourful street markets – it could only be Aix en Provence! Turn a deaf ear to the noise, steel yourself to the heat and immerse yourself from head to toe in the charm of this hotel's tiled floors and painted furniture, only a step from the graceful little square of the Quatre Dauphins.

Access : *In a quiet, small street in the Mazarin area*

ARLES - 13200

CALENDAL
Mme Jacquemin

5 rue Porte-de-Laure
13200 Arles
Tel. 04 90 96 11 89
contact@lecalendal.com
www.lecalendal.com
Langues : Eng., Ger., It., Sp.

Closed Jan • 38 rooms, all have bath/WC or shower/WC and television • €45 to €104; breakfast €7 • Restaurant only open at lunchtime in season; buffet €14 • Garden. No dogs admitted

 Proof that France also drinks tea!

Teatime, something of an institution in this establishment, means tasty pastries and a wonderful selection of teas from one of France's most famous tea houses, served in a light, airy room with veranda, which also doubles as a breakfast room when the weather is not fine enough to enjoy the shade of the palms on the terrace. The rooms overlook either the garden, the Antique theatre, or, for a lucky few, the Arena; ask for one with a view when booking. All are decorated in bright, warm colours.

Access : *Between the Antique theatre and arena*

AURONS - 13121

LE CASTELAS
M. Brauge

Vallon des Eoures
13121 Aurons
Tel. 04 90 55 60 12
lecastelas@aol.com
www.le-castelas.com
Langues : Eng.

Open all year • 3 rooms with bath/WC • €75 to €95, breakfast included • Table d'hôte €25 (by reservation in high season) • Garden, car park. Credit cards not accepted, no dogs admitted

 Discovering the joys of cased binding and picture framing during a theme stay.

Formerly an inn on the way out of the village, this spacious house still welcomes travellers. Decorated with a profusion of knick-knacks and antique furniture, each of the three rooms named after plants used in dyeing has a direct access to the outside. Upstairs the sitting room is the pride and joy of the owners, former antique dealers. Breakfasts and meals are served on the veranda that commands a magnificent view of the countryside with the Étang de Berre in the distance.

Picture framing weekend

Access : *North exit out of the village*

BARBENTANE - 13570

CASTEL MOUISSON
Mme Mourgue

Quartier Castel-Mouisson
13570 Barbentane
Tel. 04 90 95 51 17
contact@hotel-castelmouisson.com
www.hotel-castelmouisson.com
Langues : Eng.

Closed 15 Mar to 15 Oct • 17 rooms, all with bathrooms and television • €48 to €64; breakfast €8 • No restaurant • Terrace, park, private car park. Dogs not admitted • Outdoor swimming pool, tennis

The utter peace and quiet.

This mas-inspired hotel, built at the foot of the Montagnette, boasts a lovely shady park complete with swimming pool. All the bedrooms, decorated in a rustic, understated Provençal style, overlook the garden. The welcoming lady of the house can suggest any number of leisure activities either in the park (tennis, golf) or nearby (walking, mountain biking, horse riding, jet skis, etc).

Access : *Avignon sud motorway exit, follow Chateaurenard, Rognonas and Barbentane*

CABRIÈS - 13480

LA BASTIDE DE LA CLUÉE
M. Christian Perrier

Route de la Césarde
13480 Cabriès
Tel. 04 42 22 59 00
bastide.cluee@wanadoo.fr

Open all year • 5 rooms with bath/WC or shower/WC • €70 to €78, breakfast included • Table d'hôte €22 • Garden, car park. Credit cards not accepted, dogs not admitted • Outdoor swimming pool

The splendid green setting.

This 19C house, located in the heart of a residential neighbourhood, must undoubtedly be one of the oldest. A sentiment further reinforced by the collection of furniture and artefacts that adorn the dining and sitting rooms. Upstairs, the four individually decorated rooms make for stunning contrasts: four-poster bed in one room and Indonesian furniture in another. Attractive garden lounge around the swimming pool, beneath the terrace, pleasantly shaded by age-old trees.

Access : *Near the town*

CASSIS - 13260

LA GARRIGUE
M. Nederveen

22 impasse des Brayes
13260 Cassis
Tel. 04 42 01 17 98
nederveen@voila.fr
www.captainprod.com/valerie
Langues : Ger., Eng., Sp., Du., It.

Open all year • 5 rooms, 2 of which on the ground-floor, all with bath/WC • €90 to €110, breakfast included • Table d'hôte €20 to €40 • Terrace, garden, car park. Credit cards not accepted, no dogs admitted • Outdoor swimming pool, table tennis, petanque

 Friendly chats with the lady of the house.

Situated as it is on the heights of Cassis, this house commands a matchless view of the sweet-scented garrigue, at its most attractive in this site. The rooms, decorated with an appealing mixture of old and new, combine antiques, warm southern colours and the comfort of modern fixtures and fittings. Taller guests may choose to avoid the beams which adorn the ceilings of the rooms upstairs, preferring one of the two ground-floor rooms with direct access to the outside.

Access : *800m past the Super-U supermarket*

CEYRESTE - 13600

LE SORBIER DES OISELEURS
M. Centino

Chemin des Lavandes
13600 Ceyreste
Tel. 04 42 83 71 55
jj.centino@wanadoo.fr
www.lamusarde.com
Langues : Eng., It.

Closed Oct to Mar • 3 rooms with bath/WC, television and terrace • €65 to €70, breakfast included • No table d'hôte • Garden, car park. Credit cards not accepted, no dogs admitted

Cherry picking at the start of summer.

This attractive ground-floor mas, set amidst greenery and mimosas, has three fully independent rooms in the outhouses. The rooms are simple and unpretentious, but offer all the comfort you could desire and are enhanced by the appeal of direct access to private terraces. Those in the upper reaches of the garden have a pleasant view of the wooded hillsides. The owner, a former teacher, is more than happy to give you good ideas for walks in the vicinity and excellent restaurants.

Access : *1.5 km north-east from Ceyreste on the D 3 Castelet road*

FONTVIEILLE - 13990

VAL MAJOUR
M. et Mme Güell

22 avenue d'Arles
13990 Fontvieille
Tel. 04 90 54 62 33
contact@valmajour.com
www.valmajour.com
Langues : Eng., Ger., It.

Open all year • 32 rooms with bath/WC or shower/WC and television • €65 to €200 (€52 to €140 low season); breakfast €10 • No restaurant • Park, garage, private car park • Outdoor swimming pool, tennis, table-tennis, petanque

 The trees in the park are home to dozens of busy squirrels.

A stay in this regional house built on the doorstep of Alphonse Daudet's village is always a pleasant prospect. The spacious, rustic rooms are decorated with cheerful Provençal patterns; some have a terrace, while others have a balcony overlooking the park's many trees. On the leisure side, you can choose between a dip in the superb swimming pool or a friendly tennis match in the cool of the evening.

Access : *On leaving the town, by the Arles road*

GRANS - 13450

DOMAINE DU BOIS VERT
M. et Mme Richard

Quartier Montauban
13450 Grans
Tel. 04 90 55 82 98
leboisvert@hotmail.com
www.domaineduboisvert.com
Langues : Eng.

Closed from 15 Dec to 15 Mar • 3 rooms with shower/WC • €68 to €75, breakfast included • No table d'hôte • Terrace, park, car park. Credit cards not accepted, no dogs admitted • Outdoor swimming pool, table-tennis

 The award-winning friendly owners.

This drystone mas is surrounded by a refreshing riverside park of oak and pine trees. All the faultlessly kept ground-floor rooms share a typical local style with terracotta tiles, exposed beams and old furniture. Depending on the season and your inclination, breakfast is served in a large dining-sitting room or on the terrace overlooking the garden. Guests have the use of a library and a refrigerator.

Access : *7km southbound from Salon on the D 16 and then towards Lançon (D 19)*

GRANS - 13450

LA MAGNANERIE
Mme Caroline Dameron

Impasse de la Glacière
13450 Grans
Tel. 04 90 55 98 96
caroline@lamagnanerie-grans.com
www.lamagnanerie-grans.com
Langues : Eng.

Open all year • 3 rooms on two floors, all with bath/WC • €90 to €110, breakfast included • Table d'hôte €30 • Garden. Credit cards not accepted, no dogs admitted • Outdoor swimming pool, cooking courses

The almost magical atmosphere that pervades the establishment.

Perhaps because it was a silk farm in former times, this 18C country house seems to have retained a protective cocoon. Upstairs, each of the three comfortable rooms has been individually styled: "Africa" features ethnic motifs, "Hemingway" is dotted with travel souvenirs and "Diva" pays homage to Italian design. The superb swimming pool with its teak wood deck and shaded arbour is a feast for the eyes. Cooking courses (for adults) and painting courses (for children in the school holidays).

Cookery and painting courses

Access : *In the centre of the town*

GRAVESON - 13690

LE CADRAN SOLAIRE
Mme Guilmet

Rue du Cabaret-Neuf
13690 Graveson
Tel. 04 90 95 71 79
cadransolaire@wanadoo.fr
www.hotel-en-provence.com
Langues : Eng.

Open all year (by reservation only from Nov to Mar) • 12 rooms with bath/WC or shower/WC • €57 to €82; breakfast €8 • No restaurant • Terrace, garden, private car park

The lady of the house treats her guests like friends of the family.

A glance at the sundial on the façade of this three-hundred-year-old post house will explain the establishment's name. Not content merely to represent the timeless charm of Provence, the energetic lady of the house was determined to breathe a new lease of life into her property, and the result is impressive! Enchanting small rooms are decorated with taste and a profusion of delicate details, the bathrooms have been redone and the wrought-iron terrace surrounded by plants is a joy to behold.

Access : *In a residential area, on the way into the village*

MARSEILLE - 13008

LES SAINTES-MARIES-DE-LA-MER - 13460

LE MAS DES RIÈGES
M. Ducarre

Route de Cacharel
13460 Les Saintes-Maries-de-la-Mer
Tel. 04 90 97 85 07
hoteldesrieges@wanadoo.fr
www.hoteldesrieges.com
Langues : Eng., Ger.

Closed from 5 Jan to 5 Feb and 15 Nov to 15 Dec
• 20 rooms on the ground floor with bath/WC or
shower/WC, all have television • €64 to €79
(€58 to €74 low season); breakfast €7.50 • No
restaurant (snacks available around the pool on
sunny days) • Garden, car park • Swimming pool

 **Step out of your ground floor room and
straight into the Camargue.**

Just a few minutes from the tourist bustle of
the town centre and already surrounded by
marshes, you won't be able to miss this haci-
enda-style house set in a large garden full of
flowers and trees. The lovely rustic-inspired
rooms are adorned with Provençal fabrics and
all have a private terrace. Treat yourself to a
session in the beauty institute, complete with
hammam, balneotherapy and a sun bed. Horse-
riding possible.

Access : *In the heart of the marshes, 1km from
Saintes-Maries-de-la-Mer, on the Cacharel road,
then a minor road*

VILLA MONTICELLI
M. Paranque

96 rue du Commandant-Rolland
13008 Marseille
Tel. 04 91 22 15 20
contact@villamonticelli.com
www.villamonticelli.com

Open all year • 5 air-conditioned rooms, with
bath/WC • €85 to €100, breakfast included • No
restaurant • Garden, car park. Credit cards not
accepted, dogs not admitted • Wifi internet
access

 **The charm of the Prado, with the beach at
the end of the road.**

This Art Deco house surrounded by greenery is
only too happy to welcome guests. While the
interior decoration (red or yellow walls) can
sometimes surprise, the overall impression is
one of good taste. A handsome central staircase links the slightly elevated ground floor to
the first floor. Named after famous people
from the region, the rooms' often modest
proportions are compensated for by their genuine comfort and faultless upkeep. Each has a
bathroom and separate WC. Pleasant terrace.

Access : *Next to Bagatelle Gardens*

MARSEILLE - 13012

VILLA MARIE-JEANNE
Mme de Montmirail

4 rue Chicot
13012 Marseille
Tel. 04 91 85 51 31
Langues : Eng.

Open all year • 3 rooms, one of which has a terrace, all with shower/WC • €55 to €75, (€50 to €70 low season), breakfast included • No table d'hôte • Garden, car park. Credit cards not accepted, no dogs admitted • Outdoor swimming pool

  Not far from the famous "Stade-Vél", home of Olympique Marseille football club!

A rare pearl in the heart of a residential district that has gradually merged with the village of Saint Barnabé. The interior of this tasteful 19C house features a pleasant blend of traditional Provençal colours, old furniture, wrought-iron and contemporary works of art. The rooms are in the outbuildings and overlook the plane trees in the garden; one has a private terrace. Not to be missed!

Access : *From Marseille, take Boulevard de la Blancarde eastbound*

SAINT-RÉMY-DE-PROVENCE - 13210

CASTELET DES ALPILLES
Mme Canac-Roux

6 place Mireille
13210 Saint-Rémy-de-Provence
Tel. 04 90 92 07 21
hotel.castel.alpilles@wanadoo.fr
www.castelet-alpilles.com
Langues : Eng.

Open from late Mar to early Nov • 19 rooms in 2 buildings. Most rooms have bath/WC, all have television • €68 to €94 (€65 to €88 low season); breakfast €9 • No restaurant • Garden, private car park

  Just a five minute walk from St-Rémy, home to Nostradamus and Van Gogh.

This handsome early-20C house was built very near the antique site of Glanum. Some of the comfortable rooms possess a loggia and those on the second floor command a fine view of the Alpilles, a lovely chain of limestone hills. The immense sitting and dining rooms are decorated in true local style, but in the summer, guests generally prefer to breakfast in the lovely shaded garden.

Access : *On leaving the town drive towards the site of Villa Glanum*

BRAS - 83149

TARASCON - 13150

RUE DU CHÂTEAU
Mme Laraison

24 rue du Château
13150 Tarascon
Tel. 04 90 91 09 99
ylaraison@wanadoo.fr
www.chambres-hotes.com
Langues : Eng., Sp.

Closed from Nov to Jan • 4 rooms, one of which is air-conditioned, with shower/WC • €75 to €86, breakfast included • No table d'hôte • Credit cards not accepted, no dogs admitted

Faultless, down to the tiniest detail.

A porch and heavy door guard the entrance to this 18C edifice in a quiet side street leading up to the castle of Good King René - a truly great Renaissance man. The beautifully restored rooms are of an extremely high standard; two are reached via a lovely medieval-style staircase. As soon as the sun is warm enough, breakfast is served on a lovely flowered patio with ochre-red walls.

Access : *Near the castle*

DOMAINE LE PEYROURIER
« UNE CAMPAGNE EN PROVENCE »
M. Fussler

Chemin du Petit-Temple
83149 Bras
Tel. 04 98 05 10 20
info@provence4u.com
www.provence4u.com
Langues : Eng., Ger.

Closed Jan and Feb • 6 non-smoking rooms, all with bath/WC • €100 to €115, breakfast included • Table d'hôte €24 to €30 • Terrace, park, kitchenette, garage. No dogs admitted • Open-air swimming pool, sauna, hammam, internet

Countless walks around the extensive grounds.

This immense estate bordered by vineyards and meadows is an ideal chance to discover the charm of Provence's countryside. The tastefully decorated apartments and rooms are located in former farm buildings which date back to the Knights Templar; each room is individually decorated and enjoys either a view of the countryside or the garden. Home-made and local produce take pride of place on the table d'hôte.

Provençal cooking, provençal bedspreads, feldenkreis

Access : *3km southeast by the D28, then turn left onto lane to Le Peyrourier*

BRIGNOLES - 83170

LA CORDELINE
Mme Isabelle Konens

14 rue des Cordeliers
83170 Brignoles
Tel. 04 94 59 18 66
lacordeline@ifrance.com
www.lacordeline.com
Langues : Eng.

Open all year • 3 rooms with bath/WC and 2 rooms with shower/WC • €70 to €105, breakfast included • Table d'hôte €29 (evenings only during the week, by reservation) • Terrace, garden • Jacuzzi

We most liked
Listen to the birds singing and the fountain murmuring in the garden.

A haven of well-being right in the heart of town. This splendid 17C mansion offers immense rooms furnished with family heirlooms; all have new bathrooms and a small private sitting room. As soon as the sun begins to shine, breakfasts are served outside on the terrace under the trellis.

Access : *In the town centre*

CARQUEIRANNE - 83320

L'AUMÔNERIE
M. et Mme Menard

620 avenue de Fontbrun
83320 Carqueiranne
Tel. 04 94 58 53 56
pierrotdominique@free.fr
www.guidesdecharme.com
Langues : Eng.

Open all year • 3 rooms and 1 gîte, all with shower/WC • €75 to €125, breakfast included • No table d'hôte • Garden, car park. Credit cards not accepted, no dogs admitted • Direct access to the beach

We most liked
Take a seat in the garden and dangle your feet in the Mediterranean!

The total lack of signposts, in fact signs of any kind, bears witness to this establishment's desire to preserve the quiet tranquillity that reigns within its walls. The rooms are tastefully appointed and breakfast will be served either in your room or, whenever the weather permits, under the shade of the terrace's tall pine trees. The garden which has a tiny staircase down to the sea, was what we liked best, however. All that now remains is to enjoy the luxury of your very own private beach.

Access : *In a park by the seaside, 5km from Hyères*

DRAGUIGNAN - 83300

COTIGNAC - 83570

LES OLIVIERS
M. Thierry Chaillard

Route de Flayosc
83300 Draguignan
Tel. 04 94 68 25 74
hotel-les-oliviers@club-internet.fr
www.hotel-les-oliviers.com

Closed 5 to 20 Jan • 12 ground-floor rooms with shower/WC and television, 1 with disabled access • €56 to €60, (€51 to €55 low season); breakfast €8 • No restaurant • Terrace, garden, car park • Outdoor swimming pool

DOMAINE DE NESTUBY
M. et Mme Roubaud

Route de Montfort
83570 Cotignac
Tel. 04 94 04 60 02
nestuby@wanadoo.fr
www.sejour-en-provence.com
Langues : Eng.

Closed from 15 Nov to 1 Mar • 5 rooms with shower/WC • €70 to €80, breakfast included; half-board available • Table d'hôte €23 (closed weekends) • Car park. Credit cards not accepted • Sauna, fitness centre

 What better start to a summer's day than breakfast on the terrace overlooking the garden?

The nearby road will vanish as soon as you put down your suitcase in this recently-built hotel inspired by regional architectural traditions. Its cosy rooms are all excellently soundproofed and some sport the warm bright colours of Provence. A few overlook the swimming pool and a well-tended garden, planted, unsurprisingly enough given the establishment's name, with Mediterranean plants including olive trees!

 Nathalie and Jean-François love introducing guests to their estate's red, white and rosé wines.

You know you're in for a treat as soon as you catch sight of this lovely 19C property surrounded by vineyards. The pastel coloured rooms, furnished with items picked up in second-hand and antique shops, are named after the region's grape varieties. The large country dining table is in the old cow-shed, surrounded by mangers and a fireplace. In the summer, you will appreciate the shade of the plane trees and the cool spring water of the large pond.

Access : *4km on the road to Flayosc then the D 557*

Access : *5km southbound from Cotignac towards Brignoles*

ENTRECASTEAUX - 83570

59

BASTIDE NOTRE-DAME
M. et Mme Bonnichon

Au bourg
83570 Entrecasteaux
Tel. 04 94 04 45 63
mariethevalentin@aol.com

Closed 1 week in winter • 4 ground floor non-smoking rooms, 3 with shower/WC and 1 with bath/WC • €92, breakfast included • No table d'hôte • Terrace, garden, car park. Credit cards not accepted, dogs not admitted • Outdoor swimming pool

 The pleasant view over the valley.

This large house, built on a steep slope rises several storeys high on the façade side. The four rooms with independent access located in the rear and reached by a long corridor are in fact almost at ground level. Each room is decorated in a different colour scheme from the bedspread and curtains to the tiles in the bathroom. Outdoors, guests can relax in the summer sitting room or around the pool.

Access : *20km eastbound from Draguignan*

FOX-AMPHOUX - 83670

60

LE MAS D'AIMÉ
M. et Mme Aimé

D 32
83670 Fox-Amphoux
Tel. 04 94 80 72 03
contact@masdaime.com
www.masdaime.com

Open all year • 4 rooms, 3 with shower/WC and 1 with bath/WC • €75 to €115, breakfast included • Table d'hôte €30 including drinks • Terrace, park, car park. Credit cards not accepted • Outdoor swimming pool

 Olive groves and truffle oaks.

This former restaurant owner welcomes guests to a former olive oil factory tucked away in the Var hinterland. Immersed in peace and quiet, the old stone house possesses an attractive covered terrace that is perfect for breakfast and evening meals. The rooms, all of varying sizes, sport the same Provençal-style decoration. Given his experience in the trade, the owner naturally proposes a menu that will appeal to epicureans.

Access : *15km southeast from Aups by Sillans-la-Cascade*

GRIMAUD - 83310

FRÉJUS - 83600

LES VERGERS DE MONTOUREY
M. Artaud

 Vallée du Reyran
83600 Fréjus
Tel. 04 94 40 85 76
arttotof@orange.fr
http://perso.wanadoo.fr/vergers.montourey

Open from Easter to 1 Nov • 6 non-smoking rooms with bath/WC and television • €59, breakfast included • Table d'hôte €20, drinks included (Mon, Wed and Fri) • Terrace, garden, park, car park. Credit cards not accepted, dogs not admitted • Table-tennis, children's bicycles, slide

 Getting into the spirit of life on the farm.

This delightful maison d'hôte in the Reyran Valley does full justice to its former farming function. The spacious, beautifully cared-for rooms are named after and decorated in the colours of fruit grown on the estate: strawberry, cherry, plum, peach, almond and fig. Home-grown produce takes pride of place on the great breakfast and dinner table, where owners and guests all sit down together, either in a country-style dining room or on the terrace. Excellent advice for tourists. Children welcome.

Access : *In Montourey neighbourhood*

LA TOSCANE
M. et Mme Leroy

 RD 44- quartier de l'Avelan
83310 Grimaud
Tel. 04 94 43 24 11
chambreshoteslatoscane@wanadoo.fr
www.la-toscane.com
Langues : Eng., It.

Open 1 Apr to mid-Oct, closed 1 week in Nov, open in low season on request • 4 non-smoking rooms with bathroom and wifi internet access • €80 to €85 (€65 to €75 low season), breakfast included • No table d'hôte • Terrace, garden, car park. Credit cards not accepted, no dogs admitted • Swimming pool

 The care taken with the outdoor fixtures and interior decoration.

The roughcast ochre-orange walls, the patio (complete with well) of this lovely villa all bring Tuscany to mind. Relax in one of the exquisitely decorated rooms (stained wood furniture, quilted bedspreads, glazed lava tiles), each one named after a colour: off-white, yellow, orange and lavender. All have a pergola and terrace equipped with deckchair and wrought-iron furniture. Teak sun beds await guests around the pool, and there is a beautifully tended garden. (Well-behaved) children welcome!

Access : *4km north-east of Grimaud on the D 14 and the D 44 towards Plan-de-la-Tour*

HYÈRES - 83400

LA BUANDERIE
Mme Putz

36 avenue des Colibris
83400 Hyères
Tel. 04 94 38 30 98
la-buanderie@wanadoo.fr
www.la-buanderie.com

Closed during Christmas holidays • 3 non-smoking rooms with shower/WC • €95, breakfast included • No table d'hôte • Garden, car park. Credit cards not accepted, dogs not admitted • Outdoor swimming pool

The pine forest and the magnificent view.

This house, perched on a hill overlooking the sea, was a laundry in the early 20C. Cleverly decorated by an interior decorator, the ground floor is home to a large sitting room, which also doubles as a dining room in winter, and three handsome rooms. The "Moroccan" is primarily red, the "Boat" has a parquet floor, and the "Suite" is divided into two parts separated by the bathroom. Around the swimming pool with its wooden deck is a terrace, furnished with attractive benches of Asian origin.

Access : *4km southbound at l'Almanarre*

LA CROIX-VALMER - 83420

CANTE CIGALO
M. Watine

Rond-point de Sylvabelle
83420 La Croix-Valmer
Tel. 06 80 21 05 85
info@cantecigalo.com
www.cantecigalo.com

Closed from 20 Oct to Easter and Jul-Aug • 7 non-smoking rooms all with bathrooms • €70 to €90, breakfast included • No table d'hôte • Garden, terrace, car park. Dogs not admitted

The refreshing shade of the wooded park surrounding the house.

Even though it is run more on the principle of a hotel than a maison d'hôte, this house, which appears to have been purpose-built for guests, cannot fail to charm. The rooms, laid out along an outdoor gallery, which doubles as a terrace, are decorated in an elegantly understated style. The Moroccan tiles in the bathrooms add an exotic touch to the attractive combination of comfort and good taste.

Access : *3km southbound from La Croix-Valmer, Cigaro road*

LA MOTTE - 83920

LA CROIX-VALMER - 83420

LE MAS DU PÉRÉ
M. et Mme Hut

280 chemin du Péré
83920 La Motte
Tel. 04 94 84 33 52
le.mas.du.pere@club-internet.fr
www.lemasdupere.com

Closed from 16 to 31 Dec • 4 rooms with bathrooms • €70 to €78, breakfast included • No table d'hôte • Garden, car park. Credit cards not accepted, dogs not admitted • Outdoor swimming pool

LA SULTANINE
M. Chauvet

Quartier la Galiasse
83420 La Croix-Valmer
Tel. 04 94 79 72 07

Open all year • 4 non-smoking rooms, with bathrooms, direct access to outside • €90 to €110, breakfast included • No table d'hôte • Park, terrace, car park. Credit cards not accepted, dogs not admitted

 It is impossible not to feel at home here.

In the upper reaches of the village, this maison d'hôte is home to pretty rooms, pleasingly decorated with warm Provence-inspired colours and regional furniture, each of which boasts its own small terrace. Generous breakfasts comprised of three different sorts of breads, yoghurts and local honey are served on the terrace. Swimming pool in the midst of the flower-filled garden. Kitchen available for the use of guests.

 The great many species of trees in the vicinity.

Tucked away in the countryside, amid vineyards and fields of lavender, this single storey mas boasts generously proportioned, elegantly decorated rooms. Each of the three rooms has direct access to the outside, but it is impossible not to fall in love with the fully refurbished cabin with its private terrace and attractive bathroom. An enthusiastic wine producer, the owner of the house takes great pleasure in genially introducing guests to his vintages.

Access : *Southeast of Draguignan on the N555*

Access : *2.5km northeast of La Croix-Valmer, Brost road then lane on the right*

LE BEAUSSET - 83330

67

LES CANCADES
M. et Mme Zerbib

1195 chemin de la
Fontaine-de-Cinq-Sous
83330 Le Beausset
Tel. 04 94 98 76 93
charlotte.zerbib@wanadoo.fr
www.les-cancades.com

Open all year • 3 rooms and 1 apartment overlooking the pool, all with shower/WC or bath/WC • €75, breakfast included • No table d'hôte • Garden, car park. Credit cards not accepted, no dogs admitted • Outdoor swimming pool

 Breathe in the scent of pine, olive and cypress trees.

A steep, narrow lane takes you up to this Provençal villa surrounded by pine and olive trees in a quiet, wooded residential district. Designed by the owner, a retired architect, the tasteful rooms are of varying sizes; two have a terrace overlooking the sumptuous swimming pool. The summer kitchen is in a cabin in the pleasant garden.

"Back in shape" course

Access : *Northbound out of the town on the N8 towards Aubagne, then chemin de la Fontaine de Cinq-Sous, opposite the Casino supermarket*

LE CASTELLET - 83330

68

LE MAS DES OLIVIERS
M. Tokatlian

12 chemin des Puechs
83330 Le Castellet
Tel. 04 94 32 71 80
le.mas.des.oliviers@wanadoo.fr

Open all year • 5 air-conditioned rooms, all with a terrace and bathrooms • €60 to €78, breakfast included • No table d'hôte • Terrace, garden, car park. Credit cards not accepted • Outdoor swimming pool

 The attractive view over the fields and of the sea in the distance.

Built in the upper part of the village, the tranquillity of this typically Provençal-style house is happily protected by a park planted with age-old oak trees. Each of the rooms, which sport a happy mixture of local colours (lavender, mimosa, etc), has its own small private terrace and direct access to the park. During the summer months, breakfasts are served outdoors on the covered terrace, near the swimming pool and small summer kitchen.

Access : *10km northbound from Bandol*

LE LUC - 83340

LE HAMEAU DE CHARLES-AUGUSTE
Mme Gaudin

Chemin de Baraouque
83340 Le Luc
Tel. 04 94 60 79 45
margaud@wanadoo.fr
www.provenceweb.fr/83/charles-auguste

Open all year • 4 non-smoking rooms with shower/WC • €65 to €85 (€55 to €75 low season), breakfast included • Table d'hôte €25 to €40 (by reservation) • Terrace, garden, car park. Credit cards not accepted • Swimming pool

 Listening to the owner's tales of the house.

Not a real hamlet as such, it is more a collection of buildings built over time around the original 18C farmhouse. All have been restored with a great deal of taste and warmth, and the comfortable, individually decorated rooms are most appealing, furnished with old family heirlooms and pieces picked up here and there. In fine weather, breakfast is served by the swimming pool in the shade of plane and chestnut trees. A perfectly charming spot and a faultless welcome.

Access : *Southbound of Luc, towards the public swimming pool, turn right before the pool towards the Source de la Pioule*

LES MAYONS - 83340

DOMAINE DE LA FOUQUETTE
M. et Mme Aquadro

83340 Les Mayons
Tel. 04 94 60 00 69
domaine.fouquette@wanadoo.fr
www.domainedelafouquette.com
Langues : Eng.

Closed from Nov to Feb • 4 non-smoking rooms, 1 with disabled access, all with shower/WC • €60, breakfast included • Table d'hôte €20 (evenings only except Sun) • Terrace, garden, car park

 Diving into this oasis of tranquillity and recharging our batteries.

A wine-growing estate surrounds this isolated but welcoming farm on the edge of the Maures mountain range. The quiet bedrooms are simply decorated in a Provençal style and the rustic restaurant sports a fireplace and a terrace commanding a superb view. A number of the aperitifs and some respectable little Côtes de Provence wines are produced on the estate and local delicacies have naturally found pride of place on the table d'hôte. Nearby are Tortoise Village and the Mayons Forest.

Access : *10km south-east of Luc on the D 33 and the D 279 on the edge of the Maures mountains*

LORGUES - 83510

LES PINS
Mme Perin

3630 route de Saint-Antonin
83510 Lorgues
Tel. 04 94 73 91 97

Open from 15 Mar to 15 Nov • 5 non-smoking rooms with bath/WC and shower/WC • €44 to €58, breakfast included • Table d'hôte €22 (evenings only except Sun and in summer), beverages included • Terrace, car park. Credit cards not accepted, no dogs admitted • Swimming pool, play area

> The family atmosphere and bursts of laughter from the children in the pool.

A grove of pines shades this sprawling villa built in the style of a mas next to a small vineyard. The terraces of the three suites in the annex overlook the swimming pool. The other two rooms, more basic but equally immaculately kept, are located in the main building and also decorated in the same Provençal style as the three suites. Countless leisure activities for children who are made particularly welcome by this establishment.

Access : *4km north-west of Lorgues on the D 50 towards Entrecasteaux*

PLAN-DE-LA-TOUR - 83120

LA BERGERIE
M. Caranta

Route de Grimaud
83120 Plan-de-la-Tour
Tel. 04 94 43 74 74
labergeriecaranta@wanadoo.fr

Closed from Oct to mid-Dec and mid-Jan to early Feb • 3 rooms upstairs, 2 with shower/WC and 1 with bath/WC • €70 to €78, breakfast included • No table d'hôte • Park, car park. Credit cards not accepted, dogs not admitted • Outdoor swimming pool

> The delightful combination of simplicity and friendliness.

Nestled between cork trees and vineyards, this old sheepfold boasts a genuine well-being centre with a Jacuzzi, sauna and well-equipped fitness room. The owners, a couple of wine-growers, also organise wine courses out of season. In terms of accommodation, you have the choice between three unpretentious rooms upstairs, and two gîtes in another wing with a private terrace.

Oenology courses out of season

Access : *10km northeast of Sainte-Maxime*

PUGET-VILLE - 83390

PUGET-SUR-ARGENS - 83480

LE MAS DE CENTAURE
M. Bret

2281 chemin de Bagnols
83480 Puget-sur-Argens
Tel. 04 94 81 58 25
bret.family@wanadoo.fr
www.lemasducentaure.fr.st

Closed 2 weeks in Sep • 2 non-smoking rooms and 1 apartment, with bath/WC or shower/WC • €63 to €78, breakfast included • Table d'hôte €30 including drinks • Terrace, park, car park. Credit cards not accepted, dogs not admitted • Outdoor swimming pool (except Sundays)

 The arid wilderness of the surrounding countryside.

Peace and quiet reign through this stone-built house, tucked away in the garrigue, and which seems far older than its thirty years. Only one room, the smallest, is upstairs, while the two others (one of which is an apartment) are located in the outbuildings. Here and there choice pieces of old furniture enhance the generous proportions of the different rooms. Outdoors a swimming pool and summer kitchen are available to make the most of the quiet of the site whilst watching the horses nearby.

Access : *7km northwest on the RN7 and minor road on the right, chemin de la Forêt de Terre de Gastes*

LE MAS DES OLIVIERS
M. Leroy

Chemin des Grands-Prés
83390 Puget-Ville
Tel. 04 94 48 30 89
guy.leroy18@wanadoo.fr
www.masdesoliviers.sup.fr
Langues : Eng., It.

Open all year • 2 rooms with bath/WC • €68, breakfast included • Table d'hôte €24 • Terrace, garden, car park. Credit cards not accepted, no dogs admitted • Fitness room, sauna, outdoor swimming pool, horse-riding, cycling

 The unmistakable stamp of Provence.

Situated in the heart of the Vars countryside and in the midst of nearly 10 acres of vineyards and olive groves, this mas will delight travellers in search of peace and quiet. Good-sized, well-kept rooms sport the colours of southern France and the bathrooms are very pleasant. The distinctive flavour of Provence can also be tasted in the ochre colours and terracotta decoration of the sitting rooms. Bicycling and horse-riding can be organised on request.

Access : *2.5km on the N 97 Cuers road*

RAMATUELLE - 83350

75

LEÏ SOUCO
Mme Nathalie Giraud

Le Plan - Plaine de Camarat
83350 Ramatuelle
Tel. 04 94 79 80 22
www.leisouco.com
Langues : Eng., Ger., Sp.

Closed from mid-Oct to late Mar • 9 air-conditioned rooms with shower/WC or bath/WC and television • €82 to €114 (€71 to €94 low season), breakfast included • No table d'hôte • Terrace, park, car park. Credit cards not accepted • Tennis

 A quiet night's sleep, far from the hubbub of the coast.

Olive, pine and other Mediterranean trees surround this Provençal house set in a wine-growing estate off the main road between Ramatuelle and St Tropez. Most of the rooms are on the ground-floor and enjoy private terraces overlooking the vineyards. The interior decoration is pleasantly sober and understated with immaculate walls, red tiles, bare beams, rustic furniture and bathrooms which sport Salernes tiles.

Access : *3.5km east of Ramatuelle, on the D 93 towards Saint-Tropez*

ROQUEBRUNE-SUR-ARGENS - 83520

76

AU BOIS FLEURI
M. Repaux

Route de Marchandise
83520 Roquebrune-sur-Argens
Tel. 04 94 45 42 28
www.auboisfleuri.com

Open all year • 2 ground floor studios and 3 rooms upstairs, air-conditioning, wifi, baleno bathtubs and shower/WC • €70 to €110, breakfast included • No table d'hôte • Garden, terrace, car park. Dogs not admitted • Outdoor swimming pool

The attention lavished by the owners on their guests.

This couple of former hoteliers didn't want to "throw the towel in" completely, so they decided to continue to exert their sense of hospitality in their home in the forest. There are two small studios with private terraces on the ground floor, and three other rooms upstairs. The whole of the brand new site is equipped with lovely homemade larch wood furniture. The balneo-style bathrooms are distinctly modern. Outside, the well-tended lawn lined with pine trees stretches to the swimming pool.

Access : *8.3km northbound from Roquebrune-sur-Argens, towards la Bouverie*

SANARY-SUR-MER - 83110

SALERNES - 83690

LA BASTIDE ROSE
M. et Mme Henny

Chemin Haut Gaudran
83690 Salernes
Tel. 04 94 70 63 30
labastiderose@wanadoo.fr
www.bastide-rose.com
Langues : Eng., Ger., Du.

Closed mid-Oct to mid-Mar • 6 non-smoking rooms with shower/WC • €70 to €88, breakfast included • Table d'hôte €25 • Terrace, park, garden, car park. Credit cards not accepted, no dogs admitted

 The rustic charm of the spot.

A stony path leads up to this delightful farm, deep in a landscape of vineyards, orchards and sweet-smelling hillsides. Enjoy a quiet night or two in its rooms and suites fitted out with bathrooms decorated with Salernes tiles; some of the rooms are split-level and have their own private terrace. The Dutch farming couple extends a warm friendly welcome to all. Delicious home-made produce features prominently on the table d'hôte: chicken, goose, olives, wine, eggs, fish, apricots, plums.

Access : *3km south-west of Salernes on the D 31 towards Entrecasteaux, go through la Bresque towards La Colle or Riforan*

VILLA LOU GARDIAN
M. et Mme Castellano

646 route de Bandol
83110 Sanary-sur-Mer
Tel. 04 94 88 05 73
annie-bruno.castellano@wanadoo.fr
www.lou-gardian.com

Open all year • 4 rooms, 2 of which are in the garden, 3 with shower/WC, 1 with bath/WC • €82 (€72 low season), breakfast included • No table d'hôte • Garden, car park. Credit cards not accepted, no dogs admitted • Outdoor swimming pool, tennis

 Conveniently located near the sandy beach of La Gorguette.

Despite the nearby road, this recent villa surrounded by palm trees and a pleasant garden is quiet and peaceful. The bedrooms are colourful and well-soundproofed and all have lovely bathrooms; we preferred those near the large swimming pool. Meals are served on the patio. Tennis courts and table-tennis available in the grounds.

Access : *On the Bandol road*

SEILLANS - 83440

MAS DES COMBES LONGUES
M. et Mme Vliet

Les Hautes Combes Longues
83440 Seillans
Tel. 04 94 47 65 27
www.leshautescombes@wanadoo.fr

Open all year • 3 non-smoking rooms with shower/WC • €60 to €90, breakfast included • Table d'hôte €27.50 • Park, car park. Credit cards not accepted, dogs not admitted

 With a little luck, you'll be able to see the sea in the distance.

Totally isolated in the heart of the forest, this 18C stone farmhouse still relies on the milk from a dozen or so goats and the produce from its large garden to supply the organic table d'hôte meals that the owners are rightly proud of. The largest room, in the former stables, commands a superb view of the valley. The other two, in the main house, both have an independent entrance. An ideal retreat for those hoping to get away from it all!

Access : *7km eastbound from Fayence on the D19*

TARADEAU - 83460

LA BERGERIE DU MOULIN
M. et Mme Guillot

Chemin du Vieux-Moulin
83460 Taradeau
Tel. 04 94 99 91 51
bergerie.moulin@wanadoo.fr
www.bergeriedumoulin.com
Langues : Eng., It.

Closed Jan • 6 non-smoking rooms, air-conditioned upstairs, with bath/WC or shower/WC, satellite television and mini-bar • €90 to €110, breakfast included • No table d'hôte • Terrace, garden, private car park. Credit cards not accepted, no dogs allowed • Outdoor swimming pool, jacuzzi, billiards

 The owners' excellent tourist and gastronomic tips.

This characterful house nestles in a peaceful village not far from Arcs-sur-Argens and Lorgues. Rustic outer stone walls overgrown with climbers, Provençal-style bedrooms, kitchen-cum-dining room in the former sheepfold and a lovely outdoor sitting room overlooking the pool and arbour, where meals are sometimes served in the summer. The chirping of the crickets and murmuring stream which used to turn the millwheel are likely to be the only sounds you will hear!

Access : *6km from Arcs-sur-Argens on the D 10*

ANSOUIS - 84240

VINS-SUR-CARAMY - 83170

UN PATIO EN LUBERON
M. Michel Cuche

Rue du Grand-Four
84240 Ansouis
Tel. 04 90 09 94 25
patio-en-luberon@wanadoo.fr
www.unpatioenluberon.com
Langues : Eng., It.

Closed 1 Jan to 14 Feb • 5 rooms all with shower/WC or bath/WC • €55 to €60, breakfast included • Table d'hôte €20 • Patio. Credit cards not accepted, no dogs admitted • Walking

CHÂTEAU DE VINS
M. Bonnet

Les Prés du Château - au bourg
83170 Vins-sur-Caramy
Tel. 04 94 72 50 40
contact@chateaudevins.com
www.chateaudevins.com
Langues : Eng.

Closed from Nov to Mar • 5 non-smoking rooms with bathrooms with shower/WC or bath/WC • €73 to €120, breakfast included • No table d'hôte • Garden, car park. Credit cards not accepted • Cultural events organised, music courses and summer concerts

> **We most liked** The Luberon at its best.

The painstaking restoration has preserved, even enhanced the original charm of this 16C inn situated in the heart of a medieval village. Each of the gaily decorated rooms has been personalised, featuring a happy blend of old and new. Tiled floors and old stone walls add to the character of the vaulted dining room, while a refreshing fountain plays on a delightful little patio to cool down hot summer days.

> **We most liked** A listed historic castle with an emphasis on culture, music in particular.

Saved from ruin and lovingly restored by its owner, this 16C château, complete with towers on all four corners, now offers moderately sized, but beautifully appointed and utterly peaceful rooms, each of which is named after a musician. The former hunting room is now the dining room. Art exhibitions, concerts and music courses take place throughout the year in the other elegantly restored rooms.

> *Cultural events organised, music courses and summer concerts*

Access : *At the foot of the castle*

Access : *9km from Brignoles on the D 24, Thoronet road*

AVIGNON - 84000

DE BLAUVAC
Mme Chapron

11 rue de la Bancasse
84000 Avignon
Tel. 04 90 86 34 11
blauvac@aol.com
www.hotel-blauvac.com
Langues : Eng.

Open all year • 16 rooms, most have bath/WC and a mezzanine, some have shower/WC, all have television • €70 to €80 (€60 to €70 low season); breakfast €7 • No restaurant • No dogs admitted

 A stay in the heart of Avignon without the fuss of a busy town.

The Marquis de Blauvac built this 17C house in a quiet street near the Palais des Papes, from where Avignon's medieval "antipopes" defied Rome for almost 70 years. Its elegant wrought-iron balustrade and thick stone walls are typical of the period: the breakfast room is decorated in a Louis XV style. Most of the rooms, simply furnished but full of character, have a mezzanine with an extra bed.

Access : *In the town centre, in a side street leading to Place de l'Horloge (town hall)*

BÉDOIN - 84410

LA GARANCE
M. et Mme Babinet

Hameau de Sainte-Colombe
84410 Bédoin
Tel. 04 90 12 81 00
info@lagarance.fr
www.lagarance.fr
Langues : Eng.

Closed from 15 Nov to 1 Apr • 13 rooms located upstairs and on the ground floor, with bath/WC or shower/WC, all have television • €55 to €70 (€50 to €65 low season); breakfast €7.50 • No restaurant • Car park • Swimming pool

 Take on the ascent of Mont Ventoux on foot... or by car!

It is a pleasure to drive into this pretty hamlet surrounded by vines and orchards and up to the front door of the farmhouse. Inside, the rooms' furnishings are modern and the tiles are old. You will be able to wake up and feast your eyes on Mont Ventoux, before tripping down to breakfast on the terrace or in the brightly-coloured dining room. Afterwards embark on the assault of this "giant of Provence" along signposted footpaths. Well worth writing home about.

> *Watercolour course, hiking course, bicycling course in the region.*

Access : *Head for Bédoin on the D 19 from Malaucène or the D 974 from Carpentras, then drive towards Mont-Ventoux*

CADENET - 84160

BUISSON - 84110

85

LA TUILIÈRE
M. et Mme Borgarino

Chemin de la Tuilière
84160 Cadenet
Tel. 04 90 68 24 45
clo@latuiliere.com
www.latuiliere.com

Open all year • 5 rooms with bath/WC or shower/WC • €65 to €81, breakfast included • Table d'hôte €20 including drinks • Garden, terrace, car park. Dogs not admitted • Outdoor swimming pool, hiking

LE MAS DE GRATELOUP
M. Peillot

84110 Buisson
Tel. 04 90 28 17 95
masgrateloup@wanadoo.fr
www.mas-grateloup.com
Langues : Eng.

Open all year • 2 rooms and 3 apartments with bath/WC or shower/WC • €65 to €75, breakfast included • Table d'hôte €25 • Park, car park. Credit cards not accepted • Outdoor swimming pool

 The tranquillity of the site.

This 18C country house, surrounded by 12ha of vineyards and orchards, welcomes guests in the heart of the Regional Nature Park of the Luberon. Each of the five individually decorated comfortable rooms is a picture of good housekeeping. Outdoors, guests can take a refreshing dip in the swimming pool or simply relax on the terrace as they gaze at the hilly landscape. Provençal-inspired table d'hôte meals, by reservation.

 The pine forest and its ancient trees.

Originally built as a rampart against the wind, this 18C farmhouse is a pure product of Provençal architecture, despite its rather unusual layout. Behind the old walls hides a small courtyard, where guests are served local specialities in the cool of the evening. The rooms (including three apartments ideally suited to families) are of varying sizes and are dotted around the building; all have direct access outside. Attractive swimming pool on the hillside.

Access : *In Cadenet head towards the Centre-Ville, at the church follow the signs to ''Site du château la Tuilière''*

Access : *On the Coopérative de Villedieu road*

CHÂTEAUNEUF-DE-GADAGNE - 84470

87

LE CLOS DES SAUMANES
M. et Mme Lambert

519 chemin des Saumanes
84470 Châteauneuf-de-Gadagne
Tel. 04 90 22 30 86
closaumane@aol.com
www.closaumane.com
Langues : Ger., Eng., It., Sp.

Open all year • 5 non-smoking rooms, all with bathrooms • €80 to €120, breakfast included • No table d'hôte • Garden, car park. Credit cards not accepted • Outdoor swimming pool

 Nothing is too much trouble for the owners.

This elegant 18C bastide, poised between pine forest and vineyards, is an invitation to wind down and take things easy. Don't even attempt to resist the charm of the bedrooms furnished in an old-fashioned Provençal style; one has a terrace. At the end of the day, head for the swimming pool to admire the sunset. The following morning, breakfast is served under an enormous chestnut tree in a paved courtyard.

Access : *1km along the D 97 Morières road*

ENTRECHAUX - 84340

88

LA BASTIDE DES GRAMUSES
M. Reynaud

84340 Entrechaux
Tel. 04 90 46 01 08

Open all year • 3 rooms with bath/WC or shower/WC • €100, breakfast included • No table d'hôte • Park, car park. Credit cards not accepted • Outdoor swimming pool

 Lazing in the sun in the company of the grey lizards after whom the house is named.

Lost in the midst of vineyards and olive groves, this 17C farmhouse has retained its simple character. The three rooms, directly accessible from a small square courtyard, are authentically decorated with a few modern touches. Colourful mini fridges, attractive shower rooms, good quality bedding and some fine old furniture. Wifi Internet access to surf under the arbour.

Access : *On the Buis-les-Baronnies road*

GORDES - 84220

GORDES - 84220

AUBERGE DE CARCARILLE
M. Rambaud

Route d'Apt
84220 Gordes
Tel. 04 90 72 02 63
carcaril@club-internet.fr
www.auberge-carcarille.com
Langues : Eng., It.

Closed 25 Nov to 28 Jan • 20 rooms with bath/WC or shower/WC and television • €62 to €95; breakfast €10; half-board available • Menus €20 to €45 • Private car park, garden, terrace. No dogs admitted in rooms • Swimming pool

 Taking life easy on the private terrace of your room.

The beauty of Gordes is no longer a secret, but this discreet country inn is worth keeping to yourself! Installed in a dry-stone construction on the edge of a garden, painted furniture and an elegant Provençal style set the scene for the impeccably kept rooms. Regional dishes take pride of place on the menu and are served in the light, colourful dining room. The terrace is equally appealing.

Access : *Beneath the village towards Apt*

LA BADELLE
Mme Cortasse

84220 Gordes
Tel. 04 90 72 33 19
badelle@club-internet.fr
www.la-badelle.com
Langues : Eng., Ger.

Open all year, by reservation in Jan and Feb • 5 rooms with bath/WC and 3 with shower/WC • €92 to €108 (€82 to €98 low season), breakfast included • No table d'hôte • Garden, car park. No dogs admitted • Outdoor swimming pool, table-tennis, hiking, petanque

 A beautiful combination of old and new.

A tiny country road leads to this ancient farmhouse. The rooms in the outbuildings have been entirely redone and all feature the same white-washed walls, rustic earthenware tiles, old furniture and excellent bathrooms. Four open onto the swimming pool. In the summer guests are offered the use of a practical kitchen.

Access : *7km southbound from Gordes on the D 104 towards Goult*

GORDES - 84220

LA BASTIDE-DES-JOURDANS - 84240

MAS VAL - CHÊNAIE
M. et Mme Contri

Les Sauvestres
84220 Gordes
Tel. 04 90 72 13 30
masvalchenaie@yahoo.fr
www.mas-val-chenaie.com
Langues : Eng.

Closed from 15 Nov to late Feb • 4 rooms all with bath/WC • €95 to €115, breakfast included • No table d'hôte • Terrace, car park. Credit cards not accepted, No dogs admitted • Outdoor swimming pool

AUBERGE DU CHEVAL BLANC
M. Moullet

Le Cours
84240 La Bastide-des-Jourdans
Tel. 04 90 77 81 08
provence.luberon@wanadoo.fr
Langues : Eng.

Closed in Feb and on Thu • 4 rooms with bath/WC, air-conditioning and television • €70 to €90; breakfast €10; half-board available • Air-conditioned restaurant; menus €17 (weekdays) to €37 • Terrace, private car park

Without doubt the most beautiful house in "one of the prettiest villages of France".

A little out of the way in the midst of a pleasant oak wood, this handsome stone mas is home to four spacious rooms, each of which is decorated according to a different colour scheme. Exposed beams, tasteful decoration and private bathrooms with Italian-style showers complete the picture. Outside a large swimming pool surrounded by trees and a summer kitchen will ensure that you make the most of the Provençal sunshine. A delightful place.

The Luberon Regional Park is riddled with paths.

In just a few years, this former post house has been elegantly transformed into an up-to-date country inn. Exposed beams, thick stone walls and tiled floors set the scene for the spacious, welcoming rooms, some of which have a small cane-furnished sitting room. Warm, sunny colours adorn the elegant dining room which leads into the dappled shade of a quiet terrace.

Access : *7km south-east of Gordes on the D 2 and the D 156*

Access : *On the main road of the village*

LAURIS - 84360

LAGNES - 84800

LA MAISON DES SOURCES
Mme Collart

Chemin des Fraisses
84360 Lauris
Tel. 04 90 08 22 19
contact@maison-des-sources.com
www.maison-des-sources.com
Langues : Eng., Sp., It.

Closed 15 Nov to early Jan • 4 rooms with bathrooms • €85 to €87, breakfast included • Table d'hôte €25 (evenings) • Garden, car park. Credit cards not accepted

LA PASTORALE
Mme Negrel

Route de Fontaine-de-Vaucluse
84800 Lagnes
Tel. 04 90 20 25 18
Langues : Eng., Ger.

Open all year • 4 rooms with bath/WC or shower/WC • €76, breakfast included • No table d'hôte • Garden, garage. Credit cards not accepted

The chirping of the cicadas announcing the break of day.

An immense plane tree throws a welcome shade over the lawn as it stands guard over this old farmhouse. And in a region where life takes place out of doors, even in the hot summer sun, any shade is particularly sought after. The interior, including the bedrooms, is simply and sparingly decorated with white walls and a few pieces of furniture, so as to not detract from the relaxing atmosphere. Small fitted kitchen and locked garage available to guests.

Breakfast in the welcome shade of acacia trees.

This old farmhouse, built against a cliff face riddled with caves, is hidden in the midst of vineyards, orchards and olive groves in the Luberon foothills. After some major restoration work it was saved from ruin and now offers brightly coloured rooms, the most curious of which features no less than four four-poster beds. The sitting and dining rooms have fine old vaulted ceilings and the somewhat unruly garden only adds to the appeal.

> *Discovering grape picking, initiation of Côtes du Rhône wines, Nyon olives and truffles*

Access : *4.5km to the south-west of Lourmarin on the D 27*

Access : *5.5km southeast of l'Isle-sur-la-Sorgue*

LE BARROUX - 84330

MAS DE LA LAUSE
M. et Mme Lonjon

Chemin de Geysset
84330 Le Barroux
Tel. 04 90 62 33 33
maslause@provence-gites.com
www.provence-gites.com
Langues : Eng., Ger.

Closed from late Nov to early Mar • 5 rooms with shower/WC • €61, breakfast included • Table d'hôte €18.50 • Garden, car park

 Apricot rooms, apricot trees, apricot jam and nectar of apricot.

Nestled among vineyards and apricot trees, this mas built in 1883 has been renovated in true Provençal fashion. The bright sunny rooms, recently repainted, echo their evocative names. Sunflower and Iris overlook the castle of Barroux and the Comtat plain, while Apricot faces the orchards. How about a quick game of pétanque before sampling the tasty regional cooking under the shade of the arbour or the vaulted ceiling of the dining room?

Access : *800m from Le Barroux, towards Suzette*

LE CRESTET - 84110

LE MAS DE MAGALI
M. et Mme Bodewes

Quartier Chante-Coucou
84110 Le Crestet
Tel. 04 90 36 39 91
masmagali@wanadoo.fr
www.masdemagali.com/formhtml
Langues : Ger., Eng., It., Du.

Open from 31 Mar to 1 Oct • 11 rooms with bath/WC and television, 8 with terrace • €85 to €98; breakfast €10; half-board available • Restaurant closed Wed; menus €27 • Terrace, garden, car park • Outdoor swimming pool

 The heady perfume of Provence's vegetation.

The utter peace and quiet, magnificent view of Mont Ventoux and the remote Vaucluse landscape, colourful blue and yellow dining room and spacious rooms, some with terraces: this modern mas captures all that is best in Provence. Magali, the lady of the house, oversees every aspect of your stay from pétanque and pastis to a quiet afternoon nap.

Access : *Leave Vaison-la-Romaine on the D 938 (towards Malaucène) and after 3.5km, turn right (D 76)*

MURS - 84220

MORNAS - 84550

LES HAUTS DE VÉRONCLE
M. et Mme Pouget

84220 Murs
Tel. 04 90 72 60 91
hauts.de.veroncle@wanadoo.fr
http://hauts.de.veroncle.free.fr

Closed from 4 Nov to 29 Mar • 3 rooms with shower/WC • €51 to €53, breakfast included • Table d'hôte €21 (evenings) except Sun and Wed • Terrace, garden, car park. Credit cards not accepted, no dogs admitted in dining room

LE MANOIR
M. ou Mme Caillet

Avenue Jean- Moulin
84550 Mornas
Tel. 04 90 37 00 79
linfo@lemanoir-mornas.fr

www.hotel-le-manoir.com
Langues : Eng., Sp.

Closed 2 Jan to 10 Feb • 25 rooms located in 2 wings with bath/WC or shower/WC, 11 have air-conditioning and television • €48 to €75; breakfast €7; half-board available • Restaurant closed Mon and Tue lunchtimes from Jun to Sep; Sun evening, Mon and Tue lunchtime from Oct to May; menus €25 to €45 • Terrace, car park, garage

 Ever longed to be somewhere no-one could find you?

In the middle of nowhere – there is no other way to describe the peaceful tranquillity of this blue-shuttered mas with its dry stone walls, fragrant garrigue and chirping cicadas. A sophisticated cuisine is served by the fireside in winter or under the wisteria in the summer. If you feel like a walk, ask Mr or Mrs Del Corso to point you towards the path of the seven mills which runs alongside the gorges of the Véroncle.

 Wining and dining by candlelight on the patio.

This impressive 18C mansion stands at the foot of a steep cliff, dominated by the outline of Mornas fortress. The new owners have so far concentrated their restoration efforts on the restaurant, but they plan to redo the rooms shortly. That said, beautiful old wardrobes and marble fireplaces add a great deal of old-fashioned charm to the rooms. The verdant patio and flowered terrace echo to the light-hearted, sunny disposition of Provence.

Bicycling and mountain-biking weekends (by reservation)

Access : *Beside the N 7 through the village*

Access : *2km to the east on the D 15 Gordes road, then a lane to the right*

ROAIX - 84110

99

LES AUZIÈRES
M. et Mme Cuer

84110 Roaix
Tel. 04 90 46 15 54
alain @ auzieres.fr
www.auzieres.fr

Closed 15 Oct to 15 Mar • 5 rooms with bathrooms, separate WC and television • €77, breakfast included • No table d'hôte • Car park • Outdoor swimming pool, petanque, table-tennis, billiards

 A sweeping view of the valley.

It would be hard to find a more secluded spot than this Provençal farm perched on a hillside in the midst of vineyards, olive groves and lavender fields. The spacious, cool bedrooms are spotless and utterly tranquil. Sample the traditional cooking at a huge wooden table in the dining room or on the terrace, facing Mont Ventoux and the jagged peaks of the Dentelles de Montmirail.

Access : 6km westbound from Vaison on the D 975 towards Orange

ROBION - 84440

100

MAS LA FAUSSERANNE
M. et Mme Rigaut

Chemin des Mulets
84440 Robion
Tel. 04 90 20 93 48
fausseranne @ wanadoo.fr
www.fausseranne.com

Open all year • 3 non-smoking rooms with shower/WC • €75 to €90, breakfast included, half-board available • Table d'hôte €30 drinks included • Terrace, park, car park. Credit cards not accepted, no dogs admitted • Outdoor swimming pool

 The friendly atmosphere created by the owners for whom nothing is too much trouble.

This former silk farm, in the heart of a flower garden with shaded terrace, nestles among plane trees and mulberry bushes. An old stone staircase leads up to the unpretentious spacious and comfortable rooms, furnished with lovely old wardrobes; all the rooms command a fine view of the Luberon. Table d'hôte meals served in a dining room under immense beams or, in summer, under an arbour. Ideal to rest and relax before setting off to visit the region.

Access : 4km northwestbound from Robion on the D 31 then a minor road

ROUSSILLON - 84220

LES SABLES D'OCRE
M. Hilario

Les Sablières
84220 Roussillon
Tel. 04 90 05 55 55
sablesdocre@free.fr
www.roussillon-hotel.com
Langues : Eng., Ger., Sp.

Closed from early Nov to late Mar • 22 rooms with balcony, or terrace on the ground floor, 2 have disabled access, all have bath/WC or shower/WC, air-conditioning and television • €64 to €77; breakfast €10 • No restaurant • Garden, car park • Outdoor swimming pool

Walk along the "ochre footpath" to the breathtaking Giants' Causeway.

The colourful walls of this modern hotel pay homage to the "red villages" of Roussillon and their picturesque houses. The mas built in 1998 on the outskirts of the village offers rooms which are handsomely equipped and have a balcony or garden-level terrace, even though they do rather lack character; some have brass beds. 400m away, the old Mathieu factory has been turned into a pigment conservatory – tours and courses.

Access : *Around 10km from Apt, towards Avignon, leave the N 100 and turn right onto the D 149 for 4.5km*

SAIGNON - 84400

CHAMBRE DE SÉJOUR AVEC VUE
M. Jaccaud-Regent

Rue de la Bourgade
84400 Saignon
Tel. 04 90 04 85 01
info@chambreavecvue.com
www.chambreavecvue.com

Open all year • 3 rooms and 2 apartments with bathrooms • €80 to €100, breakfast included • No table d'hôte • Garden, credit cards not accepted

The unusual but attractive concept.

This house, located in a high-perched mountain village, regularly welcomes live-in artists for whom it sets aside a workshop. The owners, art collectors and patrons, have a clear preference for contemporary art, which can be admired in the sober and unusual decoration of their home. The rooms combine comfort with fault-less upkeep. The breakfast room, definitely a little out of the ordinary, is well worth the detour. Refined delicate table d'hôte meals by request.

Access : *4km southbound from Apt on the D48, Saignon road*

SARRIANS - 84260

LE MAS DE LA FONTAINE
M. et Mme Leroy

Route de Vacqueyras
84260 Sarrians
Tel. 04 90 12 36 63
lemasdelafontaine@wanadoo.fr
www.lemasdelafontaine.com

Closed from mid-Nov to Feb • 3 rooms with bath/WC or shower/WC • €65 to €90, breakfast included • Table d'hôte €25 • Park, car park. Credit cards not accepted, dogs not admitted • Outdoor swimming pool

 The three-hundred-year-old plane tree has become one with the fountain over time.

The owner of this immense restored building surrounded by vineyards has two passions in life. In addition to automobile rallies (don't miss his proudly displayed trophy collection), he also loves making jam which is served at breakfast. All the variously sized rooms are upstairs and each is decorated in the same unpretentious vein and has its own private entrance. The more spacious apartments are particularly attractive. Provence-inspired menu.

Access : *At Sarrians turn left towards Vacqueyras, drive for 5 km, take a lane on the left, continue for around 500m on a stone lane*

VAISON-LA-ROMAINE - 84110

L'ÉVÊCHÉ
M. et Mme Verdier

Rue de l'Évêché
84110 Vaison-la-Romaine
Tel. 04 90 36 13 46
eveche@aol.com
http://eveche.free.fr

Closed from 15 Nov to 15 Dec • 3 rooms and 2 apartments with shower/WC • €78 to €85, breakfast included • No table d'hôte • Terrace. Credit cards not accepted, no dogs admitted • Wifi internet access, bicycles

 A warm country welcome after a hard day's sightseeing.

This former Episcopal palace, dating from the 16C, stands in the medieval part of town. Most of its countless rooms, on a variety of levels, overlook a tiny terrace. The breakfast room is the largest and it offers a wonderful view of the lower town. A lovely spiral staircase winds up to the well-furnished and tasteful rooms. Don't forget to take a look at the interesting collection of prints originally from a treatise on lockmaking.

Access : *In the old town*

VIOLÈS - 84150

LA FARIGOULE
Mme Favrat

Le Plan-de-Dieu
84150 Violès
Tel. 04 90 70 91 78
www.la-farigoule.com

Closed from Nov to Mar • 5 rooms, including one studio, with shower/WC • €45 to €55, breakfast included • No table d'hôte • Garden, car park. Credit cards not accepted • Play area, table-tennis

The erudite atmosphere of this characterful house.

This 18C wine-growers' house has lost none of its authenticity over the years. A fine staircase leads up to antique furnished rooms, each of which is named after a writer with Provence connections, including Frédéric Mistral, Alphonse Daudet and Marie Mauron; you won't be surprised to discover that your hosts used to own a book shop. Breakfasts are served in a lovely vaulted room. As for free time, there is a play area for children and the hotel rents out bicycles (including tandems).

Access : 10km westbound from Gigondas on the D 80 towards Orange, then the D 8 and the D 977 towards Violès

VISAN - 84820

LE MAS DES SOURCES
M. Barnouin

Chemin Notre-Dame-des-Vignes
84820 Visan
Tel. 04 90 41 95 90
contact@mas-des-sources.com
www.mas-des-sources.com

Closed during the Nov half-term holidays • 3 rooms, all with bath/WC • €70, breakfast included • Table d'hôte €25 • Garden, car park. Credit cards not accepted, no dogs admitted • Outdoor swimming pool, bicycles lent out

The whole of Provence rolled into one.

Located in the heart of a 25ha wine-growing estate, this fully restored farmhouse offers four rooms, one of which is a family room and one an apartment. The tasteful sophisticated decoration features the lovely warm colours of Provence and antique furnishings. A mouth-watering selection of spices and flavours awaits you for the table d'hôte. Theme weekends organised in honour of local specialities: wine, olives and truffles.

Côtes du Rhône wine tasting courses; discovering truffles and olive oil

Access : At Visan, head towards Vaison-la-Romaine, on leaving the village, take 1st left to crossroads then take dirt track on right

Ain - 01
Ardèche - 07
Drôme - 26
Isère - 38
Loire - 42
Rhône - 69
Savoie - 73
Haute-Savoie - 74

A land of contrasts and a crossroads of culture, the Rhône-Alpes region offers visitors a thousand different faces. Its lofty peaks are heaven on earth to skiers, climbers and hikers attracted by the sublime beauty of its glittering glaciers, torrential streams and tranquil lakes, while its fashionable resorts, like Chamonix and Courchevel, set the tone in alpine chic. If you can tear yourself away from the roof of Europe, venture down past the herds of cattle grazing on the rich mountain grass and into the intense bustle of the Rhône valley, symbolised by its fast-flowing waters. From Antique Roman roads to high-speed inter-city trains, the main artery between north and south has forged the reputation of this region's economic drive. Rhône-Alpes lies on the route taken by hordes of holidaymakers every summer, and those in the know always make a point of stopping in the region to taste its culinary specialities. The area abounds in restaurants, from three-star trend-setters to Lyon's legendary neighbourhood *bouchons*, whose standards and traditions have made the region the kingdom of cuisine.

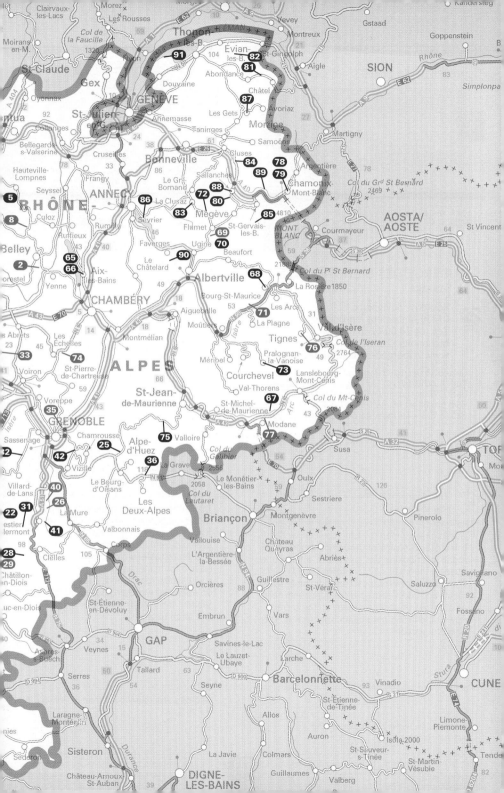

AMBÉRIEUX-EN-DOMBES - 01330

AUBERGE DES BICHONNIÈRES
M. Sauvage

Route de Savigneux
01330 Ambérieux-en-Dombes
Tel. 04 74 00 82 07
bichonnier@wanadoo.fr
www.aubergedesbichonnieres.com

Closed 15 Dec to 15 Jan, Sun evening (Mon and Tue lunchtimes in Jul-Aug) • 9 rooms with bath/WC or shower/WC and television • €54 to €64; breakfast €8; half-board available • Menus €25 to €33 • Terrace, garden, private car park

The charm of the "Route des étangs" (Pond Route).

Guests are pampered within the cob walls of this old farm, typical of the Dombes region. The rooms overlooking the courtyard, although a little on the small side, are refreshingly quiet. The cuisine draws on local traditions and ingredients and is served in a rustic dining room near an old stove or under a canopy on the terrace. Rows of crimson geraniums brighten up the peaceful garden.

Access : *On leaving the town, on the Ars-sur-Formans road*

BRENS - 01300

FERME DES GRANDS HUTAINS
M. et Mme Veyron

Le Petit Brens
01300 Brens
Tel. 04 79 81 90 95
Langues : Ger.

Closed in Nov and on Sun • 4 non-smoking rooms with bath/WC • €45, breakfast included • Table d'hôte €14 • Terrace, car park. Credit cards not accepted, dogs not admitted

Enjoyable meals of beautifully cooked garden-fresh vegetables.

The farmhouse and pergola are delightful. The rooms under the eaves are snugly welcoming, furnished with family heirlooms and decorated in an old-fashioned style; all are non-smoking. The dining table, which shows the chef's preference for home-grown produce, is located in a welcoming room where a fire is lit in winter, or when the weather allows, around a stone table in the garden under the shade of an oak and birch trees.

Access : *3km southbound from Belley on the D 31A*

CHÂTILLON-LA-PALUD - 01320

AUBERGE DE CAMPAGNE DU MOLLARD
M. Decré

01320 Châtillon-la-Palud
Tel. 04 74 35 66 09
f.decre@wanadoo.fr
www.aubergedumollard.com

Open all year by reservation • 4 rooms with shower/WC • €65, breakfast included • Menus €17 to €34 • Car park. Credit cards accepted in restaurant, no dogs admitted

The religiously preserved rustic appeal.

A tiny country lane will take you up to this attractive farmhouse and courtyard-garden bedecked with flowers – a sight to behold in the spring. The four rooms in an outbuilding have wonderful carved wooden beds, but have a shared bathroom. Meals are served in a country-style dining room with a fireplace and a huge cauldron. The tasty family cooking focuses on local produce.

Access : *14km north-east of Pérouges on the D 984 and the D 904, towards Chalamont, then a lane on the left*

CHÂTILLON-SUR-CHALARONNE - 01400

L'INATTENDU
M. et Mme Jacquet

150 place du Champ-de-Foire
01400 Châtillon-sur-Chalaronne
Tel. 04 74 55 06 86
amrjacquet@inattendu-hotes.fr
www.inattendu-hotes.fr
Langues : Eng.

Closed from 22 Dec to 8 Jan • 11 rooms with shower/WC • €58 to €63, breakfast included • Table d'hôte €24 (by reservation) • Garden, car park. No dogs admitted

A breakfast worth getting up for!

Old wardrobes, a wooden staircase, huge beams and floral wallpaper: the stage is set and the curtain can rise on this welcoming home. Bunches of fresh flowers and well-polished wooden furniture greet you in the rooms. Make sure you get up early and have had time to work up an appetite, if you want to do justice to the substantial mounds of croissants, walnut bread, pancakes and no less than thirty home-made jams!

Access : *In the town centre*

MIRIBEL - 01700

ÉVOSGES - 01230

LA VILLA DU RHÔNE
M. et Mme Cabardi

Chemin de la Lune
01700 Miribel
Tel. 04 78 55 54 16
contact@lavilladurhone.com
www.lavilladurhone.com
Langues : Eng.

Open all year • 4 rooms with shower/WC • €80 to €100, breakfast included • Table d'hôte €30 (evening only) • Garden, car park. Credit cards not accepted • Outdoor swimming pool

L'AUBERGE CAMPAGNARDE
Mme Merloz

Le Village
01230 Évosges
Tel. 04 74 38 55 55
auberge-campagnarde@wanadoo.fr
Langues : Eng.

Closed from 2 Jan to 2 Feb, 5 to 13 Sep and 13 to 29 Nov • 15 rooms with bath/WC or shower/WC, all have television • €42 to €77; breakfast €8; half-board available • Menus €21 to €50 • Terrace, garden, car park • Outdoor swimming pool, mini golf, table tennis, play area, fishing

 Ideal for nature lovers with energetic children.

This old family farmstead in a remote village of Bugey has been turned into a lovely country inn with rustic or modern-style rooms and an inviting restaurant with stone walls and a fireplace. Children however generally prefer the shaded garden with play area, mini-golf and swimming pool.

Peace and quiet on the threshold of Lyons.

This modern villa on the heights of Miribel commands a superb view of the Rhône and the valley. Two of the three rooms overlooking the swimming pool have their own private terrace with a view of the landscape. The redbrick walls of the sitting room on the veranda, complete with indoor garden and fireplace, are full of appeal. Breakfast on the terrace in the summer is a pure joy.

Access : *12km to the north-east of Lyon, A 46, Eastbound round Lyon, Rillieux exit, then D 71 towards the Mas-Rillier and Miribel*

Access : *Leave the N 504 (Ambérieu-Belley) between St Rambert-en-Bugey and Argis and follow the D 34*

NEUVILLE-SUR-AIN - 01160

CHAMBRE D'HÔTE DE BOSSERON
Mme Rivoire

325 route de Genève
01160 Neuville-sur-Ain
Tel. 04 74 37 77 06
arivoire@free.fr
http://arivoire.free.fr
Langues : Eng., Ger.

Closed from 15 Oct to Easter • 4 rooms with bathrooms • €60, breakfast included • No table d'hôte • Park, car park. Credit cards not accepted, no dogs admitted • Table tennis, billiards, bicycles

 Immaculately decorated.

You won't regret your decision to stay here when you see the impressive manor house and the five acres of parkland on the banks of the Ain. Good taste and a flair for interior decoration have resulted in comfortable, well-sound-proofed rooms. A fitness room and billiards table in the outbuildings are for the sole use of guests. Your gracious hostess certainly knows how to make visitors feel welcome.

Access : *8km to the north-east of Pont-d'Ain on the N 84*

SAINT-MARTIN-DE-BAVEL - 01510

SNC LES CHARMETTES
Mme Vincent Juliette

La Vellaz
01510 Saint-Martin-de-Bavel
Tel. 04 79 87 32 18
juliettevincent@cherea.com

 Langues : Eng., Ger.

Open all year • 3 rooms, one of which has disabled access, all with shower/WC • €44, breakfast included • No table d'hôte • Car park. Credit cards not accepted • Hiking and mountain biking

 Mother Nature at her best.

Why not treat yourself to a stay in this lovely farmhouse and enjoy the superb surrounding countryside? The snug, comfortable rooms are in the beautifully restored stables and one is equipped for disabled guests. Visitors have the use of a fitted kitchen and dining and sitting rooms in a separate wing. The owner is extremely knowledgeable about his region's tourist attractions.

Access : *11km northbound from Belley on the N 504 as far as Chazey-Bons, then take the D 31C*

SERVAS - 01960

LE NID À BIBI
Mme Bibus

Lieu-dit Lalleyriat
01960 Servas
Tel. 04 74 21 11 47
lenidabibi@wanadoo.fr
www.lenidabibi.com
Langues : Eng., Ger., It.

Open all year • 5 non-smoking rooms, all with bath/WC, 1 with balneo bathtub • €100 to €130, breakfast included • Table d'hôte €20 to €30 (evenings only) • Park. Dogs not admitted in rooms • Indoor counter-current swimming pool, fitness facilities, sauna, tennis, table tennis, mountain bikes

 The very high standard of facilities.

This carefully restored farmhouse offers comfortable accommodation, furnished in a mixture of old and new. Countless leisure activities available on site including a keep-fit room, sauna, covered swimming pool, table-tennis, tennis courts in the grounds and bicycles for rides in the forest. The generous breakfast (free range eggs, cheese, etc) will give you all the energy you need to throw yourself into one or other of the activities available.

Access : *7km south of Bourg-en-Bresse on the N 83, then 2km on the D 22 and minor road to the left*

ALBA-LA-ROMAINE - 07400

LE JEU DU MAIL
M. et Mme Arlaud

07400 Alba-la-Romaine
Tel. 04 75 52 41 59
lejeudumail@free.fr
http://lejeudumail.free.fr
Langues : Eng., It.

Closed 15 Nov to 15 Mar • 5 rooms with shower/WC • €54 to €75, breakfast included • No table d'hôte • Garden, terrace, car park. Credit cards not accepted, no dogs admitted • Outdoor swimming pool

 A lengthy lunch under the trellis or in the shade of the plane tree.

The owners of this former 19C Templar stronghold were among the precursors of the Ardèches chambre d'hôte phenomenon in the 1970s. Since then, they have never stopped taking great pleasure in entertaining guests. All the rooms are very pleasant and each has been given a name which relates to the property's history, including Émilie, Jesuit's suite and Servants Quarters. In the summer, breakfast and lunch, served under a shaded trellis or plane tree, are sheer delight.

Access : *In the village*

BEAULIEU - 07460

LA SANTOLINE
M. et Mme Espenel

07460 Beaulieu
Tel. 04 75 39 01 91
info@lasantoline.com
www.lasantoline.com
Langues : Eng., It., Sp.

Open from 1 May to 20 Sep • 7 rooms (some have a balcony), one of which is an apartment, all have bath/WC, some have air-conditioning • €65 to €135; breakfast €10; half-board available • Terrace, garden, car park. Dogs not admitted in restaurant • Outdoor swimming pool, billiards

The lovely view of the Ardèche countryside and the Cévennes foothills.

Farm? Stronghold? Hunting lodge? Whatever the case, these 16C walls now house a hotel in a remote spot of garrigue that will appeal to urbanites in search of authenticity and tranquillity. The cheerful Provençal rooms would be quite at home in a glossy home-decoration magazine. Some have air-conditioning, but to our mind the thick dry-stone walls are more than sufficient to keep the scorching heat firmly outside. Vaulted restaurant, pretty terrace and a swimming pool surrounded by greenery.

Access : *To the south-east, 1km along a gravel drive*

CHANDOLAS - 07230

AUBERGE LES MURETS
M. Rignanese

Lengarnayre
07230 Chandolas
Tel. 04 75 39 08 32
dominique.rignanese@wanadoo.fr
www.aubergelesmurets.com
Langues : Eng.

Closed from 2 Jan to 2 Feb, 19 Nov to 7 Dec, Mon and Tue from 15 Nov to 30 Mar and Mon lunchtimes • 7 air-conditioned rooms with bath/WC or shower/WC and television • €58; breakfast €7; half-board available • Menus €17 to €28.50 • Car park, park, terrace. No dogs admitted in rooms • Swimming pool

The restful swimming pool overlooking the Ardèche landscape.

Vineyards and 5 acres of grounds provide the setting for this lovely regional farm built in the 18C and recently turned into a family hotel. Attractive warm colours and bamboo furniture grace the majority of the rooms. Depending on the season, meals are served in vaulted dining room or on the terrace under the welcome shade of an old mulberry tree. The cuisine does full justice to the region's renowned culinary reputation and the buffet breakfast makes a perfect way to start the day.

Access : *6km northbound on the D 208, the D 104, then a minor road*

LYAS - 07000

CHÂTEAU DE LIVIERS
M. et Mme Humbert

07000 Lyas
Tel. 04 75 64 64 00
château.liviers@wanadoo.fr
www.chateau-de-liviers.com

Open all year • 5 non-smoking rooms with bath/WC • €55 to €60, breakfast included, half-board available • Table d'hôte €19 • Terrace, garden, park, car park. No dogs admitted

> **The panoramic view that stretches for nearly 300km.**

A haven of peace and quiet for nature lovers and enthusiasts of old stones: a 12C castle perched in the midst of oak and chestnut trees. A rustic style prevails throughout the sitting rooms, the stone vaulted dining room and in the beautifully quiet bedrooms. Warm, friendly atmosphere. The owner will be more than happy to open up his library that includes a substantial number of works on the Ardèche, countless guides to the region and nearly 3000 comic strip books, which are his passion.

Access : *7km north-west of Privas on the D 2*

MERCUER - 07200

LE MAS DE MAZAN
M. Croze

07200 Mercuer
Tel. 04 75 35 41 88
masdemazan@wanadoo.fr
http://au.masdemazan.com

Closed 15 Nov to 15 Mar • 5 rooms with shower/WC • €47, breakfast included • No table d'hôte • Car park. Credit cards not accepted, no dogs admitted

> **The owner takes guests round his pride and joy, a silk-worm farm.**

This typical Cévennes farm has been lovingly restored by a farming couple, who enthusiastically greet all new guests. The spot is stunningly tranquil and the view of the valley, wooded hills and the village is matchless. The rooms are inviting and well restored but all, sadly, do not enjoy the wonderful view. The owner breeds silk worms and loves explaining the finer points of his "hobby".

Access : *5km to the north-west of Aubenas on the D 104 and the D 435*

SAINT-DÉSIRAT - 07340

LA DÉSIRADE
M. et Mme Mennier

07340 Saint-Désirat
Tel. 04 75 34 21 88
contact@desirade-fr.com
www.desirade-fr.com
Langues : Eng.

Closed 25 Dec and 1 Jan • 6 rooms with shower/WC • €49, breakfast included • Table d'hôte €18 • Terrace, garden, car park. Credit cards not accepted

We most liked **The lady of the house's culinary skills.**

This fully renovated 19C mansion among Saint Joseph's trees and vineyards is a feast for the eyes. The simple, light and airy rooms overlook the magnolia tree in the courtyard, or the park and vineyard. Your cordon-bleu hostess loves surprising her guests with tasty regional recipes. A perfect base camp from which to explore the Ardèche.

Access : *15km eastbound from Annonay on the D 82, towards Andance, then take a minor road*

SAINT-JULIEN-DU-SERRE - 07200

MAS DE BOURLENC
M. et Mme Ventalon

Route de Saint-Andéol
07200 Saint-Julien-du-Serre
Tel. 04 75 37 69 95
bourlenc07@free.fr
http://bourlenc.com

Closed from Nov to Feb (open weekends by reservation) • 5 rooms with shower/WC • €60, breakfast included • Table d'hôte €19 to €25 (reservation) • Garden. Credit cards not accepted, no dogs admitted

We most liked **A chance to taste forgotten varieties of fruit and vegetables.**

It is impossible not to wind down during a stay at this house perched on a rock and surrounded by acacias. Colourful wardrobes, whitewashed walls and earthenware tiles add a delightful southern accent to the interior. The Pass of Lescrinet can be seen from the light, airy and generously proportioned rooms. Farm-grown fruit and vegetables take pride of place on the appetising dining table.

Access : *3.5km from Saint-Julien-du-Serre on the D 218*

SAINT-PAUL-LE-JEUNE - 07460

LA PASSIFLORE
Mme Luypaerts

Sauvas
07460 Saint-Paul-le-Jeune
Tel. 04 75 39 80 74
godeliva.luypaerts@wanadoo.fr

www.ardeche.com.lapassiflore
Langues : Eng., Ger.

Closed 15 Dec to 15 Jan • 3 rooms with shower/WC • €42, breakfast included • No table d'hôte • Garden, car park. Credit cards not accepted, no dogs admitted

The owners bend over backwards to make their guests feel at home.

This Flemish couple clearly care about their guests and want to make sure their stay in the Vans region is memorable. Despite the nearby road, the well-isolated house is a haven of peace. The agreeable rooms are extremely well-soundproofed and guests can choose from countless delightful sitting rooms. As to the breakfasts, served under an arbour near the mulberry tree and aviary, you'll certainly pass your plate for more...

Access : *13km southbound from Vans on the D 901, then the D 104 towards Alès*

SAINT-PONS - 07580

HOSTELLERIE « MÈRE BIQUETTE »
Mme Bossy

Les Allignols
07580 Saint-Pons
Tel. 04 75 36 72 61
merebiquette@wanadoo.fr
www.logis-d-ardeche.com/merebiquette
Langues : Eng., Sp.

Closed 15 Nov to 12 Feb and Sun eve from Oct to Mar • 15 rooms in a separate wing, with bath/WC and television • €63 to €107; breakfast €8 to €9.50; half-board available • Rest closed Mon and Wed lunchtimes (except public holidays); menus €19.50 to €42 • Terrace, garden, car park • Outdoor swimmingpool, tennis

Tucking into the appetising breakfast buffet.

This old country farm is named after a goat's cheese formerly produced here: "la mère biquette" (a biquette is a kid goat) was sold by the current owners' parents in the local markets. It's a perfect hideaway to build up your strength in well-appointed rooms overlooking the chestnut trees or vineyards, a stone and wood rustic-styled restaurant, a shaded terrace overlooking the valley and a superb swimming pool.

Access : *Leave the N 102 between Villeneuve-de-Berg and Le Teil, take the D 293, through Saint-Pons and on for 4km*

CHÂTILLON-SAINT-JEAN - 26750

MAISON FORTE DE CLÉRIVAUX
M. et Mme Josquin

Clérivaux
26750 Châtillon-Saint-Jean
Tel. 04 75 45 32 53
contact@clerivaux.com
www.clerivaux.com
Langues : Eng., Ger.

Closed 3 Jan to 3 Mar • 4 rooms, all have bath/WC or shower/WC • €60, breakfast included • No table d'hôte • Terrace, park, car park. Credit cards not accepted, no dogs allowed

An ideal spot to recharge your batteries.

Anne and Pierre Josquin harnessed all their enthusiasm and talent to reviving this estate nestled in a tiny valley of the Drôme. The splendid 13C stronghold is surrounded by out-houses, gardens and 11ha of farming and wood-land. Four rooms, located in a 17C farmhouse, combine contemporary comforts with the warmth of yesteryear. In fine weather, break-fasts of fruit from the orchard and home-made jams are served under the trellis, opposite the delightful "garden of Julie".

Heritage seminar 3rd weekend of November

Access : *In Châtillon-Saint-Jean, head towards Parnans. 1km further on, turn left towards Saint-Michel and follow signs*

CLIOUSCLAT - 26270

LA TREILLE MUSCATE
M. Delaitre

26270 Cliousclat
Tel. 04 75 63 13 10
latreillemuscate@wanadoo.fr
www.latreillemuscate.com
Langues : Eng.

Closed from 5 Dec to 11 Feb • 12 rooms with bath/WC or shower/WC, most have television • €60 to €130; breakfast €10; half-board avail-able • Menu €15 (weekdays) to €34 • Terrace, small garden, private car park. No dogs admit-ted in restaurant

The fruit trees in blossom in the spring.

Midway between Valence and Montélimar just off the A 7 motorway, this village lying in the hills of the Drôme valley is home to an inn, made up of two old stone houses with lilac shutters. Terracotta tiled floors and second-hand furniture adorn the uncluttered, indi-vidually styled bedrooms. Sunny Provence can be felt in the dining room and the lovely terrace is hidden in a secret garden. However, if you are unable to resist the temptation of a motor-way hotel, then have it your own way...

Access : *Leave the Valence-Montélimard road (N 7) between Loriol-sur-Drôme and Saulce-sur-Rhône for a minor road eastbound*

ÉTOILE-SUR-RHÔNE - 26800

LA MARE
Famille Chaix

Route de Montmeyran
26800 Étoile-sur-Rhône
Tel. 04 75 59 33 79
http://la.mare.free.fr

Open all year • 4 rooms with shower/WC • €47, breakfast included • No table d'hôte • Garden, car park. Credit cards not accepted, no dogs admitted

 The warm-hearted hospitality of this farming family.

On the threshold of the south of France, this lovely stone house run by a farming family is a unique chance to taste the legendary "savoir-vivre" of the region first-hand. The comfortable, appealing rooms are fitted with home-made furniture. Garden-produce features prominently in the delicious, generous helpings of home cooking. We also appreciated the friendly greeting and the modest prices.

Access : 15km to the south-east of Valence on the D 111 and the D 111B

LA CHAPELLE-EN-VERCORS - 26420

BELLIER
Mme Bellier

Avenue Goulets
26420 La Chapelle-en-Vercors
Tel. 04 75 48 20 03
www.hotel-bellier.fr

Closed Jan to 1 Apr, Tue evening and Wed out of season • 13 rooms with bath/WC and television • €58 to €65 (€46 to €55 low season); breakfast €6; half-board available • Menus €15 to €30 • Terrace, garden, car park • Outdoor swimming pool. In winter, cross-country skiing, snowshoe hiking

 Right in the heart of the Vercors, in nearly 450 000 acres of Regional Park.

Air raids and fires took their toll on the village in 1944, which explains why the spruce chalet on a rocky outcrop over the road only dates from 1946. The majority of the spacious, welcoming rooms have a balcony. A mountain flavour adds warmth to the dining room and the fireplace in the sitting room is very welcome after a long day's skiing. In the summer, tables are laid round the swimming pool.

Access : In the village, on a rocky outcrop overlooking the road

LA GARDE-ADHÉMAR - 26700

GÎTE DU VAL DES NYMPHES
M. et Mme Andruejol

Domaine de Magne
26700 La Garde-Adhémar
Tel. 04 75 04 44 54
www.valdesnymphes.com

Open all year • 5 rooms with shower/WC • €48 to €65, breakfast included • Table d'hôte €18 (evening only) • Terrace, garden. Credit cards not accepted, dogs not admitted in restaurant • Outdoor swimming pool

 We most liked **Filling a basket with fruit from the estate.**

This mouth-watering fruit farm is built on a hillside in immense grounds which formerly included the Chapelle des Nymphes. The rooms are located in a small independent house overlooking the orchards. Meals are served in a vaulted dining room where old farm tools and family photos hang on the walls. Music lovers can try the family piano, while others may prefer to lounge in the garden. Before leaving, fill your basket with freshly picked peaches and apricots.

Truffles, grape picking and ice skating weekend

Access : *1km on the Chapelle du Val des Nymphes road*

NYONS - 26110

LA CARAVELLE
M. et Mme Allignol

8 rue des Antignans
26110 Nyons
Tel. 04 75 26 07 44
www.guideweb.com/provence/hotel/caravelle

Closed Nov to Mar • 11 non-smoking rooms with bath/WC or shower/WC and television • €75 to €95; breakfast €8.50 • No restaurant • Garden, private car park. No dogs admitted

 We most liked **A quiet read in the unusual garden.**

The sign outside and a series of portholes from the battleship 'Jean-Bart' are the legacy of the former hotel owner who had a reputation as something of an old seadog. If you then add the unusual architecture of this 1900 villa and its curious garden full of Indian bean trees, you will be prepared for a stay in the earthly paradise of the olive kingdom but minus the traditional Provençal style. Quiet, well-cared for rooms.

Access : *On the Promenade de la Digue*

ALLEMONT - 38114

GINIÈS
M. et Mme Giniès

Le Plan
38114 Allemont
Tel. 04 76 80 70 03
hotel-ginies@wanadoo.fr
www.hotel-ginies.com
Langues : Eng.

Closed Jan, Apr and Dec, Sun eve and Mon (except school holidays) • 15 rooms, one of which has disabled access, all have bath/WC or shower/WC and television • €55; breakfast €6; half-board available • Menu €11 to €20 • Terrace, garden, car park. No dogs admitted in restaurant • Mini-golf

 Ideally located near some of the best skiing domains in the Alps.

A sleepy village in the valley of the Eau d'Olle is home to this inn and its recent wing. The rooms are spacious, practical and well looked-after and some have balconies. You will have a choice of dining rooms, ranging from stones and beams in a rustic room to two more modern rooms with a view of the garden. A recently redone mini-golf course completes the picture.

Access : *In the village, 9km northbound from Bourg-d'Oisans on the N 91 then right on the D 526*

AVIGNONET - 38650

CHÂTEAU DES MARCEAUX
M. et Mme Rocca

38650 Avignonet
Tel. 04 76 34 18 94
eric.rocca@wanadoo.fr
http://monsite.wanadoo.fr/chateaudesmarceaux
Langues : Eng., Sp.

Closed from Jan to mid-Apr and from Nov to late Dec • 2 rooms with shower/WC • €67 to €74, breakfast included • No table d'hôte • Park, car park. Credit cards not accepted, dogs not admitted

 Superbly original rooms.

The diversity of architectural styles in this 18C château is such that the ensuing variety of bedroom styles seems perfectly natural. The first room, in the old dovecote, is most spectacular with a superb staircase and walls adorned with hundreds of roosting places. Original parquet floors and high ceilings set the tone for the second in the square tower, while the third in an independent cottage is simply enormous. Look out for the fresco in the dining room, painted by the owner-artist himself.

Access : *From the road, take the lane to the castle gates*

CHARETTE - 38390

AUBERGE DU VERNAY
M. Sallemand

Route d'Optevoz
38390 Charette
Tel. 04 74 88 57 57
reservation@auberge-du-vernay.fr
www.auberge-du-vernay.fr
Langues : Eng., Ger., Sp.

Open all year • 7 rooms, one of which has disabled access, all have shower/WC and television • €80 to €100 (€70 low season); breakfast €9; half-board available • Restaurant closed Sun evening; menus €24 to €52 • Terrace, car park

Halcyon days in the countryside.

The spruce white stonewalls of this 18C farmstead have been given a new lease of life. All the delightful rooms are decorated individually. In the restaurant, old flagstones, a huge fireplace large enough to roast a whole cow, sandblasted beams, cheerful paintings and multi-coloured modern chairs provide an amusing and appealing mixture of tastes and styles. Outside, the old bread oven can still be seen from the shaded terrace. Aromatic garden.

Access : *After the town hall drive towards Optevoz*

CHICHILIANNE - 38930

CHÂTEAU DE PASSIÈRES
M. et Mme Perli

38930 Chichilianne
Tel. 04 76 34 45 48
www.chateau-de-passieres.fr.cx
Langues : Eng., Ger., It.

Closed from mid-Nov to late Feb and Sun evening and Mon out of season • 23 rooms, all have bath/WC or shower/WC, half have television • €50 to €72; breakfast €8; half-board available • Menus €20 • Terrace, garden, car park. No dogs admitted in restaurant • Outdoor swimming pool, tennis

Watch a climbing party make the ascent of Mont Aiguille (3842m) from the comfort of your deck-chair!

The turrets of this small 14C manor house look out onto a hamlet in the shadow of Mount Aiguille. Most of the 23 bedrooms are contemporary in style, but three furnished with old pieces and lined in dark wood have more character. The owner, a professional footballer in his day, is a fan of 19C art as the numerous oils on the restaurant and sitting room walls illustrate.

Access : *Leave the N 75 after 12km southbound from Monestier-de-Clermont, at "La Gare" take the D 7*

ESTRABLIN - 38780

CHICHILIANNE - 38930

LA GABETIÈRE
M. Neyret

D 502
38780 Estrablin
Tel. 04 74 58 01 31
www.la-galetiere.com
Langues : Eng., It.

Closed 1 to 10 Jan • 12 rooms with bath/WC or shower/WC and television • €47 to €67; breakfast €9 • No restaurant • Park, private car park • Outdoor swimming pool

FERME DE RUTHIÈRES
M. Sauze

Lieu-dit Ruthières
38930 Chichilianne
Tel. 04 76 34 45 98
fsauze@aol.com
www.fermederuthières.com

Closed from 20 to 27 Dec • 4 rooms upstairs with shower/WC • €47; breakfast included; half-board available • Meals only by reservation and for guests • Garden, car park. Credit cards not accepted

An easy-going 16C manor.

On the outskirts of Vienne, trees and parkland surround this little 16C manor. A stone staircase in the tiny tower leads up to individually decorated boudoir bedrooms, recently equipped with double-glazing which cuts out the noise of the nearby road. Character also abounds in the exposed beams and late 17C fireplace in the breakfast room.

A strong focus on farm-grown produce.

This young farming couple extends a warm, unaffected welcome to guests to their farmhouse. The cow-shed has been turned into enormous guest bedrooms furnished in a country style; two enjoy a view of the Vercors. Regional art exhibitions are regularly held in the vaulted dining room complete with fireplace and columns: try the delicious home-grown produce.

Access : *8km eastbound from Vienne on the D 41, then the D 502*

Access : *4km to the north-west of Chichilianne on a minor road*

GRESSE-EN-VERCORS - 38650

31

LE CHÂLET HÔTEL PRAYER
M. Prayer

Le Village
38650 Gresse-en-Vercors
Tel. 04 76 34 32 08
lechalet@free.fr
http://lechalet.free.fr
Langues : Eng.

Closed from 11 Mar to 5 May, 7 Oct to 22 Dec and Wed except school holidays • 20 rooms and 5 apartments, all have bath/WC or shower/WC and television • €56 to €82; breakfast €10; half-board available • Menus €20 to €50 • Terrace, garage, car park. No dogs admitted • Outdoor swimming pool, tennis, petanque

 Botanical walks in the high mountain pastures.

Despite its name and warm atmosphere, this hotel bears more resemblance to a prosperous farm than a chalet. The bedrooms are being progressively renovated and all have a view of the village and the mountains. Take a seat in one of the comfortable dining rooms and tuck into large helpings of traditional cuisine. A glance at the visitors' book reveals a number of famous patrons, including actor Gérard Dépardieu and Albert II of Belgium.

Access : *In the centre of the village*

LANS-EN-VERCORS - 38250

32

LE VAL FLEURI
M. Bonnard

730 avenue Léopold-Fabre
38250 Lans-en-Vercors
Tel. 04 76 95 41 09
levalfleuri@aol.com
www.le-val-fleuri.com
Langues : Eng., Ger., Sp.

Open from mid-May to 20 Sep and from 20 Dec to 20 Mar • 14 rooms, all have bath/WC and television • €36 to €65; breakfast €8.80; half-board available • Menus €18.85 (weekdays) to €30 • Terrace, garden, garage, car park. No dogs admitted in restaurant

 An action-packed resort perfect for energetic children!

The old belfry of the church stands guard over the blue shutters of the Val Fleuri Hotel, built in the 1920s. Almost as if defying time to take its toll of the delightfully old-fashioned interior, the decoration of the dining room is exactly as it was when the establishment opened and some of the beautifully-kept bedrooms still boast their original Art Deco furniture or lamps. The fresh mountain air on the terrace, under the lime trees in the flowered garden, will whet your appetite.

Access : *On the main road, behind the church*

LE PIN - 38730

LES BALCONS DU LAC
M. Ferrard

145 chemin de Béluran Lieu-dit
Vers-Ars
38730 Le Pin
Tel. 04 76 06 68 82

Closed during Christmas school holidays
• 5 rooms with bathrooms • €44, breakfast
included • Table d'hôte €16 (evenings only)
• Credit cards not accepted

 Watch Lake Paladru change colour throughout the day.

Half the windows of this gradually restored old farmhouse face Lake Paladru, while the other half gaze out over fields and woods. The majority of the snug, simple bedrooms enjoy a view of the lake's deep waters; three have a kitchenette and all have spanking-new bathrooms. In the morning, you will breakfast in an enormous living room, in the centre of which stands a pyramidal fireplace. Warm and friendly.

Access : *1km to the south-west of Paladru Lake on the D 50*

L'ISLE-D'ABEAU - 38080

LE RELAIS DU ÇATEY
M. Ducrettet

10 rue du Didier - Le Bourg
38080 L'Isle-d'Abeau
Tel. 04 74 18 26 50
relaiscatey@aol.com
www.le-relais-du-catey.com
Langues : Eng.

Closed 30 Jul to 22 Aug, 24 Dec to 2 Jan • 7 rooms with bath/WC or shower/WC and television • €55 to €64; breakfast €6.40; half-board available • Restaurant closed Sun; menus €29 to €51 • Terrace, garden, car park

 Sample the chef's creative recipes on the terrace.

This elegant Louis XV house surrounded by trees and flowers lies in a residential district, only 10min from the international airport of Lyons. The cosy comfort of the bedrooms has recently been enhanced following high-quality renovation work. Wrought-iron and tasteful paintings adorn the contemporary restaurant, further set off by the original flagstones. Lime and Indian bean trees shade the pleasant terrace. Excellent, imaginative cuisine.

Access : *North-west of Bourgoin-Jallieu*

MEYLAN - 38240

MIZOEN - 38142

LE MAS DU BRUCHET
M. et Mme Ferguson

Chemin du Bruchet
38240 Meylan
Tel. 04 76 90 18 30
anne-marie.ferguson@wanadoo.fr

Closed from 15 Aug to 1 Sep • 4 rooms upstairs with bathrooms and modem • €55 to €65, breakfast included • No table d'hôte • Dogs not admitted

LE PANORAMIQUE
M. Keesman

Route des Aymes
38142 Mizoen
Tel. 04 76 80 06 25
info@hotel-panoramique.com
www.hotel-panoramique.com

Closed from 15 Apr to 16 May and 23 Sep to 20 Dec • 9 rooms, 5 of which are non-smoking, all have bath/WC or shower/WC and television • €70 to €80; breakfast €10; half-board available • Evenings only except weekends, public and school holidays; menus €20 to €28 • Non-smoking establishment, terrace, garden, car park. No dogs admitted • Sauna

 The splendid site on the Meylan heights, opposite the valley and at the foot of St-Eymard.

This 18C farmhouse was the home of the grandparents of Estelle Fournier, with whom Hector Berlioz fell hopelessly in love. Four attractive rooms are located in the former barn with wooden floors and wrought-iron bedsteads. Each room bears the name of a type of grape and commands a magnificent view of the Alps. The owner, a keen oenologist, runs a small vineyard and will be more than happy to show you his cellar and have you taste his produce.

 If you're lucky, you may catch a glimpse of the chamois who live in the mountains.

In the summer, window boxes laden with geraniums adorn the balconies of this hillside chalet. Recently purchased by a young couple from the Netherlands who speak Dutch, French, English, German and Spanish, the atmosphere is decidedly polyglot. Among the establishment's numerous appeals are the warm mountain-style adopted in the bedrooms, a south-facing terrace, sauna and a superb panoramic view of the town, Oisans Valley and surrounding mountains.

Access : *3km northeast of Grenoble on the N 90*

Access : *Between Le Freney-d'Oisans and the Barrage du Chambon tunnel, leave the N 91 and take the D 25*

MOISSIEU-SUR-DOLON - 38270

DOMAINE DE LA COLOMBIÈRE
Mme Carle

Château de Moissieu
38270 Moissieu-sur-Dolon
Tel. 04 74 79 50 23
colombieremoissieu@hotmail.com
www.lacolombiere.com

Closed from 24 to 30 Dec, Feb school holidays, Sun evening and Mon (except public holidays) • 21 air-conditioned rooms, 2 of which have disabled access, all have bath/WC or shower/WC and television • €79 to €118; breakfast €12; half-board available • Air-conditioned restaurant; menus €29 to €67 • Car park, park, terrace • Swimming pool

Ideal for nature-lovers.

This handsome abode, built in 1820, stands in over 10 acres of well-tended grounds. Cleverly restored and turned into a hotel, the establishment offers spacious, brightly coloured rooms, each of which is named after a famous painter and a copy of each artist's paintings, painted by the lady of the house, hangs on the walls of the rooms. The restaurant, located in the estate's only contemporary construction, has a terrace overlooking the idyllic countryside.

Access : *Near the village*

LES BASSES PORTES
M. et Mme Giroud-Ducaroy

Torjonas
38118 Saint-Baudille-de-la-Tour
Tel. 04 74 95 18 23
mirvinc@wanadoo.fr
www.basses-portes.com
Langues : Eng., Sp.

Closed 15 Nov to 15 Jan • 3 rooms with shower/WC • €52 to €54, breakfast included • Table d'hôte €19 • Terrace, park, car park. Credit cards not accepted, no dogs admitted • Swimming pool

A happy marriage of past and present.

Extensive renovation work has restored this old farmhouse without removing any of its rustic charm. Whenever possible, the old stones, beams and parquet floors have been preserved. The somewhat surprising style of the bedrooms features a happy blend of old and new, in addition to brand-new bathrooms. A perfect base camp to explore the Île Crémieu.

Access : *2km northbound on the D 52B*

SAINT-LATTIER - 38840

39

LE LIÈVRE AMOUREUX
M. Lapeyre

La Gare
38840 Saint-Lattier
Tel. 04 76 64 50 67
contact@lelievreamoureux.com
www.lelievreamoureux.com
Langues : Eng., Ger.

Closed Jan • 3 rooms and 2 apartments, all have bath/WC or shower/WC • €70 to €75; breakfast €7 • Table d'hôte €30 to €45 • Terrace, garden, kitchenette

The professionalism of the owner.

This former hunting-lodge and former star establishment has been brought back to life by the renovation works carried out by the welcoming owner. Three spacious and personalised bedrooms and two split-level apartments will ensure that your stay is comfortable. The table d'hôte is a feast of local recipes and savours: fresh local produce (truffles, ravioles, walnuts) served with wines that guests can choose themselves from the cellar, served either in the dining room with an open fire or on the terrace.

Access : *Head towards A 49, exit no 8, Baume d'Hostun, go through Eymeux, beyond the bridge, turn right, at the roundabout, head towards Saint-Lattier*

SAINT-MARTIN-DE-LA-CLUZE - 38650

40

LE CHÂTEAU DE PÂQUIER
M. Rossi

38650 Saint-Martin-de-la-Cluze
Tel. 04 76 72 77 33
hrossi@club-internet.fr
http://chateaudepaquier.free.fr
Langues : Eng., Ger.

Open all year (by reservation in winter) • 5 rooms with shower/WC • €65 to 80, breakfast included • Table d'hôte €22, beverages included • Garden, car park. Dogs not admitted.

Unaffected and welcoming.

The owners have clearly put their body and soul into the restoration of the Renaissance castle and pretty garden and the result happily does justice to their efforts. Countless decorative features have been preserved, such as the exposed beams, wooden ceiling, spiral staircase and mullioned windows. The spacious rooms are beautifully decorated and furnished; one affords you a rare opportunity of sleeping in an old chapel. Garden produce and meat chargrilled on the open fire.

Access : *12km northbound from Monestier-de-Clermont on the N 75 and a minor road*

TREFFORT - 38650

LE CHÂTEAU D'HERBELON
M. Castillan

Lac de Monteynard
38650 Treffort
Tel. 04 76 34 02 03
chateaudherbelon@wanadoo.fr
www.chateau-herbelon.fr
Langues : Eng.

Closed from 20 Dec to 4 Mar, Mon and Tue except Jul-Aug • 9 rooms, all have bath/WC and television • €61 to €84; breakfast €8.50; half-board available • Menus €22 to €37 • Terrace, garden, car park. No dogs admitted in rooms • Ideal for wind-surfing

 The 20km-long lake is renowned for its windsurfing.

This traditional country house covered in Virginia creeper and climbing roses stands on the banks of the Monteynard reservoir lake. A great deal of care and attention has clearly been lavished on the sizeable, usefully equipped rooms. An old stone fireplace adds character to the restaurant, while a lovely vaulted room in the basement is regularly rented out for weddings, communions and other family banquets. Children's play area in the walled garden.

Access : *By the lake, 3km on the D 110E*

URIAGE-LES-BAINS - 38410

LES MÉSANGES
M. Prince

Route de Bouloud
38410 Uriage-les-Bains
Tel. 04 76 89 70 69
prince@hotel-les-mesanges.com
www.hotel-les-mesanges.com
Langues : Eng.

Closed from 20 Oct to 1 Feb • 33 rooms with bath/WC or shower/WC and television • €60 to €75; breakfast €8.50; half-board available • Menus €22 to €55 • Terrace, garden, car park. No dogs admitted • Swimming pool, table-tennis, petanque, play area

 Savouring the utter peace and quiet.

The villa overlooks the spa resort and castle. Ask for one of the renovated, practical rooms with balcony and enjoy the view over the Chamrousse or Vercors mountain ranges. A light, airy dining room in a modern style, pleasant terrace shaded by plane trees, peaceful garden with a play area and swimming pool complete the facilities of this family-run establishment.

Access : *Avenue des Thermes, drive along the park, turn left onto the Chamrousse road, then at the spa hospital, turn right on Bouloud road*

VIGNIEU - 38890

CHÂTEAU DE CHAPEAU CORNU
M. Regnier

Le Rual
38890 Vignieu
Tel. 04 74 27 79 00
chapeau.cornu@wanadoo.fr
www.chateau-chapeau-cornu.fr
Langues : Eng.

Closed from 23 Dec to 3 Jan and Sun evening except in Jul and Aug • 21 rooms (and 2 apartments) with bath/WC or shower/WC and television • €67 to €170; breakfast €9 to €12; half-board available • Menus €22 (weekdays) to €68 • Terrace, park, private car park. No dogs admitted • Outdoor swimming pool

 If only a night in this fairy-tale castle could turn our fortunes from rags to riches!

The names of the former owners of this 13C fortified castle, Capella and Cornutti, explain the origins of the castle's amusing name which translates as Battered Hat. The rooms, which are gradually being treated to a new coat of paint, tasteful fabrics and wrought-iron furniture all have antique wardrobes; some also boast a four-poster bed. A stone-vaulted dining room, attractive inner courtyard terrace and a 10-acre park with ornamental pools and tree-lined paths complete the picture.

Access : *From Bourgoin-Jallieu take the N 6 (towards Lyon), then right on the D 522 as far as Flosaille, then the D 19 and 5km after Saint-Clef, turn right*

COMMELLE-VERNAY - 42120

CHÂTEAU DE BACHELARD
M. et Mme Noirard

440 route de Commelle
42120 Commelle-Vernay
Tel. 04 77 71 93 67
bachelard@worldonline.fr
www.chateaubachelard.com
Langues : Eng.

Open all year • 4 non-smoking rooms and 1 apartment, all with bath/WC or shower/WC • €93, breakfast included • Park, car park. Credit cards not accepted • Outdoor swimming pool, pond with fishing

 The owner's warm hospitality.

A peaceful relaxed atmosphere reigns throughout this elegant 17C manor house on the doorstep of Roanne. The personalised bedrooms, including the most unusual "Peintre" and the apartment which can sleep 6, are full of character and floral frescoes in a particularly immaculate setting. The vast dining room opens onto the park, swimming pool and teak furnished terrace where breakfast is served when the weather permits.

Access : *3km south of Roanne*

FEURS - 42110

LA BUSSINIÈRE
M. et Mme Perrin

Route de Lyon
42110 Feurs
Tel. 04 77 27 06 36
la-bussiniere@wanadoo.fr

www.labussiniere.com

Open all year • 3 rooms with shower/WC • €41, breakfast included • Table d'hôte €16 (evenings only) • Garden, car park. Credit cards not accepted

We most liked **The lady of the house's ceaseless quest for perfection.**

The comfort of this renovated farmhouse leaves nothing to be desired: everything has been designed with the welfare of the guest in mind, from the digicode-access on the main gate and the excellent soundproofing to the high quality bedding. Huge beams and tasteful colours adorn the stylish bedrooms, which have immaculate bathrooms. Meals are taken around the large table in the dining room.

Access : *3km eastbound from Feurs on the D 89, towards Lyon*

NOAILLY - 42640

CHÂTEAU DE LA MOTTE
M. et Mme Froumajou

42640 Noailly
Tel. 04 77 66 64 60
chateaudelamotte@wanadoo.fr
www.chateaudelamotte.net
Langues : Eng.

Open all year • 6 non-smoking rooms, all with bath/WC, television and Internet access • €74 to €105, breakfast included • Table d'hôte €24, including beverages • Terrace, park, car park, reading and games room. Dogs not admitted in dining room • Outdoor swimming pool, fitness facilities and sauna

 We most liked **The graceful south façade.**

This stunning 18C château, tucked away in five hectares of grounds with swimming pool, is home to spacious, well cared for rooms, each of which is named after a famous writer. The "George Sand", capable of sleeping four people, is ideal for families, while "Lamartine" with a lovely round bathtub and four-poster bed, is a favourite with newly weds. The owners' friendly welcome cannot be faulted, nor can their authentic cooking in which fresh produce takes pride of place.

"Initiation to gastronomy" course, keep-fit course

Access : *In the town*

PANISSIÈRES - 42360

LA FERME DES ROSES
M. Barthélémy

Le Clair
42360 Panissières
Tel. 04 77 28 63 63
jednostka.arabians@free.fr
www.gites-de-France-loire.com
Langues : Ger., Eng., It.

Open all year • 5 non-smoking rooms, all with bath/WC or shower/WC and television • €52 to €57, breakfast included • Table d'hôte €16 • Terrace, garden, car park. Credit cards not accepted, dogs not admitted • Outdoor swimming pool

 The enchanting floral decoration.

The rooms of this old farmhouse, built in 1813, are all named after roses, the owner's second passion after horses. All are furnished in a contemporary style and two, "Rose des peintres" and "Rose de Resht" can sleep up to five people. Local produce features prominently on the menu and meals are served either by the fireside or on the terrace; don't miss the traditional "Forézien snack" served at breakfast time.

Possibility of "clay" courses on the theme of ceramics, pottery or painting

Access : *Go through Feurs, towards Panissières on the D 60*

RENAISON - 42370

PLATELIN
M. et Mme de Bats

42370 Renaison
Tel. 04 77 64 29 12
contact@platelin.com
www.platelin.com
Langues : Eng.

Open all year • 2 non-smoking rooms and 1 apartment, all with bath/WC, television and kitchenette • €60 to €75, breakfast included • No table d'hôte • Garden, car park. Credit cards not accepted • Sitting room-library with piano, outdoor swimming pool

 The view of the Roannais mountains.

Those in search of peace and quiet will fall in love with this former wine-growers' family estate tucked away in the countryside. The apartment, in the converted henhouse is called "Poules" (hens), while the "Lapins" (rabbits) and "Vaches" (cows) rooms are equally bucolic in inspiration; all are tastefully decorated and each has its own secluded garden area with deckchair and access to the swimming pool. The large sitting room, also home to the reception area, boasts a pleasant library corner and a grand piano.

Access : *On the way into the village from Roanne*

SAINT-PIERRE-LA-NOAILLE - 42190

SAINT-MAURICE-SUR-LOIRE - 42155

L'ÉCHAUGUETTE
M. et Mme Alex

Ruelle Guy-de-la-Mûre
42155 Saint-Maurice-sur-Loire
Tel. 04 77 63 15 89
contact@echauguette-alex.com
www.echauguette-alex.com
Langues : Ger., Eng., It.

Open all year • 4 rooms with shower/WC • €65 to €75 breakfast included • Table d'hôte €25 (evening only) • Credit cards not accepted, no dogs admitted

DOMAINE DU CHÂTEAU DE MARCHANGY
Mme Grandeau

42190 Saint-Pierre-la-Noaille
Tel. 04 77 69 96 76
contact@marchangy.com
www.marchangy.com
Langues : Eng.

Open all year • 3 rooms with bath/WC and television • €85 to €98, breakfast included • No table d'hôte • Park, car park. Credit cards not accepted • Swimming pool

 Watch the pleasure boats on the lake.

It is difficult to resist the charm of these three houses hidden in a medieval village opposite the peaceful waters of Lake Villerest. All the tastefully decorated rooms are different: one has a fireplace, the other enjoys a view of the lake encircled by hills, while the last overlooks the keep and church. Breakfasts are served on the terrace or behind the kitchen's bay windows: a feast for the palate, and the eyes.

A life of luxury - for just a few euros!

An oak-lined drive leads up to this idyllic 18C château in front of which is a large courtyard. The rooms, located in the former outhouses of the estate, are quiet and brimming with charm: restored parquet floors, family furniture, rugs, canopy beds, curios and paintings. The park, overlooking the countryside, is home to hundred-year-old trees and a splendid swimming pool. A few rows of vines produce a table wine that can only be tasted on the property.

Access : *5.5km north-west of Charlieu on the D 227 then a minor road*

Access : *12km to the south-west of Roanne on the D 53 and the D 203*

SAINT-ROMAIN-LE-PUY - 42610

SOUS LE PIC - LA PÉROLIÈRE
M. Perol

20 rue Jean-Moulin
42610 Saint-Romain-le-Puy
Tel. 04 77 76 97 10
laperoliere@wanadoo.fr
www.laperoliere.com

Closed 8 Jan to 5 Mar • 4 non-smoking rooms, 1 with handicapped access, all have bath/WC or shower/WC, television and modem access • €55 to €70, breakfast included • No table d'hôte • Terrace, car park. Credit cards not accepted, dogs not admitted • Golf, fishing, tennis nearby

We most liked **The charming welcome of the mistress of the house.**

This tastefully restored farmhouse stands at the foot of an 11C priory, attractively lit up in the evenings. After a restful night's sleep in one of the unpretentious inviting rooms, you will be ready to do full justice to a generous breakfast table laden with fruit salad, home-made cakes and jams, etc, before lingering in the sitting room, whose decoration and book shelves pay homage to the Forez region. There is no table d'hôte, but the owner can recommend a host of excellent restaurants.

Access : *7km from Montbrison on the D 8, then right onto the D 107*

ST-JULIEN-MOLIN-MOLETTE - 42220

LA RIVOIRE
M. et Mme Thiollière

42220 Saint-Julien-Molin-Molette
Tel. 04 77 39 65 44
info@larivoire.net
www.larivoire.net
Langues : Eng.

Open all year • 5 rooms with shower/WC • €57 to €62, breakfast included, half-board available • Table d'hôte €19 drinks included • Terrace, garden, car park. Credit cards not accepted, no dogs admitted

We most liked **Cottage-garden vegetables and local meats on the menu.**

A circular stone tower and enormous kitchen garden contribute to the appeal of this lovely stately home, thought to date from the 15C. It enjoys a lovely position in the Nature Park of Pilat, overlooking the fir trees of the Ardèche hillsides, which is the view you will have from the cheerful rooms. Three sitting rooms, complete with piano, board games and a television, are reserved for the use of guests.

Access : *5km eastbound from Bourg-Argental on the N 82*

VILLEMONTAIS - 42155

DOMAINE DU FONTENAY
M. et Mme Hawkins

42155 Villemontais
Tel. 04 77 63 12 22
hawkins@tele2.fr
www.domainedufontenay.com
Langues : Eng.

Open all year • 4 non-smoking rooms, all with bath/WC or shower/WC • €65, breakfast included • No table d'hôte • Terrace, car park, kitchenette. Dogs not admitted • Wine tasting

We most liked **The owners' matchless kindness.**

A small lane winding up through the vines leads to this guesthouse set in a 10ha wine-growing estate. All the rooms of the handsome property command stunning views of the vineyards and the Roanne plain. The spacious, light and tastefully decorated rooms look out over the surrounding vineyards. The friendly owners offer wine tasting sessions of their excellent wine, made according to ancient traditions.

Access : Leave Roanne by Clermont, follow the D 53 for 10km, at the roundabout turn left towards the motorway and follow signs to Domaine du Fontenay

FLEURIE - 69820

DOMAINE DU CLOS DES GARANDS
Mme Yves

Les Garands
69820 Fleurie
Tel. 04 74 69 80 01
contact@closdesgarands.fr
www.closdesgarands.fr
Langues : Eng.

Open all year • 4 non-smoking rooms, all with bath/WC or shower/WC • €84 to €104, breakfast included • No table d'hôte • Park, car park. Dogs not admitted

 We most liked **The stunning view of Fleurie and the Beaujolais mountains.**

A path winding through the vines leads to this superb 6ha fully walled estate. The house and terrace command a striking view of the village and vineyards. Great attention has clearly been lavished on the interior decoration (1930's, Louis XVI and contemporary furniture) and the rooms, named after flowers, are attractively personalised. The owners offer wine tasting sessions in their sumptuous vaulted cellar.

Access : At Romanèche-Thorins, turn right onto the D 32 towards Fleurie. Before the "Fleurie" signpost, turn right and follow the "Gîtes de France" sign

JULLIÉ - 69840

LE DOMAINE DE LA CHAPELLE DE VÂTRE
M. Capart

Le Bourbon
69840 Jullié
Tel. 04 74 04 43 57
vatre@wanadoo.fr
www.vatre.com
Langues : Eng., Sp., Du.

Closed during grape harvest • 3 non-smoking rooms, 2 in a different wing, all with bathroom and WC • €60 to €95, breakfast included • No table d'hôte • Terrace, car park. Dogs not admitted • Outdoor swimming pool

 The happy marriage between modern interior design and old walls.

This estate, perched on the top of a hill, commands an outstanding panorama over the vineyards and the Saône Valley. A couple of Belgians, who fell in love with the property and bought it on the spot, have restored it and created three characterful rooms which combine old and new, as well as an equally attractive gîte. In the upper part of the estate, an overflow swimming pool looks down on the castle of La Roche.

Wine tasting and oenology

Access : *3km southbound of Jullié, at Moulin-Aujas, take the Émeringes road and the lane to the right*

LANCIÉ - 69220

LES PASQUIERS
M. et Mme Gandilhon

69220 Lancié
Tel. 04 74 69 86 33
lespasquiers@wanadoo.fr
www.lespasquiers.com
Langues : Eng., Ger.

Open all year • 4 rooms, 1 with disabled access, all with shower/WC • €80, breakfast included • Table d'hôte (closed Mon evening and Sun) €25 • Garden, car park. Credit cards not accepted, no dogs allowed • Outdoor swimming pool

 A step back in time to Second Empire France.

High walls protect this lovely old house and garden from prying eyes. Many of the decorative features inside are original, such as the moulded ceilings, fireplace, carpets, library and grand piano in the sitting room. The rooms in the main house are furnished with 19C antiques, while those in the outbuilding have been reworked to a more modern design with coconut matting, bathrooms hidden by Japanese screens and children's drawings. The terrace is laid next to the swimming pool.

Access : *2km southbound from Romanèche-Thorins*

LES HALLES - 69610

LES ARDILLATS - 69430

M. ET MME BONNOT
M. et Mme Bonnot

Le Bourg
69430 Les Ardillats
Tel. 04 74 04 80 20
www.beaujeu.com

Closed in Jan • 5 rooms with shower/WC • €45, breakfast included; half-board available • Table d'hôte €17 • Garden, car park. Credit cards not accepted, no dogs admitted

MANOIR DE TOURVILLE
M. et Mme Goubier

69610 Les Halles
Tel. 04 74 26 66 57
tourville@manoirdetourville.com
www.manoirdetourville.com
Langues : Eng.

Open all year • 6 non-smoking rooms and 1 apartment, all have bath/WC or shower/WC • €65 to €120, breakfast included • Table d'hôte €23 to €45 (evenings only and by reservation) • Park, car park. No dogs admitted in rooms

Pamper your taste-buds in this lovely Beaujolais home.

This handsome farm on the doorstep of a sleepy country village is the sort of place you dream of. Its thick stone walls and natural wooden shutters immediately catch the eye, which is further treated to the vision of a lovely country interior. Bright colours and thick beams paint the juicy picture of the rooms, each of which is named after a fruit – raspberry, pineapple, plum, grapefruit and mandarin. Sample the delicious home cooking, washed down with a fruity glass of Beaujolais.

Access : *5km to the north-west of Beaujeu on the D 37*

The immense 20hectare grounds.

Tree-lined grounds, dotted with small lakes which are home to swans and ducks, surround this mansion which dates back to the 14C. Handsome staircases lead up to the bedrooms and to the apartment fitted out with antiques. French breakfasts and delicious family cooking made with home-grown or local produce are served in a beautiful dining room complete with wood panelling and floors.

Access : *On the D 4 between Ste-Foy-l'Argentière and St-Laurent-de-Chamrousset*

LUCENAY - 69480

59

LES TILLEULS
Mme Vermare Michèle

31 route de Lachassagne
69480 Lucenay
Tel. 04 74 60 28 58
vermare@hotmail.com
www.lestilleuls.org
Langues : Eng.

Open all year • 3 non-smoking rooms on two floors, one of which in a separate wing, all have bath/WC or shower/WC • €90 to €105, breakfast included • Table d'hôte €30 • Terrace. Credit cards not accepted, dogs not admitted • Golf, water-sports centre

 The delightful warm welcome.

This former wine-grower's house, parts of which date from the 17C, stands opposite the village church. The interior decoration is an elegant combination of old and new (bare stone walls, timber beams and modern furniture), both in the dining room and sitting room, as in the three cheerful personalised bedrooms. The owner, a keen cook, adores concocting mouth-watering dishes to the delight of her guests and is planning on running cooking courses taught by a chef.

Access : *In the town*

QUINCIÉ-EN-BEAUJOLAIS - 69430

60

GÉRARD LAGNEAU
M. et Mme Lagneau

Huire
69430 Quincié-en-Beaujolais
Tel. 04 74 69 20 70
jealagneau@wanadoo.fr
www.domainelagneau.com
Langues : Eng.

Open all year • 4 non-smoking rooms upstairs, all have bathrooms • €58, breakfast included • No table d'hôte • Garden, car park. Credit cards not accepted

 A genuine wine-growing atmosphere.

A hamlet encircled by vineyards is the scene for the pleasant stone-built home of this wine-growing family who bend over backwards to make you feel at home with them. The rooms upstairs are simply decorated and spotlessly clean. You will breakfast under the beams of a rustic room. The icing on the cake is, however, the 16C cellar. Where better to sample the house vintages?

Access : *In the middle of the vineyards*

QUINCIÉ-EN-BEAUJOLAIS - 69430

DOMAINE DE ROMARAND
M. et Mme Berthelot

69430 Quincié-en-Beaujolais
Tel. 04 74 04 34 49
Langues : Eng.

Closed 25 Dec and Jan 1 • 4 rooms with shower/WC • €58 to €60, breakfast included • Table d'hôte €22 (evenings only by reservation) • Garden, car park • Outdoor swimming pool. Wine tasting and sales

 The overwhelming bouquet of fine wines.

This lovely stone house run by a wine-growing couple is set in a U-shaped courtyard overlooking a flowered rock garden, vineyards and the surrounding mountains. All the modern, comfortable rooms enjoy the same panoramic view. The rafters, fireplace, huge wooden table and maps of the Beaujolais region add character to the dining room. A profusion of home-made pastries and jams adds that little extra to breakfast time.

Access : *9km to the south-east of Beaujeu on the D 37 and the D 9, then drive towards Varennes*

SAINT-LAURENT-DE-MURE - 69720

HOSTELLERIE LE SAINT-LAURENT
M. Lavault

8 rue Croix-Blanche
69720 Saint-Laurent-de-Mure
Tel. 04 78 40 91 44
le.st.laurent@wanadoo.fr
www.lesaintlaurent.fr
Langues : Eng.

Closed from 9 to 15 Apr, 7, 18 and 20 May, 29 Jul to 19 Aug, 26 Dec to 1 Jan, • 30 rooms with bath/WC or shower/WC, all have television • €62 to €115; breakfast €7 • Menus €22 to €60 • Terrace, park, 2 car parks, one of which is private. No dogs admitted in rooms

 Entirely devoted to guests' welfare.

This 18C mansion and its flowered park make an ideal stopover for weary travellers. It offers small, comfortable rooms – those in a separate wing are more modern. At mealtimes, you can choose between the warmth of maple wood or immense bay windows overlooking the greenery. In fine weather, the shade of the three-hundred-year-old lime tree is sheer bliss.

Access : *15km from Lyon, set back from the N 6*

THIZY - 69240

VAUX-EN-BEAUJOLAIS - 69460

LA TERRASSE
M. et Mme Arnette

Le Bourg - Marnand
69240 Thizy
Tel. 04 74 64 19 22
francis.arnette@wanadoo.fr
www.laterrasse-marnand.com
Langues : Eng., Sp.

Closed during Feb and Nov half-terms, Mon (except the hotel) and Sun evening (except in summer) • 10 rooms, one of which has disabled access, with bath/WC and television • €46; breakfast €6.50; half-board available • Menus €14 (weekdays) to €60 • Terrace, car park • Children's games room

 Just six kilometres from the water-sports of Lake Sapins.

This old textile factory, typical of the Beaujolais region, has been turned into a hotel. The agreeable rooms with terraces open directly onto the garden; each is named after a flower or aromatic plant and the decoration, even the fragrance, matches the theme. Two modern, soberly decorated dining rooms and a spacious terrace overlooking the mountains of the Lyonnais complete the picture: their modern menu features regionally inspired recipes.

Access : *2km to the north-east on the D 94, on the way into Bourg-Marnand, opposite the town hall*

LES PICORETTES
M. et Mme Blettner

Montrichard
69460 Vaux-en-Beaujolais
Tel. 04 74 02 14 07
francis.bletner@picorettes.com
www.picorettes.com
Langues : Eng.

Open all year • 4 non-smoking rooms and 1 apartment, all with bath/WC and shower/WC • €65 to €100, breakfast included • Table d'hôte €25 (evenings only) • Car park. Dogs not admitted • Outdoor swimming pool

 The amiable welcome.

The handsome Beaujolais-style house of Josette and Francis Blettner has three bedrooms and one family apartment. All are treated to fresh flowers every day. On the second floor, the "Vigne" room commands the best view of the village. Extremely generous breakfasts (cheese, eggs, bread, home-made jam) are followed by more traditional dishes in the evenings (blanquette de veau, Bresse chicken).

Access : *1.5km westbound from Vaux-en-Beaujolais on the D49 to a place known as Montrichard*

AIX-LES-BAINS - 73100

AIX-LES-BAINS - 73100

AUBERGE SAINT-SIMOND
M. et Mme Mattana

130 avenue Saint-Simond
73100 Aix-les-Bains
Tel. 04 79 88 35 02
auberge@saintsimond.com
www.saintsimond.com
Languages : Eng., It.

Closed in Jan, Nov school holidays, 22 to 31 Dec and Sun evening • 28 rooms, 2 of which have disabled access, all have bath/WC or shower/WC and television • €55 to €75; breakfast €9; half-board available • Menus €25 to €35 • Car park, terrace, garden. No dogs admitted in restaurant • Swimming pool

 The garden lined with trees and flowers.

For over a century, travellers have been resting their weary legs in this former post house then inn, just a few minutes from the Lac du Bourget. Eight rooms have been renovated and treated to soundproofing and new furniture, bedding and decoration. The others are comfortable if a little plain; some have a balcony; we recommend those overlooking the garden. Local dishes are served in the dining room-veranda which extends onto a terrace shaded by lovely old plane trees.

Access : *Near the town centre*

LA CROIX DU SUD
Mme Collot

3 rue du Docteur-Duvernay
73100 Aix-les-Bains
Tel. 04 79 35 05 87
ecrire@hotel-lacroixdusud.com

 www.hotel-lacroixdusud.com
Languages : Eng., Port.

Closed from 4 Nov to 5 Apr • 16 rooms, some have bath/WC or shower/WC and television • €30 to €42; breakfast €6 • No restaurant • Small courtyard-garden. Credit cards not accepted • Television room with a small library

 The old-fashioned charm of this early 20C bourgeois home.

Could it be to conjure up memories of his trips to distant lands that the former owner built up this collection of hats from the world over? Equally popular with tourists and "patients" come to take the waters, this hotel is renowned for its faultless hospitality. The generously-dimensioned bedrooms sport a stylish old-fashioned blend of moulded ceilings and marble fireplaces.

Access : *In the town centre, in a small, quiet street*

AUSSOIS - 73500

BOURG-SAINT-MAURICE - 73700

SOLEIL
M. Montaz

15 rue de l'Église
73500 Aussois
Tel. 04 79 20 32 42
hotel-du-soleile@wanadoo.fr
www.hotel-du-soleil.com

Closed from 21 Apr to 15 Jun and 30 Sep to
17 Dec • 22 rooms, one of which has disabled
access, with bath/WC or shower/WC, all have
television • €71.80 to €83.80, breakfast €8.50;
half-board available • Menus €20 to €22 (evenings only) • Terrace, car park. No dogs admitted in rooms • Cinema room, sauna, hammam,
jacuzzi, souvenir shop, billiards, skiing in season

 **Discover the thrill of the 2 560m Via
Ferrata rock-climbing course – the longest
in France.**

Next door to the church, whose bells are con-
siderate enough to remain silent after nightfall, the walls of this austere chalet hide a
warm interior. The rooms enjoy superb views
of the village and the Vanoise range; ask for one
of the renovated chalet-style rooms with light
wood and pretty fabrics. There is no lack of
outdoor activities from the roof terrace sun
deck, open air jacuzzi, giant chess board and
skittles, while indoors, you can sample the
sauna, hammam and home cinema facilities.

Access : *Near the church*

L'AUTANTIC
Mme Bourgeois

69 route d'Hauteville
73700 Bourg-Saint-Maurice
Tel. 04 79 07 01 70
bonjour@hotel-autantic.fr

 www.hotel-autantic.com

Open all year • 29 rooms, 2 of which have
disabled access, with bath/WC (2 have
shower/WC) and television • €40 to €130;
breakfast €8 • No restaurant • Car park • Indoor
swimming pool, sauna

**Tasting the thrills of white-water rafting on
the Bourg.**

The stone walls and narrow windows of this
sturdy house, in the style of a traditional
mountain chalet, were built recently in a quiet
district of Bourg St Maurice, near the futuristic
funicular railway up to the Arcs resort. The
rooms, decorated with roughcast walls and
pine furniture, overlook the peaceful valley
and four have a balcony. Friendly staff and
breakfast on the terrace are among the other
perks of this modern chalet.

Access : *On the way into the village, a little set
back from the road*

CREST-VOLAND - 73590

CREST-VOLAND - 73590

LES CAMPANULES
Mme Chevreton

Chemin de la Grange
73590 Crest-Voland
Tel. 04 79 31 81 43
chanteline@wanadoo.fr
www.lescampanules.com

Open from 6 Sep to 25 Aug • 2 non-smoking rooms and 1 apartment, with bath/WC • €57 to €65, breakfast included, half-board available • Table d'hôte €20 • Car park. Dogs not admitted

LE CAPRICE DES NEIGES
Famille Borrel

Route du Col des Saisies
73590 Crest-Voland
Tel. 04 79 31 62 95
info@hotel-capricedesneiges.com
www.hotel-capricedesneiges.com
Langues : Eng.

Closed from mid-Apr to mid-Jun and mid-Sep to mid-Dec • 16 rooms with bath/WC, some have television • €74 to €90; breakfast €9; half-board available • Menus €15 to €40 • Terrace, garden, car park. Dogs not admitted • In summer: tennis, fly fishing, mini-golf; in winter: skiing and snowshoe hiking

The splendid view of the Aravis range and Mont Charmin from the flower-decked balconies.

This contemporary chalet, designed in a style typical of the second half of the 20C, in the Crest-Voland skiing resort on the sunny slopes of Mont Lachat, is heaven to those who love peace and quiet and the outdoors. The comfortable rooms are tastefully decorated and adorned with patchwork quilts, the work of the lady of the house. Generous breakfasts, served on the balcony surrounding the dining room in summer. Local specialities and produce take pride of place on the menu. Warm welcome.

Little teddy bears adorn some of the rooms of this friendly, family establishment.

The soft warm hues of wood greet the eye wherever you look in this exquisite chalet, just outside the village but at the foot of the slopes. Step into its welcoming doll's house interior and feast your eyes on the lovely fabrics, ornaments and Savoyard furniture. The rooms on the second floor have been renovated and it is planned to refurbish the others in the near future. All offer spectacular views of the Aravis and the mountain pastures. Regional delicacies.

Access : *On the road from Col des Saisies, 1km from the resort and 50m from the ski lift*

Access : *6km southbound from Flumet on the N212*

LA CÔTE-D'AIME - 73210

LA GIETTAZ - 73590

CHALET LE PARADOU
M. Hanrard

Pré Bérard
73210 La Côte-d'Aime
Tel. 04 79 55 67 79
hanrard@aol.com
www.chaletleparadou.com
Langues : Eng., Ger.

Closed from 2 May to 30 Jun and from 5 Sep to 1 Dec • 5 rooms, 4 of which overlook a large terrace • €70, breakfast included; half-board available • Table d'hôte €23 • Garden, terrace, car park. Dogs not admitted

FLOR'ALPES
M. Bibollet

73590 La Giettaz
Tel. 04 79 32 90 88
mary-anne.schouppe@wanadoo.fr
www.hotelfloralpes.free

Closed from 15 Apr to 15 May and 20 Oct to 15 Dec • 11 rooms, 7 with balcony, all with bath/WC or shower/WC • €38 to €45; breakfast €7; half-board available • Menus €16 to €30 • Garden. Dogs not admitted in restaurant

We most liked **An impeccably-run mountain chalet.**

This superb wooden chalet perched at an altitude of 1 000m commands a stunning view of the Tarentaise Valley and Mount Pourri. The spotlessly clean, comfortable rooms open onto a large terrace. The wood-lined sitting room, complete with piano, matches the alpine spirit that prevails throughout the establishment. Skiing packages are available in the winter, and in the summer, you can laze about in the flowered garden.

We most liked **The authentic Savoyard character of this village.**

Tucked away between the village church and school, this welcoming boarding house owes its success to the faultless care and attention that the lady of the house lavishes on all her guests. The rooms, simple but pristine, all have a flower-decked balcony and a wonderful view, which more than compensates for the absence of television! Simple, home cooking with a regional tang is served in a rustic dining room overlooking the garden.

Ski and snowshoe courses, hiking and water-sports courses

Access : *3km to the north-east of Aime on the D 86*

Access : *On a small square between the town hall and the school*

SAINT-CHRISTOPHE-LA-GROTTE - 73360

PRALOGNAN-LA-VANOISE - 73710

LES AIRELLES
M. Boyer

Rue des Darbelays - BP 25
73710 Pralognan-la-Vanoise
Tel. 04 79 08 70 32
hotellesairelles@free.fr
www.hotel-les-airelles.fr
Langues : Eng.

Closed from 21 Apr to 2 Jun and from 16 Sep to 22 Dec • 22 rooms with bath/WC or shower/WC and television • €72 to €92; breakfast €8; half-board available • Menus €20 to €24 • Terrace, garage, car park. No dogs admitted • Swimming pool, sauna, Jacuzzi, billiards, shuttle to the ski lifts

 Pralognan combines the charm of a village with the facilities of a top-class ski resort.

This chalet, built on the outskirts of the resort, is encircled by the ridges and crests of the Vanoise massif. The mountain view from the rooms and balconies never fails to bring gasps of admiration. In the kitchen, the talented young chef's recipes provoke further cries of approval. On the leisure side, the swimming pool is heated, and the owner, an enthusiastic hiker, never tires of indicating paths and trails to eager guests.

Access : *In the upper part of the resort, next to the Granges forest*

LA FERME BONNE DE LA GROTTE
M. Amayenc

73360 Saint-Christophe-la-Grotte
Tel. 04 79 36 59 05
info@ferme-bonne.com
www.gites-savoie.com
Langues : Eng.

Open all year • 5 rooms, some have mezzanines, all with shower/WC • €68 to €89, breakfast included • Table d'hôte €19 to €27 • Terrace, park, car park. No dogs admitted

 Irresistibly Savoyard in spirit and flavour.

In the space of a year, this three-century-old farm at the foot of the Échelles caves has become a must in the region. The renowned cuisine has remained true to its Savoyard roots and the gourmet chef takes great pleasure in watching his guests devour his tasty home cooking. The immense but still cosy rooms are all graced with painted furniture; some also boast a mezzanine.

Access : *4km to the north-east of Échelles on the N 6, Chambéry road*

SAINT-SORLIN-D'ARVES - 73530

BEAUSOLEIL
M. et Mme Vermeulen

73530 Saint-Sorlin-d'Arves
Tel. 04 79 59 71 42
info@hotel-beausoleil.com
www.hotel-beausoleil.com
Langues : Eng., It.

Closed from 15 Apr to 30 Jun and 1 Sep to 15 Dec
• 21 rooms on 3 floors, all have bath/WC or shower/WC and television • €52 to €65; breakfast €9.50; half-board available • Menus €13 to €28 • Terrace, garden, car park. No dogs admitted in the restaurant • Sauna, hammam, jacuzzi, walks in the Croix de Fer Pass and mountain sports

 Sunshine and powdery snow: what more could you want?

You know you're in for a treat right from the moment you begin to climb the road by the Combe Genin or the Croix de Fer Pass, driving past snowy peaks or pastures of wild mountain flowers up to this remote mountain chalet. Families are welcome in the practical, attractively furnished rooms. After a long day out in the open air, you will be ready to feast on the delicacies rustled up by your cheerful host.

Access : *Away from the centre of the resort, towards the Col de la Croix-de-Fer*

TIGNES - 73320

CHALET COLINN
M. et Mme Charrière

 Le Franchet route du Val d'Isère
73320 Tignes
Tel. 04 79 06 26 99
contact@chaletcolinn.com
www.chaletcolinn.com

Open all year by reservation • 5 ground floor non-smoking rooms, with shower/WC, Modem, telephone and television • €90, breakfast included • Table d'hôte €25 (except Thu) • Library, car park. Dogs not admitted • Scandinavian tub and sauna

 Access to one of the finest skiing domains in the world.

Bought in 1998 by two friends, this chalet took six years of restoration before it reopened its doors to guests. The result was worth the wait though. Guests are invited to choose their own pair of slippers from the splendid collection "displayed" in the main hall. The immense picture window, which steals the limelight from the original barn door, commands a superb view from the sitting room. The five ground floor rooms open onto a terrace complete with a Scandinavian tub. Half-board in winter.

Access : *9.5km northeast from Tignes on the Val d'Isère road*

VILLARODIN-BOURGET - 73500

L'AIGUILLE DU MIDI
M. et Mme Farini

 479 chemin Napoléon - Les Bossons
74400 Chamonix-Mont-Blanc
Tel. 04 50 53 00 65
hotel-aiguille-du-midi@wanadoo.fr
www.hotel-aiguilledumidi.com
Langues : Ger., Eng.

Closed from 10 Apr to 15 May and 20 Sep to
20 Dec • 40 rooms with bath/WC and television
• €70 to €80; breakfast €12; half-board available • Menus €21 (weekdays) to €45 • Terrace,
garden, car park. No dogs admitted in restaurant • Outdoor swimming pool, tennis, fitness
room, sauna, jacuzzi

CHÉ CATRINE
Mme Finas

 88 rue Saint-Antoine
73500 Villarodin-Bourget
Tel. 04 79 20 49 32
info@che-catrine.com
che-catrine.com
Langues : Eng., It.

Open all year • 4 rooms and 2 apartments, all
have bath/WC • €79, breakfast included; half-
board available • Table d'hôte €30 • Garden.
Credit cards not accepted • Sauna

 **The view of the Bossons glacier from the
shade of the park.**

 **Savour the good things of life in this superb
mansion.**

This country house, built in 1524, and restored
in keeping with Savoyard traditions, is a gem of
a find. You will immediately feel at home in the
rooms and suites, decorated with solid pine
furniture. Meals are served in the vaulted
stables and the lounge-bar – hewn out of solid
rock – is a delight for the eyes. The chef makes
it a point of honour to use only garden vegetables and meat from the Maurienne Valley.
Definitely worth writing home about, unless
you'd rather keep it to yourself!

This impressive old country chalet has been a
hotel since 1908. Behind the Tyrolean-style
frescoes are wainscoted rooms, most a little
faded, but all overlooking the wonderful Mont
Blanc range. The circular dining room and the
terrace with wooden furniture and a giant
parasol give onto a lovely flowery park. Make
sure you look up and admire the beautiful
carved ceiling in the sitting room. Numerous
leisure activities.

Access : *3km southbound from
Chamonix-Mont-Blanc*

Access : *A 43 motorway , exit Modane, then
after Modane 2km on the RN 6 towards the Haute
Maurienne*

CHAMONIX-MONT-BLANC - 74400

BEAUSOLEIL
M. et Mme Bossonney

Le Lavancher
74400 Chamonix-Mont-Blanc
Tel. 04 50 54 00 78
info@hotelbeausoleilchamonix.com
www.hotelbeausoleilchamonix.com
Langues : Eng., Ger., It.

Closed fortnight in spring and from 20 Sep to 20 Dec • 17 rooms on 2 levels, with bath/WC or shower/WC and television • €86 to €100, (€70 to €80 low season); breakfast €10; half-board available • Menus €14 to €28 • Terrace, garden, car park. No dogs admitted in restaurant • Tennis, table-tennis

 The tranquillity of this secluded chalet.

Are you more of a winter- or a summer-mountain type? The Bossonney family, who have run the hotel for three generations, are guaranteed to make you feel at home in their inviting chalet, whatever the season. The small, wainscoted, refreshingly simple rooms are faultlessly kept and a few boast balconies with a view of snow-capped peaks or green pastures. Tasty home cooking and cheese-based specialities are served in a country-style dining room which opens onto the terrace and garden.

Access : *6km on the N 506, towards Argentière, then minor road on the right*

CORDON - 74700

LE CORDONANT
M. et Mme Pugnat

Les Darbaillets
74700 Cordon
Tel. 04 50 58 34 56
lecordonant@wanadoo.fr
http://lecordonant.free.fr
Langues : Eng.

Closed from mid-Apr to mid-May and from Oct to Dec • 16 rooms with bath/WC (2 have shower/WC) and television • €80 to €85; (€80 low season); breakfast €8; half-board available • Menus €23 (weekdays) to €32 • Terrace, car park. No dogs admitted in restaurant • Fitness room, sauna, jacuzzi

 The ear-splitting silence and stunning view from the valley windows.

The pink roughcast walls and creamy coloured woodwork of this smart chalet stand on the heights of the "Mont Blanc balcony". The rooms have been refurbished in a contemporary Savoyard style with wood-lined walls, painted furniture and pretty fabrics. From the dining room, you will be able to enjoy a breathtaking view of the "rooftops of Europe" as you sample the appetising, generous cooking, before settling down for a nap in the sun in the flowered garden.

Access : *4km to the south-west of Sallanches on the D 113*

LA CHAPELLE-D'ABONDANCE - 74360

LES GENTIANETTES
M. et Mme Claude Trincaz

Route de Chevenne
74360 La Chapelle-d'Abondance
Tel. 04 50 73 56 46
bienvenue@gentianettes.fr
www.gentianettes.fr

Closed out of season from Easter to 1 Nov and 20 Sep to 18 Dec • 32 rooms with bath/WC or shower/WC and television, 2 have disabled access • €75 to €100; breakfast €10; half-board available • Menus €20 to €61 • Terrace, car park • Indoor swimming pool, sauna, fitness room, hammam

 Sampling the chef's mouth-watering cooking after a day in the open air.

A faultless welcome, well-proportioned cheerful bedrooms with wainscoting and balconies, a pleasant dining room and carnotzets (sitting-rooms), impeccable regional cuisine and generous breakfasts – what more could one ask from this pretty chalet built in 1994? Those lucky enough to come to La Chapelle-d'Abondance in the summertime may catch sight of a gentian flower, the high-altitude herbaceous plant which gave the hotel its name. In winter, alpine sports are more the order of the day!

Access : *North of Chapelle-d'Abondance*

LA BEUNAZ - 74500

LE BOIS JOLI
M. et Mme Birraux

74500 La Beunaz
Tel. 04 50 73 60 11
hboisjoli@aol.com
www.hotel-bois-joli.com
Langues : Eng.

Closed from mid-Oct to 20 Dec and 18 Mar to 28 Apr • 29 rooms, 8 of which are in a separate wing, all have bath/WC or shower/WC and television • €75 to €85 (€68 to €78 low season); breakfast €9.50; half-board available • Restaurant closed Sun evening and Wed; menus €22 (weekdays) to €48 • Terrace, garden, car park • Outdoor swimming pool, tennis, sauna, table-tennis, billiards

 The country appeal of this panoramic chalet.

The bedrooms, dining room and terrace all enjoy a view of the Dent d'Oche, Mount Billiat and the summits of the Chablais. In the summer, activities include a swimming pool surrounded by foliage and a tennis court, in the winter the ski slopes are nearby while year-round activities include a children's play area and billiards room with Lake Léman and its prestigious spa resorts just a few kilometres away. Idyllic in any season.

Access : *Below the road, 1.5km from Bernex on the D 52*

LA CLUSAZ - 74220

FLORALP
Mmes Pollet

79 chemin du Pré-de-Foire
74220 La Clusaz
Tel. 04 50 02 41 46
info@hotel-floralp74.com
www.hotel-floralp74.com
Langues : Eng.

Open from 28 Jun to 15 Sep and from 20 Dec to 14 Apr • 20 rooms, all have bath/WC or shower/WC and television. Front-facing rooms have balconies. • €60 to €100 (€50 to €75 low season); breakfast €8; half-board available • Menus €18 (weekdays) to €26 • Car park. No dogs admitted in restaurant • Billiards room

 A traditional mountain chalet.

The simple rooms at the front have an east-facing balcony and are much sought after by all the chalet's numerous regular guests. The region is riddled with beautiful, immaculate peaks, dales covered in rhododendron bushes and high rocky ranges. Tangy Tomme and Reblochon cheeses tempt the palate at lunchtime and dinners enable your hostesses to show off the full scope of their culinary skills. The sitting room with bar, billiard table and fireside is the perfect place for a nightcap.

Access : *At the entrance to the resort, coming from Annecy on the D 909, take a right*

LES CARROZ-D'ARACHES - 74300

LA CROIX DE SAVOIE
M. et Mme Tiret

768 route du Pernand
74300 Les Carroz-d'Araches
Tel. 04 50 90 00 26
info@lacroixdesavoie.fr
www.lacroixdesavoie.fr
Langues : Eng.

Closed Sun evening and Mon lunchtime • 19 rooms with shower/WC, most have a balcony • €86 to €99 (€64 to €69 low season); breakfast €8; half-board available • Menus €18 to €38 • Terrace, garden, car park

 Savour the tranquillity and the view of the Aravis and lose track of time.

This establishment, ideally located in the ski resort, is a haven of friendliness. The rooms, nearly all of which have a balcony, are an excellent combination of simple comfort and warm wood-panelling. Wood is also the predominant feature of the restaurant which serves regional dishes. Winter guests can head for the immense skiing domain and in the summer, walkers set off to explore the mineral kingdom of Platé. If you're lucky, you may catch a glimpse of a wild ibex following your climb.

Access : *In the upper part of the resort, 1km from the centre, towards Flaine*

MENTHON-SAINT-BERNARD - 74290

LES CONTAMINES-MONTJOIE - 74170

GAI SOLEIL
Mme Mermoud

 288 chemin des Loyers
74170 Les Contamines-Montjoie
Tel. 04 50 47 02 94
gaisoleil2@wanadoo.fr
www.gaisoleil.com
Langues : Eng., Sp.

Closed from 20 Apr to 14 Jun and 15 Sep to 20 Dec • 19 rooms with bath/WC or shower/WC, no television • €62 to €74 (€58 to €70 low season); breakfast €10; half-board available • Menus €20 to €28 • Garden, car park. Dogs not admitted in restaurant • Fondue evenings and films on mountain life

 Mount Joly and the snowy peaks of the Miage greet you in the morning.

The painting on one of the beams bearing the date 1823, was the work of the chalet's original owner. The Gai Soleil's website joyfully relates this family farm's intriguing history – an English version is in the pipeline, we're told. Ask for one of the rooms refurbished in a mountain style with wood walls and pine furniture. The south-facing terrace is popular in winter and summer alike. Attractive garden.

Access : *In the upper part of the resort*

BEAU SÉJOUR
M. Blanc

 Allée des Tennis
74290 Menthon-Saint-Bernard
Tel. 04 50 60 12 04
h.beau-sejour@laposte.net
www.hotelbeausejour-menthon.com
Langues : Eng., Sp.

Open from 15 Apr to late Sep • 18 rooms, 14 of which have shower/WC, 4 have bath/WC, some have a balcony • €66 to €75; breakfast €8 • No restaurant • Garden, private car park. Credit cards not accepted • Table-tennis, reading room. Tennis, golf and water sports nearby

 Visit the fairy-tale castle of Menthon.

One hundred metres from Lake Annecy, this early-20C villa stands in an enormous park. The bedrooms with balcony, the most spacious, have recently been renovated, doing away with the distinctive hallmarks of the seventies. The bay windows of the breakfast room overlook the flowered garden where meals are served whenever the weather is warm enough. Friendly, family service.

Access : *100m from the lake*

MORZINE - 74110

87

FLEUR DES NEIGES
M. Archambault

74110 Morzine
Tel. 04 50 79 01 23
fleurneige@aol.com
www.fleurdesneiges.com
Langues : Eng.

Closed from 10 Apr to 1 Jul and 5 Sep to 15 Dec
• 31 rooms, all have bath/WC or shower/WC and
television • €70 to €90 (€50 to €60 low season);
breakfast €10; half-board available • Menu
€20 to €25 • Terrace, garden, car park. No dogs
admitted in restaurant • Indoor swimming pool,
tennis, fitness room, sauna, table-tennis, petanque

 **Soothing your aching muscles in the pool
after a day on the slopes.**

This chalet-style building is a little out of the
centre of Chablais' tourist capital, Morzine.
When booking, ask for one of the renovated
rooms with wood-lined walls, pine furniture
and matching fabrics; plans are afoot to
redecorate the rather dour dining room in the
near future. The hotel's facilities – fitness
room, sauna, tennis court, swimming pool
(indoor in winter) – reflect the resort's combination of sport and leisure activities.

Access : *Slightly out of the centre, on the
Thonon-les-Bains road*

SALLANCHES - 74700

88

AUBERGE DE L'ORANGERIE
M. Liboureau

3 carrefour de la Charlotte
74700 Sallanches
Tel. 04 50 58 49 16
auberge-orangerie@wanadoo.fr
www.aubergedelorangerie.com

Closed from 19 Jun to 3 Jul • 8 rooms with
bath/WC or shower/WC and television • €54;
breakfast €8.50 • Restaurant closed Sun
evening, Mon all day and Tue, Wed and Thu
lunchtimes; menus €28 to €58 • Private car
park, garden, terrace

 **Gazing up at the mountains from one of
the snug rooms.**

In the summertime, the façade of this chalet at
the foot of the Côte de Passy is a riot of flowers.
The well-renovated rooms guarantee that your
nights will be quiet and peaceful: pine-panel-
ling, excellent soundproofing against the noise
of the road, big beds piled high with duvets,
inviting armchairs and fully tiled bathrooms.
Some have a balcony. The owner-chef's cuisine, served in the rustic dining room, displays
his creative flair for mixing traditional recipes
and local dishes.

Access : *Outside the town at the foot of the
Côte de Passy*

SERVOZ - 74310

GORGES DE LA DIOSAZ
M. Fraipont

« Sous le Roc »
74310 Servoz
Tel. 04 50 47 20 97
info@hoteldesgorges.com
www.hoteldesgorges.com
Langues : Eng., Sp., It.

Closed from 15 to 30 May and from 15 to 30 Nov • 6 rooms with bath/WC or shower/WC and television • €55 to €65; breakfast €7; half-board available • Menus €19 to €44 • Terrace. No dogs admitted in restaurant

Francine and Sébastien greet guests energetically and warmly.

This traditional mountain chalet decked in flowers stands on the edge of the gorges of the Diosaz. The restful rooms have been refurbished in a sober, contemporary alpine style and the windows of the inviting rustic dining room overlook the Mont Blanc range. Wood prevails in the sitting room and bar, where you can gratefully relax with a glass of mulled wine after a hard day on the slopes.

Access : *In the centre of the village, near the post office*

SEYTHENEX - 74210

AU GAY SÉJOUR
M. et Mme Gay

Le Tertenoz
74210 Seythenex
Tel. 04 50 44 52 52
hotel-gay-sejour@wanadoo.fr
www.hotel-gay-sejour.com

Closed from 15 Nov to 15 Dec, Sun evening and Mon (except public holidays) • 11 rooms with bath/WC and television • €82 to €92; breakfast €12; half-board available • Menus €22 (weekdays) to €60 • Terrace, car park. No dogs admitted • Snowshoe hiking and ski slopes nearby

 A summer vista of lush mountain pastures or a winter picture of fields of snow.

This 17C farm, nestling in a peaceful medium-altitude hamlet, has been turned into a pleasant family inn where you can be sure of a lung-full of pure mountain air. Though hardly stylish, the rooms are nonetheless wonderfully peaceful and some enjoy a lovely view of the valley. In the restaurant, the focus is on immaculate service and well-judged traditional cooking.

Access : *4km to the south-east of Faverges*

YVOIRE - 74140

91

LE VIEUX LOGIS
M. Jacquier-Durand

Rue des Remparts
74140 Yvoire
Tel. 04 50 72 80 24
contact@levieuxlogis.com
www.levieuxlogis.com

Closed from 1 Jan to 15 Feb • 11 rooms, all have bath/WC and television • €70 to €80; breakfast €8.50; half-board available • Menus €14.80 (weekdays) to €45 • Terrace, private car park

The Maze-Garden of the Five Senses in the medieval village.

This "old abode" of character, run by the same family for four generations, is set right in the ramparts. The rooms are practical and those on the first floor have a balcony; thick 14C walls keep the interior cool, even during the hot summer months. Under the vaulted ceiling and well-worn beams of the dining room, you will be invited to sample the house speciality of fillets of perch. In the summer, meals are also served on the lovely shaded terrace.

Access : *On the way into the old town, set in the ramparts*

 So that you can treat yourself without having to break open your piggy bank, we have selected hotels and chambres d'hôte which offer a warm welcome, pleasant setting and character combined with affordable prices. The coin symbol next to an establishment indicates that it is a hotel or maison d'hôte with rooms at a maximum price of €50 per night for two (breakfast included in the maisons d'hôte, but extra in hotels).

Feel like getting away from it all? Ready for a change of scenery? Want to get out into the countryside and work off some stress or extra pounds? The hotels and maisons d'hôte listed below all have a swimming pool at the very least and generally one or several other sports facilities or activities, either on site or very nearby. These include themed or signposted walks, fishing, tennis, golf, a fitness room/mini-gym, or riding, so check out each establishment to discover what is on offer.

The guesthouses in this section do more than welcome guests gracefully. They also organise courses in a wide range of activities: pottery, music, wine tasting, cooking, etc. Some also organise weekends devoted to regional heritage. You will learn how to prepare a foie gras traditionally, go mushroom picking or visit a historic monument.